1984	1985	1986	1987	1988	1989	1990	1991	1992	1993	1994	1995	1996	1997
236	238	241	243	245	247	250	253	255	258	261	263	265	268
74.7	74.7	74.7	74.9	74.9	75.1	75.4	75.5	75.8	75.5	75.7	75.8	75.9	—
3,902	4,181	4,422	4,692	5,050	5,439	5,744	5,917	6,244	6,558	6,947	7,265	7,636	8,083
5,778	5,984	6,168	6,350	6,593	6,814	6,897	6,834	7,019	7,182	7,431	7,578	7,788	8,083
24,446	25,093	25,632	26,154	26,907	27,549	27,595	27,049	27,484	27,828	28,514	28,811	29,338	30,173
3,841	4,020	4,180	4,308	4,478	4,581	4,657	4,628	4,756	4,896	5,056	5,179	5,313	5,489
865	855	843	853	860	896	846	766	820	896	1,013	1,029	1,110	1,238
1,165	1,236	1,299	1,334	1,351	1,389	1,431	1,439	1,446	1,433	1,433	1,433	1,439	1,454
−187	−217	−241	−230	−168	−122	−91	−33	−43	−103	−154	−145	−168	−209
3,342	3,472	3,588	3,732	3,883	3,948	4,026	3,994	4,097	4,178	4,291	4,397	4,515	4,703
1,343	1,371	1,364	1,428	1,529	1,561	1,560	1,506	1,512	1,590	1,689	1,770	1,864	1,854
4.6	3.8	3.7	4.9	6.0	5.0	4.0	2.4	0.8	2.8	5.4	5.7	6.0	—
7.5	7.2	7.0	6.2	5.5	5.3	5.6	6.8	7.5	6.9	6.1	5.6	5.4	4.9
105	107	110	112	115	117	119	118	118	120	123	125	127	130
35.2	34.9	34.8	34.8	34.7	34.6	34.5	34.3	34.4	34.5	34.7	34.5	34.4	34.6
12.97	12.92	12.99	12.86	12.79	12.71	12.51	12.39	12.33	12.29	12.31	12.29	12.36	12.54
64.7	67.0	68.3	70.8	73.7	77.3	81.4	84.9	87.4	90.0	92.3	95.0	97.8	100.0
4.3	3.6	1.9	3.6	4.1	4.8	5.4	4.2	3.0	3.0	2.6	2.8	3.0	2.3
9.6	7.5	6.0	5.8	6.7	8.1	7.5	5.4	3.5	3.0	4.3	5.5	5.0	5.1
1,261	1,355	1,382	1,359	1,390	1,433	1,505	1,530	1,553	1,543	1,563	1,581	1,592	1,601
987	1,051	1,073	1,156	1,187	1,242	1,239	1,218	1,227	1,264	1,346	1,410	1,482	1,579
−274	−304	−309	−203	−203	−191	−266	−311	−326	−279	−217	−171	−110	−22
22.3	23.1	22.6	21.8	21.5	21.4	22.0	22.6	22.5	21.8	21.4	21.1	20.7	20.1
17.5	17.9	17.6	18.6	18.4	18.5	18.2	18.0	17.8	17.8	18.4	18.8	19.3	19.8
−4.9	−5.2	−5.1	−3.3	−3.1	−2.8	−3.9	−4.6	−4.7	−3.9	−3.0	−2.3	−1.4	−0.3
1,797	1,877	1,947	1,995	2,027	2,080	2,163	2,194	2,321	2,351	2,369	2,422	2,466	2,511
1,694	1,774	1,832	1,934	1,981	2,057	2,073	2,056	2,103	2,172	2,272	2,347	2,461	—
−102	−103	−115	−61	−46	−23	−89	−139	−219	−179	−96	−74	−5	—
31.1	31.4	31.6	31.4	30.7	30.5	31.4	32.1	33.1	32.7	31.9	32.0	31.7	31.1
29.3	29.7	29.7	30.5	30.0	30.2	30.1	30.1	30.0	30.2	30.6	31.0	31.6	—
−1.8	−1.7	−1.9	−1.0	−0.7	−0.3	−1.3	−2.0	−3.1	−2.5	−1.3	−1.0	−0.1	—
111,830	105,935	109,509	114,337	117,440	122,090	126,893	125,331	128,344	132,228	134,196	138,186	132,121	—

Introduction To

MACROECONOMICS

② Second Edition

Alan C. Stockman
University of Rochester

THE DRYDEN PRESS
Harcourt Brace College Publishers

Fort Worth   Philadelphia   San Diego   New York   Austin   Orlando   San Antonio
Toronto   Montreal   London   Sydney   Tokyo

Executive Editor: Gary Nelson
Product Manager: Debbie Anderson
Developmental Editor: Amy Schmidt
Project Editor: Jim Patterson
Art Director: Bill Brammer
Production Manager: Eddie Dawson

Credits appear on page C-1, which constitutes a continuation of the copyright page.

ISBN: 0-03-021832-2
Library of Congress Catalog Card Number: 98-71886

Address for orders:
The Dryden Press
6277 Sea Harbor Drive
Orlando, FL 32887-6777
1-800-782-4479

Address for editorial correspondence:
The Dryden Press
301 Commerce Street, Suite 3700
Fort Worth, TX 76102

Web site address:
http://www.hbcollege.com

The Dryden Press, Dryden, and the Dryden Press logo are registered trademarks of Harcourt Brace & Company.

Printed in the United States of America

8 9 0 1 2 3 4 5 6 7   048   9 8 7 6 5 4 3 2 1

The Dryden Press
Harcourt Brace College Publishers

To Cindy, Gwendolyn,
Madeleine, and Rebecca

The Dryden Press Series in Economics

Baldani, Bradfield, and Turner
Mathematical Economics

Baumol and Blinder
Economics: Principles and Policy
Seventh Edition—Updated 1998
(also available in Micro and Macro
paperbacks)

Baumol, Panzar, and Willig
*Contestable Markets and the Theory
of Industry Structure*
Revised Edition

Breit and Elzinga
*The Antitrust Casebook: Milestones
in Economic Regulation*
Third Edition

Brue
The Evolution of Economic Thought
Fifth Edition

Edgmand, Moomaw, and Olson
Economics and Contemporary Issues
Fourth Edition

Gardner
Comparative Economic Systems
Second Edition

Gwartney and Stroup
*Economics: Private and Public
Choice*
Eighth Edition
(also available in Micro and Macro
paperbacks)

Gwartney and Stroup
*Introduction to Economics: The
Wealth and Poverty of Nations*

Hess and Ross
*Economic Development: Theories,
Evidence, and Policies*

Hirschey and Pappas
*Fundamentals of Managerial
Economics*
Sixth Edition

Hirschey and Pappas
Managerial Economics
Eighth Edition

Hyman
*Public Finance: A Contemporary
Application of Theory to Policy*
Sixth Edition

Kahn
*The Economic Approach to
Environmental and Natural Resources*
Second Edition

Kaserman and Mayo
*Government and Business: The
Economics of Antitrust and Regulation*

Kaufman
The Economics of Labor Markets
Fourth Edition

Kennett and Lieberman
*The Road to Capitalism: The
Economic Transformation of Eastern
Europe and the Former Soviet Union*

Kreinin
*International Economics: A Policy
Approach*
Eighth Edition

Mankiw
Principles of Economics
(also available in Micro and Macro
paperbacks)

Nicholson
*Intermediate Microeconomics and
Its Application*
Seventh Edition

Nicholson
*Microeconomic Theory: Basic
Principles and Extensions*
Seventh Edition

Ramanathan
*Introductory Econometrics with
Applications*
Fourth Edition

Rukstad
*Corporate Decision Making in the
World Economy: Company Case
Studies*

Rukstad
*Macroeconomic Decision Making in
the World Economy: Text and Cases*
Third Edition

Samuelson and Marks
Managerial Economics
Third Edition

Scarth
*Macroeconomics: An Introduction to
Advanced Methods*

Sexton
*Exploring Economics: Pathways to
Problem Solving*
(also available in Micro and Macro
paperbacks)

Stockman
Introduction to Economics
Second Edition
(also available in Micro and Macro
paperbacks)

Walton and Rockoff
History of the American Economy
Eighth Edition

Welch and Welch
Economics: Theory and Practice
Sixth Edition

Yarbrough and Yarbrough
*The World Economy: Trade and
Finance*
Fourth Edition

I'll confess: This book has a secret agenda. I wrote this book to teach students how to think like economists, but my ultimate motive for writing it was my own satisfaction—I seek the delight that arises in me when a student becomes enthusiastic about economics; when he proudly explains his new application of economic reasoning; when she decides to major in economics because of my course. These occasions generate feelings (with less intensity) similar to my immense joy in sharing some beautiful aspect of the world, such as the emotions of music or the pride of accomplishment, with my own children. The gratification of teaching occurs when students rekindle their natural curiosities to feed the appetite that curiosity creates.

Students who enroll in a principles of economics course seldom have more than the vaguest idea of its subject, let alone why they should care about it. Many of them expect economics to be boring and enroll in the course only to satisfy a requirement. They have no awareness of the market, let alone any sort of *awe* of the market. It has never occurred to them that our economy, without any central plan or direction, somehow coordinates the activities of millions of people to produce efficiently the goods and services that they want. Most students have never been exposed to the kinds of questions that economics answers. Although the results of those questions and answers profoundly affect their lives, they take them for granted.

Introduction to Economics inspires students not to take those results for granted but to think like economists instead. It does so by leading them on a path of inquiry and discovery, fostering the experience of its joys. Of course, the book does teach the substantive results of economics, such as the effects of an increase in demand on price, for example. More importantly, though, the book helps students acquire *new skills* that they can apply in their own lives. It teaches students the answers, but first and foremost, it helps them learn to formulate the questions. If this book accomplishes its goal, it will evoke in students an excitement of economics and appreciation for the power of economic analysis. They will share (with those of us who love economics) that "Aha!" feeling of new discovery, and their newfound abilities to think like economists will change their lives.

Information and Analysis

The relative price of facts and analysis has changed. Since the first edition of *Introduction to Economics*, the information revolution has swept our society, reducing the price of facts. Students can obtain data at a vastly lower time cost than ever before. But facts and analysis are complements. Without tools for analysis, students may drown in a sea of facts. The widening gulf between wages of unskilled workers and wages of skilled, "knowledge workers" is one outcome of the information revolution. The gulf may widen even further in coming decades as the information age continues to raise the marginal product of analysis.

This second edition of *Introduction to Economics* reflects these changes with a fresh focus on helping students learn how to *apply* economics to solve new problems and analyze new issues, ask new questions, formulate new ideas, and view old issues in new ways. It separates explanations and examples from main points. It employs examples as memory aids and develops applications to deepen understanding. The best way to learn how to think analytically and apply economics is to practice, and then to practice again. Students learn by practicing applying concepts that relate to their own daily lives and to the greater world around them. This book provides that opportunity, and makes it both easier and fun. It helps students to venture beyond the description of economic models to the *uses* of those models. It encourages them to explore new vistas and supports their explorations by providing them with the maps and tools to do so.

A Personal Note

I expected to become a physicist or political scientist when I entered college in the fall of 1969. My interest in political science sprang from my fascination with political philosophy and broad social issues, but most political science courses appeared to focus more on the institutions of government than on fundamental questions. Meanwhile, outside reading led me to the works of Milton Friedman, Friedrich Hayek, and Ludwig von Mises, and inspired me to learn more economics. However, I found my introductory economics course dry and intellectually unsatisfying. The textbook required for the course never discussed (or even raised) the many fundamental questions to which economics applies. Rather than show me how to apply logical reasoning, the book implied that experts had already resolved most economic issues. It implied that these authorities armed with technical skills could manage government policies to correct the failures of markets and fine-tune the economy. How boring! Even if it were true (something I could not evaluate at the time), that approach to economics rejected the joy of discovery; the process of learning to think; the crucial ability to raise new questions.

Despite that experience, my outside reading (and some good professors in my classes at Ohio State University) sustained my interest in economics. When I decided to pursue economics in graduate school, I promised myself that someday I would write a better introductory economics textbook through which I could share with other people the fun and intellectual excitement I found in economics. After getting my Ph.D. at the University of Chicago and spending two years at UCLA, I found myself teaching a principles course at the University of Rochester in the fall of 1979. I have taught principles every year since then (two decades that have gone by very quickly!). The first edition of this book grew from my attempt to fulfill my promise to myself. The second edition, which you hold in your hands, grew from my desire to improve it. I hope you find that I have succeeded.

Applied, Analytical Approach to Macroeconomics

This book takes an applied analytical approach to macroeconomics. Students learn to construct models, or logical stories, of the operation of the economy and the effects of government policies. They learn how to begin with simple stories to explore key logical points, before embellishing those stories with additional features. This book begins with a long-run, neoclassical model before adding short-run complications associated with sticky prices. Numerous applications help to illustrate the relevance of these logical stories to real-life issues, including historical case studies as well as recent macroeconomic news stories, such as banking crises and recessions in Asia and Russia, introduction to the Euro and the new European Central Bank, and Federal Reserve policies to maintain economic growth with low inflation in the United States.

Fundamental Issues and Everyday Applications

Discussions or questions about important social and political issues appear throughout the book, enticing students to broaden the set of questions that they ask about the world, to understand both sides of controversial issues, and to combine economic analysis with their own value judgments as they think about current events and fundamental social issues. The book also strives for a real-life flavor through the use of data, examples, applications of economics to personal and business decisions, and the extensive use of news clippings.

Chapter-by-Chapter Changes from the First Edition

Part 1: Issues and Methods

Chapter 1 Mysteries and Motives: What Economics Is About Chapter 1 has been rewritten to place students directly into the center of economic analysis. Consistent with this edition's enhanced focus on thinking skills, the chapter now opens with a simple but very important economic model of gains from trade. The implications of this model will surprise many students. Discussion of the model leads to a discussion of what economics is about, with key facts about the world economy presented in easily-digestible form and key issues of economic analysis appearing in clear examples.

Chapter 2 Solving Puzzles: The Methods of Economics This revised chapter contains a new discussion of economic models as artificial economies, similar to simulations in computer games. The new chapter also has more concise explanations and examples of logical fallacies.

Part 2: Fundamental Tools

Chapter 3 Let's Make a Deal: The Gains from Trade This substantially rewritten chapter now presents production possibility frontiers within the chapter rather than in an appendix. The two-student example of gains from trade in this chapter complements the shoe-store example of gains from trade from the beginning of Chapter 1, and it is thoroughly integrated with the discussion of production possibility frontiers.

Chapter 4 Supply and Demand This chapter has been streamlined for even easier reading and clarity than in the first edition. The chapter contains a new early section on the concept of price-taking behavior. Some more difficult material has been omitted from this edition. (All such omitted material will be available on the Web pages for the book for instructors who wish to cover those more advanced topics. However, the second edition focuses more strongly than ever on basic skills.)

Part 3: Macroeconomics: Mysteries, Measurement, and Models

Chapter 5 Macroeconomic Issues and Measurement This revised introduction to macroeconomics provides a shorter, yet more comprehensive introduction to main concepts and issues, with the same strong real-life focus present in the first edition. Growth rates, the rule of 72, the circular flow, and coverage of AS/AD have

been moved to later chapters. This revised chapter has a stronger focus on macroeconomic questions and measurement of GDP, its components, the price level, employment, and unemployment.

Chapter 6 Simple Economic Models of GDP, Prices, and Employment This is an almost entirely new chapter that builds a basic macroeconomic model. The chapter focuses on the models as logical stories, and need for models to think about real-life economic issues.

The chapter begins with an essay from Professor Robert E. Lucas, Jr., "What Economists Do," which describes:

1. how economists think about the economy, and how they answer "what-if" questions about the economy, by telling logical stories (constructing models)

2. the creation of a recession in an amusement park

Next, the chapter develops a story (model) of a Robinson Crusoe economy to examine the factors determining real GDP. This model illustrates:

1. production functions and diminishing returns to labor effort

2. factors that affect investment

3. real GDP as the sum of consumption and investment

Finally, the chapter extends the model to a large number of people, like Crusoe, who trade with each other. This extension adds two new features to the model:

1. money, with the circular flow to illustrate the equation of exchange

2. labor markets

The chapter includes new discussions of:

1. the neutrality of money

2. why money is *not* neutral in Lucas's amusement-park model

3. labor markets, employment, and unemployment

Part 4: Savings, Investment, and Growth

Chapter 7 Interest Rates, Savings, and Investment This chapter (formerly Chapters 7 and 8) contains an entirely reorganized discussion of interest rates, savings, and investment, with new, streamlined discussions of:

1. the distinction between real and nominal interest rates

2. investment decisions

3. connections between goods-market equilibrium and loan-market equilibrium

After summarizing the basic macroeconomic model, the chapter applies the model to answer "what-if" questions on the effects of changes in:

1. consumer patience (or confidence)

2. technology

3. taxes

Each discussion is newly rewritten and significantly shorter and easier.

New material includes greater emphasis on the supply-side effects of changes in tax rates.

Chapter 8 Economic Growth This chapter has been rewritten for greater clarity and to emphasize use of the macroeconomic model developed in previous chapters. New material includes graphs of production functions to help illustrate the basic economic model of growth and the key issue of diminishing returns.

Part 5: Inflation, Money, and Banks

Chapter 9 Inflation This streamlined chapter now includes a focused discussion of the demand for money, and a new section on foreign exchange rates.

Chapter 10 Money and Financial Intermediaries This newly rewritten and reorganized chapter now begins with the advantages of monetary exchange over barter, followed by a streamlined discussion of the history of money. While maintaining coverage of basic issues such as the money supply, and the role of the banking system in the money multiplier, this edition places a new focus on the economics of financial intermediation. Recent financial crises in Asia illustrate the connections between the banking system and GDP, employment, and the exchange rate.

Part 6: Business Cycles

Chapter 11 Business Cycles 1: Aggregate Demand and Supply This first of two chapters on business cycles, substantially rewritten and shortened in this edition, introduces the AS-AD model and its applications.

Chapter 12 Business Cycles 2: Applications of Aggregate Demand and Supply This second chapter on the applications of the AS-AD model and the Phillips Curve is substantially rewritten and reorganized. Discussions of aggregate supply, the multiplier, and the Phillips Curve are easier to understand. The new chapter places greater emphasis on real-world applications and contains increased discussion of financial crises with applications to recent episodes in Latin America and Asia.

Part 7: Macroeconomic Policies

Chapter 13 Monetary Policy This shorter, streamlined chapter includes new material on the design of monetary systems and institutions, with applications to the new European currency and monetary institutions and to major monetary policy issues in Asia and elsewhere (connecting these monetary-policy issues to financial crises).

Chapter 14 Fiscal Policy This revised fiscal policy chapter contains new applications to issues such as the current Japanese recession, fiscal reform in Russia, and the issue of social security that looms over official U.S. government budget surpluses.

Part 8: Advanced Topics in Macroeconomics

Chapter 15 Financial Markets This shorter chapter on financial markets continues to introduce key facts and basic skills (such as reading financial news). However, this revised chapter also places a greater focus on *skills* of logical thinking about financial markets.

Chapter 16 International Trade This streamlined international trade chapter is reorganized for better comprehension and a stronger focus on the basic principles.

Pedagogical Features

In-Chapter Examples and Exercises Paired with Explanations

EXAMPLE

1. *Personal decisions on spending money* Is it cheaper to buy or rent? Should you repair your old car or buy a new one?

This book maintains a reader-friendly organization that helps students by pairing main points with explanations and examples. This organization increases student understanding by "walking" readers step-by-step through the main concepts of economics. In addition, this delivery method helps students review material with less study time. Some sections deviate from this organization, but always for a reason.

Main Points to Understand and Thinking Skills to Develop Sections

New to this edition, "Main Points to Understand" and "Thinking Skills to Develop" sections now appear at the beginning of every chapter. Written in an outline format, these sections provide a quick walk-through of the chapter's core concepts, guiding students toward the important ideas about to be discussed.

News Clippings

The book makes extensive use of real news clippings to help students practice applying economic principles as they read about or listen to reports of current or historical events. The news clippings also increase student familiarity with news stories on economic topics, alleviating fears that such stories are beyond their comprehension and elevating their self-confidence not only to read but also to evaluate such stories. Chapter-by-chapter links to late-breaking news stories can be found on the Web site for this book.

Review Questions and Thinking Exercises

"Review Questions" and "Thinking Exercises" appear at the ends of sections, not just the ends of chapters. Some questions are mainly for review, while others require student analysis. This placement of the questions allows students to query themselves about the material in each section before continuing to the next. These questions and problems cover each level of learning, helping students learn to restate main points, to work through applications in the text and through genuinely *new* applications, and to apply economics to everyday life, current events, and broad social issues. Many problems help students learn to work with graphs (and some with numerical examples) and to state verbally the conclusions of the graphical analysis.

Decision-Making and Social and Economic Issues Boxes

Many chapters also contain boxes presenting the main arguments on both sides of important social and economic issues. The book's strong emphasis on how economics relates to major social issues and political debates stimulates student interest and ties economics to students' lives. Some chapters also have boxes applying economic analysis to business decision making or personal decision making, showing students how they can use economics to help achieve their own goals.

Marginal "Advice" and "Making Smart Decisions" Boxes

New boxes on "Advice" and "Making Smart Decisions" appear in the margins of this edition. The "Advice" boxes offer students helpful hints on economic reasoning and common pitfalls. "Making Smart Decisions" boxes show students how economics can help them in their daily lives. Marginal boxes provide students with information on how economics can help in making predictions, diversifying risks, and making strides toward personal improvement.

Internet References

Internet references available at the Web site for this book, http://www.dryden.com, and at the author's Web site, http://www.economics101.org give students the opportunity to enhance their learning. Unlike many Internet resources that simply point to the latest data, Internet resources for this edition guide students on how to *use* the information and data. References to Internet sites that *apply* economic analysis supplement references to data from government agencies, think tanks, and private industry. This book's Internet resources include advanced topics and additional text-related explanations and examples.

Conclusion

The concluding sections of each chapter are organized by section, making it easier for students to identify sections that they need to reread. On a second reading, many students will find that they can skip explanation and example sections if they already understand the issues.

IN THE NEWS

Japanese tell U.S. that their banks are in big trouble

WASHINGTON—Japan's top financial officials told their American counterparts this weekend that their country's banking system was acutely short of capital, with the top 19 banks in deeper trouble than Tokyo has ever before admitted, according to officials familiar with the discussions.

Source: New York Times

PERSONAL DECISION MAKIN

Diversifying Risks

The key to diversifying risks is to choose inv
returns move in opposite directions. An inve
versified if some of that person's investmen
returns in those situations where her other i
vide low returns, and vice-versa. This mi:
ments protects the investor, rather like insur:
least some investments are likely to do we

Advice

Don't make the common mistake of thinking that competition always creates a winner and a loser. Remember that *both* sides win in a voluntary trade—as Lisa and Mitch did.

Inquiries for Further Thought

35. Should the United States adopt policies to reduce consumption spending and increase savings? What are the benefits and costs of a policy like this? Why did earlier chapters imply that an increase in savings raises productivity and future output, while according to this chapter, an increase in savings reduces aggregate demand and real GDP?

Inquiries for Further Thought

"Inquiries for Further Thought" are one of the most important features of the book. These distinctive inquires supplement other end-of-chapter questions and problems. They challenge students to use economic analysis to formulate positions on issues of fundamental social importance. The inquiries raise positive and normative questions on important public issues related to economics, teaching students (a) how to raise new questions and think about issues in new ways, (b) to distinguish between the positive and normative components of such questions, (c) that these positive and normative components are related to each other, (d) that economic analysis helps provide a logical way to approach many questions, and (e) that big-issue questions make economics interesting and important. The inquiries help students practice combining economic analysis with their own values and opinions about fundamental issues. Because most of the inquiries involve value judgments, they have no "correct" answers.

Supplements

Student Study Guide

Written by John Dodge (Indiana Wesleyan), the study guide utilizes numerous strategies for active learning and practice, thereby helping students improve their grades. Elements of this supplement include: learning goals, key-term quizzes, true-false questions, multiple-choice questions, fill-in-the-blank problems, priority lists of concepts, short-answer questions, and basic and advanced problems. All the problems have been checked for accuracy.

Web Sites

Located at http://www.dryden.com/econ, the Web site for the book has been newly reorganized on a chapter-by-chapter basis. This new organization makes the vast and sometimes overwhelming array of resources found on the Web intelligible. Each Web chapter provides a mini-learning module that students can learn from as they work their way chapter-by-chapter through the printed textbook. The new organization also enables professors to find more readily the material related to any particular chapter. The following are among the teaching and learning materials that can be found on the Web site:

For Instructors and Students:
Late-breaking news articles augmenting the textbook's "In the News" feature
Chapter-by-chapter links to economic Web sites
An economic URL database
Discussions of advanced topics

For Instructors:
Instructor's Manual
Overhead transparency masters
PowerPoint presentation slides

For Students:
Career listings
Chapter summaries
Chapter notes
Chapter-by-chapter, automatically graded, practice quizzes
Interactive learning graphs
"Cyber" problems
Glossary from the textbook

Additional resources for students are available at the author's online site at http://www.economics101.org

Tutorial, Analytical, and Graphical (TAG) Software

Created by Andrew Foshee (McNeese State University) and Tod Porter and Teresa Riley (both of Youngstown University), this award-winning educational software for students consists of extensive chapter-by-chapter tutorials. Included are practice exams, hands-on graphic sections in which students are required to draw or adjust curves, "news" articles with word-substitution choices to evaluate their comprehension, and an "Econoquest" feature that requires them to solve economic problems by choosing among various economic data tools. TAG can be obtained at no additional charge with the purchase of the textbook from the publisher. Instructors can now customize TAG for their students, by requesting a copy of the TAG Editing System software. This software allows them to modify, add, and delete questions. The Dryden Press is also happy to grant permission to instructors wishing to use the software in a lab setting.

On-Line Course Management

The Dryden Press is proud to offer a new course offering and delivery software package that helps instructors build sophisticated Web-based learning environments for their students. This nontechnical software package can be used to create on-line courses or simply to post office hours or materials on-line that supplement the instructor's course. Instructors can design their own Web sites that provide a full array of educational tools including communication, testing, student tracking, access control, database collaboration tools, on-line searching and navigation tools and much more. Instructors interested in taking their courses to the Web can learn more about this important new resource by contacting their Dryden Press sales representative.

PowerPoint Presentation Software

Developed by Anthony Zambelli (Cuyamaca College), this easy-to-use, overhead lecture software has been vastly improved for the second edition, with the graphs now perfectly replicating those found in the textbook. Professors can now edit the graphs and the text to customize their presentations as they please. The PowerPoint presentation covers all of the essential materials found in the book. Colorful graphs, tables, lists, and concepts are developed sequentially at the click of the button.

Wall Street Journal Edition

Instructors can enhance the real-life applications in the text by using the special *Wall Street Journal* Edition. This special edition of the textbook is the same as the standard edition but includes a discounted ten-week subscription to the *Wall Street Journal*. The addition of the *Wall Street Journal* to the study program of students provides a nice tie-in with the "In the News" boxes found in the text, since new examples of economic principles can be found in each day's paper. Students can activate their subscriptions by simply completing and mailing the business reply card found in the back of the book. Instructors interested in finding out more about this program can contact their Dryden sales representative or simply call 1-800-782-4479 and reference the following ISBN: 0-03-021837-3.

Instructor's Manual

This supplement contains valuable outlines, teaching tips, and answers to all of the review questions, thinking exercises, and problems in the book. This information is also available on disk and the Web site, which allows instructors to customize their lecture notes.

Test Bank

Revised and organized by Dean Croushore (Federal Reserve Bank of Philadelphia), the test bank contains more than 3,500 multiple-choice and critical-thinking questions. Each question is graded by level of difficulty and all questions new to this edition are highlighted. All questions were checked for accuracy.

Computerized Test Bank

The test bank is available electronically in DOS, Windows and Macintosh versions. The ExaMaster system accompanying the computerized test banks makes it easy to create tests, print scrambled versions of the same test, modify questions, and reproduce any of the graphing questions.

Acknowledgments

How can I begin to thank all of the people who have directly or indirectly helped me create this book? I owe a great debt to my former teachers at the University of Chicago, particularly Milton Friedman, George Stigler, Gary Becker, Robert Barro, Jacob Frenkel,

Robert E. Lucas, Jr., Tom Sargent, and my fellow students, particularly Tom MaCurdy and Dan Sumner. I also owe special debts of thanks to current and former colleagues, most notably Mark Bils, John Boyd, Mike Dotsey, Jim Kahn, Steve Landsburg, and Ken McLaughlin. I also am greatly indebted to Rao Aiyagari, Irasema Alonso, Jeff Banks, Karl Brunner, Jeff Campbell, Stan Engerman, Lauren Feinstone, Marvin Goodfriend, Jeremy Greenwood, Eric Hanushek, Ron Jones, Robert King, Per Krusell, Tony Kuprianov, Walter Oi, Charles Phelps, Sergio Rebelo, and Michael Wolkoff. I also owe special thanks to Jim Irwin, Andy Atkeson, Richard Rogerson, Masao Ogaki, Belton Fleisher, Peter Rupert, Lee Ohanian, and Craig Hakkio for their comments on parts of the book.

No successful principles of economics textbook could be written without the help of astute reviewers. I am very much indebted to the following people for their insightful recommendations, which helped me immensely to improve the second edition:

Michael P. Aarstol
University of Georgia

Michael J. Applegate
Oklahoma State University

Paul M. Comolli
University of Kansas

Harry Ellis, Jr.
University of North Texas

Soumen Ghosh
New Mexico State University

James D. Hamilton
University of California at San Diego

Charlotte Denise Hixson
Midlands Technical College

Beth F. Ingram
The University of Iowa

James R. Kearl
Brigham Young University

Benjamin J.C. Kim
University of Nebraska at Lincoln

Don R. Leet
California State University at Fresno

Larry T. McRae
Appalachian State University

Robert S. Rycroft
Mary Washington College

Donald J. Schilling
University of Missouri at Columbia

Tayyeb Shabbir
University of Pennsylvania

Stephen Shmanske
California State University at Hayward

Christopher J. Waller
Indiana University

The following people contributed greatly to the development of the first edition of the text, either as reviewers, class testers, or as focus-group participants: David Altig, *Cleveland State University;* Michael Anderson, *Washington and Lee University;* Richard Ballman, *Augustana College;* David Bivin, *Indiana University—Purdue University, Indianapolis;* David Black, *University of Toledo;* Robert T. Bray, *California State Polytechnic University, Pomona;* James A. Bryan, *North Harris Community College;* Tom Carr, *Middlebury College;* John Chilton, *University of South Carolina;* Daniel S. Christiansen, *Albion College;* Richard Claycombe, *Western Maryland College;* Kenneth A. Couch, *Syracuse University;* Mike Dowd, *University of Toledo;* Swarna D. Dutt, *Tulane University;* Catherine Eckel, *Virginia Polytechnic Institute and State University;* Sharon Erenburg, *Eastern Michigan University;* Paul Farnham, *Georgia State University;* David Gay, *University of Arkansas;* Lynn Gillette, *Northeast Missouri State University;* Gerhard Glomm, *Michigan State University;* Stephen F. Gohmann, *University of Louisville;* Philip J. Grossman, *Wayne State University;* Craig Hakkio, *Rockhurst College;* David L. Hammes, *University of Hawaii at Hilo;* Y. Horiba, *Tulane University;* William Hunter, *Marquette University;* Jim Irwin, *Central Michigan University;* Stephen L. Jackstadt, *University of Alaska at Anchorage;* Nasir Khilji, *Assumption College;* Janet Koscianski, *Shippensburg University;* Carston Kowalczyk, *Tufts University;* Stephen Lisle, *Western Kentucky University;* John Lunn, *Hope College;* Elaine S. McBeth, *College of William & Mary;* Catherine McDevitt, *Central Michigan University;* Michael Meurer, *Duke University;* Joanna Moss, *San Francisco State University;* Norman Obst, *Michigan State University;* Lee Ohanian, *University of Minnesota;* James A. Overdahl, *George Mason University;* Deborah J. Paige, *McHenry County College;* Jim Payne,

Kellogg Community College; James Price, *Syracuse University;* Sunder Ramaswamy, *Middlebury College;* Kevin Rask, *Colgate University;* John Reid, *Memphis State University;* Christine Rider, *St. John's University;* Jose-Victor Rios-Rull, *University of Pennsylvania;* Peter Rupert, Federal Reserve Bank of Cleveland; Robert S. Rycroft, *Mary Washington College;* Michael D. Seelye, *San Joaquin Delta College;* Dorothy R. Siden, *Salem State College;* Larry Singell, *University of Oregon;* David L. Sollars, *Auburn University at Montgomery;* John C. Soper, *John Carroll University;* Todd P. Steen, *Hope College;* Michael Taussig, *Rutgers University;* Abdul M. Turay, *Radford University;* Ivan Weinel, *University of Missouri;* James N. Wetzel, *Virginia Commonwealth University;* Mark Wilkening, *Blinn College;* Edgar W. Wood, *University of Mississippi;* Kakkar Vikas, *Ohio State University;* Joseph A. Ziegler, *University of Arkansas.*

My deep gratitude goes out to the thousands of my students in introductory economics at the University of Rochester who have helped me with this project either directly (with comments on the manuscript) or indirectly, who have been experimental subjects in pedagogy, and who have helped me learn how to teach economics. I owe a great debt to all my former teaching assistants, who have taught me new ways to teach and showed me how to improve explanations and examples. I am also grateful to my former Ph.D. students at the University of Rochester, from whom I have learned more than they realize.

I have been extraordinarily fortunate to work with a number of outstanding people at The Dryden Press. I am indebted to a great team of professionals, including Gary Nelson, Acquisitions Editor, who encouraged me to use my own judgment in this revision. Special thanks go to Jim Patterson, Senior Project Editor; Eddie Dawson, Senior Production Manager; Bill Brammer, Senior Art Director; Linda Blundell, Picture & Rights Editor; Debbie Anderson, Product Manager; and Kimberly Powell, Manufacturing Coordinator. They all did a terrific job attending to each and every detail necessary to turn the manuscript into a book. The fine product before you is a testament to their expertise, ingenuity, and dedication. I am particularly indebted to my editor, Amy Schmidt, Associate Editor, for her outstanding professional work, superb advice, and sustained encouragement and support throughout the production and revision of this book. No author could wish for a better editor.

My greatest debt is to my wife, Cindy, and my children, Gwendolyn, Madeleine, and Rebecca, who sacrificed a lot of time with me and endured many burdens while I worked on this book.

Alan C. Stockman

About the Author

Alan C. Stockman is the Marie Curran Wilson and Joseph Chamberlain Wilson Professor of Economics at the University of Rochester, and Chairman of the Department of Economics. He also serves as Research Associate at the National Bureau of Economic Research and Consultant at the Federal Reserve Bank of Richmond. He has taught introductory economics for two decades and has been honored for his outstanding teaching of that course.

Professor Stockman received his Ph.D. at the University of Chicago in 1978, and has published widely in the leading professional journals, such as the *Journal of Political Economy, American Economic Review, Journal of Monetary Economics, Journal of International Economics,* and *Journal of Economic Theory.*

He specializes in macroeconomics and international economics, although his research also extends to other areas such as the economics of philosophy. He serves on editorial boards of several professional journals and presents frequent talks at universities and professional conferences around the world. In his spare time, he enjoys music, skiing, and spending time with wife and three daughters.

BRIEF CONTENTS

CONTENTS

MACROECONOMICS

ISSUES AND METHODS

How to Study Economics

Economics takes a little work to learn—but it can be *fun*—and it can help you achieve your goals in life and understand the world around you. You will do best if you follow this advice on studying economics:

1) *Don't memorize* the material in the chapter. Instead, think about the logic and the main points.

2) *Practice drawing graphs* without looking at the book.

3) *Explain* to yourself *out loud* the main points of each chapter and the meanings of the graphs. Research on learning suggests that you should repeat this two to three times per day for two to three days, then do it once more before an exam.

4) *Do the "Review Questions" and "Thinking Exercises"* at the end of each section before reading further. Try to do them *without looking* back at the chapter. If you need to look, that's okay, but do them again later without looking.

5) *Do the Problems*. This is the best way to learn to apply economics to real-life issues.

6) Discuss the *Inquiries for Further Thought* (at the end of each chapter) with your friends. Form your own opinions, and use economics to help you explain and support them.

7) *Read the newspaper clippings* in the book and identify the associated economic reasoning. Find your own news examples and *apply economics to your everyday life*. Ask yourself questions such as: "Why didn't the bookstore charge me $300 for this book? What affects the price and quality of food at my college? What makes college a good or bad investment? What are the costs and benefits of the way I spend my time each day?" Add your own questions and keep a list of them.

8) *Get on the Internet* site for this book at http://www.dryden.com/econ/stockman/ for additional learning help—explanations, examples, applications, problems, updates, and more. Also see the author's course web site at http://www.econ.rochester.edu/eco108/ for additional resources and help.

Many people believe that economics is only the study of business, stocks, and bonds. Follow the advice here and you will soon find that economics is much broader—and much more *fun*—than that.

CHAPTER 1

MYSTERIES AND MOTIVES: WHAT ECONOMICS IS ABOUT

In this Chapter. . .

Main Points to Understand

▶ People benefit from voluntary trades.

▶ Every action has a cost—an *opportunity cost*.

▶ People's material standard of living depends on what they produce.

Thinking Skills to Develop

▶ Recognize opportunity costs of your actions.

▶ Formulate your own questions about economic events in the world around you.

▶ Recognize gains from trade in everyday life.

We live in the information age. The Internet has made facts and data easier to access than ever before. As a result, remembering facts is less important than ever before.

In contrast, *knowing how to think* and use facts, to analyze issues and solve problems, is *more* useful than ever before. That is why education has become increasingly valuable, and one reason why college-educated people now earn wages 40 percent higher on average than those of people with only a high-school education. It is one reason that wages of unskilled workers have stagnated for the last two decades while salaries of educated workers have risen.

A good way to learn how to think is to read a simple case study and then apply the reasoning and lessons of that case to new situations. This process of reasoning by analogy can help you to analyze new situations that you will encounter in the future, in your work, and in your everyday life. And so we begin . . .

Lisa and Mitch own a shoe store. Lisa runs the women's section and Mitch runs the men's section. Each year as shoe styles change, they rearrange their displays at the front of the store and count the shoes remaining in their inventory back in the storage room. Until a few years ago, Lisa did all the work in the women's section and Mitch did all the work in the men's section. One evening at dinner, they discovered a better way.

GAINS FROM TRADE: A THINKING EXAMPLE

Table 1 shows the number of hours Lisa takes to do each job in her section of the store. She spends 4 hours to take inventory and 3 hours to rearrange the display in the front of the store. She would take just as long to do each task in Mitch's section of the store—4 hours to take inventory and 3 hours to rearrange the display. As she pointed out to Mitch at dinner, it would take her 8 hours to take inventory in *both* sections of the store, or 6 hours to set up the new displays in both sections.

Table 1 also shows how long Mitch takes for those same tasks. Mitch needs 5 hours to count inventory in either section of the store, so it would take him 10 hours to inventory *both* sections. He would take 6 hours to rearrange the display in either section of the store, or 12 hours to rearrange the displays in *both* sections. As Lisa pointed out to Mitch at dinner, she works faster than Mitch does at *each* job; in that sense, she outperforms Mitch at both tasks.

Each year at this time, Lisa spent 7 hours working in her section of the store (4 hours on the inventory and 3 hours on the new display), and Mitch spent 11 hours working in his section (5 hours on the inventory and 6 hours on the new display). Then Mitch had an idea.

Lisa and Mitch decided to trade: Lisa would set up the displays in *both* sections of the store, and Mitch would take inventory in both sections. Now that they trade, Lisa finishes her work in 6 hours (3 hours in each section) and Mitch finishes his work in 10 hours (5 hours in each section). Lisa works 6 hours instead of 7; Mitch works 10 hours instead of 11. *They each* gain 1 hour of leisure time. Even though Lisa outperforms Mitch at *both* tasks, each partner gains from trade.

WHAT ECONOMICS IS ABOUT

Economics is largely about trades—how people produce, trade, and consume goods and services. Economists study the gains that people get from trading; who trades with whom and at what prices; which goods and services people produce, in what amounts, and by what methods (using which inputs and technologies); who consumes how much of each good; who invests how much in which new tools, skills, and ideas.

Table 1 | Lisa and Mitch Gain from Trade

	Hours of Work Required for	
TASK	Lisa	Mitch
Taking inventory in one section of the store	4 hours	5 hours
Setting up a new display in one section of the store	3 hours	6 hours
TOTAL TIME SPENT		
Without a trade	7 hours	11 hours
With the trade	6 hours	10 hours

THE TRADE

Mitch trades 5 hours of his time (taking inventory in the women's section) for 3 hours of Lisa's time (setting up the display in the men's section). Mitch pays 5 hours of his time for 3 hours of Lisa's time; Lisa pays 3 hours of her time for 5 hours of Mitch's time.

Lisa and Mitch both gain 1 hour of leisure time from the trade.

Economics is about the effects of scarcity:

Economics is the study of people's choices and what happens to make everyone's choices compatible.

Because people's choices sometimes conflict with one another, something must happen to make their decisions compatible with one another. If Lisa and Mitch want to finish all the work at the store, *someone* must do each job—their choices must be compatible. They can make their choices compatible by talking with each other and deciding who will do each job.

Compatibility of the decisions of the 6 billion people on earth, or even a few thousand people in a small community, is much harder to achieve. Some people must choose to practice medicine, others to produce food, build houses, teach children, manufacture toys, push the frontiers of science, engineer new products, and entertain. People's career choices must fit together in a compatible way. Similarly, a construction crew building a house may need supplies of wood, bricks, mortar, glass, electrical wire, and other materials. The right kinds of materials, in the right sizes and quantities, must arrive at the construction site at the right times. Hundreds of people around the country work to produce and deliver these supplies. Individual people make their own choices, and these choices and activities must be compatible to construct the house. The compatibility of these individual choices results mainly from billions of voluntary trades.

The trade between Lisa and Mitch is only one of the many trades that people around the world make every day, in every culture, under every kind of conditions. Most involve exchanges of money for goods and services; some involve formal contracts written by lawyers; others involve simple promises between friends. People trade to improve their own situations in life.

Trades generate jobs, and they change the jobs that people do. The trade between Lisa and Mitch created an inventory job for Mitch and a display job for Lisa. Trades create incentives for people to improve their skills, their knowledge, and their tools. They provide the driving force behind increases in material standards of living. People today live in vastly better material conditions than did people 100, or 1,000, years ago because of the effects of voluntary trades.

WORLD: 6 billion people; Production of goods and services—$36 trillion; Average income—$6,000 per person. USA: 270 million people; Average income—$32,000 per person.

Today's average American is twice as rich as the average American 40 years ago (even *after* adjusting for price increases since then). If economic growth continues at this rate, by 2040, income per person in the United States will double again, to about $64,000 per person (higher than that if prices increase).

The logic of choices and trades applies to many types of questions. The following sections introduce a few important topics of economics.

Poverty, Wealth, and Growth

What makes our material standard of living rise over time? The average American today is twice as rich as 40 years ago. Total output of goods and services *per person* in the United States is currently about $32,000 per year. Will it double to about $64,000 over the next 40 years of your life? Can you expect to be much richer than your parents and grandparents?

Why do countries like the United States, Japan, and Germany produce so many more goods and services per person than countries like Bangladesh and Ethiopia? Why do 36 million people in the United States, including 14 million children, live below the government-defined poverty line (about $16,000 per year for a family of four)? Why does nearly one-fourth of all U.S. children under 6 years old live in families with incomes below that poverty line? What can governments do about poverty? Why do many highly educated and hard-working people earn below-average incomes, while some sports stars, entertainers, and business executives earn millions of dollars each year? How much will *you* earn and how will your future income depend on the choices you make starting today?

Production and Its Composition

What leads our economy to produce enough food and housing for us? Why do we produce millions of video games and several billion ounces of soft drinks? Why do we produce about $32,000 per person in goods and services rather than half that amount or twice that amount? Why do about 130 million Americans hold paid jobs outside the home? Why are 6 million unemployed? What goods or services will you provide in the economy?

Even average people in the United States and other rich countries have material standards of living vastly greater than those of the rich in previous centuries. Billions of people live in poor countries that produce, on average, only a few hundred dollars worth of goods and services per person each year.

The average Bangladeshi is only slightly richer now than 100 years ago. People in some countries, such as Ethiopia, Madagascar, Mozambique, and Zambia, are poorer today than they were several decades ago.

Income, Spending, and Their Composition

Who gets which of the goods and services worth $32,000 per person that are produced each year in the United States? Why? How does *production* of goods and services translate into people's *incomes?*

What affects the amount of money that you and other people spend on food, housing, and other goods and services? What happens when people decide to spend more money and save less, or to save more and spend less?

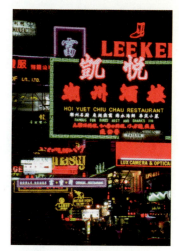

Other fast-growth countries in the last half of the 20th century include Hong Kong, South Korea, Singapore, and Taiwan.

Government Policies and World Conditions

How do government economic policies—taxes, regulations, and spending—affect your life? How about economic events in Russia, China, Japan, Mexico, and other countries? What can the government do about unemployment, poverty, the environment, and other economic problems? What *should* it do?

In the United States, a Typical ...	Earns about ...
Family with two married adults working for pay	$58,000 per year
Married couple with only one person working for pay	$34,000 per year
Adult male living alone	$24,000 per year
Adult female living alone	$15,000 per year

R e v i e w   Q u e s t i o n s

1. Define *economics*.

2. *Approximately* how large is the total annual output of goods and services per person in the United States? *Approximately* how many years ago was the average American only about half as rich as today?

3. List at least four questions about economic topics.

Thinking Exercises

4. Change the numbers in the example of gains from trade in the following way: Assume that Lisa takes *6 hours* (rather than 4 hours) to complete an inventory count. Then Table 1 changes to:

Hours of Work Required for:	Lisa	Mitch
Taking inventory in one section of the store	6 hrs	5 hrs
Setting up a new display in one section of the store	3 hrs	6 hrs

(a) How much would Lisa and Mitch each gain from a trade in which Lisa sets up displays in both sections of the store and Mitch takes inventory in both sections?

(b) How would your answer to part (a) change if Lisa took 10 hours to count inventory in one section of the store?

5. Change the numbers in the example of gains from trade in the following way: Assume that Mitch takes 2 hours (rather than 5 hours) to count inventory in one section of the store. Then Table 1 changes to:

Hours of Work Required for:	Lisa	Mitch
Taking inventory in one section of the store	4 hrs	2 hrs
Setting up a new display in one section of the store	3 hrs	6 hrs

(a) How much would Lisa and Mitch each gain from a trade in which Lisa sets up displays in both sections of the store and Mitch takes inventory in both sections?

(b) How would your answer to part (a) change if Mitch took 1 hour to count inventory in one section of the store?

6. Review your list of questions from Question 3, and explain how the answers to these questions could affect your life.

SCARCITY AND OPPORTUNITY COST

Most of the goods that people want are scarce. People face tradeoffs. They cannot have everything they want—they can have more of one thing only by accepting less of another. Economists say that a good is *scarce* (or *limited)* when people would like to have more than the total available quantity. Tangible products like videotapes, services like haircuts, natural resources like oil and human creativity, and more abstract goods like inner peace and friendship—all are scarce. Your time is scarce. Space on earth is scarce. Goods that are *not* scarce are free goods. Air is a free good, though *clean* air is sometimes scarce. Scarcity requires people to make choices. How will you spend your limited income? How will you spend your time today? How will you spend your life?

Before reading further, ask yourself "What would I do with my extra time if I decided not to read this book?" Whatever you would choose to do—whatever you sacrifice by spending your time to read this book—is your *opportunity cost* of reading this book.

> Your **opportunity cost** of something is the value of whatever you must sacrifice to obtain it.

Every scarce good or activity has an opportunity cost. This is a basic principle of economics: The cost of any action is its opportunity cost.

Each week, millions of people nationwide carefully sort their trash, putting, say, cans in one container, bottles in another, newspapers in a third. Most people feel good about recycling, convinced that they are helping the planet, and their communities, by conserving resources and saving landfill space.

What they're also doing, though, is taking money away from health care and other basic services. As experts in municipal government and garbage disposal point out, the market value of those cans, bottles, and newspapers does not come close to meeting the costs of collecting and processing them.

"Recycling is a good thing, but it costs money," said David Gatton, the senior environmental adviser to the United States Conference of Mayors. "Money that could go for schools is being absorbed by increasing disposal costs."

Source: New York Times

The opportunity cost of money spent on the environment can be money spent on health and education.

Examples of Opportunity Costs

1. Your opportunity cost of buying a T-shirt might be buying a compact disc.

2. Your opportunity cost of 4 years in college might be 4 years at Disney World, where you could work part-time waiting tables, learn about the amusement-park industry without paying tuition, and have a good time.

3. A society can have a cleaner environment, but only by forgoing other values— producing fewer consumer goods that people want, reducing the use of automobiles, or adopting other measures that require people to sacrifice things they want.

Application: Recycling

Recycling often costs cities and towns more money than they would spend to dispose of the recycled materials in landfills. A few years ago, studies showed that recycling plastic, glass, aluminum cans, and paper costs about $20 more per ton than disposal would cost, not including the higher costs of collecting recyclables. Because local governments could have spent that money for other purposes such as health care and education, the opportunity cost of recycling is less government spending on these other services (or higher taxes to pay for them).

As the definition of *economics* suggests, economists study two types of closely related issues:

1. *Decisions*—factors that affect people's choices

2. *Markets*—how people's decisions fit together or *coordinate* with each other to become compatible.

TWO TYPES OF ECONOMIC ISSUES

Scarcity of sophisticated equipment forces decisions about its use.

Decisions

Goods have opportunity costs because they are scarce, and these opportunity costs require you to make decisions. You must decide whether to watch more television or go to sleep, whether to eat dessert, whether and when to get married or have children, whether to put a hotel on Marvin Gardens or spend the cash for another house on Boardwalk, whether to keep what you have or trade it for what's behind the curtain, whether to major in economics or engineering, and whether to keep reading this book.

Opportunity costs affect people's incentives, and their incentives affect their decisions. One issue in economics involves the study of incentives and decisions—how people's tastes and opportunities affect their decisions.

EXAMPLES

1. *Personal decisions on spending money* Is it cheaper to buy or rent? Should you repair your old car or buy a new one?

2. *Personal decisions on spending time* Should you go directly from college to business school, or work for a few years first? Should you become a lawyer or an engineer?

3. *Business decisions* Should a business upgrade its equipment? Hire more workers? Cut prices to attract more customers?

4. *Government/social decisions* How do environmental regulations affect decisions of automakers? How do government welfare programs affect people's decisions to work? How do they affect decisions on having children?

Markets to Coordinate Decisions

Every day, people buy corn from Iowa, clothes from New Jersey made from cotton grown in Texas, and televisions from Japan. They make products using parts from distant countries, and they ship their finished products across the country and around the world. People seldom stop to think how amazing this activity is. Although no one directs the economy, the activities of billions of people—all making their own decisions—fit together.

What would life be like if you had to produce all of your own food, your own shelter, and all of the other goods you use? Even with access to every book ever published on modern technology, no single person could make many of the goods available in our economy. Millions of people would die if food, medical supplies, and energy for heat stopped flowing from around the world into the cities where they live. Few people ever pause to worry about this prospect, though. Most never doubt that stores will continue to offer goods for sale. Shoppers buy all kinds of goods without knowing who made them or how. Meanwhile, people around the world are working right now to produce goods for others they have never met, who speak different languages and practice different cultures in places they will never go. How do all these people know which goods to produce and how much? How do they know where to ship the goods? These questions lie at the heart of economics. Although the details of the answers vary across societies and situations, they almost always involve competition for scarce resources, usually based on the market process.

Competition

Not every team can win. Not everyone can be first in line, use the tennis court at noon, or live in a beachfront house. When people, businesses, or sports teams try to get something that not all of them can have, they compete. Scarcity inspires competition, the process by which people try to get scarce goods for themselves.

Competition takes many forms. Sports teams compete for a scarce good—victory. Students compete for grades and honors, and later for good jobs. Workers compete for promotions. Stores compete for customers. Cities compete for tourists and new businesses. People compete for attention and affection from others.

In a common form of competition, business firms compete for customers by trying to offer the most desirable goods and services on the best terms (such as the lowest price or most flexible payment schedule). Colleges, for example, compete for students by offering attractive campuses, strong academic programs, interesting features of nonacademic life for students, and scholarships that reduce costs for students who might not otherwise attend. Restaurants compete by offering enticing combinations of price, food quality, selection, service, atmosphere, and convenience.

When two sports teams compete, one wins and one loses. But the *process* of competition provides entertainment to people. When two business firms compete for your patronage, one firm may win your business while the other loses it. But the *process* of competition provides you with better goods at lower prices.

Advice
Don't make the common mistake of thinking that competition always creates a winner and a loser. Remember that *both* sides win in a voluntary trade—as Lisa and Mitch did.

Market Process

Economists use the term *market* for the activity of people buying and selling goods. For example, the real-estate market refers to the activities of people trying to buy and sell houses. The term *market process* refers to the coordination of people's economic activities.

Adam Smith, an 18th-century philosopher regarded as the founder of modern economics, pointed out two important features of the market process:

1. When people trade voluntarily, all parties expect to benefit.

2. Because people trade, each person's actions affect other people. Even selfish actions often help other people.

The first point observes that people expect to benefit from a trade, or else they would not trade. This point is obvious, but it is still important to remember.

Smith's second point is more subtle. Think of a baker who cares only about his own income. The baker can spend his time baking either bread or cakes, but which should he bake? If his customers want bread, it would be foolish to bake mostly cakes; he could earn more money by baking bread. Even though he cares only about his own income, he has an incentive to bake the goods that customers want most, measured by how much those customers are willing to pay. Though the baker acts from a selfish motive, the market process gives him an incentive to help his customers by producing the goods that those customers want most.

In his landmark book, *The Wealth of Nations,* published in 1776, Adam Smith explained:

> It is not from the benevolence of the butcher, the brewer, or the baker that we expect our dinner, but from their regard to their own interest. We address ourselves not to their humanity but to their self-love and never talk to them of our own necessities but of their advantages.

Through voluntary trades, each person helps others when he attempts to help himself. Even in acting selfishly, a person is often "led by an invisible hand to promote an end which was no part of his intention." That unintended end is to help other people. Smith pointed out that, "By pursuing his own interest he frequently promotes that of society more effectually than when he really intends to promote it."

The market process is an example of a *self-organizing system.* A self-organizing system creates a complex pattern from simple rules, without any central direction. Biologists have studied self-organizing systems of mutation and reproduction. Similar concepts apply to artificial intelligence, ecology, and traffic flows. Certain computer algorithms, called *genetic algorithms,* exploit the power of self-organizing systems. The Web page for this textbook can direct you to more information on self-organizing systems (and to sites where you can play the simulation game Life, which was at the forefront of the science of artificial life). This book concentrates on one such system—the market process. As economist Friedrich Hayek said, coordination by the market process creates a "spontaneous order" that is "the result of human action but not of human design."

The market process coordinates people's economic actions by providing them with incentives to do things that benefit others. A story written as the autobiography of a pencil demonstrates the remarkable coordination of activities that arises from the market process.[1] A pencil is a simple good, but making one from scratch would be difficult. Pencils are made because the market process coordinates the activities of many people, fitting them together for a purpose. Some people grow trees and cut them for wood. They use saws, axes, motors, and ropes made by others. They transport the cut logs to a mill using equipment made by a third group of people. Other people convert the logs into slats at the mill, and still others ship the slats to pencil companies. Meanwhile, people in another country mine the graphite (the "lead") for the center of the pencil, and other people transport it to the country where it will be sold. Another group of people mine zinc and copper to manufacture the brass collar that holds the eraser at the top of the pencil. Still other people manufacture that eraser.

People from around the world work together to make the pencil. They do not know one another; few even know that they helped to make a pencil. The pencil was not made because any one person planned the whole operation and directed it from start to finish; the pencil was made because the market process coordinated the activities of many people who live in different lands with different languages, cultures, and religions. They may not understand or like each other. Most of them work mainly to serve their own self-interests. Still, the market process provides them with incentives and coordinates their actions to produce a pencil. The same process operates to produce nearly every good or service you can name.

Adam Smith was thinking about this coordination of the activities of people who don't even know each other, let alone care about each other, when he wrote of an "invisible hand" in the market process.

Property Rights

People can trade only things that they own. As a result, property rights are necessary for the market process.

> **Ownership** means the right to make decisions about a scarce resource (whether and how to use it or to sell it); that resource is the owner's property.

Owners have property rights in all kinds of goods, including land, various products, their bodies, and sometimes their ideas. When people trade, they exchange property rights.

The results of competition depend on property rights. The following example shows one reason why.

Cookie-Jar Economics: A Thinking Example

Contrast two cases, in which four children want to eat cookies while they watch a video:

1. One big cookie jar contains 40 cookies. Each child can take as many as she wants, competing for cookies by grabbing them and eating them. Each child can bake more, but newly baked cookies must go into the common jar.

2. Each child has her own cookie jar with 10 cookies, and she can eat cookies only from her own jar. Each child can bake more cookies and put them into her own jar.

---

[1]Leonard E. Read, "I, Pencil: My Family Tree as Told to Leonard E. Read," *The Freeman,* December 1958.

In the first case, no single child *owns* the cookies. As a result, they are likely to eat all the cookies quickly. No child has an incentive to leave cookies in the jar to save for later, because she knows that any cookies she doesn't take and eat now will be eaten by the other children. If a child bakes more cookies, the other children are likely to eat most of them, leaving her with little incentive to bake more.

In the second case, each child *owns* her cookies. As a result, she has an incentive to eat the cookies slowly to make them last throughout the video. Further, any child who bakes more cookies gets them all, providing a stronger incentive to bake more. Ownership provides incentives to conserve resources, and to create more goods.

This simple example illustrates a principle that applies to competition everywhere. One important application concerns fishing. Because no one *owns* the fish in the oceans, competition gives people an incentive to overfish and deplete the waters. As the example shows, property rights provide incentives for people to maintain and conserve scarce resources. When no one owns a lake or stream, few people have sufficient incentives to prevent its pollution. In contrast, the owner of a lake or stream that is private property has an incentive to care for it to maintain its value. Water pollution has not been a serious problem in Scotland because people own streams there. Forests around the world have been destroyed because no one owned the trees that were cut, so no one had an incentive to balance the gains from maintaining the forests with the gains from harvesting the wood and replenishing the forests.

Laws and government regulations often limit property rights, restricting owners' choices about whether and how to use their property. Various laws limit property rights by prohibiting people from opening retail businesses (even on land they own) in certain areas, taking illegal drugs (into their own bodies), or selling medical advice (their own ideas) without licenses. Taxes on money that people earn also limit their property rights, because they cannot keep all the money for which they sell their labor services. To see the effects of this limitation, look back at the trade between Lisa and Mitch described at the beginning of this chapter. Suppose the government imposes a $10 tax on their trade: If Lisa and Mitch trade, they must *each* send a $5 tax payment to the government. Lisa and Mitch must now decide whether the trade is worthwhile. If they trade, each gains an hour of leisure time and loses $5. As a result, they may decide *not* to trade. They may prefer to sacrifice the gains from trade (and spend more time working) to avoid paying the tax. As you study this book, you will encounter many examples that show how property rights play an essential role in the market process.

Review Questions

7. What is an opportunity cost? Give an example.

8. Who wrote *The Wealth of Nations* and what important point did it make?

9. What was the point of the pencil story?

10. What was the point of the cookie-jar example?

Thinking Exercises

11. (a) What is your opportunity cost of attending this economics course?
  (b) What is your opportunity cost of attending college?
  (c) What was your opportunity cost of the last meal you ate?
  (d) What is society's opportunity cost of producing pizzas?

12. The beginning of this chapter discussed a trade between Lisa and Mitch.
    Look back at Table 1 and identify:
    (a) Lisa's opportunity cost of taking inventory in one section of the store
    (b) Lisa's opportunity cost of setting up a new display in one section of the store
    (c) Mitch's opportunity cost of taking inventory in one section of the store
    (d) Mitch's opportunity cost of setting up a new display in one section of the store

13. List five trades you have recently made. Explain your gains from the trades and
    the gains to the people with whom you traded.

Conclusion

Some important issues in economics include:

▶ What creates wealth, causes poverty, and leads
  to differences in people's incomes?

▶ What affects the prices of goods and services?

▶ What affects the amounts of money that people
  spend and save, how they spend money, and the
  quantities of goods and services that the economy produces?

▶ What affects business costs, business profits, and
  job opportunities for workers?

▶ How do government policies affect the economy?

Gains from Trade: A Thinking Example

People gain from trades, as Lisa and Mitch gain in the
shoe-store example. They gain even when one person outperforms the other person at every task.

What Economics Is About

Economics studies people's choices and what happens to
make everyone's choices compatible. What goods do people produce? How? How much do they produce? What do
they trade and at what prices? How much do they gain from
their trades? Who consumes how much of which goods?

These key questions lead to important issues of wealth and
poverty, economic growth, and government policies.

Scarcity and Opportunity Cost

Every scarce good has an opportunity cost. Your opportunity cost of a good is the value of whatever you must
sacrifice to obtain it.

Two Types of Economic Issues

Economics concerns two types of issues: decisions and
their coordination. Opportunity costs affect people's incentives and decisions. Markets coordinate people's decisions
through a process of competition and voluntary trades.
That market process in turn affects opportunity costs, incentives, and decisions.

When people trade voluntarily, they expect to benefit. The market process can lead people pursuing only
their own interests to do things that help others. Adam
Smith described the market process in *The Wealth of
Nations* with a metaphor: People acting in their own self-
interest are "led by an invisible hand" to help others.

Because people can trade only things that they own,
property rights are necessary for the market process to
operate. Limits on property rights affect the outcomes of
the market process.

Key Terms

economics   opportunity cost   ownership

Problems

14. Read the news article, "Clashing Priorities: Cancer
    Drug May Save Many Human Lives—At Cost of
    Rare Trees," and explain how its topic relates to
    scarcity and opportunity costs.

15. Comment on this statement: "The opportunity cost
    of AIDS research is cancer research."

16. What is the opportunity cost of:
    (a) Getting married
    (b) Freedom of speech
    (c) A law prohibiting college-age students from
        drinking alcohol
    (d) A policy to reduce global warming
    (e) The war on illegal drugs

IN THE NEWS

Clashing priorities: Cancer drug may save many human lives—at cost of rare trees

That angers conservationists, who say taxol extraction endangers the prized yew

Right now, medical researchers say, the only way to produce quickly all the taxol that is needed for treatment and testing would be to chop down tens of thousands of yews. And conservationists are successfully opposing any large-scale sacrificing of the tree, which grows in the ancient forests that are refuge to the endangered Northern spotted owl and other wildlife.

"This is the ultimate confrontation between medicine and the environment," says Bruce Chabner of the National Cancer Institute, sponsor of the studies. "It's the spotted owl vs. people. I love the spotted owl, but I love people more."

Source: The Wall Street Journal

Opportunity costs can create political conflicts.

(f) Protecting children from pornography on the Internet

(g) Preventing terrorists from acquiring chemical, biological, or nuclear weapons

17. Explain how the market process can lead people who act out of selfish interests to do things that help others.

18. What is the "invisible hand" in economics?

19. Explain how limitations on property rights can lead people to waste scarce resources.

20. Explain how a tax can interfere with people's incentives to gain from a trade.

21. A baker is willing to bake a cake if he can sell it for at least $6 (to cover the costs of ingredients, the use of his oven, and his time and effort). A customer is willing to pay $10 for a cake.
    (a) Would some trade help both the baker and the customer? What trade?
    (b) How much do the baker and the customer gain from the trade you proposed in part (a)?
    (c) How would your answer to part (a) change if the government imposed a $2 tax on every cake sold?
    (d) How would your answer to part (a) change if the government imposed a $5 tax on every cake sold?

22. How can someone own a song? How can someone own an idea?

23. Comment on this claim: "People who say that the Gulf War [between the United Nations and Iraq in 1991] cost the United States billions of dollars are wrong. Most of those billions of dollars were spent on military equipment sold by American businesses. The arms manufacturers got money that would otherwise have gone to beer manufacturers, but the United States as a whole did not pay a big cost for the war." What was the United States' opportunity cost of the war?

Inquiries for Further Thought

24. Reread the news article from Problem 14. How do you think our society should make decisions on matters like this? Can you think of any general principles that would apply to all similar kinds of decisions?

25. Do people always benefit from voluntary trades?

Why might voluntary trades leave them worse off rather than better off?

26. Should the government prohibit people from trading some goods or services? Why or why not? Defend your answer.

CHAPTER 2

SOLVING PUZZLES: THE METHODS OF ECONOMICS

In this Chapter...

Main Points to Understand

▶ Positive statements are about what *is*. Normative statements are about what *should be*.

▶ Models represent logical thinking.

▶ Certain fallacies, which appear repeatedly in the media, create errors in logical arguments and interpretations of statistical evidence.

Thinking Skills to Develop

▶ Distinguish between positive and normative statements.

▶ Formulate models to help think about complex issues.

▶ Recognize logical fallacies in news articles and discussions.

A detective creates a logical story of how a crime took place, explaining a suspect's opportunity and motive. A court examines how well available evidence supports that story. A doctor examines a patient's symptoms for evidence to support a medical diagnosis and prescribe treatment. Late at night, a driver stops at the side of the road to look at a map. Where is he?

The detective, the doctor, and the driver have something in common. Each uses a *model*—logical thinking—and seeks evidence to judge the model. The detective's model involves an imaginary reenactment of the crime; the doctor's model involves the logic of biological processes in a human body; the driver's model is his interpretation of the map. Every model leaves something out—the detective's story ignores how long the suspect waited in hiding; the doctor's diagnosis omits the path by which the virus entered the body; the map leaves out the slopes of the roads together with the trees and driveways alongside. Evidence may support the models despite their imperfections. These imperfections may not affect the best course of justice, the best medical procedure, or the best direction to drive.

Economists use models and evidence, too. Like detective work, economics involves logical thinking to solve puzzles and evidence to support that logic.

POSITIVE AND NORMATIVE ECONOMICS

An economist recently told the U.S. Congress:

> Salaries of college graduates have increased, and wages of less-educated workers have stagnated, because of technological changes. Congress should act to curb this increasing inequality by raising subsidies to higher education.

Notice that the economist made two kinds of statements:

1. A statement of *fact:* Technological change has raised salaries of college graduates and kept wages of less-educated workers low.

2. A statement of *values:* Congress should raise subsidies to higher education.

The first statement is either a true or false assertion. It involves facts, not value judgments. It states what *is,* not what *should be.* The second statement is neither true nor false. It represents a person's opinion about what *should be,* so it involves that person's value judgments. Economics is mostly about statements of fact, though people's interest in those facts may arise from controversies over what *should be.*

> **Positive statements** are statements of fact, of what is or what would be if something else were to happen. Positive statements are either true or false.
>
> **Normative statements** express value judgments; they state what *should be.* Normative statements cannot be true or false.

EXAMPLES

Positive Statements	Normative Statements
Drugs can affect your health.	Laws should prohibit drugs.
If drugs were legal, then more people would take drugs.	The country needs a stronger antidrug policy.
A reduction in the corporate income tax would raise investment, but it would also raise the budget deficit.	Government should cut the corporate income tax.

Sometimes no one knows for sure whether a positive statement is true or false, and opinions on it differ. For example, consider this positive statement: Simple forms of life inhabit other planets in our solar system. No one knows (yet) whether this statement is true or false, and scientists have different opinions about it. Someday, perhaps, we will learn who is right. On the other hand, consider this normative statement: Classical music is better than popular music. It is neither true nor false. People disagree about it, but neither side is right or wrong.

Economics as a science involves positive statements about the economy. Knowledge about the economy gained by studying these positive statements can help people make intelligent decisions. For example, positive statements about the effects of international trade on the economy can help us decide whether the government should sign a new trade agreement.

Advice

Some statements in the media combine positive *and* normative components. Others are simply *ambiguous* claims, and need to be more precise to have any *meaning.* Beware of such statements.

You study almost any subject in two ways:

1. Think logically about it.

2. Gather evidence about it.

When economists think logically about an economic problem, they produce economic models:

> An **economic model** is a description of logical thinking about an economic issue. It may express its conclusions in words, graphs, or mathematical symbols.

Logical thinking by itself is not sufficient to reach reliable conclusions about economics; logic needs the support of evidence.

> Economic **evidence** is any set of facts that helps convince economists that some positive statement about the economy is true or false.

Many sciences gather evidence through controlled experiments. Sometimes scientists gather evidence simply by observing nature. Physicists learn about stars and galaxies by observing them and measuring their emissions of radiation; medical researchers learn about diseases by observing differences in their incidence in different societies and applying statistical analysis to draw inferences about those observations.

> **Statistical analysis** is the use of mathematical probability theory to draw inferences in situations of uncertainty.

Economists gather most of their evidence from observation followed by statistical analysis. An economist might examine inflation and interest rates in ten countries over the last 40 years (or the last century) to gather evidence about the connections between inflation and interest rates. This evidence could help the economist decide which of several economic models most effectively portrays the true relationships.

The rest of this chapter discusses economic models and evidence, logical fallacies and statistical fallacies, and how to interpret graphs. Much of the material in this chapter applies not only to economics but to other subjects as well.

Assumptions and Conclusions

Every economic model requires *assumptions* about how people behave. The model works from these assumptions to draw logical conclusions. These conclusions often take the form of "If . . . then . . . " statements that say what will happen *if* someone does something. These conclusions are the *predictions* of the model.[1]

Though you may not realize it, you use models in everyday life. Your models rely on assumptions, and you use them to make predictions. Here are some examples of simple models:

---

[1] A prediction, or the model that generated it, is sometimes called an *hypothesis*.

MODELS AND EVIDENCE

Figure 1 | Model of a Play in American Football

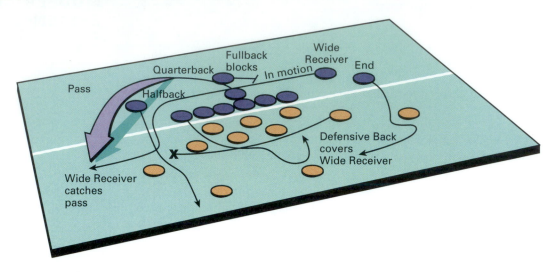

This diagram shows a model of a football play in which a wide receiver goes in motion across the field intending to fool the defensive back and break open to catch a pass.

EXAMPLES

1. "All the other people who interview for the job will *talk* about their experiences and qualifications, but this company wants to find someone different, with innovative ideas. If I prepare a *written summary* of my goals on this job and give it to them at the interview, I will impress them. Then I'll probably get the job offer."

2. "She would want me to kiss her if the time and place were right. She likes walks in the moonlight. If everything goes well tonight, I'll take her for a walk and then . . . "

Figure 1 shows a model of a play in American football. The lines show where players on the offensive team are supposed to go on the play, and where that team *assumes* that the defensive players will go. If these assumptions are correct, the quarterback can complete a pass to the wide receiver. This statement is the model's prediction. If the assumptions are wrong, then one of the defensive players may break up the play.

Each of these examples uses assumptions to derive a prediction or hypothesis. You can think of a model as a daydream based on logical reasoning.

Good and Bad Models

A model is good if it achieves its purpose. The models in the previous examples are good if the actions that they suggest raise the chances of getting the job, the kiss, or the completed pass.

You might think it is easy to find out whether a model is good or bad: simply do what the model says and see what happens. But the predictions of a bad model might turn out to be true (someone might get the job, the kiss, or the completed pass) simply by luck. Also, the predictions of a good model might be wrong by chance. (Perhaps the quarterback throws a bad pass or the intended receiver drops the ball.) No easy test can separate good and bad models. However, a good model is more likely than a bad model to lead to a successful outcome. Economists apply statistical analysis to control for luck and decide how good or bad their models are.

Purposes of Models

Economic models serve three purposes:

1. *Understanding.* A model simplifies an issue to help people understand it.

2. *Prediction.* A model helps people to predict, so they can answer questions like "What will happen . . . " and "What will happen *if* . . . " to resolve complicated, real-life issues.

3. *Interpretation.* A model helps people to interpret data as evidence about positive economic statements.

1. Models Simplify an Issue

Models are simpler than the real-life situations they represent. Many real-life situations are too complicated for the limited abilities of human minds to comprehend. Consequently, we create models—simplified versions of reality—to help think logically about real life.[2] A model assumes that some features of an issue are important to think about while other features are unimportant enough to ignore.

EXAMPLES

Imagine explaining to someone how a car works. You might give a general explanation of how the engine works and ignore details like the chemistry and physics of combustion. This simplified explanation, or model, may do the job. Similarly, suppose you are teaching a friend to play tennis. You cover the most important points about how to swing the racket, ignoring subtle details. Your *model* of tennis ignores these details to help focus your friend's attention on the most important aspects of the game; this model is useful because it helps your friend to understand the game and learn to play it.

2. Models Help Us to Predict

Economists may want to predict next year's inflation rate or the effect of a cut in military spending on unemployment. *Unconditional predictions* answer questions of the form, "What will happen?" *Conditional predictions* answer questions of the form, "What will happen *if* . . . ?" (For example, how would unemployment change if the government were to cut military spending by $20 billion?) Conditional predictions are particularly important because they help people to make good decisions: They tell people the likely results of alternative choices. Economists use models for both conditional and unconditional predictions.

EXPLANATION

If you want to predict your grade in a course, you need a model. Your model might say that because you are smart and motivated to study, you are likely to receive a good grade. (This is an unconditional prediction.) You may be confident that your model is good

Making Smart Decisions
Conditional predictions are necessary for good decisions. How much should you study for your courses? You need conditional predictions to make good decisions about this—to predict how your grades and future opportunities will change if you study more. To make these conditional predictions, you need a *model*. Your model might predict that your grade will rise by one letter, and your future salary by $1,000 per year, if you study an extra 30 minutes every day. You can use such conditional predictions to make good decisions on how much to study.

Economists use models to make conditional predictions about issues such as how employment would respond to a change in government policies. The predictions from these models can help the government make good policy decisions.

---

[2]Models help to economize on a scarce resource—our time and ability.

because you have received good grades in the past when you have been motivated to study.[3] Economists use models to make unconditional predictions about matters such as next year's inflation rate or foreign trade.

3. Models Help Us to Interpret Data as Evidence

Models can suggest which pieces of information to obtain as evidence—which statistical data are relevant for analysis of a particular economic issue. Models also indicate how to use data, clarifying questions like which numbers to add or multiply together to obtain a prediction. If a model makes accurate predictions, this accuracy is evidence that the model is a good representation of reality and that it gives reliable positive economic statements. Inaccurate predictions are evidence that the model is bad.

Evidence can prove that a theory is false by contradicting its predictions. Evidence that is consistent with such predictions can increase confidence in the truth of the theory, but evidence cannot conclusively prove a theory. No matter how much evidence supports a theory, a possibility always remains that new evidence will contradict it.

EXAMPLES

Why is a disease more common in one country than another? Medical researchers need a model to answer this question. Logical thinking about the disease can tell them which information is relevant (such as dietary intake of a particular substance) and which is not (such as exercise and sleep habits). In this way, the model helps researchers choose which data to collect and analyze. The model may also suggest how to analyze the data; perhaps the researchers should examine dietary intake above a threshold level. If the model accurately fits the data, scientific confidence in the model rises. If the model does not accurately fit the data, scientists search for ways to modify the model or construct alternative models.

Why is inflation lower in Argentina than in Brazil? Economists need a model to answer this question. Which economic data on Argentina and Brazil are relevant to explain inflation and which data are not? How should economists use those data? A model may tell the economist to:

1. Check the amount of new money each country's government has printed in the previous 2 years

2. Divide by the total amount of money in each country

3. Subtract the country's economic growth rate (the increase in its output of goods and services) over the last 2 years

These calculations would give the economist a number for each country. The model may predict that these numbers will roughly equal the inflation rates in the two countries. If data confirm the accuracy of this prediction, they provide evidence that the model is good; if not, the data indicate that economists need a better economic model to explain inflation.

Economists apply the "permanent income model" to explain how much money people spend and how much they save. The logical thinking in the model tells economists to collect data on a person's average income over many years to explain that person's spending in any particular month, say April 2001. The model says that two people of the same age, with the same education and average income over many years, will spend about the same amount of money in April 2001, even if one person earns more than the

---

[3]A different model might say that grades are completely random. Evidence from your past experience, showing that your grades are connected to your abilities and the amount of time you study, would be evidence against the random grade model.

other in *that* particular month. (The theory says that income in April 2001 is not very relevant to spending, but average income over many years before that month is relevant.)[4] Economists have found that the permanent income model gives reasonably accurate predictions, though certain inaccuracies have led economists to modify it slightly.

Models Are Artificial Economies

Imagine building 1,000 robots with computers inside them, programmed to direct the robots' behavior in various situations. You design each robot to produce a certain kind of toy, sell these toys to other robots, and spend the money to buy other kinds of toys from other robots. You could program each robot to respond to changes in the conditions it faces; for example, you might program a robot to buy a certain toy only if its price were sufficiently low. If you were to put the robots together in a room and let them interact, you could watch an entire artificial economy made up of robots.

You could change the way the robots behave by changing the computer program. In this way, you could see what happens to unemployment, wages, inflation, and interest rates in the robot economy, or what happens when you change taxes or government regulations. If the robot economy has features that are similar to our human economy, you might conclude that the robot economy is a good model of our real, human economy.

Building these robots would be expensive. Instead, you might use mathematics to describe the projected robot behavior and calculate what would happen in the robot economy. Economists do just that when they build models. Sometimes economists do the mathematical calculations by hand, and sometimes they use computers. The mathematical description of the robots' behavior and the results of their interactions is an economic model. Economic models are artificial economies that an economist invents and writes on paper or programs into a computer.[5]

---

[4]This summary oversimplifies the permanent income model a bit. The person who earns a higher income in April may also be more likely to earn a higher average income in future years, so that person would spend more in April.

[5]Scientists in other disciplines such as physics and biology use similar methods.

Models of Behavior

Economics deals with actions by real people, not robots, so economic models require assumptions about how people behave. Economists usually assume that people behave *rationally*. This term has a very specific meaning in economics.

> **Rational behavior** means that people do the best they can, *based on their own values and information,* under the circumstances they face.

In the words of the Nobel-prize-winning economist Gary Becker, people may be "selfish, altruistic, loyal, spiteful, or masochistic," but they "try as best they can to anticipate the uncertain consequences of their actions" and "maximize their own welfare *as they conceive it.*"[6]

People who dislike your values may call you *irrational,* but there are no "rational" or "irrational" values according to our definition of rational behavior. Even criminals and thoroughly disgusting people may behave rationally. Rational behavior refers to the actions people take to further their own goals, whatever those goals are. A rational person's values need not be materialistic; they may involve caring about family, friends, and poor or oppressed people around the world.

People must act based on limited information about the future results of their actions. How many times have you done something that seemed like a good idea at the time but that you later regretted? If you do what seems best to you at the time, based on your limited information, you are acting rationally, even if you later regret your actions.

People who behave rationally can make mistakes. Rational behavior does not preclude mistakes, but it implies that a person does not repeatedly make the same simple mistake; *rational behavior* means that people learn from past mistakes. It also means that their beliefs about the future reflect whatever information they have.

Most economic models assume that people behave rationally. Economists usually make this assumption with confidence because it has been successful in the past; it is a key part of many good economic models. Some economic models, however, assume *irrational* behavior, particularly in cases where evidence supports that assumption. Economists continually look for new ways to improve their models to make them better tools for understanding, predicting, and interpreting real-life economies.

Review Questions

1. What are positive statements? What are normative statements?

2. What is a model, and what purpose does it serve?

3. What do economists mean by the term *rational behavior?*

Thinking Exercises

4. Develop a model to explain the weather (such as why it rains some days and not others).
   (a) Discuss how your model simplifies the real-world situation to make it more understandable.

---

[6]Gary Becker, Nobel Lecture, "The Economic Way of Looking at Behavior," *Journal of Political Economy,* June 1993, pp. 385–409.

(b) What are some assumptions of your model?

(c) Discuss how your model can help you to predict the weather in various circumstances.

(d) Discuss how your model can help you to interpret data as evidence for or against the model.

Most of this book discusses economic models. Because these models involve logical reasoning, you must understand common logical fallacies to apply the models effectively. Unfortunately, logical fallacies are common in popular economic discussions in the news media and elsewhere. Awareness of these fallacies will help you to identify invalid arguments when you hear them (and help you to improve your own reasoning).

COMMON LOGICAL FALLACIES

Fallacy of Composition

> A **fallacy of composition** occurs when someone says that "what is true for one person must be true for the economy as a whole."

In fact, what is true for one person is *not* necessarily true for society as a whole.

EXAMPLES

Each of the following examples shows something that is true of an individual, but not true of a larger group:

1. When a professor grades exams on a curve, an individual student can increase her grade by studying more, but the class as a whole cannot increase its grades by studying more.

2. An individual at a sports event can see better by standing up than by remaining seated, but spectators as a whole cannot see better if everyone stands.

3. An individual can borrow money, but the world economy as a whole cannot borrow.

Advice
You can find more examples of each fallacy on the Web pages (www.dryden.com) for this book.

Post-Hoc Fallacy

> A **post-hoc fallacy** occurs when someone says that "one event happened before another, so the first event must have *caused* the second event."

In fact, there is no necessary relation between the timing of events and which event causes which.

EXAMPLES

1. Every year, Adrian sends Christmas cards to his friends before Christmas. He would commit the post-hoc fallacy if he concluded that his cards *caused* Christmas.

2. It always gets dark soon after the street lights begin to shine. Some street lights

have automatic timers that turn them on before dark. You commit the post-hoc fallacy if you conclude that it gets dark *because* the street lights shine.

3. Business firms often borrow money to expand their operations. A conclusion that increased borrowing *causes* business expansion would illustrate the post-hoc fallacy. Instead, the desire to expand causes business firms to borrow.

Other-Conditions Fallacy

> The **other-conditions fallacy** occurs when someone says that "if two events always occurred together in the past, they will always occur together in the future."

In fact, two events may occur together under some but not all conditions. When conditions change, incentives may change. When incentives change, past behavior is not necessarily a reliable guide to future behavior.

EXAMPLES

1. All season long, a football team punts on fourth down when it has more than one yard to go for a first down. It would be wrong to conclude that the team will always punt in this situation in the future, however, because conditions may change. If the team is losing by three points near the end of the championship game, it may pass the ball on fourth down with five yards to go. Why? Because conditions have changed: If it punts, it will lose the game, but if it passes the ball, it may win.

2. For many years, the government of a small country collected an extra billion dollars in tax revenue every time it raised the tax on business profits by 1 percent. Recently, the government increased the tax by 1 percent, but its tax revenue did not increase. Why? Because increases in world economic integration made it easier for business firms to move to other countries with lower taxes, and some firms responded to this tax increase by doing so.

STATISTICS

Economists use statistical analysis to draw inferences from economic data. The application of statistical analysis to economics is called *econometrics* or *empirical economics*.

You may have heard that people can lie with statistics. It is important to understand some basic statistical fallacies so that you can identify invalid arguments and correctly interpret statistical evidence.

Statistical Fallacies

Misleading Comparisons

One important statistical fallacy involves misleading comparisons:

> A **misleading comparison** occurs when someone compares two or more things in a way that does not reflect their true differences.

IMPORTANT EXAMPLE: FAILURE TO ADJUST FOR INFLATION

People sometimes compare dollar amounts in different years without adjusting for inflation. Someone may tell you "When I was your age back in 1950, I was happy to work hard for $1 an hour!" This statement may imply that you are lazy if you will not work for $5.25 an hour. But it may be a misleading comparison because of inflation: $1 in 1950 is equivalent to about $6.75 today. Similarly, politicians sometimes say a tax increase or tax cut is "the biggest in history"; this rhetoric is often misleading, because they fail to adjust for inflation.

Every few years, someone claims that a new movie is the highest-grossing movie of all time (the one that has earned the most money); this is usually misleading, because the person seldom adjusts for inflation. In fact, *Gone with the Wind* is the highest-grossing movie of all time after adjusting for inflation. When it was released in 1939, prices were much lower than they are today. After adjusting for inflation, *Gone with the Wind* has earned about $2.1 billion in today's dollars, more than twice the earnings of *Star Wars,* which occupies second place. The appendix to this chapter shows some misleading comparisons on graphs.

Highest Grossing Movies Adjusted for Inflation
1. Gone With the Wind
2. Star Wars
3. Jaws
4. E.T.
5. The Empire Strike Back
6. Titanic
7. Return of the Jedi
8. Raiders of the Lost Ark
9. Jurassic Park
10. Beverly Hills Cop

Source: Entertainment Weekly Online

Selection Bias

A second important statistical fallacy is selection bias:

> **Selection bias** occurs when people use data that are not *typical*, but *selected* in a way that biases results.

EXAMPLES

1. Suppose you want to calculate the average income of rock musicians. If you use data on the average income of rock stars with hit videos on MTV, you would *not* get an accurate answer to your question. Your data would reflect only *successful* rock musicians with (on average) higher incomes. The data would not reflect the lower incomes of typical rock musicians without music videos on MTV. By looking only at the most successful performers, you cannot find out about the average income of all rock musicians.

2. Suppose you want to study the investment advice of stock analysts. You gather data on the results of investment advice given by all stock analysts who have been in business in your city for the last ten years. Did the analysts give good advice to their customers? You might find that the advice was good, on average: People who listened to these stock analysts may have earned more money on their investments (on average) than other people earned. Does this imply that stock analysts give good advice, on average? Not necessarily. The problem is selection bias: You probably lack data on stock analysts who went out of business because they gave less successful advice. Therefore, you would commit a fallacy if you draw conclusions about the average performance of investment advisors from your study.

Discussion An illegal business scheme may help you to understand selection bias. First, buy a large mailing list (a list of potential customers and their addresses) and divide it into two parts. Write to people on the first part telling them that you predict stock prices will *rise* next month. Write to the people on the second part of the list telling them that you predict stock prices will *fall* next month. Next month, throw away the part of your list reflecting an incorrect prediction and keep the part reflecting an accurate prediction. For example, if stock prices fall, throw away the first part of your list, and keep

IN THE NEWS

Data called misleading in rating contraceptives

Most methods can be effective, but bias clouds comparisons.

By Gina Kolata

The available data on the comparative effectiveness of different contraceptives is misleading and only marginally useful in helping people choose which method to use, according to a new study and a growing number of health experts.

Source: New York Times

'Selection Bias' Cited

A universal drawback of the contraception studies, the scientists said, is "selection bias." Women who are most anxious to avoid pregnancy will select methods they believe are most effective, so the group using pills, for example, is always more motivated to use the method correctly than those using contraceptive foams. Even if the foam were just as effective as the pill, more women using foam would become pregnant.

This bias is a problem "because it cannot be corrected in the analysis stage," Dr. Trussell and Dr. Kost reported.

Sample selection bias can occur in any kind of research.

the second part. Divide that list in two parts and repeat. After several months, you will have a small mailing list of people who have seen your predictions come true several times in a row, with no mistakes. You are now ready to charge them a high price for advice (unless they understand selection bias)!

Correlations

When two variables (such as interest rates and inflation) tend to change together, economists say they are correlated.

> Two variables exhibit **positive correlation** if they tend to increase and decrease together. (They move in the same direction.) They exhibit **negative correlation** if one increases when the other decreases and vice versa. (They move in opposite directions.) The correlation of the variables is a number that measures how closely they are related.

EXAMPLES

Education level and income are positively correlated; people with more education tend to have higher incomes. (See Figures A4 and A5 in the appendix to this chapter.) Interest rates and inflation are positively correlated; they tend to rise and fall together. Automobile size and mileage per gallon of gasoline are negatively correlated; larger cars get fewer miles per gallon, on average.

Interpreting Correlations

Economists need models to interpret correlations. A correlation often allows several possible interpretations. For example, many studies have found that married men earn higher wages than single men of the same age and race with the same education and experience. One interpretation states that married men work harder than single men, because they are more motivated. Another interpretation states that employers discriminate against single men; perhaps employers view married men as more reliable employees. Either interpretation might lead a man to believe that he could earn more money by getting married. This move might raise his earnings by motivating him to work harder or by persuading employers of his reliability. But there is a third interpretation of the correlation: Perhaps women tend to marry men whose personal characteristics enable them to earn high wages. If the third interpretation is correct, then a man would not be able to increase his earnings by getting married. No one knows which interpretation is correct. Until more evidence becomes available about the best model to explain this correlation, room for disagreement remains.

Evidence in Economics

Economists work with two main types of data. *Time series* are data on a single person, business, industry, or country over some period of time. For example, data on the average starting salary of college graduates over the last 20 years would be time-series data. *Cross sections* are data on many people, businesses, industries, or countries at one particular time. For example, data on last year's average starting salary for college graduates in each state would be cross-section data. Time-series data provide evidence on which variables change together over time. Cross-section data provide evidence on how people or countries differ from one another at a moment in time.

Most evidence in economics comes from nonexperimental data: data gathered by observation rather than controlled experiments like those carried out in a science laboratory. Economics is not the only science that uses nonexperimental data. Scientists gather nonexperimental data when they study stars and galaxies through telescopes or the behavior of animals in their natural environments. If economists could experiment with the economy, they could change government policies to examine the results, perhaps changing one policy at a time to isolate the separate effects of each policy. Since economists cannot do this, they usually rely on statistical analysis of nonexperimental data to produce evidence for their economic models.[7]

WHY ECONOMISTS DISAGREE

Economists do not always agree with each other about economic issues. Disagreements arise for two reasons:

1. Economists may disagree about the truth of positive economic statements. Sometimes available evidence portrays mixed results for a model, with some evidence supporting the model and other evidence failing to support it. Sometimes there is simply not enough information, and the evidence is too weak to tell whether a model is a good reflection of reality. Economists are not alone; scientists in every field have such disagreements. Disagreements over positive statements can be resolved only by accumulating more evidence.

2. Economists, like other people, disagree about values. Even if they agree about the truth of positive economic statements, they may disagree about normative

---

[7]Some evidence in economics does come from experiments. Economists create small, artificial economies and study their operation. For example, they may pay a group of students to participate in an artificial stock market to examine the behavior of stock prices in the experiment. The economist can manipulate conditions in the artificial economy to see what happens.

IN THE NEWS

Impasse delays proposal to cut diet guidelines

*By Robert Pear
Special to
The New York Times*

WASHINGTON, Oct. 7—
In an unusual move, the National Academy of Sciences announced today that some of the nation's most eminent scientists were in an irreconcilable conflict over proposals to alter the recommended levels of certain vitamins and minerals in the human diet.

Despite "exhaustive deliberation," Dr. Press said, the experts were unable to agree on the interpretation of scientific data and the recommended allowances for several nutrients.

Source: New York Times

In all sciences, experts disagree in some areas.

statements such as what the government *should* do. Economists, like everyone else, want to convince people that they are smart and that their views on normative issues are correct, so, economists who make public statements to the media are not always as honest as they should be. An economist who believes that the government should do something may exaggerate the evidence for positive economic statements that support this opinion. This exaggeration may be deliberate or unintentional, but it can create disagreements with economists who have other values.[8]

Review Questions

5. Explain and give examples of:
   (a) the fallacy of composition
   (b) the post-hoc fallacy
   (c) the other-conditions fallacy
   (d) a misleading comparison
   (e) selection bias

6. Why don't economists always agree with one another?

Thinking Exercises

7. Develop a simple model to explain the spread of influenza (the flu). Contrast the problem of predicting exactly who catches influenza and when each victim catches it with the problem of predicting the average number of influenza cases in a month.

8. By age 30, the average college graduate earns about $10,000 more per year than the average high-school graduate. Does this imply that a person who did not attend college could have earned that much more if he had done so?

A NOTE ON GRAPHS

Economists use many graphs, and you will need to use them to understand this book. The key point to remember is this: *Every graph answers a question.* If you are not completely familiar with the use of graphs, you should read the appendix to this chapter.

Conclusion

Positive and Normative Economics

Positive statements are assertions about facts; normative statements express value judgments.

Models and Evidence

Economic models describe logical thinking about economic issues: They are artificial economies written on

---

[8]Nobel laureate economist Robert Solow put the matter this way: Economists, he said, "feel an apparently irresistible urge to push their science farther than it will go, to answer questions more delicate than our limited understanding of a complicated economy will allow. Some of the pressure comes from the outside. Your friendly financial journalist is frequently on the phone, and nobody likes to say 'I don't know,' or even 'nobody can know.' Some of the pressure comes from the inner drive to push against the frontiers of knowledge, to find answers. When the answer is very faint, you can hear what you want to hear" (*New York Times*, December 29, 1985, p. 2F).

paper or programmed into computers. Evidence about economics consists of facts that help to convince economists that some positive statement is true or false. Statistical analysis uses mathematical probability theory to draw inferences in situations of uncertainty. Economic models can help with understanding, predicting, or interpreting. A model may simplify an economic issue to help us understand it, help us make unconditional or conditional predictions about the economy, or help us interpret data as evidence about positive economic statements.

Economic models require assumptions about behavior. Economists usually assume that people behave rationally, which means they do the best they can for themselves, based on their own values and information, under the circumstances they face.

Common Logical Fallacies

Someone commits the fallacy of composition if he reasons that what is true for one person must be true for the economy as a whole. Someone commits a post-hoc fallacy if she reasons that because one event happened before another, the first event must have caused the second. Someone commits the other-conditions fallacy if he reasons that two events must always be related in the future if they have been related in the past.

Statistics

Economists use statistical analysis to draw inferences from economic data. Positively correlated variables tend to change in the same direction. Negatively correlated variables tend to change in opposite directions. The correlation between them measures how closely the variables move together. Models are required to interpret correlations.

A misleading comparison occurs when someone compares two things in a way that does not reflect their true differences. A common misleading comparison involves comparing dollar amounts from different years without adjusting for inflation. Selection bias occurs when people use data that are not typical, but are selected in a way that biases the results.

Why Economists Disagree

Disagreements can arise among economists for two reasons. They may disagree about the truth of positive economic statements when they lack sufficient evidence to decide which of several economic models best portrays reality. They may also disagree about values, which can create disagreement about normative economic statements.

Key Terms

positive statement	statistical analysis	other-conditions fallacy	negative correlation
normative statement	rational behavior	misleading comparison	correlation
economic model	fallacy of composition	selection bias	
evidence	post-hoc fallacy	positive correlation	

Problems

9. Are the following statements positive, normative, or a combination? Explain your answer.
   (a) "College tuition is too high and needs to be cut."
   (b) "The Yankees and Braves will probably be in the World Series."
   (c) "The distribution of income has deteriorated in the last decade."
   (d) "Foreign competition hurts American workers."
   (e) "Government regulations make it harder for U.S. businesses to compete with foreign sellers."

10. According to the *Bill James Baseball Almanac*, professional baseball players lose ability to hit as they get older (batting averages peak at age 27), yet the batting averages of older players are no lower than those of younger players. Bill James says that this fact illustrates selection bias.[9] Explain why.

11. To start a business, you make up a wild story about how to control whether a newly conceived baby is male or female, and you sell this advice to prospective parents. All customers pay you in advance, but you offer a money-back guarantee: If your procedure does not work, you refund their money.
    (a) How is your business related to selection bias?
    (b) Does your reasoning apply to businesses that sell advice on lottery numbers or sports betting?

---

[9]Bill James, *Bill James Baseball Almanac* (New York: Villard Books, 1987), pp. 60–64.

12. Develop a model to explain the effects of diet on health. Why don't nutritionists always agree about the effects of vitamins and other nutrients on health?

13. Develop a model to explain:
    (a) How the classes that college students choose affect their future salaries
    (b) How the amounts of time that college students spend studying affect their future salaries

    (c) How levels of punishment for convicted criminals affect crime
    (d) How gun controls affect crime
    (e) The average birth rate in a country
    (f) How increased practice time affects performance in sports, music, or the arts. In each case, discuss how you could use statistical data as *evidence* about the quality of your model.

Inquiries for Further Thought

14. This chapter suggested several possible theories to explain why married men earn higher incomes than single men. How would you use statistical evidence to identify the correct theory? If you could perform experiments, what experiments would you choose and why?

15. Do people behave rationally? How would you obtain *evidence* for or against your view?

Appendix: How to Use Graphs in Logical Thinking

Every graph answers a question. You will understand a graph if you understand the question that it answers.

BASIC EXAMPLE

How much money has the average family in the United States earned in recent decades? The answer can be graphed, as in Figure A1.[10] To find the answer to the question, find a year on the graph's horizontal axis, say 1990. Go straight up until you reach the curve, then straight left until you reach the vertical axis. The number on the vertical axis shows how much money an average family earned in 1990: $41,224. You can do the same thing for other years.

Each point on the curve indicates two numbers, a year and an income. Point A in Figure A1 indicates 1990 and $41,224. The two numbers allow each point to answer the question for a particular year.

The year and the income level are variables.

> **Variables** are names for sets of numbers analyzed with a graph or with mathematics.

Every graph measures one variable along the horizontal axis and another variable along the vertical axis.

MISLEADING GRAPHS

Figure A1 shows incomes adjusted for inflation to indicate how much money a family made in each year, measured in 1995 dollars. Adjusting for inflation prevents a misleading comparison; it allows accurate comparisons of family incomes in different years.

---

[10] The graph shows *median family income*, meaning that half of all families earn more and half earn less than the indicated amounts. The numbers are adjusted for inflation by expressing all incomes in 1995 dollars.

Figure A1 | Median Family Income Adjusted for Inflation

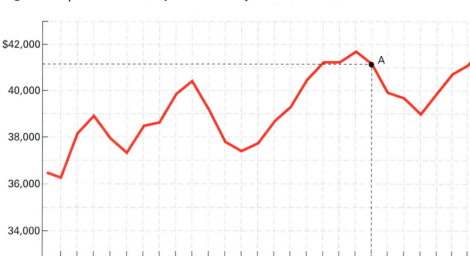

1. Find a year.
2. Go straight up until you hit the curve. Make a dot at that point (Point A).
3. Go left until you hit the Y-axis, indicating the average family income for that year: $41,224.

Source: Current Population Reports, Series P-60, No. 184, updated by author.

Figure A2 shows a graph that makes a misleading comparison among different years, because it does *not* adjust for inflation. Figure A3 shows that a typical good worth $10.00 in 1998 cost only about $8.15 in 1990, $5.14 in 1980, and only about $2.42 in 1970; prices have roughly quadrupled since 1970. Figure A2 misleads, because it fails to adjust for this inflation. Notice that the correct graph (Figure A1) conveys a very different impression than the misleading message of Figure A2.

A More Subtle Point

Figure A1 can mislead, as well, but for another, more subtle reason: The typical family of today includes fewer people than families did in the past. Median income *per person* has risen faster than Figure A1 suggests. If you remember to think critically about statistical evidence such as misleading graphs, you can protect yourself against mistakes in personal and business decisions, and you will improve your analysis of social and political issues.

Figure A2 | Median Family Income Not Adjusted for Inflation

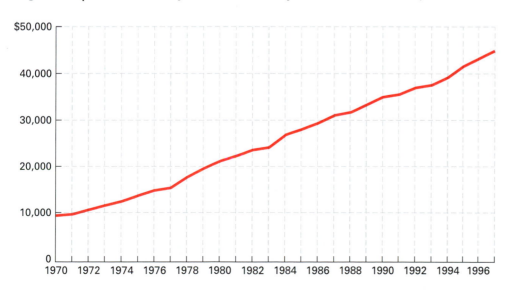

Average family income measured in dollars has risen over time, but this diagram illustrates a misleading comparison. Prices of goods have also risen over time, so families have not become as rich as quickly as the graph implies.

Source: Current Population Reports, Series P-60, No. 184, updated by author.

Figure A3 | Typical Price of a Good Worth $10 in 1998

A typical good that cost $10.00 in 1998 cost only about $8.15 in 1990, $5.14 in 1980, and only about $2.42 in 1970.

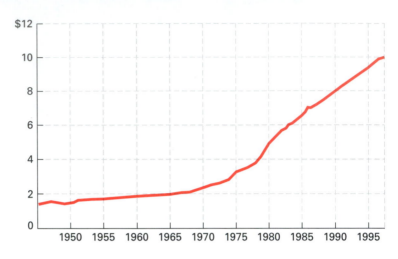

MANY CURVES ON THE SAME GRAPH

When more than one curve appears on a single graph, each curve answers a different question.

> **EXAMPLE**

Figure A4 shows five curves. The highest curve answers the question, "How much money can an average person with some graduate school education expect to earn at different ages?" The second-highest curve answers the question, "How much money can an average college graduate expect to earn at different ages?" The other three curves repeat the

Figure A4 | Earnings of Full-Time Workers

Each curve tracks income for a certain level of education.

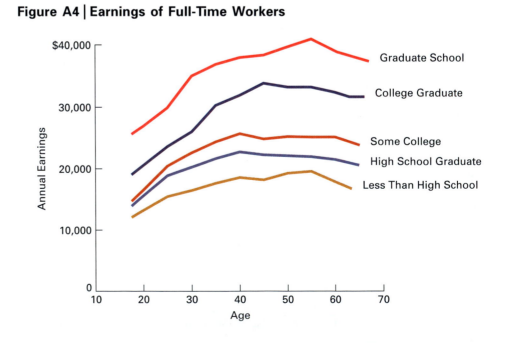

Figure A5(a) | Earnings of Males with Full-Time Jobs

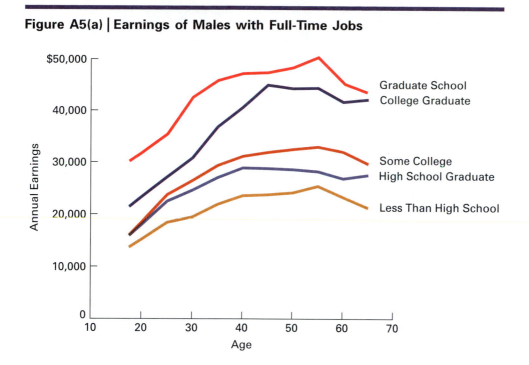

question for people with some college, high-school graduates, and people with less education. The horizontal axis measures age and the vertical axis measures income, in thousands of dollars. Figure A4 shows that a person with a college education can expect her income to rise until around age 50, after which it shows a slight decline. The average high-school graduate earns more each year until around age 40, and income falls slightly after that. This graph is adjusted for inflation; you can expect inflation to raise your future *dollar* income above the numbers in the graph.

Figures A5(a) and A5(b) show the same information separately for men and women. Compare these graphs to see that men earn, on average, more than women do.

Figure A5(b) | Earnings of Females with Full-Time Jobs

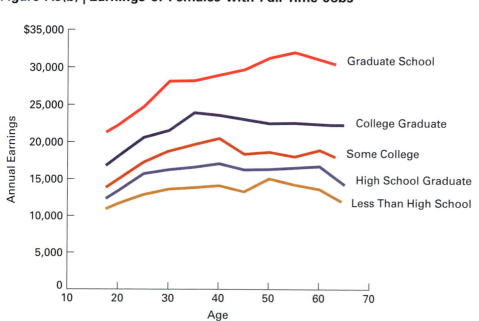

SHIFTING CURVES

Logical thinking with graphs often requires us to shift curves.

> A **shift** in a curve is a change in its position on a graph.

A curve on a graph shifts when a change in conditions changes the answer to the graph's question.

Figure A6 | The Earning Curve Shifts When a Student Goes to College

The arrow shows the shift in the curve.

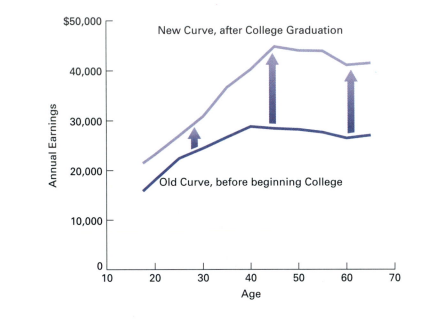

Figure A7 | Shifting a Curve: Reduced Sex Discrimination Raises the Earnings of Women

A fall in sex discrimination would shift the curve upward. (Both curves are drawn for a woman with a high-school education.)

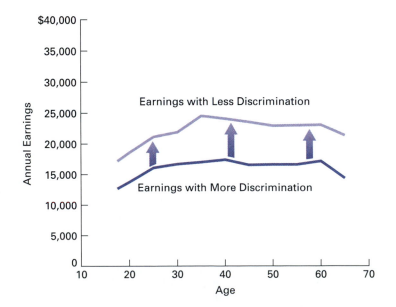

Consider a man who has just graduated from high school. The lower curve in Figure A6 shows the income that he can expect at various ages. Now suppose he goes to college. This decision raises his likely earnings at every age, so it shifts the curve in Figure A6. The curve shifts because a change in conditions (more education) changes the answer to the question, "What income can this man expect over his lifetime?"

Figures A5(a) and A5(b) showed that women earn less (on average) than men of the same age with the same education. Many people blame part of this difference on discrimination against women. If this is true, a fall in discrimination against women would shift the curves upward in Figure A5(b). Figure A7 shows the shift in one of these curves when a fall in discrimination changes the answer to the question, "How does the likely annual income of a female high-school graduate vary with her age?"

SLOPES OF CURVES

Figure A8 shows the answer to the question, "How does a change in time spent studying affect a typical student's grade on a biology exam?" The figure shows a positive correlation between the two variables, indicating that they move in the same direction. More time spent studying correlates with a higher grade. A curve with a positive slope shows the positive correlation between the two variables.

A **positive slope** refers to a shape that runs upward and to the right.

Figure A9 answers the question, "How does the time you have for watching television tonight depend on the amount of time you study?" The curve shows a negative correlation between the two variables, indicating that they move in opposite directions. A curve showing a negative correlation between two variables has a negative slope.

A **negative slope** refers to a shape that runs downward and to the right.

Figure A8 | Relation between Grade and Studying Time

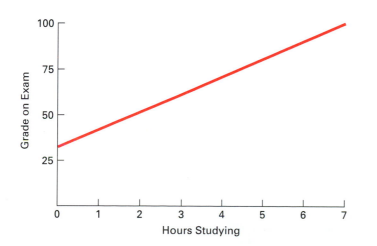

The line has a positive slope.

Figure A9 | More Studying Time Leaves Less Time for Television

The line has a negative slope. How would you choose to spend your time?

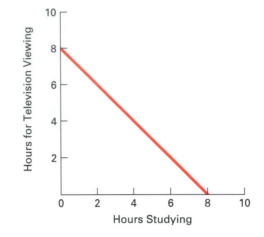

The slope of a curve is a number that measures its steepness:

> The **slope of a curve** is the distance by which the curve goes up or down as it moves 1 unit to the right.

The slope measures how much the variable along the vertical axis changes as the variable along the horizontal axis increases by 1 unit. If the curve rises as it moves to the right, the slope is a positive number; if it falls as it moves to the right, the slope is a negative number. Increasing numbers indicate ever steeper slopes.[11]

Figure A10 | Calculation of Slope

As you study one more hour, your likely grade rises by 2 points, so the slope of the line is 2.

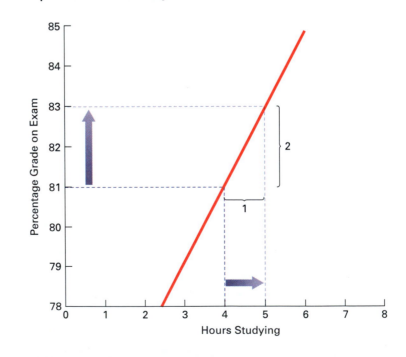

---

[11]Lines with slopes of 10 or −10 are steeper than lines with slopes of 3 or −3.

EXAMPLES

Figure A10 shows a line with a slope of 2; for every additional hour you study, your likely grade rises by 2 points. Figure A9 showed a line with a slope of −1; for every additional hour you spend studying, you lose an hour in front of the television.

The slopes of the curves in Figures A5(a) and A5(b) change at different ages. The curves are steeper for younger people than for older people. The slopes are positive at most ages: Increases in age usually lead to increases in earnings. The slopes are negative for older people, though; at advanced ages, further increases in age reduce earnings.

Logical thinking sometimes involves evaluating areas in regions of graphs.

AREAS

> An **area** of some region in a graph is a number that measures the size of that region.

Here are two formulas to calculate areas:

1. The area of a rectangle equals its base times its height. In Figure A11, the base of the shaded rectangle is 5 and the height is 6, so the area is 30 (5 times 6).

2. The area of a triangle is ½ the area of an associated rectangle. To calculate the area of a triangle, follow these steps:
   (a) Make a rectangle out of the triangle; one side of the triangle must become a side of the rectangle.
   (b) Calculate the area of the rectangle.
   (c) Divide by 2 to get the area of the triangle.

Figure A11 | Area of a Rectangle: The Base Times the Height

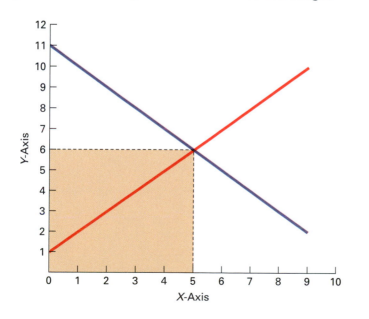

The base of the shaded rectangle is 5 and the height is 6, so the area is 5 times 6 or 30.

Figure A12 | Area of a Triangle

To calculate the area of Triangle A: *First,* make a rectangle out of Triangles A and B. *Second,* find the area of Rectangle AB. Its base is 5 and its height is 5, so its area is 5 times 5, or 25. *Third,* divide by 2 to get the area of Triangle A: 25/2 = 12½.

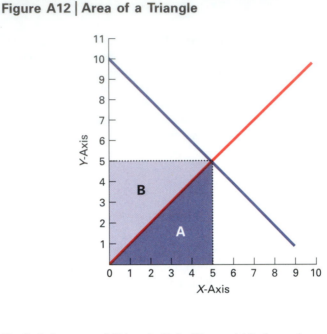

To find the area of Triangle B in Figure A12, form the rectangle with Areas A and B. This rectangle has a base of 5 and a height of 5, so the area of the rectangle is 25 (5 times 5). Dividing by 2 gives the answer 12½ for the area of Triangle B.

You will use these formulas later in this book for calculations such as how much money people pay in taxes and the losses in economic efficiency from restrictions on international trade.

Conclusion

Every graph answers a question. When a change in conditions changes that answer, the curve in the graph shifts. Curves with positive slopes show that variables move in the same direction. Curves with negative slopes show that variables move in opposite directions. Steeper curves have larger slopes (measured in absolute value). The area of a region in a graph measures the region's size.

Key Terms

variable   positive slope   slope
shift   negative slope   area

Problems

A1. Draw a graph to show the profits that U.S. manufacturing businesses earned after taxes on each dollar's worth of sales between 1973 and 1996.

A2. What makes a curve in a graph shift?

A3. Draw graphs of curves with:
   (a) Positive slope
   (b) Negative slope
   (c) Slope equal to 3
   (d) Slope equal to -2
   (e) Changing slope

A4. (Harder Problem) How might you use data to analyze how much the curve in Figure A7 would rise if discrimination against women were eliminated?

	Profit after Taxes per Dollar of Sales
1973	5.6 cents
1974	5.5
1975	4.6
1976	5.4
1977	5.3
1978	5.4
1979	5.7
1980	4.8
1981	4.7
1982	3.5
1983	4.1
1984	4.6
1985	3.8
1986	3.7
1987	4.9
1988	6.0
1989	5.0
1990	4.0
1991	2.4
1992	0.8
1993	2.8
1994	5.4
1995	5.7
1996	5.8
1997	5.7

FUNDAMENTAL TOOLS

LET'S MAKE A DEAL: THE GAINS FROM TRADE

In this Chapter...

Main Points to Understand

▶ The *production possibilities frontier* shows what the economy *can* produce.

▶ When people have different opportunity costs, they can gain from trade and consume amounts that would be impossible without trade.

▶ Different economically efficient situations are possible, with different distributions of income.

Thinking Skills to Develop

▶ Recognize limits to opportunities, and tradeoffs among opportunities; distinguish between limits and choices.

▶ Find trades in which all participants gain; recognize the gains from trade and how people share those gains.

▶ Understand why fairness is a subtle concept, and that people differ on its meaning.

Whatever you do, you face limits—constraints on your time, your spending ability, your opportunities. You can expand some of those limits. You can invest in skills that enable you to earn more money or save money to expand your future spending options. Almost everyone expands their limits, almost every day, through trade. You probably don't make your own clothes—you trade your work effort for money to buy them. You probably don't grow your own food, and you probably didn't build your own shelter. Like nearly everyone, you trade for these things. Your life would be very different without these trades. Trades vastly expand your limits and create new opportunities.

Whenever you voluntarily trade with someone, you expect to gain. The other person also expects to gain, of course. Some gains from trade are easy to understand: You have cookies and your friend has an apple, but you want the apple and your friend wants the cookies, so you trade. Other trades create much less obvious benefits, however, and this chapter explains them.

Some trades, like the cookie-apple trade, give people more of what they want by reshuffling goods that we already have. Other trades, as in the shoe-store example of Chapter 1, increase the total amounts of goods available.

Historically, standards of living rose when people started to trade, and today trade plays a larger economic role than ever before. People trade their services as carpenters, accountants, lawyers, teachers, or doctors for meal preparation and cleanup, child care, and other goods and services that people once provided mainly for themselves. If you are like most people in the United States, you spend more money on meals at restaurants than on meals at home. International trade involves a growing fraction of world output, as a single global economy develops. While the term *international trade* often evokes images of travel and excitement, its principles boil down to the basic ideas of this chapter.

LIMITS AND POSSIBILITIES

Everyone faces limits. Your time each day is limited; your budget is limited. The time you spend studying reduces the time you can spend on other activities. When you spend more on pizzas, you reduce the money you have available for other things.

Figure 1 shows a graph of your limited time. You have 24 hours every day, and every hour you spend studying leaves you with one hour less for other activities. Each point on the downward-sloping line shows one possible way to spend your time. You can choose Point A, at which you study for 2 hours and spend 22 hours on other activities. Or you can choose Point B (4 hours studying and 20 hours on other things), or Point C (8 hours studying and 16 hours on other things), or any other point on the line. But you cannot choose Point D, which indicates 8 hours of studying and 20 hours of other activities every day. Point D and other points above the line are impossible. The line shows all your possibilities.

Figure 2 shows a person's limited spending power on a graph. The graph applies to a person with $10 available to spend in a week, who can buy sodas for $1 each or rent videotapes for $2 each. Every dollar spent on one good leaves the person with $1 less for other goods. If the person spent all $10 on sodas, he could buy ten per week. (This is Point A in Figure 2.) If he spent all $10 on videotape rentals, he could rent five tapes per week. (This is Point B in Figure 2.) The person can choose any other point on the line in Figure 2, such as Point C (6 sodas and 2 videotapes per week). But the person cannot choose Point D, because he cannot afford six sodas and four videotape rentals per week. Point D and other points above the line are impossible. The line shows all the person's possibilities.

Figure 1
Your Limited Time

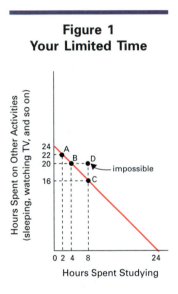

Figure 2
A Person's Limited Budget

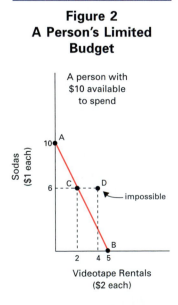

Production Possibilities Frontier

The economy as a whole also faces limits. The production possibilities frontier shows how many goods the economy can produce with its available inputs and technology.

> An economy's **production possibilities frontier,** or **PPF,** graphs the combinations of various goods that it can produce with its limited resources and technology.

Real economies produce millions of goods, and a computer can describe a PPF mathematically. To understand the PPF, imagine an economy that produces only two goods: videotapes and cars. Figure 3 shows its PPF. If the economy uses *all* its resources to produce videotapes, then it can produce 40 million videotapes and no cars. If it uses all its resources to produce cars, then it can produce 5 thousand cars and no videotapes. Alternatively, it can produce various combinations of videotapes and cars. Table 1 shows some of these possible combinations.

Main Facts about the PPF

1. *Scarcity:* The PPF shows the combinations of goods that an economy *can* produce with its current technology and resources—the economy's *possibilities*. Each point

Figure 3 | A Production Possibilities Frontier

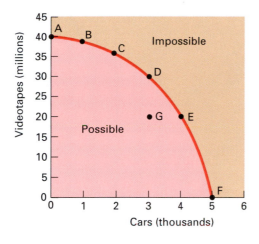

The production possibilities frontier shows the possible combinations of goods that the economy can produce if it uses its resources and technology efficiently. This combination depends on the resources and technology available to the economy, to the PPF shifts when resource availability or technology changes.

Table 1 | An Economy's Production Possibilities

Number of Videotapes Produced (millions)	Number of Cars Produced (thousands)	Point in Figure 3
40	0	Point A
39	1	Point B
36	2	Point C
30	3	Point D
20	4	Point E
0	5	Point F

on the PPF shows one possible combination of goods. All points under the PPF (such as Point G in Figure 3) are also possible. However, because resources are scarce, points above the PPF are *impossible*.

2. *Technical efficiency:* Points *on* the PPF are technically efficient combinations of output.

> **Technical efficiency** means that it is impossible to produce more of one good without producing less of another.

Technical efficiency means that the economy does not waste resources. Points A through F lie *on* the PPF, so each shows a technically efficient combination of outputs. On the other hand, Point G lies *below* the PPF, indicating a technically *in*efficient situation, because the economy could produce additional videotapes without reducing output of cars, or produce more cars without reducing output of videotapes.

1. *Decisions:* People's decisions and government policies determine which point on the graph shows the economy's *actual* output. In that sense, a society chooses some point on the PPF.

2. *Tradeoffs and opportunity costs:* The downward slope of the PPF shows the economy's tradeoff between producing cars and videotapes. The absolute value of the *slope* of the PPF shows how many videotapes the economy must sacrifice to expand production of cars. In other words, it shows the economy's opportunity cost of producing cars.

Everyone faces tradeoffs because of limited time.

Advice

If you don't yet understand why the absolute value of the slope of the PPF shows the economy's opportunity cost of cars, come back to this point after reading the two-student example below, or see the examples and explanations on the Internet site (www.dryden.com).

EXAMPLE

Suppose the economy is at Point D in Figure 3, producing 3,000 cars and 30 million videotapes. If the economy were to increase car production by 1,000 (to produce 4,000 cars altogether), it would have to produce 10 million fewer videotapes (20 million instead of 30 million). The economy would move from Point D to Point E. The slope of the PPF between Points D and E equals 10 million videotapes divided by 1,000 cars, or 10,000 videotapes per car. The economy's opportunity cost of producing a car is 10,000 videotapes.

General Point

The absolute value of the *slope* of the PPF shows the economy's opportunity cost of producing the good on the *X*-axis. In other words, it shows how many units of the good on the *Y*-axis the economy sacrifices when it produces a little more of the good on the *X*-axis.

Shifts in the PPF

The PPF shifts in response to any change in the economy's available resources or technology. The economy's resources include its available capital, labor, education and skills, and natural resources. Technical progress or an increase in resources shifts the PPF outward, as in Figure 4a. An economy's PPF shrinks inward, as in Figure 4b, if it loses resources or if its technology declines.

By expanding the economy's PPF, technical progress or accumulation of resources expands people's *consumption opportunities*. Growth in production increases the goods and services available for people to consume. As the PPF expands, people can consume more.

Application: Economic Growth

Economic growth refers to an increase in the economy's output of goods and services per person. A growing economy's PPF expands faster than its population grows. Economic growth can occur because the economy either gains new resources or discovers better technologies.

The U.S. economy has grown for both reasons. U.S. business capital (such as machines, tools, plants, and equipment) has roughly doubled since 1970 to about $6.3 trillion. (This number is already adjusted for inflation to avoid a misleading comparison with current conditions, as discussed in Chapter 2.) At the same time, U.S. technology has advanced (most visibly in computers, medicine and biotechnology, but also in thousands of other areas).

Figure 5 shows U.S. economic growth over the century from 1890 to 1990, with a prediction for 2010. The U.S. PPF for consumption and investment goods has expanded rapidly over time. Growth in total output of goods and services in the United States and western Europe averaged less than 0.2 percent per year in the years 1500 to 1750. Since that time, economic growth has increased dramatically:

▶ Growth rose to about 1.0 percent per year by 1850.

▶ It accelerated to between 1.0 and 1.5 percent per year between 1850 and 1950.

▶ Growth has continued at about 1.8 percent per year since 1950 (faster on average before 1973 and slower on average since then).

There is a huge difference between the 0.2 percent annual growth in the third quarter of the millennium and the more recent growth of 1.8 percent per year. When the economy grows at 1.8 percent per year, output doubles every 39 years. When the economy

Technological change contributes to economic growth.

Figure 4 | Shifts in a PPF

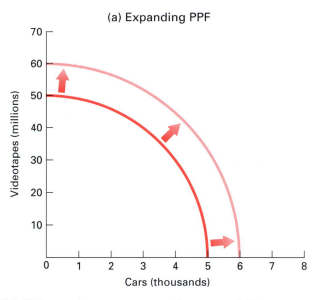

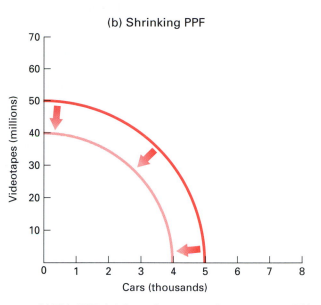

(a) This PPF expands as more resources become available to the economy or as technology improves.

(b) This PPF shrinks as the economy loses resources. This could occur if the economy failed to produce enough new machines and tools to replace those that became worn out. It could also result from an earthquake, a war, or another disaster that destroyed resources.

Figure 5 | Expansion of the U.S. PPF Since 1890

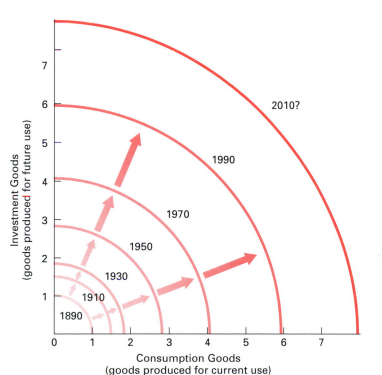

The shifts in the U.S. production possibilities frontier show the expansion of total output per person in the United States, adjusted for inflation. Each PPF represents a different year. Over each 20-year period, the United States has experienced economic growth, raising output to nearly six times the level of 100 years ago. It is now more than double the level of output in 1950, more than 50 percent larger than the level in 1970.

grows at 0.2 percent per year, output takes 350 years to double! Output per person in the United States (and most other developed countries) has more than doubled since 1950. Unfortunately, a few countries have experienced negative economic growth since 1950, with shrinking PPFs.

What happens to the extra goods and services that the economy produces when the PPF expands? Generally, people consume most of them: They wear the clothes, drive the cars, eat the food, and listen to the music. People also invest some of the extra goods they produce: They build new machines, tools, structures, and other new capital equipment.

Review Questions

1. Draw a graph like the one in Figure 2 to show your limited spending power if you have $10 to spend on tea and crumpets, and tea costs $0.50 per cup while crumpets cost $2.00 each.

2. How does a PPF show scarcity? Technical efficiency? Opportunity costs?

3. What causes a PPF to shift in?

Thinking Exercises

4. Explain why the absolute value of the slope of the line in Figure 2 shows the opportunity cost of buying videotapes.

5. Change the numbers in Table 1 so that the economy can produce twice as many cars. That is, change the numbers in the cars column from (0, 1, 2, 3, 4, 5) to (0, 2, 4, 6, 8, 10). Draw the new PPF. How does this change affect the opportunity cost of producing cars?

A FABLE WITH AN ECONOMIC MESSAGE

Once upon a time a brilliant businesswoman built a great factory by the sea, with high walls and tight security to protect the secrets of her new technological breakthrough.[1] Every month, she bought truckloads of grain from Midwestern farmers, and emptied the trucks inside her factory. Every month beautiful automobiles came out of her factory. "What marvelous technology has she discovered," people asked, "to make cars from grain?" Farmers were happy, because they sold more grain. Car buyers were delighted with their additional choices, and many chose the new "cars from grain." Competing car manufacturers resented the new competition, of course, but most people agreed that technological advance is generally good for society as a whole.

One day, government regulators investigated the factory and discovered the truth, which they promptly leaked to the nation's press. The "factory" was an empty shell. Behind its walls, workers exported the grain to foreign countries, using the proceeds to import cars. The miracle "technology" was simply international trade. Instead of putting grain into a machine that turned it into cars, workers put grain on ships, and

---

[1]Steve Landsburg tells a version of this well-known story in his book, *Fair Play: What Your Child Can Teach You about Economics, Values, and the Meaning of Life* (New York: Free Press, 1997), where he attributes it to Professor James Ingram of North Carolina State University.

the ships soon returned filled with cars. The moral: *Trade, like technological change, expands consumption opportunities.* The two-student example that follows will clarify this point.

TWO-STUDENT EXAMPLE:
A KEY EXAMPLE OF GAINS FROM TRADE

International trade, like technological change, expands consumption opportunities.

Two students, Lauren and Steve, move into apartments next door to each other. The apartments are exactly alike, and each needs repairs to its walls and windows. The landlords provide all supplies, so the only cost of fixing the walls and windows is the time involved. Lauren and Steve do equally good work, and neither prefers one task to the other. Each has 12 hours to spend working.

Lauren can fix one wall in 3 hours; she can fix one window in 1 hour. Steve can fix a wall in 2 hours, but he takes 4 hours to fix one window. Table 2 shows the number of hours that Lauren and Steve need for each job.

Because Lauren can fix a wall in 3 hours, she could fix 4 walls in the 12 hours she has available. Alternatively, she could repair 12 windows in those 12 hours. Steve could fix 6 walls in 12 hours, or he could repair 3 windows in that same time. Table 3 shows the number of walls or windows that Lauren and Steve can repair in 12 hours.

Panels (a) and (b) of Figure 6 show Lauren's and Steve's PPFs, which are straight lines. Lauren could fix 12 windows and no walls, or she could fix 4 walls and no windows, or she could choose some combination (such as fixing 6 windows and 2 walls). Steve could fix 3 windows and no walls, or he could fix 6 walls and no windows, or he could choose some combination (such as fixing 2 windows and 2 walls).

A Trade

Without trade, Lauren may choose Point L on her PPF, fixing 2 walls and 6 windows. Steve may choose Point S on his PPF, fixing 2 walls and 2 windows. However, suppose that Lauren and Steve trade: Lauren fixes 3 windows for Steve, and Steve fixes 3 walls for Lauren. After Lauren spends 3 hours to fix 3 windows for Steve, she spends her other 9 working hours to fix 9 of her own windows. After Steve spends 6 hours to fix 3 walls for Lauren, he spends his other 6 working hours to fix 3 of his own walls. Figure 7 shows their trade.

Table 2 | Two-Student Example

Time Required to:	Lauren	Steve
Fix one wall	3 hours	2 hours
Fix one window	1 hour	4 hours

Table 3 | Productivity in 12 Hours

Work Done in 12 Hours	Lauren	Steve
Walls fixed	4 walls	6 walls
Windows fixed	12 windows	3 windows

Figure 6 | Production Possibilities Frontier for Steve and Lauren Together

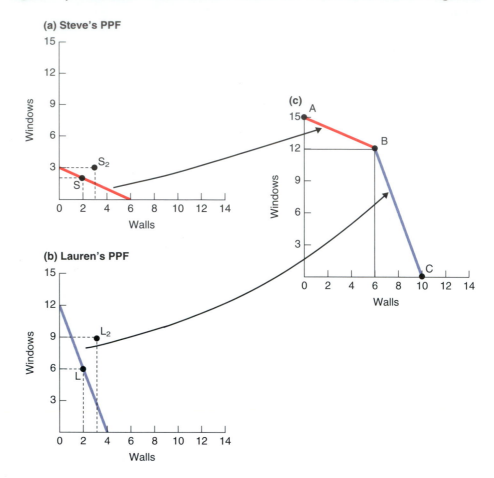

(a) Steve's PPF

(b) Lauren's PPF

(c)

Figure 7 | The Two Students Trade

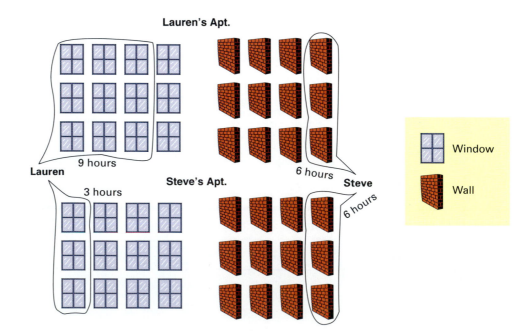

Lauren's Apt.

Lauren — 9 hours

6 hours — Steve

Steve's Apt.

3 hours

6 hours

Window

Wall

This trade places Lauren at Point L_2 in Figure 6b—she ends the day with 3 walls and 9 windows repaired. She could not possibly have reached this point on her own, without trading. Similarly, the trade places Steve at Point S_2 in Figure 6a—with 3 walls and 3 windows repaired. He could not have reached this point on his own. By trading, Lauren and Steve produce more (wall and window repairs) than they could without trading. Trade, like an improvement in technology, expands their possibilities.

Figure 6c shows the *combined* PPF for Steve and Lauren together. If they both work on windows, they repair 15 windows in a 12-hour day (Point A). If they both work on walls, they repair 10 in one day (Point C). If Lauren works only on windows while Steve works only on walls, they fix 12 windows *and* 6 walls in one day (Point B). The combined PPF also shows other possible combinations of repaired walls and windows when Lauren and Steve trade.

Gains from Trade

The trade just described moves Lauren to Point L_2 instead of Point L in Figure 6b. In other words, she gets 3 walls and 9 windows fixed, instead of 2 walls and 6 windows. Lauren's gain from the trade is 1 fixed wall and 3 fixed windows. Similarly, Steve reaches Point S_2 (3 walls and 3 windows fixed) instead of Point S (2 walls and 2 windows fixed), so he gains 1 fixed wall and 1 fixed window from the trade.

In the shoe-store example described at the beginning of Chapter 1, Lisa and Mitch share the gains from trade equally: They each gain one hour of free time from their trade. In contrast, Lauren gains more than Steve from the trade just described.

Trading Resembles Improved Technology

The fable about producing cars from grain made the point that *trade, like technological change, expands consumption opportunities*. The two-student example illustrates this point numerically. Trade allows Lauren and Steve to consume at Points L_2 and S_2, points outside their individual PPFs. This result would be *impossible* without trade or some improvement in technology that expands their PPFs as in Figures 4a and 5.

Opportunity Costs

In 3 hours, Lauren can fix a single wall. If, instead, she spent that time working on windows, she could fix 3 windows. Therefore, her *opportunity cost* of fixing a wall is fixing 3 windows. Similarly, in the time she takes to fix a window (1 hour), she could fix one-third of a wall. So Lauren's opportunity cost of fixing a window is fixing one-third of a wall.

In 4 hours, Steve can fix a single window. If, instead, he spent that time working on walls, he could fix 2 walls. His opportunity cost of fixing a window is fixing 2 walls. Similarly, in the time he would take to fix a wall (2 hours), he could fix one-half of a window. So Steve's opportunity cost of fixing a wall is fixing one-half of a window. Table 4 summarizes these opportunity costs.

Gains from the Trade

If Lauren fixes 3 windows for Steve, and Steve fixes 3 walls for Lauren, then:

▶ Lauren reaches Point L_2 instead of Point L. She gains 1 fixed wall and 3 fixed windows.

▶ Steve reaches Point S_2 instead of Point S. He gains 1 fixed wall and 1 fixed window.

Table 4 | Opportunity Costs in the Two-Student Example

Opportunity Cost of:	Lauren	Steve
Fixing one wall	Fixing 3 windows	Fixing ½ of a window
Fixing one window	Fixing ⅓ of a wall	Fixing 2 walls

Case Study: Production Possibilities during World War II

During World War II, the U.S. government required the auto industry to convert from producing cars to producing military equipment. Figure 8 shows the automakers' production possibilities frontier between civilian automobiles and military equipment. In 1941, the auto industry produced and sold about 4 million cars and only a small amount of military equipment (Point A in the figure). During World War II, the U.S. government announced that the U.S. auto industry would convert to making military equipment. The government expected it to produce 117,000 tanks, 185,000 airplanes, and 28 million tons of merchant ships in 1942 and 1943 (Point G in Figure 8).

The government underestimated the curvature of the industry's PPF, however, so Point G was impossible. Some conversion to military production was easy: Producing a small amount of military equipment required only a small cut in auto production. Massive conversion was more difficult, though. For example, most of the auto industry's machine tools were not easy to convert to produce military equipment. The curvature of the economy's PPF meant that instead of producing at Point G, the U.S. economy produced at Point B: 56,000 tanks, 134,000 airplanes, and 27 million tons of merchant ships.

Slopes of PPFs Show Opportunity Costs

Notice that the slope of Lauren's PPF in Figure 6 is -3. The absolute value of the slope, 3, is Lauren's opportunity cost of fixing one wall. Also notice that the slope of Steve's PPF in Figure 6 is $-\frac{1}{2}$. The absolute value of the slope, $\frac{1}{2}$, is Steve's opportunity cost of fixing one wall. As noted earlier, the absolute value of the slope of a PPF shows the opportunity cost of producing the good measured along the *X*-axis (walls, in this case).

Notice that the combined PPF for Steve and Lauren in Figure 6c is not a straight line. Think of the two students together as a small economy. That economy's opportunity cost *changes* depending upon which combination of goods it produces. If the economy produces along the upper segment of its PPF, its opportunity costs are the same as Steve's. If it produces along the lower segment of its PPF, its opportunity costs match Lauren's. When an economy, like the U.S. economy, consists of *many* different people with different opportunity costs, its PPF looks like those in Figures 3 through 5. The curvature of the PPF shows that the economy's opportunity costs change as it changes the combination of goods that it produces. The appendix to this chapter explains this point in further detail.

Comparative Advantage and the Gains from Trade

The two-student example illustrates a general principle: People gain from trade whenever they differ in their *relative* abilities to produce different goods—that is, whenever they have *comparative advantages* at producing those goods.

> A person has a **comparative advantage** at producing a good if she can produce it at a lower opportunity cost than other people can.

In the example, Lauren has a comparative advantage at fixing windows, and Steve has a comparative advantage at fixing walls. In any situation like this, everyone has a comparative advantage at some task. This is true even when one person works more productively than others at every job—as in the shoe-store example in Chapter 1. (Also see Problem 21 at the end of this chapter.) You can gain from a trade that allows you to increase the time you spend in an activity at which you have a comparative advantage and decrease the time you spend on other tasks.

Figure 8 | U.S. Production Possibilities Frontier during World War II

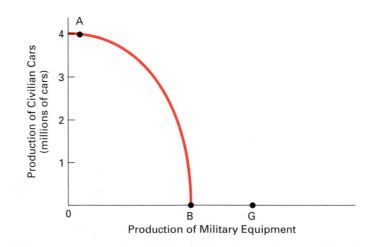

In 1941, the U.S. auto industry produced at Point A. The government expected the auto industry to move to Point G in 1942 and 1943. Because the PPF was curved, however, the industry could produce only at Point B.

Comparative Advantage in the Two-Student Example

Lauren has a comparative advantage at fixing windows. As Table 4 shows, her opportunity cost of fixing a window is fixing one-third of a wall. This is a lower cost than Steve's opportunity cost of fixing a window, which is fixing two walls. Because Lauren has a lower opportunity cost of fixing windows, that task gives her a comparative advantage.

Steve has a comparative advantage at fixing walls. As Table 4 shows, his opportunity cost of fixing a wall is fixing one-half of a window, lower than Lauren's opportunity cost of fixing a wall, which is fixing three windows. Because Steve has a lower opportunity cost of fixing walls, that task gives him a comparative advantage.

Everyone has a comparative advantage at some task. Within the two-student economy, determining that Lauren has a comparative advantage at windows immediately indicates that Steve has a comparative advantage at walls.

A Common Confusion: Comparative versus Absolute Advantage

As Table 3 showed, Lauren can fix more windows per day than Steve can, and Steve can fix more walls per day than Lauren can. Table 2 showed that Lauren can fix a window in less time than Steve would take, and Steve can fix a wall in less time than Lauren would take. Economists say that the more productive person has an *absolute advantage* at that task. Lauren has an absolute advantage at fixing windows, and Steve has an absolute advantage at fixing walls.

A common mistake is to think that Lauren and Steve gain from trade because Lauren has an absolute advantage at windows and Steve has an absolute advantage at walls. The correct statement is that Lauren and Steve gain from trade because they have different opportunity costs that give them comparative advantages. To see why, the next section changes the numbers in the two-student example. Before reading that section, though, look back at the shoe-store example at the beginning of Chapter 1. In that example, Lisa works more productively than Mitch at both jobs. (Lisa has an absolute advantage at both tasks.) Nevertheless, they gain from trade. The same logic holds in the modified two-student example.

> **Advice**
> Don't confuse *comparative advantage* (differences in opportunity cost) with *absolute advantage* (differences in productivity). The important concept is *comparative advantage*.

Modified Two-Student Example

Table 5 changes Table 2 so that *Steve now takes twice as long* to do either job. He needs 4 hours (instead of 2 hours) to fix a wall and 8 hours (instead of 4) to fix a window. The numbers in Table 5 give Lauren an absolute advantage at both jobs. Nevertheless, Steve still has a comparative advantage at fixing walls. Steve's opportunity cost of fixing one wall is fixing one-half of a window. (In the 4 hours Steve takes to fix a wall, he could fix half of a window.) Lauren's opportunity cost of fixing a wall is fixing three windows. (In the 3 hours Lauren takes to fix a wall, she could fix three windows.) Because Steve's opportunity cost of fixing walls is lower than Lauren's, Steve still has a comparative advantage at fixing walls. Lauren still has a comparative advantage at fixing windows.

Lauren and Steve continue to gain from trade, even though Lauren has an absolute advantage at both jobs. Working for 12 hours *without* trading, Lauren may choose Point L on her PPF (as before), fixing two walls and six windows. Changing the numbers for Steve shrinks his opportunities and shifts his PPF inward to the one in Figure 9. Without trade, Steve may choose Point T on his new PPF, fixing one wall and one window.

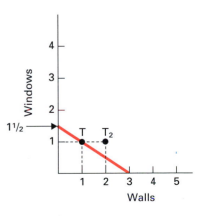

**Figure 9
Steve's PPF in the
Modified Example**

Table 5 | Modified Example

Time Required to:	Lauren	Steve
Fix one wall	3 hours	4 hours
Fix one window	1 hour	8 hours

Now suppose that Lauren and Steve trade: Lauren fixes two windows for Steve, and Steve fixes two walls for Lauren. After Lauren spends 2 hours to fix two windows for Steve, she spends her other 10 working hours to fix ten of her own windows. After Steve spends 8 hours to fix two walls for Lauren, he spends his other 4 working hours to fix one of his own walls.

With this trade, Lauren ends the day with two walls and ten windows repaired. Steve ends the day with one wall and two windows repaired (Point T₂ in Figure 9). Lauren gains 4 extra repaired windows from the trade. Steve gains 1 extra repaired window.

Diversity and Values

The modified two-student example, like the shoe-store example from Chapter 1, shows that differences in opportunity costs create possibilities for gains from trade.

> People do not gain from trade because they are more or less productive than others. People gain from trade because of diversity in their opportunity costs.

Diversity of opportunity costs creates diversity in comparative advantage. If Lauren and Steve had the *same* opportunity costs, their PPFs would be parallel lines and they would not gain from trading with each other. Diversity is not merely the spice of life, but the source of gains from voluntary trade.

The modified two-student example measured the gains from trade in terms of the extra production (fixed walls and windows) that the trade created. The shoe-store example from Chapter 1 measured gains from trade in terms of the extra hours of leisure time that the trade created. As this comparison shows, gains from trade need not be materialistic. People can also gain leisure time or other values.

Review Questions

6. Explain why people can gain from voluntary trades.

7. What is comparative advantage? How does it differ from absolute advantage?

8. Define an economically efficient situation. Define an economically inefficient situation.

9. The cars-from-grain fable shows that trade resembles technological change. How does the two-student example illustrate this point?

Thinking Exercises

10. Suppose that Argentina can produce 14 bottles of wine or 40 pounds of beef in one day, while Chile can produce 12 bottles of wine or 30 pounds of beef in one day. Which country has a comparative advantage in wine and which in beef?

11. Discuss: "If a situation is economically inefficient, everyone involved has an incentive to change it."

12. Use Table 1 from Chapter 1, reproduced here, to answer these questions:
    (a) What is Lisa's opportunity cost of taking inventory? What is her opportunity cost of setting up the display?
    (b) What is Mitch's opportunity cost of taking inventory? What is his opportunity cost of setting up the display?
    (c) Who has a comparative advantage in taking inventory? In setting up the display?

Hours of Work Required for:	Lisa	Mitch
Taking inventory in one section of the store	6 hrs	5 hrs
Setting up a new display in one section of the store	3 hrs	6 hrs

Some people believe that whenever one person gets richer, another person must become poorer. They think the economy is like a pie; if one person gets a bigger piece, less remains for other people. Those ideas are false. *Everyone* involved can gain from a voluntary trade, as the two-student example shows.

> An environment in which one person's gain is another person's loss is called a **zero-sum game.**[2]

Dividing a cake between several people is a zero-sum game: a bigger piece for one person leaves less for someone else. Most economic situations are *not* zero-sum games, though. They are positive-sum games.

> An environment in which everyone can gain at the same time is called a **positive-sum game.**

People can all gain if they produce the same amount of goods with less effort or more goods with the same effort. They gain when each person produces goods at which he has a comparative advantage and then trades with others. The two-student example is a positive-sum game: Both students gain from the trade. The world economy consists of billions of people like those two students, though the details of their lives differ in countless ways. The world economy is a positive-sum game.

Economic Efficiency

The two-student example shows how people can gain from an increase in economic efficiency.

> A situation is **economically efficient** if there is no way to change it so that everyone gains, or so that some people gain while no one else loses.

An economically efficient situation leaves no unexploited opportunities that can benefit everyone; people have *already* made use of every such opportunity.

> A situation is **economically inefficient** if there is some way to change it so that everyone gains, or so that someone gains while no one else loses.

An economically inefficient situation leaves potential, *unrealized* gains from possible changes. It is economically inefficient to fail to exploit all the potential gains from trade.

---

[2]The term means that if some people enjoy positive gains, other people must suffer negative gains (i.e., losses) so that all the gains sum to zero.

EXAMPLES

1. Susie likes yogurt and Johnny likes peanut butter. If Susie has peanut butter and Johnny has yogurt, the situation is economically inefficient because a change could help them both: They could trade lunches. After the trade, Susie has yogurt and Johnny has peanut butter. That situation is economically efficient because any further change that would help one of them would hurt the other. (If Johnny takes some of Susie's yogurt, he gains and she loses.)

2. In the two-student example, it would be economically inefficient for Lauren and Steve not to trade. A change in the situation—choosing to trade after all—could help them both. When Lauren and Steve trade as described earlier in this chapter, the trade creates an economically efficient situation because no *further* change can help one person without hurting the other.

3. In the shoe-store example in Chapter 1, it is economically inefficient not to trade. When Lisa and Mitch trade, the situation becomes economically efficient.

Technical and Economic Efficiency

Technical efficiency and economic efficiency are different, but related concepts. Recall that technical efficiency means that the economy produces on its PPF, so that it cannot produce more of one good without producing less of another. *Every economically efficient situation is also technically efficient. However, not every technically efficient situation is economically efficient.*

EXPLANATION

1. **Every economically efficient situation is technically efficient.** If a situation were technically *in*efficient, then the economy could produce more of something without producing less of anything else. This change could help someone without hurting anyone, so a technically inefficient situation must also be economically inefficient.

2. **Some technically efficient situations are not economically efficient.** It would be technically efficient for the economy to produce only pizzas, as long as it produced as many pizzas as possible, given its PPF. However, this production choice would not be economically efficient because people would gain if the economy produced a few beverages and other goods rather than only pizzas. Similarly, it would be technically efficient to produce at Point A in Figure 3, producing only videotapes. However, people might gain if the economy produced at Point C or D instead of Point A. Point A would be technically efficient but not economically efficient.

Comparative Advantage and Efficiency

In an economically efficient situation, people tend to produce goods at which they have comparative advantages. In the two-student example, it is economically efficient for Steve to fix walls, at which he has a comparative advantage, while Lauren fixes windows, at which she has a comparative advantage.

Sometimes, however, it is economically efficient for someone to produce a good at which he does *not* have a comparative advantage. If the walls don't need repair, for example, it can be efficient for Lauren and Steve both to fix windows (even though Steve has a comparative advantage at walls). Similarly, it can be efficient for Lauren and Steve both to fix windows if they fixed all the walls yesterday, but some windows remain to be fixed. It would *not* be economically efficient for Steve to fix windows while Lauren fixed walls, though; they could both gain by switching jobs.

People have incentives to trade when the trade can create economic efficiency. They can share the gains from changing an inefficient situation into an efficient one. Voluntary trades produce economic efficiency without anyone else directing them.

Suppose Lauren and Steve each have *one* window and *one* wall in need of repair. Table 6 repeats the information from Table 2 for this case. If Lauren and Steve do not trade, Lauren works 4 hours in her apartment (3 hours to fix her wall and 1 hour to fix her window) and Steve works 6 hours in his apartment.

Now suppose Lauren and Steve trade one fixed wall for one fixed window: Lauren fixes Steve's window and Steve fixes Lauren's wall. Then Lauren works 2 hours (1 hour fixing the window in each apartment) and Steve works 4 hours (2 in each apartment). They each gain 2 hours of leisure time from this trade.

In this example, Lauren and Steve share the gains from trade equally. They could have made many other trades, however, any of which would have helped them both. In fact, there are *many* economically efficient situations. Each economically efficient situation has a different distribution of income; some situations give more goods to Lauren, while others give more to Steve.

SHARING THE GAINS FROM TRADE

EXAMPLE: HOUR-FOR-HOUR TRADE

In the trade discussed above, Lauren fixes Steve's window and Steve fixes Lauren's wall. While this trade leads to economic efficiency, notice that Steve spends 2 hours fixing Lauren's wall, while Lauren spends only 1 hour fixing Steve's window. In other words, Lauren trades 1 hour of her time for 2 hours of Steve's time.

Suppose, instead, that Steve and Lauren agree to trade their time on an hour-for-hour basis: Steve will spend 1 hour fixing Lauren's wall and she will spend 1 hour fixing his window. In that 1 hour, Lauren will finish fixing Steve's window, but Steve will not finish fixing Lauren's wall—the complete job would take 2 hours. Steve will get the wall *half done* in 1 hour, leaving the other half of the job for Lauren. Since Lauren can fix a wall in 3 hours, it will take her 1½ hours to finish the job. Table 7 summarizes the work the students do when each trades an hour's time.

Table 6 | Two-Student Example with One Wall and One Window to Repair

Time Required to:	Lauren	Steve
Fix one wall	3 hours	2 hours
Fix one window	1 hour	4 hours

When Lauren and Steve *each* have 1 wall and 1 window to fix:	Lauren works	Steve works
Without a trade	4 hours	6 hours
With the trade	2 hours	4 hours

Table 7 | Hour-for-Hour Trade

Lauren	Steve
Fixes her own window in 1 hour, completing the work	Fixes his own wall in 2 hours, completing the work
Fixes Steve's window in 1 hour, completing the work	Spends 1 hour fixing Lauren's wall, completing half of the work
Spends 90 minutes fixing her own wall after Steve leaves	
Total work time: 3½ hours	Total work time: 3 hours

With the hour-for-hour trade, Lauren works 3½ hours and Steve works 3 hours. Without any trade, Lauren would have worked 4 hours in her own apartment and Steve would have worked 6 hours in his. Each gains from the hour-for-hour trade; Lauren gains half an hour of leisure time, and Steve gains 3 hours. Although they do not share the gains from trade equally, the trade creates economically efficiency.

Comparison of the Two Trades

Table 8 compares these two trades. In the first trade, Lauren trades 1 hour of her work effort for 2 hours of Steve's. In other words, they trade one fixed window for one fixed wall. In the second, Lauren trades 1 hour of her work effort for 1 hour of Steve's. In other words, they trade one fixed window for *half* of a fixed wall. A comparison of the trades leads to four main conclusions:

1. Lauren benefits from either trade. So does Steve.

2. Each trade involves a different *price* at which fixed walls exchange for fixed windows.

3. The price affects how they share the gains from trade. Lauren gains more from the first trade; Steve gains more from the second trade.

4. Each trade leads to a different economically efficient situation.[3]

Lauren prefers the first trade because she gains 2 hours of leisure time, while she gains only 30 minutes from the second (hour-for-hour) trade. Steve prefers the second (hour-for-hour) trade because he gains 3 hours of leisure time, while he gains only 2 hours from the first trade.

Lauren and Steve could also choose many other trades that would help them both and that would lead to economically efficient situations. Each economically efficient situation has a different distribution of income—some are better for Lauren, and some are better for Steve.

Fairness, Equity, and Justice

Which trade is fairer? Any answer to this question requires criteria for fairness. It might seem fair for Lauren and Steve to share the gains from the trade equally, so the 1-hour-

---

[3]Both trades create economically efficient situations, even though the total amount of time spent working is larger in the hour-for-hour trade (6½ hours) than in the first trade (6 hours).

Table 8 | Comparison of the Two Trades

First Trade: One Hour for Two Hours	Second Trade: Hour for Hour	No Trade
Price: One fixed window for one fixed wall	Price: One fixed window for one-half of a fixed wall	
Economically efficient Lauren works 2 hours; Steve works 4 hours	Economically efficient Lauren works 3½ hours; Steve works 3 hours	Economically inefficient Lauren works 4 hours; Steve works 6 hours
Compared with no trade: Lauren gains 2 hours of time; Steve gains 2 hours of time	Compared with no trade: Lauren gains ½ hour of time; Steve gains 3 hours of time	
Lauren spends 1 hour working in Steve's apartment; Steve spends 2 hours working in Lauren's apartment	Lauren spends 1 hour working in Steve's apartment; Steve spends 1 hour working in Lauren's apartment	

for-2-hour trade might seem fair because Lauren and Steve each gain 2 hours of leisure time. Or it might also seem fair for Lauren to exchange 1 hour of her time for 1 hour of Steve's time, so the hour-for-hour trade might seem fair.[4] Alternatively, it might seem fair for Lauren and Steve to have equal amounts of leisure time, in which case they must spend equal time working. Each opinion would make a *different* trade seem fair.[5]

These three ideas of fairness conflict with each other. Each leads to a different conclusion about which trade is fair and which are unfair. Unfortunately, no definition of what is fair (or just or equitable) satisfies everyone. Many people use these words loosely without clear, precise ideas of what they mean. Even philosophers have failed to agree on criteria for fairness. Consider some different ideas of fairness:

▶ There should be an equal distribution of income.

▶ People who need high incomes for important purposes, such as medical expenses or to support large families, should have more income than others with less pressing needs.

▶ Incomes should not be equal, but no one should live in extreme poverty.

▶ People who work harder than others should have higher incomes.

▶ People should get whatever incomes they can earn by working.

▶ There is no such thing as a fair distribution of income. Fairness applies only to *rules* (such as laws).

Fairness and Rules

Among people who believe that fairness applies only to rules, some say that rules are fair if everyone would agree on them in advance, not knowing whether they will be lucky or unlucky, beautiful or ugly, smart or dumb, talented or not, or born into rich or poor

---

[4]Suppose that Lauren pays Steve $20 for his work and Steve pays Lauren $20 for her work. Then the hour-for-hour trade would give them equal wage rates.

[5]Lauren and Steve would work the same number of hours if Steve were to fix his own wall (which would take him 2 hours) and spend 1 hour and 12 minutes working on Lauren's wall. Since it would take Steve 2 hours to fix Lauren's wall, he would get 3/5 of the job done in 1 hour and 12 minutes. Lauren would fix the remaining 2/5 of her wall, which would take her (2/5)(3 hours), or 6/5 hours (1 hour and 12 minutes). She would also fix the windows in both apartments, which would take her 2 hours. Then Lauren and Steve would each work for 3 hours and 12 minutes. This situation is economically efficient. (Notice that in this situation, Steve spends 1 hour and 12 minutes working in Lauren's apartment, while Lauren spends only 1 hour working in Steve's.)

families. Before an American football game, for example, the teams accept the result of a coin toss to see who will receive the ball first. According to this view, it is neither fair nor unfair that one team wins the coin toss. Outcomes are not fair or unfair. Only the rules that produce those outcomes can be fair or unfair.[6] The rule requiring a coin toss may be fair (or, if the coin is weighted to come up heads most of the time, unfair). Some people who believe that fairness applies only to rules say that rules are fair if they allow each person to keep her own property and make any desired peaceful, voluntary trades.[7]

Economics deals with positive statements (statements of fact); it does not say anything about fairness.[8] However, economics can help people to understand the results of various laws, regulations, and government policies. This understanding helps people to apply their own ideas of fairness to decide what laws, regulations, and government policies they think are best.

COMPETITION AND THE GAINS FROM TRADE

Which trade would people like Lauren and Steve make in real life? When people can choose any one of several trades, their actual choices depend on their alternative opportunities. If one person has good opportunities for alternative trades, the other person faces strong competition for his services and bargains from a weak position. The trades people choose depend on their relative bargaining positions, which depend on their alternative opportunities for trading.

EXPLANATION

Table 8 compared two of the many possible trades that Lauren and Steve might have made. Each trade would lead to a different economically efficient situation, with a different distribution of income. Lauren prefers some trades and Steve prefers others. The trade that they actually choose depends on their alternative opportunities, which affect each party's bargaining power. Steve might convince Lauren to trade time on an hour-for-hour basis by telling her that if she refuses, he will trade with Linda instead, who *will* agree to his terms. In that sense, Lauren would face competition from other potential window-repair services. In the same way, Steve might agree to a trade that Lauren prefers because he faces competition from other potential wall-repair services.

IS ECONOMIC EFFICIENCY GOOD?

Economics deals with statements of fact, not value judgments. Still, economic efficiency is good in one sense, independently of individual values. In any economically inefficient situation, a change in the economy can create gains for everyone, or gains for some people without losses for anyone else. Economic efficiency is good in the sense that waste is bad; eliminating inefficiencies improves people's conditions according to their own values. In an economically inefficient situation, people usually have incentives to make changes to achieve efficiency and share the gains.

---

[6]In most real-life situations, we already know the outcomes: Some people are born to rich families, others to poor families. Some are smarter, more talented, and more beautiful than others. No one can say for sure what rules people would have accepted if they could have decided which were fair before knowing these outcomes. One can only guess. This approach to fairness was pioneered by economist John Harsanyi in 1953 and by Harvard philosopher John Rawls in his book, *A Theory of Justice* (Cambridge, Mass.: Harvard University Press, 1971). Most of Rawls's book discusses his guesses about which rules people would say are fair before knowing these outcomes.

[7]This position grows out of a long tradition in philosophy asserting that people have natural rights. (The U.S. Declaration of Independence was influenced by this tradition.) For one statement of this libertarian position, see Robert Nozick, *Anarchy, State, and Utopia* (New York: Basic Books, 1974).

[8]See Chapter 2 for a discussion of positive statements.

Many people believe that the government should redistribute income to some degree from the rich to the poor. With this view of fairness or equity, the economy faces a trade-off between equity and efficiency: To distribute income more equitably, according to this view, the government must often create economic inefficiencies. The government may tax people with high incomes and give the money to poorer people. The tax creates economic inefficiency by changing people's incentives to trade, as the next example will explain.

How Taxes Create Economic Inefficiency: An Example

Suppose that the government places a $5 tax on purchases of wall or window repairs. Anyone who buys repair services must pay $5 to the government. This tax can create an economically inefficient situation.

Economic efficiency implies that Steve should buy window-repair services from Lauren, and Lauren should buy wall-repair services from Steve. The tax may create economic inefficiency by causing them *not* to trade. If Lauren buys Steve's services, she gains leisure time at the cost of paying the $5 tax. She may decide that the extra leisure time is not worth paying the tax. Steve faces the same decision. If the tax prevents the trade, it creates an economically inefficient situation. In addition, if they do not trade, the government does not collect the tax revenue from them. The government collects tax revenue only from people who continue to buy repair services despite the tax.

An economic inefficiency usually creates incentives for people to find voluntary trades that change the situation and make it efficient. They can then share the gains from eliminating the inefficiency. Taxes change this result. Taxes alter incentives so that people do not always gain from eliminating inefficient situations. In this way, taxes create economic inefficiency.

A Tradeoff between Equity and Efficiency?

The government can use tax revenue to increase equity (at least according to some views of equity) at the cost of economic inefficiency. Economic inefficiency may be an opportunity cost of increasing equity (and vice versa). In other words, the economy may face a tradeoff between equity and economic efficiency. Many notions of equity, though not all, lead to conflicts with economic efficiency, at least in certain cases. It would be remarkable if a well-developed idea of fairness or equity never conflicted with economic efficiency.[9]

If economic efficiency and other values (including equity) conflict, people must choose whether to sacrifice equity or efficiency. Choosing involves value judgments about which people's opinions may differ, but it also involves economics. Economic analysis can help people to understand how much economic inefficiency they must accept to achieve some other goal, thereby helping them to evaluate tradeoffs and to make more intelligent decisions.

The two-student example showed how two people can each gain by trading. The same reasoning shows that nations can each gain from *international trades*. (Think, for instance, of two countries named Laurenland and Steveland producing cars and wheat

A NOTE ON INTERNATIONAL TRADE

---

[9]For an attempt to create such a theory, see Richard Posner, *The Economics of Justice* (Cambridge, Mass.: Harvard University Press, 1983).

rather than wall and window repairs.) By specializing in goods that it can produce at a comparative advantage and trading them with other countries, a nation can obtain more goods and services than it could produce on its own without trading. The reason is simple: Every trade between nations is really a trade between people living in those nations, so the lesson of the two-student example essentially applies to every trade. Some people compare international trade to a war, but that comparison misleads, because the world economy is a positive-sum game.

Review Questions

12. (a) Explain why every economically efficient situation is technically efficient.
    (b) Explain why a situation can be technically efficient but not economically efficient.

13. Briefly discuss alternative ideas of fairness.

14. In what sense is economic efficiency good?

15. Discuss this statement: "The economy faces a tradeoff between equity and economic efficiency."

Thinking Exercises

16. Explain why there are many economically efficient situations. How do they differ?

17. Discuss: "The hour-for-hour trade requires $6\frac{1}{2}$ total hours of work from Steve and Lauren, while the original trade required only 6 hours of work, so the hour-for-hour trade is economically inefficient."

18. How do taxes cause economic inefficiency?

Conclusion

Limits and Possibilities

Everyone faces limits. The production possibilities frontier or PPF graphs the limits on the economy's production with its available inputs and technology. The PPF shows scarcity because it separates possible economic situations from impossible ones. The PPF shows technical efficiency (absence of waste) because only points *on* the PPF are technically efficient combinations of output. It shows the role for economic choices: People's decisions and government policies determine at which point in the graph the economy *actually* produces. It shows the economy's tradeoff between producing various goods: The absolute value of the *slope* of the PPF shows the economy's opportunity cost of producing the good on the *X*-axis. An economy's PPF shifts when its resources or technology change. Economic growth occurs when an economy's PPF expands faster than its population grows.

A Fable, and the Two-Student Example of Gains from Trade

The fable about producing cars from grain illustrates the point that trade, like technological change, expands consumption opportunities. The two-student example shows additional details of the gains from trade. Trade allows the students to consume at points *outside* their individual PPFs, which would be impossible without trade.

People can gain from trades by producing goods at which they have comparative advantages. A person has a comparative advantage at a task if his opportunity cost of that task is lower than other people's. Everyone has a comparative advantage at some task, even if they are less productive than others at *all* tasks. The modified two-student example and the shoe-store example of Chapter 1 illustrate why. People gain from trade *not* because they are more or less productive than others, but because they differ in their opportunity costs. Gains from trade can consist of increased production of material goods or enhancement of other values.

Efficiency and the Gains from Trade

In a zero-sum game, one person's gain is another person's loss. In contrast, a positive-sum game permits a win-win situation in which everyone gains. The economy is a positive-sum game: One person's gain is *not* another person's loss. Both participants gain in voluntary trades.

A situation is economically efficient if there is no way to change it so that everyone gains or some people gain while no one else loses. Economic efficiency leaves no unexploited opportunities that can benefit everyone, because people have already made use of all such opportunities. A situation is economically inefficient if there is some way to change it so that everyone gains or someone gains while no one else loses. The situation remains economically inefficient until that change actually occurs. In other words, an economically inefficient situation has potential but unrealized gains from a change.

Every economically efficient situation is technically efficient. However, not every technically efficient situation is economically efficient.

In an economically efficient situation, people tend to produce goods at which they have comparative advantages. Everyone can share the gains from changing an economically inefficient situation into an efficient one.

Sharing the Gains from Trade

There are many economically efficient situations, each with a different distribution of income. In an economically inefficient situation, people can usually choose from *many* mutually beneficial trades. Each involves a different price and a different division of the gains from trade.

People have many different and conflicting ideas about fairness. Economics deals with positive statements and does not say anything about fairness. Both economic analysis and value judgments are required for intelligent decisions on public policy.

Competition and the Gains from Trade

Alternative trading opportunities affect the trades that people choose. A person with better opportunities for alternative trades holds a stronger bargaining position. As a result, alternative opportunities affect the prices at which people trade and the way they share the gains from trade.

Is Economic Efficiency Good?

Economic efficiency is good in the sense that waste is bad. Eliminating inefficiencies benefits people according to their own values. Some ideas of equity imply an inverse relationship between equity and economic efficiency: The opportunity cost of greater equity is reduced economic efficiency, and the opportunity cost of greater economic efficiency is reduced equity. Taxes create economic inefficiency by changing people's incentives to trade.

A Note on International Trade

Nations gain from international trade just as individuals gain from trade. The world economy is a positive-sum game.

Key Terms

production possibilities frontier, or PPF	technical efficiency comparative advantage	zero-sum game positive-sum game	economically efficient economically inefficient

Problems

19. Explain why the economy is a positive-sum game.

20. Give an example of an economically inefficient situation, and explain how to make it efficient.

21. Consider the shoe-store example from Table 1 of Chapter 1. Change the numbers so that Lisa needs 8 hours (instead of 4) to take inventory. How does this change affect who has a comparative advantage at which task and the gains from trade?

22. You are the chief executive officer (CEO) of a major corporation. You face two urgent tasks: defending against product-liability lawsuits and finding tax loopholes for your company. You have two employees who can do these jobs. How will you choose to allocate these important tasks to them? Explain how the economic principles discussed in this chapter can help you, and illustrate your point with a numerical example.

23. (Harder Problem) Some people have suggested that the government should guarantee equal pay for workers at different jobs with "comparable worth," that is, jobs that are equally important or require similar levels of education and skill. Suppose that the government were to decide that window and wall repair are jobs of comparable worth. Consider the two-student example in Table 6, when Lauren and Steve each have one wall and one window to fix. If Steve pays Lauren $10 to fix his window (which takes her 1 hour), and Lauren pays Steve $10 to fix her wall (which takes him 2 hours), Lauren's wage is $10 per hour and Steve's wage is $5 per hour. What alternative trade could the government suggest to Steve and Lauren? Can the government suggest a trade with equal hourly pay for Steve and Lauren that Lauren would approve? Explain.

Inquiries for Further Thought

24. Do you believe that the distribution of income in our economy is equitable or inequitable, fair or unfair? What could be done about it? What should be done? What would be the opportunity cost?

25. Describe your own view of fairness or equity in as much detail as you can.

Appendix: Changing Opportunity Cost along a Curved PPF

The chapter explained that an economy composed of many people with different opportunity costs has a curved PPF. The PPF for Lauren and Steve together, in Figure 6c, shows how this may happen.

More generally, think of an economy that produces food and computer software. If it produces a small amount of software and a large amount of food, then only the best programmers work on software, and others, who have a comparative advantage at food production, work on the farms. If the economy wants to produce more software and less food, it must recruit people less skilled at programming (and better at farming). This raises the opportunity cost of software as its production rises, creating curvature in the PPF.

A similar argument applies to other inputs, such as land and capital (equipment). Suppose that all the land in a country is equally good for housing, but some land is better than other land for farming. If the economy produces only a small amount of farm products, it can cultivate only the best farmland. To produce more farm products, the economy must bring some less fertile land into production. As the economy adds more acres of farmland, average output per acre falls because the economy begins using larger quantities of less productive land.

Figure A1 illustrates an economy that can produce 40 million houses and no food (Point A) or 39 million houses and 1 million tons of food (Point B). As the economy moves from Point A to Point B, it gains 1 million tons of food and loses 1 million houses, so the opportunity cost of 1 million tons of food is 1 million houses.

The opportunity cost changes along the PPF in Figure A1. If the economy moves from Point B to Point C, it raises output of food by 1 million tons per year (from 1 million to 2 million tons) while reducing output of houses by 2 million (from 39 million to 37 million). The opportunity cost of the additional 1 million tons of food is 2 million houses. If the economy moves from Point C to Point D, the opportunity cost of 1 million tons of food rises to 3 million houses; if it moves from Point D to Point E, the opportunity cost of food reaches 5 million houses. Opportunity cost changes along a curved PPF. The opportunity cost of food rises as the economy produces larger quantities of it.

Figure A1 | Production Possibilities Frontier

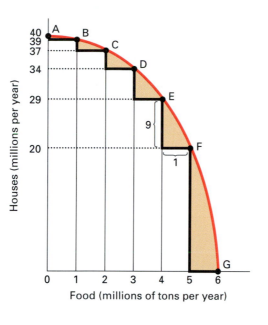

The base of the triangle between Points E and F shows an increase in food output of 1 million tons (from 4 million to 5 million). The height of the triangle shows a fall in house production of 9 million houses (from 29 million to 20 million). This is the opportunity cost of producing 1 million more tons of food.

The negative slope of the PPF shows that as the economy produces more food, it can produce fewer houses. The curvature of the PPF shows that the opportunity cost of food rises when food output increases.

Problems

A1. Explain why the negative slope of a production possibilities frontier shows the opportunity cost of producing the good measured along the horizontal axis (*X*-axis). What is the opportunity cost of 1 million tons of food as the economy moves from Point F to Point G in Figure A1?

A2. An old machine powered by natural gas can produce either 4,000 backpacks or 2,000 bicycles in a month. A newer machine that runs on solar power can produce either 2,000 backpacks or 4,000 bicycles in a month. Table A1 shows the amount of each good that can be produced with a single machine of each type in a month.
  (a) Draw the production possibilities frontier for an economy with ten old, natural-gas-powered machines and no new, solar-powered machines. What is the opportunity cost of backpacks? Of bicycles?
  (b) Draw the production possibilities frontier for an economy with no old, natural-gas-powered machines and ten new, solar-powered machines. What is the opportunity cost of backpacks in this economy? Of bicycles?
  (c) Draw the production possibilities frontier for an economy with ten machines of each type. What is the opportunity cost of backpacks? Of bicycles?
  (d) Suppose that buyers want the same number of backpacks as bicycles. How many months of each year would an economy with one natural-gas-powered machine spend producing backpacks to produce an equal number of backpacks

Table A1 | Monthly Production from One Machine (thousands)

	Natural-Gas-Powered Machine	Solar-Powered Machine
Backpacks	4	2
Bicycles	2	4

and bicycles? How many backpacks per year would it produce? What if the economy had one solar-powered machine instead?

(e) Suppose that Country A has ten old, natural-gas-powered machines and no new, solar-powered machines, while Country B has ten new, solar-powered machines and no old, natural-gas-powered machines. People still want the same number of backpacks as bicycles. Explain why the two countries would gain from trade. (*Hint:* Calculate the number of backpacks and bicycles the world economy can produce with international trade and compare your answer to the number each country can produce alone without international trade.)

CHAPTER 4

SUPPLY AND DEMAND

In this Chapter...

Main Points to Understand

▶ *Demand curves* describe the behavior of buyers.

▶ *Supply curves* describe the behavior of sellers.

▶ Prices adjust to create equilibrium between supply and demand.

Thinking Skills to Develop

▶ Recognize forces that change the behavior of buyers (demand) and the behavior of sellers (supply).

▶ Understand how a market equilibrium coordinates buyers' and sellers' individual decisions.

▶ Recognize how changes in underlying conditions change a market equilibrium.

▶ Use graphs of supply and demand for logical thinking.

W hy does a pair of shoes cost more than a compact disc? Why do entertainment stars earn more than mathematicians? Why do airline tickets cost more around holidays? Why have prices of personal computers and video equipment fallen?

What persuades farmers and manufacturers to produce all the food that people want to buy? What ensures that a city has enough apartments for people to rent? What prevents companies from making more computers than people want to buy?

Chapter 3 showed that people can gain from specialization and trade. This chapter explores which trades they choose and the prices they agree upon. The model of supply and demand presented in this chapter is among the most important models in economics.

As Chapter 3 explained, people can choose from many possible trades, and the trades they decide to make depend on their alternative opportunities. Everyone wants to make the best possible trades for herself. This chapter studies the trades that people make when their opportunities for trading are described by the *price-taking* model:

TRADING OPPORTUNITIES: THE PRICE-TAKING MODEL

1. Each buyer is a *price taker*—he can buy as much (or as little) of the good as he wants at some price, but he cannot affect that price.

2. Each seller is a *price taker*—she can sell as much (or as little) of the good as she wants at some price, but she cannot affect that price.

A price-taking consumer can buy as much of a product as she wants, without affecting its price.

For example, you can buy as many drinks as you want for 75 cents each, but no one will sell you a drink for less. You are a price taker in the market for drinks. A farmer can sell as much wheat as she wants at $5.24 per bushel, but no buyer will pay more than that amount. The farmer is a price taker in the market for wheat.

How does the price-taking model apply to the two-student example of Chapter 3? Suppose that Lauren could find *many* people like Steve, each of whom is willing to trade one repaired wall for one repaired window. No one is willing to give Lauren a better price—no one will repair more than one wall in return for one repaired window. Similarly, Steve can find *many* people like Lauren, each of whom is willing to trade one repaired window for one repaired wall. No one is willing to give Steve a better price—no one will repair more than one window in return for one repaired wall. In that case, Lauren and Steve are price takers. The price is one wall for one window, and neither Lauren nor Steve can get a better price from anyone. You might ask why the price is one window for one wall, rather than one window for *half* a wall (as in the hour-for-hour trade of Chapter 3), or some other price. That question is the topic of this chapter.

The price-taking model applies (at least approximately) to buyers of most products and to many sellers such as farms, retail stores, pizza parlors and fast-food restaurants, dry cleaners and laundromats, and gas stations. It does not apply as well to some traders, such as sellers of cable-television services or airline services. Competition among price takers is often called *perfect competition*. Competition among traders who are not price takers can take various forms: monopoly, monopolistic competition, or oligopoly. Later chapters will explore these issues. Because the price-taking model applies very accurately to many real-life situations (even when buyers and sellers are not exactly price takers), the associated model of *supply and demand*, which assumes that traders are price takers, lies at the center of economic analysis.

INTRODUCTION TO DEMAND

How many movies will you see this month? Your answer depends on many conditions, such as:

▶ The price—How much do movie tickets cost?

▶ Your tastes—How much do you like movies?

▶ Your income—Do you have enough money to pay for tickets?

▶ Prices of other goods—How much would you have to spend to rent videos or attend concerts?

Other conditions also influence the choice, such as whether you have a video recorder, how many parties you could attend, what your friends want to do, and how much studying you have to do. How many movie tickets would you buy this month if each ticket cost $1? What if it cost $3, $5, or $10? (In each case, you are a price taker; nothing you can do will change the price of a ticket.) Before you continue reading, briefly

Figure 1 | The Author's Demand Curve for Movie Tickets

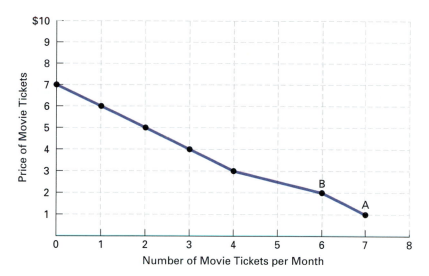

Each point is a row from Table 1.

Table 1
The Author's Demand
Schedule for Tickets

Price of Tickets	Number I Would Buy
$1	7
2	6
3	4
4	3
5	2
6	1
7	0

answer these questions based on your own tastes and circumstances. Write your answers as in Table 1, which shows *my* answers.

The table you made is your demand schedule for movie tickets this month. Your demand schedule for a good lists the quantities you would buy at various possible prices. My demand schedule in Table 1 shows that my *quantity demanded* at a price of $1 is seven tickets, and my quantity demanded at a price of $2 is six tickets. Look at your demand schedule: What is your quantity demanded at a price of $1?

Figure 1 graphs my demand schedule for tickets. The vertical axis measures the price of a ticket, and the horizontal axis measures my quantity demanded at that price. If tickets cost $1 each, I would buy seven this month, placing me at Point A on the graph. If they cost $2 each, I would buy six, placing me at Point B. Each point on the graph shows a row from my demand schedule in Table 1. The curve that connects these points is my demand curve for tickets.

Now graph your demand schedule for tickets. Indicate various prices along the vertical axis. On the horizontal axis, mark your quantity demanded at each price. Each row of your demand schedule defines a point on your graph. Connect these points to draw your demand curve for movie tickets.

Every discussion of demand must specify a time period: Will we discuss demand over a week? A month? A year? Any time period will do, but we must specify it in advance. This chapter will discuss demand (and supply) during one month, unless otherwise indicated.

DEMAND

Roughly, a person's quantity demanded of some good is the amount she wants to buy.[1] More precisely:

> A person's **quantity demanded** of a good at some price is the amount she would buy at that price.

Notice that this definition involves hypothetical, "what if?" situations. It does not say what price buyers actually pay. Instead, it indicates how much a person *would* buy *if* the price were a certain level.[2]

A table (such as a spreadsheet on a computer) that lists various possible prices and quantities demanded is called a *demand schedule*. Table 1 shows an example of a demand schedule. Graphing a demand schedule gives a *demand curve*.

> A **demand curve** graphs the relation between the price of a good and the quantity demanded.

Figure 1 shows an example.

Market Demand

We can draw *one person's* demand curve for a good, or the demand curve by several people, or *all buyers* in the market. Chapter 1 explained that the term *market* refers to the activity of people buying and selling goods. Some markets, like the market for wheat, span worldwide networks of buyers and sellers; others, like the market for haircuts, cover local regions. Whatever the size of a particular market, the demand model can apply to that market.

> The **market quantity demanded** of a good at some price is the total amount that *all buyers* in the market would buy at that price.

To obtain the total amount that *all* buyers would buy, simply add together the amounts that individuals would buy.

A table (or spreadsheet) showing various possible prices and market quantities demanded is a *market demand schedule*. A graph of the market demand schedule is the *market demand curve*.

> A **market demand curve** graphs the relation between the price of a good and the market quantity demanded.

When economists talk about *the* demand curve for a good, they mean the market demand curve.

Straight Line or Curved?

Is a demand curve a straight line, or does it curve in some way? The answer is: it all depends! When you graphed your demand for movie tickets, did you get a straight line? The answer depends on how many tickets you would be willing to buy at various possible prices.

---

[1]Do not confuse the amount of a good you would like to *have* with quantity demanded (the amount you want to *buy*). You may want more of something, but you may be unwilling to pay the price. You may want more of almost everything, but this has nothing to do with your quantity demanded. Your quantity demanded shows the amount of a good you are willing to buy, given your limited budget.

[2]Because a person's demand schedule lists many hypothetical prices, that person may not know his demand schedule. For example, he may not know for sure how many shirts he would buy each year if shirts cost $1 each or $80 each. A person's quantity demanded at some price refers to the amount that the person would actually buy if the good were available at that price. Unless shirts actually cost $1 or $80 each, however, the person might not know how he would behave under those conditions.

EXAMPLE

Figure 2 shows how to sum individual demand curves to get a market demand curve. Panel (a) shows Archie's demand schedule and his demand curve for sodas. Panel (b) shows Veronica's demand schedule and her demand curve for sodas. Panel (c) shows the market demand schedule and demand curve for sodas, assuming that Archie and Veronica are the only possible buyers.

At a price of 80 cents, Archie wants to buy 20 sodas and Veronica wants to buy 10, so the total market quantity demanded is 30. At a price of 40 cents, Archie wants to buy 40 sodas and Veronica wants 50, so the market quantity demanded is 90. Notice that even if each *individual's* demand curve is a straight line, the market demand curve can develop kinks as in Panel (c). Also notice that the demand curves add *horizontally*—the market demand curve lies further to the right than either individual demand curve.

Conditions that Affect the Quantity Demanded

The amount of a good you choose to buy—your quantity demanded—depends on many conditions besides its price. It also depends on your tastes (what you like and dislike), the usefulness of the good (a coat is more useful in cold weather than in warm weather), your income and wealth, and prices of related goods. The *market* quantity demanded also depends on the number of potential buyers.

EXAMPLES

Four main conditions affect your demand for video rentals.

Your Demand for Video Rentals	
Your tastes	How much do you like watching videos?
Usefulness of the good	Do you have access to a VCR and television?
Your income and wealth	Do you have money to spend on videos?
Prices of related goods	How much does it cost to see a movie at a theater instead of renting a video?
	How much is pay-per-view on cable television? How much does a VCR cost?

The *market* demand for children's books depends not only on tastes (for books versus television) and the other factors listed above, but also on the number of people with children (which affects the number of potential buyers).

Law of Demand

An increase in the price of a good, with *no change in other conditions*, generally reduces the quantity demanded. Thousands of economic studies support a generalization about the behavior of buyers:

> *Law of Demand:* When the price of a good rises, holding constant other conditions, the quantity demanded falls.

Figure 2 | Individual Demands and Market Demand

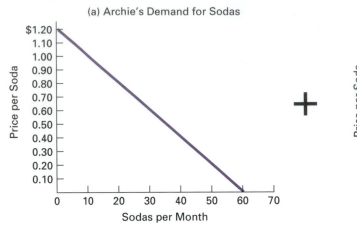

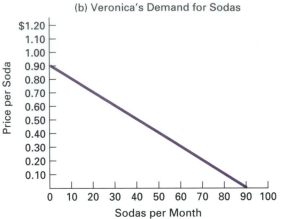

Archie's Demand Schedule for Sodas (sodas per month)

Price per Soda	Quantity Demanded
$1.20	0
1.00	10
0.90	15
0.80	20
0.60	30
0.40	40
0.20	50
0.10	55

Veronica's Demand Schedule for Sodas (sodas per month)

Price per Soda	Quantity Demanded
$1.00	0
0.90	0
0.80	10
0.60	30
0.40	50
0.20	70
0.10	80

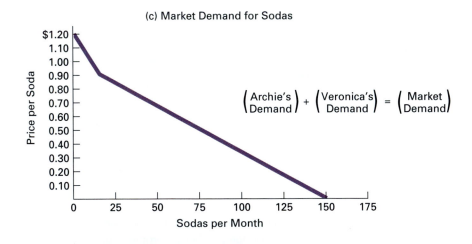

Market Demand Schedule for Sodas (sodas per month)

Price per Soda	Market Quantity Demanded
$1.20	0 (= 0 + 0)
1.00	10 (= 10 + 0)
0.90	15 (= 15 + 0)
0.80	30 (= 20 + 10)
0.60	60 (= 30 + 30)
0.40	90 (= 40 + 50)
0.20	120 (= 50 + 70)
0.10	135 (= 55 + 80)

To state this another way:

Demand curves have negative slopes.

Demand curves slope downward, as in Figure 1.[3]

EXAMPLES

1. Suppose the price of milk increases, with no change in your tastes, your income or wealth, or the prices of related goods such as other beverages or goods you might consume with milk (cookies, chocolate mix, etc.). You would be likely to buy less milk. Only rarely would anyone choose to buy *more*. If the price were to rise enough, everyone would certainly buy less.

2. Points A and B in Figure 1 both lie on my demand curve for movie tickets. My tastes (my likes and dislikes) are the same at Points A and B. I would buy more tickets at Point A than at Point B because the price is lower, not because my tastes are different. My income also remains the same at Points A and B. The only difference in conditions between these two points is the lower price at Point A, which raises my quantity demanded.

Why Demand Curves Slope Downward

Two separate logical reasons underlie the generalization that an increase in price (holding constant other conditions) reduces quantity demanded. First, buyers can replace that good with other, cheaper goods. If the price of corn rises, people tend to substitute broccoli and carrots for corn. The second reason is that people cannot afford to buy as much after a price increase. People must buy either less of the more expensive good or less of something else.[4] For both reasons, a price increase generally reduces the quantity demanded.

R e v i e w   Q u e s t i o n s

1. What is a demand curve? Why does it slope downward?
2. List conditions that affect a good's quantity demanded.

T h i n k i n g   E x e r c i s e s

3. Draw graphs to explain the difference between an increase in demand and an increase in the quantity demanded.

4. Draw a graph of your demand for leisure time. How can you buy more leisure time?

5. Comment on the following statement: "We lowered our price, which caused the demand for our pizzas to increase."

---

[3]Sometimes a price change does not affect the quantity demanded; then the demand curve is a vertical line.
[4]They could save less, but they would then buy fewer goods in the future.

CHANGES IN DEMAND

The quantity demanded of a good depends on its price and on *other* conditions such as people's tastes, the good's usefulness, people's income and wealth, prices of related goods, and (for the market quantity demanded) the number of buyers. Any change in one of these *other* conditions causes a change in demand.

> A **change in demand** means a change in the numbers in the demand schedule and a shift in the demand curve.

> An **increase (or rise) in demand** means an increase in the quantity demanded at a given price and a rightward shift in the demand curve, as in Figure 3 from D_1 to D_2.

Figure 3 | Increase in Demand

An increase in demand is a rise in the quantity demanded at each price. At each price, the new demand curve, D_2, shows a higher quantity demanded than the old demand curve, D_1.

Price	Old Quantity Demanded	New Quantity Demanded
$10	5	8
9	6	10
8	8	12
7	10	15
6	14	18
5	20	24

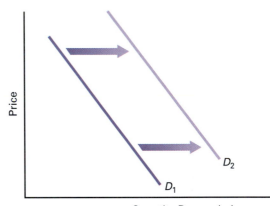

Figure 4 | Decrease in Demand

A decrease in demand is a fall in the quantity demanded at each price. At each price, the new demand curve, D_2, shows a lower quantity demanded than the old demand curve, D_1.

Price	Old Quantity Demanded	New Quantity Demanded
$10	5	2
9	6	3
8	8	4
7	10	6
6	14	9
5	20	15

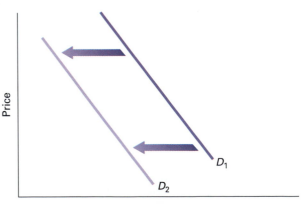

An **decrease (or fall) in demand** means a decrease in the quantity demanded at a given price and a leftward shift in the demand curve, as in Figure 4 from D_1 to D_2.

When demand changes, the *horizontal* (leftward or rightward) shift in the demand curve shows the change in the quantity demanded. Figures 3 and 4 show changes in demand.

Changes in Quantity Demanded versus Changes in Demand

Economists distinguish between changes in the quantity demanded and changes in demand. A change in the quantity demanded occurs when the price changes, moving the economy from one row to another in the demand schedule. This appears as a movement along a demand curve, as from Point A to Point B in Figure 1.

A **change in quantity demanded** means a movement *along* a demand curve due to a change in price.

The demand curve does *not* move when the quantity demanded changes, and the numbers in the demand schedule do *not* change. Buyers and sellers simply jump from one row of the demand schedule to another row. Figure 5 shows a change in the quantity demanded. When the price rises from $5 to $10, the quantity demanded falls from 20 to 10 units per month. In contrast, Figures 3 and 4 show changes in demand.

A change in price changes the quantity demanded. It does not change demand. A change in conditions *other than the price of the good* can change the demand for that good.

Changes in Conditions that Cause Changes in Demand

Table 2 summarizes the changes in conditions that can change demand.

Figure 5 | Change in Quantity Demanded

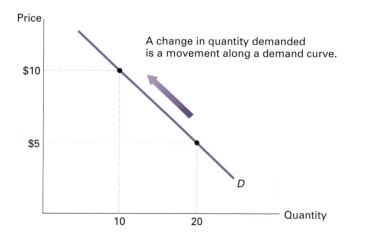

Table 2 | Effects on Demand of Changes in Conditions

Changes in Conditions That *Increase* Demand	Changes in Conditions That *Decrease* Demand
1. Change in tastes: people like the good more.	1. Change in tastes: people like the good less.
2. The good becomes more useful.	2. The good becomes less useful
3. For normal goods, buyers' incomes or wealth levels increase; for inferior goods, buyers' incomes or wealth levels decrease.	3. For normal goods, buyers' incomes or wealth levels decrease; for inferior goods, buyers' incomes or wealth levels increase.
4. The price of a substitute rises.	4. The price of a substitute falls.
5. The price of a complement falls.	5. The price of a complement rises.
6. The number of buyers grows.	6. The number of buyers diminishes.

Putting it mildly, more consumers prefer only products that are "pure," "natural"

Shift in Behavior

The trend represents a significant shift in consumer behavior. For years, consumers were motivated mainly by manufacturers' claims of convenience, performance, or prestige. Now, many people are avoiding products that contain harsh or unnecessary chemicals, especially in their homes.

The growing allure of pure products is paying off for marketers. Sales of Tom's of Maine natural toothpaste in supermarkets and drugstores soared 55 percent to $12.1 million during the 12 months ended Feb. 28.

Source: The Wall Street Journal

Demand for "natural" products rises as consumers' tastes and beliefs about safety change.

Tastes

Tastes (or *preferences)* are people's underlying likes and dislikes. Economists do not explain why people develop certain tastes or what forces change them; those are subjects for psychologists. People's tastes affect their demands, though, and changes in tastes can cause changes in demand. For example, the demand for chocolate candy increased in the United States (as in Figure 3) after World War I: U.S. soldiers developed a taste for eating chocolate because the government gave them chocolate bars during the war.

Usefulness

People often use goods they buy to create (or produce at home) the products they really want. A good's usefulness is its benefit in creating the products people ultimately want. For example, the demand for coats rises at the beginning of winter not because people's tastes change (people always want to be comfortable) but because coats are more useful in the winter than in summer; in cold weather, they help people to create comfort (the really desirable product). Similarly, ground beef is more useful if you have a stove to cook it than if you don't.

Changes in usefulness cause changes in demand. The demand for Christmas cards rises in November (as in Figure 3) and falls in January (as in Figure 4). The demand for air conditioners rises each summer and falls afterward. The demand for low-fat foods increased when people learned that these foods could help them to produce good health.

Income and Wealth

Changes in buyers' income or wealth cause changes in demand.

Income is the amount of money a person earns each year from working, interest on savings, and other sources such as gifts.

Economists always measure income in units of money per year (or some other time period). Increases in income raise the demand for most goods, such as restaurant meals and vacations.

If a rise in income raises the demand for a good, as in Figure 3, economists call it a **normal good.** If a rise in income reduces the demand for a good, as in Figure 4, economists call it an **inferior good.**

Economists identify normal goods and inferior goods by statistical analysis. Normal goods include airline travel, big houses, and swimming pools. Long-distance bus travel and bologna are inferior goods. (When income rises, people tend to substitute other goods for bologna and bus travel.)

> **Wealth** is the accumulated value of a person's savings.

Wealth includes money in savings accounts, stocks and bonds, and the value of possessions like cars, houses, and record collections. Wealth also includes *human wealth:* the value of education and skills.[5] Economists measure wealth as a stock rather than a flow—as an amount of money, *not* money *per year.* Changes in wealth affect demand in the same way as changes in income: An increase in wealth raises demand for normal goods and reduces demand for inferior goods.

Prices of Related Goods

The demand for a particular good can change due to changes in the prices of related goods. These related goods fall into two categories: substitutes and complements.

Substitutes Goods are substitutes if they can be used in place of each other. Coke and Pepsi are substitutes, as are Fords and Chevys, or Wheaties and Cheerios. When the price of coffee rises, some people switch to tea or cocoa, so the demands for these substitutes rise. The general rule states:

> When the price of a good rises, the demands for its **substitutes** increase.

This rule defines the term *substitutes*. Similarly, demand decreases when the price of a substitute falls.

Complements Goods are complements if people tend to use them together. Cameras and film are complements, as are gasoline and cars, or compact disc players and compact discs.

> When the price of a good falls, the demands for its **complements** increase.

This rule defines the term *complements*. Of course, when the price of a good rises, the demands for its complements decrease.

Economists apply statistical analysis to identify pairs of goods that are substitutes, pairs that are complements, and pairs that are unrelated (neither substitutes or complements).

Number of Potential Buyers

A *market* demand curve shifts when the number of potential buyers changes. Demographic changes, such as the fractions of the population in various age groups, can cause changes in demand.

EXAMPLES

The U.S. Census Bureau projects that within the next 20 years, the fraction of the U.S. population over 55 years old will rise dramatically, and the fraction over 75 will roughly double. This change is likely to raise the demands for medical care, retirement

CD players and CDs are complements. A decrease in the price of one raises demand for the other.

> **IN THE NEWS**
>
> Some buyers were even shrewder.
> Karen Mastin of Portland, Ore., eyed a Chevrolet pickup for eight months. "I knew the interest rates would come down. I waited it out," said Mastin, an apartment manager.

Intertemporal substitution (see box on page 80) leads car buyers to wait for interest rates on car loans to fall.

---

[5]Human wealth is the value of all future income that a person's education and skills will help to create.

Expectations of the Future Also Affect Demand

One substitute for buying a good now is to buy it later—a few days or a few months from now. You may postpone a vacation to take advantage of low, off-season prices, because a vacation later is a substitute for a vacation now. The current demand for a good falls when people expect its price to decline; they buy less now and plan to buy more later, after the price has fallen. Similarly, the current demand for a good increases when people expect its price to rise; they buy now before the price jumps. *Intertemporal substitution* (substitution over time) occurs when a change in the expected future price of a good causes a change in the current demand for that good. No one can predict future prices exactly, but people's guesses, or expectations, about future prices affect their demands.

Other expectations also affect demand. If you expect your income to rise, your demand for new clothes or a vacation may increase. When you buy a food that you have never tried, you may expect to like it. Of course, events sometimes confirm expectations and sometimes contradict them.

IN THE NEWS

Beef prices at record highs as cattle shortage continues

By Eben Shapiro

With barbecue season around the corner, a near 30-year low in the nation's cattle herd has resulted in the highest prices ever for steak, hamburger, and other cuts of beef.

Faced with the high meat prices, many grocers say they are promoting chicken breasts, which average $2.04 a pound, or less than half the price of a T-bone steak, and that more and more shoppers are choosing chicken.

Growing Popularity of Chicken

Last year, for the first time, Americans consumed more poultry than beef, an Agriculture Department survey found.

"Forget about nutrition; it is just plain old economics," said William Roenigk, vice president of the National Broiler Council in Washington.

Mr. Boehlje, the agriculture economist, said poultry would continue to gain market share at the expense of beef as meat prices rise. "The higher beef prices move, the more people are going to switch," he said. "We have seen substantial switching in the past and I think that is going to continue."

Source: New York Times

Chicken and beef are substitutes.

properties, old-age homes, and other services that satisfy the wants of elderly people more than young people. Increased international trade has raised the number of potential buyers for U.S. products and thereby raised market demands for those products.

Review Questions

6. What is a normal good? An inferior good?

7. What happens to the demand for a good if the price of a substitute for it rises?

8. What happens to the demand for a good if the price of a complement for it rises?

Thinking Exercise

9. Draw a graph of your demand curve for vacation days on a Caribbean beach. What conditions would affect your demand? How?

INTRODUCTION TO SUPPLY

Demand curves describe the behavior of buyers, summarizing the trades that buyers are willing to make. Similarly, supply curves summarize the behavior of sellers by describing the trades that they are willing to make.

Figure 6 | Supply Curve: Rebecca's Supply Curve for Painting Services

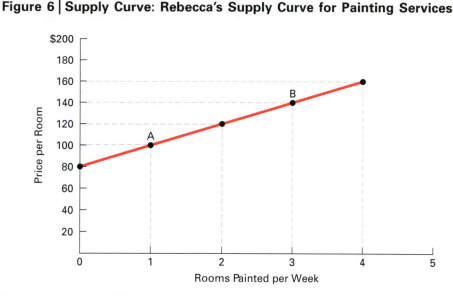

Each point is a row in Table 3.

Table 3
Rebecca's Painting Services Supplied

Price per Room	Rooms Painted per Week
$ 80	0
100	1
120	2
140	3
160	4

Suppose that your college offers you a job painting dormitory rooms next week for $100 per room, with the condition that you provide your own paint and brushes. You may choose how many rooms to paint. What choice would you make? How many rooms would you paint if the price were $80 per room, or $120, or $200? Your answer probably depends on conditions such as the cost of paint, your painting skills, how much you dislike painting, and how busy you are (the alternative uses of your time). Your answers form your supply schedule.

Table 3 shows Rebecca's supply schedule, that is, her quantity supplied of painting services at various prices. Rebecca is unwilling to paint at all for $80 per room. She will paint one room for a price of $100, two rooms for $120 each, three rooms for $140 each, or four rooms for $160 each. Figure 6 shows her supply curve of painting services. This curve graphs her supply schedule, measuring price along the vertical axis and her quantity supplied along the horizontal axis.

SUPPLY

Stated roughly, a seller's quantity supplied of a good is the amount she wants to sell. More precisely:

> A seller's **quantity supplied** of a good at some price is the amount she would sell at that price.

Notice that the quantity supplied describes the behavior of *sellers;* it is unrelated to the behavior of buyers. The definition involves hypothetical "what if?" situations. It does not say what price sellers actually receive. Instead, it indicates how much the person *would* sell *if* the price were at a certain level.

A table (such as a spreadsheet on a computer) that lists various possible prices and quantities supplied is a *supply schedule.* Table 3 shows an example of a supply schedule. Graphing a supply schedule gives a *supply curve.*

Straight Line or Curved?

Is a supply curve a straight line, or does it curve in some way? As in the case of demand curves, it all depends! In real life, some supply curves are straight lines, while many others curve. Chapters 11 and 12 will explain how technology affects the shapes of supply curves.

> A **supply curve** graphs the relation between the price of a good and the quantity supplied.

Figure 6 shows an example.

Market Supply

A graph can display *one person's* supply curve for some good, or the supply curve by several people, or by *all sellers* in the market. Whatever the size of a particular market, the supply model can describe its sellers' choices.

> The **market quantity supplied** of a good at some price is the total amount that *all sellers* in the market would sell at that price.

To obtain the total amount that *all* sellers would sell, simply add together the amounts that each individual would sell.

A table (or spreadsheet) showing various possible prices and market quantities supplied is a *market supply schedule*. A graph of a market supply schedule is a *market supply curve*.

> A **market supply curve** graphs the relation between the price of a good and the market quantity supplied.

When economists talk about *the* supply curve for a good, they mean the market supply curve.

EXAMPLE

Figure 7 shows how to add individual supply curves to get a market supply curve. Supply curves, like demand curves, add horizontally. The figure shows how to add Papa's supply of pizzas to Mama's supply of pizzas to get the market supply curve, assuming that Papa and Mama are the only sellers in the market. The market quantity supplied is the total of the quantities supplied by the individual sellers.

Conditions That Affect the Quantity Supplied

Quantity supplied, like quantity demanded, depends on several conditions. The two main conditions are input prices and technology. The *market* quantity supplied also depends on the number of potential sellers.

An increase in the price of a good, with *no change in these other conditions*, generally raises the quantity supplied. A basic generalization about the behavior of sellers states:

> *Law of Supply*: When the price of a good rises, holding constant other conditions, the quantity supplied rises.

Later chapters will discuss exceptions to this law of supply, but it holds in most cases. To state this another way:

> Supply curves usually have positive slopes.

Figure 7 | Individual and Market Supplies

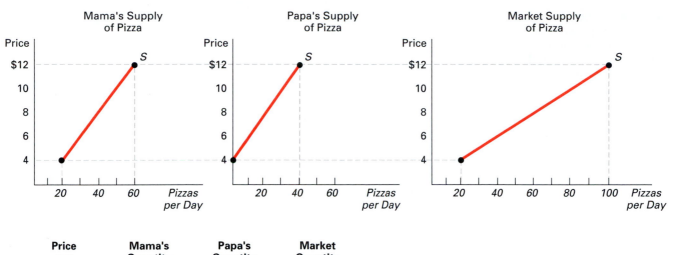

Price per Pizza	Mama's Quantity Supplied	Papa's Quantity Supplied	Market Quantity Supplied
$12	60	40	100
10	50	30	80
8	40	20	60
6	30	10	40
4	20	0	20

Supply curves usually slope upward, as in Figure 6, because an increase in price raises the incentive to produce and sell the good.

Market supply curves usually slope upward because individual sellers' supply curves slope upward and because more potential sellers become actual sellers when the price rises. For example, everyone with a ticket to a sold-out concert or football game is a potential seller—each could sell a ticket. Increasing numbers of these potential sellers become *actual* sellers as buyers offer to pay higher prices for the tickets. Consequently, the market supply curve for tickets sold outside the stadium slopes upward, even though each seller has only one ticket to sell.

CHANGES IN SUPPLY

The quantity supplied of a good depends on its price and on *other* conditions, specifically, input prices, technology, and (for the market quantity supplied) the number of potential sellers. A change in one of these *other* conditions causes a change in supply.

A **change in supply** means a change in the numbers in the supply schedule and a shift in the supply curve.

An **increase (or rise) in supply** increases the quantity supplied at each possible price, and the supply curve shifts to the right as in Figure 8, from S_1 to S_2.

Figure 8 | Increase in Supply

An increase in supply is a rise in the quantity supplied at each price. At each price, the new supply curve, S_2, shows a higher quantity supplied than the old supply curve, S_1.

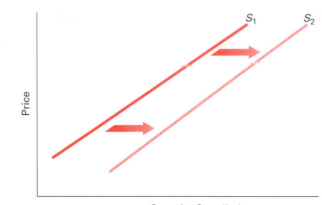

Price

Quantity Supplied

> A **decrease (or fall) in supply** decreases the quantity supplied at each possible price, and the supply curve shifts to the left as in Figure 9, from S_1 to S_2.

When supply changes, the *horizontal* (leftward or rightward) shift in the supply curve shows the change in the quantity supplied. Figures 8 and 9 show changes in supply.

Changes in Quantity Supplied versus Changes in Supply

Economists distinguish between changes in the quantity supplied and changes in supply. A change in the quantity supplied occurs when the price changes, moving the economy from one row to another in the supply schedule. This change appears as a movement *along* a supply curve, as from Point A to Point B in Figure 6.

> A **change in quantity supplied** means a movement *along* a supply curve due to a change in price.

When quantity supplied changes, the supply curve does *not* move and the numbers in the supply schedule do *not* change. The economy simply moves from one row to another in the supply schedule.

> A change in price changes the quantity supplied; it does not change supply. A change in conditions *other than the price of the good* can change the supply for that good.

Changes in Conditions Causing Changes in Supply

Table 4 summarizes the changes in conditions that can change supply.

Prices of Inputs
Increases in the prices of inputs (such as materials, equipment, labor, energy, and natural resources) decrease supply as in Figure 9, by reducing the incentive to produce and sell the good. Similarly, a fall in input prices raises the incentive to produce and sell the good, increasing supply as in Figure 8.

IN THE NEWS

Rising rents threaten theater companies

Source: New York Times

Increases in the prices of inputs reduce supply.

Figure 9 | Decrease in Supply

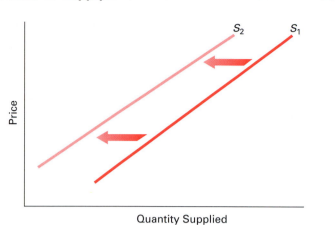

A decrease in supply is a fall in the quantity supplied at each price. At each price, the new supply curve, S_2, shows a lower quantity supplied than the old supply curve, S_1.

Technology

If an advance in technology lowers the cost of producing a good, it raises the incentive to produce and sell it. In this way, advances in technology can increase supply, as in Figure 8.

Number of Potential Sellers

Market supply increases with growth in the number of potential sellers. For example, the supply of workers increased when the baby-boom generation graduated from high school and college in the 1960s and 1970s. The supply of mail-delivery services fell in 1845 when the U.S. government prohibited anyone except the government-operated post office from delivering first-class mail; this edict reduced the number of potential sellers. The supply of telecommunications services increased dramatically in the last decade as the U.S. government deregulated the telecommunications industry, allowing new firms to enter the industry.

Expectations of the Future Also Affect Supply

One substitute for selling a good now is to wait and sell it in the future, when its price may be higher. *Intertemporal substitution* (substitution over time) affects supply when a change in the expected future price of a good causes a change in its current supply. The supply of a good falls if its expected future price increases. Freezing weather in Florida may kill orange trees and raise the expected future price of orange juice; this decreases the current supply of orange juice as producers hold already-made juice off the market, waiting to sell it in the future at a higher price.

R e v i e w   Q u e s t i o n s

10. What is a supply schedule? A market supply schedule?

11. What is a supply curve? Why does it usually slope upward?

Table 4 | Effects on Supply of Changes in Conditions

Changes in Conditions That *Increase* Supply	Changes in Conditions That *Decrease* Supply
1. Fall in the price of an input	1. Rise in the price of an input
2. Improvement in technology that lowers the cost of production	2. Decrease in available technology (e.g., a new law prohibits a certain technology)
3. Increase in the number of potential sellers	3. Decrease in the number of potential sellers

12. Draw graphs to explain the difference between a change in supply and a change in the quantity supplied.

EQUILIBRIUM OF SUPPLY AND DEMAND

Demand curves summarize the behavior of buyers. They also summarize the opportunities available to sellers by showing the trades that buyers are willing to make. Supply curves summarize the behavior of sellers. They also show the opportunities available to buyers because they show the trades that sellers are willing to make. These opportunities determine the trades that people really do make—the amounts they buy and sell and the prices they pay or receive.

This section combines supply and demand to examine these issues, beginning with a definition of *equilibrium:*

> An **equilibrium** occurs when quantity supplied equals quantity demanded.

> The price in an equilibrium is the **equilibrium price,** and the quantity is the **equilibrium quantity**.

A graph marks equilibrium at the point where the S (supply) and D (demand) curves intersect: Point A in Figure 10. The equilibrium price is P_1. The equilibrium quantity Q_1 shows the amount of the good bought and sold: the quantity traded. Buyers buy Q_1 units of the good from sellers, and pay P_1 dollars for each unit.[6]

Total spending on the good appears as the area of the shaded rectangle in Figure 10. This shaded area equals the quantity that people buy, Q_1, multiplied by the price per unit, P_1.[7] Of course, the area of this shaded rectangle also shows the total receipts of sellers, since they collect the money that buyers spend.

Why the Intersection of the Curves Shows Equilibrium

The demand curve in Figure 10 shows that at a price of P_1, the quantity demanded is Q_1. The supply curve shows that at a price of P_1, the quantity supplied is Q_1. At a price of P_1, the quantity demanded equals the quantity supplied, that is, the amount that buyers want to buy equals the amount that sellers want to sell. Equilibrium occurs at Point A, where the supply and demand curves intersect.

At any price other than P_1, however, the quantity demanded does not equal the quantity supplied, and the market is not in equilibrium.

> **Disequilibrium** is the opposite of equilibrium; it occurs when the quantity demanded does not equal the quantity supplied at the current price.

---

[6]The X-axis of the graph now measures both the quantity demanded and the quantity supplied, so its label reads simply *Quantity.*

[7]The area equals the base of the rectangle times its height, or Q_1 times P_1.

Figure 10 | Market Equilibrium

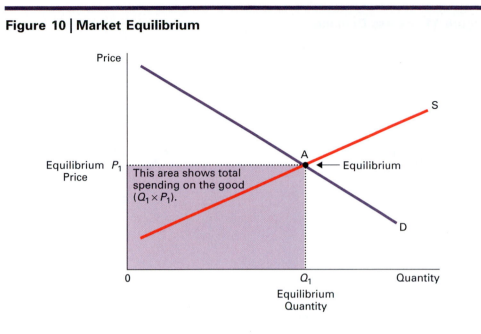

Market equilibrium is a situation in which the quantity supplied equals the quantity demanded. This occurs where the supply and demand curves intersect. Point A is the equilibrium, P_1 is the equilibrium price, and Q_1 is the equilibrium quantity traded. At price P_1, the quantity supplied and quantity demanded both equal Q_1.

A disequilibrium situation creates an inherent tendency for change. The price tends to change, and this change moves the economy toward equilibrium. To understand how, consider two kinds of disequilibrium situations: excess demand and excess supply.

Excess Demand

Suppose that the price is P_0, below the equilibrium price of P_1 in Figure 11. The supply curve shows that the quantity supplied at the price P_0 is Q_0^s units of the good. The demand curve shows that the quantity demanded at the price P_0 is Q_0^d units of the good. So the quantity demanded exceeds the quantity supplied; at price P_0, buyers want to buy more than sellers want to sell. There is a shortage of the good.

> **Excess demand,** or a **shortage,** is a situation in which the quantity demanded exceeds the quantity supplied.

A shortage occurs when the price of a good is below its equilibrium level. The size of the shortage, or the amount of excess demand, equals the quantity demanded minus the quantity supplied. At a price of P_0, Figure 11 shows a shortage of $Q_0^d - Q_0^s$.

A shortage creates pressure for the price to rise. Some buyers cannot buy the good, and stores run out of it. Sellers have an incentive to raise the price, because enough buyers are willing to pay the higher price. The price tends to rise until it reaches the equilibrium price P_1, where the quantity demanded equals the quantity supplied.

> A price below the equilibrium price creates a shortage, and the price tends to rise toward the equilibrium.

The shortage shrinks when the price rises. When the price reaches the equilibrium level, the shortage vanishes for two reasons. First, the quantity supplied increases when the price rises, helping to eliminate the shortage. Second, the quantity demanded falls when the price rises, also helping to eliminate the shortage.

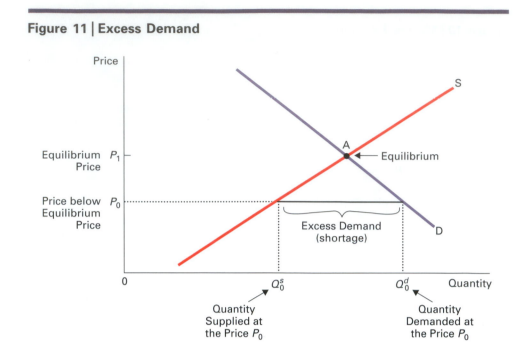

Figure 11 | Excess Demand

At a price, P_0, below the equilibrium price, buyers want to buy Q_0^d units of the good, and sellers want to sell only Q_0^s units, so there is a shortage or excess demand equal to $Q_0^d - Q_0^2$.

Excess Supply

The second type of disequilibrium involves excess supply. Suppose that the price is P_2, above the equilibrium price of P_1 in Figure 12. The quantity supplied at the price P_2 is Q_2^s units of the good. The quantity demanded at the price P_2 is Q_2^d units of the good. So, the quantity demanded is less than the quantity supplied at the price P_2; that is, buyers want to buy less than sellers want to sell, causing a surplus of the good.

> **Excess supply,** or a **surplus,** is a situation in which the quantity supplied exceeds the quantity demanded.

A surplus occurs when the price of a good exceeds its equilibrium price. The size of the surplus, or the amount of excess supply, equals the quantity supplied minus the quantity demanded. At a price of P_2 in Figure 12, the surplus equals $Q_2^s - Q_2^d$.

A surplus creates pressure for the price to fall. Sellers hold extra units that they cannot sell, and they would rather sell the goods at a lower price than not sell them at all. As sellers reduce the price to compete for customers, it tends to fall until it reaches the equilibrium price P_1, where the quantity supplied equals the quantity demanded.

> A price above the equilibrium price causes a surplus, and the price tends to fall toward the equilibrium.

A fall in the price of a good reduces a surplus in two ways: It decreases the quantity supplied and increases the quantity demanded. Sellers want to sell less while buyers want to buy more—both helping to eliminate the surplus.

Surpluses of automobiles show up as rising inventories at car dealers. The dealers respond by lowering car prices and sometimes by giving rebates, low-interest financing, or free options. Surpluses of clothing occur when people don't buy the styles that sellers expected them to buy. These surpluses lead stores to put the clothes on sale at reduced prices.

Figure 12 | Excess Supply

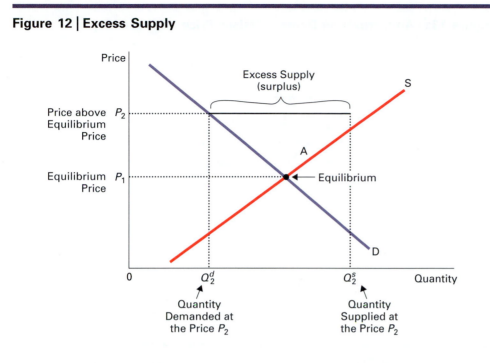

At a price, P_2, above the equilibrium price, buyers want to buy only Q_2^d units of the good, while sellers want to sell Q_2^s units, so there is a surplus or excess supply equal to $Q_2^s - Q_2^d$.

Summary of Equilibrium

At a price below the equilibrium price, a shortage occurs, and the price tends to rise. At a price above equilibrium, a surplus occurs, and the price tends to fall. At the equilibrium price, the quantity supplied equals the quantity demanded; without any shortage or surplus to disturb it, the price tends to remain constant unless supply or demand changes.

> At the equilibrium price, there is neither a shortage or a surplus, so the price shows no tendency to change unless demand or supply changes.

Changes in demand and supply cause changes in the equilibrium, as Figures 13a through 13d show. In each figure, the original equilibrium price and quantity (before the change in demand or supply) are P_1 and Q_1. The new equilibrium price and quantity (after the change) are P_2 and Q_2. Always remember the distinction between demand and supply: Demand describes buyer behavior, and supply describes seller behavior. Some changes in conditions cause changes in demand, while other changes in conditions cause changes in supply.

EFFECTS OF CHANGES IN DEMAND OR SUPPLY

Increase in Demand

An increase in demand raises the equilibrium price and the equilibrium quantity, as in Figure 13a. At the original equilibrium, Point A, the original demand curve D_1 intersects the supply curve at an original equilibrium price of P_1 and an original equilibrium quantity of Q_1. At the new equilibrium, Point B, the new demand curve D_2 intersects the unchanged supply curve at a new equilibrium price of P_2 and a new equilibrium quantity of Q_2. The increase in demand raises both the price and the quantity that people buy and sell.

Gasoline prices rise as drivers flock to road

Source: The Wall Street Journal

An increase in demand raises the price.

Figure 13a | An Increase in Demand Raises Price and Quantity

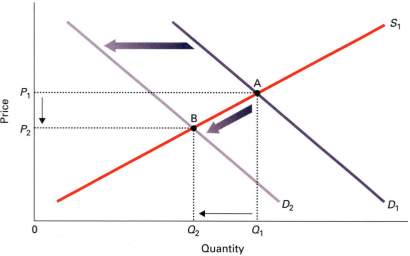

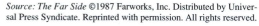

Figure 13b | A Decrease in Demand Lowers Price and Quantity

Notice that an increase in demand implies a shift in the demand curve *without* a shift in the supply curve. The supply curve stays at S_1. The quantity supplied rises, however, because the price increase from P_1 to P_2 causes movement along the supply curve from Point A to Point B.

Prices rise quickly sometimes; at other times they rise slowly. Stores may learn that demand for a product has increased and raise its price only after a shortage develops or inventories of the good decline. A seller may raise the price only after receiving more orders for a product than expected. Sellers may apply trial-and-error methods over time to find the new equilibrium price, but eventually the price will rise to P_2.

Figure 13c | An Increase in Supply Lowers the Price and Raises the Quantity

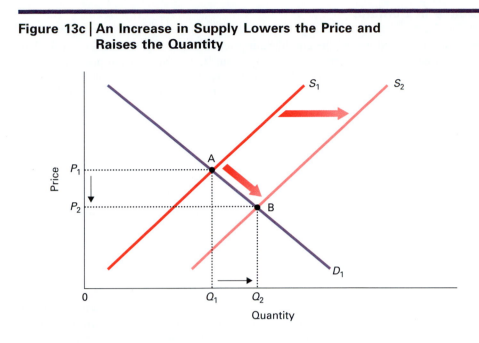

Figure 13d | A Decrease in Supply Raises the Price and Lowers the Quantity

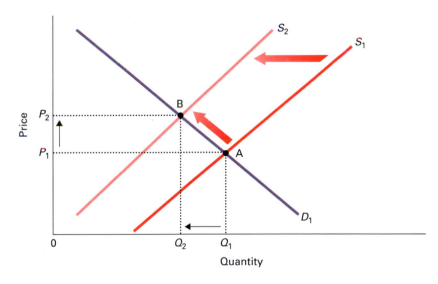

EXAMPLES

Concern over the spread of AIDS has increased the demand for both condoms and rubber gloves for health-care workers, leading to increases in quantities sold. The market demand for child-care centers increased when it became more common for both parents in families with children to work outside the home. This trend raised the number of child-care centers as well as the prices they charged.

Decrease in Demand

A decrease in demand lowers the equilibrium price and quantity, as in Figure 13b. The equilibrium point then moves from Point A to Point B. The equilibrium price falls from P_1 to P_2, and the equilibrium quantity traded falls from Q_1 to Q_2. The fall in price reduces the quantity supplied, causing movement along the supply curve from Point A to Point B.

EXAMPLE

The demand for fur coats has decreased in recent decades because of increased sensitivity to animal-rights issues. This change reduced the prices of fur coats and the quantity bought and sold.

Increase in Supply

An increase in supply lowers the equilibrium price and raises the equilibrium quantity traded, as in Figure 13c. The increase in supply shifts the supply curve from S_1 to S_2 and moves the equilibrium from Point A to Point B. The equilibrium price falls from P_1 to P_2 and the equilibrium quantity rises from Q_1 to Q_2. Notice that an increase in supply means a shift in the supply curve *without* a shift in the demand curve, which stays at D_1. The fall in price from P_1 to P_2 raises the *quantity demanded;* that is, it causes movement along the demand curve from Point A to Point B.

EXAMPLE

An increase in the number of community recycling programs in the early 1990s increased the supplies of recyclable glass, plastic, and paper, reducing their prices.

Decrease in Supply

A decrease in supply raises the equilibrium price and lowers the equilibrium quantity traded, as in Figure 13d. The equilibrium moves from Point A to Point B as the equilibrium price rises from P_1 to P_2 and the equilibrium quantity falls from Q_1 to Q_2.

Market Process and Economic Coordination

Chapter 1 described the puzzle of market coordination. People buy goods from all over the world—goods that they could never produce by themselves, goods made by people they will never meet, sometimes in cultures they will never experience. No one directs all this activity of billions of people; the market coordinates decisions so that they all fit together. It provides enough soap, food, and footballs for those who want (and can afford) to buy these goods. Enough people become doctors, plumbers, and comedians. No one has to tell people, "Joe, you must become an accountant," and "Alison, you must become an engineer." People make their own decisions about which products to buy and how much to buy. People make their own decisions about occupations to choose, and what products their businesses should make. The market process provides the amazing coordination of activities to produce even a simple good like a pencil (see Chapter 1) through the operation of supply and demand, without any central direction.

Maple sap is running, but fitfully in another 'off' year

It's driving up prices as much as $4 a quart

By Bob Bickel

CASTILE—When asked to perform, sugar maples can be as temperamental as opera singers. And recently, they have been particularly recalcitrant about giving up their sap.

Throughout the Northeast, production is down for the second year in a row. . . .

At the retail level, consumers are now paying about $10 a quart for pure maple syrup—up $3–$4 [per] quart from prices two years ago.

Source: Rochester Democrat and Chronicle

A decrease in supply raises the price.

Prices influence all these decisions. What would happen if no one wanted to be a doctor? Wages of doctors would rise until people changed their minds. The cost of medical care would rise in the process, but the prospects of high incomes would induce people to produce medical services. What happens when many people want to become movie stars or musical performers? Wages of these occupations fall to low levels, except for the few who find success. Low wages induce people to choose other occupations instead, and pursue acting and music as hobbies rather than professions.

Prices play the key role in the market process. Whenever a good becomes increasingly scarce, the fall in supply raises its price. This price increase gives consumers an incentive to conserve the good—to use less of it and to substitute other, less scarce goods in its place. The price jump also gives producers an incentive to boost production as quickly as they can. No one needs to know why the good became scarce, and only a few people may know, but the market adjusts to the change. The price increase affects incentives and changes the quantities demanded and supplied. Similarly, an emergency that raises demand for a medicine in the Third World raises its price, giving people who live elsewhere an incentive to conserve it and to substitute alternatives. The price increase also gives people an incentive to transport the medicine quickly to locations where it is needed and to produce more. The operation of supply and demand described in this chapter underlies the insight of Adam Smith that, even in acting selfishly, a person is often "led by an invisible hand to promote an end which was no part of his intention."

Review Questions

13. What is an equilibrium? What is a market equilibrium?

14. Why does excess demand tend to raise the price of a good, while excess supply reduces the price?

15. How does an increase in demand affect the equilibrium price and quantity traded? How does an increase in supply affect the equilibrium price and quantity traded?

With mandatory recycling programs in place in many areas of the country, materials brokers said, glass, aluminum, and plastic containers continue to pour into collection centers, regardless of demand. With excess supply chasing inadequate demand, prices took a beating.

The price paid by brokers for aluminum cans fell from almost 30 cents a pound at the beginning of the year to barely more than 20 cents by the end, according to the survey. The value of clear polyethylene terepthalate, which is used in large soda bottles, fell from almost 7.0 cents a pound to 1.2 cents.

Source: New York Times

An increase in supply lowers the price.

16. Use demand and supply curves to predict changes in the price of a rental car in Florida at different times of the year (winter, spring break, summer, Labor Day, Christmas). Do the same analysis for motel rates at ski resorts in the Rocky Mountains.

17. Translate the following newspaper headlines into statements about supply and demand:
(a) "Sweets Cost More Due to Sugar Price Rise"
(b) "Pork Prices Rise as Farmers Cut Output"
(c) "Profits from Popcorn Attract Farmers"

RELATIVE PRICES AND NOMINAL PRICES

Prices in the United States today are about twice as high as in 1980, on average, and about four times higher than prices in 1970. This rise in the average level of prices—inflation—makes it important to distinguish between two kinds of prices: nominal prices and relative prices.

> The **nominal price** of a good is its money price.

Everyone is familiar with nominal prices: If a hamburger costs $2.50, that is its nominal price. Inflation is an increase in the average level of nominal prices.

> The **relative price** of one good in terms of another good is its opportunity cost measured in units of that other good.

The rule to calculate the relative price between two goods is:

If the nominal price of one good is P_1 and the nominal price of another good is P_2, the relative price of the first good in terms of the second good is P_1/P_2.

The relative price of a sweater in terms of candy bars is the number of candy bars that you sacrifice each time you buy a sweater. Relative prices are important because they measure *opportunity costs*.

EXAMPLE

Suppose that a sweater costs $30.00 and a candy bar costs $0.50 (both nominal prices). The relative price of the sweater in terms of candy bars is 60 candy bars per sweater. You sacrifice 60 candy bars (and a monster stomach ache) when you buy the sweater.

The relative price is the ratio of the nominal prices:

Relative price of a sweater = Nominal price of a sweater/Nominal price of candy bar
in terms of candy bars

= $30.00/$0.50 = 60 candy bars per sweater

Similarly, the relative price of a candy bar in terms of sweaters is 1/60 of a sweater per candy bar.

Which Price Is on the Graph?

When economists use the term *relative price* without saying "measured in terms of" some other good, they mean the relative price in terms of all other goods in the economy. When a good's nominal price rises faster than the average of the nominal prices of other goods, its relative price rises. For example, the relative price of wooden furniture has increased in recent years, while the relative prices of computers and home electronics equipment (video and audio components) have fallen. If all nominal prices rise by the same percentage, relative prices do not change.

Which price—the nominal price or the relative price—appears on the graph in a supply-and-demand diagram? It is the relative price.

The price on a graph of demand or supply is the good's relative price.

Demand is affected by the relative prices of substitutes and complements; supply is affected by the relative prices of inputs and other goods. Relative prices are inflation-adjusted prices. All analysis of demand and supply in this chapter applies to relative prices.

Review Question

18. Which kind of price—a nominal or relative price—appears on the vertical axis in a supply-and-demand graph?

Thinking Exercises

19. How is the relative price of tacos in terms of Frisbees related to the nominal prices of tacos and Frisbees?

20. If sneakers cost $30 and a hamburger costs $3, what is the relative price of sneakers in terms of hamburgers? What is the relative price of hamburgers in terms of sneakers?

Conclusion

Trading Opportunities: The Price-Taking Model

The price-taking model describes trading opportunities. It states that each buyer and seller can buy or sell as much (or as little) of a good as desired at a given price, but no individual can affect that price. This price-taking model leads to the model of supply and demand, which works well in many real-life situations (even when buyers and sellers are not exactly price takers).

Demand

Demand models the behavior of buyers. A person's quantity demanded of a good at some price is the amount she would buy at that (hypothetical) price. A demand curve graphs the relation between the price of a good and the quantity demanded. The market quantity demanded and market demand curve are defined in the same way, but apply to all buyers in the market.

Four main factors besides price affect the quantity demanded: tastes, usefulness, income and wealth, and prices of related goods. The Law of Demand states that a rise in the price of a good, holding constant these other conditions, reduces the quantity demanded. This implies that demand curves slope downward.

Changes in Demand

A *change in demand* refers to a shift in the demand curve. A *change in quantity demanded* refers to a movement along a fixed demand curve due to a change in price.

Changes in demand result from changes in tastes, usefulness, income and wealth, and prices of related goods. Changes in market demand also result from changes in the number of potential buyers.

An increase in income raises demand for normal goods and reduces demand for inferior goods. Two goods are substitutes when a rise in the price of one increases demand for the other. Two goods are complements when a rise in the price of one decreases demand for the other.

Supply

Supply models the behavior of sellers. A seller's quantity supplied of a good at some price is the amount she would sell at that (hypothetical) price. A supply curve graphs the relation between the price of a good and the quantity supplied. The market quantity supplied and market supply curve are defined in the same way, but apply to all sellers in the market.

Two main factors besides price affect the quantity supplied: input prices and technology. The Law of Supply states that a rise in the price of a good, holding constant these other conditions, raises the quantity supplied. This implies that supply curves slope upward.

Changes in Supply

A *change in supply* refers to a shift in the supply curve. A *change in quantity supplied* refers to a movement along a fixed supply curve due to a change in price. Changes in supply result from changes in input prices and technology. Changes in market supply also result from changes in the number of potential sellers. An increase in the price of inputs decreases supply. An increase in technology that lowers the cost of producing a good raises supply.

Equilibrium of Supply and Demand

An equilibrium occurs when quantity supplied equals quantity demanded. That quantity is the equilibrium quantity, and the price is the equilibrium price. A graph marks equilibrium at the point where the supply and demand curves intersect.

If a price is *below* its equilibrium level, the resulting excess demand (shortage) causes the price to rise toward its equilibrium level. If a price is *above* its equilibrium level, the resulting excess supply (surplus) causes the price to fall toward its equilibrium level. In an equilibrium, there is no tendency for the price or quantity to change unless changes in underlying conditions cause demand or supply to change.

Effects of Changes in Demand or Supply

An increase in demand raises the equilibrium price and quantity. A decrease in demand lowers the equilibrium price and quantity. An increase in supply lowers the equilibrium price and raises the equilibrium quantity. A decrease in supply raises the equilibrium price and lowers the equilibrium quantity.

Relative Prices and Nominal Prices

The nominal price of a good is its money price. The relative price of a good in terms of another good is its opportunity cost measured in units of that other good. The relative price of a good is often expressed in terms of all goods produced in the economy. The price measured along the vertical axis of a supply or demand graph is a relative price.

Key Terms

quantity demanded	change in quantity demanded	supply curve	equilibrium quantity
demand curve	income	market quantity supplied	disequilibrium
market quantity demanded	normal good	market supply curve	excess demand (shortage)
market demand curve	inferior good	change (increase or decrease) in supply	excess supply (surplus)
change (increase or decrease) in demand	wealth	change in quantity supplied	nominal price
	substitute	equilibrium	relative price of one good in terms of another
	complement	equilibrium price	
	quantity supplied		

Problems

21. A national newspaper reported: "Increased retail demand for roasted and ground coffee because of lower prices . . . has contributed to a higher price for coffee." What's wrong with this reasoning?

22. Suppose that three companies sell lawnmowers. Their supply schedules appear in the following table.
   (a) Make a table of the market supply schedule.
   (b) Draw the supply curve for each company and the market supply curve.

If the Price Is	Alright Co. Wants to Sell	Better Co. Wants to Sell	Cut-It Co. Wants to Sell
$400	28	45	65
350	24	43	65
300	20	38	60
250	16	32	45
200	12	25	20
150	8	18	0
100	4	11	0
50	0	5	0

23. A change in the price of one good can affect demand and supply of other goods.
    (a) How is an increase in the price of bologna likely to affect the price of peanut butter and the amount of peanut butter that people buy?
    (b) How is an increase in the price of charcoal grills likely to affect the price of charcoal and the amount of charcoal that people buy?

24. Discuss this statement: "They're building too many hotels in this city. They think this town will become a big convention city. If they're wrong, we will have too many hotels and loads of empty rooms. It'll cost more to spend a night in a hotel here, because the hotels will charge more to make up for all the empty rooms."

25. How would the following changes affect demand curves, supply curves, and equilibrium prices and quantities? (Discuss as many economic implications of these changes as you can imagine.)
    (a) People learn about health benefits of cutting the amount of fat they eat.

    (b) Global warming raises the average world temperature by 5 degrees.
    (c) Scientists discover a cure for AIDS.
    (d) The NCAA allows college athletes to collect salaries.
    (e) A college improves its dormitories and enhances the desirability of dorm living.
    (f) California legalizes gambling.
    (g) Scientists perfect high-definition television (HDTV) and discover how to build a large-screen HDTV set for $300.

26. Suppose that a genetically engineered hormone were to raise the milk output of cows by 40 percent. How would this innovation affect the price of milk, the quantity of milk produced, and the number of dairy farmers?

27. Read the following news headlines and excerpts and interpret them in terms of supply and demand:
    (a) "Prices Soar as Everyone Wants Beanie Babies"
    (b) "Crude Oil, Petroleum Product Prices Rise after Explosion at Large Shell Refinery"
    (c) "Digital Camera Prices Fall as More People Buy, Contradicting the Law of Supply and Demand"
    (d) "Computer Prices Fall Again as Chip Technology Improves"
    (e) "Tuition Rises and College Enrollments Fall"
    (f) "Demand is increasing moderately, but with yields per acre rising, farmers have seen little change in prices."

28. If the average price of goods rises 5 percent and the price of tortillas rises 8 percent, what happens to the relative price of tortillas?

Inquiries for Further Thought

29. Which relative prices do you believe will rise over the next 20 years? Which relative prices will fall? Explain why. What conditions will cause the changes in demand or supply? Do your answers suggest that some types of businesses will become more profitable and expand, while others will become less profitable and shrink? How might you use these insights to make money?

30. How much money would you be willing to pay to become more physically attractive? Translate this into a demand curve for physical attractiveness. What products would rise in price if the demand for physical attractiveness were to increase?

31. How could you obtain evidence to support or refute the Law of Demand?

Appendix: Algebra of Equilibrium

Economists often express demand and supply curves as equations. If the demand curve is a straight line, it can be expressed as:

$$Q^d = a - bP$$

Example: $Q^d = 10 - 2P$

where Q^d is the quantity demanded, P is the price of the good, and a and b are positive numbers that depend on buyers' tastes and incomes, the prices of complements and substitutes, and the other conditions that affect demand. For example, a might be 10 and b might be 2.

The equation for the supply curve, if it is a straight line, can be written as:

$$Q^s = c - dP \qquad\qquad \text{Example: } Q^s = -5 + 3P$$

where Q^s is the quantity supplied, P is the price, and c and d are numbers that depend on technology, input costs, and the other conditions that affect supply. The number d is generally positive, which means that the supply curve slopes upward. The number c can be positive or negative. For example, c might be -5 and d might be 3.

Graphs show the equilibrium price and quantity as the intersection of the supply and demand curves. At the equilibrium price, P_1, the quantity demanded equals the quantity supplied. In algebraic terms, that means:

$$Q^d = Q^s$$

Now substitute the two equations for Q^d and Q^s into this last equation (called the *equilibrium condition,* since it says that quantity supplied equals quantity demanded):

$$a - bP = c + dP \qquad\qquad \text{Example: } 10 - 2P = -5 + 3P$$

To solve for the equilibrium price, begin by adding bP to both sides:

$$a = c + dP + bP \qquad\qquad \text{Example: } 10 = -5 + 5P$$

Subtracting c from both sides:

$$a - c = dP + bP \qquad\qquad \text{Example: } 15 = 5P$$

Collect terms on the right-hand side:

$$a - c = (b + d)P$$

Divide both sides by the quantity $(b + d)$ and rearrange terms:

$$P_1 = (a - c)/(b + d) \qquad\qquad \text{Example: } P_1 = 3$$

To find Q_1, the equilibrium quantity, substitute the solution for P_1 into either the demand curve equation or the supply curve equation. After simplifying the algebra, either equation gives the same answer for Q_1. For example, substituting the equilibrium price P_1 into the demand curve equation gives:

$$Q_1^d = a - bP \qquad \text{Example: } Q_1^d = 10 - (2 \times 3)$$
$$= a - b(a - c)/(b + d) \qquad \text{Example: } Q_1^d = 4$$

This is the formula for the equilibrium quantity.

Notice that changes in the numbers a, b, c, and d affect the equilibrium price and equilibrium quantity. Those numbers change in response to changes in tastes, technology, or other conditions that affect demand and supply.

Problems

A1. Suppose that the demand curve for rental cars is:

$$Q^d = 500 - 2P$$

and the supply curve is

$$Q^s = 100 + 6P$$

where Q^d is the quantity demanded (in cars per day), Q^s is the quantity supplied, and P is the rental price per day. Find the equilibrium price and quantity.

A2. Suppose that the demand curve for movie tickets is:

$$Q^d = 250 - 20P$$

and the supply curve is

$$Q^s = 50 + 30P$$

where Q^d is the quantity demanded, Q^s is the quantity supplied, and P is the price. Find the equilibrium price and quantity.

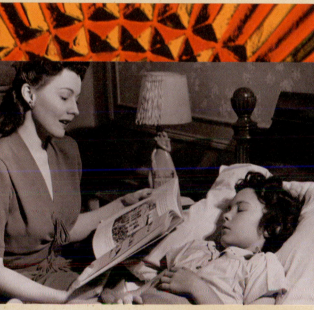

PART 3

MACROECONOMICS: MYSTERIES, MEASUREMENT, AND MODELS

CHAPTER 5

MACROECONOMIC ISSUES AND MEASUREMENT

In this Chapter...

Main Points to Understand

▶ Macroeconomics is the study of the economy as a whole—total production of goods and services, total employment and unemployment, the average level of prices, foreign exchange rates, interest rates and financial market activity, and the overall effects of government policies.

▶ GDP measures the economy's total production of final market goods and services

▶ The GDP deflator, consumer price index, and producer price index are three measures of the average level of prices.

Thinking Skills to Develop

▶ Recognize the connection between the economy's total production of final goods and services, its total income, and its total spending.

▶ Distinguish between nominal and real GDP.

▶ Recognize key issues in measurement and interpretation of economic statistics.

When you finish college and look for a job, your employment opportunities will probably depend on the nation's overall economic situation. If the economy is growing rapidly with low unemployment rates, your chances of finding a good job will be higher than if the economy is in a recession with low growth and high unemployment. In the first half of 1998, the unemployment rate in the United States was 4.5 percent, down from 7.5 percent only six years earlier. What will happen when you look for a job?

If your job has an international flavor—as many do through world trade, international business connections, or foreign competition—then international factors such as financial crises and recessions in Asia, inflation in Latin America, and high unemployment in Europe may directly impact your career. Even middle-class Americans will see their lives dramatically altered in the coming decades by economic growth in China, Africa, Mexico and Latin America, Russia, and eastern Europe. Distant as these places may seem, events there will affect your job opportunities, your salary, the prices you pay, and the products available to you. They will affect the interest rates at which you can borrow money for cars and vacations, the taxes you will pay, and the new technologies that drive the goods and services you consume in the coming decades.

Momentous economic events have transformed people's lives over the last 100 years. The 20th century saw the highest inflation rates in history; the Great Depression of the 1930s, with the highest unemployment rates ever recorded; and interactions of economics and politics that led to war—as economic penalties imposed on Germany after World War I helped bring hyperinflation and the rise of Adolf Hitler. The 20th century saw dramatic increases in government spending and taxes. In the United States, federal government spending rose from under 3 percent of the total U.S. income in 1900 to almost 20 percent in 1998. Economic catastrophes in the former Soviet Union and eastern Europe helped to bring down communism, ending the cold war and spreading freedom and democracy. The century also saw the development of new financial markets around the globe, along with the fastest growth in living standards in all of history, the biggest drops in national death rates and infant mortality rates, and the biggest increases in life expectancy. No one was isolated from these events—economic issues affected not only people's jobs and incomes but the challenges and opportunities that shaped their lives. Economics shaped the 20th century, and it will probably help shape your life in the 21st.

Macroeconomics is the study of the economy as a whole—*total* production of goods and services, rather than production of individual goods such as pizzas and painting services; *total* employment and unemployment rather than employment in the computer industry or unemployment in the auto industry; the *average* level of prices rather than the prices of haircuts and hats. You will see that macroeconomics also involves interest rates, foreign exchange rates, stock markets and other financial markets, and the overall effects of government policies. You need to understand macroeconomics before you can understand many of the major social and political issues that affect our lives. You must understand macroeconomics if you want to contribute to the design of thoughtful government policies, and to the solutions to economic problems impacting people around the globe.

This book explores the key issues of macroeconomics, including:

▶ What affects a country's living standards?

▶ Why do standards of living differ across countries?

▶ Why are average standards of living higher now than in the past? What affects the speed at which living standards *grow*?

▶ What affects available job opportunities, total employment, unemployment, and wages?

▶ What causes *business cycles* in which periods of rising incomes and low unemployment are followed by *recessions* in which incomes fall and unemployment rises?

▶ What affects the average level of prices and the increases in this average that we call *inflation?*

▶ How does international trade affect our economy? What affects exchange rates between moneys in different countries, and how do changes in foreign exchange rates affect the economy?

▶ What creates changes in interest rates and stock prices, and how do these changes affect our lives?

▶ How do government policies affect the economy? What policies are best?

TOTAL PRODUCTION OF GOODS AND SERVICES

In 1997, the U.S. economy produced final goods and services that sold for $8,080 billion (or about $8 trillion). This is the economy's *GDP,* or *gross domestic product.* With a population of 268 million, U.S. GDP per capita (per person) was $30,149.

> **Gross domestic product (GDP)** is the value of a country's production of final market goods and services during some time period (usually a year).

World GDP is currently about $36 trillion per year. With a world population of about 6 billion people, this amounts to about $6,000 per person each year.[1]

> **Nominal GDP** refers to GDP measured in money (dollars, yen, pesos, Euros, etc.).

Real GDP, to be defined formally below, refers to *inflation-adjusted* GDP.

Notice the phrase "final market goods and services." Final goods are products or services intended for sale to consumers, such as hamburgers or tattoo services. Products such as steering wheels, that become inputs into the production of other goods such as cars, are *not* final goods. In other words, GDP includes the economy's production of french fries, but it does not separately include the production of potatoes that were inputs into those french fries. The term *market goods* refers to products that people sell to others; GDP does not include the food you eat from your own garden or services that people perform without explicit pay, such as housework, child care by parents, and volunteer work.

Four decades ago, in 1960, U.S. nominal GDP was only $527 billion, or about $2,915 per person, as Figure 1 indicates. What explains the change since then? Two factors are at work: (1) increases in production, and (2) increases in prices.

Increases in Production

If prices had been the same in 1997 as in 1960, then the final goods and services produced in the United States in 1997 would have sold for $1,728 billion. In other words, U.S. GDP in 1997, *measured in 1960 prices,* was $1,728 billion.

> **Real GDP** refers to GDP measured in the prices of a certain *base year*.

Figure 2 shows U.S. real GDP measured in *base year 1960 prices*. In 1960, U.S. real GDP in 1960 prices was $527 billion; by 1997, it was $1,674 billion. The scale on the right-hand side of Figure 2 shows U.S. real GDP measured in *1997 prices*. Measured in *1997 prices*, U.S. real GDP was $2,544 billion in 1960 and $8,080 billion in 1997. As Table 1 shows, the choice of a base year affects only the scale of measurement; it does not affect the picture of how real GDP changes over time. Figure 2 shows that U.S. real GDP more than tripled between 1960 and 1997.

The U.S. population increased from 181 million in 1960 to 268 million in 1997, so real GDP per person in 1997 dollars rose from:

$$\frac{\$2,544 \text{ billion}}{181 \text{ million people}} = \$14,055 \text{ per person in 1960}$$

to

$$\frac{\$8,080 \text{ billion}}{268 \text{ million people}} = \$30,149 \text{ per person in 1997}$$

In other words, U.S. real GDP per person more than doubled during that time.

[1] Estimates of world GDP differ, ranging from about 10 percent below this estimate to about 20 percent above it.

GDP Update
In the first half of 1998, U.S. GDP reached $8,435 billion at an annual rate, meaning that GDP for the year would equal $8,435 billion, or $31,177 per person, if production in the second half of the year continued at the same pace as in the first half. See the Web pages for this book (www.dryden.com) for the latest economic statistics.

Only Final Goods Appear in GDP
To see why GDP includes only *final* market goods and services, consider an example. Suppose that National Sugar sells sugar to Nabisco for $1,000, and Hershey sells chocolate to Nabisco for $500. Nabisco uses sugar and chocolate to produce final goods: 100,000 Oreo cookies. If cookies sell for 3 cents each, people spend $3,000 to buy 100,000 cookies. If these cookies were the *only* final market good in the economy, nominal GDP would be $3,000. It would not make sense to include the $1,000 of sugar and the $500 of chocolate in GDP *in addition* to the cookies, because they are *part* of the cookies. (Should we also add the value of the cocoa beans that were used to produce the chocolate?) Only the value of *final* market goods appears in GDP.

Figure 1 | Nominal GDP in the United States, 1929–1998

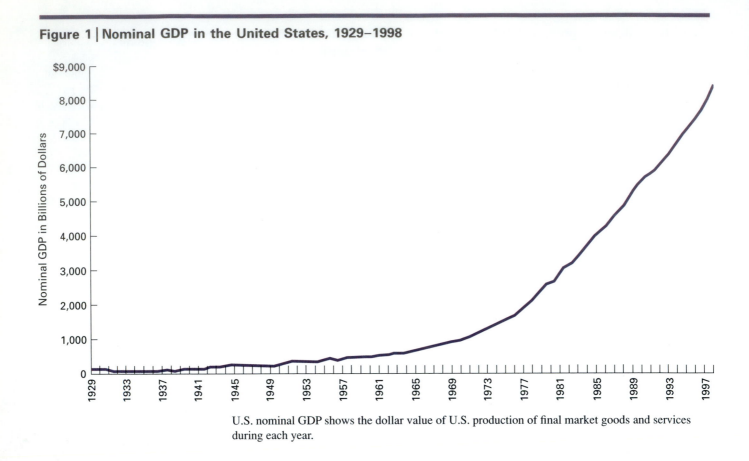

U.S. nominal GDP shows the dollar value of U.S. production of final market goods and services during each year.

Figure 2 | U.S. Real GDP, 1929–1998

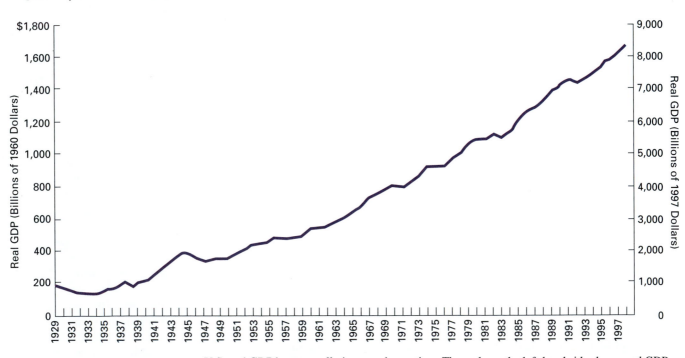

U.S. real GDP has generally increased over time. The scale on the left-hand side shows real GDP measured in base year 1960 prices; the scale on the right-hand side shows real GDP measured in base-year 1997 prices.

Table 1 | Measuring U.S. GDP in Base-Year Prices

U.S. GDP	Nominal GDP	Real GDP, Measured in 1960 Prices	Real GDP, Measured in 1997 Prices
In 1960	$527 billion	$527 billion	$2,544 billion
In 1997	$8,080 billion	$1,674 billion	$8,080 billion
Percentage increase	1,433 percent	218 percent	218 percent

Increases in Prices

Most nominal (money) prices increased between 1960 and 1997. (Chapter 4 explained the difference between nominal prices and relative prices.) One way to measure the average increase in prices over that period is to compare two figures:

▶ The money value of the economy's production in 1997 (nominal GDP in 1997)

▶ The money value of the economy's production in 1997 *if prices had been at their 1960 levels* (real 1997 GDP measured in 1960 prices)

The ratio of these two numbers shows the average increase in prices between 1960 and 1997. If prices had remained constant over that period, then these two numbers would be the same, and their ratio would equal 1. If every price had doubled between 1960 and 1997, then the first number would be twice as high as the second number, and their ratio would equal 2, indicating that prices had doubled. The *GDP deflator* measures the average change in prices between two years:

The **GDP deflator** equals nominal GDP divided by real GDP:

$$\text{GDP deflator} = 100 \times \frac{\text{Nominal GDP}}{\text{Real GDP}}$$

Figure 3 shows the U.S. GDP deflator, sometimes called the *implicit price deflator*, from 1960 to 1998. The scale on the left side shows the GDP deflator with base year

---

IN THE NEWS

Big Upward Revision in 1st-Qtr Growth

A 5.4% GDP surge shows the economy was even hotter than thought

The nation's economy roared in the first quarter, with the fastest growth in nearly 2 years.

Gross domestic product grew at a 5.4% annual rate in the first quarter, revised up from the previous estimate of 4.8%, the Commerce Department re-

ported. That's the fastest growth since the second quarter of 1996, when the economy rose at a 6% pace.

Source: Investor's Business Daily

News reports, like this one, usually mean "real GDP" when they refer to GDP.

Figure 3 | U.S. GDP Deflator, 1929–1998

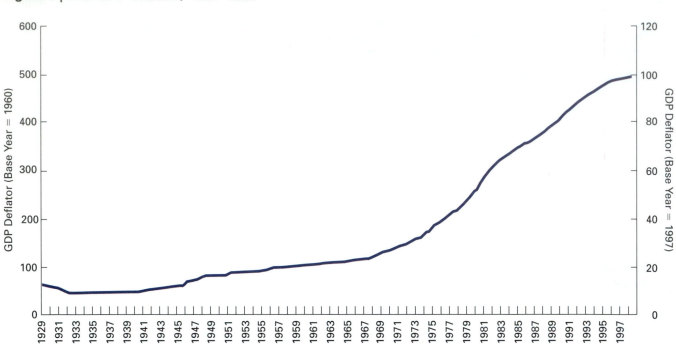

The GDP deflator, or implicit price deflator, equals nominal GDP divided by real GDP.

1960. In other words, it shows the GDP deflator when the denominator of the formula is real GDP measured in 1960 prices. The GDP deflator equaled 100 in 1960 by definition; it rose to 483 by 1997. In other words, the average level of nominal prices in the United States in 1997 was about 5 times as high as the level in 1960.

The scale on the right-hand side of Figure 3 shows the GDP deflator for base year 1997. In other words, it shows the GDP deflator when the denominator of the formula is real GDP measured in 1997 prices. With this scale, the GDP deflator equals 100.0 in

IN THE NEWS

GDP up, inflation at bay

NEW YORK (CNNfn) - The American economy grew by a stronger-than-expected 1.4 percent in the second quarter, the Commerce Department said Friday. Real gross-domestic product, or the total value of goods and services produced by the U.S. economy, expanded at a 1.4 percent annual rate from April through June, down sharply from a revised 5.5 percent growth spurt in the first quarter.

Inflation, meanwhile, appeared to be held in check. The implicit price deflator, a key inflation measure, rose only 0.9 percent in the second quarter.

Source: http://cnnfn.com/hotstories/economy/9807/31/gdp/

GDP and the GDP deflator, often called the implicit price deflator, frequently appear in the news.

1997 by definition, and it rose from 20.7 in 1960. Conclusions about changes in the average level of nominal prices do not depend on which scale we choose.

EXAMPLE: MEASURING REAL GDP IN BASE-YEAR PRICES

Suppose that the economy produces six videos and eight pillows in 2002, as Table 2 shows, and that videos cost $20 each and pillows cost $10 each in that year.

Nominal GDP in 2002 = (Output of videos in 2002)(Price of videos in 2002)
+ (Output of pillows in 2002)(Price of pillows in 2002)
= (6 videos)($20 per video) + (8 pillows)($10 per pillow)
= $120 + $80 = $200

Now choose a base year, such as 1990, and calculate real GDP.

Real GDP in 2002 measured in 1990 dollars
= (Output of videos in 2002) (Price of videos in 1990)
+ (Output of pillows in 2002)(Price of pillows in 1990)

Suppose that, as Table 2 shows, videos cost only $10 each in 1990, and pillows cost only $5 each. Then real GDP in 2002 measured in 1990 dollars equals:

(6 videos in 2002)($10 per video in 1990)
+ (8 pillows in 2002)($5 per pillow in 1990)
= $60 + $40 in 1990 dollars
= $100 in 1990 dollars

Real GDP in 2002 is $100 measured in 1990 dollars. Table 2 shows similar calculations for other years.

This measurement of real GDP allows sensible comparisons of the economy's output of goods and services in different years. To see why, suppose that the economy produces the same number of videos and pillows in 2002 as it did in 1998, but that prices are higher in 2002 than in 1998. Then nominal GDP rises between 1998 and 2002, while real GDP remains unchanged at $100, measured in 1990 dollars. This is a sensible conclusion: real GDP remains constant because production of goods does not change.

Now suppose that the economy produces 9 videos and 12 pillows in 2005, 50 percent more of each good than in 2002. In this case:

Real GDP in 2005 measured in 1990 dollars
= (9 videos in 2005)($10 per video in 1990)
+ (12 pillows in 2005)($5 per pillow in 1990)
= $90 + $60 in 1990 dollars
= $150 in 1990 dollars

Table 2 | Measuring GDP in an Economy with Videos and Pillows

	Videos	Price of Videos	Pillows	Price of Pillows	Nominal GDP	Real GDP in 1990 Dollars
1990	4	$10	4	$ 5	$ 60	$ 60
1998	6	18	8	8	172	100
2002	6	20	8	10	200	100
2005	9	21	12	10	309	150
2010	9	21	16	10	349	170

Real GDP in 2005 is $150 measured in 1990 dollars. Real GDP rises by 50 percent from 2002 to 2005, because production of each good rises by 50 percent. Finally, suppose that the economy produces 9 videos and 16 pillows in 2010. Real GDP in 2010 rises to $170 in 1990 dollars.

The change in real GDP between any two years is an average of the changes in output of the goods that the economy produces, weighted by their base-year prices. The price deflator in 2002 becomes:

$$\text{GDP price deflator in 2002 (base year 1990)}$$

$$= \frac{\text{Nominal GDP in 2002}}{\text{Real GDP in 2002 in 1990 dollars}}$$

$$= \frac{\$200}{\$100 \text{ in 1990 dollars}}$$

$$= 2 \text{ (relative to base year 1990)}$$

In this case, the price level doubles from 1990 to 2002. Notice that the equation for real GDP applies to this example: Nominal GDP in 2002 is $200, the price deflator is 2, and real income in 1990 dollars is $100.

Review Questions

1. What is the difference between real GDP and nominal GDP?

2. Roughly how large is the U.S. GDP? Roughly how large is world GDP? How big is GDP per person in the United States? GDP per person in the world?

Thinking Exercises

3. Use the numbers in Table 2 to calculate real GDP in 2010 measured in 1998 dollars.

4. A nation of elves produces only one good: cookies. In 1990, cookies sold for 2 cents each; in 1998, they cost 3 cents each; in 2000, they cost 4 cents each. How is this nation's real GDP related to the number of cookies it produces? How does your answer depend on your choice of the base year for measuring real GDP?

THE ECONOMY'S TOTAL SPENDING AND INCOME

What happens to all the goods and services the economy produces? People *consume* some of them—they wear clothes, eat pizzas, and watch movies. *Consumption* refers to the goods and services that people buy and use. Business firms *invest* some of them—they build new machinery, equipment, and office buildings. *Investment* refers to the creation of new *capital*—machinery, equipment, tools, buildings, and new knowledge (such as the technical knowledge of how to build a computer chip). The *government purchases* some of the goods and services. Finally, we may *export* some goods to people in foreign countries, perhaps more than we *import* from them. As a result, GDP equals the sum of consumption, investment, government purchases, and net exports (exports minus imports):

$$GDP = C + I + G + NEX$$

where C is consumption, I is investment, G is government purchases, and NEX is net exports (exports minus imports). Table 3 and Figure 4 show that consumption accounts for

Table 3 | GDP in the United States, 1997

	Total ($ billions)	Dollars Per Person	Percent of GDP
Nominal gross domestic product (GDP)	$8,080	$30,149	
Consumption	5,486	20,469	68%
Investment	1,243	4,636	15
Government purchases	1,453	5,421	18
Net exports	−101	−377	−1

about two-thirds of GDP in the United States, investment accounts for about 15 percent, government purchases account for 18 percent, and net exports account for −1 percent (because the United States imports more than it exports). The percentages are very similar for most other countries.

Definitions and Discussion

People consume goods when they use them—when they eat, wear, or drive them:

> **Consumption** is spending by people on final goods and services for current use.

People often buy goods, such as cars and houses, partly for future use. Official government statistics measure consumption as total household spending on goods and services except for purchases of new housing, which the official statistics count as investment.

Advice to Students
Don't be confused by the *NEX* part of this equation. *Net* exports (exports *minus* imports) appears in the GDP equation, because consumption and investment already include imports from other countries. For example, suppose GDP is $10, consumption is $8, investment is $1, government spending is $2, and exports are zero. How can consumption, investment, and government purchases sum to $11 when the nation produces only $10 in goods? Easy—the country imports $1 worth of goods, making *net* exports equal to *minus* $1. Then $C + I + G + NEX = 10, which equals GDP.

Figure 4 | Categories of Spending in GDP

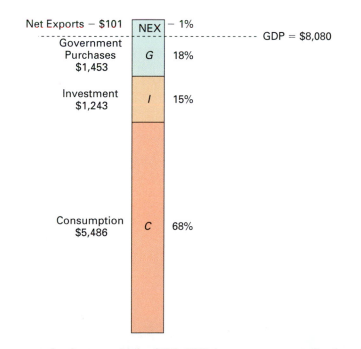

Consumption accounts for about two-thirds of U.S. GDP; investment accounts for about 15 percent; government purchases account for 18 percent.

Consumption.

Advice: Understanding Investment

In everyday life, people say they *invest* if they buy stocks or bonds. However, when you buy stocks or bonds, someone else sells them. In that case, the economy as a whole does not invest. The economy as a whole invests when it increases its capital stock (machinery, tools, knowledge, etc.). Economists use the term *investment* to refer to such increases in the economy's capital stock.

In principle, whenever you buy a durable good, such as a stereo or a car, part of that spending is investment, because you will continue to use the good in the future. However, official statistics count spending on durable goods, except new houses, as consumption.

Business firms *invest* when they buy new machines, computers, office buildings, and lab equipment. They also invest when they build new factories, train their workers, and add to knowledge through research and development.

> **Capital** is the stock of equipment, structures, inventories, human skills, and knowledge available to help produce goods and services. **Investment** is spending to create new capital.

Capital also includes inventories—stocks of spare parts and unsold final goods. For example, an auto dealer may invest in cars for its showroom or oil filters for its repair shop. In principle, you invest when you acquire skills by attending school or when you buy a durable good; however, these kinds of investments appear in official consumption statistics rather than investment statistics. The government also invests when it spends money on roads and buildings, but all government spending falls in a separate category. The term *investment* means *private* (nongovernment) investment spending.

The government purchases goods and services when it buys military equipment, builds roads, and pays school teachers and police.

> **Government purchases** include total spending on goods and services by federal, state, and local governments.

Not all government *spending* consists of government *purchases*. Government spending also includes *transfer payments* of money to people—payments that simply transfer money without any exchange of goods and services. The social security program is the largest transfer payment program in the United States. This spending is *not* included in the GDP category of government purchases of goods and services.

> **Exports** are goods and services sold to people and firms in other countries.

Investment creates new capital.

Imports are purchases of goods and services from people and firms in other countries.

Net exports, or the **balance of international trade,** equals exports minus imports.

A country with positive net exports (its exports exceed its imports) has an international trade surplus; one with negative net exports (its exports fall short of imports) has an international trade deficit.

Every good produced in the economy is consumed, invested, purchased by the government, or exported.[2] If a firm produces a good that no one buys, it becomes an investment in the firm's inventory of goods not yet sold.

Figure 5 and Table 4 show flows of money and goods in the United States in a year. All numbers in the figure show *average* amounts *per person*.[3] The figure shows four types of actors in the economy: people, firms, the government, and foreign countries. The arrows show flows of money between these actors; the green arrows show flows of money to buy *final goods*. In 1997, nominal GDP was about $30,000 per person. People spent about $20,500 per person for consumption; an arrow from people to firms shows

Figure 5 | GDP per Person in the United States

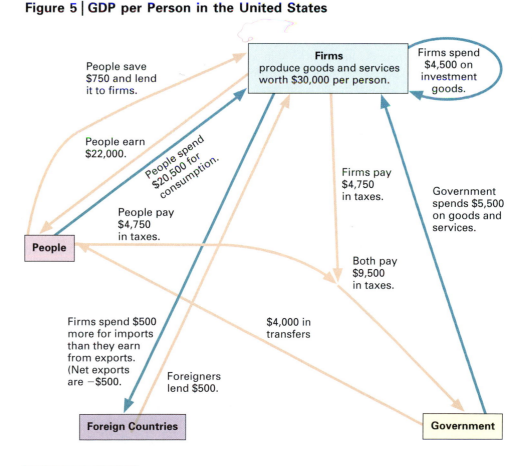

People save $750 and lend it to firms.

Firms produce goods and services worth $30,000 per person.

Firms spend $4,500 on investment goods.

People earn $22,000.

People spend $20,500 for consumption.

People pay $4,750 in taxes.

Firms pay $4,750 in taxes.

Government spends $5,500 on goods and services.

People

Both pay $9,500 in taxes.

Firms spend $500 more for imports than they earn from exports. (Net exports are −$500.

$4,000 in transfers

Foreigners lend $500.

Foreign Countries

Government

The numbers show *dollars per person* for flows in the U.S. economy. For example, wages and other income from firms averages about $22,000 per person, and consumption spending averages $20,500 per person.

[2] If you buy an ice cream cone and it melts before you eat it, you might not want to say that you consumed it. Still, this spending counts as consumption in economic data.

[3] All per-person amounts refer to the entire U.S. population—about 268 million people in 1997.

Table 4 | Flows of Money in Figure 5ᵃ

People		Firms		Government	
MONEY IN	MONEY OUT	MONEY IN	MONEY OUT	MONEY IN	MONEY OUT
$22,000 wages and profits	$20,500 consumption	$20,500 consumption $4,500 investment $5,500 government purchases	$22,000 wages and profits $4,500 investment		$5,500 government purchases
$4,000 transfer payments	$4,750 taxes		$4,750 taxes	$9,500 taxes	$4,000 transfer payments
	$750 loaned to firms	$750 borrowed from people $500 borrowed from foreign countries	$500 for imports in excess of exports		
TOTAL = $26,000	**TOTAL = $26,000**	**TOTAL = $31,750**	**TOTAL = $31,750**	**TOTAL = $9,500**	**TOTAL = $9,500**

ᵃAll Figures in dollars *per person* in the United States, 1997.

payments of $20,500 for this purpose. Firms spent about $4,500 per person on investment. The curved arrow leading from firms back to firms shows $4,500 per person in payments for that investment. Government purchases were $5,500 per person in 1997, and the arrow from government to firms shows the payment for those goods. Notice that the sum of consumption, investment, and government purchases, $30,500 per person, is $500 *more* than GDP. Where did the other $500 in spending go? The answer is that net exports totaled *minus* $500 per person; imports exceeded exports by that amount. In sum, the U.S. economy produced $30,000 in goods per person and imported $500 more, so total spending on consumption, investment, and government purchases was $30,500 per person.

The Economy's Total Income

Where did people get the $20,500 that they spent on consumption? Gold arrows show other flows of money in the economy. On average, each person earned $22,000 by working at firms and by sharing in firms' profits. In addition, the government provided money to people through *transfer payments* that averaged $4,000 per person. In total, then, an average person acquired $26,000 from these sources. After subtracting $20,500 in consumption spending and $4,750 per person in taxes, people had $750 per person left (on average) in savings. They loaned this money to firms (usually with banks acting as intermediaries).

Where did firms get the $4,500 that they spent on investment? They obtained $20,500 per person by selling goods to people for consumption. They also earned $4,500 per person by selling goods to other firms for investment. Finally, they earned $5,500 per person by selling goods to the government. In total, then, firms obtained $30,500 per person from these sources. In addition, they borrowed $1,250 per person, partly from foreign countries. Firms spent $22,000 to pay people wages and profits, $4,500 for investment, $4,750 in taxes, and $500 for imports in excess of exports.

The economy's total income—*national income*—is less than its total production, because some of that production replaces capital that wears out over the year. In 1997, two-thirds of the money that firms spent on investment, or $3,000 per person, paid for replacing capital that *depreciated* (wore out) during the year. As a result, gross investment of $4,500 per person increased the capital stock by about $1,500 per person. Figure 6 illustrates this point. If you build 4½ new machines, and 3 old machines explode or wear out (depreciate), then you have increased the number of machines by 1½.

Figure 6 | Gross and Net Investment

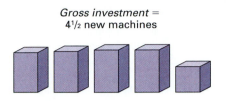

Gross investment =
4¹/₂ new machines

Minus *depreciation*
(3 old machines explode)

Leaves *net investment*
(increase in the capital stock) =
1¹/₂ additional machines

Income and GDP

Figure 5 and Table 4 suggest another way to calculate GDP—by adding incomes instead of expenditures. Income and spending are closely related: When you spend $5 for a movie, your spending creates $5 of income for the theater. Because every trade involves a buyer and seller, the buyer's spending equals the seller's income. Each person's income is connected with someone's spending:

> GDP = total value of production of final market goods and services
> = total spending on those goods and services
> = total income from selling those goods and services

U.S. firms produced $30,000 in final market goods and services per person in 1997. After replacing capital that depreciated ($3,000 per person), the economy was left with $27,000 per person in final market goods and services. Firms sold those goods, and the revenues from those sales created income for people and the government, as shown in Figure 5 and Table 4.[4]

Measuring Employment and Unemployment

Over six million adult Americans were *unemployed* in 1998, while 131.2 million had jobs, and 68 million adults were *not in the labor force*. These terms represent some simple basic concepts: People with jobs are *employed;* people are *unemployed* if they are jobless and looking for jobs; other people are *not in the labor force*. Official statistics on total employment, unemployment, and the labor force in the United States come from the government's Current Population Survey. Each month, the Census Bureau interviews about 60,000 households and classifies the members as employed, unemployed, or not in the labor force. The *unemployment rate* is the percentage of unemployed people in the labor force.

> The **unemployment rate** is the percentage of unemployed people in the labor force.

$$\text{Unemployment rate} = 100 \times \frac{\text{Number of unemployed people}}{\text{Number of employed people} + \text{Number of unemployed people}}$$

---

[4]Details of the tax system complicate the precise calculations. The appendix to this chapter shows more details on the connections between production and income in the National Income Accounts. Also see the Web page (www.dryden.com) for this book.

The last recession in the United States occurred in 1990 and 1991. When do you expect the next one?

With 6.2 million people unemployed and 131 million employed, the unemployment rate is $100 \times 6.2/(137.2) = 4.5$ percent.

Key Economic Issues about GDP, Unemployment, and Prices

Figure 7 shows the unemployment rate in the United States; Figure 8 shows total employment. Key economic issues call for explanations:

▶ Why did the U.S. unemployment rate average 5.7 percent in the last half of the 20th century, rather than 2.0 percent or 10.0 percent?

▶ Why is the unemployment rate in Europe about twice as high as in the United States? Why is the unemployment rate in Japan only about half as high as the U.S. rate?

▶ Why does the unemployment rate change over time? Why did it reach nearly 10 percent in 1982 and fall almost to 4 percent in 1998? Why did it reach almost 25 percent during the Great Depression of the 1930s?

▶ Why does unemployment increase as the growth of real GDP slows its growth or declines, as in the *recessions* of 1975, 1982, and 1991 (see Figures 2 and 7) and the Great Depression?

A **recession** occurs when real GDP is unusually low relative to its trend value. Some economists define a recession as a period when real GDP falls for two consecutive quarters (3-month periods), although official recession dates set by the National Bureau of Economic Research are based on more sophisticated criteria.

▶ Why do total employment and real GDP grow over long periods of time (see Figures 2 and 8)? What economic forces create additional jobs and additional production?

▶ How can government policies contribute to long-run growth of real GDP and employment? What can policies help to prevent recessions and maintain low unemployment?

▶ What causes prices to rise over time (as in Figure 3)? What causes foreign exchange rates to change? How can government policies contribute to low inflation?

These and other related issues will be the subjects of later chapters. Before beginning those discussions, this chapter discusses some reasons for cautious interpretations of the data and alternative measures of the average level of prices.

Problems with Measurement and Interpretation

Economists lack ideal measurements for most economic data. Three big problems complicate measurement and interpretation of gross domestic product.

First, GDP figures omit production of goods and services that are not sold on markets, such as housework, meals cooked at home, and child care provided by parents, as well as services volunteered for charities and other groups. When you repair your own apartment, your repair services do not appear in GDP. However, if two people repair each other's apartments, and each pays the other $100, the exchange adds $200 to GDP. When parents care for their own children, the value of their care does not appear in GDP. However, when parents pay for child care, those services appear in GDP. When volunteers take a group of scouts to camp, their services do not appear in GDP; however, when a camp hires paid leaders, their services appear in GDP.

Second, GDP includes only a very imperfect estimate of production of goods and services sold on the underground economy (or black market). This activity includes production of illegal goods and services (such as drugs and prostitution). It also includes production of legal goods that goes unreported to avoid taxes. Many estimates suggest that the underground economy in the United States amounts to between 5 and 10 percent of GDP; this figure is even larger in many other countries. In some episodes (such as experiences in Peru and Russia), underground economies may have been as large as above-ground (official) economies, creating huge errors in GDP measurement.

Third, special measurement problems result when GDP includes certain goods that are

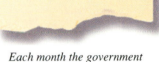
Each month the government reports the unemployment rate calculated from its survey. As Figure 7 shows, the U.S. unemployment rate fell from 1992 through 1998.

Exchange-rate crises have hit many countries in recent years, including Russia, Mexico, Indonesia, and South Korea. One key issue of macroeconomics involves the causes and prevention of crises like these. When do you expect the next one?

Figure 7 | Unemployment Rate in the United States

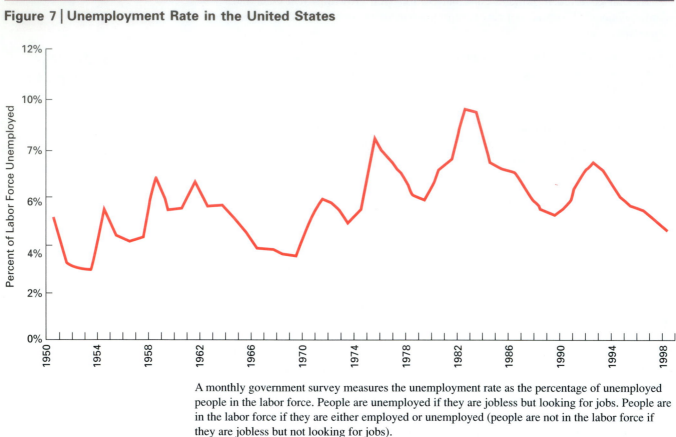

A monthly government survey measures the unemployment rate as the percentage of unemployed people in the labor force. People are unemployed if they are jobless but looking for jobs. People are in the labor force if they are either employed or unemployed (people are not in the labor force if they are jobless but not looking for jobs).

not sold on markets. When you rent a house or apartment, your expenses appear in GDP as payments for housing services. However, if you *own* your house or apartment, GDP includes the government's estimate of the rent that you *would* pay if you were renting.

Figure 8 | Total Employment in the United States

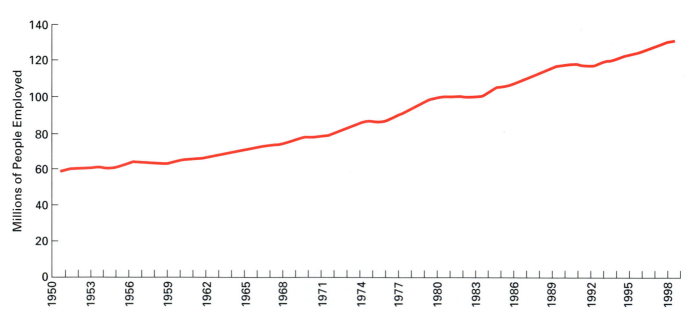

Similarly, the costs of environmental cleanups present special problems. Ideally, GDP would include the value of the improvement to the environment—the amount of money that people would be willing to pay for the cleaner environment (as measured by the equilibrium prices at which these benefits would be sold on markets). Instead, GDP includes the *costs* of environmental cleanups, which may differ significantly from their benefits. Similarly, GDP includes the *costs* of government services, such as police and public-school services, rather than their market values.

Measurement of unemployment also suffers from imperfections, and its interpretation requires caution. First, unemployment tends to be understated by official numbers, which ignore *discouraged workers,* who do not have jobs but have given up hope of finding them and stopped looking. The government classifies these people as not in the labor force. Second, unemployment tends to be understated, because it counts *underemployed* workers (mathematicians driving cabs, and so on) as fully employed. Similarly, official statistics count people who work part-time as employed, although they may want full-time jobs. Third, official statistics overstate unemployment to the extent that people are not truthful or not serious about looking for work.

Despite imperfections with measurement of GDP and unemployment, statistics on these and other economic concepts provide important evidence about the economy. It is important to remember that GDP is intended to measure production, not human happiness. GDP does not measure pollution, crime, leisure time, health, beauty, values, the qualities of goods, the qualities of relationships, or the quality of life. GDP is merely a convenient, if incomplete, summary measure of the total production of final goods sold on markets. Nevertheless, increases in GDP have been associated with increases in life expectancy, improvements in health, and increases in leisure time, as well as with increases in material comforts such as food, shelter, and entertainment. While interpreting changes in GDP and other economic statistics requires care, we can learn much about the economy from these statistics. Before turning to *how* we can use these concepts to learn about the operation of the economy, we turn to the concepts of the price level and inflation.

Review Questions

5. Consumption is (roughly) what fraction of GDP?

6. How is the unemployment rate measured in the United States?

7. What is a recession? What happens to unemployment during a recession?

8. List three main problems in measurement (or interpretation) of GDP.

9. List three main problems in measurement (or interpretation) of unemployment.

Thinking Exercise

10. Explain how you could try to estimate a broader concept of GDP that would *include* final goods and services that are currently omitted or measured poorly.

MEASURING THE PRICE LEVEL

The economy's *price level* is an average of the prices of its goods and services. We have already encountered one measure of the price level: the GDP deflator. Other common measures are the *consumer price index (CPI)* and the *producer price index (PPI).*

Due to compounding, a monthly rise of 0.2 percent equals an annual increase of about 2.7 percent per year. A monthly rise of 0.1 percent equals an annual increase of about 1.3 percent per year.

The consumer price index measures the average nominal prices of goods and services that a typical family living in an urban area buys. The CPI is a weighted average; goods such as salt and shoelaces (on which people spend small fractions of their incomes) receive less weight in the average than goods like cars and televisions, on which people spend more money. The PPI is a weighted average of the prices of inputs—crude goods and intermediate goods (sometimes called *wholesale prices*)—that producers buy to make final goods. On average, the CPI has doubled every 25 years in the 20th century, meaning that consumer prices now are 16 times higher than they were 100 years ago. The PPI and GDP deflator, on the other hand, are about 10 times higher than a century ago.

Figure 9a shows the price level in the United States as measured by the CPI, PPI, and GDP deflator; Figure 9b shows *inflation rates*—annual percentage changes in the price level—using the same three measures. The GDP deflator includes all final market goods and services produced in the country, while the CPI includes only the goods and services that an average household buys, and the PPI includes only those that an average producer buys. The CPI and PPI include the goods we import, but not those we export. The GDP deflator, in contrast, measures prices of goods we produce rather than goods we buy, so it includes the goods we export, but not those we import.

The CPI and PPI result from government survey data. Every several years, the U.S. Census Bureau conducts a Consumer Expenditure Survey to see what goods and services the typical family buys. Each month the Bureau of Labor Statistics (BLS) sends researchers to stores to find out the prices of about 400 goods and services, recording a total of about 90,000 prices. The BLS computes the total cost of buying the quantities of these goods that the typical family buys. The BLS also computes the total cost of buying these goods at base-year prices. It then calculates the consumer price index from the formula:

$$\text{CPI} = 100 \times \frac{\text{Total cost of the goods now}}{\text{Total cost of the goods in the base year}}$$

EXAMPLES

Suppose that the typical family buys ten pizzas, eight half-gallons of ice cream, and two bottles of antacid tablets every month, and that pizzas cost $10, ice cream costs $4 per half-gallon, and antacids cost $3 per bottle. (See Table 5.) The family's total spending is:

$$(10)(\$10) + (8)(\$4) + (2)(\$3) = \$138$$

Suppose that *in 1990* pizzas cost $8, ice cream cost $3, and antacids cost $3. At these 1990 base-year prices, ten pizzas, eight half-gallons of ice cream, and two bottles of antacids would have cost:

$$(10)(\$8) + (8)(\$3) + (2)(\$3) = \$110$$

The CPI, measured in 1990 dollars, is then:

$$\text{CPI} = 100 \times \frac{\$138}{\$110} = 125$$

A typical family spends $138 today to buy goods that cost only $110 in 1990. In other words, it must spend about $125 today to buy the same goods that it could have bought for only $100 in 1990. In other words, the average level of prices has increased by about 25 percent.

Figure 9 | Three Measures of the Price Level and Inflation

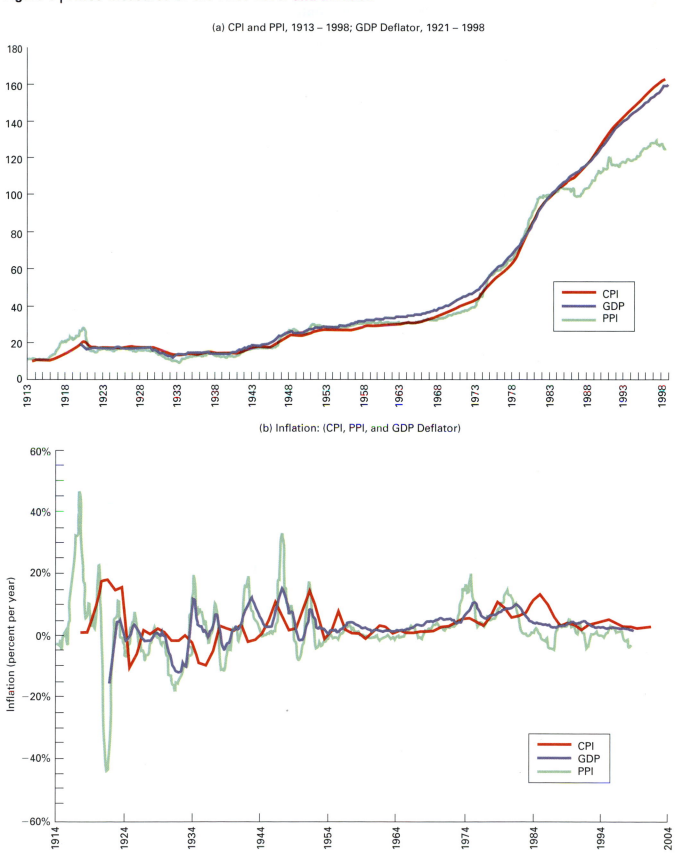

(a) CPI and PPI, 1913 – 1998; GDP Deflator, 1921 – 1998

(b) Inflation: (CPI, PPI, and GDP Deflator)

Table 5 | Measuring the CPI in an Economy with Pizzas, Ice Cream, and Antacids

Good	Price in 1990	Current Price	Quantity Purchased
Pizza	$ 8	$ 10	10
Ice cream	3	4	8
Antacids	3	3	2
Total cost of goods	110	138	

Limitations of Price Indexes

The right measure of the price level for *you* is a weighted average of the goods that *you* buy. For example, the cost of tuition, room, board, and fees for an undergraduate at Harvard increased by 343 percent over the last two decades, while the CPI increased by 171 percent over the same period.

The GDP deflator, the CPI, and the PPI all measure average prices only imperfectly, and each has limitations. Together, these sources of bias may lead the CPI to overstate inflation by about 1 percent per year. The three main problems are substitution bias, new-good bias, and quality-change bias. These measurement issues are important because they affect people's incomes. For example, changes in the CPI affect the amount of income elderly people receive in social security.

Substitution Bias

The first problem with price-level measurement is *substitution bias*. When a decrease in the supply of coffee raises its price, people buy less coffee and buy more tea. However, the CPI measures the increase in the cost of buying the *same amounts* of coffee (and other goods) as before. Obviously, when an increase in the price of coffee leads people to substitute cheaper goods (such as tea) for the more expensive good (coffee), they spend less than if they had continued to buy the same amounts of the goods. As a result, the change in the CPI *overstates* the increase in the cost of living.

IN THE NEWS

Wholesale-Price Fall Sets 11-Year Record

Washington—Inflation has rarely been so scarce.

In 1997, prices paid by wholesalers fell by 1.2%, the sharpest drop since they were pushed down 2.3% by collapsing oil prices in 1986, the Labor Department said.

The report showed no evidence of inflationary pressures in the pipeline. Consider the cost of a dress, which is influenced by the price of the cloth used to make it, called an intermediate good, and of the yarn used to make the cloth, called a crude good. In December, the prices of intermediate goods dropped 0.2%, after climbing 0.2% in November, while prices of crude goods plunged 5.6%, after rising 1.6% the month before.

Source: The Wall Street Journal

The PPI, CPI, and GDP deflator give slightly different results for inflation, because they measure different prices and because substitution bias, new-good bias, and quality-change bias affect each price index differently.

Suppose people buy a lot of orange juice and very little apple juice when orange juice costs $2.00 and apple juice costs $1.00. Now suppose that the price of orange juice doubles, while the price of apple juice falls 20 percent, leading people to buy mainly apple juice and very little orange juice. Did the price level double, or did it fall by 20 percent? A reasonable answer is something between the two. However, the CPI would show that the price level almost doubled, overstating the increase in the cost of living by ignoring consumer substitution to apple juice.

New-Good Bias

What do Viagra, CDs, Internet service, personal computers, cellular phones, Prozac, snowboards, personal satellite dishes, in-line skates, and DVDs have in common? They all emerged as new consumer products within the last decade or two, and they all create problems for the consumer price index. How can anyone compare the average level of prices today with the average level before introduction of these new goods? After all, the prices of these goods were *infinite* before they were invented—no one could buy them at *any* price. In fact, the government actually puts new goods into the CPI with a delay (typically several years). If a new good appears in the CPI for the first time in 1999, the government calculates inflation from 1998 to 1999 without including the new good, overstating the rate of inflation for that period.

Quality-Change Bias

George de Mestral and his dog returned from a country walk one beautiful day, both covered with burrs. Before removing them, the Swiss engineer looked through his microscope to see why the burrs stuck so stubbornly to his clothes and his dog's fur. Thus was born the hook and loop fastener that he called Velour Crochet (since the burrs stuck to his velour pants) and that we know as velcro, which he patented in 1955. Consumers certainly noticed quality improvements when velcro fasteners began appearing on a wide variety of consumer products. But how much better is a product that uses velcro rather than some other fastening method (zippers, etc.)? How much better is a "new, improved" laundry detergent, breakfast cereal, or computer program? If the prices of products rise by 10 percent but their qualities also improve, by how much have prices really increased? The government tries in a variety of ways to adjust the CPI for changes in quality. Sometimes the government can use statistical methods to estimate the effect of a change in quality; other times, the people collecting the data must use their subjective judgments.

The invention of a new service or good, such as in-line skates, creates a bias in the consumer price index.

Review Questions

11. Explain three problems with measurements of the average price level.

12. How is the consumer price index calculated?

Conclusion

Macroeconomics is the study of the economy as a whole—total production of goods and services, total employment and unemployment, the average level of prices, foreign exchange rates, interest rates and financial market activity, and the overall effects of government policies.

Total Production of Goods and Services

Gross domestic product (GDP) is the value of a country's production of final market goods and services during some time period (usually a year). Nominal GDP refers to GDP measured in money (dollars, yen, pesos, Euros, etc.). Real GDP refers to GDP measured in the prices of a certain base year. The GDP deflator, a measure of the average level of prices in the economy, equals nominal GDP divided by real GDP.

The Economy's Total Spending and Income

GDP equals the sum of consumption, investment, government purchases, and net exports (exports minus imports). Consumption is spending by people on final goods and services for current use. Investment is spending to create new capital, which is the stock of equipment, structures, inventories, human skills, and knowledge available to help produce goods and services. Government purchases refers to total spending on goods and services by federal, state, and local governments. Total government *spending* includes government purchases plus transfer payments (payments that simply transfer money without any exchange of goods and services). Exports are goods and services sold to people and firms in other countries; imports are purchases of goods and services from people and firms in other countries. Net exports, or the balance of international trade, equals exports minus imports.

Income and spending are closely related: Every trade involves a buyer and seller, so the buyer's spending equals the seller's income. GDP equals the total value of production of final market goods and services, which equals total spending on those goods and services, and also equals the total income created by that spending.

GDP, Employment, and Unemployment

People with jobs are employed. People are unemployed if they are jobless but looking for jobs. Other people are not in the labor force. The unemployment rate is the fraction of unemployed people in the labor force. The unemployment rate in the United States is measured with a monthly survey.

Key issues involving GDP, employment, and unemployment include the causes of recessions (periods in which real GDP falls for two consecutive quarters) and associated increases in unemployment, long-run growth of real GDP and employment, and the effects of government policies on recessions and long-run growth.

Measuring the Price Level

Like the GDP deflator, the consumer price index (CPI) and producer price index (PPI) measure the economy's price level. The CPI measures the average price of goods and services that a typical consumer buys, while the PPI measures the average price of goods that a typical producer buys. No price indexes measure price levels perfectly; all have limitations. Three main problems include substitution bias, new-good bias, and quality-change bias.

Key Terms

gross domestic product (GDP)	consumption	government purchases	net exports (balance of international trade)
nominal GDP	capital	exports	unemployment rate
real GDP	investment	imports	recession
GDP deflator			

Questions and Problems

13. Which issues of macroeconomics listed in the introduction to this chapter involve *normative* judgments?

14. Roughly what fractions of U.S. GDP are spent on consumption, investment, and government purchases of goods and services?

15. Why doesn't GDP include *all* government spending, including transfer payments (such as social security)?

16. How is GDP affected when (a) you buy a used textbook? (b) You buy a video? (c) You rent a video? (d) A town cleans up after a tornado? (e) Microsoft introduces a new computer operating system? (f) Someone buys cocaine from Colombia? (g) The government raises taxes? (h) A town builds a new school?

17. Purchases of cars and stereo systems are part of consumption spending. Why might someone sensibly decide to count them as investment instead of consumption?

18. Do the three main problems in measuring price indexes also create problems in measuring real GDP? Explain whether and how each problem applies to real GDP.

19. Why should we adjust a price index, like the CPI, for changes in the *quality* of goods? What is wrong with simply measuring price changes and ignoring changes in quality?

20. Why does substitution bias always lead the CPI to *overstate* inflation? Why doesn't it lead the CPI to understate inflation?

Inquiries for Further Thought

21. What factors do you think might cause changes in consumption? Investment? Government purchases? Net exports?

22. How will the main issues of macroeconomics affect your life in the next year? In the next 10 years?

Appendix: Measuring Production and Income: National Income Accounting

Table A.1 shows a more detailed accounting table for U.S. GDP in 1997 than the data that appears in the chapter text. This table reports data in the form adopted by the government and with the government's terminology. The table shows GDP as total spending, $C + I + G + NEX$, and the main categories of consumption and the other components. The table then adds "Receipts of factor income from the rest of the world," which mean payments of money to Americans who worked or invested in other countries. The table also subtracts "payments of factor income to the rest of the world." The result is *gross national product,* or GNP. While GDP measures the total output of final market goods and services by people and property within the country, GNP measures the country's total income.

Subtracting depreciation (called *consumption of fixed capital* in the table) from GNP gives *net national product.* Subtracting indirect business taxes (mainly sales taxes) and some other small items from net national product gives *national income.* The table makes some adjustments to national income to obtain *personal income* (which is mainly wages and salaries). Subtracting personal taxes (and nontax payments such as fees for auto licenses) gives *disposable personal income,* which is essentially the after-tax income of ordinary people. The table shows that people spend most of their after-tax income for consumption, and they save most of the rest.

IN THE NEWS

Consumer Spending Rose Faster in April Than Income, and the Savings Rate Fell

By John Simons
Staff Reporter of
The Wall Street Journal

Washington—Undaunted by foreign financial crises— or even by their own poor savings habits—Americans continue to spend, spend, spend.

While personal income

rose 0.4% in April to a seasonally adjusted annual rate of $7.18 trillion, following March's 0.3% increase, consumer spending jumped 0.5% to $5.72 trillion, the Commerce Department said. Disposable after-tax incomes were up 0.4% in April, but adjusted for in-

flation, they posted a mere 0.2% increase, the smallest in nine months.

The earn-it-and-spend-it cycle lowered personal savings as a portion of disposable income to 3.5% in April.

Source: The Wall Street Journal

Many of the concepts in Table A.1 appear regularly in news articles.

Table A.1 | U.S. NATIONAL INCOME AND PRODUCT, 1997

United States GDP, 1997	Total ($ billions)	Per Person ($)
Nominal gross domestic product (GDP)	$8,080	$30,149
Personal consumption expenditures	5,486	20,469
Durable goods	659	2,460
Nondurable goods	1,592	5,940
Services	3,235	12,069
Gross private domestic investment	1,243	4,636
Fixed investment	1,174	4,381
Change in business inventories	68	255
Government consumption expenditures and gross investment	1,453	5,421
Federal	524	1,954
State and local	929	3,466
Net exports of goods and services (exports minus imports)	−101	−377
Exports	957	3,571
Imports	1,058	3,948
GDP	$8,080	$30,149
Plus: Receipts of factor income from the rest of the world	262	978
Less: Payments of factor income to the rest of the world	282	1,052
Equals: Gross national product	$8,060	$30,075
Less: Consumption of fixed capital (i.e., depreciation)	868	3,238
Equals: Net national product	7,192	26,837
Less: Indirect business taxes, business transfer payments, and statistical discrepancy; Plus: Subsidies minus surpluses of government enterprises	543	2,024
Equals: National income	$6,650	$24,812
Less: Corporate profits	805	3,004
Less: Net interest	449	1,674
Less: Taxes for social insurance	733	2,736
Plus: Personal interest and dividend income	1,090	4,068
Plus: Government Transfer Payments to Persons	1,094	4,082
Plus: Business Transfer Payments to Persons	27	101
Equals: Personal Income	$6,874	$25,649
Wages, salaries, and other labor income	4,294	16,022
Proprietors' income	545	2,032
Rental income	148	552
Personal interest and dividend income	1,090	4,068
Transfer payments to persons minus taxes for social insurance	797	2,975
Personal income	$6,874	$25,649
Less: Personal tax and nontax payments	989	3,689
Equals: Disposable personal income	$5,885	$21,960
Less: Personal outlays	5,659	21,114
Personal consumption	5,486	20,469
Interest payments	155	578
Transfer payments to foreigners	18	67
Equals: Personal saving	$ 227	$ 846

Notes: The national income and product accounts of the United States are prepared by the Bureau of Economic Analysis, a division of the U.S. Department of Commerce. The data come from tax returns and surveys of people and business firms. For further information, see the Web pages (www.dryden.com) for this textbook.

CHAPTER 6

SIMPLE ECONOMIC MODELS OF GDP, PRICES, AND EMPLOYMENT

In this Chapter...

Main Points to Understand

▶ Economic models—logical stories about the economy—are necessary for serious thinking about our real-life economy.

▶ Technology and inputs of labor, capital, and natural resources determine the economy's total production of goods and services.

▶ The equation of exchange defines the velocity of money.

▶ Equilibrium wages equate the quantity of labor demanded with the quantity supplied.

Thinking Skills to Develop

▶ Create simple economic models to think about economic issues.

▶ Develop the implications of simple economic models.

▶ Reason by analogy from economic models to real-life issues.

Picture yourself: ten years from now. You're vice-president of a business, listening to e-mail from the company president. She wants you to report on how the latest recession in Europe will affect your company's profits and whether the situation will improve if the European Central Bank loosens its monetary policy. First, though, you have to decide whether to invest in a new facility near Beijing. Will the Chinese economy continue to grow as rapidly as it has over the past two decades, making the new facility a profitable investment?

Fortunately, you are prepared to formulate answers to questions like these, because you have learned how to think logically about economic issues. (Your coworkers vaguely remember studying current economic conditions in their economics courses, but the boss seldom asks about conditions way back in 1999 or 2001.) This chapter introduces simple models of GDP and the price level; later chapters will use these basic models as building blocks for more sophisticated analysis.

A good way to begin learning a craft is to watch an expert. Similarly, a good way to begin learning economic analysis is to listen to an expert. The following section reprints the text of a commencement speech delivered at the University of Chicago by Professor Robert E. Lucas, Jr., who won the 1995 Nobel Prize in Economic Sciences for his work on macroeconomics. His talk on "What Economists Do" introduces some new terms, which are highlighted in bold type and explained briefly nearby in the margin.

Robert E. Lucas, Jr.

IN THE NEWS

Chicago professor wins Nobel

For the fifth time in six years, a University of Chicago professor has won the Nobel Memorial Prize in economics. This year's winner, announced Tuesday, is Robert Lucas, 58. Lucas won for his research 25 years ago that showed the ineffectiveness of government attempts to use monetary and fiscal policies as cures for economic ailments such as poverty or rising inflation.

He "has had the greatest influence on macroeconomic research since 1970," the Royal Swedish Academy of Sciences said Tuesday in announcing the $1 million award.

He says he doesn't know yet what he'll do with the money. "I'm already doing what I really want to do: teaching and research."

Source: USA Today

You can find out more about Professor Lucas and other famous economists on the Web site (www.dryden.com) for this book.

Before reading Lucas's essay, recall from Chapter 2 that economic models are like artificial, robot economies. You can think of Professor Lucas's story of the Kennywood amusement park in this way.[1]

WHAT ECONOMISTS DO

The term *money supply* refers to the amount of money available for the economy to use; this term will appear later in this chapter, and a more detailed discussion will follow in Chapter 10.

Economists usually use the term *depression* for a particularly severe recession (such as the Great Depression of the 1930s); here, Professor Lucas uses it in the sense of any typical *recession.*

Essay by Robert E. Lucas, Jr.

Economists have an image of practicality and worldliness not shared by physicists and poets. Some economists have earned this image. Others—I and many of my colleagues here at Chicago—have not. I'm not sure whether you will take this as a confession or a boast, but we economists are basically story-tellers, creators of make-believe economic systems. Rather than try to explain what this story-telling activity is about and why I think it is a useful, even essential, activity, I thought I would just tell you a story and let you make of it what you like.

My story has a point: I want to understand the connection between changes in the **money supply** and economic **depressions.** One way to demonstrate that I understand this connection—I think the only really convincing way—would be for me to engineer a depression in the United States by manipulating the U.S. money supply. I think I know how to do this, though I'm not absolutely sure, but a real virtue of the democratic system is that we do not look kindly on people who want to use our lives as a laboratory. So I will try to make my depression somewhere else. The location I have in mind is an old-fashioned amusement park—roller coasters, fun house, hot dogs, the works. I am thinking of Kennywood Park in Pittsburgh, where I lived when my children were at the optimal age as amusement park companions—a beautiful, turn-of-the-century place on a bluff overlooking the Monongahela River. If you have not seen this particular park, substitute one with which you are familiar, as I want you to try to visualize how the experiment I am going to describe would actually work in practice.

Kennywood Park is a useful location for my purposes because it has an entirely independent monetary system. One *cannot* spend U.S. dollars inside the park. At the

---

[1]Often economists tell their stories in the language of mathematics instead of the languages of English or Spanish. That choice doesn't change the fact that the models are stories like this one. (As Chapter 2 explained, that is what economic models *are.*)

gate, visitors use U.S. dollars to purchase tickets, then they enter the park and spend those tickets. Rides inside are priced at a certain number of many tickets per ride. Ride operators collect these tickets, and at the end of each day tickets are cashed in for dollars, like chips in a casino.

For obvious reasons, business in the park fluctuates: Sundays are big days; July 4 is even bigger. At most attractions—I imagine each ride in the park to be independently operated—there is some flexibility: An extra person can be called in to help take tickets or to speed people getting on and off the ride, on short notice if the day is unexpectedly big or with advanced notice if it is predictable. If business is disappointingly slow, an operator will let some of his help leave early. So "GDP" in the park (total tickets spent) and employment (the number of man hours worked) will fluctuate from one day to the next due to fluctuations in demand. Do we want to call a slow day—a Monday or a Tuesday, say—a depression? Surely not. By an economic depression we mean something that ought not to happen, something pathological, not normal seasonal or daily ups and downs. This, I imagine, is how the park works. (I say "imagine" because I am just making most of this up as I go along.) Technically, Kennywood Park is a **fixed exchange rate system,** since its **central bank**—the cashier's office at the gate—stands ready to exchange **local currency**—tickets—for **foreign currency**—U.S. dollars—at a fixed rate. In this economy, there is an obvious sense in which the number of tickets in circulation is economically irrelevant. No one—customer or concessioner—really cares about the number of tickets per ride except insofar as these prices reflect U.S. dollars per ride. If the number of tickets per U.S. dollar were doubled from 10 to 20, and if the prices of all rides were doubled in terms of tickets—6 tickets per roller coaster ride instead of 3—and if everyone understood that these changes had occurred, it just would not make any important difference. Such a **doubling of the money supply** and of prices would amount to a 100 percent inflation in terms of local currency, but so what?

Yet I want to show you that changes in the quantity of money—in the number of tickets in circulation—have the capacity to induce depressions or booms in this economy (just as I think they do in reality). To do so, I want to imagine subjecting Kennywood Park to an entirely operational experiment. Think of renting the park from its owners for one Sunday, for suitable compensation, and taking over the functions of the cashier's office. Neither the operators of concessions nor the customers are to be informed of this. Then, with no advance warning to anyone inside the park, and no communication to them as to what is going on, the cashiers are instructed for this one day to give 8 tickets per dollar instead of 10. What will happen?

We can imagine a variety of reactions. Some customers, discouraged or angry, will turn around and go home. Others, coming to the park with a dollar budget fixed by mom, will just buy 80 percent of the tickets they would have bought otherwise. Still others will shell out 20 percent more dollars and behave as they would have in the absence of this change in "**exchange rates.**" I would have to know much more than I do about Kennywood Park patrons to judge how many would fall into each of these categories, but it is pretty clear that no one will be induced to buy more tickets than if the experiment had not taken place. Many people will buy fewer, so the total number of tickets in circulation—the "**money supply**" of this amusement park economy—will take a drop below what it otherwise would have been on this Sunday.

Now how does all this look from the point of view of the operator of a ride or the guy selling hot dogs? Again, there will be a variety of reactions. In general, most operators will notice that the park seems kind of empty for a Sunday and that customers don't seem to be spending like they usually do. More time is being spent on "freebies," the river view or a walk through the gardens. Many operators take this personally. Those who were worried that their ride was becoming passé get additional confirmation. Those who thought they were just starting to become popular, and had had thoughts of adding some capacity, begin to wonder if they had perhaps become overoptimistic. On many concessions, the extra employees hired to deal with the expected Sunday crowd are sent home early. A gloomy, "depressed" mood settles in.

An economy has a *fixed exchange rate system* when its government fixes the price at which its money *(local currency)* trades for foreign money *(foreign currency)*. The government agency that fixes the exchange rate is the *central bank*. For example, the Central Bank of Argentina fixes the exchange rate between the Argentine peso and the U.S. dollar at one peso per dollar; the Hong Kong Monetary Authority fixes its exchange rate at about 7.75 Hong Kong dollars per U.S. dollar. Similarly, the management of Kennywood Park fixes the price of tickets in terms of dollars at 10 tickets per dollar.

The change in *exchange rates* means the change in the price of tickets in terms of dollars—from ten tickets per dollar to eight tickets per dollar for this particular day.

Real output *means real GDP*.

The *money supply* in Kennywood Park is the number of tickets that customers have available to spend on rides. Doubling the money supply in the park means doubling the number of tickets. Notice Professor Lucas's point here: No one cares whether tickets cost 10 cents each and the roller coaster costs 3 tickets or tickets cost 5 cents each and the roller coaster costs 6 tickets. (In either case, you pay 30 cents for a ride.) Doubling the prices of rides in terms of tickets (which amounts to 100 percent inflation in the park), while simultaneously doubling the number of tickets that a person can buy for $1, makes no difference to customers or to the park. This concept is the principle of *neutrality of money* defined later in this chapter.

What I have done, in short, is to engineer a depression in the park. The reduction in the quantity of money has led to a reduction in **real output** and employment. And this depression is indeed a kind of pathology. Customers are arriving at the park, eager to spend and enjoy themselves. Concessioners are ready and waiting to serve them. By introducing a glitch into the park's monetary system, we have prevented (not physically, but just as effectively) buyers and sellers from getting together to consummate mutually advantageous trades.

That is the end of my story. Rather than offer you some of my opinions about the nature and causes of depressions in the United States, I simply made a depression and let you watch it unfold. I hope you found it convincing on its own terms—that what I said would happen in the park as the result of my manipulations would in fact happen. If so, then you will agree that by increasing the number of tickets per dollar we could as easily have engineered a boom in the park. But we could not, clearly, engineer a boom Sunday after Sunday by this method. Our experiment worked only because our manipulations caught everyone by surprise. We could have avoided the depression by leaving things alone, but we could not use monetary manipulation to engineer a *permanently* higher level of prosperity in the park. The clarity with which these effects can be seen is the key advantage of operating in simplified, fictional worlds.

The disadvantage, it must be conceded, is that we are not really interested in understanding and preventing depressions in hypothetical amusement parks. We are interested in our own, vastly more complicated society. To apply the knowledge we have gained about depressions in Kennywood Park, we must be willing to argue by analogy from what we know about one situation to what we would like to know about another, quite different situation. And, as we all know, the analogy that one person finds persuasive, his neighbor may well find ridiculous.

Well, that is why honest people can disagree. I don't know what one can do about it, except keep trying to tell better and better stories, to provide the raw material for better and more instructive analogies. How else can we free ourselves from the limits of historical experience so as to discover ways in which our society can operate better than it has in the past?

In any case, that is what economists do. We are story-tellers, operating much of the time in worlds of make believe. We do not find that the realm of imagination and ideas is an alternative to, or a retreat from, practical reality. On the contrary, it is the only way we have found to think seriously about reality.

Economists tell stories, like Professor Lucas's story about the amusement park. Then they reason by analogy from the stories to real-life economies.

IN THE NEWS

Japanese Slip into Recession; Outlook is Dim

TOKYO—Japan's once-mighty economic engine has ground into reverse for the second time this decade, and there are few signs that the world's second-largest economy will pick up soon. Economic output fell for the second quarter in a row, throwing Japan into recession by the common yardstick of two consecutive quarterly contractions. Preliminary economic data for April also suggests that consumer demand and business investment may be continuing to worsen.

Source: The Wall Street Journal

Japan is one of several Asian countries that slipped into recessions in 1997 and 1998. To understand real-life recessions, economists build models that mathematically describe stories similar to the Kennywood Park story.

In a way, there is nothing more to this method than maintaining the conviction that imagination and ideas matter. I hope you can do this in the years that follow. It is fun and interesting and, really, there is no practical alternative.

R e v i e w   Q u e s t i o n s

1. Professor Robert Lucas said in his essay that we can reason by analogy from Kennywood Park to our own, vastly more complicated society. In his analogy (his story), what plays the role of U.S. GDP?

2. In his thought experiment, Professor Robert Lucas considered a change in underlying conditions at Kennywood Park. What was that change in underlying conditions? What were its *effects?*

T h i n k i n g   E x e r c i s e s

3. Why do you think Professor Lucas decided to "make" a depression and "let you watch it unfold" rather than stating his "opinions about the nature and causes of depressions in the United States"? Why would he think this method is more valuable to you?

4. Professor Lucas says that "by increasing the number of tickets per dollar we could as easily have engineered a boom in the park." Explain how that could happen by retelling his story with an *increase* in the number of tickets that customers can purchase for each dollar.

What determines the economy's GDP? Rather than simply stating an answer—which would give you little help in learning to *use* economic analysis to solve real-world problems that you will confront in your life—this chapter follows Professor Lucas and constructs a *model*. We examine a model precisely because we are interested in understanding *real-world* GDP in the United States and other countries. If we simply listed data about the U.S. economy in a spreadsheet, without a model, we would not be able to answer *"what if" questions* that interest us: *What if* technology changes? *What if* people decide to consume more and save less? *What if* the government cuts taxes? A model suggests how the various bits of data are interrelated—it tells us how changing *some* numbers in a spreadsheet are likely to change *other* numbers. As Professor Lucas asks, how else can we free ourselves from the limits of historical experience (the U.S. economic numbers in the spreadsheet) and discover ways to do better than in the past, by seeing how the numbers would *change* in various *"what if"* scenarios?

It is usually easier to begin with very simple models, and then to add more realistic features, than to dive in to a complicated model that may be difficult to understand. Therefore, we begin with a very simple model of an economy in which no one trades— a Robinson Crusoe economy.

A Robinson Crusoe Economy

Robinson Crusoe lives in his own economy. He produces goods for his own consumption by picking berries from trees. Crusoe's *real GDP* each day equals the number of berries he picks that day, and depends on the number of hours he works that day.

A VERY SIMPLE MODEL OF GDP

Spreadsheet with data for the U.S. economy:

LABOR	GDP	MONEY	CPI
136,206	8,013.6	1,080.8	121.5
137,169	8,103.5	1,065.4	121.9
137,447	8,204.2	1,073.7	122.6
137,962	8,340.7	1,075.0	123.1

We need a *model* to help us interpret economic data and tell us how changing *some* numbers in the spreadsheet are likely to change *other* numbers. We need to answer such *what-if* questions in order to formulate good economic policies and make good business decisions.

Table 1 shows Crusoe's *production function*—the first two columns show how his real GDP (berries picked per day) depends on the number of hours he works at picking berries.

A **production function** is a mathematical description of an economy's technology, showing the total production that an economy can obtain from its inputs of labor, capital, and natural resources.

Crusoe's input of labor is his work effort; his capital is a basket he has woven to carry berries back to his camp, his skills at picking, and his knowledge of which berries are safe to eat; the natural resources are the bushes and trees on which berries grow. Figure 1 graphs Crusoe's production function, with hours worked on the X-axis and total production on the Y-axis.

The third column of Table 1 shows Crusoe's *average product of labor:*

The **average product** of a person's labor equals total production divided by the number of hours worked.

For example, the table shows that Crusoe picks 3,000 berries if he works 3 hours, making his average product of labor equal to 1,000 berries per hour.

The fourth column of Table 1 shows Crusoe's *marginal product of labor:*

The **marginal product** of labor is the *additional* production obtained from *increasing* labor a little, without changing the amounts of capital or natural resources.

For example, the table shows that Crusoe can pick a total of 1,200 berries if he works 1 hour or a total of 2,200 berries if he works 2 hours. If he *increases* his work time from 1 hour to 2 hours, he picks 1,000 *additional* berries (2,200 − 1,200), meaning that his marginal product of labor is 1,000 berries per hour.

Similarly, the table shows that Crusoe can pick a total of 3,000 berries if he works 3 hours or a total of 3,500 berries if he works 4 hours. If he *increases* his work time from 3 hours to 4 hours, he picks 500 *additional* berries (3,500 − 3,000), meaning that his marginal product of labor is 500 berries per hour.

Table 1 | Crusoe's Production Function

Hours Worked Picking Berries (per day)	Real GDP per Day (total berries picked per day)	Average Product of Labor (berries per hour, on average)	Marginal Product of Labor (*additional* berries from one *additional* hour of work)
0	0		
1	1,200	1,200	1,200
2	2,200	1,100	1,000
3	3,000	1,000	800
4	3,500	875	500
5	3,800	760	300
6	4,000	667	200
7	4,100	586	100
8	4,150	519	50
9	4,160	462	10
10	4,165	416	5

Figure 1 | Robinson Crusoe's Production Function

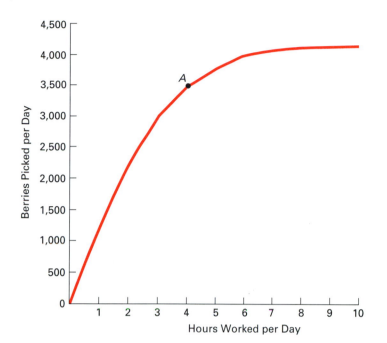

Diminishing Returns

Notice that Crusoe's marginal product of labor is higher if he only works a few hours than if he works many hours. This illustrates the important concept of diminishing returns.

> The **law of diminishing returns** is the principle that raising the quantity of an input eventually reduces its marginal product, if the quantity of some other input remains fixed.

Holding fixed the number of trees and bushes, as well as the size of Crusoe's basket and his knowledge and skills, Crusoe faces diminishing returns as he works additional hours. As Table 1 shows, his marginal product of labor falls as his hours of work rise. Several factors contribute to diminishing returns. Crusoe may get tired as he works, working more slowly in each additional hour. If he works only a few hours, he picks the berries that are easiest to reach; however, if he works many hours, he must pick hard-to-reach berries, reducing his marginal product of labor. The curved shape of Crusoe's production function in Figure 1 illustrates diminishing returns.

Production Possibilities Frontier

Crusoe must choose: He can work a lot and eat a lot of berries, or he can increase his leisure time and eat less. His *production possibilities frontier (PPF)* in Figure 2 illustrates that choice. He can take 24 hours of leisure time each day and have nothing to eat, or he can work 24 hours and have 4,175 berries to eat each day. He can also choose positions such as Point A, in which he takes 20 hours of leisure time each day, working 4 hours and eating 3,500 berries each day. In this way, Crusoe chooses his real GDP.

Notice that Crusoe's PPF and his production function (in Figure 1) show the *same* information, but in different ways.

Investment

Now add some additional realism to the model. Crusoe is not likely to spend all his time picking berries with the tools provided by nature; instead, he is likely to realize that he can build some tools. In other words, he can *invest*. Crusoe can build an automatic

Figure 2 | Robinson Crusoe's Production Possibilities Frontier

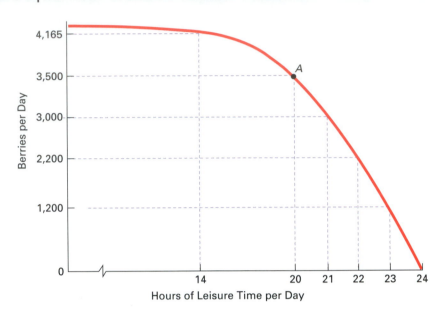

berry-picker by spending less time picking berries or relaxing by the shore. When he completes his new machine, he will be able to pick more berries in less time than before. By investing, Crusoe sacrifices consumption and leisure time *today* to obtain more consumption and leisure time *in the future*. Whether he is willing to build the machine depends on the terms of that tradeoff—how much can he gain in the future by sacrificing consumption and leisure today? How much is he *willing* to sacrifice?

If automatic berry pickers are highly productive, and if Crusoe is sufficiently willing to sacrifice consumption today for future consumption, then he might even build several berry-picking machines. The amount of investment Crusoe undertakes, and the *capital stock* that he ends up with, depend on his choices.

Suppose that Crusoe must sacrifice 3,000 berries for each automatic berry-picking machine he builds. In other words, the time he requires to build each machine is the same as the time he requires to pick 3,000 berries. Then Crusoe can, in essence, "buy" a machine for 3,000 berries—the relative price of a machine is 3,000 berries per machine. (Recall the discussion of relative prices in Chapter 4.)

Real GDP

Crusoe's production function depends not only on his labor input (hours worked) and the natural resources available to him but also on his *capital* stock. The production function can take the form of an equation:

$$\text{Real GDP} = F(l, k)$$

where l represents the number of hours that Crusoe works, k represents his capital stock (the number of machines he uses), and real GDP is *total* production of berries and machines, counting each machine as equivalent to 3,000 berries.

For example, Crusoe may work 8 hours, building one machine and picking 1,150 berries. If he had not built the machine, he would have picked 4,150 berries in 8 hours of work. Building the machine took time—the same amount of time in which he *could have* picked 3,000 of those 4,150 berries. Because he built the machine, he could pick only 1,150 berries in his 8-hour work day.

Crusoe's production function describes how his real GDP depends on his inputs of labor and capital.

Crusoe's real GDP is also the sum of his consumption and investment:

$$\text{Real GDP} = c + i$$

where c is Crusoe's consumption and i is his investment (measured in the number of berries he gave up for his machines). In the example, Crusoe's consumption is 1,150 berries and his investment (building one machine) is 3,000 berries, for a total real GDP of 4,150 berries.

The numbers in Table 1, graphed in Figures 1 and 2, showed Crusoe's production of berries when he had no automatic berry-picking machines. Once he has those machines, however, they can help him boost berry production, changing the numbers in Table 1 and shifting the curves, as in Figure 3.

Changes in GDP

Each evening, Crusoe spends time thinking about how to improve his economic situation. Eventually, he figures out how to build a better automatic berry-picker. Over the next weeks or months, he spends time building that new, better machine. To make time for this investment, he works more hours and spends a little less time picking berries. As a result, his GDP rises, although his consumption of berries falls. Finally, he completes his new machine. Now he can stop working so many extra hours per day. Although this decrease in work hours for investment tends to reduce his real GDP, the new machine helps him pick more berries per hour than before. As a result, his real GDP rises to a new, higher level. Technical change, which resulted from Crusoe's investment of time in thinking about new ideas for a better machine, raises investment and real GDP in the short run, and raises consumption and real GDP in the long run.

Crusoe's production changes over time for other reasons, as well. The weather varies, and he picks fewer berries per hour on a stormy day than on a pleasant one. Seasons change, and in the winter he finds fewer berries to pick than in the summer. Some days he doesn't feel energetic, and his production is lower than usual. Other days, he wants to avoid working at all, taking time to sleep, write in his journal, or explore the island. As a result, Crusoe's real GDP fluctuates over time, and an observer might interpret these fluctuations as booms and recessions.

Figure 3 | Effects of an Increase in Capital

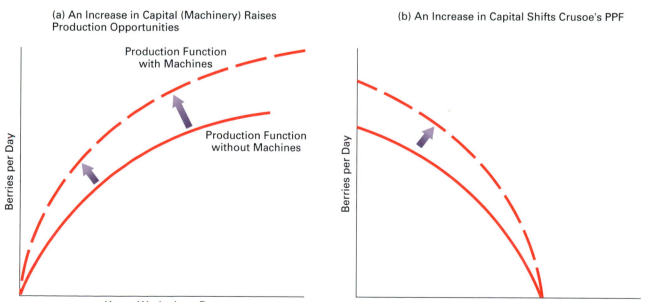

(a) An Increase in Capital (Machinery) Raises Production Opportunities

Production Function with Machines

Production Function without Machines

Berries per Day

Hours Worked per Day

(b) An Increase in Capital Shifts Crusoe's PPF

Berries per Day

Hours of Leisure Time per Day

In fact, some economists *do* interpret real-life booms and recessions in this way. They note that Crusoe is "unemployed" on days that he doesn't work, making his "unemployment rate" high when his real GDP is low, as in recessions. Most economists, however, believe that a simple model like this cannot explain key features of real-life recessions. (For example, people who are unemployed in a real-world recession may struggle to find jobs. In contrast, Crusoe is self-employed and he can stop being "unemployed" simply by deciding to pick berries.)

So far, it is impossible to examine *nominal* GDP and nominal prices in this model, because Crusoe doesn't use money. In fact, he doesn't even *trade* with anyone. The next sections extend the model to include trade and nominal prices.

Review Questions

5. How does Table 1 show diminishing returns to Crusoe's labor?

6. In what way does Crusoe choose his real GDP?

Thinking Exercises

7. How would the shape of the production function in Figure 1 change if there were *not* diminishing returns, so that Crusoe would pick 1,200 berries per hour *regardless* of how many hours he worked? Draw the production function for that case.

8. The text claimed that Crusoe's production function (in Figure 1) and his PPF (in Figure 2) show the same information in different ways. Explain why.

A Model with Trade

Imagine an economy with a large number of people just like Crusoe, except that they produce and sell different goods. Everyone wants to consume a little bit of each good. Some people have comparative advantages in producing food, and other people have comparative advantages creating housing, entertainment, and other goods and services. As a result, people specialize in production and then trade with one another. They receive gains from trade as discussed in Chapters 1 and 3. Trade will create two other changes in the model: labor markets, and the use of money.

Labor Markets
Trade among people will create a labor market in our model, in which people buy and sell labor services. Some people will form business firms and hire workers, and other people will decide to work for those firms. Unlike Crusoe, who was self-employed, many people in the model will participate in labor markets. The desire by firms to hire workers creates a demand for labor, and the desire by some people to work for firms instead of becoming self-employed creates a supply of labor.

Figure 4a shows the supply of labor by people who want to work, as well as the demand for labor by firms that want to hire workers. The price of labor services is the *wage* rate. Equilibrium occurs at Point A, with an equilibrium wage of w_0 and equilibrium employment of l_0.

At the equilibrium wage, everyone who wants to work has a job. In equilibrium, there is no surplus or shortage of labor. When labor demand or supply change, the wage adjusts to restore equilibrium.

Although barter sometimes occurs, as in Russia in recent years, most trades in most economies involve exchanges of goods and money.

Labor Markets and Real GDP

Our model determines real GDP in two steps. First, equilibrium in the labor market determines equilibrium employment, l_0 in Figure 4a. Second, the economy's *aggregate* production function, which relates *total* real GDP in the economy to *total* labor hours worked, determines equilibrium real GDP as in Figure 4b.

Money

People in our model economy will want to use *money* for their trades, rather than bartering like the two students in Chapter 3. We will assume that they form a government,

---

Figure 4 | Equilibrium Employment and Real GDP

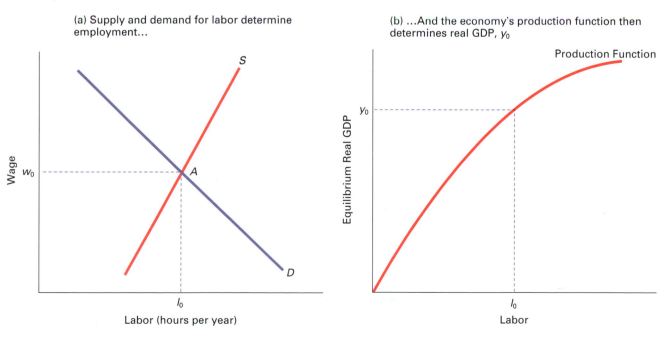

(a) Supply and demand for labor determine employment...

(b) ...And the economy's production function then determines real GDP, y_0

whose sole task is to print some dollar bills and distribute them equally to every person in the economy. Sellers are willing to accept these dollar bills as payments for goods and services, because they know that they can later exchange those dollars for goods and services from *other* sellers. The *nominal money supply* in this model is the total amount of money that the government has printed and distributed.

> The **nominal money supply** is the total amount of money in the economy, measured in monetary units such as dollars or yen.

The term *nominal* refers to measurement in money units such as *dollars*. For example, the government may print 1,000 $1 bills for people to use, making the nominal money supply equal to $1,000.

Circular Flow

Figure 5 shows the *circular flow* of economic activity in the model; it resembles a simple version of Figure 5 from the preceding chapter (which showed a circular flow for the U.S. economy).

The outside circle shows the flow of money in the economy. People pay money to firms in exchange for goods and services. Firms pay people to work for them, and they pay profits to their owners for providing capital (tools and machines). Money travels clockwise around the circle.

The flow of money from firms to people shows this economy's nominal GDP, which equals total spending on goods and services (for consumption or investment), that is, the total monetary value of the economy's production of goods and services. The inside circle in Figure 5 shows flows of physical goods and services. The arrow from people to firms represents flows of labor and capital services from people to firms. The arrow from firms to people represents the final goods that people buy from firms. While the outside circle shows aggregate nominal income and spending, measured in money terms, the inside circle shows the economy's *real GDP* measured in terms of actual goods and services. It represents a weighted average of berries, automatic berry-picking machines, and other goods and services, using relative prices of the goods as weights in the average (as explained earlier with berries and berry-picking machines in the Crusoe model).

Equation of Exchange

Suppose that the circular flow in Figure 5 occurs *once per year.* The money in the economy flows once each year from people to firms and back to people. Each dollar in the

Figure 5 | Circular Flow of Economic Activity

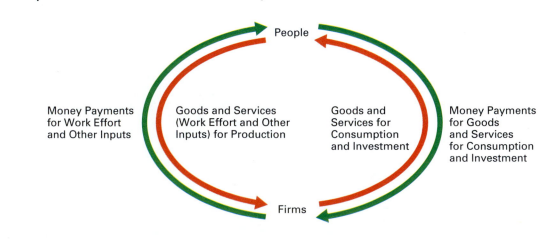

economy is used once each year by people to buy goods, and once each year by firms to pay people. In this case, the flows of money in Figure 5 show the economy's nominal GDP for one year, and the flows of goods show its real GDP for that year. (If the circular flows in the figure occurred *twice* each year, then the money in the economy would flow from people to firms and back twice each year. In that case, annual GDP would be *twice* the amount shown by the arrows in the figure.)

With the circular flow in Figure 5 occurring once annually, each dollar in the economy is spent once per year. As a result, this economy's nominal GDP equals its nominal money supply. Both the nominal GDP and the money supply equal the flow of money shown by the outer arrows in Figure 5. If, instead, the circular flow occurred *twice* each year, then each dollar would be spent *twice* per year on goods, so the economy's nominal GDP would be *twice* its nominal money supply. The number of times that each dollar bill gets spent each year is the *velocity* of money.

> The **velocity of money** is the average number of times per year that money is spent in the circular flow; velocity equals nominal GDP divided by the nominal money supply.

If the circular flow occurs once annually, then the velocity of money equals 1 per year. If the circular flow occurs twice per year, then velocity equals 2 per year. In that case, nominal GDP equals twice the money supply. More generally:

Nominal GDP equals the nominal money supply multiplied by the velocity of money.

Using the letter M for the nominal money supply and the letter V for velocity, this relationship gives the equation:

$$\text{Nominal GDP} = MV$$

Recall that nominal GDP equals real GDP multiplied by the GDP price deflator. Using the letters P for the GDP deflator and y for real GDP:

$$MV = Py$$

This equation is called the *equation of exchange*.

> The **equation of exchange** says that $MV = Py$.

In words, the equation of exchange says that the nominal money supply multiplied by the velocity of money equals the GDP price deflator multiplied by real GDP.

Now rewrite the equation of exchange to express the GDP deflator in terms of the money supply, velocity, and real GDP:

$$P = MV/y$$

This equation shows that the economy's price level equals the nominal money supply times its velocity, divided by real GDP. Note that the nominal money supply is determined by the number of dollar bills that the government has printed, and real GDP is determined as in Figure 4, by the economy's equilibrium level of employment and production function. After determining the velocity of money—the number of times per year each dollar is spent in the economy—the equation of exchange gives the economy's price level.

Your true height does not change if we switch our units of measurement from feet to inches; only the units of measurement change. Similarly, the economy's real GDP and employment do not change if we switch our units of measurement by raising the nominal money supply and all nominal prices and wages in the same proportion. Nominal GDP may rise from $1,000 to $2,000, but every dollar is worth only one-half of its previous value.

Real wages adjust nominal wages for inflation. Real wages are measured in *base-year* dollars, like real GDP. To compute the real wage in 1999, measured in 1992 base-year dollars, we divide the 1999 *nominal* wage, W, by the consumer price index measured in 1992 base-year dollars:

real wage (in 1992 base-year dollars)

$$= \frac{\text{nominal wage}}{\text{CPI (in 1992 base-year dollars)}}$$

Neutrality of Money

We can use the equation of exchange to find the effects of an increase in the money supply. Suppose the money supply rises permanently from $1,000 to $2,000, because the government prints up additional dollar bills and distributes them equally to every person in the economy. This 100 percent increase in the money supply raises all *nominal* prices (prices measured in monetary units) by 100 percent. Because all prices rise in the same proportion, *relative* prices remain unchanged. Similarly, the 100 percent rise in the money supply raises *nominal* wages (wages measured in monetary units) by 100 percent. However, *real wages*—wages measured in *base-year* dollars to adjust for inflation—remain unchanged, because nominal wages and prices rise proportionally.

> **Nominal wages** are payments for labor services, measured in monetary units like dollars or yen.

> **Real wages** are wages measured in *base-year* dollars.

Because the increase in the money supply does not affect real wages, it does not affect the quantities of goods and services that people can afford to buy. After the 100 percent increase in nominal prices and nominal wages, goods and services cost twice as many dollars as before, but people earn twice as many dollars per hour as before. Only our *unit of measurement* has changed (the value of a dollar has fallen in half), but nothing real—nothing of importance to people—has changed. The 100 percent increase in the money supply leaves consumption, employment, and real GDP unchanged. This result is called the *neutrality of money:*

> **Neutrality of money:** The implication of an economic model that an increase in the nominal money supply raises all *nominal* prices and wages but leaves real GDP, employment, and *relative* prices unaffected.

Doubling the money supply from $1,000 to $2,000 doubles the price level; people spend twice as many dollars to buy the same goods and services, at twice the prices.[2] The economy's technology is unaffected by printing pieces of paper for use as money, so the aggregate production function in Figure 4b is unaffected by a change in the money supply. Similarly, printing money does not affect the supply of labor or the demand for labor in Figure 4a, so it does not affect equilibrium employment or the equilibrium real wage. What happens in Figure 4a when an increase in the money supply raises nominal wages? The answer is *nothing*. Chapter 4 explained that the price on the Y-axis of a supply-demand diagram is the *relative price* of the product, *not* the *nominal* price. The relative price of labor services is the *real wage*, so the *real wage* appears on the Y-axis in Figure 4a. Because an increase in the money supply raises the nominal wage and the CPI in the same proportion, it leaves the real wage unchanged. Because the increase in the money supply does not affect equilibrium employment or technology, it does not affect real GDP.

Because equilibrium employment remains at l_0 and the production function does not change, real GDP remains at y_0 in Figure 4. In Professor Lucas's words, raising the money supply from $1,000 to $2,000 would not make any important difference. "Such a doubling of the money supply and of prices would amount to a 100 percent

---

[2] For now, we *assume* that the velocity of money does not change. A later chapter will discuss velocity in more detail, reaching the conclusion that a permanent change in the level of the money supply does not affect the long-run level of velocity. However, even if velocity were to change, this change would *not* affect the neutrality-of-money conclusion that real GDP is unaffected by doubling the money supply.

inflation in terms of local currency, but so what?" No one in the economy would really care, because they would work the same number of hours as before, and they would consume the same goods and services as before.

In summary, this model says that real GDP and employment are determined by the labor market and the economy's production function, as in Figure 4. Knowing real GDP, the equation of exchange allows you to solve for the equilibrium price level in terms of the nominal money supply and its velocity.

Recessions: Return to Kennywood Park

The story that Professor Lucas told early in the chapter about Kennywood Park leads to the conclusion that a decrease in the money supply causes a recession. In other words, that model does *not* predict the neutrality of money. Why not? What is different about the Kennywood Park story and the model developed in this chapter? There is one key difference: In the Kennywood Park story, prices do not fall along with the money supply.

Recall the reactions of customers in Kennywood Park when they learn that they can get only eight tickets per dollar instead of ten. They were disappointed, and the total number of tickets sold at the park decreased that day. In Professor Lucas's story, the number of tickets people need for each ride remains unchanged. Imagine how different the story would be if the number of tickets needed for each ride were to fall by 20 percent along with the exchange rate of tickets for dollars, publicly announced to customers at the park entrance. Although people could get only eight tickets per dollar instead of ten, rides that previously required ten tickets would now require only eight tickets; rides that required five tickets before now would require only four. In that case, customers would not care about the changes. They would say, in Lucas's words, "So what?" The change would not affect the number of people in the park or how many rides they choose to buy. This change in the money supply would be *neutral*, with no effect on real GDP.

A fall in the money supply creates a recession in Professor Lucas's Kennywood Park model because prices inside the park (the number of tickets per ride) do *not* adjust to the change in the money supply. In Professor Lucas's story, prices fail to adjust because no one inside the park becomes informed about the change in the money supply. Later chapters will discuss other reasons for prices not to change, and for violations of the *neutrality of money*.

Real wages (inflation-adjusted wages) have grown more rapidly in the past several years than in previous years.

Review Questions

9. What determines real GDP in the model with many people specializing and trading? Use graphs to help explain your answer.

10. Explain the equation of exchange and how it relates to the circular flow of economic activity.

11. What is the *neutrality of money*?

Thinking Exercises

12. Suppose the nominal money supply is $4,000, velocity equals 2 per year, and real GDP is 1,000 goods per year. What is the equilibrium price level?

13. Suppose your nominal wage rises by 10 percent and the consumer price index rises by 5 percent. What happens to your real wage?

14. Explain why doubling the nominal money supply and all nominal prices is similar to changing units of measurement from gallons to half-gallons, or miles to half-miles.

EQUILIBRIUM EMPLOYMENT AND UNEMPLOYMENT

Although the macroeconomic model developed in this chapter is very simple, many of its conclusions carry over to the more complicated models that economists analyze using computers. This chapter's model assumes equilibrium in the labor market (Figure 4a); as a result, *unemployment* occurs in the model only when people choose not to work, as when Crusoe decides to take a day off from picking berries. However, real-life unemployment often occurs when people have lost their old jobs and have not yet found suitable new jobs. Fortunately, the logic in this chapter also applies when the economy experiences unemployment. To see why, think about the causes of unemployment.

Some unemployment results from continuing economic changes. Changes in demand and supply cause some industries to expand and others to contract, raising the demand for labor in some parts of the economy and reducing labor demand in other parts. For example, steel manufacturers lay off workers when the demand for steel falls; computer firms hire workers when the demand for computers rises. Some people suffer unemployment as they take time to search for suitable jobs. Although someone who is willing to take a low-paying job can usually find one quickly, it takes longer for people to find good jobs that suit their interests and skills. Unemployment occurs partly because continuing changes always force some people to look for new jobs.

Some jobs go unfilled while people are unemployed and looking for work. Job vacancies occur because firms, like people, need time to find suitable employees who match their needs for skills, experience, and other characteristics. This *matching* process takes time. While firms are looking for suitable workers, and workers are looking for suitable jobs, unemployment and job vacancies occur together. Meanwhile, continuing changes in technology, consumer tastes, population, weather, government policies, international competition, and other factors, create new unemployment.

> **Equilibrium unemployment** refers to unemployment that results from continuing changes in supplies and demands and the costs of searching for and matching jobs in labor markets.

IN THE NEWS

Labor Day Reflects a Changing World for Job Seekers and Employers

With the passage of Labor Day, the hiring outlook for employers is daunting as they face the tightest employment market in three decades. Since unemployment is hovering at historically low levels, employers are devising new and creative methods, including technology-based solutions, to help them find, attract and hire new candidates. And employees on the hunt for a new job are quickly adapting to a new set of rules to succeed in today's job market. Now and in the future, employers and employees alike can expect a remarkably different playing field in their hiring and job-hunting quest.

Source: PRNewswire

Changes in technology have made it easier than in the past for people to obtain information about jobs, and for firms to obtain information about prospective workers. Will these new technologies help reduce the equilibrium level of unemployment?

The equilibrium rate of unemployment is often called the *natural* rate of unemployment (though there is little *natural* about it). When economists refer to *full employment,* they do not mean an economy with *zero* unemployment; they mean an economy with unemployment equal to its equilibrium (or natural) rate.

Full employment refers to a situation with equilibrium unemployment.

Determinants of Equilibrium Unemployment

Equilibrium unemployment occurs when the rate of job creation equals the rate of job destruction.[3]

The **rate of job creation** is the number of new workers hired each month.

The **rate of job destruction** is the number of people who quit or lose their jobs each month.

The rate of job destruction depends on the size and speed of changes in technology, government policies, and other factors that reduce the demand for labor in certain industries. The rate of job creation depends partly on the speed with which workers can learn about job opportunities and the speed with which firms can learn about candidates for hiring. The rate of job creation also depends on the number of people unemployed at the time; when the number of people looking for jobs and the number of firms looking for workers increase, so does the rate of new job matches each month. For example, if 20 percent of unemployed workers find jobs each month, then the rate of job creation is 1 million jobs per month if 5 million people are unemployed, or 2 million jobs per month if 10 million people are unemployed.

Equilibrium unemployment occurs when job destruction equals job creation, that is, when the number of people who lose their jobs each month equals the number of unemployed people who find jobs, leaving total unemployment unchanged. If unemployment exceeds its equilibrium level, then the rate of job creation exceeds the rate of job destruction, and unemployment falls. If unemployment falls below its equilibrium level, then the rate of job creation falls below the rate of job destruction and unemployment rises. In this way, the rate of unemployment tends to move toward its equilibrium level.

EXAMPLES

Suppose that continuing changes in demand and supply cause 1 million job losses each month, and each month one-third of all unemployed people find jobs. In this case, equilibrium unemployment is 3 million people. Each month one-third of these 3 million people find jobs, so the rate of job creation is 1 million jobs per month. Because 1 million jobs are destroyed each month, unemployment stays at 3 million people, composed of 2 million people who were already unemployed and did not find jobs plus 1 million newly unemployed people.

To see why unemployment tends toward its equilibrium level, suppose that 6 million people are unemployed at the beginning of January. Because one-third of them find jobs in January, only 4 million remain unemployed by February. Because 1 million other

Jobless Rate Held Steady in August

The U.S. unemployment rate held steady at 4.5% in August as job losses in other industries outweighed the return to work of laborers affected by strikes at General Motors earlier this summer. Net job growth across all employment sectors in August was 365,000.

Source: USA Today

The unemployment rate remains the same when the rate of job creation equals the rate of job destruction.

---

[3]When the labor force—the number of people who have or want jobs—grows over time, perhaps due to population growth, equilibrium unemployment occurs when the rate of job creation equals the rate of job destruction *plus* the increase in the labor force. Employment then rises along with the size of the labor force and unemployment is constant.

people lose their jobs, however, total unemployment in February falls to 5 million, 1 million less than in January. One-third of these 5 million people (about 1,667,000 people) find jobs in February, and 1 million new people lose their jobs, so unemployment falls by 667,000 people, to 4.33 million, by March. Each month, unemployment falls toward its equilibrium level of 3 million people, although the process takes time.

What If the Economy Lacks Enough Jobs?

What if the economy does not create enough jobs to employ everyone who wants to work? What if the number of workers looking for jobs exceeds the number of firms looking for workers? People and firms then create new jobs. Jobs are not products like houses and food; the number of jobs available in the economy is not limited by available resources. Jobs are *trades*—voluntary agreements in which people exchange labor services and money. The only limit to the number of jobs the economy can create comes from the number of voluntary trades that people are willing to make. As long as a person can produce goods or services that are valuable to other people, that person can create a job by offering to work for a wage below the value that the other people place on those goods or services. The economy can always create enough jobs for everyone who can produce something valuable and who is willing to accept a wage equal to or below the value of his production.

> Jobs are trades; the number of jobs the economy can create is limited only by the number of trades that people are willing and able to make.

Unemployment results as people take time to find the trading opportunities that provide them with the greatest benefits. You may decide *not* to hire Mark to paint your house, even if you would gain from that trade, if you expect to find *someone else* who offers to paint it for a lower price that Mark charges. By waiting, you may find a *better* trade. Meanwhile, your house goes unpainted. Similarly, an unemployed person may not accept a job offer if he expects that an even *better* offer may soon arise; meanwhile, he remains unemployed.

Think about a person who drops out of college to look for a job. This person's work effort may be worth $8 per hour to many businesses, and yet the person may have difficulty finding a job. What creates this difficulty? Why don't business firms offer him a job at $6 per hour—leaving the firm with a $2 per hour profit from hiring the worker? Two reasons may prevent firms from hiring this person. First, firms may believe that the worker will soon quit to go back to school or look for a different job. Firms do not want to spend money to hire and train workers whom they will soon lose. Second, firms may expect to find other job applicants with better or more appropriate skills or experience. Even if the job applicant meets the basic qualifications for the job, these firms may prefer to wait for an even more suitable job applicant. Factors like these increase the time required to match people to jobs. These factors reduce the rate of job creation and create equilibrium unemployment.

Why don't unemployed people create jobs by becoming self-employed, like Crusoe? They might offer services as barbers, carpenters, caterers, designers, painters, plumbers, maintenance workers, baby-sitters, consultants, or taxi drivers. They might sell handicrafts or provide lawn and landscape care, music lessons, tutoring services, or laundry services; they could open restaurants or video-rental stores. (Centuries ago, when most people were self-employed, unemployment was virtually unknown.) Self-employment has several drawbacks. Although it eliminates the need for a person to find a job at a firm, self-employment requires people to find other things, such as suppliers (of inputs) and customers. A self-employed person may need to find and arrange a business location (for a barber shop or restaurant); tools (to work as a carpenter or computer repairer), and money for machinery, office space, and advertising. A self-employed person may need organizational skills, marketing skills, and other inputs that an employer would have provided. Self-employment requires potentially difficult and costly efforts to buy all these inputs, organize them, and make key business decisions. As a result, many people prefer to remain unemployed while they search for suitable jobs at established firms.

Automation

Throughout history, many people have worried about automation causing unemployment, as new machines gain capabilities to replace workers at lower cost. How does the economy create new jobs to replace those that automation destroys? The answer does not come from jobs producing the new machines, because one worker may produce a machine that replaces ten workers. Instead, the economy solves this problem by creating new jobs through new trades; firms are willing to hire the people who lose their jobs to automation, because those people offer valuable labor services. Because firms and workers need time to create suitable matches, automation temporarily drives unemployment above its equilibrium level. In time, however, it falls back toward its equilibrium level. People who lose their jobs may suffer greatly from unemployment, and the new jobs they find may not be as good as the jobs they lost, but the new machines raise the economy's aggregate GDP. The economy produces more goods and services for people than before technology improved. Although automation creates losses for some people (particularly those who lose their jobs), the average person gains from automation and other technical progress.

Unemployment in Kennywood Park

In the Kennywood Park story, ride operators become partially "unemployed" as fewer customers buy their rides after the money supply falls. As explained earlier, the fall in the money supply creates a recession in Kennywood Park because prices (tickets per ride) do *not* fall along with the money supply. As a result, customers make fewer trades with ride operators. This decrease in trading creates unemployment.

Unemployment in the Kennywood Park story illustrates another type of unemployment that economists often call *cyclical unemployment*. Cyclical unemployment refers to unemployment created by the economic forces that cause recessions, in contrast to the unemployment resulting from job destruction and creation in normal times. Because the distinction between cyclical unemployment and other unemployment is based on its *cause*, economists need *models* to distinguish cyclical unemployment from other unemployment in real-life data.

Chapter 2 explained that models have three purposes: understanding, prediction, and interpretation. This chapter has explained how a simple economic model helps with *understanding*, and why it helps with *prediction* by helping economists answer "what-if" questions; we now see that economists also need a model to *interpret* real-life unemployment data. The next chapter develops the model further by introducing financial markets and then using the model to answer some basic "what-if" questions.

Review Questions

15. List some reasons for unemployment.

16. Explain why the rate of unemployment tends to move toward its equilibrium level.

Thinking Exercises

17. Discuss this statement: "Advances in technology that replace workers with machines are likely to raise the rate of unemployment over the next several decades by reducing the number of jobs available in the economy."

18. Consider the Kennywood Park story. (a) Explain how changes in consumer tastes might create unemployment among ride operators in the park. (b) How would you identify job destruction and job creation in the park? (c) Explain how the fall in the money supply described by Professor Lucas creates unemployment among ride operators. (d) What could ride operators do to become re-employed in the park, after a fall in the money supply? (e) How would you estimate equilibrium unemployment in the park? How would you estimate cyclical unemployment?

Conclusion

What Economists Do

Economists construct models, which are like logical stories, and then reason by analogy from those models to real-life economies. They construct models *because* they want to understand *real-world* economies. Models allow economists to answer *"what if"* questions about the economy, understand the economy, make real-life decisions, and give advice about government policies.

In the Kennywood Park story told by Professor Lucas, a decrease in the money supply and a proportional decrease in prices inside the park (the number of tickets per ride) would not make any difference to customers. Professor Lucas considers an experiment in which the money supply in the park decreases and prices do *not* decrease because the fall in the money supply was a surprise. He explains why this combination creates a recession. This "story" is an example of an economic model.

A Very Simple Model of GDP

In the Robinson Crusoe economy, Crusoe's real GDP is determined by his production function and the number of hours he chooses to work. Crusoe also decides how much to invest in building new capital. His investment decisions depend on his willingness to sacrifice consumption or leisure time today to increase his consumption in the future, and his opportunities for doing so. Crusoe's real GDP fluctuates over time. These fluctuations may resemble recessions and booms, but they may also differ from them in important ways.

In a model with many people who specialize and trade, equilibrium in labor markets determines employment and the real wage. Given equilibrium employment, the aggregate production function determines real GDP.

The circular flow diagram illustrates the equation of exchange, which says that the nominal money supply, multiplied by its velocity, equals the price level multiplied by real GDP. This equation *defines* velocity. The equation of exchange shows how the price level depends on the nominal money supply, velocity, and real GDP.

In this chapter's basic model (which *assumes* a constant velocity of money), doubling the nominal money supply causes nominal prices to double without changing real GDP and employment. The prediction that real GDP does not depend on the money supply is called the *neutrality of money*. Economic controversies about business cycles and recessions surround discussions of the neutrality of money. The Kennywood Park story is one example of a model without the neutrality of money.

Equilibrium Employment and Unemployment

Unemployment results from continuing changes in underlying conditions such as technology, consumer tastes, population, weather, government policies, international competition, and other economic factors. Some industries contract while others expand. Unemployed people require time to find jobs that suit their interests and skills. Firms also require time to find workers who match their needs. Unemployment occurs because this matching process takes time.

Economists use the term *full employment* to refer to an economy with the equilibrium level (or natural rate) of unemployment, resulting from continuing changes in labor markets. Unemployment reaches it equilibrium level when the rate of job creation equals the rate of job destruction. At this level, the number of people who lose their jobs each month equals the number of unemployed people who find jobs, so total unemployment does not change. If unemployment exceeds its equilibrium level, then the rate of job creation exceeds the rate of job destruction and unemployment falls. If unemployment falls below its equilibrium level, then the rate of job creation falls below the rate of job destruction and unemployment rises. This activity moves the rate of unemployment toward its equilibrium level.

Jobs are trades, not products with limited supplies. The only limit to the number of jobs the economy can create is the number of profitable, voluntary trades to which people can and will agree. Anyone who can produce something of value to other people can obtain a job at some wage. Unemployment occurs because searching and matching take time; some people choose unemployment while they search for better opportunities. Cyclical unemployment results from additional factors that cause recessions, as in the Kennywood Park story.

Key Terms

production function
average product
marginal product
law of diminishing returns

nominal money supply
velocity of money
equation of exchange

nominal wages
real wages
neutrality of money

equilibrium unemployment
rate of job creation
rate of job destruction

Questions and Problems

19. Explain the Kennywood Park story of Professor Robert Lucas.

20. Why do you think Professor Lucas says that "we could *not* use monetary manipulation to engineer a *permanently* higher level of prosperity in the park"? What might happen if the park tried to do that?

21. In what ways are fluctuations in Robinson Crusoe's real GDP like recessions and booms in the U.S. economy? In what ways do they differ?

22. Suppose the nominal money supply is $2,000, velocity equals 1 per year, and real GDP is 1,000 goods per year. What happens to the equilibrium price level if real GDP rises to 2,000 goods per year?

23. How large is equilibrium unemployment if the rate of job destruction is 300,000 workers per month, and one-tenth of unemployed workers find jobs each month? Suppose that 10 million people are currently unemployed, and explain why unemployment falls over time toward its equilibrium level.

24. A professor at Stanford University, Alvin Rabushka, suggested that the government of Japan should try to end its 1998 recession by organizing a "national fire sale" in which all businesses, large and small, would be subsidized to reduce the nominal prices of their products.[4] Use the economic analysis of this chapter to explain why and how this policy might end a recession.

Inquiries for Further Thought

25. Professor Lucas says, "In any case, that is what economists do. We are storytellers, operating much of the time in worlds of make believe. We do not find that the realm of imagination and ideas is an alternative to, or a retreat from, practical reality. On the contrary, it is the only way we have found to think seriously about reality." Do you agree, or not? Defend your answer.

26. Why are people unemployed? Why don't unemployed people create their own jobs by going into

business for themselves? What could governments do to reduce unemployment? What government policies add to unemployment?

27. Why don't people buy unemployment insurance like they buy fire insurance?

---

[4]"On Sale Now," Alvin Rabushka, *The Wall Street Journal*, August 19, 1998.

SAVINGS, INVESTMENT, AND GROWTH

CHAPTER 7

INTEREST RATES, SAVINGS, AND INVESTMENT

In this Chapter...

Main Points to Understand

▶ The supply of loans by savers and demand for loans (mainly for investment) jointly determine the equilibrium interest rate and equilibriums levels of savings and investment.

▶ Equilibrium in the loan market is equivalent to equilibrium in the market for goods and services.

▶ The real (inflation-adjusted) interest rate affects saving and investment decisions.

▶ The economy's responses to changes in underlying conditions (such as technology or taxes) depend on the willingness of consumers to sacrifice current consumption for additional future consumption.

Thinking Skills to Develop

▶ Develop skills in working with economic models.

▶ Add new features to a simple model to address new issues.

▶ Use an economic model to examine changes in underlying conditions.

▶ Recognize the role of Adam Smith's "invisible hand" in macroeconomic issues.

As a college student, you are making a sacrifice. By attending school rather than working full time, you sacrifice income and consumption. You have probably made this choice on purpose, because you expect (quite correctly, on average) that a college education will raise your *future* income and consumption. In this and many other decisions in life, you make "now or later" choices that require current sacrifices for future gains or provide current gains at the expense of the future. Everyone regularly makes this kind of decision: A child decides whether to eat all her candy now or save some for next week; a worker decides whether to take time away from work and family to upgrade his skills; a business firm decides whether to pursue short-term profits or sacrifice them by investing in research and development in pursuit of increased long-term gains; every society somehow makes decisions about using natural resources or conserving them for future generations.

These "now or later" decisions affect the economy as a whole: They affect the amounts that people work, consume, and save. They affect the economy's current GDP and the opportunities that it will offer to future generations of workers and consumers. This chapter explains how a basic financial market and an important price—the market for loans and the interest rate—coordinate these decisions.

Think about the basic model of real GDP, employment, and the price level discussed in the previous chapter. In that basic model, each person produces and sells a good or service, and each buys goods and services from other people. (Some people work for

As a student, you sacrifice income now to improve your future. Similarly, the economy as a whole can sacrifice consumption now to invest in its future.

firms rather than producing goods as individuals, but that distinction does not affect our story.) People in the basic model have opportunities to invest in new tools, equipment, buildings and factories, skills, and technical knowledge, just as Robinson Crusoe had the opportunity to invest in automatic berry-picking machines. Robinson Crusoe's situation differs in two important ways from the situation of people in the basic model.

1. When Robinson Crusoe invests, he must either spend more time working or spend less time picking berries for consumption. As a result, Crusoe can invest only by reducing consumption or leisure time. In contrast, a person in the basic model can *borrow* to invest without reducing consumption or sacrificing leisure time.

2. Sometimes Robinson Crusoe enjoys a large berry harvest, because random changes in the weather or seasons allow him to pick a lot of berries in a short time. On those days, Crusoe has a high income (a high real GDP), and he can either eat a lot of berries, or work fewer hours and take more leisure time. On bad-harvest days, Crusoe has a low income; even by working extra hours, he picks fewer berries than normal to eat. If he could, Crusoe would like to store berries on days when he earns a high income for use on days when he has a low income. However, he cannot store berries (because they spoil quickly in the island heat). As a result, each day, Crusoe eats whatever he picks that day. In contrast, a person in the basic model can *save* on days when she has a high income. She saves by spending less than her income and lending the difference.

In the basic model, some people want to borrow money to spend on investments. Other people want to save money. As a result, people can gain from trades, and their trades create a *loan market* in which people borrow and lend.

INTEREST RATES AND LOAN-MARKET EQUILIBRIUM

Figure 1 shows equilibrium in the loan market. The price of a loan is the *interest rate*. The *demand for loans* shows the behavior of borrowers: *Borrowers demand loans*. The demand curve slopes downward because a rise in the interest rate raises the cost of borrowing. The *supply of loans* shows the behavior of lenders: *Lenders supply loans*. The supply curve slopes upward because a rise in the interest rate raises the interest income that lenders receive when loans are repaid.

Borrowers demand loans. Lenders supply loans.

Equilibrium in the loan market occurs at Point A in the figure, where the quantity of loans supplied equals the quantity demanded. The equilibrium interest rate is R_0 and the equilibrium quantity of loans is L_0. At interest rates above R_0, the quantity of loans supplied exceeds the quantity demanded, leading interest rates to fall toward the equilibrium. At interest rates below R_0, the quantity of loans demanded exceeds the quantity supplied, leading interest rates to rise toward the equilibrium.

Interest Rates

> An **interest rate** is the price of a loan, expressed as a *percentage per year* of the amount loaned.

EXAMPLES

If you borrow $100 for one year at an interest rate of 12 percent per year, you owe the lender $112 at the end of the year. The interest on the loan is the extra $12 you must pay; the interest rate expresses this amount as a percentage of the $100 loan; paying $12 on a loan of $100 gives an interest rate of 12 percent per year. If you borrow $200 for one year at an interest rate of 8 percent, you owe the bank $216 at the end of the year. You pay $16 in interest, which is 8 percent of the $200 loan.

If you borrow $100 for *two* years at an interest rate of 10 percent per year, you will owe $121 at the end of two years. The interest rate is 10 percent per year, *each year.* Your debt is $110 after one year ($100 plus $10 interest), so the interest on the second year of the loan is $11 (10 percent of $110), and you owe $121 at the end of two years. The $21 interest that you pay reflects an interest rate of 10 percent per year for two years.

Interest Rate Formula

If you borrow X dollars for one year, you must pay back:

$$X(1 + R)$$

dollars the next year, where R is the interest rate on the loan, measured as a decimal. In other words, an 8 percent interest rate means R is 0.08, and a 10 percent interest rate means R is 0.10.

Discounted Present Value

One of the most useful formulas in economics is the formula for a discounted present value. The discounted present value of some amount of money in the future is its value today.

> The **discounted present value** of a future payment of money is its market value *today.*

In other words, the discounted present value of $100 paid next year is *today's* equilibrium price of the right to receive $100 next year.

The general formula for a discounted present value is:

$$X \text{ dollars payable 1 year from now is worth } \frac{X}{1 + R} \text{ dollars now}$$

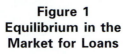

Figure 1
Equilibrium in the Market for Loans

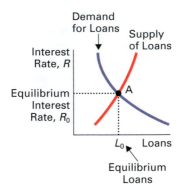

Equilibrium occurs at Point A, with an equilibrium price of R_0 per year and an equilibrium quantity of L_0 per year.

where R is the interest rate, measured as a decimal. For example, 12 percent per year is the number 0.12.

EXPLANATION AND EXAMPLES

Applying the Discounted Present Value Formula

Suppose an investment will pay $1,000 two years from now (but nothing before or after that time). Find the discounted present value of $1,000 paid two years from now by applying the formula *twice*. Suppose that in 2000 the interest rate is 10 percent per year. Your investment will pay you $1,000 in 2002, and you want to find the discounted present value, in 2000, of that money. First, apply the formula to find out how much $1,000 payable in 2002 is worth in 2001; the formula shows that this amount is worth $1,000/(1.10), or $909.09 in 2001. Then apply the formula again to find out how much $909.09 in 2001 is worth in 2000. (This time, substitute $909.09 for X in the formula.) The formula shows that it is worth $909.09/(1.10), or $826.45. The discounted present value of $1,000 paid two years from now is $826.45 if the interest rate is 10 percent per year.

Using this logic, you can apply the formula N times to find the discounted present value of $1,000 in N years from now. The formula for the discounted present value of X dollars paid N years from now is:

X dollars payable N years from now is worth

$$\frac{X}{(1 + R)^N} \text{ dollars now}$$

The idea of discounted present value is very simple: A dollar today is worth more than a dollar in the future, because if you have the dollar today you can save it and earn interest. For example, suppose the interest rate is 10 percent per year. If you have $91 today and you save it and earn interest on it, then you will have $91 + $9.10 = about $100 next year. Therefore, $91 *today* is worth about $100 paid next year. In other words, if the interest rate is 10 percent per year, then the *discounted present value* of $100 paid next year is about $91 today.

Notice that, with an interest rate of 10 percent per year, you can *trade* $91 today for about $100 next year by saving and earning interest. Similarly, you can trade $100 payable next year for about $91 *today* by *borrowing*. Suppose you will earn $100 next year. You can trade that money for $91 *today* by borrowing $91 now, for 1 year. You will owe the lender about $100 next year, and you can pay off the loan, with interest, by using the $100 that you will earn next year. In this way, you can trade $100 next year for $91 today. In summary, when the interest rate is 10 percent per year, people can trade $91 today for $100 next year, or they can trade $100 next year for $91 today. As a result, these amounts have the same value. We say that (when the interest rate is 10 percent per year) the discounted present value of $100 payable next year is about $91.

Consider some more examples: If the interest rate is 12 percent per year, then the discounted present value of $112 payable next year is $100 now. A person with $100 now can trade it for $112 next year, and a person who will have $112 next year can trade it for $100 today. If the interest rate is 8 percent per year, then the discounted present value of $20,000 payable next year is $20,000/1.08 = $18,518.52.

Investment and the Demand for Loans

The demand curve for loans in Figure 1 slopes downward because a rise in the interest rate raises the cost of borrowing. Think about a firm that wants to borrow to invest $1,000 in a new machine. Suppose that the new machine would add $1,200 to the firm's production next year, and would fall apart immediately after that. Borrowing $1,000 to invest in this machine is profitable if the interest rate is less than 20 percent per year, but not profitable if the interest rate is above 20 percent. For example, if the interest rate is 10 percent per year, then the firm will owe $1,100 to repay its loan. Because the firm gains $1,200 from the machine, the firm can repay the loan and keep $100 in profit. If the interest rate were 25 percent, however, the firm would owe $1,250 to repay its loan, and the revenue from the machine would not be enough to repay the loan. Loosely speaking, borrowing to invest is profitable only if the *rate of return* on the investment—20 percent per year in this example—exceeds the interest rate. More precisely:

> An investment is profitable if the discounted present value of the benefits from the investment exceeds the expenditure on the investment.

Suppose, in the example, that the interest rate is 10 percent per year ($R = 0.10$). Then the discounted present value of the benefit from the investment is $1,200/1.10 = $1,091. This amount exceeds the expenditure on the investment ($1,000), so the investment is profitable. However, if the interest rate were 25 percent per year ($R = 0.25$), then the discounted present value of the benefit would be only $1,200/1.25 = $960. This amount is less than $1,000, so the investment is *not* profitable.

A nearby box shows how to calculate discounted present values of more complicated investments. Notice that a rise in the interest rate reduces the discounted present value of the benefit from the investment. In this example, the firm will borrow and invest if the interest rate is less than 20 percent, but not if the interest rate exceeds 20 percent. Other firms have their own investment ideas. Some of those ideas would be profitable even with a 30 percent interest rate; many more would be profitable if the interest rate were only 5 percent per year. The result is a downward-sloping demand curve for loans, as in Figure 1.

For example, suppose a firm has an idea for building new equipment that would cost $100,000 but would add $130,000 to the firm's revenue next year (and nothing in years after that). Then the investment is profitable—the discounted present value of the benefit exceeds the initial expenditure on the investment—if the interest rate is less than 30 percent per year, but not if the interest rate is higher than 30 percent. Suppose another firm has an idea for an investment that would cost $100,000 and would add $110,000 in revenue next year (and nothing in years after that). This investment is profitable only if the interest rate is less than 10 percent per year. Both firms would want to borrow if the interest rate is below 10 percent per year; only the first firm would want to borrow at an interest rate between 10 percent and 30 percent; neither

---

The Powerball Payout Dilemma

Every player has to choose whether he would prefer to take any winnings up front or over a number of years. Making the right choice is tougher than it seems.

When a machinist from Westerville, Ohio, drove 100 miles recently to buy Powerball tickets for himself and a dozen buddies, he—like every other player in the huge lottery—faced a decision about how to get paid if he happened to win. He could either take the prize as a single lump sum—or as a stream of payments stretched out over 25 years.

As it happened, he chose the lump sum. And that's why, when the "Lucky 13," as they call themselves, claim their winnings, they will collect only $161.5 million, rather

than a total of $295.7 million over the next 25 years.

Did they make the right choice? Answering that question turns out to be more difficult than it might appear, financial planners told *Money Daily* on Thursday. But the answer has implications for how people facing more commonplace financial dilemmas—such as whether to take an annuity or a lump sum upon retirement—ought to analyze their situation.

In the case of Powerball, the choice works like this. You must decide when you buy your ticket whether to take the full prize—in this case, a total of $295.7 million over 25 years—or a much smaller sum ($161 million) up front. Yet the two are really equivalent. That's because

the way the lottery pays the $295 million is to buy a series of government bonds timed to mature in one year, two years, three years and so forth up to the full 25-year period. Buying those bonds costs about $161 million. So in either case, the lottery will pay out only $161 million.

Which type of payment is better for you depends critically on what you do with the money. "The difference between the lump sum and the annualized payout is equivalent to the government paying you 5.35% yearly interest on your money," says tax attorney Walker Arenson of Austin, TX. "So if you can beat that rate by investing the money, then you come out ahead."

Source: Money Daily

The article goes on to explain how tax laws complicate the calculation. Additional information can be found on the Web pages for this book.

---

where R is the interest rate *per year.* The previous example shows how this formula applies when $N = 2$.

You can easily extend this logic to find the discounted present value of more complicated future payments. For example, suppose that someone will pay you $1,000 one year from now and another $1,000 two years from now. What is the discounted present value of these two payments? The discounted present value of $1,000 paid one year from now is $1,000/(1 + R)$. The discounted present value of $1,000 paid two years from now is $1,000/(1 + R)^2$. So the discounted present value of both payments is:

$$\frac{\$1,000}{(1 + R)} + \frac{\$1,000}{(1 + R)^2}$$

If the interest rate is 10 percent per year, the result is $909.09 plus $826.45, or $1,735.54.

Finally, you can apply this logic to payments that occur every year without stopping. The discounted present value of $1,000 per year paid *every year, forever* turns out to be:

$$\frac{\$1,000}{R}$$

If the interest rate is 10 percent per year, this amount equals $10,000. This result is also a rough approximation to the discounted present value of $1,000 paid every year for more than about 30 years ($9,370 if the interest rate is 10 percent per year).

Opportunity Cost and Investment

Firms in the U.S. economy sometimes pay for investments with money they already have (from sales of their products) rather than by borrowing. Firms face an opportunity cost of using their money in this way, because they *could have* loaned the money to someone, earning interest on it. As a result, the interest rate affects investment decisions in the same way regardless of whether firms borrow money to fund investments or whether they use money they already have. Consequently, you can think of firms that use their own money for investments as *borrowing the money from themselves*. This borrowing appears as part of the demand for loans in Figure 1, and this saving and lending by firms appears as part of the supply of loans in Figure 1.

firm would want to borrow at an interest rate above 30 percent. This creates the demand curve for loans in Figure 2. With additional firms and additional investment ideas, the demand for loans appears as in Figure 1.

Adjustments to the Logic of Investment

These criteria for profitability of investments require three adjustments for many real-life applications. First, the future benefits of investments in real life are uncertain, so the logic above applies to *expected* benefits rather than actual benefits (which are unknown at the time a firm invests).

Second, firms must often pay taxes on returns from their investments, so they must adjust the logical reasoning for the effects of taxes. Essentially, the logic above applies to *after-tax* costs and benefits.

Third, people tend to dislike risk. A firm may have a 6/10 chance of gaining $1,000 on an investment and a 4/10 chance of losing $1,000. Although the chance of winning is better than the chance of losing, a firm may not want to accept the risk of this investment. In real-life investment decisions, firms adjust the logic of the decision to account for risk. Essentially, the discounted present value of the expected future benefits from the investment must exceed the required expenditure by an amount sufficient to repay people for taking risks. The fundamental logic of investments is not affected by these adjustments.

Government Budgets and the Demand for Loans

The demand for loans shows the amount of money that *everyone* in the economy—people, firms, and the government—would want to borrow at various possible interest rates. In the U.S. economy, the demand for loans is *mostly* demand by firms to pay for investments. Until recent years, however, the second-largest part of the demand for loans came from the *government budget deficit*.

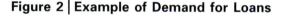

Figure 2 | Example of Demand for Loans

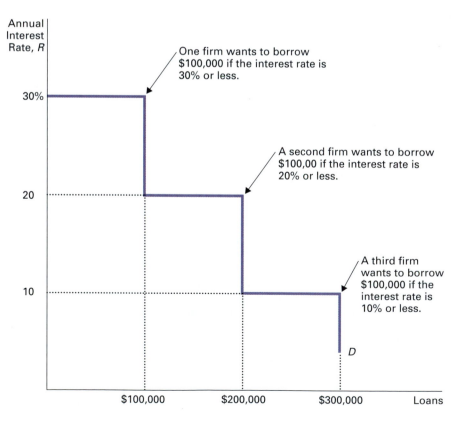

IN THE NEWS

American dream is back

Low interest rates light up home sales

Falling mortgage rates are adding fuel to an unseasonably hot market for home sales. Not since the 1960s has the housing market been so uniformly strong across the USA.

From Boston to San Francisco, Charleston, S.C., to Des Moines, people are buying homes at a record rate. Behind the boom: a strong economy, low interest rates and easy credit as more banks offer low- or no-down-payment loans.

"I never thought I could have a home of my own," says Mary Kutsch, who moved from El Segundo, Calif., to Las Vegas last year. Lured by low interest rates, the family first looked to buy a new home. And mortgage applications are at near-record levels, lifted by lower interest rates.

Source: USA Today

Decreasing interest rates raise investments in housing as well as investments in factories, equipment, and research.

The **government budget deficit** equals government spending in excess of tax receipts during some period of time.

A government budget deficit creates a demand for loans. When the government spends more than it collects in taxes, it borrows money to *finance* its deficit. If the government spends $2,500 billion, and collects $2,400 billion in taxes, it borrows the other $100 billion. As recently as 1996, the U.S. government's annual budget deficit exceeded $100 billion. However, state and local governments had budget surpluses that year (revenues that exceeded their spending), so the combined budget deficit of U.S. federal, state, and local governments was only $5 billion in 1996, meaning that units of government in the United States borrowed $5 billion. Back in 1992, the combined government budget deficit was almost $200 billion; by 1998, even the federal government had a *surplus* rather than a deficit. While U.S. government budget deficits may appear to be a topic of history, economists expect them to reemerge in future years as the baby-boom generation retires and begins collecting social security. Figure 3 shows the connection between investment demand, the government budget deficit, and the demand for loans.

The total demand for loans equals demand by firms for investment plus the government budget deficit.

Review Questions

1. Who supplies loans? Why does the supply curve for loans slope upward?

2. What is a discounted present value? Explain this concept in words. What is the formula for it?

Figure 3 | Equilibrium in the Market for Loans

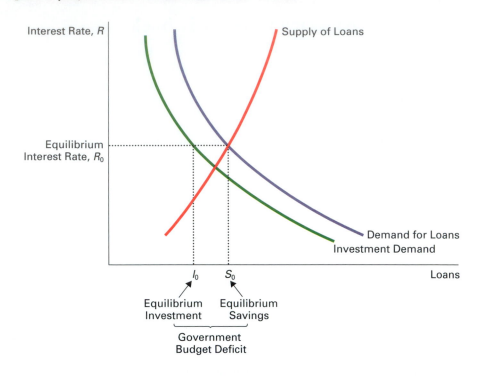

Thinking Exercises

3. If the interest rate is 10 percent per year, what is the discounted present value of $200 paid one year from now? What if the interest is 5 percent?

4. How does an increase in the interest rate affect the discounted present value of a certain future payment?

5. If the interest rate is 10 percent per year, what is the discounted present value of $20,000 paid two years from now?

SAVINGS AND THE SUPPLY OF LOANS

People supply loans when they lend money that they have *saved* by spending less than their incomes:

$$\text{Savings} = \text{Income (after taxes)} - \text{Consumption}$$

After-tax income is often called *disposable income*.

When people save, they usually put their money in bank accounts (or some similar accounts) or they buy financial assets such as stocks and bonds. When you put your money in a bank account, the bank lends your money to someone else. The bank is essentially a middleman or intermediary between savers (lenders) and borrowers. (Further analysis of the role of banks in this process appears in Chapter 27.)

You also lend money when you buy bonds; you lend to the business firms that sell those bonds. Each bond is an I.O.U.—a piece of paper printed with a promise to pay a specified amount of money at a future date. If a bond promises to pay $1,000 one year from now, and you buy that bond for $909.09, then you are actually lending $909.09 for a year at a 10 percent interest rate. The business firm that issues the bond gets the $909.09 now, and it repays you $1,000 next year. (As this example shows, the price of a bond is the discounted present value of its future payments.) A later chapter will discuss stocks, bonds, and other financial assets in greater depth. The current discussion can ignore the details of banks, stock markets, and similar complications: In the basic economic model, savers lend money directly to borrowers to fund investments.

Supply of Loans

The supply of loans slopes upward as in Figure 1 because a rise in the interest rate raises the return from lending. People gain more from lending money at a 10 percent interest rate than at a 5 percent interest rate. As a result, the quantity of loans supplied rises as the interest rate rises, creating the upward-sloping supply curve.

> The supply of loans shows the amounts of money that people would want to save and lend at various possible interest rates.

Total saving by people and businesses in the United States equals about $1.4 trillion per year. Almost all of this money is loaned to business firms for investment; a small fraction funds loans to households for cars, houses, vacations, and other purchases. (A few years ago, when the U.S. government was running a large budget deficit, the government also borrowed a portion of this money.)

Equilibrium in the Loan Market and Goods Market

Equilibrium in the loan market occurs when the quantity of loans demanded equals the quantity supplied, as at Point A in Figure 1. The equilibrium interest rate is R_0 and the equilibrium quantity of loans is L_0. The supply of loans reflects saving and lending, so *equilibrium saving equals L_0*. Similarly, the demand for loans reflects investment and the government budget deficit, so *equilibrium investment equals L_0 minus the government budget deficit*.

When business firms take out loans from banks, they borrow money that other people have saved and spend it on investments.

Equilibrium in the loans market is closely connected with equilibrium in the economy's overall market for goods and services reflected in the circular flow diagram (Figure 5 in the previous chapter). For the moment, ignore all international trade. Equilibrium in the loan market implies that the quantity of loans supplied—savings—equals the quantity of loans demanded—investment plus the government budget deficit:

$$S = I + DEF$$

where S is total savings, I is investment, and DEF is the government budget deficit. Recall that savings equals income minus taxes and minus consumption spending:

$$S = Y - T - C$$

Therefore, equilibrium in the loan market implies:

$$Y - T - C = I + DEF$$

However, the government budget deficit equals government spending minus taxes, so

$$DEF = G - T$$

Therefore, loan-market equilibrium implies:

$$Y = C + I + G$$

In the absence of international trade, this expression is the equation for equilibrium in the market for goods and services—GDP equals consumption plus investment plus government purchases.[1] In other words, equilibrium in the loan market and equilibrium in the goods market are *the same*.

What about International Trade?

International trade fits easily into the previous analysis. The key point to notice is the connection between net exports and international trade in loans: When we export to other countries more goods than we import from them (when we have an international trade surplus), other countries *borrow* from us to pay for the difference. For example, suppose we export $500 in goods to another country, and we import $300 in goods from them; our net exports equal $200. People in the other country need to obtain $500 to pay us for their purchases; they earn $300 of that money by selling goods to us, and they borrow the other $200. Similarly, when we import more goods than we export (when we have an international trade deficit), other countries *lend* the difference to us. For example, suppose we export $500 in goods to another country, and we import $600 in goods from them; our net exports equal *minus* $100. In that case, we *borrow* $100 from people in foreign countries. Figure 5 in Chapter 24 showed that the United States currently has an international trade deficit of about $500 per person, meaning that net exports, NEX, is *negative* and foreigners lend about $500 per person to Americans.

International trade enters the loan-market analysis because lending by foreigners adds to the total supply of loans. Therefore equilibrium in the loan market implies that

---

The idea that loan-market equilibrium and goods-market equilibrium are the same is easiest to understand with no government spending, no taxes, and no international trade.

In this case, loan-market equilibrium implies that savings equals investment, or

$$S = I$$

However, savings is simply income minus consumption, so:

$$S = Y - C$$

Substituting for S and rearranging:

$$Y = C + I$$

which is the same as goods-market equilibrium.

---

[1] An alert reader might recall the difference between government *spending* and government *purchases*. *Spending* includes transfer payments (such as social security payments). This difference does not affect these conclusions, however. To see why, let G represent government purchases. Then the government budget deficit is $DEF = G +$ transfer payments $-$ taxes. Now define T as taxes minus transfer payments. (In other words, we count transfer payments as *negative* taxes, which makes sense because transfer payments add to people's incomes in the same way that taxes reduce the incomes of others.) Then $DEF = G - T$, as in the text.

the quantity of loans supplied, or savings *minus net exports (NEX)*, equals the quantity of loans demanded, or investment plus the government budget deficit:

$$S - NEX = I + DEF$$

Therefore, equilibrium in the loan market implies $Y - T - C - NEX = I + DEF$, or

$$Y = C + I + G + NEX$$

This expression is the equation for equilibrium in the market for goods and services. GDP equals the sum of consumption, investment, government purchases, and net exports. As before, equilibrium in the loan market and equilibrium in the goods market are the same thing.

Intertemporal Allocation of Resources

Why is equilibrium in the loan market the same as equilibrium in the goods market? The answer is connected with the "now or later" choices mentioned in the introduction to this chapter—choices that people make every day, such as your decision to sacrifice current consumption to invest in a college education and raise your future consumption. Economists refer to these "now or later" choices as *intertemporal* choices. These choices affect the the economy's overall use of labor, capital, and other resources to create consumption *now* versus consumption in the *future*.

Goods-market equilibrium occurs when the *current* supply of goods and services equals the *current* demand (for consumption, investment, government purchases, and net exports). Loan-market equilibrium occurs when the amount of *current* goods that some people want to trade away in return for *future* goods (by lending) equals the amount that other people want to acquire (by borrowing).

Suppose people suddenly want more consumption now—and they are willing to pay for it by having less in the future. This decision creates *excess demand* in the goods market *now,* as well as excess supply in the future goods market. It also creates excess demand for loans, as people save less than before and spend more on consumption. As a result, the interest rate rises, bringing the loan market *and* the goods market into equilibrium.

As the interest rate increases, investment falls, reducing excess demand for loans. This fall in investment also reduces excess demand in the goods market. As the interest rate adjusts to create equilibrium in the loans market, it also automatically creates equilibrium in the market for current goods and services. That reasoning expresses in *words* the logic behind the *algebra* showing the equivalence of loan-market equilibrium and goods-market equilibrium.

The logic connecting loan-market equilibrium and goods-market equilibrium points out the important role of the interest rate. It also shows that the interest rate is connected to the *relative price* of consumption now versus consumption in the future. The next section explores this important issue.

Review Questions

6. Who demands loans? Why does the demand curve for loans slope downward?

7. In what way is the demand for loans related to the government budget deficit?

8. Use equations to show why equilibrium in the loan market is the same as equilibrium in the goods market.

Thinking Exercises

9. Discuss this statement: "Investors gain from a higher interest rate. By making investments more attractive, an increase in the interest rate raises investment."

10. Suppose an increase in the supply of loans leads to a new equilibrium in the loan market, with a $100 billion increase in equilibrium savings and investment. If government purchases, net exports, and GDP do not change, what happens to keep the goods market in equilibrium—that is, what happens to guarantee that $Y = C + I + G + NEX$?

REAL AND NOMINAL INTEREST RATES

In 1990, interest rates reached more than 1,000 percent per year in Argentina and Brazil, but they were only about 35 percent per year in Mexico and 8 percent per year in the United States and Japan. Why do interest rates differ so much between countries? Are they connected with inflation, which was above 1,000 percent per year in Argentina and Brazil, much lower in Mexico, and even lower in the United States and Japan?

The interest rates that people usually talk about or read about are *nominal* interest rates.

> The **nominal interest rate** on a loan is the annual dollar interest payment expressed as a percentage of the dollar amount borrowed.

The formula for the discounted present value of a certain amount of money to be delivered in the future involves the nominal interest rate. The nominal interest rate is actually a relative price.

> The nominal interest rate (expressed as a decimal), plus one, equals the *relative price* of $1 this year in terms of dollars next year.

In other words, when a person borrows $500 for a year, he buys $500 *this year* at a price of $500(1 + R) *next year*. For example, if the nominal interest rate is 6 percent per year, then 1 plus the nominal interest rate expressed as a decimal is 1.06, so the relative price of $500 this year is 1.06 times $500, or $530 next year. This price is the amount of money that a borrower must repay on the loan.

The *real* interest rate corrects the nominal interest rate for inflation:

> The **real interest rate** is the interest rate *adjusted for inflation.*

The real interest rate plays an important economic role, because it is the *relative price* of a good at two points in time.

> The real interest rate (expressed as a decimal), plus one, is the relative price of goods *this year* in terms of the same goods *next year*.

To see how the real interest rates corrects the nominal interest rate for inflation, suppose that you lend someone $100 for one year at 10 percent interest; you get back $110 at the end of the year, which is 10 percent more money than you originally loaned. If inflation has occurred, however, the borrower repays you in dollars that have lower purchasing power than the dollars you lent. Each dollar buys less at the end of the year than

Example
If the nominal interest rate is 10 percent per year, then the relative price of $1 this year is 1.10 dollars next year: If you borrow $1 now, you will owe $1.10 next year.

it bought at the beginning of the year. The nominal interest rate shows how much you gain in dollar terms from the loan; the real interest rate adjusts for inflation to measure your gain in purchasing power.

Fisher Equation

Real and nominal interest rates are connected by a formula called the *Fisher equation,* named after the famous American economist, Irving Fisher. The Fisher equation says:[2]

$$R = r + \pi$$

where R is the nominal interest rate, r is the real interest rate, and π is the rate of inflation.

The Fisher equation shows why countries with high rates of inflation have high nominal interest rates. Whatever the level of the real interest rate, a high rate of inflation, π, causes a high nominal interest rate, R. Figure 4 shows the nominal interest rate, inflation rate, and real interest rate in the United States since 1955. Notice that decreases in the nominal interest rate in the 1980s and 1990s accompanied decreases in the rate of inflation. Rearranging the Fisher equation gives the real interest rate in terms of the nominal interest rate and inflation:

$$r = R - \pi$$

Figure 4 | Interest Rates in the United States, 1955–1998

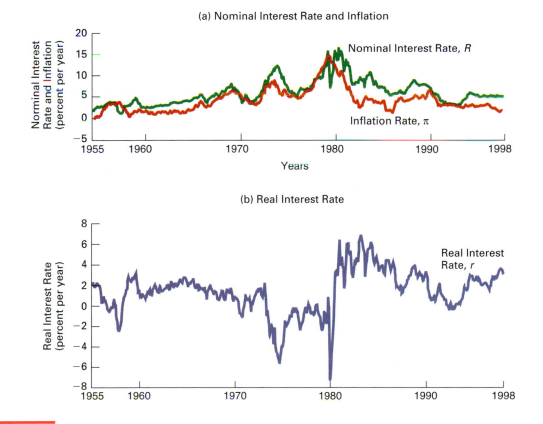

(a) Nominal Interest Rate and Inflation

(b) Real Interest Rate

---

[2] This version of the Fisher equation is an approximation for interest that is not continuously compounded; the actual equation in that case is $(1 + r) e^{\pi} - 1$ where e is the natural exponent. The formula in the text is exact for continuously compounded interest.

Inflation is driving global rates higher

Inflation and fears of inflation are driving interest rates higher around the globe.

Source: The Wall Street Journal

Higher inflation inevitably leads to higher nominal interest rates, as the Fisher equation indicates. Similarly, lower inflation rates in recent years have reduced nominal interest rates, as Figure 4 illustrates.

EXAMPLES

Suppose that the nominal interest rate is 10 percent per year. If you lend someone $100, that borrower pays you $110 next year. Without inflation, π equals 0, and the Fisher equation gives a real interest rate of 10 percent ($r = 0.10 - 0 = 0.10$). When the borrower repays the loan, you gain 10 percent more dollars and 10 percent more purchasing power than you had before you made the loan. (You can buy 10 percent more goods next year with $110 than you could buy this year with $100.) Your 10 percent gain in purchasing power means that you can buy 11 goods worth $10 each next year instead of 10 goods this year, so the relative price of each good this year is 1.10 goods next year. In other words, 1 plus the real interest rate (expressed as a decimal) is 1.10, so the real interest rate is 0.10, or 10 percent per year.

Now suppose that inflation is 10 percent per year, while the nominal interest rate remains at 10 percent per year. In this case, the Fisher equation gives a real interest rate of zero (because $r = 0.10 - 0.10 = 0$). Prices next year will be 10 percent higher than prices this year, so you will need $110 next year just to buy the *same* amount of goods you could buy for $100 this year. Lending money gives you a 10 percent gain in dollars, but no increase in purchasing power. (This shows the meaning of a zero real interest rate.) The relative price of goods now in terms of goods in the future is 1.

Finally, suppose that the nominal interest rate is 10 percent per year and inflation is 4 percent per year. In this case, the Fisher equation gives a real interest rate of 6 percent per year, because 0.10 minus 0.04 equals 0.06. If you lend $100 for one year at 10 percent interest, you collect $110 at the end of the year. The $110 gives you 6 percent more purchasing power next year than you would have with $100 this year. In other words, the relative price of goods this year in terms of goods next year is 1.06. Since this relative price is 1 plus the real interest rate, the real interest rate is 6 percent per year.

These three examples illustrate an important point: The real interest rate states the interest rate in terms of the purchasing power that a borrower pays and a lender receives on a loan.

Relative Prices over Time

Higher real interest rates mean that goods now (this year) are relatively more expensive in terms of future goods because people sacrifice more future goods for each good they buy now. This sacrifice occurs because higher real interest rates give people higher returns, measured in purchasing power, on their savings. A person who spends today, rather than saving for the future, sacrifices more future consumption when the real interest rate is high than when it is low. Lower real interest rates make goods today relatively cheaper in terms of future goods; people sacrifice fewer future goods for each good they buy now. This is the same as saying that future goods are relatively more expensive measured in terms of current goods. The real interest rate is the *relative price* that plays the key role in the economy's "now or later" decisions, and connects loan-market equilibrium with equilibrium in the market for goods and services.

EXAMPLE

Suppose that a can of soda pop costs $0.50 this year and everyone expects it to cost $0.55 next year (a 10 percent increase). Bob loans Tom $10.00 for one year at a 15 percent nominal interest rate; Tom will repay $11.50 next year. If Bob had spent $10.00 on soda pop, he could have bought 20 cans, so his opportunity cost of $10.00 is 20 cans of soda pop this year. His benefit from lending $10.00 equals the amount of soda pop that he can buy with the $11.50 that he collects from Tom next year. If soda pop really does cost $0.55 next year, he will be able to buy 21 cans, this amount is 5 percent more than the 20 cans he sacrificed this year.[3] The real rate of interest on the loan, measured in soda pop, is 5 percent per year. The relative price of soda pop this year in terms of soda pop next year is 1.05.

If the nominal interest rate were 20 percent per year instead of 15 percent, then Tom would repay Bob $12.00 next year. In this case, Bob would have enough money to buy 22 cans of soda pop next year, so the relative price of soda pop this year in terms of soda pop next year would be 1.10. A rise in the nominal interest rate, combined with the same rate of inflation of soda-pop prices, raises the real interest rate and the relative price of soda pop this year in terms of soda pop next year.

Uncertainty and Expected Inflation

In real life, future inflation is uncertain. No one knows what the rate of inflation will be over the next year. The Fisher equation applies with the term π representing the *expected* rate of inflation—the rate of inflation that people, on average, believe will occur.

Uncertainty about inflation also creates uncertainty about the real interest rate. For example, if the nominal interest rate is 10 percent and people don't know whether inflation will be 3 percent, 4 percent, or 5 percent over the next year, then they don't know whether the real interest rate will turn out to be 7 percent, 6 percent, or 5 percent. Economists distinguish the *expected* real interest rate from the *actual* real interest rate. If the nominal interest rate is 10 percent per year and people *expect* inflation of 4 percent, then the *expected* real interest rate is 6 percent per year. If inflation *turns out* to be 3 percent over the year of the loan, then the *actual* real interest rate is 7 percent.

> The *expected* real interest rate equals the nominal interest rate minus the *expected* rate of inflation. The *actual* real interest rate equals the nominal interest rate minus the *actual* rate of inflation during the period of the loan.

When this chapter refers to the *real interest rate,* it means the expected real interest rate.

Why the *Real* Interest Rate Matters

It is important to understand why the real interest rate, not the nominal interest rate, affects investment. Suppose that the nominal interest rate and expected inflation rise equally. The Fisher equation, $R = r + \pi$, indicates that these increases do not affect the real interest rate. These equal changes in the nominal interest rate and inflation do not affect a firm's investment decisions because two terms in the discounted present value formula cancel each other. First, the increase in expected inflation raises the firm's expected future income from investments. Second, the increase in the nominal interest rate reduces the discounted present value of each future dollar that the firm earns. When the nominal interest and expected inflation change equally, leaving the real interest rate constant, these two terms exactly offset each other in the discounted present value formula. As a result, only changes in the *real* interest rate affect investment.

---

[3]He is $0.05 short of the price of 21 cans. This reflects the fact that the Fisher equation is an approximation when interest is not continuously compounded. See footnote 2.

EXAMPLE

Sammy's Sports Store could spend $15,000 for a new machine that would produce 6,000 baseball caps each year for the next 3 years. More precisely, the machine would produce 6,000 caps 1 year from now, another 6,000 caps 2 years from now, and another 6,000 caps 3 years from now. After that, the machine would be worthless. The store can sell the caps for $1.00 each. Suppose there is *no* expected inflation, so the nominal and real interest rates are equal. Then the machine would provide expected income of $6,000 after 1 year, another $6,000 two years from now, and another $6,000 three years from now.

Is it profitable to invest in the machine? You can verify that investing in the machine is profitable if the interest rate (real and nominal, since they are equal) is less than 9.7 percent per year. The discounted present value of the three future receipts of $6,000,

$$\frac{\$6,000}{1+R} + \frac{\$6,000}{(1+R)^2} + \frac{\$6,000}{(1+R)^3}$$

exceeds the $15,000 cost of the machine if R is less than 0.097.[4] For example, if the (real and nominal) interest rate is 3 percent per year, then the discounted present value of these three receipts is $16,972.

Now suppose that expected inflation rises from zero to 5 percent per year, while the real interest rate remains at 3 percent per year. The Fisher equation shows that the nominal interest rate rises to about 8 percent per year. In fact, the Fisher equation is an approximation (as footnote 2 explained), and the nominal interest rate actually rises to 8.15 percent per year. With expected inflation of 5 percent per year, the expected price of baseball caps rises at 5 percent per year from its current level of $1.00 to $1.05 next year, $1.103 two years from now (another 5 percent increase), and $1.158 three years from now. Therefore, the discounted present value of the store's extra revenue from buying the machine is:

$$\frac{(6,000)(\$1.05)}{1.0815} + \frac{(6,000)(\$1.103)}{1.0815^2} + \frac{(6,000)(\$1.158)}{1.0815^3} = \$16,972$$

Notice that the discounted present value of the benefits from the investment does not change if inflation and the nominal interest rate rise together, with the real interest rate unchanged. Only changes in the *real* interest rate affect the profitability of investment.

Review Questions

11. What is the real interest rate? Explain it in words. What relative price equals 1 plus the real interest rate?

12. What is the relationship between the real interest rate, the nominal interest rate, and the expected rate of inflation?

13. What is the difference between the expected real interest rate and the actual real interest rate?

---

[4]On the other hand, if the interest rate exceeds 9.7 percent per year, then the discounted present value of the three future receipts from the investment is smaller than the cost of investment, and it is not profitable.

Thinking Exercises

14. Concert tickets cost $20 now, but the price will rise to $24 next year. The nominal interest rate is 10 percent per year. What is the relative price of concert tickets this year in terms of concert tickets next year?

15. When the real interest rate rises, do current goods become cheaper or more expensive compared to goods in the future? Explain.

SUMMARY OF THE BASIC MODEL

We now have a basic model with several parts, summarized in Figure 5. The economy has a money supply, chosen by the government, and a capital stock that has resulted from *past* investments. It also has some technology, described by its production function, which shows how its real GDP depends on its inputs of labor and capital. It has firms that demand labor. Finally, it has people who supply labor services.

The demand for and supply of labor determine equilibrium employment, as in Figure 5a. With this level of employment and with the capital that the economy has created in the past, the production function determines real GDP, as in Figure 5b. The equation

Figure 5 | The Basic Model of the Economy

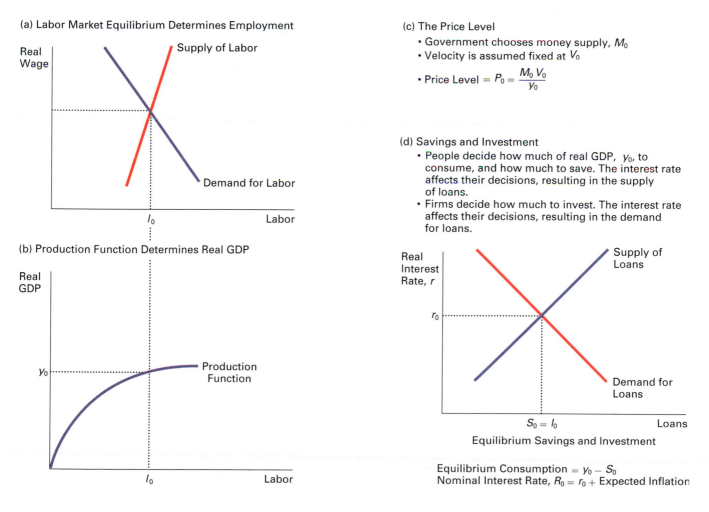

(a) Labor Market Equilibrium Determines Employment

Real Wage — Supply of Labor — Demand for Labor — l_0 — Labor

(b) Production Function Determines Real GDP

Real GDP — y_0 — Production Function — l_0 — Labor

(c) The Price Level
- Government chooses money supply, M_0
- Velocity is assumed fixed at V_0
- Price Level $= P_0 = \dfrac{M_0 V_0}{y_0}$

(d) Savings and Investment
- People decide how much of real GDP, y_0, to consume, and how much to save. The interest rate affects their decisions, resulting in the supply of loans.
- Firms decide how much to invest. The interest rate affects their decisions, resulting in the demand for loans.

Real Interest Rate, r — Supply of Loans — Demand for Loans — r_0 — $S_0 = I_0$ — Loans

Equilibrium Savings and Investment

Equilibrium Consumption $= y_0 - S_0$
Nominal Interest Rate, $R_0 = r_0 +$ Expected Inflation

of exchange determines the price level: $P = MV/y$, where y represents real GDP, M represents the money supply (the number of dollars printed by the government), and V represents the velocity of money (which we treat as a constant for now). Changes over time in M, V, and y lead to changes in the price level, creating inflation. The supply of loans and demand for loans determine the equilibrium real interest rate, savings, and investment, as in Figure 5d. Consumption equals after-tax income minus saving. The nominal interest rate equals the real interest rate plus expected inflation. Finally, next year's capital stock rises as a result of this year's investment.

APPLYING THE MODEL

We now apply this basic macroeconomic model to answer "what-if" questions about the effects of changes in underlying economic conditions, such as the economy's technology and its government's policies. We use the model to examine the effect of these changes on variables such as consumption, savings, investment, and the real interest rate.

The following results will emerge from our analysis:

▶ An increase in consumer patience, that is, an increase in people's desire to save for the future, reduces the equilibrium real interest rate and raises equilibrium savings and investment. The additional investment raises the economy's future capital stock, raising future GDP and consumption.

▶ Technical progress raises the production that the economy can obtain from its labor and capital inputs. It thereby raises investment and the real interest rate. In the long run, it raises consumption and real GDP.

▶ The effects of a tax cut on the economy depend on two main factors:

1. How the tax cut affects incentives to work, incentives to save money rather than spend it, and incentives for firms to invest

2. Whether people choose to spend or save the money from the tax cut

The next sections explain these results. We analyze the effects of each change in conditions separately, one at a time. For example, the discussion of the effects of a change in consumer tastes assumes that technology and taxes remain unchanged. In real life, of course, many changes occur at the same time. However, logical thinking benefits by studying the effects of each change separately.

Effects of an Increase in Consumer Patience

Suppose that people become more concerned about the future and decide to reduce spending on current consumption and save more for the future. This kind of change is sometimes called an *increase in consumer patience,* or a *fall in consumer confidence.* This change raises the supply of loans, as in Figure 6, lowering the real interest rate and raising the equilibrium quantity of loans. It increases equilibrium savings from S_1 to S_2, along with the equilibrium quantity of loans. For now, we ignore the government budget deficit since deficits are currently close to zero in the U.S. economy. Equilibrium investment rises from I_1 to I_2. Equilibrium investment and savings rise by the same amount because savings *equals* investment plus the (zero) government budget deficit. Firms invest more than before because the real interest rate falls, making more investment projects profitable. Equilibrium consumption falls because consumption equals GDP minus investment minus government purchases, and investment rises while GDP

Figure 6 | Increase in Consumer Patience

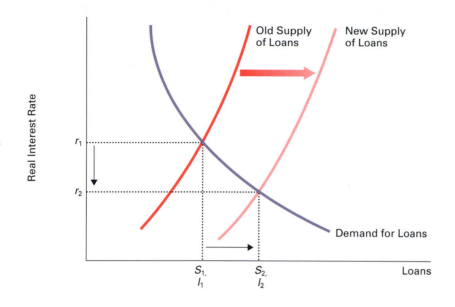

An increase in consumer patience, or desire to save, raises the supply of loans. This reduces the equilibrium real interest rate from r_1 to r_2, raises equilibrium savings from S_1 to S_2, and raises equilibrium investment from I_1 to I_2.

and government purchases remain unchanged. As a result, equilibrium consumption falls by the same amount that equilibrium investment rises.

The increase in investment eventually raises the economy's capital stock, so it eventually raises real GDP. No one has to work harder or more hours for this increase in real GDP; the economy produces more than before because each person works with more capital (such as machinery or equipment). This future increase in real GDP raises future consumption. In this way, the economy responds to the desires of consumers. When people want to reduce current consumption and raise *future* consumption, the economy increases investment, making fewer goods available for current consumption and more goods available for future consumption. When people want more *current* consumption and less future consumption, the economy provides this result through a decrease in investment. Adam Smith's metaphor of the "invisible hand" (see Chapter 1) applies here: As business firms make investment decisions to maximize their own profits, they are led "as if by an invisible hand" to provide consumers with the "now or later" choices that they *want*.

People spend less and save more if they expect lower incomes in the future. Although this news item refers to the U.S. economic situation a decade ago, the situation is likely to repeat itself when signs of the next recession occur.

Increases in confidence about the future lead consumers to raise their spending, and reduce their saving.

Effects of Technical Progress

Suppose now that technical progress permanently increases productivity, shifting the production function, as in Figure 7. This raises the quantity of output that the economy can produce with each possible level of labor and capital inputs. To simplify this analysis (without affecting its main results), we consider the case in which the quantity of labor supplied is *perfectly inelastic* (indicated by a vertical supply curve), as in Figure 8.

The increase in productivity has two main effects. First, it raises total production of goods and services, real GDP, as in Figure 9. Second, it raises the demand for loans,

Figure 7 | Technical Progress

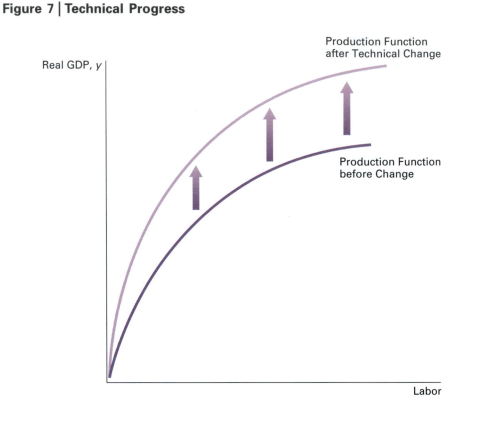

Figure 8 | Perfectly Inelastic Labor Supply

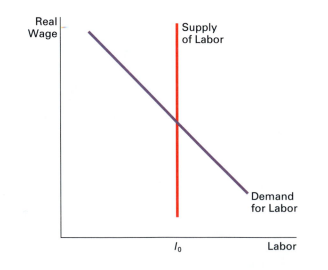

Figure 9 | Technical Progress Raises Real GDP

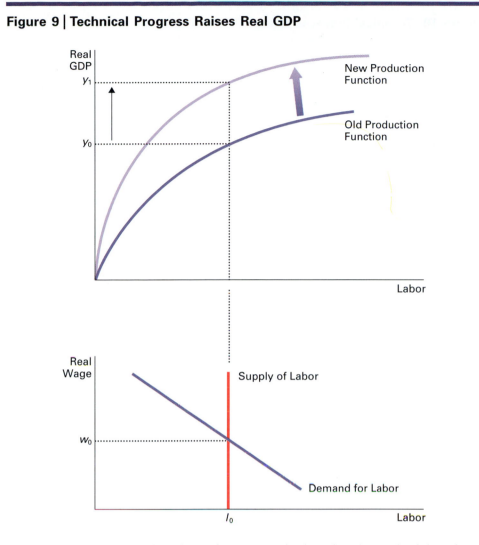

because it raises the benefits of new investments by boosting the productivity of new capital goods. For example, technical progress might allow companies to produce a new generation of computers that are faster than older computers or new farm equipment that increases output per acre. The increase in demand for loans raises the equilibrium real interest rate, and it raises equilibrium saving and investment, as in Figure 10.

The increase in equilibrium investment begins to raise the economy's capital stock. As the capital stock rises, the economy's real GDP increases, as in Figure 11. This increase in GDP allows consumption to increase along with production.

Notice that the economy's precise response to technical progress depends on the desires of consumers. The economy faces a trade-off: When its real GDP rises by $10 billion per year, consumption could rise by $10 billion per year *or* investment could rise by $10 billion per year, raising the future capital stock and creating an even larger increase in future real GDP than would otherwise occur. The economy's response to this trade-off depends on its available *opportunities* for investment and the *preferences* of consumers. These forces operate through the supply and demand for loans. Would people rather consume $10 billion more each year, starting *now,* or would they rather postpone the increase in consumption in return for a larger future increase (perhaps $12 billion more each year, starting two years from now)? The economy's investment opportunities determine the combinations of current and future consumption from which consumers can choose. Consumers decide which of these combinations of current and future consumption they like best. Consumer choices affect their savings, so they affect the supply of loans and the economy's equilibrium level of investment.

Figure 10 | Technical Progress Raises Demand for Loans

Technical progress makes investments more profitable than before, raising the demand for loans and raising equilibrium savings, investment, and the real interest rate.

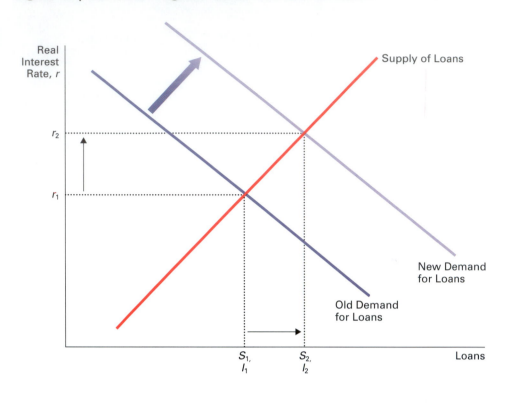

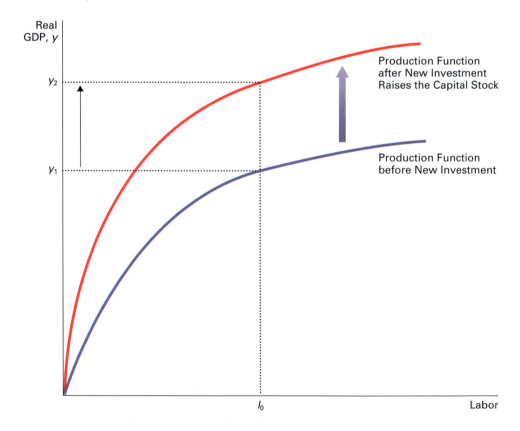

Figure 11 | Investment Raises the Capital Stock, which Raises Production

Technical progress raises investment. The increase in investment raises the economy's capital stock. The increase in capital raises production, increasing real GDP from y_1 to y_2.

Effects of a Tax Cut

Suppose that the government cuts taxes without changing its spending. The effects of a tax cut depend on two main factors: (1) how the tax cut affects incentives to work, incentives to save money rather than spend it, and incentives for firms to invest; and (2) whether people choose to spend or save the money from the tax cut.

Before-Tax Wages and After-Tax Wages

A person who earns $20,000 per year before taxes might pay $6,000 in income taxes (to federal, state, and local governments) and social security taxes. This person has a 30 percent *tax rate*.

The **tax rate** on income is the tax per dollar, as a percentage.

The tax drives a wedge between the *before-tax* wage of $20,000 and the *after-tax* wage of $14,000. Because employers pay the before-tax wage, that is the price they care about:

The demand for labor depends on the before-tax wage.

Workers, however, care about the after-tax wage they receive:

The supply of labor depends on the after-tax wage.

Figure 12 shows equilibrium in the labor market with a tax on wages. Employers pay the equilibrium wage *before* taxes of $15 per hour. Workers collect the equilibrium wage *after* taxes of $10 per hour. The government collects $5 in taxes per worker-hour, or a 33 percent tax rate (based on before-tax income). The equilibrium level of employment is 400 billion worker-hours, so the government collects $2,000 billion in revenue.

Figure 12 | The Labor Market With an Income Tax

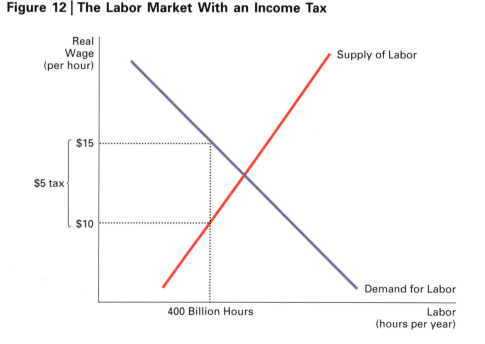

With an income tax, firms pay workers $15 per hour, and the quantity of labor demanded is 400 billion hours. Workers collect an after-tax wage of $10 per hour, and the quantity of labor supplied is 400 billion hours. The graph shows an equilibrium, because the quantity of hours demanded equals the quantity supplied.

Marginal and Average Tax Rates

Suppose you must pay taxes at a 20 percent rate on the first $20,000 that you earn each year, and a 30 percent tax rate applies to each dollar you earn above that amount. If you earn $20,000, you pay 20 percent, or $4,000, in taxes. If you earn $30,000, you pay $4,000 plus 30 percent of the *extra* $10,000, or $3,000, for a total tax payment of $7,000. Your *average* tax rate equals your taxes divided by your income: If you earn $30,000, your average tax rate is $7,000/$30,000 or about 23 percent. Your *marginal* tax rate equals the *extra* taxes you must pay if your earnings rise a little. If you earned $30,100 instead of $30,000, your taxes would rise from $7,000 to $7,030, so your marginal tax rate is 30 percent. In this example, the marginal tax rate exceeds the average tax rate, as it usually does in real life.

This distinction is important because some changes in taxes affect mainly average tax rates, and others affect mainly marginal tax rates. For example, an increase in the personal deduction on U.S. income taxes reduces the average tax rate without affecting the marginal tax rate (for most people). A drop in the average tax rate leaves people with more after-tax income than before, and they may choose to work less, reducing the supply of labor and lowering equilibrium employment and GDP. In contrast, a cut in the *marginal* tax rate, with little change in the average tax rate, means that people keep more of the

Incentive Effects of a Cut in Tax Rates

Figure 13 shows the effects of a tax cut. With a tax rate of 25 percent instead of 33 percent, the before-tax wage becomes $14 per hour, the after-tax wage becomes $10.50 per hour, and equilibrium employment rises from 400 billion to 440 billion hours. The government collects $3.50 per worker-hour (25 percent of the new $14 before-tax wage). Although the government collects less than before in taxes per worker-hour, it collects the tax on more worker-hours (440 billion instead of 400 billion). In this example, the tax cut reduces government revenue from $2,000 billion to $1,540 billion (equal to $3.50 per worker-hour times 440 billion worker hours).

The tax cut raises the equilibrium level of employment because the lower tax rate raises the gains from potential trades between employers and employees. Recall the discussion in Chapter 3 about why a tax reduces incentives to trade. A tax reduces the quantity bought and sold, because the gains from some trades are smaller than the per-unit tax that the parties would have to pay. People stop making those trades to avoid the tax. People make a trade only if it creates a total gain (to buyer and seller) that exceeds the tax. A cut in the tax rate reduces the *disincentive* to trade, raising the equilibrium quantity, as in Figure 13.

By raising equilibrium employment, as in Figure 13, a cut in the income tax rate raises employment and real GDP. Similar logic applies to other taxes. For example, a cut in the tax rate on income from savings raises the equilibrium quantities of saving an investment. Similarly, a cut in taxes that business firms must pay on income earned from their investments in new machinery raises the equilibrium saving and investment.

Figure 13 | Effects of an Income Tax Cut

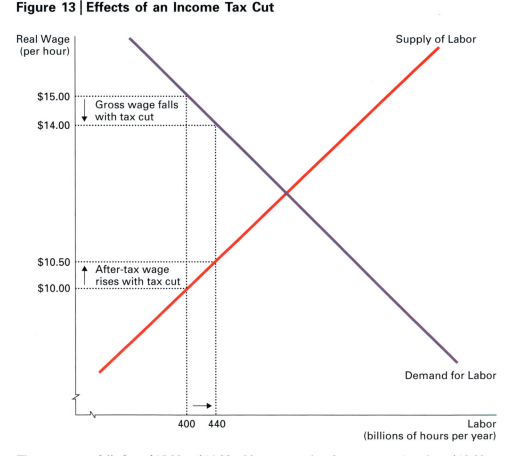

The gross wage falls from $15.00 to $14.00 with a tax cut; the after-tax wage rises from $10.00 to $10.50.

You might expect total tax payments to fall after a tax cut, as in Figure 13. In fact, a cut in a tax rate *can* (logically) raise tax revenue, although evidence indicates that *most* real-life tax cuts reduce tax revenue. Logically, a cut in a tax rate can increase total tax revenue collected by the government if demand and supply curves are sufficiently elastic. Figure 14 shows an example. The following discussion applies to the *usual* case in which a cut in the tax rate lowers government revenue from taxes, as in Figure 13.

Tax Revenue and Government Borrowing

A tax cut with no cut in government spending raises the government budget deficit if it reduces government revenue. As a result, the government must borrow more to finance the increased deficit. This increase in government borrowing raises the demand for loans, as in Figure 15. The demand for loans shifts *to the right* by the amount of the cut in tax revenue, as in the figure. If a cut in the tax rate reduces government tax revenue by $100 billion, then the government creates a $100 billion budget deficit, and the demand for loans shifts rightward by $100 billion.

Next, we must ask, "What do people do with the money they gain from the tax cut?" There are two extreme cases (as well as many in-between possibilities). First, suppose that people *spend* all the money from the tax cut on consumption. Then the supply of loans does not change. Figure 15 shows the results. Ignoring the incentive effects on savings already discussed the equilibrium moves from Point A to Point B, with the real interest rate rising from 10 percent to 12 percent. Before the tax cut, the government budget deficit was zero, so equilibrium savings and investment were equal at $1,000 billion. After the tax cut, the increased interest rate raises equilibrium savings to $1,060 billion. As a result, total loans rise to $1,060 billion. However, $100 billion of these loans go to the government, leaving only $960 billion for business

extra income they earn if they work more than before. As a result, a cut in the marginal tax rate tends to *raise* equilibrium employment as in Figure 13 and raise equilibrium real GDP. Clearly, the distinction between average and marginal tax rates is important.

Figure 14 | A Cut in the Tax Rate Can Raise Tax Revenue

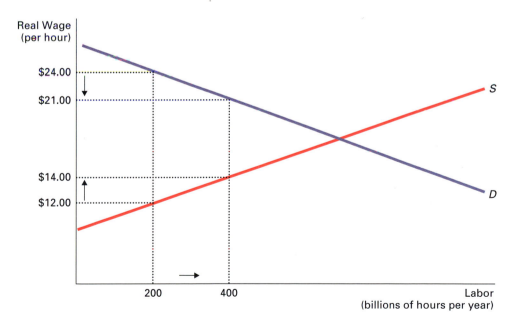

With a 50 percent income tax rate, the before-tax wage is $24 and the after-tax wage is $12. The equilibrium quantity of labor is 200 billion hours per year. The government collects a tax of $12 per hour, so it collects $2,400 billion in tax revenue. With a smaller 33 percent tax rate, the before-tax wage is $21, the after-tax wage is $14, and the equilibrium quantity of labor is 400 billion hours per year. The government collects $7 per hour in taxes, so it collects $2,800 in tax revenue. In this special case, the government's tax revenue rises when it cuts the tax rate.

Why Rational People Might Save all the Tax-Cut Money

Some (though not most) economists believe that evidence suggests people tend to *save* money from tax cuts, as in Figure 16, rather than *spend* it, as in Figure 15. A logical argument explains why people might choose to save the money from a tax cut. When the government reduces taxes without reducing spending, it collects the same amount of money from taxpayers as before! However, it *calls* some of this money it collects *loans* rather than *taxes*. People give the government less money than before in the form of taxes, but more money in the form of loans. Either way, the government collects the money required to pay for its (unchanged) spending.

The main difference between paying taxes and lending money to the government, is that the government promises to repay loans. However, where will the government get the money to repay these loans? Unless the government cuts spending some time in the future, it is likely to get that money by *raising taxes* in the future. Perhaps you loan the government some money, and it promises to repay you $100 in the future. However, you will not gain from the loan repayment if the government repays that $100 by raising your taxes by $100! In that case, lending money to the government is the same as paying taxes, because the government collects the same discounted present value of

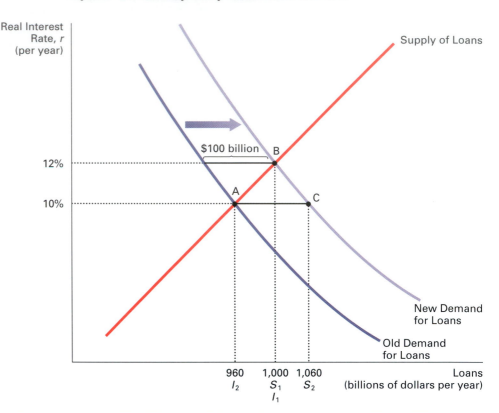

Figure 15 | Effects of a Tax Cut and Rising Budget Deficit when People Spend the Money They Gain from the Cut

firms to borrow for investment. As a result, equilibrium investment falls by $40 billion to $960 billion.

This fall in investment caused by an increase in government borrowing is called *crowding out* investment. Government borrowing crowds out borrowing for private investment by business firms. Although the tax cut raises savings, savers lend more to the government to finance the budget deficit, leaving less for business firms to borrow to finance private investments.

> **Crowding out** of private investment means that government borrowing raises the real interest rate, reducing the equilibrium amount of investment.

The increase in government borrowing in Figure 15 is the distance from Point A to Point C, that is, the $100 billion amount by which the demand curve shifts to the right. This amount exceeds the amount of the increase in the equilibrium quantity of loans, which rises by $60 billion, so part of the increase in government borrowing comes from an increase in savings, and part comes from a decrease in investment. Because government borrowing rises by $100 billion but total savings rises by only $60 billion, the government borrows $40 billion that firms would otherwise have borrowed to finance investment. In this way, government borrowing crowds out $40 billion in investment. Figure 16 shows the opposite extreme case, in which people *save* all the money they gain from the $100 billion tax cut. In this case, the supply of loans increases by $100 billion, shifting the curve rightward by exactly the same amount as demand. As a result, the equilibrium real interest rate remains unchanged. Because equilibrium savings rise by the same amount as the increase in government borrowing, investment remains unchanged.

Figure 16 | Effects of a Tax Cut and Rising Budget Deficit when People Save the Money They Gain from the Cut

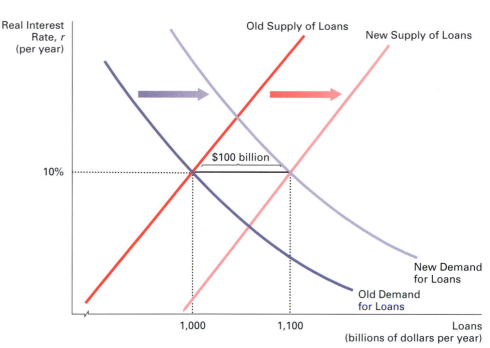

Other Changes in Underlying Conditions

Now that we have used the basic model to examine the effects of changes in the people's desires to save versus spend, advances in technology, and changes in tax rates, you can try to apply the model to other changes in underlying conditions. The next chapter will apply the basic model to help understand real-life experiences of economic growth.

I N   T H E   N E W S

Retailers see public using fall tax cut mostly for Christmas buying, not saving

What's in store?

Administration officials who expect much of the tax reduction to be saved point to the aftermath of the Kennedy-era tax cut. In 1964, 1965, and 1966, personal savings rose by an amount equaling about 75 percent of the tax cut, and

in 1967 the rise in savings equaled 121 percent of the tax cut. This time around, the Treasury Department estimates that at least 50 percent and perhaps 60 percent of the tax cut will be saved. Stephen Entin, a deputy assistant Treasury

secretary, describes this projection as "deliberately conservative."

JCPenney Co. believes it isn't nearly conservative enough. Penney expects taxpayers to save only one-third of the initial tax cut.

Source: The Wall Street Journal

If people spend part of the money from a tax cut, then the tax cut raises the equilibrium real interest rate.

---

your money in either case. Knowing this, you may save the money from a tax cut because you will need those savings to pay the increased future taxes.

For example, suppose that the government cuts taxes by $100 per person, and the interest rate is 10 percent per year. Then the government owes $110 more next year and raises taxes next year by $110 to pay its debt. If people save all the money from the tax cut and earn 10 percent interest on their savings, they will have $110 next year; that is exactly the amount that they need to pay their taxes next year. Alternatively, suppose that the government cuts taxes by $100 per person and the interest rate is 10 percent per year, but that the government *never* repays its debt—instead, it pays $10 per year interest on that debt every year, forever. The government permanently raises taxes by $10 per year to make these interest payments. If people save all the money from the tax cut and put it in bank accounts earning 10 percent interest, they earn enough interest each year to pay the permanently increased taxes. After 1 year, people have $110 each in their bank accounts; they can withdraw $10 each to pay the increased taxes and leave the $100 in the account. Next year, they will have $110 again, and they can again withdraw $10 to pay the taxes and leave $100 in the account. They can repeat this process every year for as long as the government pays interest on this debt. By saving all of the money from the tax cut, people can afford to pay their raised future taxes without reducing their future consumption spending.

While this logical reasoning shows that people may have reasons to save the money from a tax cut, other factors may lead them to spend it. For example, some people may not care about the future tax increase if those bills will be paid by *future generations*. In that case, they may spend the tax cut and let future generations worry about paying the future taxes on the government's debt.

Review Questions

16. Explain how the basic model determines equilibrium employment, real GDP, the real interest rate, consumption, and investment. Also explain how it determines the price level and the nominal interest rate.

17. Suppose that people decide that they are willing to reduce consumption now if they can increase consumption in the future. In what way does the economy respond to their wishes?

18. Explain why government borrowing may *crowd out* investment.

Thinking Exercises

19. Suppose that the government runs a budget deficit and raises taxes to eliminate that deficit. Discuss the likely effects on the real interest rate, savings, investment, consumption, employment, real GDP, and the price level.

20. What are the effects of a tax increase that creates a budget surplus? In what way does your answer depend on how people obtain the money to pay the increased taxes?

Conclusion

Interest Rates and Loan-Market Equilibrium

Savers lend money—they supply loans. Firms borrow money to pay for investments in new capital equipment, tools, buildings, skills, and knowledge—they demand loans. The government also borrows when it runs a budget deficit (when it spends more than its tax revenue), adding to the demand for loans. Equilibrium in the loan market determines the interest rate and equilibrium quantity of loans. The equilibrium quantity of loans equals savings, which equals investment plus the government budget deficit.

An interest rate is the price of a loan, expressed as an annual percentage of the amount borrowed. The discounted present value of a future payment of money is its market value today, which equals the amount of money that you would need to save and lend today to end up with that amount of future money. The discounted present value of X dollars next year is $X/(1 + R)$ dollars now, where R represents the annual interest rate (measured as a decimal, so that an 8 percent interest rate means R equals 0.08).

An investment is profitable if the discounted present value of the benefits from the investment exceeds the expenditure on the investment. A rise in the interest rate reduces the discounted present value of the benefit from an investment. As a result, the demand curve for loans slopes downward to the right: A fall in the interest rate raises the quantity of loans demanded.

Savings and the Supply of Loans

Equilibrium in the loan market is identical to equilibrium in the market for goods and services. Loan-market equilibrium occurs when saving plus lending by foreigners equals investment plus the government budget deficit. This relationship implies that GDP equals the sum of consumption, investment, government purchases, and net exports.

Real and Nominal Interest Rates

The nominal interest rate on a loan is the dollar interest payment expressed as a percentage of the dollar amount borrowed. The nominal interest rate, expressed as a decimal, plus one, is the cost a borrower must pay next year if she borrows $1 to spend this year. Therefore, the nominal interest rate plus 1 is the relative price of $1 this year in terms of dollars next year.

The real interest rate corrects the nominal interest rate for inflation. It measures the interest rate in terms of purchasing power. The real interest rate, expressed as a decimal, plus one, is the relative price of *goods* this year in terms of the same *goods* next year. Higher real interest rates mean that goods this year are relatively more expensive in terms of future goods; lower real interest rates mean the opposite.

The Fisher equation shows the connection between real and nominal interest rates: The nominal interest rate is the real interest rate plus the expected rate of inflation.

Because future inflation is uncertain in real life, economists distinguish between the expected and actual real interest rates. The expected real interest rate is the nominal interest rate minus the expected rate of inflation; the actual real interest rate is the nominal interest rate minus the actual rate of inflation during the period of the loan.

Summary of the Basic Model

The labor market determines equilibrium employment. The economy's production function shows the real GDP that the economy produces with this level of employment and the available capital stock. The equilibrium price level equals the economy's money supply multiplied by the velocity of money and divided by real GDP. The loan market determines equilibrium savings and investment and the equilibrium real interest rate. Consumption equals after-tax income minus saving. The nominal interest rate equals the real interest rate plus expected inflation.

Applying the Model

An increase in consumer patience—an increase in people's desire to save for the future—reduces the equilibrium real interest rate and raises equilibrium savings and investment. The additional investment raises the economy's future capital stock, raising future GDP and consumption. Technical progress raises the production the economy can obtain from labor and capital inputs, so it raises investment and the real interest rate. In the long run, technical progress raises consumption and real GDP. The effects of a tax cut on the economy depend on (a) how the tax cut affects incentives to work, to save money, and to invest; and (b) whether people choose to spend or save the money they gain from the tax cut. An increase in the government budget deficit raises the real interest rate and crowds out private investment, except in the extreme case in which people save all the money from the tax cut.

Key Terms

interest rate	nominal interest rate	tax rate
discounted present value	real interest rate	crowding out
government budget deficit		

Questions and Problems

21. Find the discounted present value in the following cases:
    (a) You will receive $540 one year from now and the nominal interest rate is 8 percent per year.
    (b) Your employer promises to pay you a $1,000 bonus 10 years from now, and the the nominal interest rate is 10 percent per year. Approximately what is the discounted present value of your bonus? (You may want to use a calculator.)
    (c) A state lottery promises to pay the winner $1 million, in the form of a $50,000 payment each year for 20 years. Use a calculator or computer to find the discounted present value of the prize if the nominal interest rate is 8 percent per year.
    (d) A perpetuity is a financial asset that pays interest every year, forever. If the nominal interest rate is 10 percent per year, what is the discounted present value of a perpetuity that pays $1,000 every year?

22. If the nominal interest rate is 8 percent per year and the expected rate of inflation is 5 percent per year, what is the real interest rate? If the real interest rate is 2 percent per year and expected inflation is 2 percent per year, what is the nominal interest rate?

23. Suppose that the nominal interest rate rises by 4 percent per year, because the expected rate of inflation rises by 4 percent per year. Explain why this change does not affect investment.

24. Discuss this statement: "The interest rate plays no role in the investment decisions of firms that use their own profits to pay for investments in new equipment."

25. Explain the flaw in the following argument: "A fall in the real interest rate reduces savings. But savings equals investment plus the government budget deficit, so a fall in the real interest rate must also reduce investment." (*Hint:* Recall the difference between changes in demand and changes in the quantity demanded.)

26. Show in a diagram how a tax on interest income affects the economy's savings and investment.

27. Suppose the government runs a budget surplus (it spends less than it collects in tax revenue), and it cuts taxes. Discuss the likely effect of the tax cut on the real interest rate, savings, investment, consumption, employment, real GDP, and the price level.

28. (a) Suppose the government cuts taxes by $100 million without changing its spending, and borrows $100 million to finance its deficit. Also suppose the interest rate is 10 percent per year. How much additional money will the government owe in the future? (b) If the government pays its future debts by raising taxes in the future, how much will future taxes rise? (c) What is the discounted present value of the tax increase that you calculated in part (b)? (d) Explain why this calculation may lead rational people to save all the money that they receive from a tax cut.

29. Comment on this statement: "A tax increase to reduce a government budget deficit is more likely to reduce the real interest rate if people pay the increased taxes by saving less instead of spending less."

30. A *fall in business confidence* occurs when firms reduce investments in new equipment because of increased uncertainty about future demand for their products. Discuss the effects of a fall in business confidence on the real interest rate, savings, investment, and consumption.

31. The baby-boom generation (people born in the 1950s) will retire after two or three more decades. Most retired people spend more than their incomes. The U.S. population now has about 3.4 workers for each retired person; by 2030, it may have only about 2 workers for each retired person.
  (a) Explain how this change will affect total savings in the United States.
  (b) Explain how this change will affect the real interest rate, savings, consumption, and investment.

Inquiries for Further Thought

32. Some economists believe that people in the United States do not save enough for the future.
  (a) What affects the amount of money that people choose to save? How much *should* people save? Who should decide?
  (b) Do people voluntarily save the amount that they should save, or should government policies provide incentives for people to increase saving? What government policies might lead people to increase saving? Do any current government policies encourage or discourage saving?

  (c) Discuss this statement: "Free-market economies do not provide enough savings, investment, and other resources for future generations. The government should adopt policies to raise savings and investment for future generations."

33. The social security system taxes workers' incomes and gives money to retired people.
  (a) How do you think the social security system affects the amount of money that people choose to save? Why?
  (b) How do you think the social security system affects equilibrium investment? Explain.

CHAPTER 8

ECONOMIC GROWTH

In this Chapter...

Main Points to Understand

▶ Long-run economic growth is perhaps the most important topic in economics, with the greatest effects on people's lives.
▶ Economic growth requires savings and investment.
▶ Economic growth has increased rapidly over the last two centuries. Some people speculate that diminishing returns will soon cause growth to slow down or even stop; others speculate that economies can avoid diminishing returns for many more centuries.
▶ Current evidence provides only limited knowledge about which government policies best promote long-run economic growth.

Thinking Skills to Develop

▶ Evaluate a model with evidence, and change the model with evidence as a guide.
▶ Develop speculative questions that raise new issues, and use them to guide logical thought in new directions.

Real GDP per person in the United States has doubled since 1964. Many of the products that you take for granted, such as CD players and VCRs, were not even available then. What does the future hold? Will real GDP double again in the next 30 or 40 years and give you the opportunity to use products unimaginable today?

Long-run economic growth—a continuing rise in real GDP per person over several decades—is one of the most important topics in economics. For most of history, people have lived in conditions of extreme poverty without even the basic goods that we now regard as necessities. Life was brutal, filled with hard work, little food or health care, short life spans, and high infant mortality rates.

Economic growth has lifted billions of people out of these conditions, although many people continue to live in poverty. World real GDP is about $6,000 per person today, roughly 12 times higher than the level in 1800, and 5 times higher than the level in 1900. Real GDP per person in the United States is almost $32,000 today, about 20 times higher than the level during the American Revolution, 12 times higher than the level during the Civil War, 6 times higher than the level in 1900, and twice as high as 34 years ago. The economies of some countries, such as Hong Kong (now a special zone of China), Japan, Singapore, South Korea, and Taiwan, have grown much faster than that of the United States in recent years, while others have grown much more slowly. Not only has the level of per-capita real GDP risen over time, but the rate of economic growth has also increased over most of the last 200 years. Economic growth has been much higher in the last 200 years than over all previous history.

Will the economy continue to grow rapidly in your lifetime and raise your material standard of living, or will economic growth slow down or stop? These issues have profound effects on people's lives. As one economist puts it, "The consequences for human welfare involved in questions [of economic growth] like these are simply staggering: Once one starts to think about them, it is hard to think about anything else."[1]

BASICS OF GROWTH

An economy's real GDP depends on its technology and its available inputs of labor and capital. Real GDP also depends on laws, regulations, taxes, and other factors that affect people's incentives for efficient use of technology and inputs, so that the economy produces at a point *on* its production possibility frontier rather than below it.[2]

Throughout most of history, real GDP and population grew at the same rates, leaving GDP *per person* roughly constant over time. Then, about 200 to 300 years ago, total real GDP began growing much faster than population (despite continuing increases in population), so real GDP per person began growing rapidly.

Figure 1 shows estimates of average real GDP per person in the world over the past million years. Despite some small changes, until 300 years ago, real GDP per person stayed about the same as it had been throughout all of human history—just high enough to keep people alive and reproducing. Then, things changed. Real GDP per person began to rise enormously—for example, about *1 percent per year* in the 19th century. While 1 percent per year may seem small, its cumulative effects are awesome—people's lives began to change dramatically—health improved, death rates declined, common people gained leisure time, and vast arrays of new products and services became available. Figure 2 shows the growth of world real GDP per person by century over the last millennium.

Figure 1 | World Average GDP per Capita

Source: Bradford De Long, "Estimating World GDP, One Million B.C.–Present."

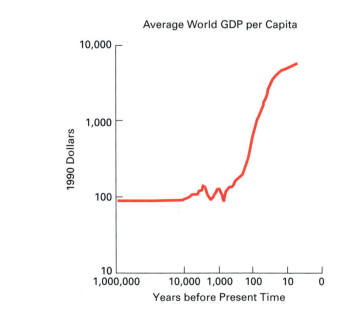

---

[1]Robert E. Lucas, "On the Mechanism of Economic Development," *Journal of Monetary Economics* 22, no. 1 (July 1988), pp. 3–42.

[2]Chapter 3 introduced production possibility frontiers.

Figure 2 | Growth of World Real GDP per Person

Source: Bradford De Long, "Estimating World GDP, One Million B.C.–Present."

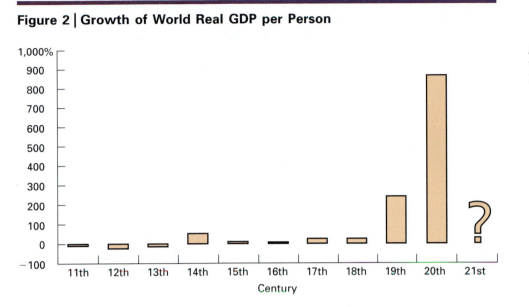

We will define economic growth as an increase in a country's real GDP per person:

Economic growth is a rise in real GDP per person.

We will measure economic growth by the *average annual growth rate* (percentage change) in real GDP per person. For example, the rate of economic growth in the 100-year period from 1900 to 2000 is:

$$\text{Rate of economic growth, 1900 to 2000} = \frac{1}{100} \times \frac{(\text{Real GDP per person in 2000} - \text{Real GDP per person in 1900})}{\text{Real GDP per person in 1900}}$$

Rule of 72

How is the actual change in real GDP per person connected to the rate of economic growth? What does growth of *2 percent per year* mean for your actual standard of living? A simple method called the *rule of 72* helps to answer these questions.

The **rule of 72** says that if the growth rate of a variable is *X* percent per year, then the variable doubles after about 72/*X* years.

For example, if GDP grows at 2 percent per year, then it doubles after about 36 years. If it grows at 3 percent per year, then it doubles after about 24 years. World economic growth of 1 percent per year in the 19th century meant that real GDP per person doubled after about 72 years. Never before in history had living standards changed by so much.[3]

Using the rule of 72, you can estimate the effect on your future standard of living of various growth rates. If economic growth in the future is only 1 percent per year, you can expect average income to have doubled 72 years from now—a long time to wait.

---

[3]You can also use the rule of 72 backwards—if some quantity doubles in *X* years, then its average growth rate is about 72/*X* percent per year. For example, the U.S. consumer price index roughly quadrupled from 1970 to 1994. Because it doubled about twice in that 24-year period, on average it doubled every 12 years, so the price level grew at a rate of about 72/12, or 6 percent per year over that period.

However, if economic growth is 3 percent per year, average income will double in 24 years and quadruple in 48 years. So the difference between 1 percent and 3 percent economic growth—which may seem small—could have a major impact on your future standard of living, and the living standards of your children and grandchildren.

MAIN FACTS ABOUT ECONOMIC GROWTH

World Economic Growth

World per-capita real GDP is about $6,000 today. In 1900, it was only $1,200 to $1,300, and in 1800, it was only about $500 (all in today's dollars). The rate of world economic growth has generally increased over time for the last 300 years, meaning that the average person has been getting richer at a faster rate than in the past. World real GDP per capita grew at about 1 percent per year in the 19th century and 1.7 percent per year in the 20th century. World economic growth averaged 1.1 percent per year from 1900 to 1950, and it has averaged 2.1 percent per year since then. Per-capita world real GDP is now almost 5 times as high as in 1900.

One major exception to this experience involves a slowdown in world economic growth starting in 1973. World economic growth averaged about 1.4 percent per year from 1973 to 1998, higher than in the 19th century, but below that earlier in the 20th century.[4]

Economic Growth in the United States and the United Kingdom

Table 1 shows economic growth in the United States for the last two centuries. The rate of U.S. economic growth has generally increased over time, although it has fallen to an average of 1.6 percent per year for the period from 1973 to 1998.

Gross domestic product per capita in the United States is approaching $32,000 today. At the time of the American Revolution, U.S. real GDP per capita was about $1,450 (in 1998 dollars). Output per person was just slightly higher in the United States than in England and France. By 1860, on the eve of the Civil War, per-capita real U.S. GDP was $2,550 (in 1998 dollars). Table 2 shows levels of real GDP per person in selected years in the United States and the United Kingdom. U.S. output of goods and services per person is now more than 20 times its level at the time of the American Revolution, about 12 times its level at the time of the Civil War, and 2½ times its level in 1950.

Table 1 | Rising Economic Growth in the United States

Time Period	Growth Rate of Per-Capita U.S. Real GDP (percent per year)
1800–1855	1.1%
1855–1900	1.6
1900–1950	1.7
1950–1998	1.9

[4]Although economists lack good statistics on economic growth in earlier centuries, we know that the rate of economic growth must have been much lower in those centuries. Here is the basic logic: In 1800, per-capita world real GDP was about $500 (in today's dollars). If economic growth had averaged 1 percent per year in earlier centuries (its rate in the 19th century), then world real GDP per person would have been only $25 in the year 1500, and about $0.16 in 1000 (measured in today's dollars). This is impossible because people need more food than this to survive. Moreover, historical records prove that incomes were higher than this at those times. Therefore, the rate of world economic growth must have been much lower before the 19th century.

Table 2 | Per-Capita Real GDP in 1998 Dollars

	United States	United Kingdom
1776	$ 1,450	$ 1,350
1860	2,550	3,000
1900	5,450	5,300
1950	12,500	8,150
1998	31,500	22,000

You can use the rule of 72 to estimate the annual growth rate of per-capita real GDP in the United States. U.S. real GDP per capita doubled in the 34-year period from 1964 to 1998. Since 72 divided by 35 is about 2, you can estimate that U.S. real GDP per capita grew at about 2 percent per year over that period. If growth continues at that rate, real GDP per capita will be twice as high as in 1998 by the year 2033.

Economic Growth in Japan

In 1860, at the time of the U.S. Civil War, per-capita real GDP in Japan was about $850—about one-third that of the United States. The Japanese economy then grew at about the same rate as the U.S. economy, so Japanese real GDP per capita stayed at about one-third the U.S. level, until World War II. That war cut Japanese per-capita real GDP in half; when the war ended, it was about one-sixth of U.S. per-capita real GDP. After the war, Japan began a period of rapid growth. By 1960, Japanese real GDP per capita was again one-third of the U.S. level. This rapid growth continued, and by 1998, per-capita real GDPs in Japan and the United States were about equal, depending on the method of comparison.[5]

Economic Growth in Other Countries

Economic growth rates differ substantially across countries. Japan's economy has grown much faster than that of the United States in recent years. Table 3 shows the rates of economic growth in several countries. (For comparison, recall that U.S. economic growth in the 20th century has averaged 1.8 percent per year.)

Per-capita real GDP has grown despite the fact that people work *less* than they did in earlier times! The number of worker-hours per person in developed countries has fallen by about one-fourth since the mid-19th century.[6] Real GDP is much higher today, despite the decrease in work per person, because people are more productive today, due to better technology and greater quantities of capital (tools, equipment, and worker skills).

Economic growth is not inevitable, however. Chapter 5 noted that India, China, Bangladesh, Indonesia, and Pakistan experienced negative economic growth from 1900 to 1950; their per-capita GDPs fell. Similarly, Afghanistan, Angola, Chad, Madagascar, Mozambique, and Zambia have experienced negative economic growth since 1960. Many other countries have experienced negative economic growth over 5-year or 10-year periods.

[5]One way to compare amounts in Japanese yen with those in U.S. dollars is to use the foreign exchange rate between yen and dollars. Another way adjusts for differences in the prices of goods in Japan and the United States.

[6]An average worker in the United States, England, France, Germany, and Japan worked about 2,600 hours per year in 1913, but only 1,700 hours by the 1980s. A higher fraction of the population worked, however, so the average number of hours worked per person (not per worker) stayed about the same from 1913 to 1950, rose from 1950 to 1973, and has fallen since 1973, except in the United States and Japan.

Table 3 | Annual Rates of Economic Growth in Various Countries

Country	Growth Rate, 1900–1998	Country	Growth Rate, 1950–1998
Japan	3.2%	Taiwan	6.1%
Finland, Norway	2.6	Japan	6.0
Canada	2.3	South Korea	5.7
Switzerland	2.0	Thailand	3.7
Belgium, Mexico	1.6	Germany	3.6
Australia	1.5	Mexico	2.3
United Kingdom	1.4	India	1.7
Argentina	1.1	Chile	1.0
Bangladesh	0.1	Bangladesh	0.3

Source: Maddison, *The World Economy in the 20th Century* (Paris: OECD, 1989). Figures updated by author.

In contrast, the so-called *four tigers of Asia* (Hong Kong, Singapore, South Korea, and Taiwan) have posted rapid economic growth. Between 1965 and 1998, annual economic growth averaged 7.8 percent in Hong Kong, 7.5 percent in Singapore, and 9.5 percent in South Korea. (Despite the economic recessions that began in many Asian countries in 1998, average real GDP per person in these countries remains far higher than in previous decades.)

Countries with low per-capita incomes are sometimes called *third-world countries* or *LDCs* (for less developed countries). Many high-income countries are members of the OECD, or Organization for Economic Cooperation and Development. The richest of these nations account for 20 percent of world population and about 60 percent of world GDP. The second-richest 20 percent of the world population produce about 20 percent of world GDP. LDCs account for 60 percent of world population and only 20 percent of world GDP. An average person in an OECD country has an income about nine times higher than an average person in an LDC. The low-income countries had faster economic growth (about 3.1 percent per year) from 1965 to 1998 than the OECD countries, which grew at about 2.4 percent per year in that period.

LOGIC OF ECONOMIC GROWTH: A BASIC MODEL

Discussions of international differences in growth rates raise questions that require a *model* of economic growth. Why do some countries grow faster than others? This section begins with a simple model of growth. It then discusses the problems with that model and adds some realistic features.

Economist Robert E. Lucas explains why economists need models of economic growth:

> At the close of World War II, South Korea was less than twice as well off as India. . . . By 1980 Korea's income was four times higher than India's. If present trends continue, by the year 2000 Korea's per-capita income will be over 10 times India's . . . comparable to those in the U.S. and Western Europe today.
>
> With such a range of experience, why do we need theoretical models? Why not simply use success stories—like Korea—as models? Why can't India send a fact-finding delegation to Korea, find out how they do it, and then go home and get Indians to do the same?

This sounds easy enough, but it is not really operational. . . . An economy is just too complex an entity—there are just too many things going on at once—for getting all the facts to be either possible or useful.

Faced with so much data, an observer who is unequipped with a theory sees what he wants to see, or what his hosts want to show him. One needs some principles for deciding which facts are central and which are peripheral. This is exactly the purpose of an economic theory: to isolate some very limited aspects of a situation and focus on them to the exclusion of all others. . . . We need to make some hard choices about what to emphasize and what to leave out before we can think in an organized way at all.[7]

Per-Person Production Function

The basic model from the previous chapter implies that the *level* of real GDP depends on technology and available inputs of labor and capital. The economy's input of labor results from equilibrium in the labor market. Its input of capital results from its previous investments—the amount of equipment and tools it has created in the past.

We can write the economy's production mathematically:

$$\text{Real GDP} = A\ F(l, k)$$

where l is the economy's labor input (measured as the total number of workers, or total worker hours per year) and k is its capital input. The function F shows how the economy combines inputs of labor and capital to produce real GDP. The variable A measures the economy's technology. Increases in A reflect improvements in technology. An increase in A raises real GDP, even if the amounts of labor and capital do not change.

Now add an assumption to the basic model: The economy's production function has *constant returns to scale*. This statement means that doubling all inputs doubles real GDP. Similarly, increasing all inputs by 20 percent boosts real GDP by 20 percent. (Evidence about real-life production functions indicates that this is a realistic assumption.) This assumption implies that we can write the economy's production function in *per-person* terms:

$$\text{Real GDP per person} = \frac{y}{l} = A\ f\left(\frac{k}{l}\right)$$

In other words, real GDP *per person* depends on technology and capital per person, $\frac{k}{l}$.

Figure 3 shows this production function—it shows how real GDP per person depends on capital per person. When capital per person is low, at $\frac{k_1}{l}$, real GDP per person is low, at $\frac{y_1}{l}$. When capital per person is higher, at $\frac{k_2}{l}$, real GDP per person is higher at $\frac{y_2}{l}$.

Figure 4 shows how an increase in technology—an increase in A—changes real GDP per person. Even with the same amount of capital per person, an increase in A raises real GDP per person. In fact, they increase in proportion: If capital per person remains constant, a 10 percent rise in A raises real GDP per person by 10 percent.

An increase in technology shifts the production function. In contrast, an increase in capital per person moves the economy *along* the production function as in Figure 5. That figure shows that an increase in capital per person, $\frac{k}{l}$, raises real GDP per person. However, diminishing returns imply that increases in capital per person create proportionally smaller increases in real GDP per person, as the economy moves from Point A to Point

Advice

Here is one way to understand constant returns to scale and the per-person production function. Remember the Robinson Crusoe economy from an earlier chapter? Crusoe's production function was obviously a *per-person* production function, because he was the only person in the economy. Think about an economy with lots of people like Crusoe, each with the same *per-person* production function. That economy's production function has constant returns to scale—if you double the number of people like Crusoe, total production doubles.

---

[7]Robert E. Lucas, 1991 Fischer-Schultz lecture, European meetings of the Econometrics Society, September 1991.

Figure 3 | GDP per Person Depends on Capital per Person

When each person has k_1 capital to work with—so that capital per person is $\frac{k_1}{l}$, real GDP per person is $\frac{y_1}{l}$. At a higher capital per person, $\frac{k_2}{l}$, real GDP per person is higher, at $\frac{y_2}{l}$. The production function is steep at Point A, so small increases in capital per person have big effects on real GDP per person. The production function is relatively flat at Point B.

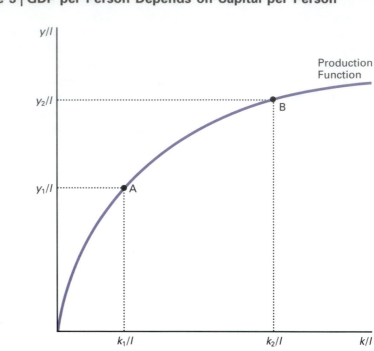

Figure 4 | Increase in Technology Raises Real GDP per Person

An increase in technology shifts the production function. It raises real GDP per person from $\frac{y_2}{l}$ to $\frac{y_3}{l}$, even if capital per person remains at $\frac{k_2}{l}$.

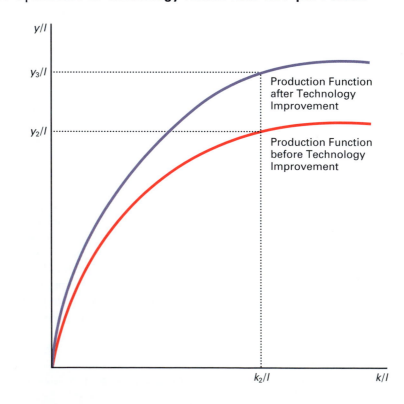

Figure 5 | Increase in Capital per Person Raises Real GDP per Person

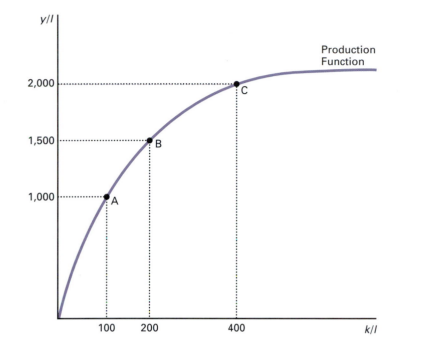

When capital per person is 100, real GDP per person is 1,000. When capital per person rises, real GDP per person rises. Because of diminishing returns, increases in capital per person raise real GDP per person in smaller proportions. In this example, when capital per person doubles from 100 to 200, real GDP per person rises by 50 percent, from 1,000 to 1,500. When capital per person expands to 400, real GDP per person rises to 2,000.

B to Point C. Doubling capital per person from 100 to 200 raises real GDP per person by only 50 percent. Doubling capital per person again, from 200 to 400, boosts real GDP by an even smaller proportion.

Economic Growth without Technical Change

Think about the logical question: Can an economy grow without technical progress? The answer is *yes,* because capital per person can grow, raising real GDP per person as in Figure 5. The economy can increase its capital by investing. The loan-market equilibrium discussed in the previous chapter shows the equilibrium amount of savings and investment. Each year, investment adds to the economy's capital, raising real GDP, as in Figure 5. With sufficiently high equilibrium investment, capital per person and real GDP per person rise over time. The economy grows.

The rate of economic growth depends on the equilibrium amount of investment. Raising investment accelerates growth in capital per person and real GDP per person. Increases in capital per person, however, are not sufficient to create *permanent* economic growth. As capital per person rises, the benefit of additional investment falls due to *diminishing returns*, discussed in Chapter 6. Because of diminishing returns, the benefit of additional investment falls over time as the capital–labor ratio rises. As capital per person rises, the demand for loans falls, as in Figure 6, from D_1 to D_2 to D_3, reducing equilibrium investment from I_1 to I_2 to I_3. Over time, investment falls and *economic growth slows.*

Eventually, capital per person stops increasing, so real GDP per person also stops increasing. Economic growth *stops.* At this point, economists say the economy reaches a *steady state.*

A **steady state** is a long-run equilibrium in which capital per person remains constant.

Figure 6 | Economic Growth toward a Steady State

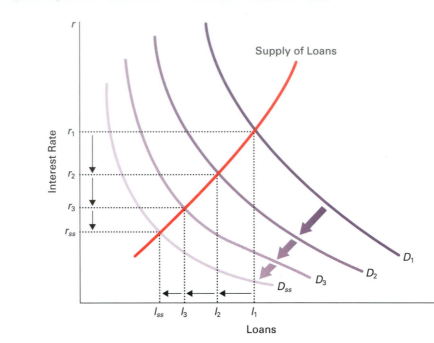

When the economy has low capital per person, investment demand is D_1, so equilibrium investment is I_1 and the equilibrium real interest rate is r_1. Investment adds to the economy's capital stock, but, because capital provides diminishing returns, investment demand falls as the economy's capital stock rises. As the economy grows and adds to its capital per person, equilibrium investment and the real interest rate fall. Eventually, the economy reaches a steady state. Steady state investment, I_{SS}, is just enough to replace capital that wears out, so the economy's capital stock stops rising. The steady state real interest rate is r_{SS}. (Note: This figure assumes that all loans fund investments, so the demand for loans is investment demand.)

In the steady state, investment of I_{SS} in Figure 6 is just high enough to replace the capital that depreciates (wears out) each year and to keep up with rising population, so that capital per person remains constant.

Will you live in a steady state world in which economic growth has slowed and finally *stopped?* Or can we extrapolate the growth of the last half-century and expect that living standards will *double* in the next 36 years? Obviously, these two scenarios lead to entirely different lives for you and your children. To examine the issues underlying these questions, this chapter first analyzes this model of growth more carefully by using a numerical example, then it discusses evidence related to the model.

Numerical Example of Growth that Stops at a Steady State

Suppose that real GDP per person, $\frac{y}{l}$, depends on capital per person, $\frac{k}{l}$, in the following way:

$$\text{IF } \tfrac{k}{l} \text{ is } \le 20 \text{ THEN } \tfrac{y}{l} = 2\left(\tfrac{k}{l}\right)$$

$$\text{IF } \tfrac{k}{l} > 20 \text{ THEN } \tfrac{y}{l} = 30 + \left(\tfrac{k}{l}\right)/2.$$

Advice

Don't get confused by the strange formula for the production function in this example. If you have trouble understanding the formula, then ignore it and concentrate on the *numbers* from that formula in Table 4 and its *graph* in Figure 7.

Figure 7 graphs this production function, and the first two columns of Table 4 show various levels of capital per person and the resulting real GDPs per person. If capital per person is 20, real GDP person is 40; if capital per worker is 40, real GDP per person is 50, and so on.

Now assume that people save exactly one-tenth of GDP per person. The third column of the table shows total savings. Finally, assume that exactly one-tenth of capital depreciates (wears out) each year. The fourth column of the table shows total depreciation—if capital per person is 20, then depreciation equals 2 per year.

Suppose the economy's capital per person equals 20. Then real GDP per person is 40, and people save 4. Equilibrium in the loans market implies that savings equals investment, so the economy invests 4. Since only 2 units of capital wear out, the economy replaces those 2 units and adds 2 more to its capital stock. Therefore, next year

Figure 7 | Production Function in the Numerical Example

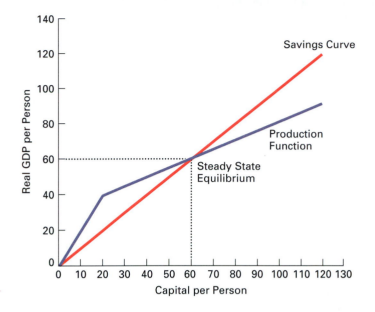

the economy's capital per person will be 22 instead of 20, and its GDP per person will rise. *The economy grows.*

The economy continues to grow as long as it saves more than enough to replace the capital that wears out each year. That is, it grows as long as the number in the savings column exceeds the number in the depreciation column. Eventually, the economy's capital per person reaches 60. When that happens, the table shows that real GDP per person also equals 60.[8] At that point, savings equals depreciation per person—each equals 6. The economy saves and invests just enough to replace the capital that depreciates each year. Therefore, capital per person stops growing, and real GDP per person stops increasing. The economy reaches a steady state, and economic growth stops.

Figure 7 shows a straight-line *savings curve* that intersects the production function at the steady state capital per person. The height of the savings curve shows the real GDP per person required to create enough savings to replace the capital that depreciates each year. When the production function lies above the savings curve (as in the left portion of the graph), real GDP per person is high enough that savings can replace all the capital that depreciates and still *add* to the capital stock. In this case, the capital stock rises over time—the economy grows.

Table 4 | Numerical Example of Growth that Stops at Steady State
(billions of base-year dollars)

Capital per person	Real GDP per person	Savings per person	Depreciation per person
0	0	0	0
20	40	4	2
40	50	5	4
60	60	6	6
80	70	7	8
100	80	8	10

[8]The numbers for steady-state capital and steady-state GDP are equal in this example purely by coincidence.

When capital per person reaches 60, GDP per person is high enough to create *just enough* savings to replace the capital that depreciates. In this case, the capital stock does not increase further, and growth stops. This is the steady state equilibrium.[9]

Figure 8 shows a more general case of a production function and a savings curve in which people save 5 percent of GDP. At the steady state equilibrium, capital per person is 1,000 and real GDP per person is 2,000. One-tenth of capital depreciates each year, so the economy needs investment of 100 per year to replace it. With GDP per person of 2,000, people save 100—just enough to replace the depreciating capital. As a result, the capital stock remains constant, and the economy remains at its steady state equilibrium.

Evidence on the Model

How well does this model of economic growth correspond to real-life experiences? It applies well to certain situations. For example, World War II destroyed a large amount of capital in Germany and Japan (buildings, machinery, and so on). At the end of the war, these countries' economies had lower levels of capital per person and real GDP per person than they had before. For several decades after the war, investment levels in Germany and Japan far exceeded those in other countries, such as the United States, where little capital had been destroyed. Germany and Japan had high rates of economic growth as they rebuilt their capital stocks. Similar increases in investment and rapid growth typically occur after cities are struck by natural disasters such as earthquakes, floods, or hurricanes.

Figure 8 | Steady State Capital per Person and GDP per Person

At Point *SS* (for *steady state* equilibrium), capital per person is 1,000. One-tenth of this capital wears out each year, so firms must invest 100 just to replace depreciated capital, and capital per person remains at 1,000. At Point *SS*, real GDP per person is high enough (2,000) that people save 100, lending this amount to firms for investment and keeping capital per person at 1,000.

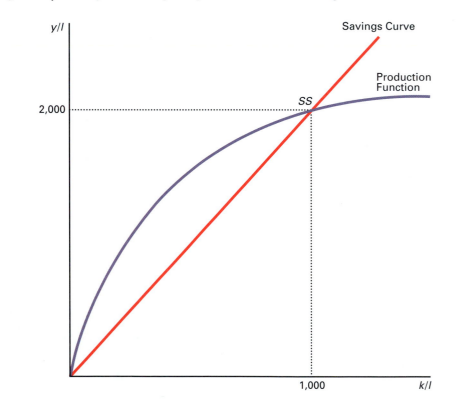

[9]When the production function lies below the savings curve (as in the right portion of the graph), real GDP per person is not high enough to create sufficient savings to replace the capital that depreciates. As a result, the capital stock falls over time, so real GDP also falls. Capital and real GDP rise when capital per person is less than 60, and they fall if capital per person exceeds 60. These forces create a tendency for the economy to move toward its steady state equilibrium.

The model does not apply so well, however, to most real-life economic growth. Two main observations about real-life growth are inconsistent with the model. First, the model implies that economic growth slows down and eventually stops. However, as Figures 1 and 2 and Table 1 indicate, the rate of economic growth has *increased* over time, except in the last quarter of the 20th century. Do people today live in an era of slowing economic growth as the economy approaches a steady state? No one knows for sure, but the overall experience of increasing rates of growth over the past two centuries does not support the predictions of the model. Second, the model predicts a falling real interest rate over time, as in Figure 6. However, evidence indicates that the real interest rate has *not* fallen over time; the real interest rate is about the same now as a century ago. Clearly, the basic model is missing certain important features of economic growth, such as technical progress.

Review Questions

1. Roughly how long does it take real GDP per person to double if it grows at 2 percent per year? What if it grew at 3 percent per year?

2. What does it mean to say that the economy's production function has constant returns to scale?

3. Draw graphs of a production function to show how real GDP per person changes when (a) capital per person rises; (b) technology advances.

4. What is a steady-state equilibrium?

5. What main observations about data contradict the basic model of economic growth without technical change?

Thinking Exercises

6. Comment on this claim: "People produce more today than in the past because they work more than in the past."

7. Explain why (a) increases in capital per person can create economic growth without technical change, and (b) without technical change, economic growth would slow down over time.

8. Change the numerical example in Table 4 to make people save ⅛ of GDP per person. How does this increase in savings affect the numbers in the table? How does it affect steady state capital per person and real GDP per person?

LOGIC OF GROWTH: EXTENSIONS

The model of growth discussed so far says that an economy grows by saving and investing. However, when its capital per worker reaches the steady state, the economy stops growing. That model is not consistent with the observations that economic growth has increased over time (except in the last quarter-century) and that the real interest rate has remained about constant over time. However, the model ignores an important fact: As time passes, our economy can produce more output than it did in the past *without* using additional inputs. In other words, the economy experiences *technical change*.

A classic study of American economic growth since 1929 found that about one-third of increases in U.S. real GDP per person resulted from increases in capital per person.

Technical Change *Rearranges* Natural Resources

Technical progress does not mean that the economy produces *more* output with the same inputs. That would violate a basic law of physics—the law of conservation of mass and energy. Instead, technical progress refers to *rearrangements* of resources that increase their *value* to people. When metals such as gold, silver, copper, and (later) iron were discovered thousands of years ago, people developed technologies to heat them and transform them into products such as ornaments, utensils, tools, and weapons. Today, advances in technology have shown people how to use silver in photographic film, and iron oxide to carry information magnetically on videotapes.

Thousands of years ago, people learned to produce glass by heating quartz or sand (often mixed with ground seashells and other materials), and then quickly cooling it. They used glass for beads and other decorations. Today, advances in technology have shown people how to use different types of glass (with various characteristics) and to use glass for fiber optics that carry messages over telephone lines and the Internet.

By rearranging natural resources in new ways, technical change can increase the *value* of those resources to people. Economic growth results not from increases in the *quantity* of resources, but from increases in the *value* of resources.

About two-thirds of increases in U.S. real GDP per person resulted from increases in technology, knowledge, education, and increases in economic efficiency (meaning that the economy improved its use of its resources). A classic study comparing economic growth in Singapore and Hong Kong also illustrates the important role of technological change. Since 1965, economic growth has averaged over 7 percent per year in both countries. However, very different factors accounted for this growth. Singapore grew almost entirely through increases in capital per person (resulting from very high rates of saving and investment). In contrast, a large fraction of economic growth in Hong Kong resulted from technical progress.

Technical changes appear as increases in the variable A in the per-person production function,

$$\text{Real GDP per person} = A\ f(\tfrac{k}{l})$$

Technical Change and Economic Growth

Think about the logical question: What does technical change add to the previous model? Technical change raises production per person without any increase in capital per person, as in Figure 4. An economy can grow indefinitely as long as technical progress continues, even if capital per person remains constant as in Figure 4. But can technical progress continue indefinitely? What creates technical change, and what policies can a country follow to promote technical change?

Investment in Technical Change

Technical change results from progress in science, engineering, and application of scientific knowledge to improve capital equipment and production methods. Some technical change occurs by accident, but most results from *investments* in research and development and in education and skills.[10]

Does technical change have diminishing returns? Do the benefits of additional knowledge fall as the economy adds to its stock of knowledge? If so, the logic from

---

[10]Practice and experience also raise productivity; economists call this learning by doing.

the last section would apply: Equilibrium investment in scientific research and its applications would fall over time. Technical change would slow down and eventually stop. As a result, economic growth would slow down and eventually stop at a steady state equilibrium. On the other hand, if knowledge does *not* have diminishing returns, then continuing technical change may cause economic growth to continue indefinitely without slowing. Economists can only speculate about the answers to these questions, although those answers will profoundly affect the lives of our children and grandchildren.

Investment in Human Capital

Future economic growth *might* not slow down, even if technical change were to slow. Economic growth could continue indefinitely if the economy could continually add to its *effective* labor input by investing in human capital through education and training. To see why, suppose that technical change stops. When the variable *A* in the production function stops growing, economic growth can continue only if inputs of capital and labor continue to grow. *Both* inputs must grow; if the economy adds to only *one* input without adding to the other input, diminishing returns to the growing input cause economic growth to slow down and eventually stop.

The economy can add to its capital stock by producing additional machinery and equipment, but how can it add to its labor input? People could try to work harder, or to work more hours per year, but there are clear limits to human effort and work hours per week. However, improvements in skills and knowledge can make people more *effective* as workers. Investments in human capital—education and training—can raise *effective* labor per person.

> An economy's **effective labor input** is its labor input adjusted for knowledge and skills.

Because one skilled, educated person may do the work of two or three less knowledgeable people, increases in human capital resemble increases in the quantity of labor. They add to the economy's effective labor input.

If the economy can increase its effective labor input per person along with its capital stock, real GDP per person can grow even without technical change. With constant returns to scale, doubling the capital stock and the *effective* input of labor per person doubles real GDP per person. By increasing *both* inputs proportionally, the economy may avoid diminishing returns. If so, economic growth could continue indefinitely without slowing. Will this happen? Like questions about diminishing returns to technical progress, the answer is a matter for speculation.

Fixed and Exhaustible Natural Resources

Diminishing returns may cause economic growth to slow and perhaps eventually stop for another reason: The economy has fixed physical quantities of natural resources. We can distinguish three types of natural resources:

> **Renewable resources** are natural resources that can be replenished, such as trees.

> **Fixed resources** are natural resources that cannot be replenished, but are not depleted in production, such as land.[11]

---

[11]Of course, *fertile* land can be replenished as well as depleted.

Exhaustible resources are resources that cannot be physically replenished and that are depleted in production, such as coal.[12]

Renewable resources play the same role that capital played in the earlier discussions. They create no complications for economic growth. In contrast, fixed resources may prevent economic growth from continuing indefinitely without slowing. By the law of diminishing returns, as the economy adds capital and labor to a fixed quantity of land and other fixed resources, the benefits of further increases in capital and labor fall. At some point, the economy reaches a steady state at which economic growth stops. In this way, fixed resources could limit per-capita real GDP. Exhaustible resources may create even more severe problems. As people use oil and other fossil fuels, the earth's remaining quantities of these resources fall over time. Some people worry that depletion of exhaustible resources will cause world real GDP to *fall* in the future.

Malthus on Population

The idea that fixed resources restrain economic growth goes back to Thomas Malthus and his famous "Essay on the Principle of Population," published in 1798. Malthus argued that as the population rises and increasing numbers of people work with a fixed amount of land, diminishing returns to land would reduce output of food per person. As a result, Malthus predicted that wages would fall over time as the population rose. When the wage fell far enough, he theorized, malnourishment and death would stop the population

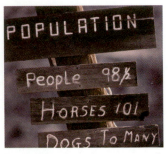

Is world population at a good or bad level?

IN THE NEWS

Losing faith: Many Americans fear U.S. living standards have stopped rising

They believe their children face a tougher future; but Boomers have hope

Alan Murray
Staff Reporter of The Wall Street Journal

For nearly three decades after World War II, the rise in American living standards was as reliable as a Maytag washer.

The march of material prosperity created the easy assurance that each generation would live better than the last.

Today, that has changed.

The economic confidence of the postwar years has faded. In a painful awareness striking at the heart of American life, many no longer assume that their children will be better off than they are.

Expectations about the future may vary—but what is that future really likely to hold? Has the American dream of ever-rising living standards vanished, dwindled to a faint hope or merely gone into hibernation?

Source: The Wall Street Journal

This news article, appeared a decade ago, when most American had more pessimistic expectations about the U.S. economy than they have today. Economists draw lessons about long-run economic growth from long-run data, rather than economic experiences of a few years.

---

[12]Economists say that people *deplete* a resource if they transform it into a *less valuable* resource.

increase, and the population would stabilize at a subsistence wage just large enough for people to live and reproduce with zero population growth. This Malthusian view of growth became very popular and led people to call economics "the dismal science."

Was Malthus right? The world population numbered about 275 million people in the year 1000. It reached 750 million by 1750, 3.0 billion by 1960, and 6 billion by 1998. Obviously, the growth rate of the world population has increased rapidly. From 1000 to 1750, the human population grew at about 0.13 percent per year; from 1750 to 1960 it grew at about 0.66 percent per year, and from 1960 to 1998 it grew at almost 1.8 percent per year. Most experts predict that world population will reach 9.3 billion by the middle of the 21st century.

Malthus assumed that the population would rise as long as people earned incomes high enough to survive. Modern studies of fertility and population growth show clearly that people *choose* family sizes in relation to their incomes, the usefulness of children (to help raise food or support parents in old age), and other factors. People do not choose to have enough children to drive their wages down to subsistence levels. Instead, wages have increased over time as the world population has grown; these wage increases have resulted from technical advances and increases in physical and human capital that have raised the demand for labor faster than population growth has raised the supply. A century after Malthus published his book in Britain, that country's population had quadrupled and people's incomes had increased greatly.[13]

Scarcity of Natural Resources

Despite the evidence against the Malthusian model of population and wages, his argument about diminishing returns to a fixed quantity of land and natural resources raises serious issues. Even with moderate population growth diminishing returns could cause economic growth to slow down and eventually stop. Many social commentators have argued that this may happen, and some have argued for government policies intended to reduce the use and depletion of resources, and to reduce the rate of world population growth. According to their arguments, population growth reduces economic growth and could even reduce the level of real GDP per person. Population increases with fixed quantities of land may also reduce quality of life through crowding, pollution, and other factors that GDP calculations ignore.

Other analysts have argued that people respond to scarcity of a resource by innovating and creating new ways to replace scarce resources with more plentiful resources. History is filled with examples, as the Social and Economics Issues box on the next page illustrates. The evidence suggests that scarcity of natural resources has not limited economic growth in the past. As people deplete the remaining quantity of an exhaustible resource, its supply falls and its price rises. If economic growth were limited by depletion of exhaustible resources, the prices of those natural resources would rise. However, the evidence suggests the opposite: Historically, relative prices of most exhaustible resources have *fallen* over time.

Prices of exhaustible resources have fallen for two reasons. First, technical progress has increased their supply (for example, by locating new mines, reducing the cost of mining, and decreasing waste). Second, technical progress has reduced the demand for these resources by creating substitutes. (For example, satellite links and fiber-optic lines have replaced copper wires for telephone calls.) If technical change provides methods to increase output with reduced inputs of fixed and exhaustible resources, then economic growth may continue indefinitely without slowing or stopping.[14]

This debate on the future of economic growth continues today. One side says that economic growth will slow down and eventually stop because of diminishing returns to

---

[13] Even in the years from 1500 to 1700, when technical progress was slow, the situation differed from Malthus's scenario. The population grew at a rate well below the biological maximum. Europeans lived in conjugal rather than extended families, and married in their mid-20s rather than at puberty to keep fertility low; priests enforced prohibitions on premarital sex with reasonable success. Average living standards remained well above the subsistence level.

[14] Though the quantity of land is physically finite, it has not inhibited economic growth in the past. The development of better techniques for land use (for irrigation, fertilization, cropping, and breeding) have reduced the importance of land for agriculture. Similarly, the developments of elevators and high-rise buildings have helped to reduce the importance of land in cities.

SOCIAL AND ECONOMIC ISSUES

Will the Finite Quantity of Natural Resources Cause Economic Growth to Slow Down or Stop?

Yes

The earth provides a finite amount of many important natural resources. Some of these, like total land area, don't change over time, but population growth reduces the amount available per person. People are using up many others, such as fossil fuels (oil and natural gas) and metals. Future generations will have diminishing quantities of these resources available, even if the population stops growing.

World population growth shows no indication of slowing any time soon. Most experts expect massive increases in world population over the next century. Population growth is already outstripping the world's supplies of fresh water, food, and minerals.

The inaccuracy of earlier warning of doom is irrelevant to today's situation. The forecasters were wrong at the time, but the real crisis will come soon.

Finite natural resources will soon get more expensive, because they are being consumed. The fact that they became cheaper in the past proves nothing, because people were not near the point of running out; the world is near that point now.

No

Scarce resources haven't run out yet, and for a good reason. When resources become scarce, people respond with innovations and substitutes. This process has continued throughout history. The Greeks moved from the Bronze Age to the Iron Age 3,000 years ago because wars in the eastern Mediterranean disrupted trade and reduced the supply of tin for bronze production. The Greeks responded to the bronze crisis by starting to use iron instead. Timber shortages in 16th-century Britain led to the use of coal as a substitute fuel. As a resource becomes scarce, people find new ways to produce its services with resources that are more abundant, and the alternatives usually turn out to be better than the old ways. The most important natural resource for production of new ideas is human ingenuity, and its supply is unlimited.

As a result, neither the finite physical quantities of natural resources nor population growth will limit economic growth. An increase in population growth causes short-term problems, because children do not produce goods, but it does not create long-term problems because adults produce both goods and new ideas.

Serious people have claimed many times in the past—wrongly—that the world was about to run out of some natural resource. The current claims are wrong for the same reason that similar warnings were wrong in the past.

Many physically finite natural resources have become cheaper rather than more expensive over time because of new discoveries that have raised their supplies or the development of substitutes that have reduced their demand. Similar changes will likely occur in the future.

Investment in new ideas is a key source of economic growth.

finite resources, and perhaps because real GDP per capita will fall as the economy depletes exhaustible resources. The other side says that economic growth can continue indefinitely, driven by technical change and accumulating knowledge and human capital. Many past predictions have incorrectly warned that the world would soon run out of some finite resource.[15] This record of inaccuracy does not necessarily imply that similar claims will be wrong in the future.

Externalities and Growth

People and firms have incentives to invest in research and development to create technical change, because the results of the research can add to their profits. These additional profits are the private benefits of investing in research and development. Other people

---

[15] In his famous book The Coal Question: An Enquiry Concerning the Progress of the Nation (London, U.K.: Macmillan, 1865), economist Stanley Jevons warned that the world would soon run out of coal. The U.S. Federal Oil Conservation Board said in 1926 that the United States had only a 7-year supply of oil left. In The Population Bomb (New York: Ballantine Books, 1968), Paul Ehrlich warned that "The battle to feed humanity is over. In the 1970s the world will undergo famines—hundreds of millions of people are going to starve to death." Ehrlich warned that "nothing can prevent a substantial increase in the world death rate." He predicted that "America's vast agricultural surpluses are gone." In Ehrlich's book with Anne Ehrlich, The End of Affluence, the authors warned of a "nutritional disaster that seems likely to overtake humanity in the 1970s (or, at the latest, in the 1980s)," and said that "before 1985 mankind will enter a genuine age of scarcity" in which "the accessible supplies of many key minerals will be nearing depletion." These predictions were all wrong.

A Famous Bet

In 1980, economist Julian Simon offered a bet to environmentalist Paul Ehrlich. For years, Ehrlich had been forecasting doom as the world runs out of resources. Simon had been arguing that continual innovations would prevent resource depletion, and that the prices of natural resources would continue to fall as in the past.

Simon offered to bet on the *relative prices* of natural resources. Ehrlich could choose any five metals for the bet, with quantities chosen so that they cost a total of $1,000 in 1980. If the relative prices of the metals increased by 1990, so the total value of the metals (adjusted for inflation) exceeded $1,000 in 1990, then Ehrlich would win the bet. If the

relative prices of the metals fell by 1990, so their total value (adjusted for inflation) was less than $1,000 in 1990, then Simon would win. The loser would pay the winner the difference in the total value of the metals, above or below $1,000. Ehrlich accepted the bet and chose copper, chrome, nickel, tin, and tungsten.

By 1990, the relative prices of all five metals had fallen below their levels in 1980. Ehrlich lost the bet, and sent Simon a check for $567.07. (In fact, the relative prices fell enough that Simon would have won the bet even if prices had not been adjusted for inflation.) Simon (who died in 1997) offered to renew the bets and increase the ante to $20,000, but Ehrlich was not interested.

More information on this bet, and other related bets offered by Simon and by Ehrlich, can be found on the Web site for this book.

may gain directly from these investments as well, so the social benefits of investments in research may exceed the private benefits.

> The **private benefit** of producing a good or investing in research is the benefit to the people who produce it or invest. The **social benefit** is the benefit to everyone in society of the production or investment.

Firms often copy technical changes they see in other firms or industries. Countries copy technical changes they see in other countries. New ideas often lead to even more ideas. Technical knowledge and ideas tend to spread throughout the economy, sometimes through written media in books and technical reports and sometimes through products that can be studied by reverse engineering (in which people take apart products to see how they work). You may know of many examples such as clones of brand-name computers, designer clothes, and other consumer products. Knowledge can be such a valuable asset that some firms undertake industrial espionage (spying) to gain information about technical developments at other firms.

> A **positive externality** occurs when the social benefit of producing a good or investing in research exceeds the private benefit.

Some economists believe that positive externalities play important roles in economic growth. Countries that invest more than others may grow faster partly because the new ideas generated by these investments create positive externalities that spread throughout the investors' economies.

If investments in knowledge or human capital generate positive externalities, then the economically efficient quantity of these investments exceeds the equilibrium quantity. This fact has led some economists to suggest that government policies should encourage savings and investment, perhaps through subsidies or lower taxes.

Similarly, positive externalities from investments in knowledge or human capital mean that doubling the amounts of physical and human capital may *more* than double real GDP. While doubling inputs of physical and human capital at any one firm may double *that* firm's output, the increase may also create positive externalities that raise output at other firms. Some economists cite this possibility as one reason for the increase

Externalities and Government Policies

Evidence indicates that when a typical business firm invests in research and development, it gains only about one-half of the benefits from its investments. One study found that the *private benefit* to investment in research and development has been about 25 percent per year (before taxes), while the *social benefit*, has been about 50 percent per year. When business firms decide on a level of investment in research and development, they weigh the *private* benefits of investment against the costs. As a result, businesses invest less in research and development than they would if they had an incentive to take into consideration *all* the benefits of those investments. This discrepancy has led the U.S. government to reduce taxes for businesses that invest in research and development (by about 20 cents per dollar of investment). One study found that for every $1 billion in tax revenue the government sacrifices for these tax incentives, businesses raise investment in research and development by about $2 billion. These tax policies provide one important channel through which government policies can promote economic growth.

in the rate of economic growth over time. Of course, no one knows whether the rate of growth will continue to increase in the future, but the suggestion that growth results partly from positive externalities emphasizes this possibility.

Review Questions

9. What do economists mean by an economy's *effective* labor input? What increases the effective labor input? How do these increases contribute to economic growth?

10. (a) Explain why fixed and exhaustible natural resources might cause economic growth to decrease in the future. (b) Explain how the economy might avoid decreasing growth, despite the limited physical quantities of natural resources.

11. Explain and criticize Malthus's views of population and wages.

IN THE NEWS

The pump on the well

Unforeseen consequences of technology

When a solar-powered water pump was provided for a well in India, the village headman took it over and sold the water, until stopped. The new liquid abundance attracted hordes of unwanted nomads. Village boys who had drawn water in buckets had nothing to do, and some became criminals. The gap between rich and poor widened, since the poor had no land to benefit from irrigation. Finally, village women broke the pump, so they could gather again around the well that had been the center of their social lives.

Moral: Technological advances have social, cultural, and economic consequences, often unanticipated.

Source: New York Times

With enough economic growth, they could socialize at the local gourmet coffee shop.

12. What is a positive externality and how might externalities contribute to growth?

13. Suppose economic growth were limited by the earth's finite quantities of exhaustible resources. Why would economists expect the relative prices of these resources to rise over time? Why have their relative prices not risen over time?

14. Why would economic growth eventually slow and stop if investments in knowledge and technical change had diminishing returns?

ECONOMIC DEVELOPMENT: GROWTH IN LESS DEVELOPED COUNTRIES

The term *economic development* refers to economic growth in low-income countries. Economic development is generally accompanied by increases in life expectancy, health, and literacy, and by decreases in infant mortality. In 1900, average life expectancy at birth was only 49 years in the OECD countries and 35 years in LDCs (less developed countries). Economic growth in the 20th century has raised life expectancy to 77 years in OECD countries and 64 years in LDCs. Countries with highly developed economies tend to have more political freedom; more stable governments; fewer civil wars, coups and revolutions; and fewer government restrictions on people's activities than LDCs have. Developed countries tend to have more equal distributions of income than LDCs. Although development often raises inequality in the short run, it reduces inequality in the long run.

Why are some countries poorer than others are? What can a poor country do to increase its economic growth? Why have *some* countries risen from poverty by growing rapidly and joining the developed countries of the world? What have *those* countries done that other poor countries have not? Will poor countries ever catch up with rich countries? These are some of the key questions of economic development.

Differences among Countries

Two centuries ago, no country was as rich as developed countries are today, but no one was much poorer than the poorest country today. In 1900, real GDP per person in the world's richest country was about 8 times higher than real GDP per person in the world's poorest country. By 1998, real GDP per person in the world's richest country (the United States) was about 60 times higher than real GDP per person in the world's poorest country (Ethiopia). Clearly, inequality among countries of the world has increased as some countries have grown rapidly and others have remained far behind. Inequality among *developed* economies has fallen, however. Real GDP per person in OECD countries (with the exception of Asian countries) has become more equal in the 20th century, especially since 1950. Figure 9 shows growth in various regions around the world over the past 250 years.

Conditions that Promote Growth

Evidence suggests that several factors contribute to a country's economic growth. Poor countries tend to grow faster than richer countries (they tend to "catch up" with richer countries) *given* other conditions that affect growth. One advantage that less developed countries have in economic growth involves imitation. Poorer countries can copy techniques and

SOCIAL AND ECONOMIC ISSUES

Does Economic Growth Create Problems?

Economic growth has improved people's lives enormously over time. Nevertheless, some people argue that growth has negative effects. These people often favor government policies designed to prevent or solve the problems, even if the policies reduce the rate of economic growth. Other people disagree, seeing negative aspects of growth as illusory or small issues. They favor government policies to promote fast growth. Here are some arguments on the positive and negative aspects of growth.

Positive Results of Growth

Economic growth brings people out of poverty. It raises health and expected life span, increases literacy, and opens new opportunities for people to have fulfilling lives. It gives people both the material goods they want and more leisure time. People can use this leisure time as they choose, for recreation or to pursue other goals and promote nonmaterial values.

Growth provides resources that can help the environment. A good summary measure of environmental quality as it affects people is expected life span, which has increased with economic growth, largely due to improvements in health and medicine that accompany growth. Economic growth also provides the resources that offer people some insurance against many risks, such as famine and disease. While economic growth requires change, and any change has risks, changes can produce good as well as bad effects.

Economic growth creates new opportunities for people to pursue fulfillment through work. People who want to be artists or self-dependent producers of their own food can still do so. In fact, with the increased technical knowledge made possible by economic growth, a self-dependent person can have a higher standard of living now than people could in the past. The romantic image of life and jobs before economic growth is completely different from the reality that life and work for most people are better—not worse—

Figure 9 | Real GDP per Capita around the World, 1750–1998

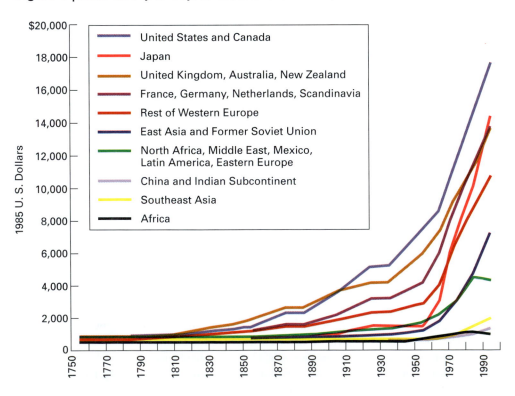

after economic growth. Future economic growth can continue to improve the quality of life.

Economic growth generates riches for some people. Although it may initially raise income inequality, it eventually reduces inequality. (For example, compare the amount of income inequality in developed countries and LDCs.) Any government policies to reduce economic growth would not reduce inequalities; they would entrench existing ones and reduce opportunities for people to advance themselves through innovation, hard work, or luck.

Problems that Some People See in Economic Growth

Some people claim that economic growth reduces the quality of life by leading people to focus on material goods that do not provide real satisfaction and to ignore the nonmaterial values that are important to satisfying lives. Others claim that economic growth increases income inequality and allows some people to get rich but not others.

Some people say that growth ruins the beauty of nature, harms the environment, and threatens a fragile ecosystem. They say it threatens the welfare of future generations of people as well as nonhuman life.

Some people assert that growth alienates people from the most important values in life. It moves them from basic, fulfilling work such as farming, craft work, and building to unfulfilling jobs in factories and offices. Economic growth reduces a worker's understanding of how his efforts fit into a larger scheme and help other people. Some jobs, like investment banking, encourage gross materialism and discourage important values like honesty and charity. The increased specialization that goes with economic growth, in this view, alienates people from each other; it reduces shared experiences, makes it harder for people to understand each other, and breaks down the social bonds that support a civilized community.

What do you think? What evidence could you obtain to support your position?

technologies that were invented in richer countries. Copying does not always create success, however, because the technologies that are most appropriate in a country with highly-paid, skilled workers may differ from the best technology in a country with lower-paid, less-skilled workers.

While evidence suggests that poor countries tend to grow faster *given* other conditions, many countries are poor precisely because these other conditions differ. Differences in these other conditions can prevent poor countries from catching up with rich countries. Several other conditions affect economic growth. First, a country tends to grow faster than others if it has a skilled, educated population. Education and skills allow people to take greater advantage of advanced technologies. Often however, people in poor countries spend more time working and less time investing in education and skills than people in richer countries.

Countries tend to grow faster if their governments place few restrictions on international trade. International trade creates incentives for the nation's producers to specialize in the goods and services in which they have a comparative advantage. International trade also provides competition for domestic producers, creating stronger incentives for efficient uses of resources. A later chapter discusses other benefits from international trade.

Countries tend to grow faster if they attract high levels of investment from foreign countries. While the savings of people living in a country can provide resources for investment, poor countries generate low levels of saving. As a result, a poor country can raise its level of investment and economic growth by attracting foreign investment.

Countries tend to grow faster if they have stable economic and political conditions. High rates of inflation (discussed in the next chapter) inhibit economic growth. Countries with more coups, civil wars, and revolutions show lower economic growth than countries with more political stability.

Finally, countries tend to grow faster if they have well-developed and well-enforced systems of property rights, commercial and contract law, and legal methods for resolving

ON ECONOMICS—

Rich in Cash, But Not in Happiness

You say money can't buy happiness? It must be you just don't know where to shop. Most economists accept, nearly as an article of faith, that individual satisfaction tracks closely with income. Their faith isn't blind, either: Most of us seek raises, wish we could afford a bigger house and dream about winning the lottery.

But a small band of economists are breaking ranks. They cite numerous studies showing paradoxically that as society grows richer over time, the average level of happiness—as measured by the percentage of people who rate themselves "happy" or "very happy" in national surveys—doesn't grow in tandem. If true, the implications are potentially enormous. These findings should challenge economists—and everyone else for that matter—to reexamine the merits and consequences of economic growth.

Richard Easterlin, now an economist at the University of Southern California,

published a seminal study reporting no clear trend in surveys of Americans' reported happiness. Average happiness rose from the 1940s to the late 1950s, then gradually sank again to the early 1970s, even as personal income grew sharply. Returning to the subject three years ago, Easterlin cited an annual U.S. survey that showed a slight downward trend in the percentage of Americans saying they were "very happy" from 1972 to 1991—even though per capita income, adjusted for inflation and taxes, rose by a third.

Even more striking evidence came from Japan, where a Dutch scholar, Ruut Veenhoven, tracked self-reported levels of satisfaction from 1958 to 1987. During that period, Japan's economy defined the "Asian miracle." Real per capita income soared nearly fivefold, taking Japan from a developing country to an industrial superpower in a generation. Yet average levels of

reported satisfaction didn't budge at all.

Psychologists find that few things permanently budge individuals from their normal level of happiness, which is determined above all by inherited temperament. But income does matter. At any given time, the higher your income, the more likely you are to report being happy, so there's still reason to envy the rich.

How can these findings be reconciled? Easterlin believes people feel more satisfied if their consumption exceeds the social norms. But as an economy grows, so do material aspirations. That moving target keeps the average person from ever feeling better.

An economy with no growth, on the other hand, can turn ugly as people continue striving to climb the social ladder. The only way for people to get more out of a fixed pie is to grab someone else's slice. A static economy promotes nasty fights over distribution; growth promotes civility and altruism.

Source: San Francisco Chronicle

What do you believe? Does economic growth contribute to human happiness? Would you be as happy if you lived in the conditions of 1000 years ago? 100 years ago? How would human happiness be affected if economic growth were to end this year, or sometime in the near future? Should governments pursue policies to promote economic growth?

legal disputes. Economic growth in Russia in the 1990s, for example, has been hindered by absence of well-developed and well-enforced property rights. Property rights, along with economic and political stability, helps ensure businesses that they can reap the returns

The development gap

Most developing countries will gain little from new technologies

Developing countries face a series of obstacles in their efforts to participate in the Third Industrial Revolution. First, a pool of highly trained scientific and technical personnel is essential for the successful diffusion of the new technologies. But only 13 percent of the world's scientists and engineers are in the third world, and they are concentrated in only a few countries in East Asia and in Brazil, India, and Mexico.

Second, new technologies require large amounts of capital. But many developing countries lack access to capital markets and already are heavily burdened by debt.

Third, shifts in world consumption and technical innovation have cut demand for traditional raw materials—bad news for the nearly 40 developing countries that depend on raw materials for at least 15 percent of their total export earnings.

Source: New York Times

of their investments. When business firms are reluctant to invest in a country, perhaps because they fear future government confiscation of the returns from their investment, that reluctance reduces economic growth.

Investment and Government Policies

Very poor countries tend to save smaller fractions of their incomes than rich countries save. Consequently, they have very low levels of investment in equilibrium unless they borrow from rich countries. Foreign investment in poor countries can increase their incomes, partly by bringing equipment to boost their workers' productivity and partly by bringing technical knowledge, organizational skills, and information about how to export their products. Foreigners have an incentive to invest in a poor country if it offers sufficiently low wages compared to worker productivity.

In practice, poor countries attract little foreign investment and wages remain much lower in poor countries than in rich ones. This difference may reflect low skill levels of workers in poor countries, which offsets the benefits of their low wages, or it may reflect risks of investing in those countries because of uncertainty about property rights. Potential investors evaluate the risk that the government of a less developed country may confiscate their property in the future, impose new taxes or regulations that reduce the returns on their investments, or limit their ability to take their profits out of the country.

Other factors further limit foreign investment in LDCs. Many LDCs have poor infrastructures with unreliable or nonexistent transportation and communication systems (roads, telephone systems, and so on). Governments of LDCs often limit foreign investment to avoid the perception that foreigners are taking over their countries or in response to political pressures from people who would lose from foreign investments. Government bureaucrats, for example, often benefit from maintaining the status quo.

Many governments of LDCs adopt economically inefficient policies such as limiting international trade and controlling domestic trade. Economists may see these inefficient policies as mistakes, but the policies may also benefit powerful special-interest groups within these countries, at the expense of reduced economic growth. Government policies also affect the extent to which people divert resources from production to economically inefficient activities such as seeking political influence through lobbying, bribes, legal battles, and other activities to increase their shares of the country's output. Countries that spend comparatively high levels of resources fighting over the distribution of output have comparatively low levels of real GDP and low rates of economic growth.

Success Stories

Among the most famous successes of economic development are the so-called *four tigers of Asia* mentioned earlier: Hong Kong, Singapore, South Korea, and Taiwan. These countries have averaged more than 7 percent annual growth of per-capita real GDP—more than four times the world average—since 1965. (The rule of 72 estimates that 7 percent annual growth would double these countries' incomes every decade.)

Why did these countries succeed so well at development? Economists do not yet have a complete answer, but the reason seems partly related to free markets and international trade. Evidence shows that economic growth is connected with increased international trade, particularly for small countries. All four Asian tigers imposed less government regulation and control than most LDCs, and all experienced large increases in international trade along with their rapid growth. Their governments left more economic decisions to free markets than did officials in low-growth countries; this policy promoted economic efficiency and probably raised economic growth. International trade promotes efficiency by allowing countries to specialize in the products at which they have comparative advantages, which raises their income, as Chapter 3 explained. In addition, increased specialization can raise a country's rate of economic growth under certain conditions. Increased international trade also raises competitive pressures on firms, which may reduce inefficiencies and raise output. Finally, increased international trade can help pressure governments to follow economically efficient policies.

Some economists look at the evidence on development and conclude that countries can develop and grow most rapidly if their governments eliminate restrictions on international trade, promote private property rights and free markets, reduce regulations and controls on the economy, and encourage foreign investment. Others believe that economic development can speed up if the government actively promotes international trade by subsidizing exports. While most agree that governments of less developed countries follow many policies that cause inefficient uses of resources, some question the extent to which changes in government policies alone can raise economic growth rates.

Review Questions

15. List some factors that promote fast economic growth.

16. How can foreign investment raise the rate of growth in a less developed country?

Conclusion

Basics of Growth

Economic growth is a rise in real GDP per person, measured by the annual percentage increase in per-capita real GDP. Throughout most of history, real GDP per person remained roughly constant until about 200 to 300 years ago, when it began a rapid increase. The rule of 72 says that if the growth rate of a variable is X percent per year, then the variable doubles after about $72/X$ years.

Main Facts about Economic Growth

World real GDP per person is about $6,000 today, 12 times higher than in 1800 and more than 4 times higher than in 1900. U.S. real GDP per person is about $32,000 today, almost 6 times as high as in 1900. It has doubled since 1964. Economic growth rates differ substantially across countries. Some countries have had annual growth rates over 7 percent in recent decades, with real GDP per person doubling every 10 years; others have roughly the same living standards as a century ago.

Logic of Economic Growth: A Basic Model

An economy can grow by saving and investing in new capital. However, without technical change, diminishing returns cause growth to slow down and eventually stop as the economy reaches a steady state equilibrium. Evidence indicates, however, that economic growth has increased over time (with the possible exception of the last quarter-century), which conflicts with the implication of this model. In addition, this basic model implies that the real interest rate falls over time, but evidence indicates a constant real interest rate.

Logic of Growth: Extensions

Technical change results from investments in research and development and in education. An economy can continue to grow indefinitely if technical change continues. If technical change were to have diminishing returns (a highly speculative question), then technical change and economic growth would slow down and eventually stop. Similarly, economic growth could continue indefinitely if the economy could indefinitely add to its *effective* labor input per person—through education—along with its capital per person.

Fixed and exhaustible natural resources cause diminishing returns for investments in physical and human capital, so they may lead growth to slow down and eventually stop. However, growth may continue indefinitely without slowing down if technical progress allows the economy to reduce its use of fixed and exhaustible resources or to substitute replenishable resources such as trees and sunlight for those resources. Some technical change may occur by accident, but the economy may be able to increase technical progress and long-run growth by increasing investments in education, research, and development.

Economic Development: Growth in Less Developed Countries

Countries tend to grow relatively rapidly if they are poor, have educated or skilled populations, limit government restrictions on international trade, and stimulate high levels of investment. Countries in Africa and Latin America have grown more slowly than similar countries elsewhere, perhaps because they have tended to suffer more political instability and less certain property rights. The fact that poor countries tend to grow faster than others does not mean that they are catching up with rich countries. Many countries remain poor because of frequent wars and inefficient government policies.

Key Terms

economic growth
rule of 72
steady state

effective labor input
renewable resource
fixed resource

exhaustible resource
private benefit

social benefit
positive externality

Questions and Problems

17. Explain why a country cannot keep growing at the same rate indefinitely simply by adding indefinitely to its physical capital.

18. Use a graph of the supply and demand for loans to help explain why an increase in savings raises the speed at which the economy grows toward its steady state.

19. How might increases in savings and investment raise the rate of economic growth as well as the level of per-capita real GDP?

20. Discuss this statement: "Poor countries are likely to catch up, eventually, with rich countries."

21. Why do some countries grow faster than others?

22. (*More difficult problem.*) Suppose the economy's per-person production function is

$$\text{Real GDP per person} = k^{4/5}$$

where k represents the capital stock per person. Also suppose that people save 2/10 of real GDP each year, and that 1/10 of the economy's capital depreciates (wears out) each year. Find the steady state capital stock and steady state real GDP.

23. Suppose that people in France begin saving more than before and people in England begin saving less. Is this change likely to raise the rate of economic growth in France and reduce the growth rate in England? (*Hint:* What happens to international borrowing and lending and to the world equilibrium real interest rate?)

Inquiries for Further Thought

24. Are we at a turning point in history beyond which economic growth is likely to decline?

25. Does economic growth create winners and losers? Who are they?

26. (a) Would further economic growth in the United States be good or bad? Why? If you are opposed to more economic growth, would you have opposed more growth in 1800? In 1900? In 1950?
(b) How fast should countries' economies grow? What general principles should guide the answer to this kind of question?

27. What government policies would you recommend for an LDC that wants fast economic growth?

28. Discuss this statement: "To feed starving populations is desirable, but if new crops help add a billion new people to a crowded globe, is that necessarily a good thing?"

29. Discuss these statements.
(a) "Population growth may raise economic growth, because it adds more brains as well as more mouths and hands."
(b) "Population growth that increases the volume of trash may increase our problems in the short run, but it bestows benefits on future generations. The pressure of new problems leads to the search for new solutions. The solutions constitute the knowledge that fuels the progress of civilization, and leaves us better off than if the original problem had never arisen. That is the history of the human race."

30. Suppose that a higher population would reduce per-capita real GDP but raise aggregate real GDP. Would this increase in population be good or bad?

31. Discuss this statement: "Allowing foreigners to immigrate to our country can raise our rate of economic growth, particularly if the immigrants are well educated."

Appendix: Mathematics of Production Functions

A realistic production function for an economy is

$$\text{Real GDP} = A l^{2/3} k^{1/3}$$

This equation provides a good approximation to real-life production functions in the United States and many other countries. The variable A represents the level of technology, with increases in A representing technical progress. Real GDP rises with increases in A, k, or l.

This production function implies constant returns to scale: Doubling all inputs, doubles real GDP. To see why, multiply labor and capital by 2 in the equation:

$$\begin{aligned}\text{Real GDP with twice the inputs} &= A(2l)^{2/3}(2k)^{1/3} \\ &= A 2^{2/3} l^{2/3} 2^{1/3} k^{1/3} \\ &= 2 A l^{2/3} k^{1/3} \\ &= \text{twice the original GDP}\end{aligned}$$

This result shows that doubling all inputs doubles real GDP. Similarly, multiplying all inputs by *any* number, such as X, multiplies GDP by that same number. This fact means the production function has constant returns to scale.

Now we let X be $1/l$. In other words, we multiply both inputs by $1/l$, which also multiplies real GDP by $1/l$. This gives an expression for real GDP per person:

$$\begin{aligned}\frac{\text{Real GDP}}{l} &= \frac{A l^{2/3} k^{1/3}}{l} \\ &= A\left(\frac{k}{l}\right)^{1/3}\end{aligned}$$

This expression shows that real GDP per person depends on capital per person, as in the chapter.

PART 5

INFLATION, MONEY, AND BANKS

CHAPTER 9

INFLATION

In this Chapter . . .

Main Points to Understand

▶ *Inflation* refers to continuing increases in the average level of *nominal* prices.

▶ Nothing affects inflation without affecting the growth rate of the money supply, the growth rate of velocity, or the growth rate of real GDP.

▶ Equilibrium between the supply of money and the demand for money determines the price level, as in the equation of exchange.

▶ No one would care about inflation if it reflected a change in units of measurement, like a reverse currency reform. Economic and social problems from inflation result from the *differences* between inflation and reverse currency reforms.

Thinking Skills to Develop

▶ Distinguish between factors that affect *relative* prices of various goods and services and factors that affect the *nominal* price level.

▶ Apply the economics of supply and demand to money.

▶ Reason by analogy (between inflation and currency reforms), and evaluate the limits of an analogy.

At the beginning of the 20th century, basketballs cost about $2 each; at the end of the century they cost about $30. Prices of most goods and services are higher now than a century ago, or even a decade ago. On average, prices in the United States in 1998 were more than 18 times higher than prices in 1900, and twice as high as in 1980.

In 1998, after years of rapidly rising prices, Russia removed three zeros from the ends of all its money, prices, wages, bank accounts, and debts. The price of cheese, for example, fell from about 30,000 rubles per kilogram to about 30 rubles. People exchanged their old 100,000 ruble bills for newly designed 100 ruble bills and other new money printed by the government.

This Russian experience was not unique. In Germany from August 1922 to November 1923, inflation averaged 322 percent per month. Prices at the end of that German hyperinflation—a term for particularly high inflation—were 10 billion times the original level. Someone who lived through hyperinflation once defined it as a situation in which it's cheaper to pay for your lunch before you start eating it than after you finish. Indeed, people have sometimes resorted to eating money itself, or burning it for heat or cooking fuel as in the picture that opens this chapter.

Less than 20 years ago, inflation reached almost 5,000 percent per year in Argentina, 2,000 percent per year in Brazil, and several hundred percent in Israel. Bolivia's inflation rate reached 60,000 percent per year in the summer of 1985. Other countries, including

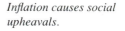

IN THE NEWS

BUENOS AIRES, May 31—Rioting over runaway inflation increased in the Argentine capital today.

Source: New York Times

Inflation causes social upheavals.

IN THE NEWS

A weary Buenos Aires family wonders how to keep afloat

By James Brooke
Special to
The New York Times

BUENOS AIRES, June 15—With his 2-year-old son squirming on his lap, Guillermo Dietrich pondered how to keep his family afloat in Argentina's rising sea of inflation.

"My wife, my mother, and my aunt are the antibodies of hyperinflation," the drawn father of two said, cracking a rare smile. "Every morning, they pool price information and try to save before prices are marked up again."

Last month, food prices jumped 78 percent, a record here. Argentina's working class neighborhoods erupted in the worst riots in a decade.

'We Live Day to Day'

This month, prices are expected to jump 100 per-cent. With businessmen projecting this year's inflation to be 12,000 percent, Argentina's middle class feel pushed to the edge.

"We live day to day," Mr. Dietrich said. "We only pay bills when the money comes in."

The descendants of immigrants from Europe, the Dietrichs grew up to think of themselves as middle class. Guillermo was a construction foreman. Elida, his wife, is a lawyer.

"We grew up with inflation of 7 to 15 percent a month," Mr. Dietrich, 31 years old, said of the annual inflation rate common to Argentina in the 1970s and 1980s. "But now, prices don't mean anything any more."

"I bought this last week at 37 australes," he said, toying with a half-smoked pack of L&M Light cigarettes. "Now it is selling for 55 australes. Next week, it will be 78 australes. What is the price?"

Elida Dietrich juggled her 4-year-old daughter, Valeria, and said: "It makes you feel very insecure."

"This morning, I went into one store, looking for detergent," she continued. "In one place, it was 140. The next place, 100. Finally, I bought it at a third store at 80. But tomorrow all the prices will change."

In late May, sudden rises of food prices triggered the sacking of hundreds of food shops across Argentina. In a shock to the nation, 15 people were killed, dozens were injured, and hundreds were arrested.

Source: New York Times

Living with inflation.

Austria, Greece, Hungary, and Peru, have had similar experiences in the last century. Around the world, the 20th century saw the biggest price increases in all of history.

Inflation—defined as a continuing increase in the price level—has a long history. Emperor Diocletian tried to stop inflation in the Roman Empire by imposing wage and price controls in A.D. 301. Despite the death penalty for violaters, inflation continued and many people were executed until Diocletian abdicated the throne in A.D. 305.

Personal hardships and social upheavals have accompanied periods of high inflation in the last century. Riots in the streets and changes in government make the news, but just as devastating are the difficulties that many families face when prices rise hourly, when their money loses value faster than they can spend it, and when increases in prices wipe out the values of their life savings.

Inflation in the United States today—about 2½ percent per year since 1991—is low by 20th-century standards, but high by standards of earlier centuries. Prices in the United States today are about one-fourth higher than in 1990. In contrast, the U.S. price level in 1940, at the beginning of World War II, was only about one-third higher than it was a century and a half earlier, when George Washington became the nation's first president. Clearly, the continuing inflation that people in the United States take for granted today is a relatively recent phenomenon.

IN THE NEWS

Hunger spreading in Peru inflation

Food is plentiful in markets but soaring prices put it out of reach for many

By Alan Riding
Special to
The New York Times

LIMA, Peru—Wandering around a street market near her home with the equivalent of just 60 cents in her pocket, Sara Chaverry seemed almost in a daze as she tried to imagine how she would provide the next three meals for the 10 members of her household.

"There's plenty of food in the stalls," the 28-year-old mother said, waving at unsold chickens and cuts of meat, "but things I could afford a couple of months ago are now out of reach. Sometimes I just buy the tail, skin, and head of a fish and boil it up with rice."

Since this country's deepening economic crisis brought a surge of inflation of 114 percent in September alone, food—or the lack of it—has become the central concern of millions of Peruvians who were already living below the poverty line.

Source: New York Times

Inflation creates winners and losers.

Who gains from inflation? Who loses? Why do some countries have higher rates of inflation than others? Why are policy makers around the world concerned about inflation? What causes inflation and what can prevent it? These are the subjects of this chapter.

One of the most basic concepts in economics involves the distinction between nominal and real variables:

> **Nominal variables** are quantities measured in units of money (U.S. dollars, Mexican pesos, etc.).

> **Real variables** are quantities measured in units of goods and services or in units of *base-year* money.

DEFINITIONS AND BASIC MODEL

A previous chapter explained one example—the distinction between nominal GDP and real GDP. Economists measure nominal GDP in units of money; they measure real GDP in units of *base-year* money. In an economic model with only one good (such as berries in the Robinson Crusoe model), real GDP represents the number of goods that the economy produces in a year.

A related distinction concerns nominal and relative prices (first discussed in Chapter 4):

> **Nominal prices** are money prices of goods and services.

> **Relative prices** are the opportunity costs of goods, measured in terms of other goods.

If a sandwich costs $3, and a drink costs $1, then the nominal prices of sandwiches and drinks are $3 and $1, and the relative price of a sandwich, measured in terms of drinks, is 3 drinks per sandwich. If we measure an average nominal price by giving equal weight in the average to sandwiches and drinks, we find that the average nominal price level in this example is $2.

These distinctions are extremely important because inflation involves nominal prices and other nominal variables, while the supply–demand model discussed in Chapter 4 involves relative prices and real variables. Many economic fallacies (some discussed later in this chapter) result from confusing relative prices and nominal prices. You should notice, for example, that the price level can change without any changes in relative prices. For example, all nominal prices may double, doubling the price level, but leaving all relative prices unaffected. Similarly, relative prices can change without any change in the price level—for example, the relative price of sandwiches can rise from 3 to 4 drinks per sandwich, with the nominal price of sandwiches rising to $3.20 and the nominal price of drinks falling to 80 cents. This change raises the relative price to 4 drinks per sandwich but leaves the average nominal price of the goods at $2.

The term *price level* refers to the average level of *nominal* prices of goods and services. An earlier chapter discussed three measures of the price level—the GDP deflator, the consumer price index (CPI), and the producer price index (PPI). Inflation refers to continuing increases in the average level of nominal prices:

> **Inflation** is a continuing increase in the (nominal) price level.

Economists measure inflation by the *percentage increase* in the CPI (or GDP deflator or PPI) over some period of time, such as a year.

The basic model discussed in previous chapters used the *equation of exchange,* represented by the circular flow diagram, to determine the equilibrium price level. We begin analyzing inflation—the *growth rate* of the price level—by examining this model in greater detail.

Equation of Exchange

Figure 1 shows the basic version of the circular flow of economic activity that Chapter 6 introduced to discuss the price level. The outer circle shows money flowing from people to firms as people buy goods and services (aggregate nominal spending). That flow of money shows the economy's total spending, or nominal GDP. Money also flows back to people as firms pay wages and distribute profits (another way to measure nominal GDP). The inner circle shows the flow of final goods from firms to people (real GDP) and the flow of work effort and other inputs from people to firms (another way to measure real GDP).

Chapter 6 defined the *nominal money supply* as the total quantity of money in the economy, measured in monetary units such as dollars or yen. That definition will continue to apply in this chapter: the nominal money supply is the total amount of dollar bills that the government has printed, minus those lost or destroyed. (The following chapter will add additional new real-life features of money and banking to the model and discuss several alternative measures of the money supply.)

> The **nominal money supply**, *M,* is the total dollar value of all paper money and coins in the economy.[1]

Example of Calculating Inflation

The U.S. CPI (measured using a base period of 1982 to 1984 = 100) was 160.3 in June 1997, and 163.0 in June 1998. Therefore the rate of inflation over this period was $100 \times (163.0 - 160.3)/160.3$, or 1.7 percent per year.

---

[1]This is the *currency* definition of money, to be discussed in the next chapter.

Figure 1 | Circular Flow

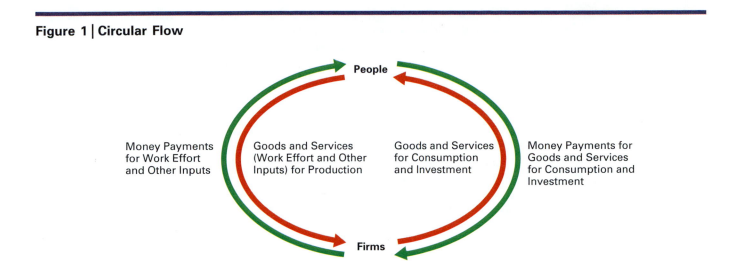

The velocity of money, *V*, equals the number of times someone spends each dollar (or yen) each year, on average. The price level, *P*, is the average nominal price of goods and services in the economy, measured by a price index such as the GDP deflator or the consumer price index.

The equation of exchange says that the nominal quantity of money (*M*) multiplied by the velocity of money (*V*) equals nominal GDP, or the price level (*P*) multiplied by real GDP (*y*):

$$MV = Py$$

This relationship implies that the price level equals the nominal money supply times velocity, divided by real GDP:

$$P = MV/y$$

The second equation shows that the price level depends on the nominal money supply, real GDP, and the velocity of money. Increases in the nominal money supply or velocity raise the price level, while increases in real GDP reduce the price level.

EXAMPLES

Think about an economy that produces 10 final goods each month, for a real GDP of 120 goods per year. Suppose also that its nominal money supply is $60. Each time the circular flow occurs, people spend $60 on goods. If people spend the money once per month, so velocity equals 1 per month (or 12 per year), then they buy 10 goods per month with $60, implying that each good costs $6. In this case, the equation of exchange becomes:

$$(\$60)(1 \text{ per month}) = (\$6 \text{ per good})(10 \text{ goods per month})$$

On an annual basis:

$$(\$60)(12 \text{ per year}) = (\$6 \text{ per good})(120 \text{ goods per year})$$

These equations can be rewritten in terms of the price level,:

$$\$6 \text{ per good} = \frac{(\$60)(1 \text{ per month})}{10 \text{ goods per month}} = \frac{(\$60)(12 \text{ per year})}{120 \text{ goods per year}}$$

Similarly, if people spend the nominal money supply *once* (rather than 12 times) per year, so that annual velocity equals 1, then they spend $60 each year to buy 120 goods, so each good must cost $0.50. In this case, the equation of exchange becomes:

$$(\$60)(1 \text{ per year}) = (\$0.50 \text{ per good})(120 \text{ goods per year})$$

SUPPLY AND DEMAND FOR MONEY

While the equation of exchange shows the relationship of the price level to the nominal money supply, real GDP, and velocity, it does not indicate the forces that affect those variables. Who controls the economy's nominal money supply? What determines the velocity of money, and what factors affect it? These questions lead to a discussion of supply and demand for money.

Money Supply

The government controls the economy's nominal supply of money, as defined earlier, printing paper money and minting coins.[2] U.S. nominal money supply, by this chapter's definition, was about $400 billion in 1998 (though people outside the United States hold much of it). This figure is about 8 times higher than a quarter century ago, and 350 times higher than a century ago. Governments of other countries have also increased their nominal money supplies. For example, the nominal money supply in Japan, by the same definition, is now about ¥50 trillion, 6 times its 1970 level.

Money Demand

Most people own some money, and carry it in their wallets. But money is just one of many assets that you can own. Other assets include stocks, bonds, bank accounts, land, art, jewelry, and Beanie Babies. When you save, you must decide what assets to own, and how much of each. You probably make your choice by comparing the benefits of each type of asset. For example, stocks, land, and Beanie Babies might increase in value; bonds and bank accounts pay interest; money is useful if you want to buy something at a store.

Costs and Benefits of Holding Money

Stocks, bonds, and bank accounts pay interest or dividends, but paper money and coins pay no direct returns. In fact, money *loses* value in times of inflation, because each dollar can buy fewer goods and services after prices increase. The *opportunity cost of owning money* is the nominal interest rate that you *could have* earned by putting that money in a bank account (or lending it by buying a bond).

Of course, holding money has benefits as well as costs. You cannot exchange a stock certificate, corporate bond, or piece of land for food at the grocery store. The special benefit of money is that you can spend it to buy goods and services.[3] The size of this benefit depends on many factors, such as the extent to which sellers accept credit cards or debit cards, and the time required for buyers to use such cards.

---

[2]The next chapter discusses other measures of the money supply and shows that the government does not have complete control over them. This result does not affect the main conclusions or logic in the current chapter.

[3]This fact ought to strike you as rather peculiar—why should other people give you goods and services you want in exchange for certain pieces of paper? Why will they accept some kinds of paper and not others? The answer to these questions are not obvious; these questions raise deep issues. Learning to raise questions, even if you cannot answer them, is an important skill that will make you a better economist.

Relative Price of Money in Terms of Goods

The relative price of sandwiches in terms of drinks is the opportunity cost of sandwiches; it equals the number of drinks you sacrifice for each sandwich. Similarly, the *relative price of money* in terms of goods is the opportunity cost of money—the number of goods you sacrifice for each unit of money. If goods cost $1 each, then you sacrifice one good for each dollar that you keep (rather than spending). If goods cost $2 each, then you sacrifice *half* of a good for each dollar that you keep (rather than spending). Clearly, the *relative price of money* in terms of goods equals the inverse of the price level (*P*):

Relative price of money in terms of goods = Inverse of price level = $1/P$

Quantity of Money Demanded

As Chapter 4 explained, your quantity of CDs demanded, at some relative price of CDs, is the amount that you would choose to buy at that price, *given* your income, wealth, tastes, the prices of related goods, and so on. Similarly, your *quantity of money demanded,* at some relative price of money, is the amount of money that you would choose to own, *given* your income, wealth, tastes, and other conditions.

> The **quantity of money demanded** at some relative price of money, is the amount of money that people would choose to own, given current conditions such as their income and wealth, the usefulness of money, and the costs and benefits of owning other assets.

Figure 2 graphs the demand for money. As usual, the demand curve slopes downward: As the relative price of money (1/*P*) falls, the quantity of money demanded rises. Because the relative price of money is the inverse of the price level, you can see that increases in the price level raise the quantity of money demanded.

Studies of money demand have drawn several conclusions:

1. The quantity of money demanded is proportional to the price level, *P*. Doubling the price level (cutting the relative price of money in terms of goods by half) doubles the quantity of money demanded. It is easy to understand why. When nominal prices double, people need twice as much money to buy the same goods and services as before, so they carry twice as much money in their wallets.

2. The quantity of money demanded rises as real GDP rises. On average, each 1 percent increase in real GDP raises the quantity of money demanded by about 1 percent. Again, it is easy to understand why. When people become 1 percent richer, they buy about 1 percent more goods and services, so they carry about 1 percent more money in their wallets.

3. The quantity of money demanded falls when the nominal interest rate rises. A rise in the nominal interest rate raises the opportunity cost of holding money, so it decreases the amount of money that people want to hold. Estimates of the magnitude of this effect vary, but an increase in the nominal interest rate from 5 percent to 6 percent per year may reduce the quantity of money demanded by about 5 percent.

4. The demand for money has changed in recent decades in the United States and many other countries. Economists do not yet fully understand the reasons for those changes.

In summary, a mathematical expression gives the demand for money:

$$M^d = Py/V$$

Advice
Don't get confused about money demand. A common confusion is to think, "My demand for money is 1 billion dollars—or maybe an infinite amount, because I would always want more." Of course you want more! So does everyone! They also want more vacations and movie tickets and CDs, but they do not have infinite quantities demanded for these things. The quantity demanded of any good refers to the amount that people would choose to buy, given their incomes and other conditions. (See Chapter 4.) Similarly, the quantity of money demanded refers to the amount that people would choose to own, given their incomes and other conditions.

   Example: You have saved a total of $1,000. If you decide to put $900 into the stock market and keep $100 in money to carry in your wallet, then your quantity of money demanded is $100. If conditions change, and you decide to put only $800 in the stock market and keep $200 cash in your wallet, then your demand for money *increases*. If conditions change, and you decide to put only $950 in the stock market and keep only $50 in your wallet, then your demand for money *decreases*.

Increasing the relative price of money in terms of goods and services, $1/P$, reduces the quantity of money demanded.

Figure 2 | Demand for Money

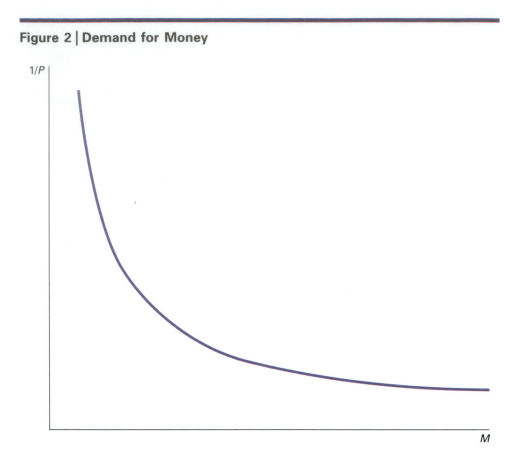

where M^d is the quantity of money demanded, P is the price level, y is real GDP (so Py is nominal GDP), and V is the velocity of money. Because the nominal interest rate is the opportunity cost of holding money, velocity is not a constant. It rises and falls with the nominal interest rate.

> Increases in the nominal interest rate raise the velocity of money; decreases in the nominal interest rate reduce velocity.

When the nominal interest rate rises, people spend their money faster than before. To see why, think about a country with a *very* high rate of inflation. That country has a very high nominal interest rate (recall the Fisher equation, discussed in Chapter 7). People in that high-inflation country spend their money very quickly after they receive it, before price increases reduce its value. As they quickly spend money, they create a very high velocity. In other words, an increase in the nominal interest rate raises the velocity of money.

An increase in the nominal interest rate raises the opportunity cost of holding money. As a result, people want to hold less money (and hold other assets, such as stocks and bonds, instead). Therefore, the quantity of money demanded falls. In the previous equation, an increase in the interest rate raises V, reducing M^d.

Equilibrium Price Level

Economists use the model of the supply and demand for money to analyze the equilibrium price level. Figure 3 shows equilibrium between the demand for money and the supply of money. The perfectly inelastic (vertical) supply of money curve shows the amount of money that the government has printed. The equilibrium relative price of money in terms of goods, $1/P_0$, gives the equilibrium price level, P_0.

> The **equilibrium price level** is the price level that equates the quantity of money demanded with the quantity supplied.

Essentially, the supply of money shows the amount of money *available* for people to hold, while the demand for money shows the amount that they *want* to hold (given their incomes, the relative price of money in terms of goods, and the benefits of holding other assets instead). Equilibrium occurs when people *want* to hold exactly the *available* amount. Mathematically, the quantity of money demanded equals the quantity supplied, M, so $M^d = M$, therefore:

$$MV = Py$$

where M is the quantity of money supplied, V is velocity, P is the price level, and y is real GDP. In other words, the equation of exchange, discussed earlier along with the circular flow, shows equilibrium between the demand and supply of money. Our analysis of the demand for money, however, shows that velocity is *not* a constant number; it rises and falls along with the nominal interest rate.

We can use the equation of exchange to examine factors that affect the equilibrium price level. We conclude that the equilibrium price level (P) rises when:

▶ The nominal money supply, M, rises
▶ The nominal interest rate rises, raising V
▶ Real GDP, y, falls

We also conclude that changes in underlying economic conditions do *not* affect the equilibrium price level *unless* they affect the nominal money supply, real GDP, or velocity.

Figure 3 | Equilibrium of Money Demand and Money Supply

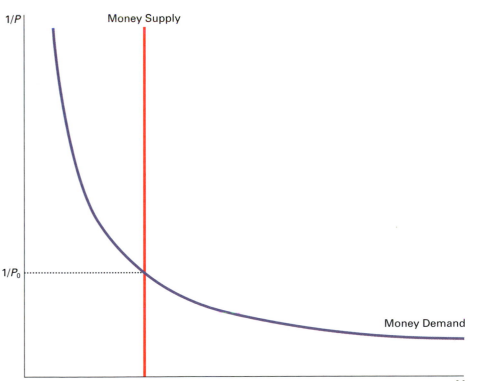

Equilibrium between money demand and money supply determines the equilibrium relative price of money in terms of goods (the inverse of the price level). Therefore, it determines the equilibrium price level.

If the price level is below its equilibrium level (P_0 is less than P_1), then the relative price of money in terms of goods exceeds its equilibrium level, creating a surplus in which the quantity of money supplied exceeds the quantity demanded. As a result, people spend the excess money, driving up prices until the price level rises to P_1, that is, until the relative price of money falls to its equilibrium.

Figure 4 | Adjustment to Equilibrium

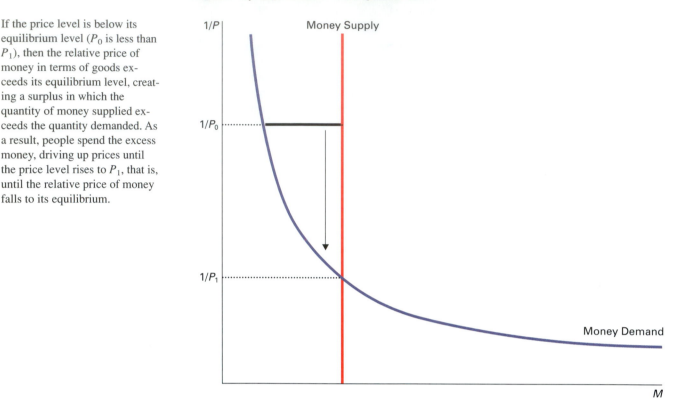

Adjustment to Equilibrium

If the price level is below its equilibrium level—so the relative price of money is *above* its equilibrium level—then the quantity of money supplied exceeds the quantity demanded, as in Figure 4. In this situation, people have more money (and fewer other assets such as stocks and bonds) than they want to hold, so they begin spending more money.

Any *one person* can trade money for stocks, bonds, and other assets, but *society as a whole* cannot trade away money.[4] Whenever one person spends the money, someone else receives it. Society as a whole is stuck with the amount of money that the government has printed—*someone* must hold it. However, as people spend more money, nominal prices rise moving the economy toward equilibrium. The relative price of money, $1/P$, falls as in Figure 4, raising the quantity of money demanded. In other words, the increase in the price level, P, raises Py/V. The price level rises until the quantity of money demanded equals the quantity supplied. At that point, the economy reaches its equilibrium.

Changes in Money Supply or Money Demand

Figure 5a shows the effect of an increase in the supply of money—the equilibrium relative price of money falls from $1/P_0$ to $1/P_1$, so the equilibrium price level rises from P_0 to P_1. Figure 5b shows the effect of an increase in the demand for money, perhaps due to an increase in real GDP, y, or a fall in velocity, V. A rise in the demand for money raises the equilibrium relative price of money from $1/P_0$ to $1/P_2$, reducing the equilibrium price level from P_0 to P_2.

---

[4]Thinking otherwise is an example of the *fallacy of composition,* discussed in Chapter 2.

Figure 5 | Effects of Changes in the Money Supply or Money Demand

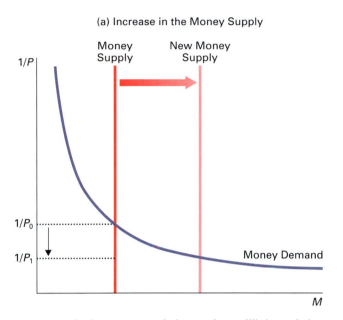

(a) Increase in the Money Supply

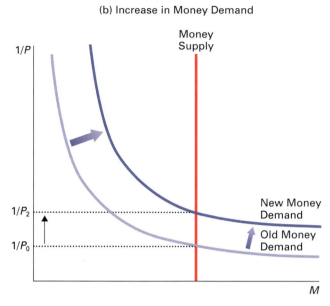

(b) Increase in Money Demand

An increase in the money supply lowers the equilibrium relative price of money in terms of goods, raising the equilibrium price level.

An increase in money demand raises the equilibrium relative price of money in terms of goods, lowering the equilibrium price level.

Review Questions

1. State and explain the equation of exchange.

2. Explain why an increase in the nominal interest rate reduces the quantity of money demanded.

3. Explain why an increase in the price level raises the quantity of money demanded.

4. Explain the relationship between the velocity of money and the quantity of money demanded. How is velocity affected by the nominal interest rate?

5. What happens if the price level is below its equilibrium? Explain why.

Thinking Exercises

6. Discuss this claim: "The quantity of money demanded is infinite because people always want more money."

7. How would the equilibrium price level react to: (a) an increase in the money supply? (b) an increase in the nominal interest rate caused by an increase in expected inflation? (c) an increase in real GDP?

An important real-life example of a change in the money supply occurs during a currency reform.

CURRENCY REFORMS

IN THE NEWS

Argentina slims peso by stripping off 0,000

By a Wall Street Journal Staff Reporter

With the Argentine peso wracked by a 210 percent inflation rate last year, the military government has decided to lop four zeros off each peso note.

Source: The Wall Street Journal

When the measure takes effect in about a month's time, a current 10,000-peso note will be called 1 peso. By the end of the year, the government hopes to phase out all the old notes and replace them with new units.

In 1967, the authorities resorted to a similar measure during a bout of inflation by converting 100 pesos into 1 peso. The new Argentine peso will be the equivalent of 1 million pesos of 1966.

A currency reform that reduced money and prices to 1/10,000 of their previous levels.

A **currency reform** occurs when the government of a country (a) replaces one kind of money with another, new kind of money, and (b) automatically adjusts all nominal values in existing contracts (such as nominal wages in employment contracts and nominal debts in loan contracts) for the change in money to keep *real* values the same.

The new money introduced in a currency reform often has a different name than the old money. Usually each unit of new money is worth many units of the old money. For example, each new dollar may be worth 1,000 old dollars. In that case, nominal values specified in existing contracts would automatically fall to one one-thousandth of their previously stated levels. If a firm owes a bank 2 million old dollars, and each *new* dollar is worth 1,000 in old dollars, then the firm owes 2,000 new dollars after the currency reform.

A currency reform does not affect real GDP. It does not affect the amount of goods and services a country produces, consumes, or invests; it leaves all *real* variables unchanged. Also, it leaves *relative* prices unchanged. It affects nominal values, however, because the nominal values are measured in the new, different money. When the new money is worth 1,000 units of the old money, all nominal prices measured in the new money equal one one-thousandth of the prices measured in the old money; nominal GDP and other nominal variables fall to one one-thousandth of their values before the currency reform. (Note one exception: The nominal interest rate does *not* change in this way.)

EXPLANATION AND EXAMPLE

The following fictional news report gives an example of exactly what happens every several years in some country, somewhere in the world: "President Announces New Money: One 'New Dollar' Worth Ten Old Dollars; Crossing off Zeros; Prices Fall," *America Today,* February 1, 2002:

> The president announced today that the United States would immediately issue "New Dollars" in place of old ones. Effective immediately, every $10 bill is now called one "New Dollar," every old $1 bill is now called

one "New Dime." Every old $5 bill is now called 50 "New Cents," and so on. People must cross a zero off each $10 and $20 bill they own (making the bills $1 and $2 bills). The same requirement applies to larger bills (a $100 becomes a $10 bill, for example). Also, people must relabel $1 bills as 10 cents, and so on. Pennies become 0.1 cent coins, and nickels become 0.5 cent coins. The government has announced that it will soon issue "New Dollars," which will look different than the familiar green paper money.

As part of the change, all wages, salaries, debts, and payments stated in all contracts will automatically fall to one-tenth of their previous levels. For example, anyone who has earned $10 per hour will now earn one New Dollar per hour. Anyone who owed a debt of $2,000 in old money automatically owes 200 New Dollars.

In a related development, major retailers announced reductions in prices to one-tenth of their previous levels. For example, a television that previously sold for $300 will now sell for 30 New Dollars. The president described the measure as a "victory for consumers." He called the policy a "currency reform" and said similar policies have been very successful in other countries.

The speaker of the House, a long-time political foe of the president, opposed the measure. "This is just a political ploy by the president," he said. "Sure, a bag of groceries that used to cost $40 will now cost $4, but so what? It still takes the same four $10 bills as before to pay for those groceries—all we've done is to cross a zero off of each bill and rename it. Now we'll call each of those $10 bills 'one dollar' and say that we pay only $4 for those groceries. Any fool can see this does not change anything except the name of the dollar bills. It doesn't change anything of real importance to American consumers."

A currency reform changes the units of measure for nominal prices and other nominal variables without affecting real prices and real variables.

If the United States were really to make this change, the move would have almost *no* effect on real GDP, real consumption and savings, real investment, and employment.[5] Everything real in the economy would continue as before, except the names of the pieces of paper money that people exchange to buy and sell. Where once people paid $10 they would pay one (new) dollar; where they once paid $4.50 they would pay 45 (new) cents.[6] The currency reform would affect only nominal values. Each person would have one-tenth as many dollars and collect one-tenth of her previous nominal wage, and all nominal prices would fall to one-tenth of their previous levels. This is what has happened in real-life currency reforms throughout the world.[7] It is also the main idea behind the *neutrality of money* discussed in Chapter 6.

Real-Life Currency Reforms

History records many cases of currency reforms. In every case, nominal prices changed by the same percentage as the nominal money supply, and the change had no perceptible effect on real variables such as real GDP or on relative prices. The most recent example of a currency reform occurred in 1998 when Russia dropped three zeros from its money, the ruble. As a result, the money supply fell to one one-thousandth of its

[5]The word *almost* appears in this sentence because a currency reform could make the economy somewhat more efficient by reducing the time required to count money and make change when people buy and sell goods. Clerks would spend less time counting the zeros on paper money after the currency reform.

[6]Where people once paid 25 cents for something, they would pay 2.5 new cents. If the government had issued no half-cent coin, then payments involving half cents would have to be rounded up or down to the nearest whole cent. The effects of this rounding on real variables, such as real GDP, would be very small.

[7]Economists' use of the term *nominal* reflects the fact that only the name of the money changes in a currency reform.

And in Bolivia: Weary from inflation that has hiked the price of a hamburger to 3 million pesos ($1.56), Bolivia will create a new currency by lopping six zeros from the peso's value and renaming it boliviano. One U.S. dollar now buys 1.9 million pesos; after Jan. 1, it will be worth 1.9 bolivianos. Argentina, Brazil, and Israel have taken similar steps.

Source: USA Today

A currency reform in Bolivia.

previous level, and nominal prices (in rubles per good) fell to one one-thousandth of their previous levels. This typical currency reform occurred, as most do, after a period of extremely high inflation.[8]

Similarly, Brazil introduced a new money in 1989, eliminating three zeros from its money and all nominal prices. As in Russia, the money supply and nominal prices fell to one one-thousandth of their previous levels, and the money's name changed. Brazil had another currency reform in 1994, introducing another new money. Bolivia had currency reforms in 1963 and 1987 (losing three zeros from its money and nominal prices in 1963 and six more zeros in 1987). Argentina had currency reforms in 1970 (losing two zeros from money and nominal prices), 1983 (losing five more zeros), 1985 (losing three more zeros), and 1992 (losing four more zeros). After several decades of extreme inflation, Argentina has had low inflation since the last currency reform. Other countries that have had currency reforms include France, in 1960, and Israel in 1980 and 1985.

Currency Reform in Reverse

Inflation resembles a *reverse* currency reform, introducing a new money worth *less* than the old money it replaces. For example, suppose that the government were to tell people to *add* a zero to every piece of money, so that $1 becomes $10, $5 becomes $50, and so

Argentina returns to peso, saving numerous zeros

By Nathaniel C. Nash
Special to
The New York Times

BUENOS AIRES, Feb. 8— For the fifth time in 21 years, Argentina has switched currencies. The country has officially stopped using the austral and returned to the peso, the name of the currency in many Spanish-speaking countries.

In leaving the austral behind last month, the administration of Carlos Saúl Menem is hoping to send a signal that stable times are here.

Introduced in June 1985, the austral, whose name refers to the southern-

most extremes of Argentina, was at first worth $1.40. Then hyperinflation took over. By the end of last year, the austral was worth one-hundredth of 1 cent. That implies that the dollar's appreciation against the austral was 1.39 million percent.

When the switch was made on Jan. 1, $1 was equal to almost 10,000 australs. With 10,000 australs converted to one peso, the dollar and the peso are equal in value.

"When we came to the point of considering the need to print a bill of a million australs, that touched

off an alarm that said we had to change," said Alvaro Otero, a spokesman for the country's central bank. "The calculator and computers we import do not have the capacity to do such large sums."

But lopping off zeros— this time four—is not new for Argentina. In the last 21 years, the national currency has lost 13 zeros. If no such changes had occurred, the price tag for a $1,400 stereo system in an electronic shop on Avenida Florida in downtown Buenos Aires would have to read 14,000,000,000,000,000.

Source: New York Times

A currency reform in Argentina.

---

[8]Some countries impose government controls on nominal prices that prevent prices from changing in proportion to the money supply. Uncontrolled prices and black-market prices, however, change in rough proportion to the money supply.

on. The nominal money supply would be ten times higher after the change, and all nominal prices would rise to ten times their previous levels. Real variables and relative prices would not change, though.

Inflation works like a reverse currency reform. The main difference is that a currency reform does not redistribute income, so it does not create winners and losers. In real-life episodes of inflation, however, some people may gain and others may lose as inflation redistributes income. A later section discusses these redistributions.

The rate of inflation is the growth rate of the price level.

EQUILIBRIUM INFLATION

> The **equilibrium rate of inflation** is the growth rate of the equilibrium price level.

Economists take growth rates of the variables in the equation $P = MV/y$ to solve for the equilibrium rate of inflation:

$$\%\Delta P = \%\Delta M + \%\Delta V - \%\Delta y$$

In this equation, $\%\Delta$ indicates the percentage change in the variable, which is its growth rate. For example, the $\%\Delta M$ from 1998 to 1999 equals the change in the money supply from 1998 to 1999, divided by its 1998 level.

This equation says that the rate of inflation equals the growth rate of the nominal money supply plus the growth rate of velocity minus the growth rate of real GDP. For example, if the growth rate of the money supply is 8 percent per year, the growth rate of V is zero (which means that velocity remains constant over time), and the growth rate of real GDP is 3 percent per year, then inflation is 5 percent per year.[9] Nothing affects the equilibrium rate of inflation unless it affects either growth rate of the money supply, the growth rate of velocity, or the growth rate of real GDP.

The equation indicates the sense in which inflation is caused by "too much money chasing too few goods," as a famous quote explains. If velocity is constant (its growth rate is zero), then inflation occurs if the growth rate of the nominal money supply exceeds the growth rate of real GDP. An increase in the growth rate of real GDP reduces the rate of inflation.

Short-Run and Long-Run Inflation and Money Supply Growth

Over short periods of time, the growth rate of the money supply often increases without raising inflation, and decreases without reducing inflation. Figure 6 shows the annual inflation rate and growth rate of money in recent years in the United States.[10] As the figure indicates, money growth and inflation are not closely related in the short run. Although large increases in the money growth rate preceded large increases in inflation in 1973 through 1975 and 1978 through 1980, short-run changes in inflation and money growth have not usually been closely connected.

Over longer periods of time, however, money growth and inflation move more closely together. Figure 7 shows the relationship between the average inflation rate and the average growth rate of the nominal money supply in the United States in various decades from 1870 to 1998. With only three exceptions (the decades of the 1880s, the

---

[9] If something remains constant, its growth rate is zero.

[10] The next chapter will discuss the definition of the nominal money supply, called *M2*, that appears in these Figures.

Figure 6 | Inflation and Money Growth in the United States (1960–1998)

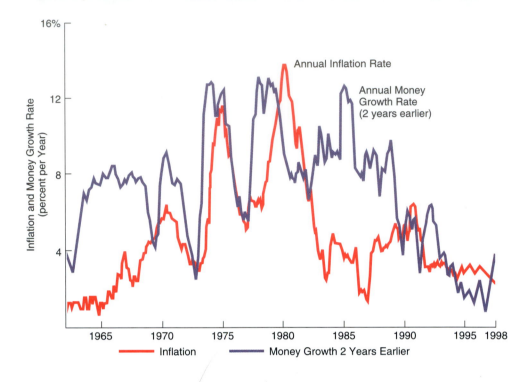

1930s, and the 1950s) the rate of inflation and the rate of money growth lie close together along the same line. This figure shows that nominal money growth and inflation are closely connected in the long run.

Similarly, differences in average inflation rates between countries over periods of several years or more are also related to differences in money growth rates. Countries whose nominal money supplies grow at high rates have high rates of inflation, and countries with low rates of nominal money growth have low rates of inflation.

Famous Episodes of Inflation

During the American Revolution, the colonies printed Continental Currency to pay for the war. The increase in the money supply caused inflation of 8.5 percent per month. Similarly, an increase in the growth rate of the money supply during the French Revolution caused inflation to average 10 percent per month.

During the U.S. Civil War, the money supply doubled in the North as the government printed paper money called *greenbacks* to pay for the war; the inflation rate was high enough that the wholesale price level doubled between 1861 and 1864.

The Confederacy (the South) also printed money to pay its cost of the U.S. Civil War. Inflation averaged 10 percent per month from October 1861 to March 1864. In May 1864, the Confederacy stopped increasing the money supply and actually reduced it with dramatic results. As one study put it, "Dramatically, the general price index dropped . . . in spite of invading Union armies, the impending military defeat, the reduction in foreign trade, the disorganized government, and the low morale of the Confederate army. Reducing the stock of money had a more significant effect on prices than these powerful forces."[11]

---

[11]Eugene Lerner, "Inflation in the Confederacy," in *Studies in the Quantity Theory of Money,* ed. by Milton Friedman (Chicago: University of Chicago Press, 1956).

Figure 7 | U.S. Inflation and Money Growth Rate by Decades, 1870s–1990s

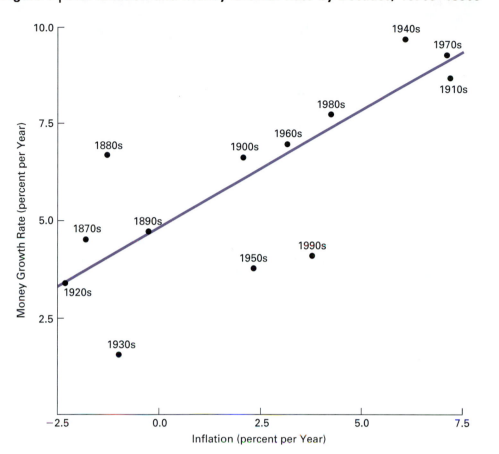

A famous case of hyperinflation occurred in Germany after World War I. The Treaty of Versailles that ended the war forced Germany to make large reparation payments to the Allied countries. The German government printed money rapidly to meet this obligation, and between August 1922 and November 1923, its money supply grew at an average rate of 314 percent per month. Inflation averaged 322 percent per month. The money supply and price level both increased by a factor of 10 million. In October 1923 alone, prices increased 32,000 percent.

In this case, as in many other times of hyperinflation, money lost value so fast that people could not wait to spend it. People would go to work, receive their pay (daily), and quickly spend the money before it lost value. Eventually, many German workers were paid two or three times a day; they would go to work in the morning, receive their pay, go out and spend the money before it lost value, then go back to work in the afternoon, receive partial pay again, and then quickly spend that money before it lost value. People took wheelbarrows full of money to stores to buy goods. Often the money weighed more than the groceries people could buy with it. Money became so worthless that people gave it to children as toys. It was cheaper to tie bundles of money together to make blocks than to buy blocks for children.

Other episodes of hyperinflation followed World War I in Austria, Hungary, Poland, and Russia. Greece experienced hyperinflation during World War II. But the biggest hyperinflation in recorded history occurred in Hungary after World War II. From August 1945 to July 1946, the money supply grew at 12,200 percent per month, and inflation averaged 19,800 percent per month. This rate amounts to 19.3 percent per day, or 0.74 percent per hour. In a year—the length of this

IN THE NEWS

When inflation rate is 116,000%, prices change by the hour

In Bolivia, the pesos paid out can outweigh purchases; No. 3 import: More pesos

LA PAZ, Bolivia—A courier stumbles into Banco Boliviano Americano, struggling under the weight of a huge bag of money he is carrying on his back. He announces that the sack contains 32 million pesos, and a teller slaps on a notation to that effect. The courier pitches the bag into a corner.

"We don't bother counting the money anymore," explains Max Loew Stahl, a loan officer standing nearby.

"We take the client's word for what's in the bag."

A 116,000% Rate?

Bolivia's inflation rate is the highest in the world. Prices go up by the day, the hour, or the customer. Julia Blanco Sirba, a vendor on this capital city's main street, sells a bar of chocolate for 35,000 pesos. Five minutes later, the next bar goes for 50,000 pesos. The two-inch stack of money needed to buy it far outweighs the chocolate.

The 1,000-peso bill, the most commonly used, costs more to print than it purchases. It buys one bag of tea. To purchase an average-size television set with 1,000-peso bills, customers have to haul money weighing more than 68 pounds into the showroom. (The inflation makes use of credit cards impossible here, and merchants generally don't take checks, either.)

Source: The Wall Street Journal

Living with hyperinflation.

Following World War I, Germany's currency became virtually worthless. Its value declined so much that parents could allow children to play with actual bundles of money more cheaply than they could buy building blocks.

period of hyperinflation—Hungary experienced an inflation rate of 3.81×10^{27} (3,810,000,000,000,000,000,000,000,000) percent. (Note that inflation compounds; a 10 percent per month inflation rate amounts to 214 percent per year, not 120 percent per year.)

Inflation and the Nominal Interest Rate

Inflation causes high nominal interest rates. The Fisher equation says that the nominal interest rate, R, equals the real interest rate, r, plus the expected rate of inflation, π^e:

$$R = r + \pi^e$$

Suppose that the real interest rate does not change when expected inflation changes. In this case, the equation shows that each 1 percentage point increase in expected inflation raises the nominal interest rate by 1 percentage point. Studies show that the real interest rate does not change, at least not very much, when inflation changes. Some studies show that the real interest rate falls slightly with higher inflation, but the fall in r is smaller than the rise in π^e, so an increase in expected inflation raises the nominal interest rate. Figure 8 shows the nominal interest rate and actual inflation in the United States from 1962 to 1998. When inflation rises, the nominal interest rate tends to rise also, because expected inflation tends to rise. For this reason, countries with high inflation also experience high nominal interest rates.

IN THE NEWS

Daily inflation struggle obsesses Brazil

Nation looks to president-elect for relief from price shock

By Thomas Kamm
Staff Reporter of
The Wall Street Journal

RIO DE JANEIRO—It was a balmy evening in Rio, the sort of weather that invites one to relax at an outdoor cafe in Copacabana or Ipanema and take in the beachfront action.

But on this particular recent evening the hottest spot in town wasn't one of the cafes, bars, or restau-

rants that line the city's coast. The place to be was the gas station.

"The price of gas is going up 60% at midnight, so I want to fill up my tank before that happens," explained a taxi driver as he pulled into the line at the Petrobras gas station on Copacabana's Avenida Atlantica. It was close to 11:30 p.m. and there were a good 30 cars ahead of him.

"I hope I reach the pump before midnight," he said. "Otherwise, my money will buy only 20 liters instead of 34."

In the 12 months ended in February, consumer prices here increased 2,751 percent. Restaurant patrons complain that the cost of their meals goes up as they eat. Shoppers complain that prices are marked up while they wait in checkout lines.

Sources: New York Times,
The Wall Street Journal

High inflation diverts people's time and resources from producing goods and enjoying life.

Inflation and Foreign Exchange Rates

From 1990 to 1997, Brazil had one of the highest rates of inflation in the world. The price level in 1997 was about *50,000 times* higher than it was in 1990. Over the same period, the price level in the United States rose only about 23 percent. As a result, the *foreign exchange rate* between Brazilian money and U.S. dollars increased by a factor of about 50,000.[12]

> An **exchange rate** is a price of one money in terms of another.

Most countries have their own forms of money. People buy and sell moneys on the foreign exchange market.

Table 1 shows foreign exchange rates between the U.S. dollar and the moneys of some other countries. The first column shows the country and the name of its money. (For example, Argentina uses pesos.) The next two columns show the price of the foreign money in terms of U.S. dollars, and the price of one U.S. dollar in terms of the foreign money. For example, one Japanese yen cost $0.0075, or about three-fourths of one cent. Stated the opposite way, one U.S. dollar cost ¥133. Similarly, one French franc costs about 17.5 cents, and $1 cost about 5.7 French francs.

For clarity, this chapter will refer to the exchange rate as the *price of foreign money*—the amount of domestic currency (such as U.S. dollars) needed to buy one unit of foreign money. This corresponds to the first column of the table. We will use the letter *e* to represent the exchange rate.

---

[12]Brazil had two currency reforms during this period, removing zeros from its money. Brazil's money is now called the *real*.

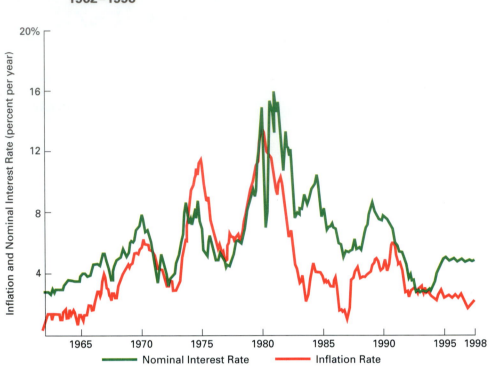

Figure 8 | Inflation and the Nominal Interest Rate in the United States, 1962–1998

The exchange rate *e* is the price of foreign money—the amount of home money required to buy one unit of foreign money.

(You will sometimes see exchange rates quoted the other way around, as in the second column in Table 1.)

When the exchange rate changes, *appreciation* means that the money becomes more valuable in terms of the other money (*e* falls); *depreciation* means that the money becomes less valuable (*e* rises).

A currency **appreciates** when less of that currency is needed to buy one unit of foreign money (*e* falls).

A currency **depreciates** when more of that currency is needed to buy one unit of foreign money (*e* rises).

For example, in January, 1996, about 100 Japanese yen were required to buy 1 U.S. dollar. By September, 1998, about 133 Japanese yen were needed to buy 1 U.S. dollar. Over that period, the yen depreciated, and the U.S. dollar appreciated.

How Exchange Rates Have Changed

Figure 9 shows the change in the exchange rate between the U.S. dollar and the Japanese yen since 1980. This graph shows the exchange rate from Japan's point of view: the Y-axis of the graph shows the *price of dollars* measured in terms of yen. An increase in the exchange rate in the figure means depreciation of the yen and appreciation of the U.S. dollar. The figure also shows the ratio of the price level in Japan to the price level

Table 1 | Exchange Rates, September, 1998

Country and Currency	US$ per Unit of Foreign Money	Units of Foreign Money per US$
	An increase in the number in this column represents *depreciation* of the U.S. dollar and *appreciation* of the foreign money.	An increase in the number in this column represents *depreciation* of the foreign money and *appreciation* of the U.S. dollar.
Argentine Pesos	1.0002	0.9998
Brazilian Real	0.8476	1.1798
British Pounds	1.6771	0.5962
Canadian Dollars	0.6596	1.5161
Chilean Pesos	0.0021219	471.20
Chinese Renmimbi	0.1208	8.2794
French Francs	0.1751	5.7126
German Marks	0.5872	1.7026
Indian Rupees	0.02355	42.451
Italian Lira	0.0005943	1682.9
Japanese Yen	0.007506	133.22
Mexican New Pesos	0.09511	10.514
Russian Rubles	0.1176	8.5000
South Korean Won	0.00072027	1388.4

Updated data are available on the Web page for this book at www.dryden.com

in the United States. Inflation was lower in Japan than in the United States over this period, so that ratio fell over time.

Exchange Rates and Prices

The exchange rate allows people to compare prices in different countries. Suppose that a compact disk costs £8.00 (8 British pounds) in England. If the exchange rate between the British pound and the dollar is $2.50 per pound, then the CD costs

Figure 9 | Exchange Rate: Japan-USA, 1980–1998

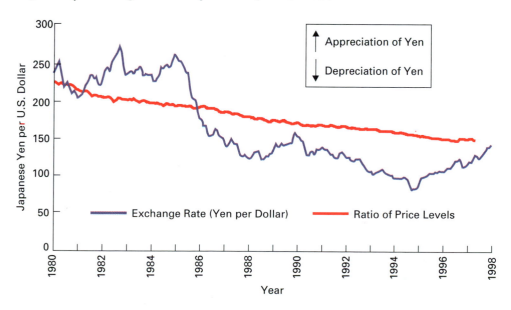

$20.00. To restate a foreign-money price in domestic money, multiply the foreign price by the exchange rate, where the exchange rate is defined as the price of foreign money.

> If P^f is an amount of foreign money and e is the exchange rate (the price of one unit of foreign money), then the equivalent amount of domestic money is eP^f.

In our example, the foreign price P^f is £8.00 and the exchange rate e is $2.50 per pound, so the equivalent dollar price is (£8.00)($2.50/£) = $20.00.

Suppose you see the same CD for sale on two Internet sites. One site, in London, quotes a price of £8.00, and the other site, in the United States, quotes a price of $20.00. Clearly, these two prices are equal if the exchange rate is $2.50 per pound. More generally, let P represent the price of a good in dollars and P^f denote the price in foreign money. The prices are the same if

$$P = eP^f.$$

If P exceeds eP^f then the good is cheaper in the foreign country; if P is less than eP^f then the good is cheaper in the United States.

The equation makes it easy to see how exchange rates are connected to inflation. Because the United States had higher inflation than Japan between 1980 and 1998, prices of goods in the United States increased faster than prices in Japan. If the exchange rate had not changed, U.S. goods would have become more expensive than Japanese goods, leading Americans to buy more from Japan at the lower prices there. Because Americans need yen to buy goods in Japan, this increase in imports raises the demand for yen, raising its price, the exchange rate. As a result, the U.S. dollar depreciated in terms of the yen between 1980 and 1998, as in Figure 9. Notice that while the exchange rate tracks the ratio of price levels on average over the period, it does not track the ratio of price levels every year.

> A country's money tends to *depreciate* on the foreign exchange market if that country has higher inflation than other countries.

Review Questions

8. Describe how a currency reform works. Explain why it changes nominal prices but not relative prices, without affecting real variables.

9. Cite examples of (a) currency reforms and (b) periods of high inflation or hyperinflation. What caused such high inflation?

10. How does a reverse currency reform resemble inflation?

11. What does it mean to say that a currency depreciates on foreign exchange markets?

Thinking Exercises

12. (a) If the growth rate of the money supply is 1 percent per year, the growth rate of velocity is 2 percent per year, and the growth rate of real GDP is 3 percent per year, what is the equilibrium rate of inflation? (b) If the growth rate of the money supply rises from 1 percent per year to 5 percent per year, what happens to the rate of inflation?

13. If the growth rate of the money supply is 5 percent per year, the growth rate of velocity is 1 percent per year, the growth rate of real GDP is 2 percent per year, and the real interest rate is 3 percent per year, what is the nominal interest rate?

14. You want to buy a T-shirt in Mexico that costs 50 pesos. If the exchange rate is $0.10 per peso, how many dollars does the T-shirt cost? A hotel in Italy charges 64,000 lira for a room for the night. If the exchange rate is 1,600 lira per dollar, what is the price of the room in dollars?

WHAT AFFECTS— AND DOESN'T AFFECT— INFLATION?

The equation of exchange, in its percentage-change form, is the key equation for inflation. Anything that raises inflation must either raise the growth rate of the money supply, raise the growth rate of velocity, or reduce the growth rate of real GDP. This section discusses commonly cited forces that do—and do not—cause inflation.

News reporters and commentators often blame inflation on some special forces that affect relative prices. However, these special forces may not affect the overall price level, which is an average of the nominal prices of the economy's goods and services. While relative prices depend on the supplies and demands for particular goods and services, the economy's price level is determined by the supply and demand for money.

A second common fallacy confuses a high price level with a rising price level. Some factor, such as a low level of real GDP, may cause the price level to be high without causing it to continue to rise. The words *high* and *rising* do not mean the same thing! For example, the equation $P = MV/y$ implies a high price level associated with low real GDP. It also implies that the price level rises when real GDP falls. It does not say, however, that the price level *rises* due to a low *level* of real GDP, so it does not say that a low level of real GDP causes inflation. An analogy may help to explain the distinction. If you maintain a high effort level in a class, you will likely receive high grades on exams. However, a high level of effort does not imply that your exam grades will *increase* as the class continues. Improving grades would require *increases* in effort as the class continues. *High* levels of effort and *increasing* levels of effort are not the same thing.

Any change in conditions can raise inflation if that change causes the government to raise the growth rate of the money supply. Similarly, any change in conditions can raise the price level, raising inflation temporarily, if it causes people to reduce the quantity of money they demand, raising velocity. Except as indicated, the following paragraphs assume that the government does not change the money supply.

Suggested Causes of Inflation

1. Greed

Business firms want high profits, but greed for high profits does not cause inflation. Two fallacies mar the reasoning that greed causes inflation. First, sellers almost always want more profits. If sellers could increase their profits by raising their prices, they would already have done so![13] While greed might make prices high, it does not cause prices to continually *increase* over time. (The assertion to the contrary is an example of the fallacy of equating high prices with rising prices.) The episodes of hyperinflation discussed earlier did not occur because sellers suddenly became greedy—they were *always* greedy, looking for the highest profits they could capture. Nor did the episodes end because sellers suddenly became

---

[13] Why doesn't a seller increase its profits by raising its prices? Because the seller would lose enough sales to competitors, including sellers of other, substitute products, that raising prices would not increase its profits. That is, sellers charge the prices that give them the highest profits they can get, so any further price increases would reduce profits by changing prices from their profit-maximizing levels.

less greedy. Similarly, the fall in U.S. inflation from over 5 percent in 1991 to 2 percent in 1998 did not occur because sellers' greed decreased; greed has nothing to do with inflation.

The second fallacy in the claim that greed causes inflation results from ignoring equilibrium between the quantity of money demanded and quantity supplied. If the nominal money supply, velocity, and real GDP do not change, then the equilibrium price level does not change. Only factors that affect the growth rates of money, velocity, or real GDP can affect inflation.

2. Monopoly Sellers

Monopoly sellers charge higher prices than sellers that face more competition, but monopolies do not cause inflation. The idea that they do suffers from the same two fallacies as the idea that greed causes inflation. First, it confuses high levels of prices with increasing prices, as discussed above. A monopoly does not continually raise prices; it charges the price that gives it the highest profit and keeps its price at that level.

Second, the idea that monopolies cause inflation ignores equilibrium between the demand and supply of money, confusing relative prices with the price level. A monopoly charges a high *relative* price, but the equilibrium price level averages *nominal* prices of goods and services. It reflects equilibrium between the quantities of money demanded and supplied, as in the equation of exchange.

3. Low Productivity

Low productivity means that real GDP is lower than it would otherwise be (with higher productivity). Low productivity, therefore, means that the price level is higher than it would otherwise be, but not that the price level is *increasing*. Low productivity does not cause inflation.

A low *growth rate* of productivity, however, may cause a low growth rate of real GDP and therefore a high rate of inflation. The percentage change equation shows that high inflation occurs with a low growth rate of real GDP. However, a change in productivity growth has only a small effect on inflation. For example, a 1 percentage point fall in the growth rate of real GDP, from 3 percent per year to 2 percent per year (a large fall in the growth rate of real GDP), raises inflation by only 1 percentage point, such as from 3 percent per year to 4 percent per year. As a result, changes in the growth rate of real GDP explain only a small fraction of changes in real-life inflation. Similarly, differences among countries' growth rates of real GDP explain only small fractions of differences in inflation rates between countries.

4. Government Regulations

Government regulations, like low productivity, may cause low real GDP and a high price level. Regulations cause a *rising* price level, however, only if they reduce the growth rate (not just the level) of real GDP. As in the case of low productivity growth, regulations have a very small effect on inflation.

5. Increase in the Price of an Important Good

News reporters and commentators often say that inflation results from an increase in the price of some particular good or set of goods. Such a statement is usually a mistake. An increase in the price of any particular good or service can cause inflation only if it raises the growth rate of money or the growth rate of velocity, or if it reduces the growth rate of real GDP.

It is easy to see why someone might make this mistake. Whenever inflation occurs, most prices rise, so someone might easily think, incorrectly, that the price increases cause inflation when, in fact, the price increases *are* inflation. Saying that a price increase causes inflation is like saying that falling raindrops cause rain.[14]

Fallacies about inflation in the news media.

---

[14]A similar fallacy states that unemployment is caused by people losing their jobs, a famous observation of President Calvin Coolidge.

Think about a change in demand. If people decide to eat more vegetables and less meat than before, then the demand for vegetables rises and the demand for meat falls. This raises the *relative* price of vegetables and reduces the *relative* price of meat, but it does not change the overall price level, because the money supply, velocity, and real GDP do not change. The nominal price of vegetables rises, but the nominal price of meat *falls,* leaving the overall price level roughly unaffected.

6. High Wages

High wages, perhaps due to strong unions, do not cause inflation. The idea that they do confuses levels with changes, as discussed earlier. High wages might cause high prices, or vice versa, but high wages do not cause *rising* prices.

Increases in wages can raise the price of a good by reducing its supply. An *increase* in union power could raise wages throughout the economy and reduce employment. Figure 10 shows the demand for labor by firms, which depends on the *real wage* (the purchasing power of the nominal wage). Figure 10 represents the real wage by the nominal (money) wage, W, divided by the price level, P. If the money wage, W, and the price level, P, rise by the same percentage (for example, if they both double), then the purchasing power of the wage, the real wage, remains unchanged.

If unions raise the nominal wage from W_1 to W_2 when the price level does not change, the real wage rises from W_1/P to W_2/P, and the quantity of labor demanded falls from L_1 to L_2. This reduces employment from L_1 to L_2 and increases unemployment. This fall in employment reduces the economy's total output of goods and services, real GDP, which raises the equilibrium price level. As a result, the economy experiences *cost-push inflation* (inflation due to an increase in wages or other costs of production) as the price level rises to reach its new, higher equilibrium level. However, this inflation is only temporary; it stops when the price level reaches a new, higher level associated with the lower level of real GDP. In addition, this effect is small in real life. Even a permanent 2 percent fall in real GDP, which would be fairly large compared to most real-life changes in real GDP, would raise the price level permanently by only 2 percent, temporarily adding 2 percentage points to inflation. This increase in inflation is small compared to most real-life inflation experiences.

Cost-push inflation may also occur for a second reason. The increase in unemployment resulting from an increase in wages above the equilibrium level might lead the government to increase the money supply.[15] Such an increase in the money supply, sometimes said to "validate the wage increase," would raise the price level. The rise in the price level in turn would reduce the real wage (the increase in P would reduce W/P), raising the quantity of labor demanded, and employment, back to L_1, and reducing unemployment. Although firms would pay higher nominal wages than before, they could also charge higher prices for their products, allowing them to hire L_1 workers.

If unions and the government act this way, a wage–price spiral can result. Unions see that the increase in the price level reduces the real wage, so they raise nominal wages again. Similarly, the government may again increase the money supply, further raising the price level. Inflation continues, and the rate may even increase, until either the unions or the government change their behavior. While the wage–price spiral may be important in some episodes of inflation, especially in countries with strong unions that operate in many industries, it is not the main explanation for most episodes of inflation. Evidence shows no strong connection between a country's rate of inflation and the strength of its unions.[16]

7. Rising Interest Rates

Sometimes people claim that inflation results from rising interest rates. They see interest

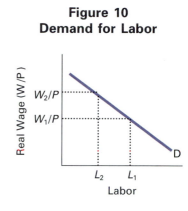

**Figure 10
Demand for Labor**

Higher pay may be pushing up prices

Our wages and benefits are rising at a faster pace and may soon land in shopping bags as slightly higher prices.

Robert Dederick, chief economist at Northern Trust Co. in Chicago, says you can bet businesses "will certainly make every effort to pass those costs on to consumers."

Source: USA Today

Another fallacy about inflation in the news media—the article never mentions the fact that the price level will increase only if the government raises the money supply.

---

[15] Later chapters will discuss possible reasons for this reaction.

[16] Of course, wages do usually rise with prices during inflation, but this effect is part of the process of inflation (as rain drops are part of the process of rain), not a cause of inflation.

> ### IN THE NEWS
>
> # Inflation Stays Under Control
>
> Washington—Inflation stayed under control in July, helped in part by falling prices for energy, produce and telephone service.
>
> Despite labor shortages that have begun to drive up wages—which can prompt price increases from companies seeking to maintain their profits—inflation has remained contained. It's running at a 1.6 percent annual rate this year, compared to 1.7 percent for all of last year. That's partly because hard times in other countries have dampened world demand for many products, lowering prices on commodities from gasoline to coffee.
>
> *Source: Associated Press*

Find the economic errors in this news article.

rates as a cost of doing business, so rising interest rates seem to them to raise business costs and create higher prices. This argument confuses relative prices with the nominal price level by forgetting that the equilibrium nominal price level is determined by the equation between the supply and demand for money. A rise in the nominal interest rate is more likely to *result* from an increase in inflation (as discussed earlier) than to cause that increase.

8. Government Budget Deficits

Government budget deficits can cause inflation in two ways. When the government spends more than it collects in taxes, it must choose from two options:

1. Print money to spend in excess of its tax revenue.

2. Borrow money to spend in excess of its tax revenue.

If the government prints money, the money supply and the price level increase. In this way, a deficit causes temporary inflation, and deficits that continue year after year can create continuing inflation, if the government finances them by printing money.

If the government borrows money to finance its deficit, the increased demand for loans can raise the interest rate, which, in turn, raises the velocity of money and therefore the price level. An earlier chapter discussed the effects of a government budget deficit, which raises the real interest rate unless people save all the money that they get from the tax cut.

Government budget deficits and inflation show no close relationship in the United States, however. For example, inflation in the United States decreased during the 1980s as government budget deficits rose. In some countries, though, particularly less developed countries, governments often finance budget deficits by printing money, and deficits and inflation tend to occur together.

9. International Competition

Sometimes people claim that increases in international competition hold down inflation, because sellers cannot then raise prices without losing business to those foreign sellers. This incorrect claim confuses relative prices with nominal prices. An increase in international competition in the automobile industry reduces the relative price of automobiles, but has no direct effect on the nominal price level, unless it affects the money supply, velocity, or real GDP.

IN THE NEWS

Keener competition among producers keeps price increases, inflation at bay

*By Erle Norton and
David Wessel
Staff Reporters of
The Wall Street Journal*

In most recoveries, companies use increased demand as an excuse to raise prices—and with them, the inflation rate. But not this time.

The difference is intense competition. In this recovery, producers have been plagued by a fear that cutthroat rivals will rob them of market share if they raise prices. That market-share mentality, particularly in industries without dominant producers, has fostered intense competition that outweighs the normal tendency toward higher prices and profit margins.

Producers in many industries—diaper makers, tire manufacturers, food companies, clothing peddlers and electronics concerns, among others—are complaining that competition has kept price increases off the books. That keeps inflation at bay.

Source: The Wall Street Journal

Find the economic errors in this news article.

Review Questions

15. Explain the effects on inflation of:
    (a) Greed
    (b) Low productivity
    (c) An increase in international competition
    (d) High wages
    (e) A fall in the government budget deficit

Thinking Exercises

16. What would happen if unions were to raise wages, sellers were to raise nominal prices to "pass along the higher wage costs to consumers," and the money supply were to remain unchanged?

17. Identify at least one error in economics in the news article, "Keener Competition among Producers Keeps Price Increases, Inflation at Bay." Explain why it is an error.

Winners and Losers

EFFECTS OF INFLATION

Some people lose from inflation, but others gain. Everyone who holds money loses, because the real value of the money (its purchasing power) falls.

The loss that people suffer when inflation reduces the purchasing power of their assets is called the **inflation tax.**

Inflation acts like a tax on holding money. Your money loses 10 percent of its value if prices rise 10 percent. You suffer the same loss as if you were required to give 10 percent of your money to the government as a tax payment.

The government gains when it prints money, because it can spend the money. Saying that "the government gains" really means that certain people gain—those people who benefit from whatever the government buys with the money. Suppose that the government raises the money supply by 10 percent, raising prices 10 percent. The government's gain from printing money equals 10 percent of the money supply. Because prices rise 10 percent, the money that people already have in their wallets loses 10 percent of its value. In this way, the people who hold money pay an inflation tax equal to 10 percent of the money supply. The gain to the government from the inflation tax equals the losses to holders of money.

Unexpected Inflation

If inflation is unexpected—if prices rise more rapidly than people thought they would—then it creates winners and losers:

▶ Debtors (people who have borrowed money) gain.

▶ Creditors (people who have loaned money) lose.

Debtors gain because they repay loans in dollars with lower purchasing power than the dollars they borrowed. They repay the same number of dollars, but each dollar buys fewer goods, so inflation reduces the purchasing power of the debt repayment. Unexpected inflation reduces the opportunity cost of paying off the loan. Creditors lose what debtors gain, because they collect dollars with lower purchasing power than those they lent.

Similarly, if inflation is lower than people had expected, debtors lose and creditors gain. The nominal interest rate reflects the inflation rate that people had expected, so unexpectedly low inflation means that the nominal interest rate overcompensates lenders for their loss in purchasing power.

Expected Inflation

When inflation is fully expected—when people correctly anticipate the actual rate of inflation—the nominal interest rate exceeds the real interest rate by the rate of inflation. In this way, the interest rate on the loan rises enough to offset the reduction in purchasing power of the dollars with which the borrower repays the loan. Even though each dollar that a borrower repays to a lender buys fewer goods due to inflation, the rise in the nominal interest rate requires borrowers to pay enough to counteract that loss in purchasing power. Neither debtors nor creditors gain or lose from fully expected inflation.

Indexing Contracts

Unexpected increases in inflation help debtors at the expense of creditors only if loans are not *indexed* to inflation. A wage is indexed to inflation if the nominal wage automatically changes with the price level (that is, if the wage contract specifies a cost-of-living adjustment, or COLA). With complete indexing, the nominal wage rises by the same percentage as the price level, keeping the real wage constant. Most wages in the United States and (most) other countries are *not* indexed to inflation. However, social security payments in the United States are indexed to inflation: Increases in the price level automatically raise nominal social security payments.

When a wage is *not* indexed to inflation, an unexpected increase in inflation reduces the real wage, so firms gain and workers lose. Similarly, an unexpected fall in inflation raises the real wage, so workers gain and firms lose.

Is Inflation Bad?

If inflation worked exactly like a reverse currency reform, no one would care much about it. After all, nominal prices are not very important. In a currency reform, all nominal prices change, but nothing real changes: relative prices, real GDP, and people's real incomes remain unaffected.

Most people think that inflation is bad because rising prices reduce the amount of goods that people can afford. This statement is true for an individual with a fixed income, but it is false for society as a whole. Inflation does not necessarily make society, as a whole, poorer. A country's real income is its real GDP, which is determined primarily by technology, available inputs, and other factors that do not respond to changes in nominal prices. In the long run, at least, the government cannot affect real GDP simply by printing *pieces of paper* called money.

Some economists, in fact, believe that inflation is *not* very important as long as it remains steady so that everyone can learn to expect it and adjust to it. In that case, inflation does not redistribute income from creditors to debtors. Although people lose from inflation as the purchasing power of their money falls (the inflation tax), the government gains by printing the extra money that causes prices to rise. In this case, the inflation tax is like any other tax, and the government must collect *some* taxes, after all, to finance its spending. According to this view, steady inflation has little or no effect on the economy's real income, so steady inflation is not a serious problem as long as the rate does not become too high (not above about 2 or 3 percent per year, for example).

Other economists believe that inflation is a serious problem that creates economic inefficiencies and harms people. Inflation differs from a reverse currency reform, because it redistributes income and continually changes the basic unit of measurement for prices, the dollar (or yen, franc, or peso). A currency reform changes the

Inflation: Some like it

Just when you thought inflation was history, here it comes again. But while most of us nervously await its arrival, some are secretly rolling out the red carpet.

They're the USA's closet inflation-lovers, the ones for whom the gains of rising prices outweigh the losses.

To the rest of us, though, inflation is still a bogeyman. "Inflation is bad and has a very insidious effect in that it erodes value while people aren't looking," says Wayne Gantt, an economist at SunTrust Banks Inc. in Atlanta. "For every winner in inflation, there's a loser."

Source: USA Today

Some people gain from inflation.

IN THE NEWS

Argentina in chaos as prices rise hourly

By James Brooke
Special to
The New York Times

BUENOS AIRES— "Weimar Germany never had an I.B.M. computer," Adrián Rodríguez Boero said today, explaining with a wry smile how he manages to keep his supermarket ahead of Argentina's annual inflation rate of 12,000 percent.

"Every four hours, these prices lose 1 percent of their value," he said, surveying the well-stocked aisles of the Disco supermarket. With all produce tagged with bar codes, the prices are adjusted daily on a central computer.

The rub for Argentines is that their salaries do not increase by 1 percent every four hours.

In the last week, food prices jumped 27 percent. With food climbing out of reach, poor people responded by sacking hundreds of food stores across the nation.

The riots have left 15 people dead and about 80 wounded. In addition, about 1,700 people have been arrested around the country.

Here, at the Disco in downtown Buenos Aires, shoppers pushed loaded carts through the aisles in panic shopping.

"People want their money in something solid," Mr. Rodríguez Boero said, grasping a box of oatmeal for emphasis.

Source: New York Times

Redistributions of income caused by inflation create social problems.

Inflation creates uncertainty and erodes confidence.

amount of money that everyone has in the same proportion, but inflation redistributes income. When the government prints additional money, most people don't get any! Furthermore, critics of inflation point out, low and predictable inflation might not be a serious problem; however, few if any real-life episodes of inflation have stayed low and predictable over any sustained period of time. While a relatively harmless low and predictable inflation is a theoretical possibility, it may be difficult to maintain in real life.

We can summarize the main points on both sides. Inflation may be *bad* for several reasons:

▶ Inflation wastes valuable time and resources as people adjust to rising prices. For example, inflation raises the nominal interest rate and reduces the quantity of money demanded, raising velocity and reducing the benefits of money as a convenient method of payment. During hyperinflation, people try to spend the money they receive very quickly before it loses value. Sometimes they resort to barter and other inefficient methods of trade.

▶ Inflation wastes resources in financial markets by creating costly new methods for people to avoid personal losses due to inflation.

▶ Inflation is like changing the length of an inch every year or continually changing the definition of a pound or a quart. Inflation distorts nominal prices and prevents people from easily comparing prices of different goods at different times. This leads people and business firms to make mistakes in their economic decisions, creating inefficiencies.

▶ Inflation creates uncertainty that causes economic inefficiency. For reasons that economists do not yet fully understand, high rates of inflation are more variable and unpredictable than low rates. People generally dislike the increased uncertainty associated with inflation.

▶ Inflation raises certain taxes in a subtle way without an open and honest government policy of raising taxes.

▶ Unexpected inflation harms people by redistributing income. It penalizes people who work and save, because savers usually become creditors who lose from unexpected inflation. Similarly, the redistributions caused by inflation take from some people and give to others with no regard for either property rights or any notions of fairness.

On the other hand, inflation may have *good* effects. People may feel happier, perhaps irrationally, when their nominal wages rise, even if their real wages remain constant (because their nominal wage increases merely compensate them for price-level increases).

Suppressed Inflation

Many governments have imposed price and wage controls to try to reduce inflation, often while they were printing money at rapid rates.

Suppressed inflation refers to inflation that would occur without government controls on wages and prices, but that does not fully occur due to those controls.

Government efforts to suppress inflation have a long history. The money supply in the Roman Empire rose rapidly starting in A.D. 296 under Emperor Diocletian, causing the Roman inflation mentioned in the introduction to this chapter. In response, Diocletian issued a famous Edict on Maximum Prices that set maximum legal prices on 900 goods and maximum legal wages for 130 types of work, imposing the death penalty for violations on both buyers and sellers. These wage and price controls failed to stop inflation, although numerous people were executed before Diocletian abdicated the throne. Almost 1,700 years later, President Nixon imposed price controls in the United States in 1971 when the country's inflation rate reached 4.5 percent per year. Between the Roman and U.S. episodes, many other tries at price controls (often during wartime bouts of inflation) nearly always created shortages and economic inefficiencies, led to black markets (illegal transactions to avoid the controls), and ultimately failed to stop inflation.[17] A recent attempt to control inflation with price controls began in Russia in 1998, when the government imposed price controls on food and other items in an attempt to prevent inflation while it began increasing the money supply more rapidly.

Review Questions

18. Who gains from inflation? Who loses? Does the answer depend on whether inflation is expected or unexpected? Why?

19. Is inflation bad? Defend both *yes* and *no* answers to this question.

IN THE NEWS

Moscow puts price controls on food

Now merchants struggle along with their customers

MOSCOW—In this time of crisis, store manager Farik Dabibov is having trouble remaining diplomatic about a decision by Moscow's mayor to control the price of baby food. "It's going to be a serious problem, and our salaries are going to get cut," said Dabibov, a store manager with a baby goods chain in Moscow. "Now we're just waiting to see what the government is going to do with us next."

Mayor Yuri Luzhkov decreed Tuesday that city retailers may not mark up basic food products by more than 20 percent, at least until Nov. 1. The list includes 27 categories such as sausage, cooking oil, sugar, matches—and baby food. Many small stores already pummeled by the crisis said the decree would push them closer to bankruptcy. "It's turning my work into a total mess," said Mikhail Kochetkov, who runs a small market. "I think about 20 percent of businesses will survive the decree. We're certainly not going to survive."

Source: Associated Press

Price controls will create shortages without stopping the underlying causes of inflation.

IN THE NEWS

Russia's New Government to Print Rubles to Pay Debts

MOSCOW—Russia's new Communist-influenced government indicated Thursday that it plans to satisfy old debts and bail out old friends by printing billions of new rubles, a decision that drew a swift and strong reaction from President Boris Yeltsin's capitalist allies.

Hours later in Washington, Deputy Treasury Secretary Lawrence Summers told a House subcommittee that Russia was heading toward a return of the four-digit inflation rates that savaged consumers and almost toppled Yeltsin's government in 1993. Russia's new leaders cannot repeal "basic economic laws," he said. "They must resist pressures to spend and lend which will doom the economy to another bout of high, perhaps hyperinflation."

Source: New York Times

As this textbook went to press, Russia had just announced that it would start increasing the supply of money. Has Russia followed through with this plan? Has inflation in Russia increased?

---

[17]Some people argue for wage and price controls in periods of high inflation on the grounds that by enacting them, a government shows people it is serious about reducing inflation. This action could help reduce expected inflation, reducing the nominal interest rate and the velocity of money and helping to hold down price increases until the government can attack inflation in other ways. However, wage and price controls can create serious distortions in the economy, and they cannot ultimately reduce inflation unless the government also reduces the rate of growth of the money supply. Moreover, if people view wage and price controls as a desperate measure or an indication that the government lacks the political will to fight inflation by reducing the rate of money growth, then wage and price controls may actually raise inflationary expectations and compound the difficulty of stopping it.

A fascinating history of wage and price controls appears in Robert Schuettinger and Eamonn Butler, *Forty Centuries of Wage and Price Controls: How Not to Fight Inflation* (Thornwood, N.Y.: Caroline House, 1979).

20. How does inflation impose a tax? What does it tax? Who collects the tax revenue?

21. Explain why fully expected inflation does not redistribute income from creditors to debtors.

Conclusion

Definitions and Basic Model

Nominal variables are quantities measured in units of money (U.S. dollars, Mexican pesos, etc.). In contrast, *real* variables are quantities measured in units of goods and services or in units of base-year money. *Nominal* prices are money prices of goods and services. *Relative* prices are the opportunity costs of goods, measured in terms of other goods. Inflation, a continuing increase in the (nominal) price level, refers to changes in *nominal* variables, not (necessarily) *real* variables such as relative prices.

The circular flow diagram of economic activity illustrates the equation of exchange, $MV = Py$, where M is the nominal money supply, V is velocity, P is the price level, and y is real GDP. The equation of exchange implies that the price level can be expressed as $P = MV/y$.

Supply and Demand for Money

The government controls the nominal money supply, defined as the total dollar value of all paper money and coins in the economy. Money is just one among many assets that people can own. Each asset has costs and benefits. A benefit of owning money is that you can spend it at a store. However, money does not pay interest. The nominal interest rate measures the opportunity cost of holding money (rather than putting the money in a bank account or lending it).

The *relative price of money* in terms of goods is the opportunity cost of money—the number of goods you sacrifice for each unit of money you keep (rather than spending). The relative price of money in terms of goods equals $1/P$, the inverse of the price level. The *quantity of money demanded* at some relative price of money, is the amount of money that people would choose to own, given current conditions such as their income and wealth, the usefulness of money, and the costs and benefits of owning other assets. Evidence shows that the nominal quantity of money demanded is proportional to the price level. It rises as real GDP rises, and falls as the nominal interest rate rises.

Economists summarize the demand for money with a formula that defines the quantity of money demanded as proportional to GDP, $M^d = Py/V$. Increases in the nominal interest rate raise the velocity of money, so they reduce the demand for money. The equilibrium price level, the price level for which the quantity of money demanded equals the quantity supplied, can be expressed as $P = MV/y$. The equilibrium price level rises with increases in the money supply and velocity, and falls with increases in real GDP.

Currency Reforms

A currency reform occurs when the government of a country replaces an old unit of money with a new unit of money and automatically adjusts all nominal values in existing contracts (such as nominal wages and debts) for the change in money to keep real values the same. Each unit of new money is usually worth more than a unit of old money. (The new money often crosses off several zeros from the old money.) A reverse currency reform would add zeros to money, effectively raising the nominal money supply and nominal prices. Inflation resembles a reverse currency reform, except that inflation may create winners and losers by redistributing income in ways that a currency reform does not.

Equilibrium Inflation

The equilibrium rate of inflation is the growth rate of the equilibrium price level. It equals the growth rate of the nominal money supply, plus the growth rate of velocity, minus the growth rate of real GDP. Over long periods of time, inflation and the growth rate of the money supply are closely related. Over short periods of time, however, they are not closely related. High rates of inflation raise the nominal interest rate.

An exchange rate is a price of one money in terms of another. A currency appreciates when its value rises in terms of foreign money, so that fewer units of the currency are required to buy one unit of foreign money. A currency depreciates when its value falls in terms of foreign money. A country's money tends to depreciate on the foreign exchange market if that country runs higher inflation than other countries.

What Affects—and Doesn't Affect—Inflation?

Anything that raises inflation must either raise the growth rate of the money supply, raise the growth rate of velocity, or reduce the growth rate of real GDP. News commentators commonly blame inflation on special forces that do not affect those variables; their assertions involve a fallacy of confusing changes in relative prices with changes in the price level, which is an average of nominal prices. In another common source of error, people often confuse a high price level with a rising price level, although the words *high* and *rising* have different meanings.

These fallacies explain why the greed of business firms, the actions of monopoly sellers, low levels of productivity, and high levels of government regulation do not cause inflation. Similarly, they explain why an increase in the price of a particular good, however important that good, need not cause inflation unless it accompanies a fall in the economy's overall real GDP. For the same reasons, high wages do not cause inflation. *Increases* in wages, however, may lead the government to raise the nominal money supply, and in this way, create inflation. Increased foreign competition reduces the relative prices of products experiencing that competition, but increased foreign competition does not directly affect the (nominal) price level or inflation.

Effects of Inflation

Some people lose and others gain from inflation. Everyone who holds money loses, because inflation reduces the purchasing power of money. This loss is the inflation tax. The government collects revenue from the inflation tax, because it prints and spends the money that causes the inflation. The government also gains from inflation, because some taxes (those not indexed to the price level) automatically rise with inflation.

Unexpected inflation redistributes income from creditors to debtors. Debtors gain from unexpectedly high inflation, because they repay loans in dollars with lower purchasing power; creditors lose what debtors gain. When people fully expect inflation, in contrast, the nominal interest rate exceeds the real interest rate by the rate of inflation, and the higher nominal interest rate offsets the reduction in purchasing power. Although each dollar that a borrower repays buys fewer goods because of inflation, borrowers pay sufficiently more dollars that they do not gain, and creditors do not lose, from fully expected inflation.

Unexpected inflation can redistribute income from workers to firms if previously-set nominal wages do not automatically rise with prices. Similarly, unexpected inflation can redistribute income away from certain people such as retirees who live on pensions fixed in nominal terms.

If inflation worked exactly like a reverse currency reform, no one would care much about it. However, high, unexpected inflation can disrupt the economy by creating massive redistributions of income. Suppressed inflation can create serious economic inefficiencies. Economists disagree, however, over the question of whether low, steady inflation poses a serious problem.

Key Terms

nominal variable	inflation	currency reform	depreciation
real variable	nominal money supply	equilibrium rate of inflation	inflation tax
nominal price	quantity of money demanded	exchange rate	suppressed inflation
relative price	equilibrium price level	appreciation	

Questions and Problems

22. How is an increase in the growth rate of the nominal money supply likely to affect the nominal interest rate?

23. Comment on this statement: "If the demand for money rises over time, then eventually the government will be forced to increase the supply."

24. Suppose that velocity rises at 1 percent per year and real GDP grows at a rate of 2 percent per year. If the money supply rises at 6 percent per year, what is the equilibrium rate of inflation?

25. Suppose that velocity is constant and real GDP grows at a rate of 2 percent per year.
(a) Explain why the government can increase the money supply at a rate of 2 percent per year without causing inflation.
(b) Note that the government can spend the new money it prints. Who loses the purchasing power that the government gets from printing money? What would happen—and who would gain—if the government did not raise the money supply at a rate of 2 percent per year?

26. A counterfeiter prints money and spends it. Does this activity hurt anyone? Explain.

27. Comment on this situation: In an old movie, Doris Day plays a teenager whose father is a banker. Her boyfriend, trying to impress her father, asks him for a $10 bill and then tears it up, saying, "See? Money is really worthless! Even though I have destroyed this money, there is no less food, clothing, cars, houses, or love in the world than there was before!" Doris's father is not impressed. Is the boyfriend correct? Who (if anyone) gained or lost when he tore up the money?

28. Discuss the following quotation from Milton and Rose Friedman:

Money is a veil. The "real" forces that determine the wealth of a nation are the capacities of its citizens, their industry and ingenuity, the resources at their command, their mode of economic and political organization, and the like.[18]

29. An airline ticket from London to New York costs $400 in the United States or £300 in England. Where is it cheaper to buy the ticket? (Use Table 1.)

30. Discuss the likely effects of suppressed inflation.

31. *Disinflation* means a fall in the (positive) rate of inflation. Who gains and who loses from disinflation? *Deflation* refers to negative inflation (a falling price level). What could cause deflation? Who would win and who would lose from deflation?

Inquiries for Further Thought

32. Is inflation good or bad? Is deflation (negative inflation) good or bad? If both are bad, why are both increases *and* decreases in the price level problems? What is so good about the current price level that makes you want to keep it?

33. Why isn't every nominal wage indexed for inflation? Why don't people have cost-of-living adjustments for everything?

34. Discuss this statement:

Inflation is a disease, a dangerous and sometimes fatal disease, a disease that if not checked in time can destroy a society. Examples abound.

Hyperinflations in Russia and Germany after World War I . . . prepared the ground for communism in one country and nazism in the other. The hyperinflation in China after World War II eased Chairman Mao's defeat of Chiang Kai-shek.[19]

35. Why do people in the United States use dollars and not Swiss francs? Why don't Canadians and Mexicans use U.S. dollars in their every day trades? Why will many Europeans soon use Euros, rather than dollars, Swiss francs, or Russian rubles?

---

[18] Milton Friedman and Rose Friedman, *Free to Choose* (New York: Harcourt Brace, 1979), p. 238.
[19] Ibid., p. 242.

CHAPTER 10

MONEY AND FINANCIAL INTERMEDIARIES

In this Chapter . . .

Main Points to Understand

▶ Money is a medium of exchange, a store of value, and a unit of account. Important measures of the money supply include M1, M2, and the monetary base.

▶ The Federal Reserve—the U.S. central bank—controls the money supply, mainly through open-market operations.

▶ Actions of banks and depositors affect M1 and M2, creating a money multiplier.

▶ Financial intermediaries play important roles in the market for loans, creating connections between the monetary system and the loan market.

▶ Actions of the Fed to change the money supply can have short-run effects on the *real* interest rate.

Thinking Skills to Develop

▶ Understand connections between different markets, such as the money market and the loans market.

▶ Understand how actions of various groups, such as the Fed, banks, and depositors, can interact to determine the sizes of M1 and M2.

▶ Recognize the roles of financial intermediaries and the economic problems associated with them.

▶ Understand the incentives created by deposit insurance and the resulting economic problems.

H ow would you like to grow your own money? In some southern colonies before the American Revolution, people did. Tobacco functioned as money, and people could literally grow their own money with which to buy other goods.

Today, people think of money mainly as paper notes printed by the government. Throughout much of the 19th century in the United States, however, people used paper money created by regular private banks. Each bank's money was a little different from others. (Imagine owning your own bank, printing your own money with your picture on it, and watching people spend your money to buy groceries!) Today, people use paper money issued by the government, as well as checks and electronic money on the Internet, but banks still affect the money supply. Banks, in fact, play important roles not only in the monetary system but also in the market for loans. When these roles are disrupted, the economic effects can devastate people's lives, as in the 1997–1998 financial crises in Japan, Russia, Indonesia, South Korea, Malaysia, the Philippines, and Thailand. Although the government's monetary policies may profoundly affect your life, few people know much about the Federal Reserve System, the independent U.S. government agency that controls that policy. This chapter will introduce the Federal Reserve, its operations, and its monetary policy tools.

HISTORY AND ROLES OF MONEY

While the economic model developed in previous chapters treats money as paper notes printed by the government, real-life "money" includes checks and other means of payment. Systems of money and payments have changed frequently throughout history, and our current system is likely to continue to change in the future.

Money and Barter

Not all civilizations have used money, and certainly not all used money as people know it today. Some primitive societies relied mainly on barter. In ancient Egypt, people paid taxes by giving goods, not money, to the government. The same was true in medieval Europe under the feudal system; serfs paid goods rather than money to lords. Barter was common during the Middle Ages, except for international trade. In America, money transactions began to replace barter during the 16th century.

Advantages of Money over Barter

People use money because it is more convenient than barter. It avoids the problem of creating a *double coincidence of wants* in which you find a trading partner who wants to sell goods that you want to buy *and* wants to buy goods that you want to sell. A modern economy cannot function well if every trade requires a double coincidence of wants. Can you imagine professors trying to barter lectures on chemistry or economics for food and rent, or computer programmers trading their services for movie tickets and gasoline? Money simplifies trading. People can sell goods for money and then spend that money to buy the goods they want from other sellers. A monetary transaction does not require a double coincidence of wants. This function is the main role of money: as a medium of exchange.

> A **medium of exchange** is an asset that sellers generally accept as payment for goods, services, and other assets.

Money also acts as a store of value and a unit of account.

> A **store of value** is any good or asset that people can store while it maintains some or all of its value.

Many goods can serve as stores of value, although goods such as gold and land function better than others, such as perishable food, by maintaining their values better over time. Any good that people use as a medium of exchange must be an effective store of value; otherwise it could lose its value between the time you earn it and the time you spend it.

Money also serves as a unit of account:

> A **unit of account** is a measure for stating prices.

The unit of account in the United States is the dollar: People quote prices in dollars. When buyers and sellers negotiate prices, they discuss dollar amounts. A unit of account requires a homogeneous good—all units of it must be roughly equivalent, like ounces of gold or paper money. In contrast, shoes would be a poor unit of account because they are not all alike. Throughout history, the kinds of goods that have served as money have been reliable stores of value and effective units of account.

Types of Money

Although people exchange paper money and coins today, cigarettes served as money in World War II prisoner-of-war camps and in Germany immediately after the war ended. People have traded shells, salt, silk, cattle, furs, dried fish, beads, and even stones as money in various societies. Gold, silver, copper, tin, iron, and other metals have been used as money. Some Native Americans used seashells (called *wampum)* as money. Tobacco served as money in the colonies of Virginia, Maryland, and North Carolina in the 1600s and 1700s. Of course, since farmers could grow tobacco, they could literally grow money, and they did, boosting the supply of money 40-fold over half a century, which caused a giant surge of inflation.

Gold and Silver Coins

Coins first circulated in China in 1091 B.C. and in Greece in about 750 B.C. Nearly 2,000 years later, the Chinese first invented and traded paper money around A.D. 900.

In economies that designated gold or silver coins as money, the money supply could increase in three ways: debasement of coins, new discoveries of gold or silver deposits, or imports of gold or silver. First, governments could *debase* coins by making more of them from the same amount of gold or silver, either by reducing the size of each coin slightly (shaving the edges and using the shavings to make new coins) or by mixing other, cheaper, metals with the gold or silver. By increasing the number of coins, debasement created inflation. Governments gained by creating more coins to spend, and people paid an inflation tax, as described in the previous chapter.

Inflation in ancient Rome resulted from frequent debasement of money. Rome first used copper coins, then switched to silver coins, and then switched again to gold coins. The government debased them all. The money supply in the Roman empire rose rapidly starting in A.D. 296 under Emperor Diocletian, who tried and failed to stop inflation with wage and price controls. In contrast, governments in ancient Athens and other Greek city-states did not debase their coins even in times of war. As a result, ancient Greece did not experience inflation. However, Greece was an exception: Debasement of coins has been common throughout history.

New discoveries of gold or silver raise the money supply in economies that use gold or silver coins as money. For example, inflation resulted from gold discoveries in the United States and Australia from 1848 to 1851 that increased world gold output by 8 percent per year for 15 years.

Finally, a country's money supply increases if it imports gold or silver from other countries to make coins. Suppose that an increase in the supply of gold money in Spain raised the Spanish price level. Goods and services would cost more gold coins than before. People in Spain would have an incentive to buy goods in other countries where prices had not changed, such as England, and bring those goods to Spain. To buy English goods, they would pay gold coins to English sellers, raising the supply of gold in England. As England exported goods and imported gold, the gold imports would raise the English money supply and price level. Meanwhile, the Spanish money supply would fall as Spaniards spent their gold coins in England. The fall in the Spanish money supply would reduce the Spanish price level. At the same time, the price level in England would rise until prices were again equal in the two countries. At that point, Spanish people would stop exporting gold to England.

During the Middle Ages, when barter was common, people often exchanged gold coins in international trade—coins minted by the Byzantine Empire before the 8th century and Moslem Arabic coins after that. Later, in medieval Europe, various feudal lords, kings, and ecclesiastics minted, and frequently debased, silver coins for local use. International trade expanded in the 13th century, and gold coins issued in Florence became the medium of exchange for international trade. By the 14th century, England, France, Germany, and other European countries had begun issuing gold coins.

PRINT YOUR OWN MONEY! It's Fun. It's Legal. But you need your own design . . .
Two kinds of paper money circulate in Ithaca, New York. One kind, printed by the U.S. government, is familiar throughout the United States. The other money, printed right in Ithaca, uses an entirely different unit of account: the "Ithaca hour." Since 1991, people in Ithaca have been using Ithaca hour notes to pay for home repairs, groceries, childcare, movies, restaurant meals, and other goods and services. The multi-colored notes are a form of *private money*, issued in five denominations: 2 Hours, 1 Hour, ½ Hour, ¼ Hour, and ⅛ Hour. Private moneys like this are completely legal, as long as they are distinct from Federal Reserve notes. The idea may spread: in recent years, several other communities have issued their own local currencies.

In modern times, European countries have begun replacing their national currencies with a new continentwide standard called the *Euro*.

Europe experienced a long period of inflation in the 16th and early 17th centuries due to gold and silver discoveries in the New World, which nearly doubled the European gold stock and more than tripled the silver stock. Although inflation rates in this period appear low by today's standards—inflation was about 2 percent per year—this *Price Revolution,* as it is commonly known, was the longest period of inflation in history up to that time, with a higher inflation rate than in any preceding century.

In the 18th century, the Bank of England began issuing paper money, which began to replace silver and gold coins. The Bank of Amsterdam did the same in Holland, and paper money began to replace coins in Spain, as well.

Gold Standard

Gold is the most historically important commodity that has served as money. Countries have adopted the gold standard in two different forms.

> In a **pure gold standard**, people use gold coins as money.

> In a **gold exchange standard**, people use paper money that is backed by gold stored in warehouses.

The gold standard is one type of *commodity standard* of money, in which money consists of some commodity, or is backed by that commodity. The silver standard, which resembles a gold standard except that it is based on silver instead of gold, is another historically important commodity standard.

A pure gold standard functioned for many centuries, before most countries replaced it with a gold exchange standard. In the gold exchange standard, paper money initially served as a sort of warehouse certificate for gold. People found paper certificates more convenient than gold coins to carry and store. Although anyone could exchange paper money for the gold that backed it, few people did so.

Imagine that the U.S. government were to adopt a gold exchange standard at a $300-per-ounce gold price. Anyone could bring $300 to a government office to buy or sell an ounce of gold for $300. The government would sell as much gold as anyone wants to buy for $300 an ounce, and buy as much as anyone wants to sell for that price. This policy would fix the price of gold at $300 per ounce, for two reasons. First, no buyer would be willing to pay more to another (non-government) seller, so the price would not rise above $300 per ounce. Second, no seller would be willing to sell for less than $300 per ounce to another (non-government) buyer, so the price would not fall below $300 per ounce. Gold would back paper money in the sense that anyone could exchange one for the other at the $300 price.

To fix the price of gold at $300, the government must have enough gold to sell to people who want to buy it at that price. If the government does not have enough gold, it cannot fix the price at $300. Under any commodity standard, paper money works like a warehouse certificate for the commodity. However, when people are willing to hold and accept paper money without exchanging it for the commodity in the warehouse, then the commodity may seem to lose its importance. Why let the commodity sit unused in a warehouse when it could be used for other purposes? When the government does *not* back its paper money with any commodity (such as gold or silver)—when people cannot trade the paper money for a commodity at a fixed price—that money becomes *fiat money*.

A government that fixes the nominal price of gold (in terms of its money) requires a sufficient quantity of gold to sell. In the same way, a modern government that tries to fix the price of its currency in terms of foreign money (the *exchange rate*) needs sufficient reserves of foreign money to sell. When a country lacks sufficient reserves, it cannot continue to fix its exchange rate. This situation has arisen in recent years in Mexico, Russia, and a number of Asian countries such as Indonesia.

> **Fiat money** is paper money that is not backed by a commodity in the sense that people cannot trade it for a particular commodity at a fixed nominal price.

Money in American History

Before the American Revolution, the 13 colonies relied on paper money denominated in British pounds. During the revolution, the colonies printed paper money known as *continental currency* to pay war expenses, causing inflation of 8.5 percent per month during that time. The continental currency was denominated in dollars, a word for Spanish pesos (pieces of eight). From 1775 to 1779, the colonial money supply rose to ten times its previous level, causing massive inflation. Prices climbed to as much as 100 times their previous levels. In a famous phrase, something utterly worthless was said to be "not worth a continental."

After 1783, the continental currency lost all its value. The United States adopted a type of silver standard until 1834, followed by the gold standard after that year. U.S. inflation remained virtually zero for the first 70 years of U.S. independence. From the time that George Washington became the first president in 1789 until the Civil War, the U.S. price level stayed about the same.

Money took several forms in the United States besides silver or gold coins, such as paper money issued by the Bank of the United States early in the 19th century and paper money issued by private banks. The federal government first printed fiat money (money not convertible to gold) in 1862 to help pay for the Civil War. These so-called *greenbacks* were measured in dollars and were designated as *legal tender,* meaning that the government required sellers to accept greenbacks in payment for goods and services (even if the sellers would rather be paid in gold or some other kind of money). The U.S. money supply doubled during this time, creating inflation that roughly doubled prices.

After the Civil War, the government began reducing the supply of greenbacks, creating *deflation* (negative inflation). By 1879, the wholesale price level had fallen all the way back to its pre–Civil War level. Once again, people could exchange paper money for gold. The United States remained on the gold exchange standard until World War I began in 1914. Countries often suspended the gold standard temporarily during wars, and World War I was no exception. Germany returned to the gold standard in 1924, after its hyperinflation discussed in the previous chapter. Britain and France returned to the gold standard in 1925 and 1928, respectively. As the United States returned to the gold standard after World War I, the new *Federal Reserve System* (discussed later in this chapter) began operation.

Review Questions

1. Why is trade based on money often more efficient than barter?

2. Name some commodities that have served as money.

3. What are three important properties of money?

Thinking Exercise

4. What is a gold standard? Use a supply–demand diagram to explain how that monetary system worked.

The basic model developed in previous chapters, defined the nominal money supply as the total nominal value of the paper money and coins created by the government. Because people in modern economies often pay for goods and services without using paper money or coins, economists have developed several alternative measures of the money supply.

MEASURING THE MONEY SUPPLY

IN THE NEWS

Overseas travels by U.S. dollar follow in tracks of world economy

In the ad, a little boy in Arab dress leads a confused American couple down side streets and through a crowded market, finally depositing them triumphantly in front of an automated teller machine.

The Americans, who'd just gotten cleaned out buying a driverless camel, gasp with amazement to discover that, no matter where they go, there's easy access to American money.

Obviously it was their first trip abroad or they wouldn't be the least bit surprised to find greenbacks in even the remotest corners of the world. In fact, to currency experts, the definition of overseas is that vast place where most American money is kept.

According to the Federal Reserve, 60 percent of all American currency in circulation—$500 billion at last count—is held somewhere outside the United States. Other experts think the number could be as high as 80 percent. What's more, the dollar outflow may be matched by a similar movement of other hard currencies.

Some of the money is in drugs and the underground economy, but most is used as legal tender.

Source: Journal of Commerce

Mystery of the Missing Money

Who has all the paper money? By 1998, U.S. currency (paper money and coins) in circulation totaled almost $500 billion. That amounts to an average of about $1,800 per person for everyone (including children) in the United States. You probably don't have that much cash. (I don't.) Where is the missing money?

Most of it is held by people in other countries. People in less developed countries, particularly countries with high inflation rates, often hold U.S. dollars. People also use dollars to buy goods on black markets in many countries. U.S. currency is also used for illegal transactions such as those in the drug trade. Some of it, obviously, has been lost at the bottom of the ocean and burned in fires. No accurate sources of data show precisely where all the currency is.

By extending the model to include new features associated with these measures of the money supply, we can use it to address important economic issues such as the causes of the 1997–98 economic crises in Korea, Japan, and other Asian countries.

The most important measures of the U.S. money supply are M1, M2, and the monetary base. These measures reflect the facts that you can pay for some goods by writing checks, and money in the bank is almost like money in your wallet. These measures distinguish between currency, demand deposits, and bank reserves:

> **Currency** is the paper money and coins owned by people and business firms.

The basic model of previous chapters has treated currency as the money supply. We now consider other measures of the money supply. The first measure adds balances in checking accounts, because people can buy goods and services with these balances by writing checks.

> **Demand deposits** are balances in bank accounts that you can withdraw on demand by writing a check.

In addition to demand deposits, *other checkable deposits* include balances in other, similar accounts on which people can write checks.

> **M1** equals the sum of currency, demand deposits, other checkable deposits, and traveler's checks.

The M1 measure of the money supply recognizes that money in a checking account is almost like cash in your wallet—you can spend it by writing checks. Traveler's checks appear in M1 because you can use them like currency to buy goods and services.

You might wonder why a definition of money should include balances in checking accounts but not balances in savings accounts. After all, you can easily transfer deposits from your savings account to your checking account or withdraw cash from your savings account. Perhaps a definition of money should include balances in money market mutual funds, because people who own them can often write checks on their account balances. A second measure of the money supply, *M2*, includes balances in these accounts:

> **M2** equals M1 plus the sum of balances in savings accounts, money market mutual funds, and similar accounts.

Figure 1 plots M1 and M2, and their growth rates, for the United States since 1960.

Choosing a measure of the money supply is somewhat like choosing a measure of intelligence. Scientists could measure a person's ability to learn mathematics, memorize poetry, recognize and deal with complex issues in human relationships, succeed in creating a happy life, and so on, but the many different ways to measure intelligence have different purposes, and not all people are intelligent in the same ways. To predict how well a person will succeed in an engineering course, one would choose some definition or measurement of intelligence that could predict that kind of success. Similarly, to predict inflation, economists want to use a measure of the money supply suited to that purpose. No one can supply a unique answer to the question of which is the best definition of money.

Basics of Bank Accounts and Money

Suppose that you have money in a checking account at a bank. When you write a check for $20 to pay for food at a grocery store, the store deposits the check at its bank. That bank gets $20 from your bank and adds it to the balance in the store's bank account. In that way, the store gets your $20.

When you deposit $100 in paper money in a bank account, the bank does not keep all of this $100 in its vault. Instead, it lends most of that money to someone who wants to borrow. The money the bank keeps (the part of the $100 that it does not lend) becomes part of its reserves.

> **Bank reserves** are the deposits that banks have *not* loaned.

Figure 1 | Measures of the U.S. Money Supply, 1960–1998

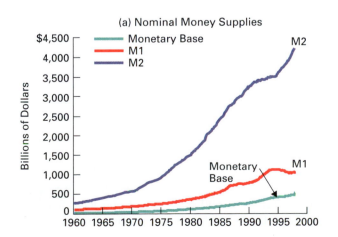
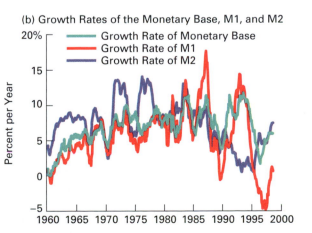

Choosing between alternative measures of the money supply is like choosing between alternative measures of *performance* in sports. You might measure a player's performance as total points that the player scores, but team cooperation and other complexities of the game may suggest other, perhaps better, measures of performance. Similarly, economists might measure money as the number of dollars the government has printed, but complexities of real-life economies suggest other, perhaps better, measures.

A simple model of a team sport—like Figure 1 in Chapter 2, showing a model of a play in American football—neglects some of a game's subtle features, such as how players respond when the other team changes its tactics. Discussing those features of the game requires adding new complexities to the model beyond the features in that figure. Similarly, our basic economic model has omitted certain aspects of real-life monetary and payments systems. By extending the model to include new features, the model can be applied to new issues such as the details of U.S. monetary policy and the causes of the recent Asian economic crises.

Bank reserves in the United States include the currency that banks keep in their offices and vaults (called *vault cash),* plus the balances they keep at the Federal Reserve (an independent agency of the federal government, discussed later in this chapter).

Banks hold reserves for two reasons. First, they need cash to give to people who withdraw from their accounts. The practice of keeping only a fraction of deposits as reserves and lending the rest is called *fractional reserve banking.* Fractional reserve banking provides banks with funds to lend, turning them into intermediaries between borrowers and lenders rather than simply safe places to store money or bookkeeping firms that record who owes how much to whom. However, fractional reserve banking also creates the possibility that people may try to withdraw more cash than a bank has available to give them. Because only a small fraction of depositors typically withdraw funds each day, banks generally have enough reserves to satisfy those depositors. Banks also hold reserves because the government *requires* them to hold a small fraction of deposits (in 1998, 3 percent of total checking-account deposits below $49 million and 10 percent of checking-account deposits above that amount). Every day, some banks find that they have more reserves than they want while other banks have less, so some banks borrow reserves from others.

Banks earn profits by lending the money that people deposit and charging higher interest rates to borrowers than the interest rates that they pay to depositors. For example, you may earn 4 percent annual interest on the money in your bank account, but the bank lends most of the money you deposited, perhaps charging 10 percent interest. The difference covers the bank's costs and provides a profit for its owners. A bank incurs an opportunity cost by holding reserves, because it could lend that money and earn interest on the loans. Banks balance the costs and benefits of reserves when they choose the amounts of reserves they choose to hold.

The Monetary Base

Because of fractional reserve banking, the government cannot directly control M1 or M2, although it can control a narrower measure of the money supply, the *monetary base.*

> The **monetary base** equals currency plus bank reserves.

Figure 2 compares the monetary base, M1, and M2.

The U.S. government—specifically, the Federal Reserve—has nearly complete control over the country's monetary base, which changes only when the Federal Reserve changes it or when money is lost (as in a shipwreck). However, the Federal Reserve cannot control the amount of the monetary base that flows outside the United States. People in other countries, particularly countries with high inflation rates, hold U.S. dollars because they provide a better store of value than local money. Dollars also serve as the main means of payment for illegal international drug trades and similar activities around the world. Only rough estimates, not precise data, are available on foreign holdings of dollars, so the Federal Reserve can only estimate the size of the monetary base held inside the United States. Nevertheless, these estimates give the Federal Reserve reasonably strong control over changes in the monetary base held within the country.

The Federal Reserve has incomplete control over M1 and M2 because these measures of money respond to actions of people and banks. To see why, you need to understand how banks help to create money.

How Banks Help to Create Money

Suppose you take $100 from your wallet and deposit it in your bank account. The bank might keep $10 of this money as reserves and lend the other $90 to your economics professor. Your professor then has $90 in cash and you have $100 in your bank account. Even though your professor has $90 of the paper money you deposited,

Figure 2 | Measures of the Money Supply

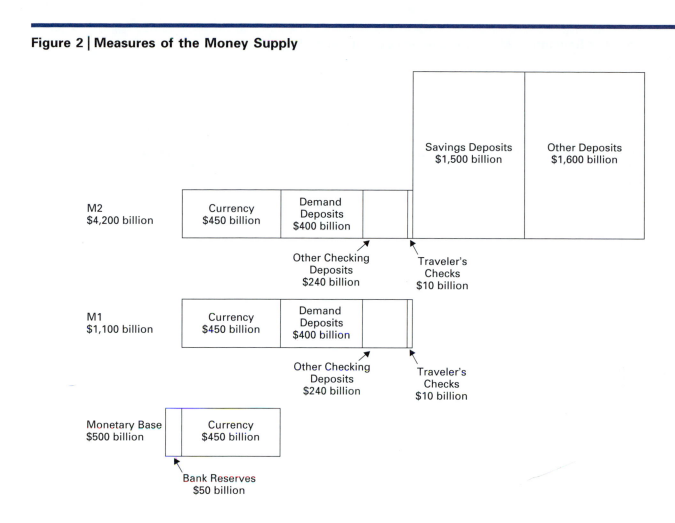

you still feel as if you have the entire $100. In a sense, you do; you have a $100 balance in your bank account. Your actions, along with those of your bank and your professor, have increased the M1 measure of the money supply by $90. M2 also increases by $90.

The story does not end there. M1 and M2 rise by more than $90 when your professor uses the borrowed money. When your professor deposits the $90 into a bank account, that bank lends most of the money to someone else. This process continues through many rounds, and eventually M1 rises by a larger amount. That amount depends on how much reserves banks hold and how people choose to divide their money between cash in their wallets and money in the bank.

EXAMPLE

Suppose that banks always hold reserves equal to 10 percent of the balances in checking accounts. Table 1 shows the results. Initially, you take $100 in cash from your wallet and deposit it in your checking account. The monetary base does not change, even though currency falls by $100, because bank reserves rise by $100 (since the bank has your money). M1 and M2 also remain unchanged, because currency falls by $100, while the balance in your checking account rises by that same amount.

The bank, however, keeps only $10 of the money you deposited and lends the other $90 to Andrea. At this point, M1 rises by $90 because you still have $100 in your bank account, but Andrea has $90 that she did not have before. Andrea spends the $90 to buy

Table 1 | How the Banking System Creates Money: An Example

Actions	Effects on Money Supply
You take $100 cash from your wallet and put it in your checking account.	No change in monetary base or M1.
The bank keeps $10 (10 percent of your $100 deposit) as reserves and lends $90 to Andrea.	No change in monetary base; M1 rises by $90.
Andrea spends the $90 to buy something from Bob, who deposits the $90 in his checking account.	No change in monetary base; M1 rises another $81, bringing its total increase to $171.
Bob's bank keeps $9 (10 percent of $90) as reserves, and lends the other $81 to Celine.	
Celine spends the $81 to buy something from Dave, who deposits the $81 in his checking account.	No change in monetary base; M1 rises another $72.90, bringing its total increase to $243.90.
Dave's bank keeps $8.10 (10 percent of $81) and lends the other $72.90 to Elaine.	
Elaine uses the money to buy something from Fran, who deposits the money in her checking account, and the process continues. . . .	Eventually, M1 rises by $900.[a]

[a]The $900 figure comes from adding:

$$\$90 + \frac{(.9)(\$90)}{\$81.00} + \frac{(.9)^2(\$90)}{\$72.90} + \frac{(.9)^3(\$90)}{\$65.61} + \frac{(.9)^4(\$90)}{\$59.05} + \ldots$$

$$= \$90(1 + 0.9 + 0.9^2 + 0.9^3 + 0.9^4 + 0.9^5 + \ldots)$$

$$= \$90/(1 - 0.9)$$

$$= \$90/0.1$$

$$= \$900$$

boots from Bob, who deposits it in his bank account. His bank keeps $9 (10 percent of the $90) as reserves and lends the other $81 to Celine. At this point, M1 rises by another $81, for a total increase of $171, because Celine now has $81 that she did not have before, while you still have your $100 in the bank and Bob still has his $90 in the bank. Celine spends the $81 to buy daggers from Dave, who deposits the money in his bank account. His bank keeps $8.10 (10 percent of the $81.00 deposit) and lends the other $72.90 to Elaine, raising M1 by another $72.90. By this time, M1 has increased by $243.90. Next, Elaine spends the money to buy flowers from Fran, and this process continues. After three more rounds, M1 rises by a total of $421.70; eventually, M1 rises by a total of $900 as a result of your initial $100 deposit.

Money Multiplier

The example showed how M1 eventually rises by $900 when a person deposits $100 in the bank, and banks hold reserves equal to 10 percent of their deposits. Because a $100 rise in deposits raises M1 by $900, economists say that the money multiplier is 9 in this case.

> The **M1 money multiplier** is the ratio of M1 to the monetary base.

For example, the money multiplier for M1 is defined as:

$$\text{M1 money multiplier} = \frac{\text{M1}}{\text{Monetary base}}$$

A similar definition applies to the M2 money multiplier.

In the example, the M1 money multiplier was 9 because the ratio of bank deposits to reserves equaled 9, that is, banks lent $9 for every $1 they held in reserves. For each dollar of deposits, banks lent $0.90 and kept $0.10 as reserves. In that example, the M1 money multiplier equaled:

$$\text{M1 money multiplier} = \frac{\text{Deposits}}{\text{Reserves}}$$

In that example, however, each seller deposited all newly received money into a bank account. More generally, a seller may keep some of that money as cash in a wallet, giving a more general formula for the M1 money multiplier:

$$\text{M1 money multiplier} = \frac{1 + \dfrac{\text{Currency}}{\text{deposits}}}{\dfrac{\text{Reserve}}{\text{deposits}} + \dfrac{\text{currency}}{\text{deposits}}}$$

(See the Appendix that follows this chapter for a derivation of this formula.) The ratio of currency to deposits shows how much currency (paper money and coins) people hold as a fraction of their total checking-account balances; the ratio of reserves to deposits shows how much reserves banks hold as a fraction of their total checking-account balances.

Using the Money Multiplier

The money multiplier measures the effect of a change in the monetary base on M1. Suppose that the government raises the monetary base by printing $1,000 in new money and spending it to buy something. The seller now has the $1,000, so the monetary base has risen by $1,000. The typical M1 money multiplier of 2.2 suggests that M1 will eventually rise by $2,200 (2.2 times $1,000). The general rule is:

$$\text{Change in M1} = \text{M1 money multiplier} \times \text{Change in monetary base}$$

> **Money Multipliers in the United States**
> The M1 money multiplier in the United States is about 2.2. The ratio of currency to deposits in the United States is about 0.70 (70 percent), and the ratio of reserves to deposits is about 0.075 (7.5 percent). Plugging in these values, the formula gives an M1 money multiplier of about 2.2. Figure 3 shows the changes in the U.S. M1 money multiplier in recent years.

Figure 3 | M1 Money Multiplier in the United States

Table 2 | How a Change in the Monetary Base Raises M1

	Starting Amount	Kept as Currency	Deposit in Bank	Bank Reserves	Bank Loans	Cumulative M1 Increase
Megan	$1,000.00	$412.00	$588.00	$44.10	$543.90	$1,543.90
Ned	$543.90	$224.09	$319.81	$23.99	$295.83	$1,839.73
Oprah	$295.83	$121.88	$173.95	$13.05	$160.90	$2,000.63
Pete	$160.90	$66.29	$94.61	$7.10	$87.51	$2,088.14
Quentin	$87.51	$36.06	$51.46	$3.86	$47.60	$2,135.74
Robert	$47.60	$19.61	$27.99	$2.10	$25.89	$2,161.63
Sandra	$25.89	$10.67	$15.22	$1.14	$14.08	$2,175.71
Tom	$14.08	$5.80	$8.28	$0.62	$7.66	$2,183.37

EXPLANATION AND EXAMPLE

Suppose that the government prints $1,000 in new currency and buys something from Megan, a typical person whose currency–deposit ratio of 0.7 indicates that she holds $0.70 in currency for each $1.00 in her bank account. Therefore, as a typical person, Megan puts $588 of her newly earned $1,000 into her checking account and keeps $412 as currency (since $412 is 70 percent of $588). These actions appear in the first row of Table 2. Megan's bank has a reserve–deposit ratio of 7.5 percent, so it keeps $44.10 of Megan's deposit as reserves and lends the other $543.90 to Ned.

Ned, another typical person with a currency–deposit ratio of 0.7, keeps $224.09 in cash and deposits $319.81 in his checking account. His bank keeps $23.99 as reserves on this deposit, and lends the other $295.83 to Oprah, another typical person. The money supply grows as the process continues down the rows of Table 2. Eventually, by the eighth round of this process (when Tom's bank has loaned $7.66 to someone), M1 has increased by $2,183.37, as shown in the last row of the table. If the table were to continue even further, it would show that M1 eventually rises by $2,200. The money multiplier simply gives a quick way to calculate the final change in M1.

Review Questions

5. If you pay for a new shirt with a check, how does the store get your money?

6. How can you (with the help of a bank) increase the money supply? Explain.

7. Define and explain who controls (a) the monetary base, (b) M1, and (c) M2.

8. Explain how the banking system creates money.

Thinking Exercises

9. Suppose that banks hold $0.10 of reserves for every $1.00 of deposits and that the currency–deposit ratio is 0.5. How large is the M1 money multiplier?

10. Suppose that people choose to increase the fraction of their money that they hold in the form of currency and reduce the fraction that they hold in the form of bank deposits. How would this change affect M1 and M2?

We now have three measures of the money supply (the monetary base, M1, and M2), with varying degrees of control by the government. We have a model to describe how the actions of banks and depositors affect the sizes of M1 and M2. We now turn to the actions of *government* that affect the money supply.

Many countries, including the United States, operate central banks that serve as banks for other banks. The U.S. central bank is the Federal Reserve System, often simply called the *Fed*.

> A **central bank** is a bank for banks. The **Federal Reserve System** is the central bank in the United States.

The Federal Reserve conducts monetary policy (controlling the money supply) and regulates banks in the United States. Similar agencies in other countries include the Bank of Canada, Bank of England, Bank of Japan, Bank of Mexico, the Bundesbank in Germany, and the new European Central Bank. These central banks conduct monetary policies and regulate banks in their countries.

The Fed was created by the Federal Reserve Act in 1913. Before that time, the United States had no central bank. Although the Fed affects the life of every citizen through its policies, most people know little about how it operates. The Federal Reserve System consists of three main parts:

1. The Board of Governors, a seven-member panel in Washington, D.C., employs a large supporting staff of statisticians and researchers. Members of the board are appointed by the U.S. president and confirmed by Congress to serve 14-year terms. The long terms are intended to help shield board members from political pressure, much as judges' life terms shield them. Board members' terms are staggered so that one becomes vacant every 2 years. The president appoints one governor to chair the board for a 4-year term. The chairman, currently Alan Greenspan, wields more influence and power than the other governors, partly through control of meeting agendas.

2. Regional Federal Reserve Banks are centered in 12 cities around the country, shown in Figure 4. Nine directors oversee each Federal Reserve Bank, three appointed by the Fed's Board of Governors and six elected by private banks in the Federal Reserve Bank's district. These nine directors choose the president of the Federal Reserve Bank. The New York Federal Reserve Bank carries out most of the Fed's monetary policy actions.

3. The Federal Reserve's Federal Open Market Committee, or FOMC, meets about every four to six weeks in Washington to discuss the economy, set the nation's monetary policy, and choose Fed policy actions. The FOMC's 12 members include the 7 governors in Washington D.C., the president of the Federal Reserve Bank of New York, and the presidents of 4 of the 11 other Federal Reserve Banks, who take turns serving on the committee. The bank presidents who do not serve on the FOMC can participate in its meetings, but they cannot vote on policy. The Federal Reserve Bank of New York is responsible for carrying out the policies chosen by the FOMC.

The Fed, unlike most government agencies, operates somewhat independently of the rest of the government. This independence is intended to isolate Fed decision making from political forces that might compromise its choices of the best policies for the economy. The Fed does not receive money directly from Congress. Instead, the Fed pays its expenses (staff salaries and so on) out of the interest it earns on its financial assets, mostly

FEDERAL RESERVE SYSTEM

One of the most powerful people in the world: Federal Reserve Chairman Alan Greenspan.

Figure 4 | Regional Federal Reserve Banks

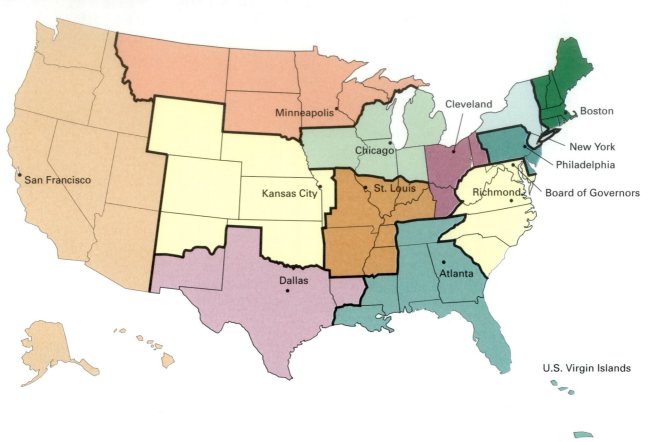

U.S. Treasury bills and government bonds.[1] After paying its expenses, the Fed returns any leftover money to Congress. In addition, the Fed does not undergo audits by the General Accounting Office, the federal accounting agency that audits the books of most other government agencies. This separation helps to reduce political pressures on the Fed.

Federal Reserve Policy Tools: How the Money Supply Changes

The Fed relies on three main tools to conduct monetary policy:

▶ Open market operations

▶ Discount window lending

▶ Reserve requirements and other bank regulations

Open Market Operations

The Fed's primary policy tool is the open market operation: Think of the Fed increasing the money supply by using newly printed money to buy government bonds.

> An **open market operation** is a Federal Reserve sale or purchase of U.S. government bonds. In an open market *purchase*, the Fed buys bonds, expanding the monetary base. In an open market *sale*, the Fed sells bonds, contracting the monetary base.

[1]Chapter 15 discusses government bonds and other financial assets.

The FOMC makes decisions about open market operations, and the Federal Reserve Bank of New York does the actual buying and selling. An open market purchase increases the monetary base, because the Fed creates money to buy financial assets. When the Fed buys bonds from a bank, the bank receives an increase in its reserves at the Fed. When the bank wants currency and coins to lend, it withdraws reserves from its account at the Fed. The Treasury Department prints currency and mints coins, and the Fed provides them to banks for lending. This increase in the monetary base sets into motion the money-multiplier process described earlier, raising M1 and M2.

An open market sale reduces the monetary base, because the Fed collects payments for the bonds it sells by taking reserves out of the accounts of the banks that buy those bonds. (Think of the Fed destroying the money that it receives for selling the bonds.) This fall in reserves sets into motion the money-multiplier process described earlier, only in reverse, so the open market sale reduces M1 and M2.

Discount Window Lending

The Fed sometimes lends reserves to banks. The bank is said to borrow at the Fed's discount window, and the interest rate the bank pays is called the *discount rate*.

> The **Federal Reserve discount rate** is the interest rate the Fed charges banks for short-term loans.

When the Fed lends reserves to a bank, the monetary base rises. Broader measures of the money supply, such as M1 and M2, then increase through the money-multiplier process. By raising and lowering the discount rate, the Fed can affect the amount of bank borrowing at the discount window.

As noted earlier, banks borrow and lend reserves among themselves every day. Banks with more reserves than they want lend to other banks with fewer reserves than they want. The interest rate that banks charge each other for short-term loans of reserves is called the *federal funds rate*.

> The **federal funds rate** is the interest rate that banks charge each other when they borrow and lend reserves for short periods.

The federal funds rate has nothing to do with the federal government, although it is often a target of Federal Reserve monetary policy.

Figure 5 shows changes in the Federal Reserve discount rate and the federal funds rate in recent years. When the federal funds rate is less than the discount rate, banks can borrow from other banks more cheaply than from the Fed. When the discount rate is less than the federal funds rate, banks would prefer to borrow from the Fed. The Fed discourages banks from borrowing too much or too often at the discount window, however, and it does not always lend to banks that want to borrow. (Banks that try to borrow from the Federal Reserve too often or too much attract increased scrutiny by its bank regulators, creating inconvenience and costs for those banks.)

The Fed lends reserves to banks at the discount window for two purposes: acting as a lender of last resort in an emergency situation and conducting monetary policy. The discount window was originally intended to make the Fed a lender of last resort—a source of loans to banks that could not easily borrow funds elsewhere and that needed reserves so depositors could withdraw their money (or for other purposes such as meeting legal reserve requirements). Banks that borrow at the discount window frequently could choose instead to borrow in the federal funds market, but only at a higher interest rate.

If only one bank needs to borrow reserves for depositors to meet withdrawal demands, it can borrow from other banks. However, if *all* (or many) banks simultaneously experience large withdrawals, they may be unable to borrow enough, because the

Figure 5 | Two Key Interest Rates for Monetary Policy

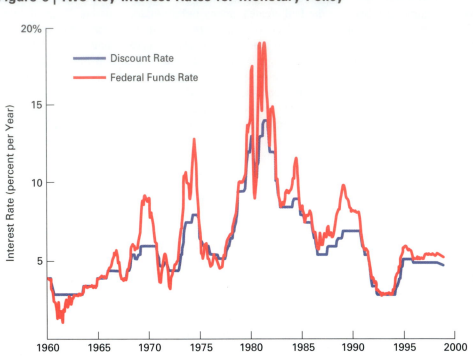

entire economy may not contain enough currency to pay all depositors who want to withdraw at once. As a lender of last resort, the Fed provides additional currency in such a situation; by assuring people that they can always withdraw their money whenever they want, it can help to prevent such a situation from developing out of panic. This function was originally intended as the main role of the Federal Reserve, and discount window lending was the main tool of Fed policy in its early years.[2]

The second purpose of discount window lending is to help conduct monetary policy, that is, to control the money supply. By lending reserves to banks, the Fed can raise the monetary base and broader measures of the money supply (such as M1 and M2).

Reserve Requirements and Other Bank Regulations

As an earlier section noted, the Fed requires banks to hold minimum proportions of reserves per dollar of deposits.

Required reserves are reserves that the Fed requires banks to hold.

The Fed can increase the M1 money multiplier by reducing required reserves. A fall in required reserves increases the fraction of deposits that banks can lend, raising the M1 money multiplier. Similarly, the Fed can reduce the M1 money multiplier by raising required reserves, reducing the fraction of deposits that banks can lend. Although changes in reserve requirements can affect M1 and M2, the Fed seldom changes money supplies in this way.

The Fed also supervises and regulates banks. Its officials make sure that banks actually hold the reserves they are required to hold. It monitors their investments to make sure that they meet certain legal requirements, such as those intended to prevent banks

---

[2]As an option, banks could give people only $0.90 for each $1.00 in their accounts. This has actually happened in many banking panics.

from choosing particularly risky investments. The Fed also enforces a variety of other bank regulations. Other functions of the Federal Reserve include acting as a clearinghouse to clear checks and distributing new currency.

Review Questions

11. Describe the Federal Reserve System and its three main policy tools.

12. Explain open market operations and how they affect the money supply.

13. What is the Federal Reserve discount rate? The federal funds rate?

Thinking Exercise

14. Why might the Federal Reserve be more effective than a private bank as a lender of last resort?

FINANCIAL INTERMEDIARIES

Earlier chapters discussed the supply and demand for loans and used these concepts as thinking tools to examine the effects of changes in consumer spending, government budget deficits, and other macroeconomic issues. The supply of loans mainly reflects lending by people who save, while the demand for loans mainly reflects borrowing by firms for investments (and by governments to finance budget deficits). In a modern economy, financial intermediaries participate in a large fraction of borrowing and lending transactions.

A **financial intermediary** gathers money from savers and lends it to borrowers.

Banks are financial intermediaries; other financial intermediaries include savings and loan associations and credit unions.

Financial intermediaries provide three main benefits to the economy. First, they essentially bring borrowers and lenders together, so that savers can find people who want to borrow money, and borrowers can find people who want to lend money. Second, financial intermediaries combine small amounts of savings by many people into large sums of money to lend. A business firm that wants to borrow $1 million can borrow directly from a bank, rather than borrowing $1,000 each from 1,000 different savers.

The third important role of financial intermediaries involves information and monitoring. Before banks lend money to a firm, they study the firm's financial position and plans, carefully estimating the likelihood that the firm will repay the loan in full and on time. After lending money, banks often monitor its use by making sure that the firm follows through with its investment plans. By obtaining information about borrowers and monitoring their activities, financial intermediaries reduce the risks involved in lending money.

While financial intermediaries were not part of the basic economic model discussed in earlier chapters, they play a key role in the real-life loan market. They *also* play a key role in the real-life money market, by affecting M1 and M2. The combination of these roles is natural. Any firm that *safeguards* a person's money, like a bank, might as well lend it and earn interest. Consequently, monetary functions of banks affects their intermediary functions. Similarly, when banks lend, they create money through the money-multiplier process, so the intermediary functions of banks affects their monetary functions. Unfortunately, this natural connection between the money system and the loan market creates some important economic problems, to which we now turn.

Russia's turmoil hammers young commercial banks

Crisis may force many to shut down

MOSCOW—Russia's financial crisis is tearing away the glittery facade of the country's young commercial banks. As the ruble falls, many have failed to meet obligations to either depositors or Western creditors, and government and central-bank officials warn that the crisis is likely to force many of the country's 1,500 banks eventually to close their doors.

The immediate reason: The collapse of financial markets has shrunk the assets of banks an average of 90% since their peak last fall, forcing some banks to default on loans to Western creditors.

Source: The Wall Street Journal

Banking Crises

If banks kept *all* their deposits as reserves—if they did *not* lend the money they receive in deposits—then the money market and loan market would not be closely connected, and banks would play no role in either creating money or lending it. Banks would simply safeguard money and transfer it to sellers' accounts when people paid for purchases by writing checks. Banks would always have enough money to give to people who came to withdraw their money. However, under the *fractional reserve* system (in which banks lend most of the money deposited with them), banks sometimes do *not* have enough currency to satisfy people who want to withdraw their deposits.

Two types of problems can arise. First, a bank may lose so much money on its loans that it becomes *insolvent*—even if all its current loans are repaid with interest, it would lack enough money to give to its depositors if they wanted to withdraw their money. This problem can occur if a bank makes a large number of bad loans—loans that borrowers simply cannot or do not repay. Some banks in Japan, Korea, and other countries faced insolvency during the Asian financial crisis of 1997–98. Most Russian banks also faced insolvency in 1998.

In the second, less severe type of problem, a bank may lack enough money to cover withdrawal demands *unless* it calls in its current loans—that is, asks borrowers to repay their loans ahead of schedule. This second type of problem is often called a *liquidity* problem—banks can obtain enough money to cover withdrawals with sufficient time, but they cannot quickly get that money. Many Asian banks did not become insolvent during the 1997–98 financial crises, but faced severe liquidity problems.

When *many* banks in the economy face either problem, the economy may experience disastrous consequences. Either type of problem reduces the supply of new loans, raising the interest rate and the cost for business firms to borrow money to finance investments. Some business firms may seek loans to continue operations despite short-run losses, and bank insolvency or bank liquidity problems may prevent them from obtaining these loans. Essentially, the *monetary* problems that can occur with fractional reserve banking can disrupt the operation of the economy's loan market. As a result, these troubles can reduce investment and disrupt normal operations of business firms. Recessions in Korea, Japan, and other Asian countries in 1998 resulted partly from the problems created by economy-wide banking crises.

Sometimes these problems lead to *bank runs*.

> A **bank run** occurs when many people try at the same time to withdraw their money from a bank that lacks enough reserves to accommodate all of them. In a **banking panic,** many banks face runs at the same time.

Banking panics frequently resulted from suspensions of convertibility in the United States prior to the beginning of the Federal Reserve System. Banking panics occurred in 1814, 1819, 1837, 1839, 1857, 1873, 1893, and 1907–08. When a bank lacked sufficient reserves to let people withdraw money from their accounts, it often suspended convertibility, that is, it stopped letting people withdraw their money. *Convertibility* means that depositors can convert bank balances into currency; in suspending convertibility, banks refused to let people make this conversion. Banking panics swept Russia in the summer of 1998, as the central bank became unable to keep the foreign exchange rate of the ruble pegged (see the nearby box) and most Russian banks became insolvent.

Banks that closed during historical U.S. banking panics were not usually insolvent; they simply faced liquidity problems. A bank closed when it lacked enough currency at the time to provide to depositors who wanted to withdraw funds. In most cases, though, banks could and did eventually allow depositors to withdraw all of their money once people had repaid their loans. Some banks went out of business permanently during banking panics, usually because people who borrowed money from them failed to repay their

A bank run in Russia in 1998 has depositors pushing and shoving to get into a bank to try to withdraw rubles and exchange them for dollars.

loans. (Loans to farmers, which were common, exposed banks to great risk, because bad weather could prevent farmers from repaying.) In these cases, depositors divided up whatever money the banks held, but they did not get their full balances.

The vast majority of banks, however, reopened after runs without any ultimate losses to depositors. Even in the worst banking panic, in 1893, 98.7 percent of banks later reopened. On average, depositors lost about $0.02 out of every dollar of their deposits in banks.[3] Of course, averages do not always accurately portray effects on people; this average loss of $0.02 per dollar reflects little or no loss for many people but major losses of lifetime savings did occur for a few people.

Banking panics often occurred with recessions. Real GDP fell 8.5 percent during the banking panic of 1907–08, convincing many people that the United States needed a cen-

IN THE NEWS

During the bank run, $250 million an hour left First Republic

By Michael J. Lyon

The silent run was accelerating at the First Republic Bank Corporation's offices in Texas—silent because retail customers

were not lining up on the streets. This run was being fueled by large institutions, including other banks, racing to electronically withdraw uninsured

deposits. Alarm bells went off around Washington, as the nation's top bank regulators met in an emergency session.

Source: New York Times

Today, bank runs can occur over electronic links.

---

[3]The banking panic during the Great Depression of the 1930s was worse than this one, however.

Fixed Exchange Rates

Many countries today operate systems of *fixed exchange rates*. A central bank keeps the price of foreign money fixed by following procedures like those described earlier in the discussion of the gold standard. For example, the central bank of Argentina pegs the exchange rate between the Argentine peso and the U.S. dollar at $1 per peso. It does this by selling as many dollars (for pesos) as anyone wants to buy at that price, and buying as many dollars (with pesos) as anyone wants to sell for that price. This is the same procedure that central banks followed to fix the price of gold under the gold exchange standard. Under the gold exchange standard, a central bank could fix the price of gold only if it had enough gold to sell to people who wanted to buy it at the fixed price. Similarly, a central bank can operate a pegged exchange rate only if it has enough *reserves* of foreign money to sell to people who want to buy it at the fixed exchange rate. When a central bank lacks sufficient reserves, it can no longer keep its exchange rate fixed. That happened in Indonesia, South Korea, Malaysia, the Philippines, and Thailand in 1997, and central banks of those countries had to stop fixing their exchange rates. The central bank of Russia lacked sufficient reserves and was forced in 1998 to stop fixing the foreign exchange rate of the ruble. Mexico went through a similar experience several years earlier.

tral bank to prevent recurrences. (To put this drop in GDP in perspective, note that no recession in the United States since the Great Depression of the 1930s has seen such a large decline.) The Federal Reserve System was intended to prevent banking panics by acting as a lender of last resort and supervising banks.

Deposit Insurance

Despite the actions of the Federal Reserve System, the United States (and many other countries) experienced banking panics in the Great Depression from 1929 through much of the 1930s. In 1934, following the banking panic associated with the Great Depression, the federal government started the Federal Deposit Insurance Corporation (FDIC) to insure bank deposits. Deposit insurance was intended to protect people from losing their deposits if a bank lacked sufficient funds to meet withdrawal demands or went out of business. If a bank lacks sufficient funds for people to withdraw their deposits, the FDIC provides those funds. Banks pay the FDIC to provide this deposit insurance.

Without deposit insurance, a bank run may occur simply because people *believe* that it will occur. Suppose you believe that a bank run will occur at your bank tomorrow, and the bank has no deposit insurance. What would you do? Most people would quickly go to the bank and withdraw all of their money while the bank still has it—before other people withdraw all their money, and the bank runs out of funds. In other words, everyone wants to be near the beginning of the line at the bank to withdraw their money, because the people at the end of the line may find the vault empty. As many people rush to the bank to withdraw simply because they expect a bank run, they cause that bank run. The bank run becomes a self-fulfilling belief—when the bank run occurs, people see their beliefs confirmed.

Deposit insurance can prevent bank runs. Even if people expect a bank run, deposit

"Yeah, but who guarantees the federal government?"
Source: *The Wall Street Journal*, August 15, 1986, p. 15.

insurance takes away their incentive to rush to the bank to be near the front of the line by guaranteeing that all of them can withdraw their money. Because people have no incentive to rush to the bank to withdraw, a bank run becomes less likely.[4]

Private Deposit Insurance

Many banks in the United States arranged private deposit insurance in the 19th century. Banks often joined together and agreed that if any one of them failed, the others would pay depositors their money. In this way, the banks jointly acted as an insurance company for one another.

These insurance arrangements differed across states because of differences in state laws. Some states prohibited branch banking and required each bank to have only one office (one bank building). These laws were intended to protect small banks by preventing large banks from opening many conveniently located branch offices that would draw customers away from small competitors. However, large banks usually took the leadership roles in creating private deposit insurance, so states that prohibited branch banking often lacked effective deposit insurance.

Bank clearinghouses began to provide deposit insurance in the mid-19th century. A clearinghouse moves money between banks to clear checks. If you wrote a $50 check to pay for a new horse, the seller would deposit the check in a local bank. The seller's bank would then collect money from your bank. If the seller's bank already owed your bank $30, then your bank would owe a net amount of $20 to the seller's bank. The clearinghouse figures out all of this detail and moves the money. Privately operated clearinghouses flourished in the 19th century, as they also acted as lenders of last resort. Unfortunately, state laws against branch banking limited the benefits of clearinghouses, including deposit insurance and lender-of-last-resort services. The creation of the Federal Reserve essentially put an end to private deposit insurance and many private clearinghouse activities. Today, the Federal Reserve and several private firms function as bank clearinghouses in the United States.

Problems with Deposit Insurance

Until the last two decades, government-provided deposit insurance seemed to most analysts like a safe way to prevent bank runs. Then the government agency that provided deposit insurance for savings and loan associations went bankrupt. (Savings and loan associations, or S&Ls, resemble banks, but are a legally distinct type of financial intermediary.) The FSLIC (Federal Savings and Loan Insurance Corporation) lacked enough money to reimburse depositors of failed institutions, and the country plunged into a savings and loan crisis that ultimately cost the government over $100 billion.[5]

This episode highlighted the fact that deposit insurance changes the incentives of banks. With deposit insurance, banks want to make riskier investments than they would choose otherwise. With good luck, these risky investments pay off well, and the banks or savings and loan associations earn high profits. With bad luck, they go out of business, and deposit insurance covers depositors' balances.

Suppose that a bank without deposit insurance can choose between investing depositors' money in a safe way or a risky way. If the risky investment pays off, the bank's owners make a big profit. If not, they suffer a big loss. If the bank goes out of business, the bank's owners lose, but so do the depositors, who lose part or all of the money in their accounts. This threat gives depositors, particularly people with large balances, an incentive to monitor the bank and prevent it from making risky investments. Any bank that began to make risky investments would lose deposits as people moved their money to other banks with safer investments.

---

[4]Some economists believe that by preventing a banking panic, deposit insurance can prevent a repeat of the Great Depression, when a large number of bank failures caused a large fall in the M1 and M2 measures of the money supply. Chapter 15 will discuss the connection between money-supply changes and the Great Depression.

[5]For various reasons, the costs are difficult to estimate and are not summarized in any convenient form in U.S. government financial accounts.

Asian Economic Crisis—1997–1998
The economic crisis in Japan, South Korea, Indonesia, Thailand, the Philippines, and Malaysia in 1997 to 1998 grew out of banking crises created by fractional reserve banking and (implicit) deposit insurance. Banks in these countries made a number of bad loans, often due to political pressures on banks. A second factor operated in Japan, where some major borrowers became unable to repay their loans to banks, after suffering losses when real estate prices fell from all-time highs. Because depositors expected governments to guarantee that they could withdraw their money, bank runs did not occur. However, insolvency at some banks and illiquidity at others contributed to recessions and created costs of bailing out depositors. The supply of loans decreased substantially in these countries, disrupting investment and the daily operations of many business firms. Similar problems have plagued many other countries in recent years.

Deposit insurance takes away the incentives of depositors to monitor their banks. Knowing that they can get their money out of the bank no matter what happens, depositors do not care whether banks make risky investments. The insurer, such as the FDIC, has an incentive to establish rules that limit the riskiness of banks' investments and to monitor banks to make sure that they follow these rules. If a bank suffers losses from risky investments, after all, the insurer must pay.

In the 19th century, private deposit insurers regulated and monitored bank investments. Similarly, when the government provides deposit insurance, it could either establish regulations that prevent banks from making risky investments or charge insurance premiums in proportion to the riskiness of investments, just as private health and life insurance companies raise insurance premiums for people who smoke.

Review Questions

15. What is a bank run and why might one occur?

16. How is deposit insurance intended to prevent bank runs?

17. What problem does deposit insurance create? How was this problem connected with the U.S. savings and loan crisis of the 1980s and the Asian financial crises of 1997–98?

Thinking Exercise

18. Suppose that a banking panic occurs and banks close, reducing the amount of bank deposits enough to raise the currency–deposit ratio from 1 to 2. If the reserve–deposit ratio is 10 percent, how does the money multiplier change? How would M1 change if the monetary base were to remain constant at its previous level?

IN THE NEWS

Perils of insuring bank deposits

By Lindley H. Clark, Jr.

Any insurance plan has to deal with a basic problem: something insurance men call "moral hazard." The idea is simple. If you have no fire insurance on your home, you are extra careful. If, on the other hand, you are insured, you relax. You may not let the kids play with matches, but you don't stay awake nights trying to smell smoke.

Similarly, when a bank deposit is insured, the depositor doesn't worry about the safety of his funds. He has little incentive to check up on the bank to try to learn if its operations are safe and sound. The bank, for its part, pays a fixed rate for deposit insurance regardless of the riskiness of its assets. If the bank's loans go bad, it knows the government will be standing by to pick up the pieces. There's a substantial incentive to make riskier loans to improve bank profits.

Source: The Wall Street Journal

Deposit insurance, like all insurance, creates a problem of moral hazard.

Connections between the monetary system and the loan market discussed in the previous sections imply connections between changes in the money supply and changes in the supply of loans. This section explains an additional *short-run* connection between the money market and the loan market.

When the Federal Reserve expands the money supply through an open market purchase, the long-run effects fall entirely on *nominal* variables, and money is neutral. In the long run, an increase in the money supply raises all nominal prices in the same proportion. For example, a 10 percent rise in the money supply eventually raises all nominal prices by 10 percent, so that relative prices do not change. Like a currency reform in reverse, an increase in the money supply has no long-run effects on real GDP, employment, or other real economic conditions.[6] Similarly, in the long run, a fall in the money supply reduces all nominal prices in the same proportion, without altering relative prices or real economic conditions.

In the short run, however, a Federal Reserve open market purchase may affect *real* variables rather than only *nominal* variables. The essay "What Economists Do," by Professor Robert Lucas (in Chapter 6) showed how a change in the money supply in Kennywood Park can affect real GDP and employment in the park. The real effects of changes in the money supply have inspired much economic research and controversy, as the next two chapters will explain. Most economists agree that one key element involves the connection between the *money market* and the *loan market*. This section discusses a simple model of this connection that explains why Fed actions affect the real interest rate in the short run.

Think about the supply and demand for short-term loans among banks. The equilibrium interest rate on these loans is the equilibrium federal funds rate. When the Fed adds reserves to the banking system through an open market purchase, the supply of loans increases, as in Figure 6a, reducing the equilibrium federal funds rate. Similarly, the supply of loans decreases when the Fed withdraws reserves from the banking system through an open market sale.

SHORT-RUN EFFECTS OF FEDERAL RESERVE POLICIES

Figure 6 | Effects of an Open Market Purchase

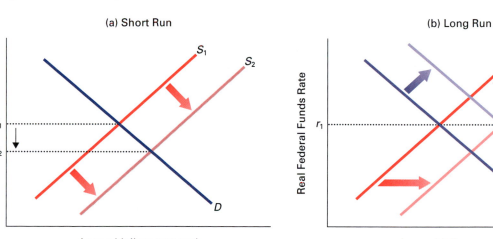

(a) Short Run

(b) Long Run

In the short run, an open-market purchase raises the money supply and the supply of loans. If the price level does not rise in the short run, as in the Kennywood Park story, then the real interest rate falls.

In the long run, the increase in the money supply raises the price level proportionately, raising the demand for loans and raising the equilibrium real interest rate back to its original level.

[6]Unlike a currency reform in reverse, however, the change in the money supply may redistribute income, creating winners and losers. In a reverse currency reform, everyone would share the increase in the money supply (essentially by adding zeros to their money). However, not everyone receives additional money when the money supply rises through an open market purchase, so the open market operation can redistribute wealth from some people to others.

Fed cuts discount rate to 6.5%; move signals concern on economy

Lower funds rate is also seen backed at earlier meeting

By David Wessel
Staff Reporter of
The Wall Street Journal

WASHINGTON—The Federal Reserve Board, signaling its concern about the weakening U.S. economy, cut the highly visible discount rate one-half percentage point to 6.5 percent.

The unanimous decision by the six Fed governors came hours after a meeting of the Fed's larger policy-making committee. The committee is believed to have authorized an immediate reduction of one-quarter percentage point in the key federal funds rate, which banks charge on loans to one another.

Market reaction to the cut in the discount rate—which the Fed charges on loans to banks—was swift

and enthusiastic. Stock and bond prices rose, driving interest rates down.

The discount-rate move, and the expected reduction in the federal funds rate to 7 percent as early as today, are likely to force banks to finally cut their lending rates.

Just two weeks ago, the Fed cut the federal funds rate one-quarter percentage point and made the unusual move of reducing the fraction of deposits that banks must hold as reserves—two moves aimed at stimulating the economy.

Symbolic Move

Moves in the discount rate have little direct effect on the economy, but are used by the Fed to send loud and clear signals. "Symbolism is important," said Mr. Moran.

"This will be on the front pages rather than the credit market columns. It will be on the evening news. It will be seen by individuals and small-business people who might not otherwise know [what the Fed is doing]. It will be a boost to confidence."

The Fed governors directly set the discount rate in response to requests from district Fed banks. But the Fed's Open Market Committee—for which the voting members consist of the six current governors plus five of the 12 district bank presidents—controls the federal funds rate by buying and selling Treasury securities. The fed funds rate is more significant in determining the level of interest rates in the economy.

Source: The Wall Street Journal

Federal Reserve policy actions affect interest rates.

Suppose the Fed raises the money supply by 10 percent, by increasing reserves that banks lend to people. If the *demand* for loans also were to increase by 10 percent, then the equilibrium real federal funds rate would not change. In the long run, a 10 percent increase in the money supply raises all nominal prices by 10 percent. As a result, the nominal quantity of loans demanded also rises by 10 percent in the long run, so equilibrium federal funds rate does not change. Figure 6b shows the long-run effect of the open market purchase on the federal funds market. An open market operation has no long-run effects on the real federal funds interest rate.

In the short run, however, an open market purchase tends to reduce the real federal funds rate. Suppose that the price level does *not change* in the short run, despite the 10 percent increase in the money supply. (Recall that a surprise decrease in the money supply in Kennywood Park left the price level in the park unaffected in the short run.) In this case, the increase in the money supply raises the *supply* of loans but leaves the *demand* for loans unchanged in the short run. As a result, the equilibrium real federal funds rate *falls* in the short run.

In this way, Federal Reserve actions affect the real interest rate in the short run. Specifically, the Fed's actions affect the real federal funds interest rate. The Fed can reduce the real interest rate through open-market purchases (which raise the money supply), or raise the real interest rate through open-market sales. These changes in the real federal funds rate also tend to be reflected in the nominal federal funds rate, unless the Fed's action has a large effect on expected inflation. As a result, the Fed lowers or raises the nominal federal funds rate through open-market purchases or sales.

The change in the federal funds rate affects other interest rates. A fall in the federal funds rate reduces the cost to banks of borrowing reserves, and competition then leads banks to reduce the interest rates that they charge to borrowers. Similarly, a rise in the federal funds rate raises the cost to banks of borrowing reserves, leading them to raise the interest rates they charge. An open market operation has no long-run effects on real interest rates. After changing in the short run, real interest rates return to their original levels.

Because open market purchases temporarily reduce the real federal funds rate, and open market sales temporarily raise it, commentators often describe Federal Reserve policies in terms of their effects on interest rates. The Fed itself usually describes its policies in this way—as raising or lowering interest rates.

> A **looser monetary policy** refers to Fed actions that increase the growth rate of the money supply or decrease the federal funds rate.

The Fed loosens monetary policy by expanding open market purchases or increasing its lending to banks at the discount window.

> A **tighter monetary policy** refers to Fed actions that reduce the growth rate of the money supply or increase the federal funds rate.

The Fed tightens monetary policy by reducing open market purchases (or expanding open market sales) or by reducing its lending to banks at the discount window.

The next two chapters discuss the short-run effects of monetary policy as they explore business cycles and recessions. A later chapter discusses alternative views of the role of monetary policy.

Review Questions

19. How does a Federal Reserve open market purchase affect the federal funds rate? Why does this effect occur? How do the short-run effects of such a policy differ from the long-run effects?

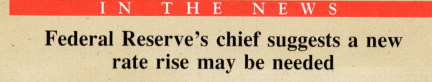

The Fed tightens monetary policy to fight inflation.

20. What does the Fed do when it loosens or tightens monetary policy?

Thinking Exercise

21. If an open market sale raises the real interest rate by 1 percentage point and reduces expected inflation by 2 percentage points, how does it affect the nominal interest rate?

Conclusion

History and Roles of Money

Many commodities have served as money, and some civilizations have not used money at all. Money offers advantages, however, because it avoids the problem with barter of creating a double coincidence of wants. In its main role as a medium of exchange, money acts as an asset that sellers generally accept as payment for goods, services, and other assets. Money also serves as a store of value and a unit of account.

The most common form of commodity standard for money has been a gold standard. In a pure gold standard, people use gold coins as money, and the economy includes no paper money. In a gold exchange standard, people trade paper money that is backed by gold stored in warehouses. A silver standard resembles a gold standard, but silver instead of gold backs paper money. Fiat money is paper money that is not backed by a commodity in the sense that people cannot trade it for a particular commodity at a fixed nominal price.

Measuring the Money Supply

Banks help to create money. An increase in bank reserves leads to an increase in bank lending, which raises broad measures of the money supply. Definitions of the money supply include the monetary base and broader measures such as M1 and M2. M1 includes currency plus traveler's checks and bank balances against which people or firms can write checks; M2 combines M1 with balances in most savings accounts and similar accounts. The money multiplier is the ratio of a broad measure of the money supply, such as M1 or M2, to the monetary base.

Federal Reserve System

A central bank is a bank for banks. The Federal Reserve is the central bank of the United States. The Federal Reserve System consists of the Board of Governors, 12 regional Federal Reserve Banks, and the Federal Open Market Committee (FOMC).

The Fed's three main tools of monetary policy are open market operations, discount window lending, and changes in reserve requirements. The primary tool of monetary policy is the open market operation, in which the Fed buys or sells financial assets, usually U.S. government Treasury bills and Treasury bonds. In an open market purchase, the Fed buys financial assets; in an open market sale, it sells them.

Financial Intermediaries

Financial intermediaries, such as banks and similar kinds of firms, gather funds from many savers to lend to borrowers. They also monitor borrowers' activities to try to ensure timely repayment of loans.

A banking panic refers to many bank runs at the same time. Deposit insurance can help to prevent bank runs, but it changes the incentives of financial intermediaries, increasing their willingness to choose risky investments and reducing the incentive of depositors to monitor banks' investments and choose low-risk banks. The U.S. savings and loan crisis resulted from these incentives, coupled with a failure of the insurer (the government, in that case) to prevent risky investments or raise insurance premiums to risky institutions. Banking crises are usually associated with recessions, as in many Asian countries in recent years.

Short-Run Effects of Federal Reserve Policies

In the long run, an increase in the money supply raises all nominal prices proportionally and does not affect relative prices or the real interest rate. In the short run, however, an open market purchase reduces the real federal funds interest rate, leading other real interest rates to fall. Nominal interest rates also fall unless expected inflation rises sufficiently.

Economists commonly describe Fed policies in terms of raising or lowering interest rates. A looser monetary policy increases the growth rate of the money supply or decreases the federal funds rate, usually by increasing open market purchases. A tighter monetary policy reduces the growth rate of the money supply or increases the federal funds rate, usually by reducing open market purchases or increasing open market sales.

Key Terms

medium of exchange
store of value
unit of account
pure gold standard
gold exchange standard
fiat money

currency
demand deposit
M1
M2
bank reserves
monetary base

M1 money multiplier
central bank
Federal Reserve System
open market operation
Federal Reserve discount rate
federal funds rate

required reserves
financial intermediary
bank run
banking panic
looser monetary policy
tighter monetary policy

Questions and Problems

22. What is a double coincidence of wants?

23. When and why was the Fed created?

24. Why do banks hold reserves?

25. Suppose that banks hold reserves equal to 20 percent of deposits in checking accounts and that people always keep equal amounts of currency and checking-account balances (making the currency–deposit ratio equal to 1). If the Fed raises the monetary base by $1 million with an open market purchase, how much will M1 increase? Explain why.

26. What does a government do when it debases coins?

27. Suppose that the United States and Russia were on a gold standard and that large quantities of gold were discovered in Russia. Explain the process by which this discovery would affect prices in the United States.

28. Suppose that prices take 6 months to increase after the Fed increases the money supply. Suppose that the Fed raises the money supply by 10 percent through open market purchases.
 (a) Explain why this action could reduce the real interest rate for 6 months.
 (b) Explain why this action would not reduce the long-run real interest rate (after nominal prices have increased by 10 percent).

Inquiries for Further Thought

29. (a) Why are sellers willing to trade goods for the pieces of paper that people call dollar bills? What makes those pieces of paper different from other pieces of paper that sellers would refuse to accept as payment?
 (b) Why do sellers in the United States usually insist on payment in U.S. dollars rather than Canadian dollars, while Canadian sellers display the opposite preference?
 (c) Why do people use the money issued by their own governments? Why not other moneys? What advantages and disadvantages might accompany attempts by people in another country to use U.S. dollars rather than their own country's money?

30. What would happen if banks were allowed to issue their own money, as they were in 19th-century America?

31. What would happen to the U.S. economy if many communities began using their own local currencies, such as the Ithaca Hours in Ithaca, N.Y.?

32. What would happen if the government were to stop providing deposit insurance to banks? What would happen if the government were to privatize deposit insurance?

33. Do you think that people will use money 50 years from now? Some people have predicted that cash will disappear as computers keep track of who owes what to whom. How might that work? Could inflation exist with that system?

34. Some people have proposed that the United States eliminate pennies. (The federal government mints about 12 billion pennies each year, about 50 for every person in the country. Sales clerks at stores take a few extra seconds to deal with pennies, and this time adds up to a large expense, in the millions of dollars, for stores. Banning the penny would eliminate these expenses.) If the penny were abolished and all prices were rounded to the nearest $0.05, would stores always round the price upward, or would they maintain the psychological advantages of a $12.98 price by rounding down to $12.95? What would happen? Who would gain and who would lose from eliminating the penny? Would it be a good or bad idea?

Appendix: The Formula for the Money Multiplier

One can derive the M1 money multiplier from the definitions of M1 and the monetary base. If C stands for currency (cash), D stands for deposits, and R stands for bank reserves, then M1 equals:

$$M1 = D + C$$

and the monetary base, B, equals

$$B = R + C$$

The M1 money multiplier equals the ratio of M1 to B:

$$\text{M1 money multiplier} = \frac{M1}{B}$$

Substituting the definitions for M1 and B:

$$= \frac{D + C}{R + C}$$

Dividing both the numerator and denominator by D:

$$= \frac{(1 + C/D)}{(R/D + C/D)}$$

This is the expression in the text. Money multipliers for broader measures of money can be derived in a similar way, with more complicated results.

BUSINESS CYCLES

CHAPTER 11

BUSINESS CYCLES 1: AGGREGATE DEMAND AND SUPPLY

In this Chapter . . .

Main Points to Understand

▶ The aggregate demand curve graphs the equation of exchange for given levels of the money supply and velocity. It shows the total amount of goods and services that people, firms, and the government would buy at each possible price level, given the money supply and velocity.

▶ The aggregate supply curve graphs the total amount of goods and services that firms would produce and try to sell at each possible price level.

▶ The long-run aggregate supply curve is a vertical line.

▶ The short-run aggregate supply curve slopes upward because of sticky prices.

▶ Decreases in aggregate demand can cause recessions.

Thinking Skills to Develop

▶ Distinguish aggregate demand and supply curves from demand and supply curves for individual products.

▶ Use a special case of a model to help understand a more general case.

From 1929 to 1933, real GDP in the United States fell by 30 percent. The price level fell by more than 20 percent, and nominal GDP fell by half. The U.S. unemployment rate rose to almost 25 percent—roughly one out of every four workers became unemployed. This period is appropriately called the *Great Depression*.

The Great Depression may seem long ago and distant from your life today, but people in Mexico, Russia, Japan, and other countries have experienced major recessions within the last few years. In 1998 alone, real GDP fell about 15 percent in Indonesia, 8 percent in South Korea, 7 percent in Thailand, 6 percent in Russia, and 2.5 percent in Venezuela. Unemployment in Japan reached a new record high in late 1998, and leaders around the world began to talk openly of policies to avoid a repeat of the 1930s. Even smaller recessions, like the United States recession of 1991 when unemployment reached 7.5 percent, brought hardships for many families.

The basic model developed in earlier chapters is not capable of explaining these recessions. This chapter will extend the model in the direction suggested by the Kennywood Park story from Chapter 6. The extended model will help explain recessions and predict complex connections between real and nominal variables. For example, economists have noted that the money supply, measured by M2, fell by one-third during the Great Depression.[1]

---

[1] The government did not purposely reduce the money supply. The Federal Reserve kept the monetary base roughly constant, but the money multiplier (discussed in the previous chapter) fell as banks failed and the currency-deposit ratio increased.

> ### IN THE NEWS
>
> ## Japan's unemployment at record high
>
> TOKYO, Oct. 1—Japan's unemployment rate bounced back to a record high 4.3 percent in August, boosted by an increase in corporate restructurings and bankruptcies, the government said Friday. The labor figures were the latest in the series of data that showed further deterioration of the Japanese economy.
>
> *Source: Associated Press*

Many economists believe that if the Federal Reserve had prevented the fall in the money supply, it would have averted the Great Depression or dramatically reduced its severity. The extended model will explain why. It will also explain the logic that the Federal Reserve uses when it decides to loosen monetary policy to help fight a potential recession, as it did in September 1998.

Connections between real and nominal variables are controversial subjects in economics. Economists do not yet fully understand these connections; evidence is less complete than economists would like; and disagreements abound on details of these issues. However, governments cannot wait for additional evidence to formulate their policies, nor can business firms postpone their decisions on operations and investments. They must act on the best available information, even if that information is incomplete. This chapter studies the logic that underlies economists' current understanding of these key issues that have such profound impacts on our lives.

BOOMS AND RECESSIONS

Economic growth does not proceed smoothly—it fluctuates in patterns called *business cycles.*[2] A typical business cycle has two parts: a recession and a recovery or expansion. During a recession, which typically lasts between two quarters and two years, real GDP falls, employment falls, and unemployment rises. Some commentators define a recession as two consecutive quarters of falling real GDP. However, the National Bureau of Economic Research, a private organization generally regarded as the authority on dates of business cycles, uses a more complex definition involving an extended period of decline in real GDP and other related variables. Figure 1 shows recessions in the United States in the last quarter-century. Note that decreases in real GDP occur along with rising unemployment.

A recession begins at the *peak* of a business cycle and continues until its *trough* (low point), when a *recovery* or expansion begins, continuing until the next peak. The last U.S. recession occurred from July 1990 (the peak of the last business cycle) until March 1991 (the trough). Since that time (at least until late 1998) the U.S. economy continued in a long expansion.

Why do business cycles occur? Economists disagree on the details of the answer to this fundamental question, because available evidence is not yet strong enough to create full agreement. The basic model of previous chapters suggests one possible reason for business cycles: Perhaps business cycles result from changes in technology or

---

[2] The economy also experiences seasonal cycles throughout each year. These seasonal variations, which are much easier to predict than business cycles, share other features of business cycles. For example, unemployment rises as real GDP falls.

Figure 1 | U.S. Business Cycles, 1950–1998

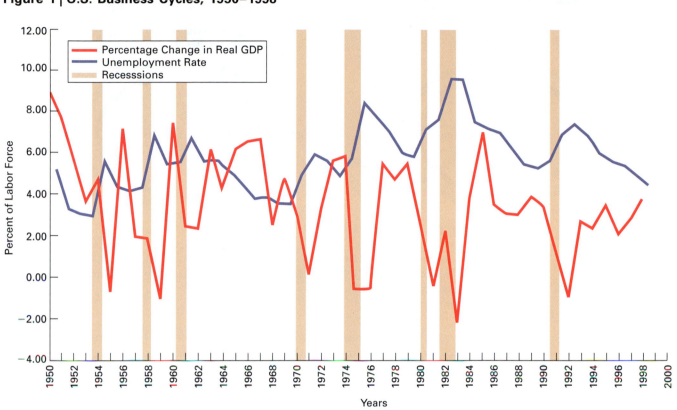

equilibrium quantities of inputs. (Chapter 8 showed how changes in technology and available capital affect real GDP.) However, available evidence leads most economists to doubt this explanation. Changes in overall technology occur too smoothly over time to cause the yearly fluctuations in GDP shown in Figure 1, or the Great Depression and the recent recessions throughout the world. Evidence indicates connections between recessions and *monetary policy,* a connection that the basic model of previous chapters cannot explain. This chapter modifies the basic model by adding *short-run* features that most economists believe are important in understanding business cycles.

A SIMPLE MODEL OF A RECESSION

We can use the circular flow diagram of Chapter 9 to create a simple model of a recession based on the equation of exchange, $MV = Py$. In Figure 2, firms produce 100 goods per year, so real GDP is 100 goods per year. The nominal money supply is $1,000, and the velocity of money is 1 per year, so people spend $1,000 per year to buy 100 goods, and the price level is $10 per good.

Suppose the money supply falls from $1,000 to $900 with no change in velocity. People spend only $900 per year, so the equilibrium price level falls from $10 to $9 per good. The 10 percent fall in the money supply reduces *nominal* variables by 10 percent, so nominal GDP falls from $1,000 to $900 per year. However, the fall in the money supply does not affect *real* variables, such as production and employment. Real GDP remains at 100 goods per year. In the language of previous chapters, *money is neutral.* Now consider a new complication to the circular-flow model. *Suppose that the price level cannot change.* Again, the money supply falls from $1,000 to $900 with constant velocity, so people spend only $900 per year. However, the price level remains at $10 per good,

Figure 2 | Key Example

Original Equilibrium

Short-Run after the Money Supply Falls, with Unchanged Price Level

At first, people spend $1,000 to buy 100 goods each year. Velocity is 1 per year, and the price is $10 per good. The money supply then falls from $1,000 to $900. The completely sticky price level keeps the cost of goods at $10 each. Unless velocity rises, people spend only $900 each year, so they can afford to buy only 90 goods each year. Firms reduce output from 100 goods per person to 90 goods per person, and a recession occurs.

so *people can afford to buy only 90 goods.* Figure 2 shows the results. Firms have enough technology and inputs to produce 100 goods, but they can sell only 90. As a result, firms reduce production from 100 to 90, laying off workers and raising unemployment. The economy enters a *recession.*

In mathematical terms, these results appear in the equation of exchange:

$$MV = Py$$

The money supply, *M,* falls and velocity, *V,* remains constant, so the left-hand side of the equation falls. In the basic model of previous chapters, a fall in the price level, *P,* reduces the right-hand side of the equation, restoring equality. The price level falls by the same percentage as the money supply. Real GDP, *y,* remains unaffected. However, if the price level *cannot* fall, then real GDP must fall to balance the equation. Even though firms *could* continue to produce 100 goods per year, they would not be able to sell all those goods. As a result, they reduce production, decreasing real GDP and raising unemployment. If the price level cannot fall, money is *not* neutral, and the economy enters a recession.

Return to Kennywood Park

The recession in Professor Lucas's Kennywood Park story, discussed in Chapter 6, occurs for a similar reason. The money supply in Kennywood Park—the total number of tickets sold at the park—decreases one Sunday. However, nominal prices—the numbers of tickets required for the rides—remain unchanged. As a result, the park's real GDP falls; people buy fewer rides, and the park enters a recession.

Short Run and Long Run

Suppose that the price level remains fixed for 6 months following a fall in the money supply, then changes to its new equilibrium level. During the first 6 months, the economy will experience a recession. After the price level falls to its new equilibrium level, the recession ends. Economists distinguish the *short run* from the *long run*: The short run is the time period *before* the price level adjusts fully to its new equilibrium level after a change in conditions (like a fall in the money supply). The long run refers to the time period *after* prices have fully adjusted to a change in conditions.[3] If the price level cannot fall in the short run, then a decrease in the money supply causes a recession in the short run, but the recession ends in the long run. Money is *neutral* in the long run, though not in the short run.

Sticky Prices

The simple model of a recession says that the price level does not change in the short run, even after a change in underlying conditions: The price level is *sticky* in the short run.

> Nominal prices are **sticky** if they take time to adjust to their new equilibrium levels following changes in supply or demand.

Some prices adjust very quickly to changes in demand or supply. Prices of homogeneous commodities (such as gold, silver, tin, wheat, and soybeans) traded on organized markets such as the Chicago Mercantile Exchange change every few seconds. Prices of some consumer goods, such as computers, change very frequently. These prices are not sticky. Other prices adjust more slowly: prices of magazines at newsstands, prices of clothing in mail-order catalogs, apartment rental prices, and prices of steel, cement, chemicals, and glass bought by manufacturing firms. Prices in some industries remain unchanged for periods of several years.

Overall, evidence suggests that the *price level* is sticky in the short run—it adjusts only slowly after changes in underlying conditions, such as the money supply. Although economists disagree about interpretations of available evidence, most believe that the price level may take one or two years to adjust to its new equilibrium after a change in the money supply. Economists also disagree about the *causes* of short-run price-stickiness. Do firms remain unaware of changes in conditions that would otherwise prompt them to adjust prices? Or do firms postpone price adjustments because they involve costly reprinting of catalogs, menus, and price tags? Fortunately, logical analysis of the *consequences* of price stickiness can proceed without full answers to those questions. That logic begins with the model of *aggregate demand and supply.*

The price level is sticky in the short run—it moves only slowly to its new equilibrium after a change in underlying conditions.

AGGREGATE DEMAND

Loosely, a country's aggregate demand is the total demand for all the goods and services produced in that country in a given year. More precisely,

> The **aggregate demand curve** shows the total amount of goods and services that people, firms, and the government would choose to buy at each possible price level, given the nominal money supply and velocity.[4]

The aggregate demand curve graphs the equation of exchange, solved for the price level:

$$P = MV/y$$

for given values of M and V. The aggregate demand curve shifts when M and V change, rising when MV rises.

---

[3]This *macroeconomic* distinction between *short run* and *long run* differs from the distinction between those terms common in microeconomics.

[4]If you take additional courses in economics, you may encounter a different, more complex definition of aggregate demand.

Figure 3
Aggregate Demand Curve

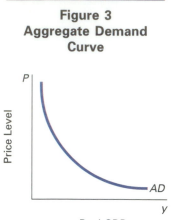

Figure 3 shows an aggregate demand curve. Given total nominal spending, *MV*, the graph shows that the price level (*P*) and real GDP (*y*) vary inversely with one another: Increases in *y* accompany decreases in *P*. For example, suppose that the money supply is $100 and velocity is 2 per year. Then *MV* is $200 per year, so *Py* must be $200 per year. At a price of $10 per good, *y* equals 20 goods per year (Point A in Figure 4). At a price of $20 per good, however, *y* equals only 10 goods per year (Point B in Figure 4).

The total amount of money you spend at a grocery store equals the sum of your spending on each type of good you buy (spending on marshmallows, plus spending on graham crackers, plus spending on chocolate). The term *MV* equals the economy's total spending in a year—the number of dollars in the economy (*M*) multiplied by the number of each times each dollar is spent in that year. This total equals the sum of spending on each type of good: consumption, plus investment, plus government purchases, plus net exports. Therefore, consumption (*C*), plus investment (*I*), plus government purchases (*G*), plus net exports (*NEX*) equals total spending.

$$MV = C + I + G + NEX$$

Both sides of this equation show total spending: both sides show the level of aggregate demand.

For example, suppose that the money supply equals $1 trillion and the velocity of money equals *7 times per year.* Then total spending on final market goods and services, *MV,* is $7 trillion per year. Perhaps people spend $5 trillion on consumption, firms spend $1 trillion on investment, the government spends $1 trillion, and exports equal imports (so net exports equal zero). Then total spending—aggregate demand—equals:

$$C + I + G + NEX = \$5 + \$1 + \$1 + 0 = \$7 \text{ trillion}$$

Figure 4
Example of an Aggregate Demand Curve

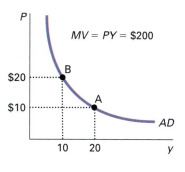

Changes in Aggregate Demand

The aggregate demand curve *shifts* when the money supply changes or velocity changes. Chapter 10 showed that Federal Reserve open market operations (and other Fed policy actions) can change the money supply, as can actions of banks and depositors. When the money supply increases, aggregate demand increases, as in Figure 5.

Our basic economic model shows how various factors can change the velocity of money. Chapter 9 explained that the velocity of money rises when the nominal interest rate rises. Many factors can affect the equilibrium nominal interest rate by affecting the demand or supply of loans. Three important sources of changes in velocity include consumption, investment, and government purchases:

IN THE NEWS

Consumption, the engine of the economy

A decline in consumer confidence often points toward recession because lower confidence is generally translated into lower sales of such things as cars and refrigerators. The effect of canceled or postponed purchases ripples through the economy as, say, the automobile salesman decides he'll wait another year to add a patio to his house and the mason's helper begins to worry about being laid off.

Source: New York Times

A change in spending has indirect effects that ripple through the economy.

A rise in uncertainty about the future can lead people to raise savings and reduce consumption, decreasing aggregate demand.

1. An increase in consumption, *C:* When people decide to consume more and save less, the decrease in savings reduces the supply of loans, increasing the equilibrium real interest rate, as in Figure 6. Given the expected rate of inflation, this increase in the real interest rate raises the nominal interest rate, raising velocity. The increase in velocity raises aggregate demand as in Figure 5.

2. An increase in investment, *I:* When firms decide to increase investment, the demand for loans rises, increasing the equilibrium real interest rate. Given the expected rate of inflation, this increase in the real interest rate raises the nominal interest rate, raising velocity. The increase in velocity raises aggregate demand as in Figure 5.

3. An increase in government purchases, *G:* If the government borrows money to pay for its additional spending, then the demand for loans rises, increasing the equilibrium real interest rate. Alternatively, the government may raise taxes to pay for its additional spending, reducing people's after-tax income. The fall in after-tax income may lead people to reduce savings, decreasing the supply of loans and raising the equilibrium real interest rate. The demand for loans rises, increasing the equilibrium interest rate. Given the expected rate of inflation, this increase raises the nominal interest rate, raising velocity. The increase in velocity raises aggregate demand as in Figure 5.

Summarizing these results:

> Increases in consumption (*C*), investment (*I*), or government purchases (*G*) raise aggregate demand, as in Figure 5.

You can personally raise aggregate demand in the U.S. economy by increasing your spending and reducing your saving. A business firm can raise aggregate demand by borrowing for new investment. The government can raise aggregate demand by boosting spending.

Review Questions

1. What do economists mean when they say that the price level is sticky in the short run?

**Figure 5
Increase in Aggregate Demand**

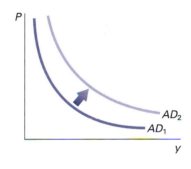

**Figure 6
A Fall in Savings Raises Velocity**

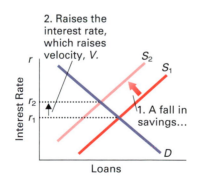

An increase in consumption spending reduces saving, which reduces the supply of loans from S_1 to S_2. This raises the real interest rate from r_1 to r_2, which raises the nominal interest rate and velocity. Therefore, aggregate demand (*MV*) rises.

An Important Reminder

The aggregate demand curve differs from the demand curves for individual products introduced in Chapter 4. Those demand curves involve *relative prices* of goods. When the relative price of a good rises, its opportunity cost increases, so the quantity demanded falls as people substitute other goods in its place. In contrast, the aggregate demand curve involves the economy's overall *nominal price level*. A rise in the nominal price level does not affect the opportunity costs of the economy's goods and services. However, it reduces the overall purchasing power of the money that people have available to spend. Understanding the distinction between relative prices and the nominal price level, and the related distinction between demand curves for individual products and the aggregate demand curve, will help you avoid logical fallacies.

"Whether the marriage lasts or not, we've certainly given the economy a boost."

A small increase in aggregate demand.
Source: The Wall Street Journal, October 25, 1988, p. A27.

2. Draw a circular-flow diagram and explain why a decrease in the money supply leads to a fall in real GDP if prices are completely sticky and velocity remains constant.

3. What does the aggregate demand curve show? Why does it slope downward? What makes it shift?

4. Why is the money supply multiplied by velocity equal to the sum of consumption, investment, government purchases, and net exports?

Thinking Exercise

5. Recall that the aggregate demand curve graphs the equation of exchange for given money supply and velocity. Explain how and why the following changes shift the aggregate demand curve: (a) a decision by people to reduce consumption and increase savings; (b) a decrease in investment demand; (c) a decrease in government purchases.

AGGREGATE SUPPLY

Loosely, a country's aggregate supply is the total supply of all the goods and services produced in that country in a given year. More precisely,

> The **aggregate supply curve** shows the total amount of goods and services that firms would produce and try to sell at each possible price level.[5]

---

[5] If you go on in economics, you may encounter a different, more complex definition of aggregate supply that distinguishes the amount that firms want to sell from the amount they want to produce.

The most important facts about the aggregate supply curve are:

The aggregate supply curve is vertical in the long run.

The aggregate supply curve slopes upward in the short run.

Long-run aggregate supply measures the total supply of goods and services after the economy has had time to adjust fully to a change in underlying conditions. *Short-run aggregate supply* refers to the total supply before that adjustment is complete.

Long-Run Aggregate Supply

The long-run aggregate supply curve is a vertical line, as in Figure 7. In the long run, a country's production of goods and services does *not* depend on *nominal* variables, such as the price level. Long-run production depends *solely* on *real* variables, such as available technology and inputs such as capital, labor, natural resources, as well as the laws, property rights, regulations, and taxes that affect people's incentives to use technology and inputs efficiently. This is an application of the idea from Chapters 6 and 8 that *money is neutral* in the long run. Changing the units by which we measure money and nominal prices, as in a currency reform, does not affect real variables such as production and relative prices.

The long-run level of real GDP in Figure 7, often called the *full-employment level of output*, y^{FE}, is the equilibrium level from the basic model of previous chapters. The supply and demand for labor determine equilibrium employment, and the production function then determines equilibrium real GDP, as in Figure 5 of Chapter 7.[6]

Changes in Long-Run Aggregate Supply
Increases in technology raise long-run aggregate supply, as in Figure 8. Long-run aggregate supply also rises with increases in the economy's equilibrium inputs of labor or capital, workers' skills, or the quality of capital equipment. Finally, long-run aggregate supply increases when changes in taxes, government regulations, or the legal system lead to more efficient use of the economy's resources. Long-run aggregate supply *decreases* when equilibrium inputs fall, workers' skills erode, or the quality of capital equipment falls, and when changes in taxes, government regulations, or the legal system lead to less efficient use of the economy's resources. Changes in the prices of imported inputs, such as oil from foreign countries, also shift the long-run aggregate supply curve. For example, a quadrupling of the price of oil a quarter-century ago contributed to the recession of 1973 to 1975 by reducing aggregate supply.

Long-Run Equilibrium of Aggregate Supply and Demand

The intersection of the long-run aggregate supply curve with the aggregate demand curve, as in Figure 9, shows the long-run equilibrium real GDP and price level. This graph summarizes the *same* equilibrium as in Figure 5 of Chapter 7. The supply and demand for labor determine equilibrium employment, and the production function then determines equilibrium real GDP; given this level of real GDP, together with the money supply and velocity, the equation of exchange determines the price level.

Changes in Aggregate Demand
Figure 10 on page 285 shows the long-run effects of a rise in aggregate demand from AD_1 to AD_2 (perhaps due to an increase in government purchases or the money supply). The price level rises from P_1 to P_2 and real GDP remains unchanged at y^{FE}, the full-employment rate of output.

---

[6]The economy's capital stock and its technology result from its past investments, as Chapters 7–8 explained.

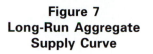

**Figure 7
Long-Run Aggregate
Supply Curve**

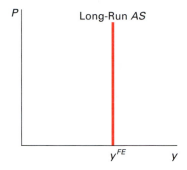

The long-run aggregate supply curve is a vertical line at the full-employment level of output, y^{FE}.

An Important Reminder, Part 2
The aggregate supply curve differs from the supply curves of individual products introduced in Chapter 4. Those supply curves involve *relative prices* of goods. In contrast, the aggregate supply curve involves the *nominal price level*.

Understanding this distinction will help you avoid logical fallacies. For example, someone might say that the aggregate supply curve must slope upward, reflecting the upward slopes of the supply curves of individual goods, like pizzas and parkas. This claim is incorrect because it ignores the distinction between the price level and relative prices of individual goods. When the relative price of pizzas

(continued)

rises, production of pizzas rises as existing pizza restaurants boost production and new firms (such as hamburger restaurants) start selling pizzas. With a rise in the *relative* price of pizzas, sellers trade each pizza for *more* units of other goods, such as T-shirts and vacations. However, when the price *level* rises, with no change in relative prices, the incentive to sell pizzas remains unchanged, because each pizza trades for the same number of other goods as before the general price increase. You must understand these distinctions to understand why the slope of the aggregate supply curve is *vertical* in the long run, *regardless* of the shapes of supply curves of individual products. Similarly, the slope of the short-run aggregate supply curve depends on factors such as the degree of price stickiness; the slope is *unrelated* to the slopes of supply curves of individual products.

Figure 8 | An Increase in Long-Run Aggregate Supply

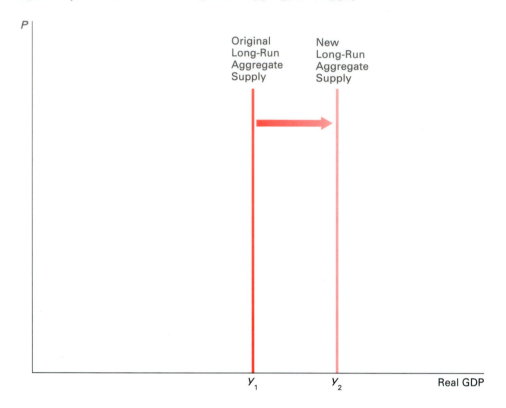

Figure 9 | Long-Run Equilibrium

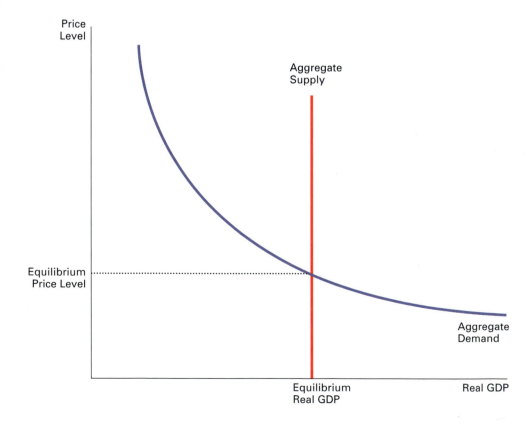

Suppose aggregate demand rises, because the government increases the money supply by 10 percent. The price level rises by 10 percent in the long run, and real GDP does not change. You may wonder how one can know that the price level will rise by 10 percent rather than 5 percent or 15 percent. To get this answer, use the equation of exchange, $MV = Py$. An increase in the money supply does not change real GDP, y, or velocity, V, in the long run, so these variables do not change; therefore, P must rise to balance the equation (raising the right-hand side by the same amount as the left-hand side). A 10 percent rise in M requires a 10 percent rise in P to balance the equation. As a result, the aggregate demand curve shifts *upward* by 10 percent, raising the equilibrium price level by 10 percent.

Now suppose an increase in government purchases raises aggregate demand. You may wonder why this increase in spending does not raise real GDP in the long run. The answer is that long-run real GDP depends on technology and available inputs, which are not affected by the increase in government purchases. When the government buys more goods and services than before, fewer remain available for people's consumption and business firms' investments. The increase in government purchases reduces the amount of goods that go to consumption and investment, and raises the price level.

The logic behind this result depends on how the government pays for its spending. If the government borrows money to pay for its additional spending, then the demand for loans rises, increasing the equilibrium real interest rate and reducing investment. Alternatively, suppose the government raises taxes to pay for its additional spending. This tax increase reduces people's after-tax income. With less after-tax income, people reduce their consumption. They also may save less, which decreases the supply of loans, raises the equilibrium real interest rate, and reduces investment. Either way, the increase in government purchases reduces consumption and investment in the new long-run equilibrium, and leaves real GDP unchanged.

Changes in Aggregate Supply

Figure 11 shows the long-run effects of a rise in aggregate supply from AS_1 to AS_2. The price level falls from P_1 to P_2, and the full-employment level of real GDP rises from y_1 to y_2.

Short-Run Aggregate Supply: Special Case

Suppose that *the price level cannot change* in the short run, as in the simple model of a recession earlier in this chapter—the price level is *completely sticky* in the short run. We can show this on a graph by drawing a horizontal line, as in Figure 12. This line shows that the price level P is completely sticky and that real GDP, y, adjusts to keep $MV = Py$ when MV changes. In this special case of a completely sticky price level, this horizontal line is the *short-run aggregate supply curve*.

Earlier, we defined the aggregate supply curve as a curve showing the total amount of goods and services that firms choose to produce and sell at each possible price level. The short-run aggregate supply curve in Figure 12 shows the total amount of goods and services that firms choose to produce and sell when the price is stuck at P_1. This is often called the simple Keynesian (pronounced *kane'-zee-en*) case of a horizontal short-run aggregate supply, after British economist and statesman John Maynard Keynes (pronounced like *canes)*, the most famous economist of the 20th century. Keynes's 1936 book, *The General Theory of Employment, Interest, and Money,* revolutionized economics and led to economic models like the model of aggregate demand and supply.[7]

---

[7]If you go on in economics, you may encounter the *IS–LM* model, which resulted from the work of Keynes and his followers. The *IS* part of that model refers to *investment equals savings,* which corresponds to loan-market equilibrium in this book's model. The *LM* part of that model refers to the equation of exchange, which appears in this book's graphs as the aggregate demand curve. Therefore, if you study the *IS–LM* model in a future course, you may recognize it as the model from this chapter expressed in a different graphical language.

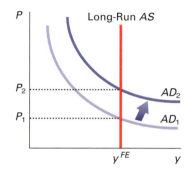

Figure 10
Long-Run Effects of an Increase in Aggregate Demand

An increase in aggregate demand raises the price level in the long run and leaves real GDP unchanged at the full-employment level of output, y^{FE}.

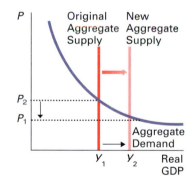

Figure 11
Long-Run Effects of an Increase in Aggregate Supply

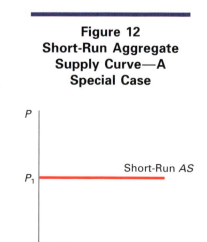

Figure 12
Short-Run Aggregate Supply Curve—A Special Case

Figure 13
Short-Run Effects of a
Decrease in Aggregate
Demand

Figure 14 | Short-Run and Long-Run Effects of a Decrease
in Aggregate Demand

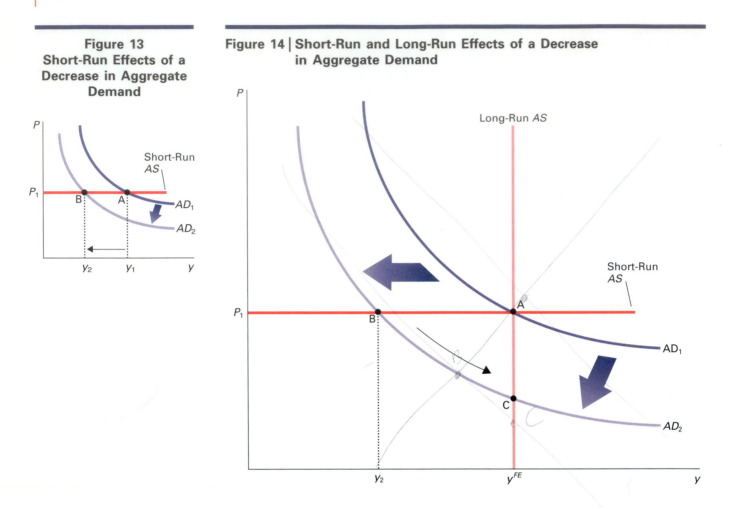

Short-Run Equilibrium of Aggregate Supply and Demand

The Kennywood Park recession in Professor Lucas's story, like the recession in the simple model discussed at the beginning of this chapter, resulted from a decrease in aggregate demand as in Figure 13. In the short run, the decrease in aggregate demand decreases real GDP from y_1 to y_2, moving the economy from Point A to Point B, creating a recession. In the long run, the price level falls and the recession ends, as real GDP returns to its full-employment level (Point C), as in Figure 14.

IN THE NEWS

Italy's GDP shrinks as Asia woes bite

ROME—Italy's economy unexpectedly shrank in the first quarter as Asia's economic slump knocked back Italian exports to the region.

Tumbling currencies and economies in Asia have eroded shoppers' appetite for Italian-made goods, notably clothing.

Source: International Herald Tribune

A fall in aggregate demand spreads
throughout the world.

A fall in aggregate demand can cause a recession.

Short-Run Aggregate Supply—General Case

The horizontal short-run aggregate supply curve illustrates a special case in which the price level is completely sticky in the short run. More generally, the price level can change *partly* but not fully in the short run toward its long-run equilibrium level after a change in aggregate demand. As a result, the short-run aggregate supply curve slopes upward as in Figure 15.

The short-run aggregate supply curve in Figure 15 generalizes the special case in Figure 12. The price level is sticky, but not completely so, in the short run. As indicated earlier, some prices are not sticky even in the short run; prices of gold and wheat change continuously in organized markets; prices of computers change almost every day. However, other prices, such as prices of hamburgers at fast-food restaurants, prices of new books, and prices of clothes from catalogs, tend to be sticky in the short run. The aggregate supply curve in Figure 15 combines the results from these different markets. An upward movement along the short-run aggregate supply curve shows a rise in the nominal price level, resulting from increases in prices for some goods, and an increase in real GDP, resulting from sticky prices and increases in production of other goods.

Figure 15
Short-Run Aggregate Supply—A More General Case

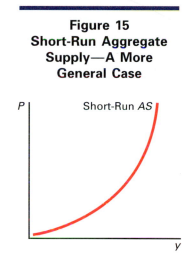

In the general case with upward sloping aggregate supply, a rise in aggregate demand raises the price level and real GDP in the short run, as in Figure 16a. A fall in aggregate demand lowers the price level and real GDP in the short run, as in Figure 16b.

If a change in aggregate demand is *temporary*, then its effects on the price level and real GDP are temporary. After moving from Point A to Point B in Figure 16 in the short run, the economy returns to Point A in the long run.

Figure 17 shows the effects of a *permanent* change in aggregate demand. Panel (a) shows the effects of a permanent rise in aggregate demand. In the short run, real GDP and the price level both rise, as the economy moves from Point A to Point B. In the long run, the economy moves to Point C, with unchanged real GDP, but a higher price level. Panel (b) shows the effects of a permanent fall in aggregate demand. In the short run, real GDP and the price level both fall (from Point A to Point B). In the long run, the forces that created sticky prices disappear. As a result, the price level falls further to its new long-run equilibrium level, and real GDP returns to its full-employment level (Point C).

SUMMARY OF CHANGES IN AGGREGATE SUPPLY AND DEMAND

SOCIAL AND ECONOMIC ISSUES

Does the United States Spend Too Much? Should the United States Save More?

Throughout the second half of the 20th century, Japan has saved a much larger fraction of its GDP than the United States has saved. As Chapter 8 indicated, the Japanese economy has also grown much faster over that period than the U.S. economy. Japan's GDP per person grew from about one-sixth of the U.S. level in 1950 to one-third of the U.S. level in 1960 (its pre–World War II ratio), to near equality with the United States today. For the past decade, Japan has saved about one-third of its GDP, more than twice as much as the United States.

Many economists argue that the United States should increase its saving. Because an economy needs savings to provide investment, which is necessary for long-run economic growth, they argue that the United States sacrifices the incomes of future generations by saving only a small fraction of GDP.

One natural response to this argument notes that people must not *want* to save more. If they would benefit by saving more and spending less, they would do so. Don't people know their own interests better than economists or government officials?

Many economists respond that government policies are partly to blame for low savings in the United States. Government policies have reduced savings in three main ways. First, government budget deficits in the last half of the 20th century contributed to low savings in the United States. Chapter 7 explained that an increase in the budget deficit

raises the demand for loans as the government expands borrowing to finance its spending. Most economists believe that U.S. government budget deficits over that period raised the real interest rate and crowded out private investment. While the equilibrium quantity of loans increased, the savings available to the private sector for investment decreased.

Second, government policies reduce savings through the social security system. That system reduces private savings by providing income for elderly people, reducing the amount that people need to save for themselves. The more a person pays in social security taxes, and expects to receive in social security benefits, the smaller the incentive for that individual to save. If savings by the government replaced savings by individuals, then total savings would remain unaffected by the social security system. However, the U.S. government does not actually *save* the money that people pay in social security taxes. Until the late 1990s, the government simply collected these taxes from workers and immediately paid that money to social security recipients. Currently, the government saves the excess of social security tax revenue over payments (although this "saving" is only an accounting entry, since the government actually spends that money in other ways, as Chapter 14 will discuss). *Most* of the money that people pay in social security taxes continues to finance current social security expenditures. As a result, the social security system reduces U.S. national savings.

Third, the government's tax policies reduce savings. People pay income taxes on the money they earn regardless of whether they spend it or save it. However, if they save, and invest, they pay additional taxes on the interest (and capital gains) that their savings generate.

Figure 16 | Short-Run Effects of Changes in Aggregate Demand

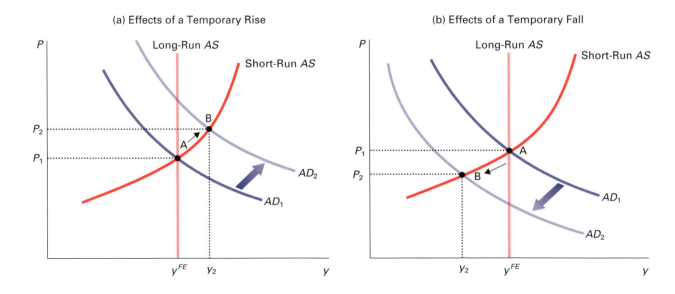

The income from investment is also taxed twice: corporations pay the corporate income tax on the income from investments, and then people pay personal income taxes (or capital gains taxes) when they receive this income. For example, suppose a person saves and buys stock in a corporation. That firm uses the money to invest in new equipment, and it earns $100, paying a corporate income tax of $40. The corporation pays the remaining $60 to the investor as stock dividends. The investor pays one-third of this income, $20, in personal income taxes. This leaves the investor with only $40 after taxes, on an investment that earned $100. Many economists have proposed changes in the tax system to reduce the features that discourage savings and investment.

Together, the government budget deficit, the social security system, and the negative effects of taxes on savings probably reduce U.S. savings below the level that people would choose without these policies. In that sense, one could say that the United States saves too little.

Suppose that the U.S. government were to adopt policies to raise savings by changing the tax system, altering the social security system, or encouraging people in other ways to increase savings. The resulting increase in savings would raise investment, which in turn would raise the economy's future productive capacity and its future real GDP. Therefore, the increase in savings would raise people's incomes in the long run.

The short-run effects of increased saving, however, could differ from the long-run effects. The model of aggregate demand and supply, with sticky prices, implies that an increase in savings would *reduce* real GDP in the short run by reducing consumption and aggregate demand, as in Figure 16b. This short-run analysis was first developed by John Maynard Keynes in his famous book, *The General Theory of Employment, Income, and Prices.* Many Keynesian economists (those who adopted Keynes's arguments) influenced governments in subsequent years. After World War II, the United States adopted policies to provide people with incentives to spend more and save less. These policies included taxes, legal limits on interest rates available to most savers, and expansion of a social security program that, by helping to provide income to retirees, reduced the incentive to save.

Increased savings clearly produce long-run benefits by raising long-run economic growth. With short-run price stickiness, however, increased savings during a recession could deepen the downturn. Choosing tax policies that encourage enough savings for rapid long-run growth while avoiding the short-run problems raised in this chapter is a difficult job, and it can raise questions of tradeoffs between short-run and long-run benefits.

Figure 17 | Effects of a Permanent Rise and Fall in Aggregate Demand

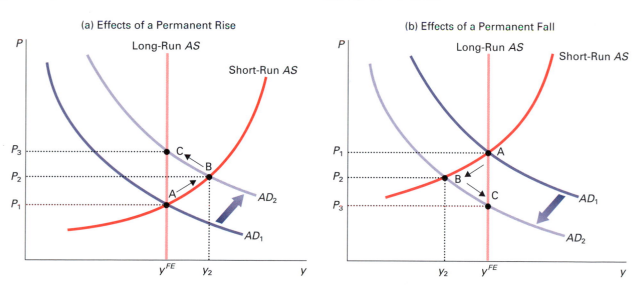

In Panel (a), aggregate demand rises from AD_1 to AD_2. In the short run, the economy moves from Point A to Point B as the price level rises from P_1 to P_2 and real GDP rises from y^{FE} to y_2. In the long run, the economy moves to Point C, where the new aggregate demand curve intersects the long-run aggregate supply curve. The price level rises all the way to P_3, and real GDP falls back to its full employment level, y^{FE}. In Panel (b), aggregate demand falls from AD_1 to AD_2. In the short run, the economy moves from Point A to Point B as the price level falls from P_1 to P_2 and real GDP falls from y^{FE} to y_2. In the long run, the economy moves to Point C, where the new aggregate demand curve intersects the long-run aggregate supply curve. The price level falls all the way to P_3, and real GDP rises back to its full employment level, y^{FE}.

Experts say a lack of hiring stems from weak spending

By Louis Uchitelle

Americans are being bombarded with explanations of why the nation cannot generate enough jobs: a shortage of skilled workers, they are told, holds down hiring, along with higher taxes, global competition, expensive government regulations, technology that automates work, and cutbacks in military spending.

American consumers—and for that matter European consumers who buy American goods—have simply not purchased with their usual gusto. As a result, fewer workers are needed to make goods or provide services to the nation. The problem, in short, is weak demand, not a new world that has found a way to prosper without workers.

Source: New York Times

This news story from 1993, as the U.S. economy began recovering from a recession, illustrates the role of aggregate demand in recessions,

This model of aggregate demand and supply forms the basis for most economic analyses of the short-run effects of changes in underlying conditions on real GDP and other variables. However, economists disagree about certain issues such as whether the short-run aggregate supply curve is very flat or very steep, the period of time over which the price level remains sticky, and the sizes of real-life shifts in aggregate demand and aggregate supply. Economists may differ about the extent to which a particular recession results from a fall in aggregate demand and the extent to which it results from a fall in aggregate supply. For example, economists disagree about the relative importance of increases in aggregate *supply*, and increases in aggregate *demand*, in creating the long

Source: *Richmond Times-Dispatch,* December 16, 1987, p. 12.

A fall in spending can contribute to a recession by reducing aggregate demand, but a rise in savings raises long-run economic growth.

expansion of the 1990s (and before that the long expansion of the 1980s). Current evidence is not sufficient to resolve these disagreements.

The next chapter explores some additional aspects of the model developed in this chapter. It also uses the model to discuss interest rates, unemployment, and recessions in the United States and other countries.

Review Questions

6. What does the long-run aggregate supply curve show? Why is it a vertical line? What makes it shift?

7. What does the short-run aggregate supply curve show? Why does it slope upward? What makes it shift?

8. Draw a graph of aggregate demand and supply to show how a fall in the money supply causes a recession in the short run, and why the recession ends in the long run.

Thinking Exercises

9. Discuss this claim: "The long-run supply curves for housing, food, and every other good in the economy are upward sloping. Therefore the long-run aggregate supply curve, which shows total supply for *all* goods in the economy, is also upward sloping."

10. Draw a graph to show the short-run and long-run effects on real GDP and the price level of an increase in aggregate demand.

11. The text said that changes in the prices of imported inputs shift the aggregate supply curve. Draw a graph to show the long-run effects on real GDP and the price level of an increase in the price of imported oil.

Typically, a slowdown in money-supply growth leads to slower overall economic growth. And indeed, Japan's economy has slowed somewhat, owing to the tight monetary policy the central bank has pursued since May 1989, when it began a series of interest-rate increases.

Source: The Asian Wall Street Journal

Japan's economic slowdown of the 1990s began with tighter monetary policy starting at the beginning of the decade.

Conclusion

Booms and Recessions

Some people define a recession as two consecutive quarters of falling real GDP, although the National Bureau of Economic Research uses a more complex definition. A recession begins at the peak of a business cycle and continues until its trough, followed by a recovery or boom until the next peak. Economists are divided on the causes of business cycles.

A Simple Model of a Recession

A fall in the money supply, with a given velocity of money, reduces the left-hand side of the equation of exchange, $MV = Py$, so the right-hand side also must fall. If the price level is sticky in the short run, P cannot fall, so real GDP, y, falls instead. Real GDP falls because the fall in the money supply reduces total spending, so people cannot afford to buy all the goods that the economy can produce.

Nominal prices are sticky if they take time to adjust to their new equilibrium levels following a change in supply or demand. The short run is the time period over which the price level has not fully adjusted to its new equilibrium level (because it is sticky) after a change in conditions. The long-run is the period after prices have fully adjusted to a change.

Aggregate Demand

The aggregate demand curve shows the total amount of goods and services that people, firms, and the government choose to buy at each possible price level, given the nominal money supply and velocity. The curve graphs the equation of exchange, $MV = Py$, for given values of M and V.

The economy's total spending each year, MV, equals the sum of spending by people on consumption, by firms on investment, by the government for purchases of goods and services, and net exports. As a result, $MV = C + I + G + NEX$. Both sides of this equation show aggregate demand.

The aggregate demand curve shifts in response to changes in the money supply or velocity, rising with an increase in *MV.* Increases in consumption, investment, and government purchases raise aggregate demand by increasing velocity.

The aggregate demand curve differs from the demand curves for individual products. Unlike those demand curves, which involve *relative prices,* the aggregate demand curve involves the economy's (nominal) *price level.*

Aggregate Supply

The aggregate supply curve shows the total amount of goods and services that firms choose to produce and sell at each possible price level. The aggregate supply curve differs from the supply curves of individual products, which involve relative prices of those individual products. In contrast, the aggregate supply curve involves the nominal price level.

The aggregate supply curve is a vertical line in the long run, because money is neutral in the long run: A country's long-run real GDP does not depend on *nominal* variables such as the price level. Instead, it depends solely on *real*

variables—available technology and inputs, and the laws, property rights, regulations, and taxes that affect people's incentives to make efficient use of inputs. Because long-run aggregate supply is vertical, changes in aggregate demand affect the price level, but not real GDP, in the long run.

The aggregate supply curve slopes upward in the short run. (In a special case with *completely* sticky prices in the short run, it is a horizontal line.) The price level is sticky in the short run; it can change *partly* but not fully to its new long-run equilibrium level following a change in conditions.

Summary of Changes in Aggregate Supply and Demand

A rise in aggregate demand raises the price level and real GDP in the short run; a fall in aggregate demand lowers them in the short run. If a change in aggregate demand is permanent, then the price level continues to rise (or fall) farther in the long run, while real GDP returns to its long-run equilibrium level. This model of aggregate demand and supply forms the basis for most economic analyses of business cycles.

Key Terms

sticky price   aggregate demand curve   aggregate supply curve

Questions and Problems

12. Explain why aggregate demand rises if:
    (a) The money supply increases
    (b) The velocity of money increases
    (c) Investment demand increases
    (c) Government spending increases

13. Suppose that people decide to save less money and increase spending on entertainment. Explain how this change affects:
    (a) The real interest rate and the nominal interest rate
    (b) The velocity of money
    (c) Aggregate demand
    (d) Real GDP and the price level in the short run and long run
    If people spend $10 million more than before on entertainment, does real GDP change by more or less than $10 million? Explain.

14. Suppose that the government raises spending by $20 billion and raises taxes by $20 billion to pay for the higher spending.

    (a) Explain how this action affects consumption and saving, the interest rate, investment, velocity, and real GDP in the short run.
    (b) How would your answer change if the government did not raise taxes to pay for increased spending, but borrowed the money instead?
    (c) How would your answer change if the government did not raise taxes to pay for increased spending, but printed money to pay for the higher spending?

15. Suppose the economy is currently in a recession. Use the model of aggregate demand and supply to explain how a tax cut could raise real GDP and reduce unemployment.

16. Suppose the money supply is $500 and velocity is 5 per year. Also suppose the long-run aggregate supply curve is represented by the equation,

$$y = 500$$

and the short-run aggregate supply curve is represented by the equation,

$$P = (1/100)\, y$$

(a) Find the long-run equilibrium price level and real GDP.

(b) Suppose the money supply increases from $500 to $720. Find the new *long-run* equilibrium price level and real GDP. Then find the new *short-run* equilibrium price level and real GDP. (*Hint:* Find the *two* equations that hold in the short-run equilibrium, then solve them for the two unknown variables.)

17. Suppose the money supply is $1,000 and velocity is 3.6 per year. Also suppose the long-run aggregate supply curve is represented by the equation,

$$y = 360$$

and the short-run aggregate supply curve is represented by the equation,

$$P = (1/36)y$$

(a) Find the long-run equilibrium price level and real GDP.

(b) Suppose velocity rises from 3.6 per year to 4.9 per year. Find the new *long-run* equilibrium price level and real GDP. Then find the new *short-run* equilibrium price level and real GDP. Your answer for the price level may be rounded to the nearest dollar.

18. How is aggregate demand likely to react to an increase in consumer confidence about the future of the economy?

Inquiries for Further Thought

19. Should the United States adopt policies to reduce consumption spending and increase savings? What are the benefits and costs of a policy like this? Why did earlier chapters imply that an increase in savings raises productivity and future output, while according to this chapter, an increase in savings reduces aggregate demand and real GDP?

20. Why are prices sticky in the short run? Does price stickiness imply inefficiency in the economy?

CHAPTER 12

BUSINESS CYCLES 2: APPLICATIONS OF AGGREGATE DEMAND AND SUPPLY

In this Chapter...
Main Points to Understand

▶ Because the price level is sticky in the short run, changes in the money supply affect the real interest rate in the short run.

▶ The short-run Phillips Curve shows an inverse relationship between inflation and unemployment, although the curve shifts frequently over time. The long-run Phillips Curve shows *no* relationship between inflation and unemployment.

▶ Three models of short-run aggregate supply have different implications for unemployment and for government economic policies.

▶ Effects of a change in aggregate demand ripple throughout the economy, leading to further changes in aggregate demand.

Thinking Skills to Develop

▶ Interpret specific economic episodes in light of a model.

▶ Develop new implications of a model by extending its logic.

▶ Use a model to answer "what if?" questions.

▶ Learn to look at the *indirect* effects of a change as well as its direct effects.

A round the world, the 1990s witnessed major economic events: the collapse of the Soviet Union and the end of socialism in eastern Europe; rapid economic growth in China; a recession in the United States in 1990 to 1991, followed by a long period of rapid growth; an economic crisis in Mexico in 1995; economic crises in Korea, Indonesia, Thailand, the Philippines, and Malaysia in 1997 to 1998; a long recession in Japan; and the beginnings of new economic crises in other countries, such as Brazil and Russia. While entire courses could focus on each of these events, this chapter examines some of these events by applying the economic model developed in previous chapters, extending the model in a few places and delving deeper into it in other places. To understand macroeconomics, you must learn more than the model of aggregate supply and demand: You must learn how to *apply* that model to real events. You must learn to analyze news reports with economic reasoning, and adopt economic reasoning as a practical tool for thinking about new issues.

It was November 1991, and the United States was in a recession. Unemployment climbed above 7 percent; real GDP remained below its level from the previous year. The Federal Reserve decided to conduct open market purchases (buying assets) to reduce the federal funds rate (the interest rate on short-term loans between banks) from 5 percent to 4.75

MONEY AND INTEREST RATES IN THE SHORT RUN

percent per year. The action was very unusual, because it was the second cut in the federal funds rate within a single week and the 13th cut within two years. It would not be the last: The Fed cut the federal funds rate twice more before the end of the year, bringing it down from 8 percent in mid-1990 to 4 percent at the end of 1991. (Figure 5 in Chapter 10 showed the federal funds rate over a longer period of time.)

These actions of the Federal Reserve in 1990 and 1991 were intended to raise aggregate demand and help pull the U.S. economy out of its recession. The model of aggregate demand and supply shows why an increase in the money supply can raise real GDP and help end a recession. We begin this chapter by examining the connection between changes in the money supply and changes in the interest rate. These connections help to explain why increases in the money supply generally reduce the real interest rate in the short run. Understanding these connections will help you to understand news reports about Federal Reserve policies, such as its more recent actions to reduce interest rates starting in 1998.

Most news reports about monetary policy focus on interest rates: Will the Fed reduce interest rates? Will it raise them? Will the Bank of Japan change Japanese interest rates? Chapters 7 and 8 explained that changes in the money supply affect inflation, which affects *nominal* interest rates. However, as Chapter 10 explained, changes in the money supply also affect *real* interest rates in the short run. The model of aggregate demand and supply can help to clarify the effects of monetary policy on the real interest rate.

Long-Run Effects of a Federal Reserve Open Market Purchase

The easiest way to understand the effects of Fed policy (or the policy of a foreign central bank) on interest rates is to think about the special case of aggregate supply in the previous chapter, in which prices are *completely* sticky in the short run. In that case, the short-run aggregate supply curve is a horizontal line. Suppose the Fed permanently raises the money supply through an open market purchase, raising aggregate demand and temporarily raising real GDP as in Figure 17a of Chapter 11. What happens to the real interest rate? To answer that question, think about the demand and supply of loans. As in Chapter 10, focus on the supply and demand for short-term loans between banks and the federal funds rate.

The Fed's open market purchases raises the supply of loans. Figure 1 shows the results. Look first at Figure 1b, which shows the *long-run* results. In the long run, the increase in the money supply will raise all nominal prices in the same proportion. The long-run results will resemble a currency reform in reverse, with real variables remaining unchanged. For example, a 5 percent increase in the money supply will raise all nominal prices by 5 percent. With 5 percent higher prices of capital goods (such as new equipment), business firms will borrow 5 percent more money for the same real investments in capital equipment. Therefore the demand for loans (measured in dollars) rises *in the long run* by 5 percent, along with the supply of loans. Because the supply *and* demand for loans (measured in nominal terms) *both* rise by 5 percent in the long run, the real interest rate does not change. Therefore the Fed's open market purchase leaves the real interest rate unchanged in the long run.

Because the Fed's action raises the money supply, it raises the price level in the long run. As Chapter 7 explained, that rise in the price level (a temporary jump in the rate of inflation) raises the *nominal* interest rate while the price level falls toward its new long-run level.

Short-Run Effects of an Open Market Purchase

In the short run, however, the price level is sticky. Figure 1a shows the short-run results of the open market purchase. The prices of new equipment and other capital goods remain unaffected in the short run, so the demand for loans remains unchanged. However, the Fed's open market purchase increases the supply of loans, *reducing the real interest rate* in the short run.

What happens to the nominal interest rate in the short run? Two opposing forces affect the nominal interest rate. First, the decline in the real interest rate tends to

Figure 1 | How Open Market Operations and Interest Rates

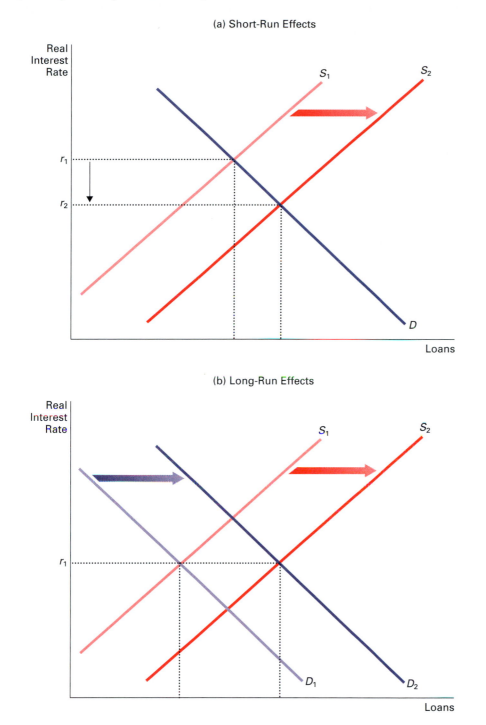

(a) Short-Run Effects

(b) Long-Run Effects

In Panel (a), an open market purchase raises the supply of money. By raising the supply of loans, it lowers the real interest rate in the short run (while the price level remains sticky). In Panel (b), a fall in the supply of money leaves the real interest rate unchanged in the long run. A 5 percent rise in the money supply raises the price level by 5 percent. As a result, the demand and supply of loans each rises by 5 percent, leaving the equilibrium real interest rate at r_1.

Money and the Nominal Interest Rate: a Complex Connection

The connection between the nominal interest rate and the money supply is complex. If the price level is sufficiently sticky in the short run, a Federal Reserve open market purchase reduces the nominal interest rate in the short run. However, that open-market purchase raises the price level in the long run, boosting inflation and *increasing* the nominal interest rate. So the same change in the money supply that *lowers* the nominal interest rate in the short run *raises* it afterwards.

reduce the nominal interest rate. Second, the jump in inflation, as the economy moves upward along its short-run aggregate supply curve (as in Figure 17a of Chapter 11), tends to raise the nominal interest rate. If the price level is sufficiently sticky, the short-run jump in inflation is small, so the nominal interest rate falls. (The first effect dominates the second effect: the nominal interest rate falls because the real interest rate falls.)

The discussion so far involves the federal funds interest rate, but the Fed's policy

U.K. cuts key interest rate

THE BANK OF ENG-LAND cut the repo rate, the lowest rate at which the central bank loans money to commercial banks, by a quarter percentage point to 7.25 percent. The rate had been at 7.50 percent since June 4 when it was raised by 0.25 percentage points. That was the sixth rise in interest rates since Labor won power.

Labor removed authority over interest rates from politicians and gave it to the Bank of England within days of taking office. The bank then tightened monetary policy in line with a government target of low 2.5 percent inflation. But as world economic turbulence worsened, Britain's treasury chief, Gordon Brown, indicated this week that recession is now a greater risk than inflation, encouraging speculation that Britain would follow the U.S. Federal Reserve and cut rates.

Source: MSNBC News

England's central bank loosened monetary policy in late 1998 to help prevent a recession. A sticky price level allows the Bank of England to reduce the real interest rate in the short run.

also affects other interest rates. When the federal funds rate rises, banks must pay more to borrow from other banks, so they raise the rates they charge on their own loans. The rise in the federal funds rate ripples through the economy, raising other interest rates in the short run. Similarly, when the Fed reduces the federal funds rate through an open market purchase that raises the money supply, interest rates throughout the economy fall in the short run.

This model of the connections between Federal Reserve policies and interest rates can help you interpret news articles on those policies and their effects. To raise the interest rate, the Fed conducts open market sales, reducing the money supply. To reduce the interest rate, the Fed conducts open market purchases, raising the money supply.

These short-run effects of Fed policies result from short-run price stickiness. In the long run, the price level adjusts to its new equilibrium level, and the real interest rate returns to its original equilibrium level as the economy moves from the short-run aggregate supply curve to the long-run aggregate supply curve.

Figure 2 shows that the federal funds rate and the interest rate on U.S. government treasury bills tend to move together. Some analysts interpret their common movements as the effects of Fed policies: changes in the federal funds rate affect the treasury bill rate. However, other analysts note that the common movements in these interest rates are more complex: changes in the federal funds rate often occur *after* changes in the treasury bill rate. Some economists say that this occurs because loan-market participants *expect* changes in the federal funds rate, changing demand and supply so that the equilibrium treasury bill rate responds to these expectations. Others say the treasury bill rate often changes before the federal funds rate because the Federal Reserve *responds* to economic events. According to this view, changes in treasury bill rates cause the Fed to change the federal funds rate, and evidence on their common movement does not reflect the ability of the Fed to control the treasury bill rate or other interest rates.

The Federal Reserve conducted open market purchases in September 1998 to reduce the federal funds rate from 5.50 percent to 5.25 percent. The 3-month U.S. treasury bill interest rate dropped from 4.9 percent to 4.4 percent during that month, but the drop occurred throughout the month, *before* the September 29 date when the Federal Reserve reduced the federal funds rate. To some extent, the drop in the treasury bill rate probably reflected expectations that the Fed would reduce the federal funds rate; to some extent, the drop in the treasury bill rate probably occurred for other reasons, with the Fed merely responding. Until economists can find evidence to distinguish these two possibilities, the *magnitude* of the Fed's influence on the treasury bill interest rate (and other interest rates) remains uncertain.

The Federal Reserve, like other central banks, decides on its monetary policy by analyzing data on recent changes in the price level, real GDP, unemployment, and other variables. When the Fed believes the economy is "slowing down," because aggregate demand is falling (or growing less rapidly than aggregate supply), it tends to follow an *expansionary* monetary policy to raise aggregate demand. It conducts open market purchases that raise the money supply and reduce interest rates. When the Fed believes the economy is "speeding up" or "overheating," meaning that aggregate demand is rising more rapidly than the Fed would like (creating a threat of inflation), the Fed tends to follow a *tight* monetary policy to reduce aggregate demand. It conducts open market sales that reduce the money supply and raise interest rates.

The Fed monitors many economic variables for signals of changes in aggregate demand. Two important areas of focus are unemployment rates and inflation; its attention to unemployment results from a set of observations about the economy and its controversial interpretation as a *Phillips Curve*, to which the next section turns.

Figure 2 | Federal Funds Rate and Treasury Bill Interest Rates, 1991–1998

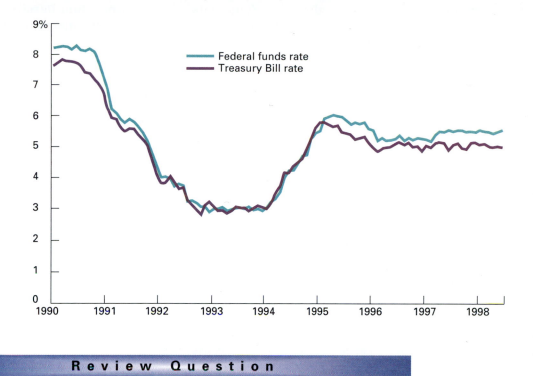

R e v i e w   Q u e s t i o n

1. What actions does the Fed take to reduce the real interest rate? Why do these actions work in the short run but not in the long run?

T h i n k i n g   E x e r c i s e s

2. Draw a graph to help show the short-run effects of a Federal Reserve open market *sale* on (a) the real interest rate, (b) the nominal interest rate, and (c) investment.

3. What factors complicate evidence on the extent to which the Fed's influence on the federal funds rate extends to the treasury bill rate and other interest rates?

PHILLIPS CURVES

Suppose an economy experiences temporary changes in aggregate demand. When aggregate demand temporarily rises, output and the price level both increase along the short-run aggregate supply curve, AS^{SR}; when aggregate demand falls again, output and the price level both decrease. Large increases in aggregate demand create a high growth rate of real GDP and high inflation, as in Figure 3; smaller increases in aggregate demand create smaller growth rates of real GDP and lower inflation, as in Figure 4. These temporary changes in aggregate demand cause inflation and the growth rate of real GDP to move together, as in Figure 5.[1]

A statistical generalization called *Okun's Law* indicates that each one percentage-point increase in the growth rate of U.S. real GDP typically accompanies a 0.5 percentage-point

---

[1]Permanent changes in aggregate demand also cause inflation and the growth of real GDP to move together in the short run.

**Figure 3
Large Rise in Aggregate
Demand**

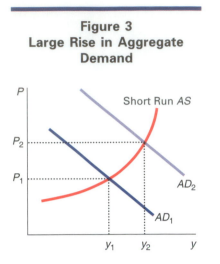

**Figure 4
Small Rise in Aggregate
Demand**

**Figure 5
Short-Run Results of Changes
in Aggregate Demand**

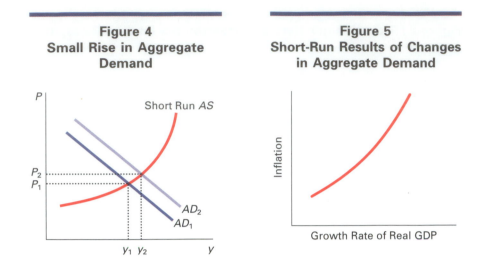

fall in the unemployment rate.[2] Because higher growth in real GDP accompanies lower unemployment, we can redraw Figure 5 as Figure 6.

Figure 6 shows the short-run relationship between inflation and unemployment predicted by the model with an upward-sloping short-run aggregate supply curve and temporary changes in aggregate demand, or the short-run effects of permanent changes in aggregate demand. In the short run, high inflation accompanies low unemployment, and low inflation accompanies high unemployment.

**Figure 6
Short-Run Phillips Curve**

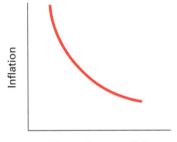

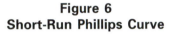

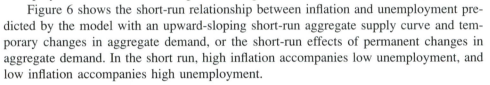

IN THE NEWS

Brazil's harsh attack on inflation is risking deep economic slump

Shrinkage of its money supply hobbles many companies, forces people to cut back. A housemaid loses her job.

SAO PAULO, Brazil— When Fernando Collor de Mello took office in March, he said he had "only one shot" to halt Brazil's hyperinflation. But instead of firing a bullet, the new president dropped a bomb.

"The monetary contraction we imposed on society is fantastic," acknowledges

Source: The Wall Street Journal

Ibrahim Eris, one of the architects of the harsh anti-inflation plan and now the president of the central bank. "It's probably the first time in the world that a country in time of peace has practically destroyed its monetary standard and replaced it."

But in stopping inflation, the government has

also stopped the economy. "To kill the cockroach, they set the apartment on fire," complains former Economic Planning Minister Antonio Delfim Netto.

Deprived of cash, consumers stopped buying, companies stopped producing, and exporters stopped exporting.

In any country, policies intended to reduce inflation risk causing a recession, as the economy moves along a short-run Phillips Curve.

[2]For example, a rise in the growth rate of real GDP from 2 percent to 3 percent per year typically occurs with a fall in the unemployment rate from 6 percent to 5.5 percent.

Most economists interpret available evidence as supporting the short-run relationship in Figure 6. They refer to it as the *short-run Phillips Curve*—a statistical relationship between inflation and unemployment.

> The **short-run Phillips Curve** is a statistical relationship between inflation and unemployment: In the short run, unemployment is low when inflation is high, and unemployment is high when inflation is low.

Figure 7 shows unemployment rates and inflation rates for the United States since 1986. While the points from 1986 through 1993 are consistent with a downward-sloping short-run Phillips Curve similar to the curve in Figure 6, the points from 1992 through 1998 would indicate an *upward*-sloping relationship. Clearly, the short-run Phillips Curve is not as simple a relationship as Figure 6 would indicate.

Two issues complicate the analysis:

▶ *Short-run* relationships between inflation and unemployment differ from *long-run* relationships.

▶ The short-run Phillips Curve *shifts* as people's *expectations* change.

The Short Run versus the Long Run

In the long run, when the price level adjusts to its new equilibrium, the economy returns to the equilibrium, full-employment level of output, y^{FE}, and the associated equilibrium level of unemployment, called the *natural rate of unemployment*.[3]

> The **natural rate of unemployment** is the unemployment rate that occurs when the economy produces the full-employment level of output.

Figure 7 | Phillips Curve for the United States, 1986–1998

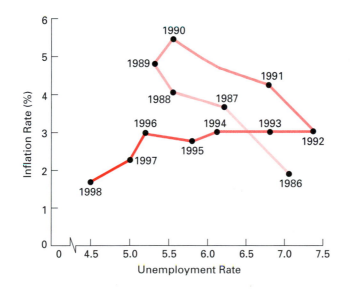

---

[3]Chapter 6 discussed the equilibrium level (natural rate) of unemployment, and the factors that affect it.

The natural rate of unemployment corresponds to equilibrium unemployment discussed in Chapter 6. Unemployment results from inevitable changes in any real economy, including changes in population, technology, consumer preferences, government policies, and world economic conditions. The natural rate of unemployment is not a constant; it changes over time. Its size depends on many factors, such as:

▶ Larger and more frequent changes in supply and demand raise equilibrium unemployment by raising the number of people who lose jobs each year.

▶ A decrease in the costs of searching for jobs and finding good matches between employers and employees reduces equilibrium unemployment.

▶ An increase in availability of good information about job opportunities reduces equilibrium unemployment by reducing the time people require to find new jobs.

▶ An increase in labor mobility reduces equilibrium unemployment by increasing the extent to which people will accept jobs in other cities.

▶ Increases in incomes of unemployed people, due to an increase in unemployment compensation or increases in incomes of other family members, raises equilibrium unemployment by reducing the willingness of people to accept new job offers.

▶ Union policies that raise wages, and increases in legal minimum wages can raise equilibrium unemployment by reducing the quantity of labor demanded.

▶ Government regulations and taxes can raise equilibrium unemployment. For example, regulations in European countries make it costly for firms to fire employees, which reduces their willingness to hire new workers.

No one knows exactly the size of the natural rate of unemployment in the United States. A decade ago, many economists estimated it to be about 5.5 percent; more recent estimates put it at about 4.5 percent.

Because unemployment returns to its natural rate in the long run, the long-run Phillips Curve is a vertical line as in Figure 8.

Figure 8
Phillips Curves

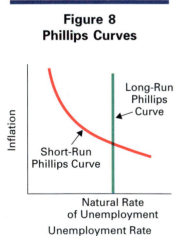

The **long-run Phillips Curve** is a vertical line at the natural rate of unemployment.

Figure 7 showed unemployment and inflation rates in the United States since 1986; Figure 9 shows them in earlier periods during the second half of the 20th century. Some periods show downward sloping short-run Phillips Curves. However, notice that scales differ among the plots in Figure 9. Consequently, a plot that combines all the data, as in Panel (f), does *not* show a short-run Phillips Curve. Apparently, the short-run Phillips Curve shifts over time.

Shifts in the Short-Run Phillips Curve

Evidence indicates that the short-run Phillips Curve shifts when expected inflation changes. An increase in expected inflation shifts the short-run Phillips Curve upward and to the right. Figure 10 shows a short-run Phillips Curve shifting upward from PC_1 to PC_2 as expected inflation rises. A fall in expected inflation shifts the short-run Phillips Curve downward and to the left. Figure 10 shows a short-run Phillips Curve shifting downward from PC_1 to PC_3 as expected inflation falls. In contrast, the long-run Phillips Curve remains unaffected by changes in expected inflation.

Suppose that the economy begins at Point A in Figure 10, in a long-run equilibrium. One day, the Federal Reserve, in a surprise policy change, permanently raises the growth rate of the money supply. As a result, inflation rises above the level that people had expected. In the short run, unemployment falls as the economy moves from Point A to Point B in Figure 10. After a while, however, people learn to expect this new, higher rate of inflation, so expected inflation rises. The rise in expected inflation shifts the short-run Phillips Curve upward and to the right, from PC_1 to PC_2, until the economy reaches Point C in the long run. Unemployment returns to its natural rate. A permanent increase

Figure 9 | Inflation and Unemployment in the United States

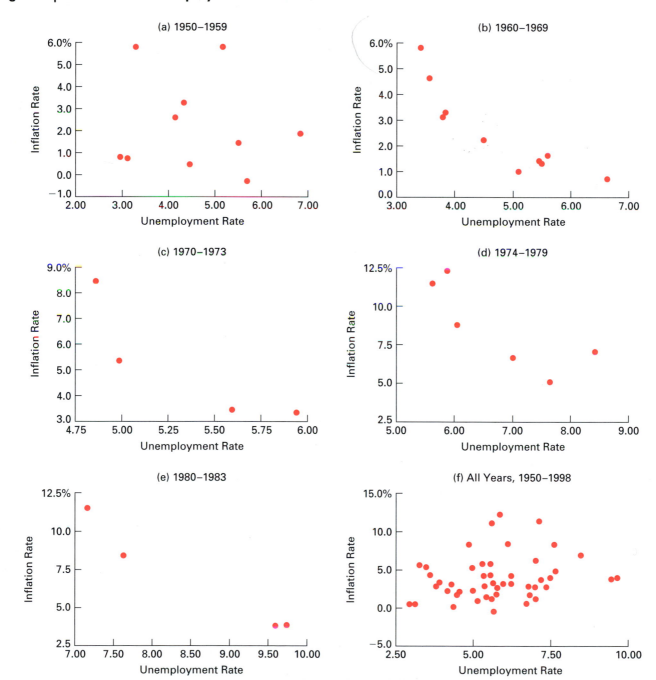

Figure 10 | Shifting Short-Run Phillips Curves

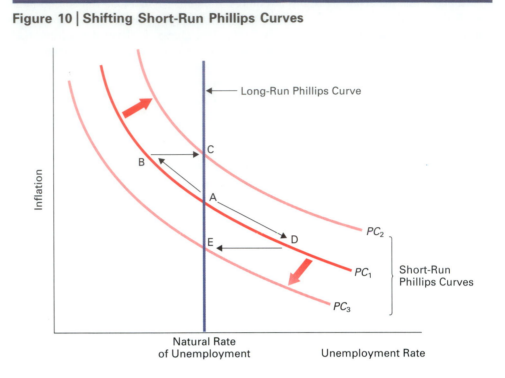

in the growth rate of the money supply raises inflation, but reduces unemployment only temporarily. It has no long-run effect on unemployment.[4]

Figure 10 also shows the effects of a permanent decrease in the growth rate of the money supply. Starting from Point A, inflation falls and unemployment rises in the short run, as the economy moves from Point A to Point D. As expected inflation falls, the short-run Phillips Curve shifts from PC_1 to PC_3. In the long run, unemployment falls back to its natural rate as the economy moves from Point D to Point E. A permanent fall in the growth rate of the money supply permanently lowers inflation, and temporarily raises unemployment. It has no long-run effect on unemployment.

Figure 11 shows the way most economists view the U.S. data on Phillips Curves. According to the standard interpretation, the figure shows a short-run Phillips Curve for the 1960s, which shifted upward when expected inflation increased in the early 1970s, and then shifted upward again in 1974 (as the world economy experienced a fall in aggregate supply due to a major increase in the price of imported oil). As inflation continued to increase in the late 1970s, expected inflation rose again, shifting the short-run Phillips Curve to an even higher level. As inflation decreased from 1980 to 1983, the U.S. economy moved downward to the right along that short-run Phillips Curve. Then, as expected inflation fell, the short-run Phillips Curve shifted downward to its 1986–94 level. Finally, as inflation remained lower in the 1990s than previous years, expected inflation declined throughout the decade as unemployment fell toward its natural rate. Some economists, questioning the standard interpretation, view Figure 11 as misleading. They argue that the figure groups years together in a way that artificially creates the *appearance* of short-run Phillips Curves. These economists argue that there is no reliable statistical relationship between inflation and unemployment that can guide policymakers in predicting the effects of alternative policies.

---

[4]If you exercise your thinking skills in economics, you may wonder *why* changes in expectations shift the short-run Phillips Curve. What economic *model* logically predicts these shifts? The answer requires a more complex analysis than the models in this book. Roughly, the short-run Phillips Curve shifts (as in Figure 10) when the short-run aggregate supply curve shifts, moving the economy from a short-run equilibrium to a long-run equilibrium (as in Figure 17 of the previous chapter). These changes are not quite the same, because the short-run Phillips Curve shifts due to changes in expected inflation, while the short-run aggregate supply curve shifts when the price level completes its adjustment to its new equilibrium. The precise logical connections between the model of aggregate demand and supply and the short-run Phillips Curve lie beyond the scope of this book.

Figure 11 | Shifting Short-Run Phillips Curves for the United States, 1960–1998

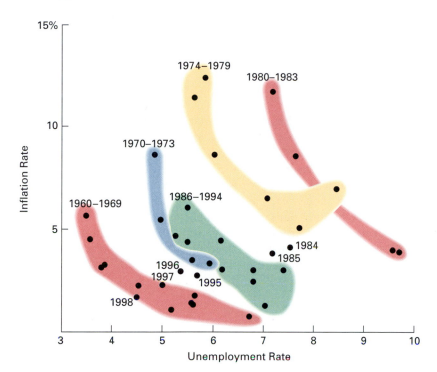

The difference between these two views of the evidence represents conflicting predictions about the answer to a "what-if" question: What would happen *if* the Federal Reserve changed its policies to raise or reduce inflation? Would a policy to raise inflation also reduce unemployment in the short run? Would a policy to reduce inflation create a recession and raise unemployment temporarily? Some economists argue that these policies would affect unemployment and real GDP; others disagree. For example, in the Kennywood Park story of Chapter 6, Professor Robert Lucas argued that changes in monetary policy could not repeatedly create recessions or expansions ("Sunday after Sunday"). He argued that monetary policy affects real GDP "only because our manipulations caught everyone by surprise." Economists will probably continue to disagree on the answers to these questions until stronger evidence on these issues becomes available.

Review Questions

4. Draw a short-run Phillips Curve and a long-run Phillips Curve.

5. What factors affect the natural rate of unemployment?

6. Summarize the evidence presented in this chapter about the short-run Phillips Curve, including criticisms of the usual interpretation of the evidence.

Thinking Exercises

7. A politician recently argued that the Federal Reserve should reduce interest rates to prevent an increase in unemployment. However, a Fed official warned that looser

monetary policy may ignite inflation. What do economic models and evidence say about the short-run and long-run effects of looser monetary policy on unemployment and inflation?

8. Economists disagree about the interpretation of the short-run Phillips Curve and its implications for policy. Explain that disagreement. What evidence would help resolve the disagreement?

THREE THEORIES OF AGGREGATE SUPPLY

The previous chapter explained that the short-run aggregate supply curve slopes upward because the price level is sticky in the short run—it does not immediately and fully adjust to its new long-run equilibrium level after a change in conditions. That chapter explained one of three alternative models of the short-run aggregate supply curve. The sticky-price model of aggregate supply is often called the *New Keynesian theory*. The other two models, the *sticky-wage model* and the *imperfect-information model*, explain the upward slope of the short-run aggregate supply curve in alternative ways. Each model differs in its explanation of unemployment and the short-run Phillips Curve. The three models also differ in their predictions about other macroeconomic variables and their implications for government policies.

Sticky Product Prices

The first model of short-run aggregate supply, the *sticky-price* or *New Keynesian* theory, states that the nominal price level is sticky in the short run. This stickiness makes the short-run aggregate supply curve slope upward, as discussed in the previous chapter.

Although evidence suggests that the price level is sticky, economists do not fully understand the causes of price stickiness. The most prominent explanation involves *menu costs*—a term for the actual costs of changing prices. Menu costs include the costs of printing new menus at restaurants, new catalogs for mail-order firms, and the costs of attaching new price tags to products at retail stores. More generally, menu costs include the costs of gathering information to decide which prices to change, and how much to change them.

When firms pay menu costs to change their prices, they must think carefully about the future when choosing their prices. For example, suppose a firm experiences an increase in demand for its product, but believes that this high demand is only temporary, and that demand will return to normal next month. The firm may leave its price unchanged, rather than paying the menu costs of raising the price today and reducing it again next month. As this example illustrates, a firm that faces menu costs must anticipate changes in future conditions when it sets prices.

Firms facing menu costs are less likely to change their prices in the short run, but they change them in the long run. If a firm's price is close to its equilibrium level, a firm may leave its price unchanged rather than pay the menu costs to change it. However, when the difference between the firm's price and the equilibrium price becomes large, the firm will change its price despite the menu costs.

Firms facing menu costs may not all change their prices at the same time, because they face different supply and demand conditions. For example, changes in the supply or demand for coffee or airline tickets may lead coffee sellers and airlines to change their prices more often, and at different times, than firms selling books. When aggregate demand falls, *some* firms will be ready to adjust their prices almost immediately, while others will leave their prices unchanged for some time. Consequently, in the short run the overall price level will fall only *part* of the way to its new long-run equilibrium level. Firms that have not changed their prices will see sales drop, and they will reduce production. As a result, the fall in aggregate demand reduces real GDP in the short run. Eventually, all firms reduce their prices to the new long-run equilibrium level, and real GDP returns to its full-employment level.

Sticky Wages

A second model, the *sticky-wage theory,* states that the short-run aggregate supply curve slopes upward because *nominal wages* are sticky in the short run. Nominal wages may be sticky because workers sign long-term employment contracts that set the levels of wages for an extended period of time (such as a year, or even longer).

Suppose the equilibrium nominal wage is $20 per hour, and a firm and its workers sign a contract fixing the nominal wage at that rate for the coming year. After the contract is signed, suppose the money supply and the price level fall by 5 percent. The new *equilibrium* wage is now $19 per hour. If all *nominal* prices and *nominal* wages fell by 5 percent, no *real* variables (such as real GDP or real wages) would change; money would be neutral. However, the employment contract creates stickiness in *nominal* wages. Because the nominal wage is sticky, the falling price level raises the *real* wage above its equilibrium level. This increase in the real wage reduces the quantity of labor demanded as in Figure 12. In that figure, the nominal wage is sticky at $20, so a fall in the price level from P_1 tp P_2 raises the real wage from $20/P_1$ to $20/P_2$. The firm sells its product for 5 percent less than before, in nominal terms, but it must pay workers the same nominal wage as before. As a result, the firm wants fewer workers—its quantity of labor demanded falls from L_1 to L_2. This decrease in employment reduces real GDP. In summary, when nominal wages are sticky, a fall in aggregate demand raises the real wage but reduces employment, raising unemployment and reducing real GDP. With short-run stickiness in nominal wages, a fall in aggregate demand creates a recession.

Nominal wages are not permanently sticky, though. Eventually, firms and workers sign new employment contracts, and nominal wages adjust to their new equilibrium levels. When the new contracts become effective, the real wage returns to its equilibrium, bringing employment and production back to their equilibrium levels. The recession ends and the economy returns to its full-employment level of real GDP.

Figure 12 | Effects of a Fall in the Money Supply With a Sticky Nominal Wage

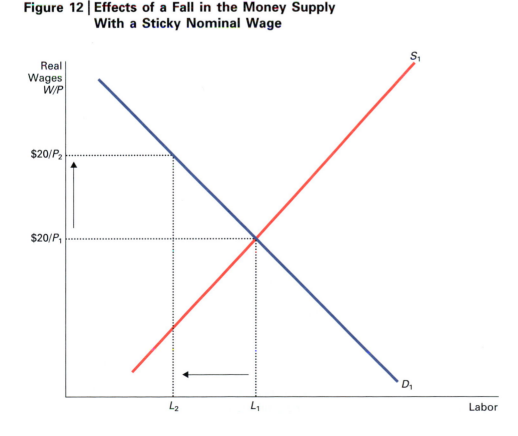

After workers sign labor contracts fixing the nominal wage at $20 per hour, the money supply falls by 5 percent. This reduces the price level by 5 percent, from P_1 to P_2. Because the price level falls by 5 percent, and the nominal wage, *W,* remains at $20, the real wage, *W/P, rises* by 5 percent. Employment falls from L_1 to L_2.

Comparing the Sticky-Wage and Sticky-Price Models

The sticky-price model and sticky-wage model differ in explaining when recessions end. Both models say that a recession ends when the short-run aggregate supply curve shifts and the economy returns to a long-run equilibrium. The sticky-price model says that this happens when the nominal price level completes its adjustment (after a change in aggregate demand). The sticky-wage model, in contrast, says that this happens when people sign new employment contracts and the nominal wage adjusts to its new long-run equilibrium.

The sticky-wage model predicts that a change in the money supply affects employment and real GDP only if it was *unexpected* at the time the nominal wage was set. Any changes in the money supply and price level that workers and firms expect when they sign the contract will affect the nominal wage. For example, suppose that workers and firms know that all nominal prices will rise 10 percent in the second year of the labor contract discussed in the last section. They could keep the real wage at its equilibrium level by writing a contract that would set the nominal wage at $20.00 per hour in the first year of the contract, and $22.00 per hour (10 percent higher) in the second year.

The prediction that only unexpected changes in the price level affect employment and real GDP receives support from evidence that surprise (unexpected) changes in the money supply have larger effects on real output than do predictable changes. This relationship remains controversial, however, because some evidence suggests that even predictable changes in the money supply or inflation temporarily affect real GDP. Still, surprise changes in the money supply and inflation seem to have larger effects on real GDP than do predicted changes. This evidence supports the sticky-wage model.

Imperfect Information

A third model of the short-run aggregate supply curve, the *imperfect-information* model, does *not* assume that menu costs make prices sticky, or that nominal wages are sticky. Instead, it states that the short-run aggregate supply curve slopes upward because sellers sometimes make mistakes: They sometimes *confuse* nominal price changes with relative price changes.

Suppose that a surprise fall in the money supply creates a surprise fall in the price level. When a firm sees an unexpected fall in the nominal price of the good it sells, it may mistakenly believe that the *relative* price of that good has fallen. Of course, in reality, the relative price may not have changed; instead, *all* nominal prices may have fallen by the same percentage. But the firm may not know that. It may incorrectly believe that the relative price has fallen, so it may reduce production. As other sellers make similar mistakes, the unexpected fall in the price level reduces real GDP.

The Kennywood Park story in Chapter 6 illustrates the imperfect-information model. Neither prices nor wages are sticky in that story. Instead, a fall in aggregate demand reduces *real* GDP and employment in the short run because each ride operator mistakenly believes that his ride is becoming passé—that the *relative* demand for his ride has decreased. If ride operators were aware that the park's money supply has decreased, they would all reduce their nominal prices and the recession would not occur.

Unemployment in the Three Models

The three models of aggregate supply differ in their interpretations of unemployment. According to the sticky-price model, people who become unemployed may not be able to find jobs even by offering to work for a reduced wage. When aggregate demand falls, firms become unable to sell all of the products that they produce. As a result, they reduce production and employment. Firms would be unable to sell the additional goods that they could produce by employing additional workers, so they are unwilling to hire additional workers regardless of the wage. In the long run, the fall in aggregate demand reduces the price level, and unemployment returns to its natural rate. With the price level sticky in the short run, government policies to raise aggregate demand would allow firms to sell additional products, thereby raising production and employment.

According to the sticky-wage theory, unemployment occurs when the real wage exceeds its equilibrium level. Unemployed people could find jobs if firms could reduce wages, but the sticky-wage model postulates that labor contracts or other forces prevent nominal wages from decreasing in the short run. In the long run, unemployment falls as the nominal wage falls to its equilibrium level. In the short run, the only way to reduce unemployment is to reduce the real wage, and the only way to reduce the real wage is to raise the price level by increasing aggregate demand.

The sticky-price and sticky-wage models both imply that increases in aggregate demand can reduce unemployment in the short run. Consequently, many economists propose government policies to raise aggregate demand in response to rising unemployment or the threat of a recession. The incomplete information model sees unemployment as a voluntary response to a situation of bad opportunities. According to that model, any unemployed worker could find a job by offering to work at a sufficiently low wage. Wages are not sticky in that model, so firms can reduce wages. Nominal prices are not sticky, so firms can sell the additional output that new workers would produce. According to the incomplete information model, people are unemployed when they prefer unemployment to their current job opportunities, which may fall short of the opportunities they expect to encounter if they continue searching for better options.

Review Questions

9. Why does unemployment develop in a recession according to the (a) sticky-price model? (b) sticky-wage model? (c) incomplete information model?

10. A recession ends when the economy moves from its short-run equilibrium (on a short-run aggregate supply curve) to its new long-run equilibrium. What change creates this movement according to the (a) sticky-price model? (b) sticky-wage model? (c) incomplete-information model?

Thinking Exercises

11. Suppose the Fed suddenly raises the money supply by 10 percent. Explain the effects on real GDP, unemployment, and the price level, according to (a) the sticky-price model; (b) the sticky-wage model, and (c) the incomplete information model. In each case, explain the *reasoning* involved, as well as the results.

12. Explain why only *unexpected* (surprise) changes in the money supply affect real GDP and unemployment in the incomplete-information model. Draw aggregate demand and supply curves to distinguish the effects of expected and unexpected changes in the money supply, according to that model.

13. How do the effects of expected and unexpected changes in the money supply differ, according to the sticky wage model? Draw aggregate demand and supply curves to distinguish the effects of expected and unexpected changes in the money supply, according to that model.

Example: Unemployment in the Sticky Price Model Recall the simple example at the beginning of Chapter 11, illustrated in Figure 2 of that chapter. The economy begins in long-run equilibrium: firms produce 100 goods per year, the money supply equals $1,000, velocity equals one per year, and the price level is $10 per good. When the money supply falls from $1,000 to $900 with no change in velocity, people spend only $900 per year, so the equilibrium price level falls from $10 to $9 per good. However, if the price level is completely sticky and remains at $10 per good, people can afford to buy only 90 goods per year (spending $900). While firms could produce more than 90 per year, they cannot sell more than that as long as the price level exceeds its long-run equilibrium. Consequently, firms would be unwilling to hire additional workers, even if their wages were low.

You might think that if you spend $100 more and save $100 less than before, you will raise aggregate demand by $100. Actually, your spending will create *ripple effects* in the economy—in the end, aggregate demand may increase by *more* than $100, or it may increase by less. The size of the total change in aggregate demand depends on the *aggregate-demand multiplier*.

THE AGGREGATE DEMAND MULTIPLIER

A change in spending creates ripple effects in the economy, which are summarized by the aggregate-demand multiplier. When you understand the logic of these ripple effects, you will learn an important lesson of economic reasoning.

> The **aggregate-demand multiplier** shows the ultimate increase in aggregate demand that results from an exogenous $1 rise in spending.

An *exogenous* change refers to a change in underlying conditions that affects other variables in a model. A model predicts *results* of exogenous changes. For example, a change in consumer tastes for pizza is an exogenous change in the model of supply and demand, which predicts the reactions of prices to that change. Similarly, a change in tastes can create an exogenous $1 rise in total spending. That exogenous increase in spending may have economic effects that lead to *further* changes in spending, which the aggregate-demand multiplier measures. For example, if spending rises exogenously by $100 and the multiplier is 2, then aggregate demand rises by $200. If the multiplier is 1, aggregate demand rises by $100. If the multiplier is ½, aggregate demand rises by $50; see Figure 13.

Direct and Indirect Effects—A Lesson in Logical Reasoning

A common explanation of the aggregate-demand multiplier involves a logical fallacy, and you can learn an important lesson in logical reasoning by studying the fallacy in the argument. That logical lesson can help you avoid making similar mistakes when you apply the logic of economics to real-life problems that you will face in the future.

The common, but incorrect, explanation of the multiplier goes like this: Suppose that Al decides to reduce his savings by $100 and increase spending by $100 to buy bread from Bill the baker. This purchase raises Bill's income by $100. Bill decides to save $50 of this extra income and spend the other $50 to buy candy from Cindy, so Cindy's income rises by $50. She decides to save $25 of this extra income and spend the other $25 to buy dishes from Dave. Dave's income rises by $25, and so on. If each person spends half of any increase in income and saves the other half, total spending eventually rises by $200. (That is, $100 + $50 + $25 + $12.50 + $6.25 + · · · = $200.) Therefore, the common argument goes, Al's $100 increase in spending has a *ripple effect* on the economy that raises total spending by $200.

The analysis in the preceding paragraph is incorrect, because it looks only at the *direct* effects of Al's spending and ignores the *indirect* effects. The *indirect* effects occur because when Al raises his spending by $100, he *reduces his saving* by $100. He puts $100 less in his bank account for the bank to lend, so someone else—say, Marcia—borrows $100 less than she would otherwise have borrowed. Marcia spends $100 less

---

Figure 13 | The Aggregate Demand Multiplier

Suppose that autonomous spending rises by $100. If the multiplier is 2, aggregate demand rises by $200, from AD_1 to AD_4. (The AD curve shifts to the right by $200.) If the multiplier is 1, aggregate demand rises by $100 and the AD curve shifts from AD_1 to AD_3. If the multiplier is ½, aggregate demand rises by only $50 and the aggregate demand curve shifts from AD_1 to AD_2.

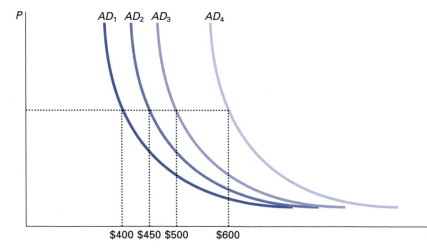

on nachos from Ned. Ned's income falls by $100, so Ned spends $50 less on oranges from Ollie. Ollie's income then falls, and so on.

Now compare the direct effects of Al's increased spending with the indirect effects. Al spends $100 more, but Marcia spends $100 less, so those changes in spending cancel each other. Bill spends $50 more, but Ned spends $50 less, so their changes in spending also cancel each other. Similarly, Cindy's increase in spending cancels Ollie's decrease, and so on. Clearly, the common argument incorrectly ignores these offsetting decreases in spending.

It is easy to notice the direct effects of Al's spending. For example, a reporter might interview Bill or Cindy, whose incomes have increased because of Al's spending. It is harder to notice the indirect effects. After all, Marcia might not know that she *could have* borrowed Al's money, if only he had saved it and deposited it in a bank account, so that the bank could have loaned it to her. These indirect effects indicate events that *would have* happened if Al had *not* increased his spending. Looking at direct effects but ignoring indirect effects is a common source of fallacies in economics. You will encounter this fallacy again in a later chapter on international trade. One of the important lessons you can learn from studying economics is not to ignore indirect effects.

> In logical thinking about economics, remember the *indirect* effects as well as the *direct* effects.

The Logic of the Multiplier

Despite the logical error in the common explanation of the multiplier, the assertion that a change in spending has ripple effects on the economy is correct. A $100 increase in spending may raise aggregate demand by more (or less) than $100. The economic model developed in earlier chapters provides a logical explanation of the multiplier. Consider the supply and demand for loans in Figure 14. When Al boosts spending by $100 and reduces savings by $100, the supply of loans falls. This fall in supply raises the equilibrium real interest rate from r_1 to r_2. This increase in the real interest rate raises the nominal interest rate, which raises velocity. The increase in velocity, in turn, raises

Figure 14 | Why the Multiplier Exceeds Zero

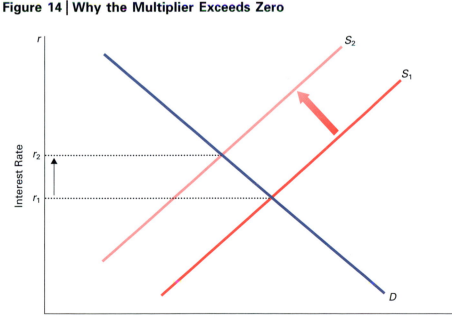

An increase in consumption spending reduces saving, which reduces the supply of loans from S_1 to S_2. This raises the real interest rate from r_1 to r_2, which raises the nominal interest rate and velocity. Therefore, aggregate demand (*MV*) rises.

IN THE NEWS

From Alaska fisheries to Australian outback, Asian crisis hits home

'Like ripples in the water'

Asia's financial crisis has taught a lesson in the world's new geography to the residents of Monroe County, the taproot of southern Alabama's pulp country.

In January, Monroe's Alabama River Pulp Mill and Alabama Pine Pulp Mill shut down temporarily, idling 700 of 900 workers. The reason: shrinking demand for their softwood pulp in Asia, especially in the gritty paper factories of Indonesia. There, in a tropical archipelago of 200 million-plus people, a savage currency depreciation has dried up demand for dollar-priced imports.

"Anyone who was aware of how trade relationships work could see this coming," says Marilyn Culpepper, a Monroe County industrial-development specialist. "It's like ripples in the water."

More like waves pounding the beach. Asia's economic woes are rocking companies, cities, and countries world-wide. Though the global economy remains stable, the pain emanating from Asia reaches nearly every corner of the world. Reduced demand from Asia has struck family-run New Zealand dairies and European petro-chemical giants. Fishermen in Alaska and the Falkland islands are struggling to keep afloat as their major buyers in Asia content themselves with cheaper fish fare processed closer to home.

Source: The Wall Street Journal

In our integrated world economy, a recession in one part of the world can spread internationally like ripples on water. Asian recessions in 1998 reduced exports from the rest of the world, decreasing aggregate demand with a multiplier effect.

---

aggregate demand, *MV*. In other words, total spending rises because an increase in the interest rate leads people to spend money faster than before. So Al's decision to increase spending and reduce savings really does raise aggregate demand.

The size of the aggregate demand multiplier depends on two factors. First, how much does the initial increase in spending (and decrease in saving) raise the real interest rate? When Al reduces saving by $100, the supply of loans shifts leftward by $100. The size of the increase in the interest rate depends upon the elasticity of demand for loans (roughly, the shape of the demand curve), with larger increases in the interest rate reflecting a more inelastic (roughly, steeper) demand for loans. Second, how much does the velocity of money increase when the interest rate rises? The larger the increase in the interest rate, and the larger the response of velocity to that increase, the larger the aggregate-demand multiplier.

This same reasoning applies to any exogenous change in spending. An increase in investment, government spending, or net exports also raises aggregate demand. The ultimate change in aggregate demand resulting from such an increase in spending can exceed that original increase.

Review Questions

---

14. Zach decides to take $300 out of his bank account and buy the latest interactive game machine. Explain (a) a common *fallacy* about the effects of this spending on aggregate demand, (b) why the reasoning in part (a) is fallacious, and (c) the true effects on aggregate demand of Zach's spending.

15. How is the size of the aggregate demand multiplier affected by the responsiveness of velocity to a change in the nominal interest rate?

T h i n k i n g   E x e r c i s e

16. Suppose the government decides to raise military spending by $25 billion, and to pay for this increase in spending by raising taxes. Explain how this change affects aggregate demand, and the factors that affect the *size* of the total response of aggregate demand.

The Great Depression

CASE STUDIES

The Great Depression, which lasted from 1929 through most of the 1930s, was the biggest recession in U.S. history. Real GDP per capita fell 30 percent from 1929 until 1933 and then rose slowly, reaching its 1929 level again only in 1940. The rise from 1933 to 1940 was interrupted by another recession in 1937 to 1938. Analysts customarily date the beginning of the Great Depression at the stock-market crash of October 1929, particularly October 24 (Black Thursday) and October 29 (Black Tuesday). Many people lost fortunes in the crash; some even committed suicide as a result. As much as some people suffered from the stock market crash, the coming depression would be far worse and affect more people. Deflation (negative inflation) occurred as the price level fell by more than 20 percent.[5] By 1933, nominal GDP was only 56 percent of its 1929 level.

The unemployment rate in the United States rose to almost 25 percent in 1933 and 1934; roughly one out of every four workers was unemployed. In September 1932, *Fortune* magazine estimated that 34 million people (28 percent of the U.S. population) had no incomes at all.[6]

A multiplier effect magnified the decline, as discussed in the last section. People without jobs or other incomes could not pay taxes or rents; landlords who could not collect rents could not pay taxes; cities that could not collect taxes could not pay for social programs or schools. People without incomes could not buy much, and many businesses closed.[7]

It is important not to let statistics hide the impact of the depression on people's lives—the depression caused considerable misery. That misery highlights the importance of economic models to analyze these events and help guide policies to prevent their recurrence. The issues in these chapters have great, direct effects on people's lives.

What Caused the Great Depression?

In 1933, the U.S. economy produced only about two-thirds as many goods as it produced in 1929, even though most of the same people, equipment, and technology remained available for production. Why did output fall so much? Although the stock market crash marks the beginning of the Great Depression, the crash did not *cause* the

---

[5]It fell 3.0 percent in 1930 and 8.7 percent in 1931 as the depression deepened, and it continued to fall until 1934.

[6]Cited in Paul Johnson, *Modern Times* (New York: Harper & Row, 1983), p. 247.

[7]Big retail stores did not suffer as badly as industry. James Thurber noted that they reduced prices and that anyone who could earn money could get bargains at these stores.

depression. After all, many recessions have occurred without major stock market crashes, and many stock market crashes (such as the crash of October 19, 1987) have occurred without recessions soon following.

Economists generally agree that the Great Depression cannot be explained with the basic model discussed in earlier chapters. Most economists believe that the sticky-price or sticky-wage models discussed in this chapter and the previous one play a major role in the explanation.

Economists generally interpret the Great Depression as the result of a huge fall in aggregate demand, but they disagree about the reasons for that fall. Perhaps the most prominent view, developed by Milton Friedman and Anna J. Schwartz in a famous study, holds that the main cause of the depression was a fall in the money supply. The M2 measure of the money supply fell by almost one-third from 1929 to 1933. Although the Federal Reserve increased the monetary base slightly during that period as the economy slid into the Great Depression, more than 9,000 banks stopped operating. People lost over $1 billion in deposits in those banks, making them poorer than before, though the loss was small compared to the $85 billion people lost in the stock market over the same period. Bank failures increased the currency–deposit ratio, which reduced the money multiplier (discussed in Chapter 10), causing M2 to fall. According to this view, this fall in the money supply reduced aggregate demand. Banking problems were related to the stock market crash. Because stock prices fell, many borrowers could not repay their loans on time, or even make scheduled interest payments. Consequently, most banks faced the liquidity problems discussed in Chapter 10. A banking panic occurred as depositors tried to withdraw their money. Many banks, lacking sufficient reserves to cover these withdrawals, closed down. Although most banks reopened later and most people recovered most of their deposits, many people lost their money for several years, and some lost it permanently.

Another prominent view holds that an exogenous fall in spending on consumption and investment reduced aggregate demand, causing the depression. Consumption spending may have fallen because people lost money in the stock market or because consumer confidence declined and people decided to increase savings and curtail spending. Some economists see unexpected deflation as a major factor, since it redistributed wealth from borrowers to lenders. Note, however, that this redistribution would reduce aggregate demand only if lenders tend to save more and spend less than borrowers.[8]

Finally, investment spending may have fallen because bank failures interfered with firms borrowing money from people who saved it. The unexpected deflation bankrupted many firms that had borrowed money and pushed other firms to the brink of bankruptcy. It became risky for people to lend money to firms, because the threat of bankruptcy increased, worrying lenders that they would not be repaid in full. With lenders increasingly cautious about lending money, firms had trouble obtaining funds to finance their operations and investments, which may have reduced aggregate demand and contributed to the depression.

Whatever the reason for the fall in aggregate demand, the result was a huge fall in real GDP and the price level from 1929 to 1933. This fall was followed by a long movement back toward the full-employment level of output.

Many, though not all, economists believe that if the Federal Reserve had prevented the fall in the M2 measure of the money supply, the action would have avoided the Great Depression or reduced its severity. Milton Friedman and Anna J. Schwartz took this position in their important book, *A Monetary History of the United States*.[9] They argued that

---

[8]Some history books attribute the fall in aggregate demand to a fall in wages, claiming that workers spent less because they earned less. This claim embodies two fallacies. First, although the average *nominal* wage fell from 57 cents per hour in 1929 to 44 cents an hour in 1933, a larger percentage fall in the price level *raised* the average real wage, for those who remained employed. Second, the claim ignores the increase in profits to firms resulting from a fall in wages. Even if the real wage had fallen, the redistribution from workers to firms' owners would reduce aggregate demand only if workers tended to spend more of their income than owners.

[9]Milton Friedman and Anna J. Schwartz, *A Monetary History of the United States* (Princeton, N.J.: Princeton University Press, 1963).

every major change in the money supply in U.S. history has led to changes in real GDP in the short run and the price level in the long run, regardless of why the money supply changed. As a result, a fall in M2 by one-third, the largest fall in U.S. history, should be expected to bring about the biggest depression in U.S. history. Friedman and Schwartz argued that if the Federal Reserve had increased the monetary base to keep M2 from falling, the Great Depression would have been, at most, a mild recession. Even if aggregate demand had fallen for some reason unrelated to the fall in M2, a stable money supply would have prevented aggregate demand from falling enough to cause a depression.[10]

International Comparisons

The Great Depression was a worldwide event. As the price level fell in the United States, international trade transmitted deflation to other countries on the gold standard. The depression became deeper in the United States, Canada, and Germany than in most other countries.

One way for economists to learn about the effects of government policies on the economy is to compare results in countries with different policies. From 1929 to 1933, countries with the biggest deflations also had the biggest recessions. Researchers have identified three groups of countries to compare. First, many countries, such as the United States and Germany, operated on the gold standard. These countries had deflations and major recessions from 1929 to 1933. Second, some countries, such as China and Spain, had no deflations because they were not on the gold standard. These countries had no major recessions.

Third, some countries stopped their deflations by abandoning the gold standard in 1931.[11] These countries put early ends to their recessions. For example, Great Britain went off the gold standard in September 1931, and its real GDP stopped falling. Figure 15a shows the results. From 1929 to 1933, aggregate demand fell in the United States, and the economy moved along the short-run aggregate supply curve, AS^{SR} from Point A to Point B to Point C, with falling prices and falling real GDP. In Great Britain, aggregate demand fell between 1929 and 1931, then stayed about constant from 1931 to 1933, so the price level and real GDP fell from 1929 to 1931 in Great Britain (from Point A to Point B in Panel (b) of the figure). As the British economy adjusted toward the long-run equilibrium, prices fell further and real GDP increased (from Point B to Point C) back to the level associated with the long-run aggregate supply curve, AS^{LR}.

Sweden also abandoned the gold standard in 1931, immediately ending its deflation. Prices and the money supply remained about constant for a year, then rose slowly for the next few years. Real GDP in Sweden fell 9.1 percent in 1931, almost as much as the 11.5 percent fall in U.S. real GDP. However, after Sweden stopped its deflation in 1932, Swedish real GDP fell only 3.2 percent, while U.S. real GDP fell another 18.7 percent.[12] By 1934, Swedish real GDP was back to its 1929 level, while U.S. real GDP remained at only ¾ of its 1929 level. These episodes suggest that the United States might have been able to end the Great Depression earlier if it had raised the monetary base to keep M1 and M2 from falling and to stop the deflation.

Some people have suggested that the Hawley-Smoot Act of 1930, which raised tariffs significantly, made the depression much worse than it otherwise would have been.

---

[10]Some economists claim that an increase in the money supply would not have helped in this situation. They say that in certain situations with low nominal interest rates, as in the Great Depression, people would be unwilling to spend increases in the money supply, so those increases would not raise aggregate demand. Instead, they argue, an increase in M would simply reduce velocity, V, so that aggregate demand, MV, would not increase.

[11]As Chapter 10 explained, the gold standard restricted growth rates of the money supply. In the early 1930s, these growth rates were low enough to cause deflation. Abandoning the gold standard gave governments the ability to raise money growth to prevent deflation.

[12]Why did Swedish real GDP not *rise*? Perhaps because depressions in other countries reduced the demand for Sweden's exports. This would have caused aggregate demand in Sweden to continue to fall, but by less than had Sweden remained on the gold standard and continued to endure deflation as in the United States, Germany, and other countries.

Figure 15 | An International Comparison of the Great Depression

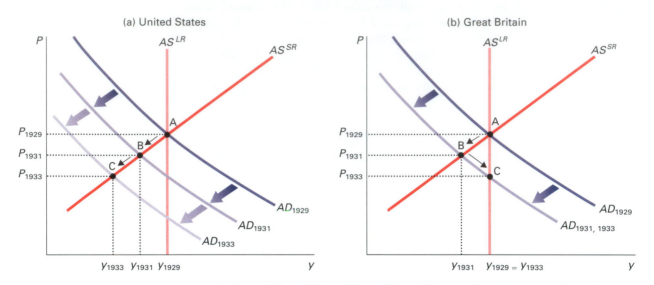

Panel (a): From 1929 to 1931, and from 1931 to 1933, the price level and real GDP fell in the United States. Panel (b): From 1929 to 1931, the price level and real GDP fell in Great Britain, but that country then abandoned the gold standard, and real GDP increased as the price level fell.

Economists generally agree that tariffs reduce economic efficiency, but most doubt that the Hawley-Smoot Act played a major role in causing the Great Depression. Its main role may have been to help spread the depression to European countries, many of which also increased their tariffs.

In the United States, the Great Depression helped Franklin Roosevelt win election over President Herbert Hoover in 1932, leading to the New Deal, Roosevelt's policies to fight the depression.[13] Real GDP started rising slowly in 1934.

The famous book by John Maynard Keynes, *The General Theory of Employment, Interest, and Money,* was published in 1936, when real GDP in the United States was still below its 1929 level. The book received immediate attention for its theory of why recessions occur and how to cure and prevent episodes like the Great Depression. Keynes's General Theory became the dominant influence on the development of macroeconomics over the next 40 years.

Credit Controls in 1980[14]

On March 14, 1980, President Carter imposed credit controls on the U.S. economy to try to reduce inflation, which had reached 12.4 percent in 1979. These credit controls subjected lenders to special regulations that effectively worked like a tax on loans.[15] They were intended to lower inflation by reducing the amount of money that consumers and businesses borrowed and spent on consumption and investment. That is, they were intended to reduce aggregate demand, and they succeeded.

---

[13] President Hoover, who had come into office in early 1929, had followed some policies to raise aggregate demand, such as cutting taxes and raising government spending (mainly for transfer payments), leading to a government budget deficit of almost 3 percent of GDP in 1931.

[14] This discussion is based on Stacey L. Schreft, "Credit Controls, 1980," *Economic Review 76* no. 6 (November/December 1990), published by the Federal Reserve Bank of Richmond. Figure 16 comes from that paper.

[15] These controls included, for example, a special deposit requirement on lenders for certain types of consumer credit that required lenders to hold non-interest-bearing deposits at the Fed equal to 15 percent of their loans.

Figure 16 | Effects of Credit Controls in 1980

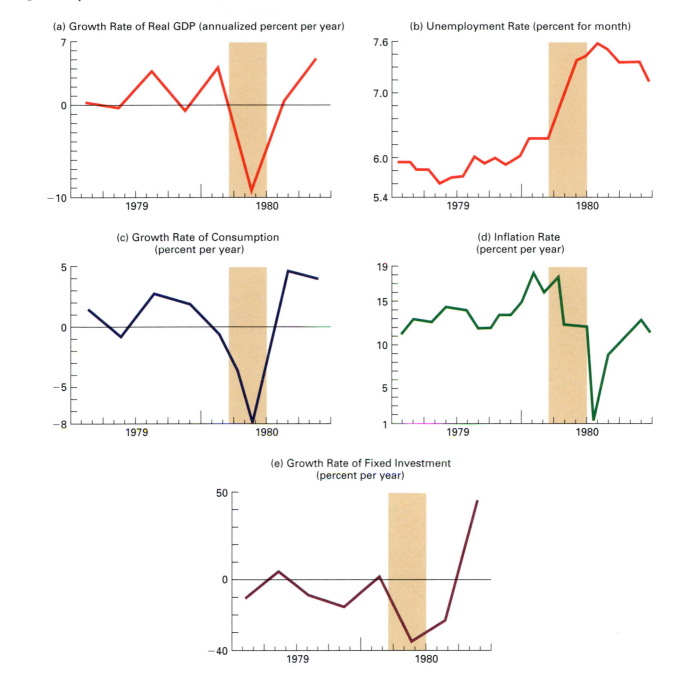

(a) Growth Rate of Real GDP (annualized percent per year)

(b) Unemployment Rate (percent for month)

(c) Growth Rate of Consumption (percent per year)

(d) Inflation Rate (percent per year)

(e) Growth Rate of Fixed Investment (percent per year)

The controls led some banks to stop accepting new credit-card applications and others to tighten requirements to get credit cards, raise annual fees for credit cards, raise interest rates on the cards, and raise minimum required monthly payments. Although other controls on consumer borrowing were mainly symbolic, the publicity and confusion generated by the credit controls caused a large fall in consumer spending. Total bank loans fell 5 percent in April 1980 alone, and retail sales fell at the fastest rate in 29 years. Figure 16 shows growth rates of consumption, investment, and real GDP, as well as the unemployment rate and inflation rate. The shaded area indicates the period of credit controls.

The credit controls led to steep falls in consumption and investment spending, reducing aggregate demand, real GDP, and the rate of inflation and raising the unemployment rate. Although the growth rate of the monetary base did not change much, the growth rates of M1 and M2 fell because the money multiplier fell as banks reduced lending. In this way, the credit policy caused reductions in M1 and M2 as well as a fall in aggregate demand. This fact shows why economists must analyze data cautiously, without drawing hasty conclusions about cause and effect. One could easily look at the graph and conclude, falsely, that the fall in the money-growth rate *caused* the fall in consumption and investment that reduced real GDP. In fact, the fall in the money-growth rate was a *result* of the decrease in borrowing and spending, due to the credit controls; it did not *cause* that fall in spending.

Recession of 1982

In October 1979, the new chairman of the Federal Reserve Board, Paul Volcker, announced that the Fed would change its operating procedures to increase its attention to the money supply and to reduce inflation. The Federal Reserve did just that, with some help from a fall in velocity. The Fed quickly reduced the growth rate of the monetary base from almost 8.0 percent per year in 1980 to about 4.5 percent per year in 1981, before letting it gradually rise in 1982. The growth rate of M1, however, changed little.[16] The velocity of M1 had been growing steadily since 1960, and it suddenly started falling in 1982 for reasons that economists do not yet fully understand.[17]

The combination of a fall in the growth rate of the money supply and lower velocity reduced aggregate demand. Figure 17 shows the results. Inflation was 12.4 percent in 1979, 11.6 percent in 1980, and 8.5 percent in 1981. It suddenly fell to 3.8 percent in 1982, as the economy entered a recession, and to 3.7 percent in 1983. Real GDP fell more than 3.0 percent from fall 1981 to fall 1982, reaching 1.6 percent below its 1979 level. The unemployment rate rose from 5.8 percent in 1979 to more than 10.0 percent in the last half of 1982. The 1982 recession was the largest in the United States since the Great Depression. (Figure 9e shows the Phillips Curve for this period.)

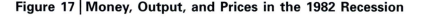

Figure 17 | Money, Output, and Prices in the 1982 Recession

Output in this graph is measured by industrial production; the money supply is measured by the monetary base. M1 also fell in 1981 prior to the 1982 recession.

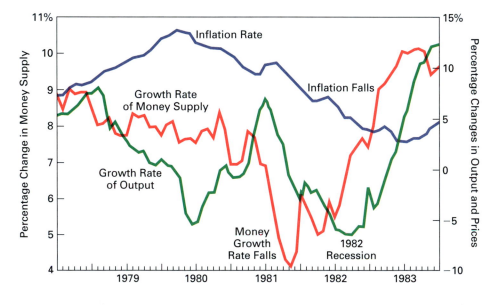

---

[16]The growth rate of M2 did not fall, but its velocity fell.

[17]The nominal interest rate fell, which helped to reduce velocity, but velocity fell by more than economists expected based on that fall in the nominal interest rate.

Recessions and Expected Inflation

Some economists believe that the short-run Phillips Curve does *not* shift quickly when expectations change. Instead, they argue, policies to reduce inflation cause a recession *even if* people expect inflation to fall. These economists cite the 1982 recession as evidence. That recession occurred after the Federal Reserve announced publicly that it would try to reduce inflation. People expected inflation to fall in 1982, argue these economists, but a recession occurred anyway. If the change in expectations had shifted the short-run Phillips Curve—if only unexpected inflation could affect real GDP—then, these economists say, the 1982 recession would not have happened.

Other economists argue that people did not expect inflation to fall despite the Federal Reserve's public announcement in October 1979. They argue that people pay attention to actions and may not believe announcements. After all, this was not the first time the government announced that it would fight inflation. Politicians and government officials (including Federal Reserve policymakers) make many announcements and people would be foolish to believe all of them. Whether a fully expected fall in inflation causes a recession remains a topic of controversy among economists.

Recession of 1990 to 1991

Economists disagree about the causes of the U.S. recession in 1990–1991. According to one view, that recession resulted from tight monetary policy, which reduced aggregate demand. Figure 18 shows the growth rate of real GDP in the United States from 1985–94, and the growth rate of M1 that had occurred 1½ years earlier. (The lag appears because changes in GDP tend to be more closely related to previous changes in M1 than

IN THE NEWS

Fed foresees slow growth in economy

More jobless the cost of curbing inflation

Source: Washington Post

Many economists believe that policies to reduce inflation also create a recession. However, others believe that those policies can avoid a recession if they also reduce expected inflation, shifting the short-run Phillips Curve.

IN THE NEWS

Busy factories revive fears of inflation

So the Fed, which has been trying since March to hold off inflation by raising interest rates, will likely push rates higher. The goal: dampen demand for loans, which would discourage spending. Then businesses would have to hold off on some price increases.

Job growth revives fears of inflation

If anyone out there knows when U.S. businesses will stop creating more than 10,000 jobs a day, please call Alan Greenspan.

The Federal Reserve chairman has been pushing up interest rates for a year, to slow the economy and head off what he fears is an onrushing wave of inflation.

Sources: USA Today

Fast growth of real GDP and falling unemployment in 1988-1989, led the Federal Reserve to conclude that the economy was moving upward along a short-run Phillips Curve. To prevent rising inflation, the Fed tightened monetary policy. Although the Fed may have been correct, its policy reaction might have caused the 1990 recession.

Figure 18 | Output and Money Growth in the 1990–1991 Recession

Economy climbs while inflation slides

WASHINGTON—The economy exploded at a 4.2% annual rate in the first quarter while inflation fell to early 1950s levels, the Commerce Department said.

The data highlight the dilemma facing the Federal Reserve. Central bankers remain convinced that, at some point, the economy can't grow at its current pace without triggering inflation. Fed officials have stressed that their job is to pre-empt inflation before waiting for signs to emerge, not to wait for prices to escalate.

Source: The Wall Street Journal

Does fast growth of real GDP necessarily trigger inflation?

to current changes in M1.) The figure shows that large decreases in the growth rate of the money supply preceded the recession, and may have caused it.

Some economists believe that the 1990–91 recession resulted at least partly from two other factors. First, banks and other financial intermediaries became less willing to lend, partly because government regulators began stricter oversight of risky loans.[18] This decrease in lending may have contributed to a fall in aggregate demand by reducing investment. Second, Iraq's invasion of Kuwait in August 1990 suddenly raised the world price of oil substantially (though temporarily). This increase in the price of imported oil may have reduced aggregate supply, and the associated increase in uncertainty about future oil prices may have reduced investment and aggregate demand.

The U.S. Recovery of the 1990s

In recent years, the U.S. economy has experienced rapid growth, with real GDP rising at 3 percent per year from 1992 to 1998, and unemployment falling from 7.5 percent in 1992 to 4.5 percent in 1998. One remarkable feature of the 1990s has been the *combination* of low inflation, as shown in Figure 19, with rapid growth in real GDP and low unemployment. Many commentators have questioned whether this combination is consistent with economic theory—doesn't the Phillips Curve show that low unemployment goes with *high* inflation, while low inflation, as in the 1990s, occurs with high unemployment?

Of course, the commentators are wrong: Economic theory does not imply that inflation and unemployment move inversely. Prominent economic models predict that inflation and unemployment tend to move in opposite directions in the *short run*, given expected inflation, in response to changes in aggregate *demand*. However, falling unemployment

---

[18] The increased strictness of government regulation began after the federal government spent about $150 billion when savings and loan associations went bankrupt in the 1980s, as mentioned in the discussion of deposit insurance in Chapter 10.

Figure 19 | U.S. Inflation, 1980–1998

may occur with low inflation (as in the 1990s) as the economy returns to a long-run equilibrium, as in the movement from Point D to Point E in Figure 10. Similarly, unemployment may fall as real GDP rises and the price level falls, as in the movement from Point B to Point C in Figure 17 of the previous chapter. Moreover, changes in aggregate *supply* can lead to falling unemployment with low inflation. Figure 20 shows the effects of an

Figure 20 | Increase in Aggregate Supply Raises Real GDP and Reduces the Price Level

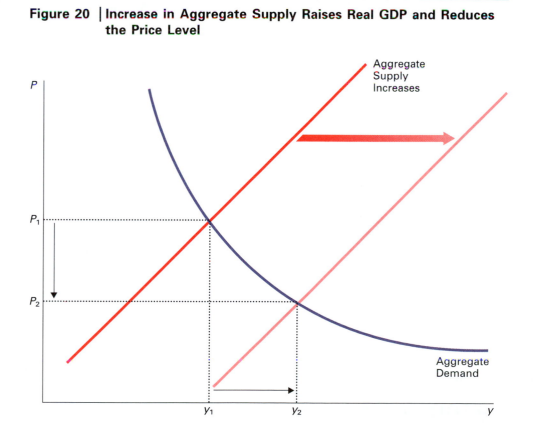

increase in aggregate supply, perhaps due to advances in technology and falling prices of imported inputs such as crude oil (which occurred in the 1990s). The increase in aggregate supply raises real GDP, reducing unemployment (by Okun's Law), as it reduces the price level.

Asian Recessions in the Late 1990s

Several Asian countries experienced severe economic crises in the late 1990s. Recessions, banking crises, and exchange-rate crises hit Japan, South Korea, Malaysia, Indonesia, and Thailand in 1997 and 1998. Along with recessions, these countries experienced bank failures, stock market crashes, devaluations of their currencies on foreign exchange markets, and corporate bankruptcies.

Economists do not yet understand fully the causes of the Asian crisis. However, they generally agree that banking crises played a key role. The banking crises grew from the problems with deposit insurance discussed in Chapter 10. Deposit insurance, or implicit promises of such insurance from the government as in most of the Asian countries, affected the incentives of banks. Deposit insurance encouraged banks to make risky loans and investments, with high chances of default. Governments of some countries encouraged lending to certain firms and industries, sometimes for political reasons and sometimes to encourage growth in certain parts of the economy, which added to the risky loans. Eventually, banks took big losses as many borrowers became unable to repay their loans. Banks became unable to extend additional loans, and many firms faced bankruptcy. Stock markets crashed. Some banks became insolvent, and closed. Decreases in lending reduced investment; decreases in wealth and financial panics reduced consumption spending. Aggregate demand decreased, and the economies fell into recessions. Concerns increased that governments would ignite inflation by loosening monetary policy to raise aggregate demand. Increases in expected inflation caused currency depreciation on foreign exchange markets.

The concept of moral hazard plays a key role in understanding the Asian crisis. *Moral hazard* refers to an effect of your actions on someone's incentives when you cannot monitor that person's actions. For example, when you pay someone $10 per hour to do a job for you, you may create an incentive for that person to work slowly, to raise the total payment. Moral hazard arises when someone can reap the rewards from their actions when things go well but do not suffer the full consequences when things go badly. When an insurance policy provides reimbursement if a car is stolen, that policy reduces owners' incentives to prevent theft. Similarly, when the government provides deposit insurance, it reduces banks' incentives to avoid risky loans and investments. If banks are lucky with their risks, they earn high profits; if they are unlucky, their losses are limited because the government bails them out with deposit insurance. That is why deposit insurance, without sufficient government regulation of banks, creates the possibility of a financial crisis. Moral hazard from deposit insurance contributed to the savings and loan crisis in the United States in the 1980s, and to the Asian crisis of 1997–1998.

Moral hazard also played other roles in the Asian crisis. The International Monetary Fund (IMF) provided loans to several of these countries to lessen the impact of the crisis, as the IMF had done in earlier years with other countries. Many economists became concerned that the moral hazard problems created by IMF assistance would reduce the incentives of governments to avoid the conditions that lead to such crises. An additional concern involves the moral hazard effect on incentives of major U.S. banks and corporations that lend to these countries. Do these lenders count on IMF bailouts to reduce their risks?

By late 1998, policymakers around the world were concerned about the spread of the Asian recessions internationally. The Federal Reserve, the Bank of Canada, the Bank of England, and other central banks loosened monetary policy to try to raise aggregate demand and prevent a world recession.

IN THE NEWS

G7 nations try to halt slide to depression

Fear of a meltdown in world stock markets and a decline into a 1930s-style economic depression has pushed the world's leading finance ministers into making an unprecedentedly strong demand for an urgent and coordinated response to the current turmoil. The Group of Seven industrialised nations is calling for immediate interest rate cuts and a rapid move towards the creation of a new international authority that would act to avert any future economic collapse.

In an effort to halt the panic that set in on world stock markets last week, Gordon Brown, the Chancellor of the Exchequer, said that the world's major powers were now co-operating to boost international demand, restructure financial systems and provide help for the victims of the world financial crisis.

Source: The Times (London)

As the 1998 Asian financial crises and recessions threatened to spread internationally, the G7 industrial countries (the United States, Canada, Japan, England, Germany, France, and Italy) began policies to raise aggregate demand.

Review Questions

18. How did credit controls in 1980 affect aggregate demand? What happened to the U.S. economy?

19. (a) What is moral hazard and what role did it play in the Asian financial crises of the late 1990s? (b) How does a banking-system crisis reduce aggregate demand, as in those Asian countries?

20. How did the stock market crash of 1929 contribute to the banking crisis in the Great Depression, and how did that crisis contribute to the change in the money supply?

Thinking Exercises

21. Draw a graph of aggregate demand and supply and use it to interpret (a) the Great Depression (b) the U.S. recession of 1982, (c) the U.S. economic expansion in the 1990s, and (d) the Asian recessions of the late 1990s.

22. Cite two hypotheses about the causes of the fall in aggregate demand that caused the Great Depression. What evidence could help determine which hypothesis is correct?

Conclusion

Money and Interest Rates in the Short Run

Because the price level is sticky, Federal Reserve open market operations affect the real interest rate in the short run. An open market purchase lowers the real interest rate in the short run, while it increases the money supply. An open market sale raises the real interest rate in the short run, while it reduces the money supply. These short-run effects on the real interest rate vanish in the long run as the price level adjusts to its new equilibrium level.

Phillips Curves

The short-run Phillips Curve describes a statistical relationship between inflation and unemployment. Unemployment falls temporarily when inflation rises, and it rises temporarily when inflation falls. Eventually, the economy returns to the natural rate of unemployment and produces the full-employment level of output, so the long-run Phillips Curve is a vertical line at the natural rate of unemployment. Evidence indicates that the short-run Phillips Curve shifts over time, perhaps in response to changes in people's expectations for inflation.

Three Theories of Aggregate Supply

The sticky-price model states that the aggregate supply curve slopes upward because nominal prices of many goods and services are sticky in the short run, creating a sticky overall price level, as well. Nominal prices may be sticky due to menu costs. When prices of individual products eventually differ sufficiently from their equilibrium levels, firms pay the menu costs and adjust prices. At that point, the economy moves from its short-run equilibrium to a new long-run equilibrium.

The sticky-wage models states that the aggregate supply curve slopes upward because nominal wages are sticky in the short run. Nominal wages may be sticky due to employment contracts. The economy moves from its short-run equilibrium toward a new long-run equilibrium when wages change as new employment contracts eventually replace old contracts.

The imperfect-information theory asserts that the short-run aggregate supply curve slopes upward because sellers mistake nominal price changes for relative price changes. When the nominal price of a product falls, its sellers falsely believe that its relative price has decreased, so they cut production. The short-run aggregate supply curve shifts and the economy moves to a new long-run equilibrium when sellers eventually realize that they have made a mistake.

All three models imply that the long-run aggregate supply curve is vertical at the full-employment level of output. They differ in their interpretations of the causes of short-run unemployment. The sticky-price model implies that unemployed people cannot find jobs, even by offering to work for reduced wages, because firms cannot sell the additional products that those workers would produce. The sticky-wage theory implies that unemployment occurs because the real wage exceeds its equilibrium level. The incomplete information model implies that unemployed workers could find jobs by offering to work at reduced wages.

The Aggregate Demand Multiplier

An exogenous $100 increase in spending can raise aggregate demand by more or less than $100, due to the aggregate demand multiplier. The logic behind the multiplier—and a common fallacy—illustrates the importance of looking at indirect effects as well as direct effects when applying economic analysis. An exogenous $100 increase in spending may raise aggregate demand by more than $100, because it raises the interest rate and, therefore, raises the velocity of money.

Case Studies

Many economists believe that the Great Depression resulted from a large decrease in the money supply from 1929 to 1933 that reduced aggregate demand. Some economists believe that the Great Depression resulted from an exogenous fall in spending on consumption and investment. Redistributions of income due to an unexpected fall in the price level may have contributed to the fall in aggregate demand by causing some business firms to go bankrupt and inhibiting others from borrowing money to finance operations and new investments.

Many countries around the world suffered from the Great Depression. However, the depression ended earlier in countries that left the gold standard and adopted monetary policies to prevent deflation than in other countries. Credit controls imposed by the U.S. government in 1980 reduced aggregate demand by decreasing consumption spending. This fall in aggregate demand reduced real GDP. Most economists believe the 1982 recession in the United States resulted mainly from tight Federal Reserve monetary policies. The Fed adopted these policies to reduce inflation from 13.5 percent per year in 1979 to 3.2 percent per year in 1983. Monetary policy may also have helped cause the U.S. recession in 1990 and 1991.

Moral hazard problems at banks, created by government deposit insurance, led to financial crises in several Asian nations in 1997–1998. These nations experienced bank failures, bankruptcies of firms, currency depreciation, and stock market crashes, as decreases in aggregate demand drove the economies into recessions. Policymakers around the world became concerned about the spread of the recessions internationally, and began taking steps to raise aggregate demand and prevent a world recession.

Key Terms

short-run Phillips Curve   natural rate of unemployment   long-run Phillips Curve   aggregate demand multiplier

Questions and Problems

23. Use the framework in this chapter to explain why a city's real GDP may rise and its unemployment may fall if it hosts the Olympics or some other major event.

24. Suppose that aggregate demand rises. Explain what happens in the short run and the long run (and why) according to the:
(a) Sticky-price model
(b) Sticky-wage model
(c) Incomplete information model

25. Use the model of aggregate demand and supply to explain the 1982 recession.

26. Use the model of aggregate demand and supply to help explain how a recession in one country can spread to other countries.

27. Why does unemployment return to its natural rate in long-run equilibrium?

28. According to the sticky-wage model, are real wages likely to rise or fall in a recession?

29. The GDP deflator in the United States fell 18 percent from 1920 to 1921 and another 8 percent from 1921 to 1922. Meanwhile, per-capita real GDP fell 11 percent from 1920 to 1921 and then rose 13 percent from 1921 to 1922. Explain, using aggregate supply and demand curves, what happened.

30. Great Britain had high inflation during and after World War I. The price level doubled from 1914 to 1918 and then rose 40 percent from 1918 to 1920. Then the British government decided to reduce the price level back to about its prewar level. From 1920 to 1921, the GDP deflator fell 11 percent, while real GDP fell 6 percent. The next year, the price level fell another 17 percent, and real GDP increased. Use the aggregate demand/aggregate supply framework to explain what happened.

31. Use aggregate supply and aggregate demand curves to discuss the short-run and long-run effects of:
(a) An exogenous increase in consumer savings
(b) An earthquake
(c) An increase in government spending for defense, paid for by a tax increase
(d) An increase in the government budget deficit caused by a tax cut without any cut in government spending

Inquiries for Further Thought

32. Some economists argue that it is incorrect to interpret the data in Figure 11 as a shifting Phillips Curve. They argue that economists see in that figure only what they *want* to see (downward sloping Phillips Curves), and that by grouping consecutive years together differently, we could produce *any* results—even upward-sloping Phillips Curves.
(a) Get annual data on inflation and unemployment from the Web site for this book. Can you find a way to group consecutive years together that makes Phillips Curves appear to slope upward rather than downward?
(b) What do you conclude about Phillips Curves from this evidence?

33. Consider the Asian countries that were subject to recessions in the late 1990s due to banking crises. What kinds of policies should these countries adopt? Why? How might other countries avoid their fates?

34. If you could guide U.S. economic policies, what would you do to try to avoid recessions?

35. Should the government follow policies that raise inflation permanently to reduce unemployment temporarily? Should they reduce inflation permanently if doing so raises unemployment temporarily?

36. Suppose you are an economic advisor for a country with high inflation. The President of that country wants to know if he can reduce inflation without causing a recession. What advice can you suggest for this country?

37. Find data on the Internet or in your library to graph Phillips Curves for other countries. What do you find?

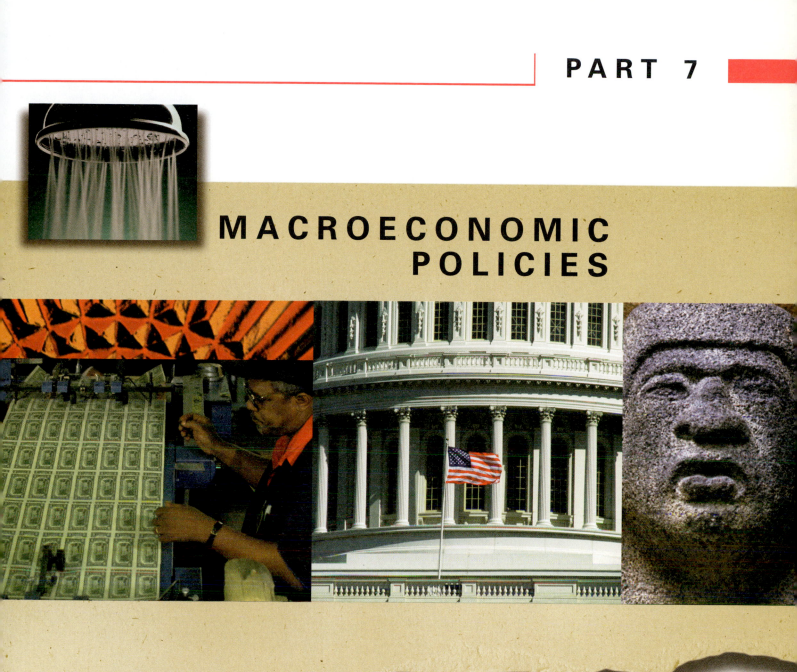

PART 7

MACROECONOMIC POLICIES

CHAPTER 13

MONETARY POLICY

In this Chapter. . .

Main Points to Understand

- ▶ Two fundamentally different views about government macroeconomic policy are reflected in the activist view, advocating discretionary policies, and the laissez-faire view, advocating policy rules.
- ▶ Monetary policy can try to offset changes in aggregate demand caused by changes in underlying conditions to stabilize real GDP and unemployment.
- ▶ Three main problems with activist, discretionary policies concern lags, information problems, and the effects of policies on expectations and incentives.

Thinking Skills to Develop

- ▶ Raise new questions about appropriate policies.
- ▶ Recognize the bases for legitimate disagreements about appropriate policies.

Not many people discuss monetary policy around the dinner table. Even news reports spend much less time reporting on monetary policy than on the latest political scandals or daily fluctuations in the stock market. Yet monetary policy has a more dramatic impact on your life than most of the issues discussed more frequently in the news. It determines whether you live in a country with stable prices or suffer through hyperinflation. It affects interest rates and redistributes income and wealth. In the short run, most economists believe, monetary policy affects the economy's output of goods and services, job opportunities for millions of workers, and unemployment. The Federal Reserve is one of the most powerful agencies in the world, perhaps with more impact on your life than the Supreme Court, but how much do you know of its policies? How many of its members can you name? (See the Web pages for this book for the answer.)

If you were in charge of the Federal Reserve or the central bank of another country, how would you make decisions?[1] How would you decide what the Fed should do this week? How would you decide whether to raise the money supply through open market purchases and by how much to raise it? How would you choose long-term goals for your policies to accomplish these decisions? What would those goals be? How would you decide whether to fight a possible recession if your actions would risk raising inflation?

---

[1]Chapter 10 discussed the Federal Reserve System and its main tools of monetary policy: open market operations, discount-window lending, reserve requirements, and other bank regulations.

If you had been in charge of designing the new monetary system for Europe, would you have chosen a single money, the Euro, for the nations of Europe? How would you have chosen operating procedures for the new European Central Bank? If you were an advisor to the British or Swiss governments, would you have advised joining the new system or remaining outside it (as these nations decided to do)? If you were a member of Congress in charge of redesigning U.S. monetary policy, would you want laws requiring the Fed to follow particular policies? Would you want to keep the Federal Reserve System at all or replace it with another system?

TWO VIEWS OF MACROECONOMIC POLICIES

Monetary policy is one of the two main types of government macroeconomic policies. (Fiscal policy, the second main type of macroeconomic policy, is discussed in the next chapter.)

> **Monetary policy** refers to changes in the nominal money supply through open market operations or other actions of a nation's central bank.

The Federal Reserve conducts monetary policy in the United States. Other countries have their own central banks, such as the Bank of Japan, the Bank of England, and the Bank of Mexico, which conduct those nations' monetary policies. Members of the European Union have created a new European Central Bank to operate European monetary policy for their new currency, the Euro.

Just as we often classify people's political views according to categories of liberal or conservative, views about the proper role of government economic policy fit into two categories: the *activist view* and the *laissez-faire view.* These categories don't fit everyone perfectly (just as the labels *liberal* and *conservative* don't), but they provide a useful contrast between two general views of government policy.

Activist View

Some economists take an activist view of policy.

> An **activist view** of policy maintains that the economy often operates inefficiently on its own and that government macroeconomic policies can improve its efficiency.

According to this view, changes in aggregate demand and supply often reduce output below its full-employment level and raise unemployment above its natural rate. Government macroeconomic policies can stabilize the economy—that is, prevent or reduce the business cycle fluctuations—by preventing or offsetting these changes in aggregate demand and supply.

Suppose, for example, that a decrease in investment demand reduces aggregate demand from AD_1 to AD_2 as in Figure 1. The Fed could *undo* this decrease in aggregate demand by raising the money supply. The increase in the money supply would raise the aggregate demand curve *back* to AD_1. To pursue this policy, the Fed would *loosen* monetary policy when it detected signs of declining real GDP and price level. The Fed, like most other central banks, usually describes its monetary policies in terms of effects on interest rates rather than effects on the money supply.[2]

---

[2]Chapters 10 and 12 discussed the effects of open market operations on the federal funds rate and other interest rates.

Figure 1 | An Activist View of Government Policy

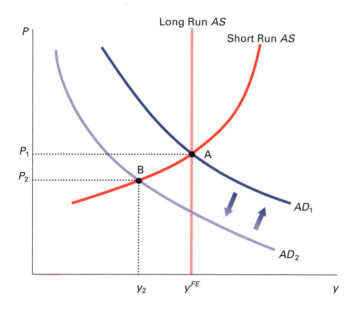

If aggregate demand were to fall from AD_1 to AD_2, an activist government policy might raise the money supply or government spending to try to raise aggregate demand back to AD_1.

> A **looser monetary policy** increases the growth rate of the money supply, decreasing the federal funds rate.

The Fed might loosen monetary policy by conducting open market purchases, lowering the discount rate, or reducing reserve requirements at banks. A loose policy is sometimes called *expansionary* policy because (by raising aggregate demand) it tends to expand real GDP.

Similarly, the Fed would *tighten* monetary policy, to decrease aggregate demand, when it believes that aggregate demand has increased beyond AD_1 in Figure 1. The tighter monetary policy is intended to bring aggregate demand back down to AD_1, preventing a short-run increase in real GDP but also preventing an increase in the price level.[3]

> A **tighter monetary policy** reduces the growth rate of the money supply, raising the federal funds rate.

The Fed might tighten monetary policy by conducting open market sales (or reducing the rate at which it conducts open market purchases), raising the discount rate, or raising reserve requirements at banks.

The Fed follows a *countercyclical* monetary policy if it loosens monetary policy to raise aggregate demand at times of low real GDP (relative to trend) and tightens monetary policy to reduce aggregate demand at times of high real GDP (relative to trend).

Figure 2 uses short-run Phillips Curves to describe countercyclical monetary policy. Many economists view the short-run Phillips Curve (discussed in the last chapter) as a short-run tradeoff between inflation and unemployment. They believe policy makers can *temporarily* choose any combination of inflation and unemployment on the short-run Phillips Curve, such as Point A, with high inflation and low unemployment, or Point B, with moderate inflation and unemployment, or Point C, with low inflation and high

Most short-term interest rates rise amid talk Fed might be tightening its policy somewhat

NEW YORK—Most short-term interest rates rose amid speculation that the Federal Reserve may be tightening credit slightly in an effort to combat inflation.

Source: The Wall Street Journal

Changes in monetary policy have almost instant effects on financial markets.

---

[3]More precisely, the Fed would tighten monetary policy if it detected a rise in aggregate demand that seemed too rapid relative to its *long-run trend* associated with long-run economic growth. In other words, both aggregate demand and aggregate supply increase with long-run economic growth. The Fed would tighten policy if aggregate demand were to begin rising *faster* than aggregate supply.

Figure 2 | Conventional View of Inflation–Unemployment Tradeoff

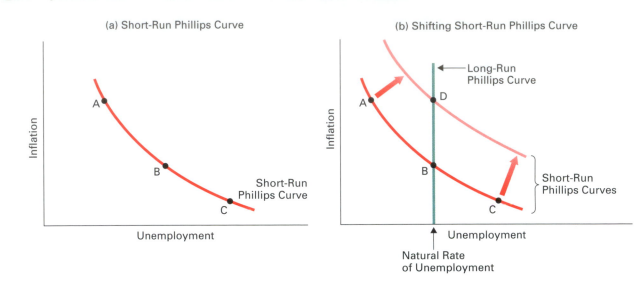

(a) Short-Run Phillips Curve

(b) Shifting Short-Run Phillips Curve

unemployment. However, if policy makers choose a combination of inflation and unemployment that lies *off* the *long-run* Phillips Curve (such as Point A or Point C), then the economy remains only temporarily at that point. Eventually, the short-run Phillips Curve shifts as in Figure 2b, so that the long run equilibrium occurs along the economy's long-run Phillips Curve, with unemployment returning to its natural rate.

If the Fed follows a countercyclical monetary policy, it loosens policy at times of high unemployment and low inflation, as at Point C in Figure 2. The Fed may try to move the economy upward and to the left *along* the short-run Phillips Curve, moving the economy from Point C to Point B. Although the policy increases inflation, it reduces unemployment. Similarly, the Fed may tighten monetary policy at times of high inflation and low unemployment, as at Point A in Figure 2. The Fed may try to move the economy downward and to the right along the short-run Phillips Curve from Point A to Point B. Although the policy raises unemployment, it reduces inflation.

The Fed must carefully avoid overreacting. Suppose that a fall in consumer spending or business investment spending causes a fall in aggregate demand. Real GDP falls and unemployment rises, as the economy moves from Point B to Point C in Figure 2. As a result, the Fed loosens monetary policy to try to increase aggregate demand and bring the economy back to Point B. The policy reduces unemployment and raises inflation. If the Fed loosens monetary policy too much, however, the economy moves past Point B to Point A, with even lower unemployment (temporarily) but higher inflation. In the long run, this overreaction may leave the economy at Point D, with the natural rate of unemployment but higher inflation than before the policy change.

Similarly, suppose that a rise in aggregate demand takes the economy from Point B to Point A in Figure 2, reducing unemployment but raising inflation. A tight monetary policy could bring the economy back to Point B. However, if the Fed overreacts by tightening too much, it creates a recession as the economy moves to Point C. The Fed faced this problem in 1989 and again in 1994 to 1995. In 1989, the Fed believed that U.S. aggregate demand was rapidly rising, so it tightened monetary policy to help prevent inflation from increasing. The tight monetary policy contributed to the 1990 to 1991 recession. Similarly, the Fed tightened monetary policy in 1994 and early 1995 because it interpreted rapid growth of real GDP as an increase in aggregate demand, and the Fed wanted to prevent inflation from rising. In this case, the Fed did not overreact, and the economy continued to grow without either a recession or an increase in inflation.

Goals of Activist Monetary Policy

As the discussion of Figure 2 indicates, monetary policy-making involves weighing the costs of low GDP and high unemployment against the costs of high inflation. Should the Fed follow policies to reduce unemployment temporarily even if the result is permanently higher inflation? Should the Fed follow policies to reduce inflation even if it creates a recession with a temporary rise in unemployment?

Economists need more statistical evidence on the effects of monetary policy to reach full agreement on its consequences. Their opinions differ on issues such as the size of the effects of monetary policy on real GDP, and the duration of those effects. Opinions also differ about the size of the short-run tradeoff between inflation and unemployment (the slope of the short-run Phillips Curve) and the duration of the tradeoff (the time before the short-run Phillips Curve shifts and unemployment returns to its natural rate). In addition, opinions differ regarding the costs of high inflation and the costs of low real GDP and high unemployment. These differences amount to disagreements over the best countercyclical monetary policy, that is, how loose or how tight the Fed should set policy in any given situation, and when it should change its policy.

As a result of these uncertainties and disagreements, advocates of activist monetary policy sometimes disagree about the best policy for the Fed to pursue. Most proponents of activist monetary policy argue that the Federal Reserve should focus on both inflation and real GDP or unemployment. Many economists advocate goals that compromise between pursuit of steady, low inflation and stable real GDP. In practice, the Federal Reserve itself usually states its goals only vaguely. Most Fed-watchers believe that the Fed compromises between these goals as it formulates policies.

Laissez-Faire View

While many economists take an activist view of economic policy, many others take a laissez-faire (hands-off) view:

> A **laissez-faire view** of policy maintains that the economy usually operates efficiently on its own and that even when it does not, active government policies will more likely aggravate inefficiencies and create new inefficiencies than alleviate problems.

Proponents of the laissez-faire view usually advocate a small role for government in the economy along with little government interference with individual freedom to make voluntary trades. Whenever possible, government policies should conform to a set of rules announced in advance rather than basing decisions on the discretion of government officials. For example, a rule might require the Federal Reserve to keep the growth rate of M1 between 2 percent and 4 percent per year; another rule might require the government to balance its budget each year.

Why do supporters of the laissez-faire view oppose activist policies? Don't they care about rising unemployment and falling real GDP when aggregate demand falls as in Figure 1? Why shouldn't government policy try to raise aggregate demand back to its original level to eliminate the rise in unemployment and fall in real GDP? Proponents of the laissez-faire view respond by arguing that activist policies usually do more harm than good. They argue that general *rules*, rather than discretionary judgment of policymakers, should govern policy.

Rules or Discretion?

Should the Federal Reserve act at its own discretion, that is, base its daily actions on its judgment of the economic situation, or should it follow a policy rule? Most proponents of activist monetary policy advocate *discretionary policy*. With discretionary policy, a group of experts, such as the people in the Federal Reserve System, watch the economy on a daily basis and use their best judgment and discretion about the most appropriate policy actions.

> **Discretionary policy** means that policy makers choose policy actions (such as open-market operations) on a daily basis, based on their own best judgments and discretion.

Most central banks around the world, including the Fed, operate in this way.
Proponents of the laissez-faire view, on the other hand, generally favor policy rules.[4]

> A **policy rule** is a specific statement of the policy actions that an agency will follow in the future.

For example, a policy rule might say that each month, the Fed will conduct open market operations to raise M1 at a constant rate of 3 percent per year. This example illustrates a *simple* policy rule.

> A **simple policy rule** requires a particular policy regardless of economic circumstances.

> A **contingent policy rule** states specifically how policies will depend on particular economic circumstances.

A contingent policy rule takes the form "if conditions are x, then policy will be y." For example, a contingent policy rule might state something like:

> Each month, the Fed will look at the most recent unemployment rate. If the unemployment rate is below 5 percent, the Fed will conduct open market operations to raise M1 at a constant rate of 3 percent per year. If the unemployment rate is 5 percent or higher, the Fed will conduct open market operations to raise M1 at a constant rate of 5 percent per year.

Contingent policy rules can specify any number of conditions and involve any level of complication.

The choice of a policy rule raises some of the same issues as the choice of a discretionary policy. What goals should monetary policy pursue? What kinds of actions would best achieve those goals? What kind of policy rule would best promote those actions? Should Congress or the Federal Reserve choose the policy rule? What happens if policymakers choose actions that violate the rule? When and how can the rule be changed? Advocates of policy rules advance three main arguments about the superiority of rules to discretion, The next section discusses those arguments.

Review Questions

1. Use a graph to help explain how a central bank can use monetary policy to stabilize real GDP.

---

[4]Questions of rules versus discretion in economic policy have analogies in criminal law. Should a judge have discretion to choose the punishment for a convicted criminal, or should the law set rules specifying punishments? The U.S. legal system sets rules for determining issues such as admissibility of evidence, but uses a combination of rules and discretion for determining punishments for various crimes. Like a legal system, a system of economic policy can be governed by either rules or discretion.

2. Use the economic analysis in this chapter to explain this newspaper headline: "Federal Reserve lowers interest rates to fight recession."

3. What is discretionary monetary policy?

4. What is a policy rule? What is the difference between a simple rule and a contingent rule?

Thinking Exercise

5. Suppose that the Fed raises the growth rate of the money supply from 3 percent per year to 6 percent per year and that people expect this new policy to last for many years. Explain the likely short-run and long-run effects of this policy change on real GDP, unemployment, the price level, the rate of inflation, the real interest rate, and the nominal interest rate.

THREE PROBLEMS WITH DISCRETIONARY POLICY

Advocates of policy rules cite three main problems with discretionary policies. They see discretionary policy as inferior to rules because:

1. Lags complicate the effects of policies, reducing the effectiveness of discretionary policies and raising the dangers of overreaction.

2. The Fed lacks enough information to follow good discretionary policies.

3. Discretionary policies affect people's incentives in ways that hinder the economy's performance.

First Problem: Lags

The first problem with discretionary policies involves lags in their implementation and effects. Any government agency, including the Fed, needs time to react to economic changes. Furthermore, the Fed gathers the economic data that tracks the economy with a lag. Try as it may, the Fed's information is never as fully up to date as it would like. These two factors create a lag in policy implementation.

The second type of lag involves the delay between a Fed policy action and its effects on the economy. Changes in the money supply take time to affect aggregate demand, real GDP, and prices. Evidence suggests that these lags are long, variable, and unpredictable. These lags make it difficult for the Fed to know when, and by how much, to act. For example, the Fed may want to loosen monetary policy to help bring the economy out of a recession, but lags might delay the effects of current actions until next year, when the recession is over and loose monetary policy only adds to inflation.

To see why lags matter, think about turning on the water to take a shower. You turn on the hot water along with the cold water, but the hot water takes time to reach the shower head; a lag separates the time when you turn on the faucet and the time when hot water arrives. After a minute, if the water feels too cold, you may turn on more hot water, but you may not have waited long enough for the hot water to arrive at the shower head. If you turn up the hot water, the shower may become too hot after a few minutes. The lag—the length of time hot water takes to arrive at the shower—may change from day to day depending on the outside temperature, how many other people in the building are using hot water, and so on. This may make it difficult to get the right water temperature. You may be better off with a simple rule such as "turn up the hot and cold water each halfway regardless of the water temperature for the first several minutes."

Remember lags, or you might get burned.

Why the Fed's efforts to forestall inflation have thus far failed

Delayed reaction It pushed up interest rates, but maybe not enough; Risk of recession grows

Why has the Fed's anti-inflation campaign failed?

In part, the answer lies in the long and unpredictable lags that always separate Fed actions from desired results.

Source: The Wall Street Journal

A decade ago, when the Fed was trying to reduce inflation while avoiding a recession, its efforts were frustrated by unpredictable lags .

EXAMPLES

The Fed is aware of the policy problems created by lags, and it tries to minimize those problems. For example, in 1994 the Fed saw signs that inflation would soon rise. Although inflation was not yet increasing, the Fed began tightening monetary policy so that, after a lag, the tight policy would prevent inflation from rising in the future. This policy sparked controversy. Critics argued that the Fed should not tighten monetary policy because inflation was not rising and, in their view, was not likely to rise. The Fed defended its policy on the grounds that real GDP was rising very rapidly and that, based on historical experiences, inflation would soon increase. Because monetary policy affects the economy with a lag, argued the Fed, it could not wait for inflation to rise before tightening monetary policy. Similarly, the Fed reduced the funds rate in September 1998 mainly to reduce the chance that recessions in Asia would spread to the United States, rather than because it saw clear signs that the U.S. economy was entering a recession yet. The Fed, taking lags into account, tries to act preemptively before problems begin.

Second Problem: Lack of Information

The second problem with discretionary policy comes from policy makers' lack of enough information about the economy. Policy makers need two types of important information that they do not have. First, they don't have enough information about current changes in the economy. Second, they don't have enough information about how their policy actions will affect the economy.

Information about the Economy

Usually neither policy makers nor economists know whether a current change in GDP occurs because of a change in aggregate demand or a change in aggregate supply, nor do they know if the change will be temporary or permanent. Economists even disagree about causes of many *past* economic changes, including the Great Depression. Without good knowledge of current changes in the economy, the Fed lacks sufficient information to conduct good discretionary monetary policy.

Economist Milton Friedman has argued that the problems of lags and insufficient information have led the Fed's discretionary policies to *deepen* recessions and to raise

Fed cuts short-term rates by 0.25 point

First cut since January '96 is a pre-emptive strike to stave off recession

WASHINGTON—The Federal Reserve cut interest rates for the first time since January 1996 in a preemptive strike against recession that reflects a sudden reversal in the central bank's outlook for the economy and new worries about a credit crunch.

The Fed trimmed its key short-term interest rate by ¼ percentage point to 5.25%, saying it sought to "cushion the effects on prospective growth in the United States of increasing weakness in foreign economies" and offset what it termed "less accommodative financial conditions domestically."

Source: The Wall Street Journal

inflation. When a fall in aggregate demand or supply raises unemployment, the Fed usually loosens monetary policy to help reduce unemployment and raise real GDP. The Fed often responds too vigorously, however, partly because it lacks sufficient information about the economy and partly because its policies affect the economy only after a lag. After the lag, when the effects of Fed policy appear, unemployment falls below its natural rate and inflation rises. However, unemployment does not remain permanently below its natural rate; it eventually begins to rise back toward its natural rate. This rise in unemployment creates political pressures for the Fed to loosen monetary policy even further. Consequently, unemployment falls in the short run again, but only at the cost of even higher inflation than before. As people begin to adjust to ever-higher rates of inflation, the Fed can keep unemployment below its natural rate only by continually accelerating money growth. Eventually, inflation rises enough that people become more concerned with price increases than with unemployment. At that point, political pressure leads the Fed to tighten monetary policy, raising unemployment above its natural rate and causing a recession. The more inflation rises, the deeper will be the recession when the Fed eventually acts to stop inflation.

Figure 3 shows Friedman's argument in terms of short-run Phillips Curves. When a fall in aggregate demand moves the economy from Point A to Point B, raising unemployment, the Fed overreacts (partly because of lags and information problems) and moves the economy to Point C, reducing unemployment and raising inflation. However, when the short-run Phillips Curve shifts from Curve 1 to Curve 2 and unemployment begins to rise again toward Point D, the Fed reacts again by loosening monetary policy, moving the economy to Point E. This cycle may repeat, as the economy moves toward Point F, but loose Fed policy takes it to Point G. Eventually, people become concerned about inflation. As the short-run Phillips Curve shifts again and the economy heads toward Point H, the Fed tightens policy and takes the economy to Point I, reducing inflation, but at the cost of a big recession.[5]

---

[5] Friedman, a winner of the Nobel Memorial Prize in Economic Science, is often called a *monetarist* due to his view that changes in the money supply are the most important causes of business cycles, and due to his view that the Fed should follow a policy rule of keeping the growth rate of M1 or M2 at a constant rate of about 3 percent per year.

A fall in aggregate demand takes the economy from Point A to Point B. The Fed loosens monetary policy, but because of lags and information problems, it may overreact, taking the economy to Point C. In the long run, the economy moves from Point C as the short-run Phillips Curve shifts. The Fed may react to the rise in unemployment by loosening policy again, taking the economy to Point E. This cycle repeats, and the economy moves to Point F and then Point G. Finally, as the economy moves toward Point H in the long run, pressures to reduce inflation lead the Fed to tighten policy and reduce inflation at the expense of a recession (Point I).

Figure 3 | When Monetary Policy Overreacts

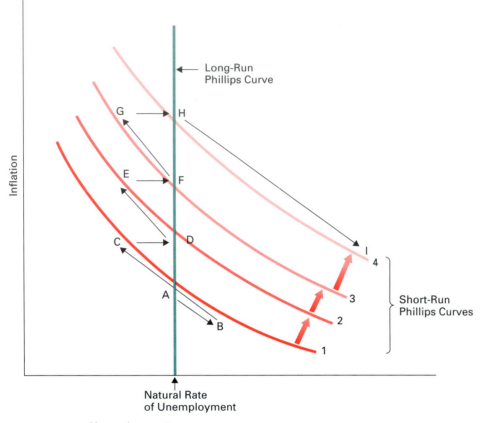

Information about the Effects of Policies

Policy makers lack a second type of information concerning the effects of their policies. Economists have constructed intricate mathematical models of the economy on computers to forecast the effects of changes in policies. The computer models use data from the past to try to predict effects of current policy changes. These models face an important problem, though: The effects of current policy changes may differ from the effects of past policy changes if people's expectations have changed. This problem leads to the Lucas critique of econometric policy evaluation.

> The **Lucas critique** says that people do not always respond the same way to a change in economic conditions or government policies, because their responses depend partly on their expectations about the future, and those expectations can change.

People's expectations about the future depend partly on their past experiences. The past responses of government policy to changes in underlying conditions affect how people expect the government to respond in the future. Therefore, past responses affect the results of current policies. For example, if the Fed has usually tightened monetary policy in the past when inflation rose by more than 2 percentage points over a 6-month period, then people may expect the same response in the future. The effects of a tight Fed policy under these conditions, when people *expect* it, may differ considerably from its effects when people expect a different policy.

The Lucas critique complicates efforts to predict the effects of a particular policy, because those effects depend on people's expectations, which change with circumstances. Then consequently, past experience does not necessarily provide a reliable guide to the effects of future policy changes. This complicates efforts of economists to obtain evidence on the effects of policies. This complication also limits the abilities of computer models to predict the effects of government policies in a reliable way. Obviously, it also complicates discretionary policymaking.

Public Information about Policy

Discretionary policy can add uncertainty to the economy. Firms and investors find it hard to predict what Fed officials will do in various situations. In contrast, a credible policy rule could reduce economic uncertainty.

> A **credible policy rule** is a rule that people believe policymakers will follow, perhaps because policymakers have incentives to follow the rule.

Some policy rules are more credible than others. The credibility of a rule increases as incentives rise for policymakers to follow that rule. A rule for monetary policy might be credible if Congress passed a law specifying a certain policy, and created mechanisms to ensure enforcement of that rule. Alternatively, policymakers themselves can try to commit to a rule.

> A policy maker makes a **commitment to a policy rule** by doing something to guarantee its implementation.

People sometimes say that a person "burned his bridges behind him" when he has done something that makes it hard to reverse some action. This phrase has its origins in war, when a general for an invading army might burn bridges after the army crosses them to prevent soldiers from retreating during a battle; burning bridges commits the army to either fight or surrender. Burning bridges increases the incentive to fight hard for the current goal; it is a method of promoting commitment. Commitment is more difficult for economic policymakers than for soldiers, but some degree of commitment may be possible through actions and public statements of policymakers.

Without a credible policy rule, people have difficulty forming expectations about policy. In a letter to the editor of *The Wall Street Journal*, Nobel Prize winning economist Milton Friedman wrote:

> I know, or can find out, what monetary actions have been: open market purchases and sales and discount rates at Federal Reserve Banks. I know also the federal funds rate and rates of growth of various monetary aggregates. What I do not know is the policy that produced those actions.
>
> The closest I can come to an official specification of current monetary policy is that it is to take those actions that the monetary authorities, in light of all evidence available, judge will best promote price stability and full employment— i.e., to do the right thing at the right time. But that surely is not a "policy." It is simply an expression of good intentions and an injunction to "trust us."
>
> I hasten to add that the present situation is not unique. On the contrary, it has persisted for nearly the entire . . . life of the Federal Reserve System. The only exception was from the outbreak of World War II to 1951, when the Fed followed an announced policy of pegging interest rates on federal government securities. For the rest, the Fed has consistently resorted to statements of good intentions . . . It has claimed credit for good results and blamed forces beyond its control—generally fiscal policy—for any bad outcomes.[6]

---

[6]"The Fed Has No Clothes," *The Wall Street Journal,* April 15, 1988, p. 28.

This third problem of information arises because discretionary policy creates uncertainty when the public lacks enough information about the Fed's policy to form accurate predictions of its future actions. This problem highlights an important benefit of rules over discretion.

Third Problem: Effects on Incentives

The third problem with discretionary policy is that it affects expectations, incentives, and behavior in ways that hinder economic performance. This leads to an important result:

> A credible rule for actions can lead to better results than even the best case-by-case (discretionary) actions.

The easiest way to understand this result is to consider an example from outside economics, in which this result is well known: Rules for dealing with terrorists.

EXAMPLE: DEALING WITH TERRORISTS

Suppose that you are a government official in charge of dealing with terrorist threats. Terrorists may take hostages and offer to trade their freedom for things like cash or armaments. A *credible* policy rule never to deal with terrorists gives them little incentive to take hostages. Terrorists will know that taking hostages has no benefits.

However, incentives are totally different without a credible policy rule against dealing with terrorists. If your policy calls for discretionary responses to terrorism—for doing whatever seems best in a particular case—then terrorists may expect hostages to be good bargaining chips. They may see at least a chance of gains by taking hostages. Consequently, terrorists are more likely to take hostages if you rely on discretionary policy than if you set a credible rule not to deal with them.

Time Consistency

The best discretionary decisions may differ from the best rules. In that case, a credible rule produces better results than discretion. To see why, consider the terrorist example. Suppose that you are a discretionary policy maker, and terrorists take hostages. You can either deal with the terrorists to try to save the hostages, or take a hard line on terrorism by not dealing with them and trying to discourage future hostage-taking. Sometimes the benefits of dealing with the terrorists and saving the hostages may exceed the costs of creating a bad precedent. In that case, you benefit by dealing with the terrorists to save the hostages. However, you would benefit from having a credible rule *not* to deal with terrorists because that rule would remove terrorists' incentives to take hostages in the first place.[7] A credible rule produces better results than discretionary policy when that policy is not *time consistent*.

> In a **time consistent policy,** the best case-by-case decisions are the same as the decisions suggested by the best policy rule.

> In a **time inconsistent policy,** the best case-by-case decisions differ from the decisions that the best policy rule would suggest.

---

[7]This statement assumes that terrorists' behavior responds to incentives. Evidence and general agreement among experts suggest that it does.

Time inconsistency occurs when a choice that *currently* seems best for today and tomorrow no longer seems best when tomorrow comes, even if no new information emerges. Consider an example of giving in to some temptation. You may sometimes benefit by committing to a rule that prevents you from giving in to temptation at the last minute, *even though* you may want to give in when the time comes. In fact, you benefit precisely *because* you want to prevent yourself from giving in at the future date.

Application to Taxes

High taxes on income from capital would discourage investment, but after someone had *already* invested in new capital equipment, the government could gain revenue by placing a very high tax on income from that capital equipment. If investors know that the government *could* do this, they have little incentive to invest. By reducing investment, expectations of a high tax actually *reduce* government tax revenue. Policy makers can raise government tax revenue by committing to a credible policy *not* to place high taxes on capital in the future. In this way, a credible commitment to a policy rule of low taxes on capital encourages investment, and provides higher revenue than even the best discretionary policy.

Application to Monetary Policy

Proponents of the laissez-faire view of policy argue that discretionary monetary policy has an inflationary bias.

Suppose the Fed follows discretionary policy. When inflation is low, and people expect low inflation to continue, the Fed has an incentive to loosen monetary policy, because the benefits of a (temporary) fall in employment may exceed the small costs of a slight increase in inflation. The Fed wants to move the economy from Point B to Point A in Figure 2. However, sophisticated business people and investors recognize the Fed's incentive for looser policy. As a result, they begin to expect inflation. This rise in expected inflation raises the short-run Phillips Curve, as in Figure 2b. This creates a problem for the Fed. If it loosens policy, it moves the economy to Point D, creating the inflation that people expected, without reducing unemployment. If it does *not* loosen policy, it prevents inflation, but unemployment *rises* temporarily above its natural rate. (The economy would move to a point below and to the right of Point D, along the higher short-run Phillips Curve.)

Discretionary policy, therefore, creates a problem for the Fed, because it allows inflationary expectations to increase. When expected inflation rises, the Fed must create the inflation that people expect simply *to prevent a rise* in unemployment. To prevent unemployment, the Fed has an incentive to respond to a rise in *expected* inflation by loosening policy to *create* the inflation that people expect. As a result, discretionary policy has an inflationary bias.

If the Fed could follow a credible rule, however, it could choose a rule that would create low inflation. A credible rule would affect expectations: it would lead people to expect low inflation. As a result, the Fed would not face the problem discussed above. With both actual and expected inflation remaining low, unemployment equals its natural rate, so the credible rule would produce better economic results than discretionary policy.

Can Credible Policy Rules Shift Short-Run Phillips Curves?

Suppose an economy has high inflation, as at Point H in Figure 3. Can the Fed reduce inflation without causing a recession? Suppose an economy is in a recession, as at Point C in Figure 2 or Point I in Figure 3. Can the Fed end a recession quickly without raising inflation?

Some economists argue that a *credible* change in monetary policy can reduce inflation without affecting unemployment or real GDP. The idea is that a credible change in policy leads people to change their expectations of inflation. The change in expectations shifts the short-run Phillips Curve (as described in the last chapter). This change allows inflation to fall without any rise in unemployment. Some economists argue that

IN THE NEWS

Economics aside, the Fed is not likely to risk its credibility by responding to political pressures, market participants said.

Source: New York Times

The Fed knows that it would benefit from credibility in its announced policies.

a government can make its policy credible by committing to a policy rule or by taking unusual and dramatic actions that would indicate a major change in policy, showing people that policy makers are not following "business as usual."

A credible policy rule could take the form of a law or a constitutional amendment stating a required policy, although even these measures leave the possibility of loopholes or simple disobedience. Unusual and dramatic actions might include major changes in fiscal policy, such as balancing a government budget that previously had run big deficits, making big changes in taxes or government regulations, and so on. History offers only a few good examples of major policy changes of the kind that may affect expectations. For example, at the end of the German hyperinflation in 1923, the central bank was separated from the government so the government could not force it to print money to finance budget deficits, as it had done during the period of hyperinflation.

Other economists argue, however, that even credible changes in policy cannot achieve these results, citing other historical experiences. For example, when Margaret Thatcher became prime minister of Great Britain in 1979, she promised to reduce inflation. Inflation fell, but Britain had a major recession. Similarly, when Alan Greenspan became Chairman of the Board of Governors of the Federal Reserve System, he stated that he would follow policies to reduce inflation. He did, and U.S. inflation fell, but the country suffered a major recession in 1982. Some economists argue that Thatcher and Greenspan made credible promises, and that these experiences show that policy makers cannot avoid the short-run Phillips Curve simply by adopting credible policies. Other economists argue that few people really believed these announcements of policy changes, so the changes in policy lacked credibility. Lacking credibility, tighter monetary policies created recessions. According to this argument, the recessions could have been avoided if both countries had been following formal, credible rules for monetary policy rather than discretionary policies.

Review Questions

6. What does it mean to say that a policy rule is credible?

7. Why do lags create difficulties for discretionary monetary policy?

8. Why can policy rules produce better results than case-by-case, discretionary policy making?

9. Why do information problems create difficulties for discretionary monetary policy?

10. Explain the Lucas critique.

Thinking Exercises

11. Explain why discretionary monetary policy has an inflationary bias.

12. Discuss this statement from a study by the Congressional Budget Office: "Inflation could be reduced relatively painlessly by lowering inflationary expectations."

TARGETS OF MONETARY POLICY

Once a society has chosen the goals for its monetary policy and decided whether to employ rules or use discretionary policy, it must choose a method for achieving those goals. If it decides on rules for monetary policy, it must decide *which* rules; if it decides on discretion, policy makers must decide *which* economic indicators they will use to guide their policy actions.

When economic signs point in different directions, the Fed may not know which way to turn.

Targeting the Federal Funds Rate

In recent years, the Federal Reserve has conducted discretionary monetary policy with an *informal* rule devoted to keeping the nominal federal funds interest rate at a *target* level. (The Fed targets the *nominal* federal funds rate, because it cannot affect the real rate in the long run.) Recall that the federal funds rate is the interest rate that banks charge each other for short-term loans of reserves. The Fed can control the federal funds rate by raising the supply of bank reserves when demand for them rises and reducing the supply when demand falls. An increase in the demand for bank reserves would ordinarily raise the equilibrium federal funds rate, but the Fed can prevent a rise by increasing the supply of reserves through open market purchases (i.e., loose monetary policy), as in Figure 4. The Fed can stabilize the federal funds interest rate by changing the supply of bank reserves to offset changes in the demand.

Targeting the Foreign Exchange Rate

The monetary policies of many nations are focused on the foreign exchange rates of their currencies. When a country chooses monetary policy to keep its exchange rate fixed, it maintains a fixed exchange-rate system.

> In a **fixed (or pegged) exchange-rate system**, the government buys or sells the country's currency in foreign exchange markets in whatever amounts are necessary to keep its exchange rate fixed (pegged) to some foreign currency.

Other countries maintain floating exchange-rate systems.

> In a **floating (or flexible) exchange-rate system**, the government does not actively trade in foreign exchange markets to try to influence exchange rates.

Figure 4 | Stabilizing the Federal Funds Rate

An increase in the demand for reserves by banks would raise the federal funds rate from i_1 to i_2, but the Fed can keep this rate at i_1 through an appropriate increase in the supply of reserves.

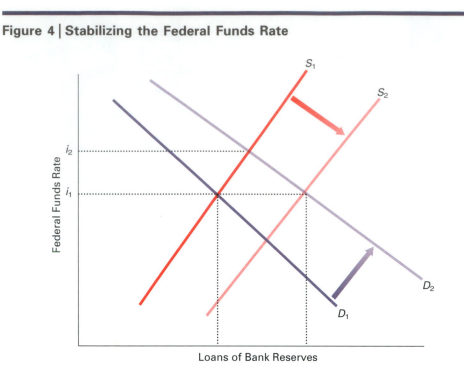

Some countries operate in-between, hybrid systems.

> A **managed-float exchange-rate system** combines elements of the other two systems; the government sometimes trades in foreign exchange markets to try to influence the exchange rate without trying to maintain a fixed rate.

Systems of Fixed Exchange Rates

The gold standard of the 19th century was one type of fixed exchange-rate system. Each country on the gold standard fixed the nominal price of gold in its currency by acting as a residual buyer or seller of gold. Because the law of one price applies to gold, this policy fixed the country's exchange rate. For example, suppose that the United States fixes the dollar price of gold at $35 per ounce, while the British government fixes the pound price of gold at £7 per ounce. Arbitrage (the law of one price) implies that the price of gold must be the same in both countries, so £7 must equal $35, implying that £1 is worth $5. The gold standard keeps the exchange rate between two countries fixed as long as each country maintains its policy of fixing the price of gold.

The gold standard evolved, and in 1944, it led to the Bretton Woods System of fixed exchange rates. The Bretton Woods agreement set the U.S. dollar price of gold and required other countries to keep their own exchange rates fixed against the dollar. For example, the British pound exchange rate was fixed at $4.80 per pound, and the Japanese yen exchange rate was fixed at 0.278¢ per yen (or ¥360 per dollar). To keep its exchange rate fixed, each country's government would sell as much of its own currency as people wanted to buy at the fixed exchange rate and buy as much as people wanted to sell. When a country sold its own money and bought U.S. dollars on the foreign exchange market, it was said to have a *balance-of-payments surplus*. When it bought its own money by selling U.S. dollars on the foreign exchange market, it was said to have a *balance-of-payments deficit*.

Under the Bretton Woods System of fixed exchange rates, governments bought and sold their own money for U.S. dollars rather than buying and selling gold, as they would under a gold standard. Whenever a government bought its own currency (with dollars) on the foreign exchange market, its money supply fell. Whenever it sold its own currency (for dollars), its money supply increased. In this way, the requirement that a government fix its exchange rate dictated the extent to which it could change its money supply, just as a requirement that you drive at 30 miles per hour would dictate the extent to which you press the accelerator pedal in a car. While a country fixed its exchange rate to the U.S. dollar, it could not use monetary policy to pursue other goals.

Devaluations

For many reasons, governments did not like the constraint that the fixed exchange rate system placed on their monetary policies. They frequently wanted to increase their money supplies more rapidly (or sometimes more slowly) than was dictated by fixed exchange rates. Countries that tried to increase their money supplies more rapidly experienced balance of payments deficits. A country with a large balance of payments deficit risked exhausting its supply of U.S. dollars to sell, which would prevent it from continuing to fix its exchange rate. This prospect often led to devaluations.

> A **devaluation** of a currency occurs when a country that fixes its exchange rate at a certain level changes that level so that its money loses value in terms of foreign money (that is, the exchange rate rises).

In the long run, a devaluation raises nominal prices of all goods and services along with the nominal money supply, without affecting relative prices, real GDP, or employment. A devaluation works like a currency reform in reverse. To see why, imagine that a country decides to add a zero to every unit of its money. A 1 peso bill becomes a 10 peso bill; a 10 peso bill becomes a 100 peso bill, and so on. The foreign exchange rate must also change. If 1 peso was originally worth $1.00, the devaluation reduces its value to only $0.10 (so that 10 pesos are worth $1.00). This currency reform in reverse, which would amount to a huge inflation that would raise prices by a factor of 10, is the same as a devaluation.

Short-Run Effects of Devaluation

In the short run, however, a devaluation can have real effects with sticky nominal prices or nominal wages. With sticky prices in the short run, a devaluation lowers the foreign-currency prices of domestically produced products and raises the domestic-currency

---

IN THE NEWS

Import prices start rising in response to ruble's fall

St. Petersburg Governor Vladimir Yakovlev's promise last Wednesday not to allow price rises on foodstuffs and consumer goods has wilted before the power of market mechanisms.

One week after the government allowed the ruble to devalue, consumers are starting to feel the effects, with shops around the city hiking prices on imported goods.

On Monday, most shops and kiosks interviewed by The St. Petersburg Times said that prices for imported goods had already risen by between 10 percent and 25 percent.

Source: St. Petersburg Times

Yen's rally might bring Japan pain, not gain

Anxiety about the effects of yen surge on profits spurs Nikkei sell-off

A strong yen makes Japanese-made products more expensive overseas, cuts exporters' yen-dominated earnings, and tends to shrink the trade surplus.

Clinton hails dollar's fall against the yen

Says tumble could help manufacturers in U.S., boosting their exports

Although some investors worry the sharp decline in the value of the dollar against the Japanese yen portends tough times for the economy, President Clinton praised the development, saying it "coud be a good thing."

Speaking briefly to reporters before a late afternoon meeting with advisers, Mr. Clinton said that "the yen got too weak," causing a flood of cheaper Japanese imports into the U.S.

Source: The Wall Street Journal

prices of foreign products. For example, suppose that a country devalues its money from 10 francs per dollar to 12 francs per dollar. A product that sells for 100 francs cost foreigners $10.00 before the devaluation, but it costs only $8.33 after the devaluation; a foreign product that sells for $100 cost 1,000 francs before the devaluation, but it costs 1,200 francs after the devaluation. These price changes may lead people to buy more domestically produced goods and buy fewer foreign goods, reducing imports, raising exports, and possibly affecting the country's employment and real GDP.

Just as unexpected inflation can redistribute income, creating winners and losers, devaluations usually redistribute income. Losers include workers whose nominal wages are fixed in the short run. By raising prices of imported products, a devaluation reduces their real wages. People whose savings or pensions are fixed in nominal units of the domestic currency also lose real income from the devaluation. Winners include owners of some firms that increase their exports as a result of the devaluation, while paying the same nominal wages and lower real wages. Indeed, countries with fixed exchange rates sometimes devalue their currencies specifically to try to increase competitiveness of their goods in world markets, intentionally creating these winners and losers.

As a whole, however, a devaluation makes a country poorer than before, because it increases the cost of foreign goods and services. In the short run, a country cannot trade its products for as many foreign products after a devaluation as before. In the long run (after prices and wages fully adjust), the devaluation does not affect relative prices or boost a country's international competitiveness, although the effects of the redistribution of income may linger.

When speculators believe that a country might devalue its money, they try to avoid losses or make profits by selling that currency and buying others instead. This speculation can create a balance-of-payments crisis, in which people rapidly sell a country's money, forcing the country's government to spend a large amount of resources to continue to fix the exchange rate. Balance-of-payments crises usually result in devaluations, because governments are unwilling to spend the resources needed to continue to fix their exchange rates.

For example, in late 1994, speculators began to expect that the government of Mexico would devalue the peso. As a result, speculators tried to sell pesos and buy other currencies, such as U.S. dollars. This raised the amount of pesos that Mexico's central bank had to buy (with U.S. dollars) to maintain a fixed exchange rate. Mexico spent billions of dollars in this effort. Finally, rather than lose more dollars, Mexico devalued the peso. More recently, Russia devalued its ruble in 1998, abandoning a fixed exchange rate system and adopting a floating rate system, though it imposed many regulations and controls on trades. Several Asian countries, including Indonesia, South Korea, the Philippines, Thailand, and Malaysia experienced financial crises and devalued their currencies in late 1997 and early 1998, as Figure 5 shows.

A government may try to maintain a fixed exchange rate by increasing regulations and controls that obstruct efforts to sell the country's money. Although these regulations and controls reduce the losses that the government incurs to keep the exchange rate fixed, they can also cause large economic inefficiencies. Also, they seldom prevent devaluation in the long run.

Currency Boards

Some countries have added credibility to their monetary policies by replacing their central banks with currency boards. A currency board, like a central bank, buys or sells currencies on foreign exchange markets to keep the exchange rate fixed. However, a currency board has only one goal—keeping the exchange rate fixed—and has political independence and a sufficient level of assets (reserves) to meet that goal.

> A **currency board** is an institution whose sole purpose is to keep a foreign exchange rate fixed by acting as a residual buyer or seller of the country's money at that price.

Figure 5 | Asian Crisis: 1997–1998: Exchange Rates against U.S. Dollar

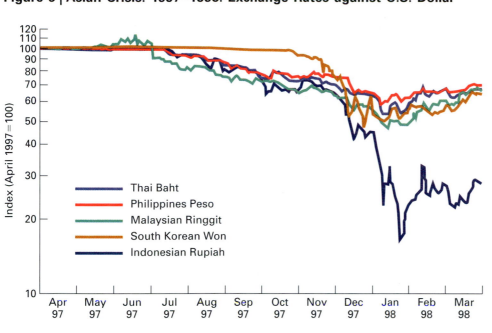

Index (April 1997 = 100)

- Thai Baht
- Philippines Peso
- Malaysian Ringgit
- South Korean Won
- Indonesian Rupiah

The reserves of the currency board must be large enough to fund any conceivable purchase of domestic money to maintain the designated fixed exchange rate.

Hong Kong has had a currency board since 1984. More recently, Argentina, Estonia, and Lithuania have created currency boards. A currency board disciplines monetary policy, adding credibility at the cost of flexibility to pursue other goals. Some economists believe that currency boards represent an attractive alternative for countries that suffer from high inflation or low credibility in their monetary policies.[8]

Which Exchange-Rate System Is Best?

Until the third quarter of the 20th century, most countries had fixed exchange rates. Then continuing balance-of-payments crises and devaluations led many countries to switch to floating exchange rates or hybrid systems. European countries have alternated between floating exchange-rate systems and managed-float systems.

Several European countries are now in the process of changing to an entirely new monetary system with a new money, the *Euro,* replacing their national currencies and a new European Central Bank to set combined monetary policy. When several nations share the same money, they have a *common currency.* A common currency has two main advantages over a pegged exchange rate system: People don't have to exchange currencies when they import goods and services, and the common currency system provides *credibility* by eliminating the risk that one of the countries may devalue its currency.

Economists disagree about the relative merits of fixed exchange rates and flexible exchange rates. Some argue for a floating exchange rate system, because it allows a government to choose its monetary policy without the restriction of keeping a fixed exchange rate. This frees a country to use monetary policy to pursue low inflation or other goals. With a fixed exchange rate, in contrast, a country cannot use monetary policy for these goals. While a country with a fixed exchange rate has the same long-run inflation rate as the country to which it fixes the exchange rate, a floating

Several European countries will soon share a common currency, the Euro.

[8] In 1998, international financier George Soros advocated a currency board for Russia.

exchange-rate system allows the country to choose its own inflation rate and monetary policies. In addition, governments do not need to spend resources to keep their exchange rates fixed under a floating-rate system, freeing resources for other uses.

Perhaps the strongest argument for floating exchange rates centers on avoiding the balance-of-payments crises that seem inevitably to occur under fixed exchange-rate systems. These crises disrupt international trade and financial flows, often cause governments to lose billions of dollars to speculators, and sometimes lead governments to adopt economically inefficient restrictions on international trade.

Other economists argue for a fixed exchange-rate system as much more convenient than a floating-rate system. Information costs fall, because the exchange rate does not change every day. As a result, people and business firms can plan more easily. This stability helps to promote international trade. In contrast, the constant change in a floating exchange-rate system creates uncertainty that may hinder international trade. A fixed-rate system also imposes discipline on governments by preventing them from raising their money supplies rapidly and creating high inflation. This fosters international cooperation in setting policies.

Advocates of fixed exchange rates argue that exchange rates change too often and by too much under a floating exchange-rate system. Speculation causes large, unpredictable changes in exchange rates. Because prices are sticky in the short run, these changes affect relative prices between domestic and foreign goods. The resulting overvaluations or undervaluations cause economic inefficiencies and may affect a country's exports, imports, real GDP, and employment. Evidence shows that the relative prices of foreign goods in terms of domestic goods varies much less under a fixed exchange-rate system than under a floating exchange-rate system. A fixed exchange-rate system can avoid the problems of overvaluation and undervaluation of currencies if countries follow appropriate monetary and fiscal policies to avoid balance-of-payments crises. Proponents of floating exchange rates respond that countries with fixed exchange rates have seldom followed the necessary policies to prevent balance-of-payments crises.

Banking Regulations

Chapter 10 discussed the important dual role of banks in the economy: They help to create money, and they act as intermediaries in the loan market. As a result, issues involving monetary policy and loan markets, including interest rates, savings, and investment, become intertwined. Because of these connections, bank regulation is one important component of monetary policy.

The importance of good bank-regulation policy is one key lesson from the 1997–1998 economic crises in Japan, South Korea, and other Asian countries. Banks in those countries made many bad loans to firms that are unlikely to repay. Some of these loans resulted from the moral hazard problems discussed in the previous chapter; others resulted from government policies that specifically encouraged those loans.

When the public became aware of the size of the bad loans in the banking systems of these countries, a financial crisis erupted in 1997, triggering currency devaluations and recessions. Devaluation of the Russian ruble in 1998 and other changes in Russian monetary policies also resulted from a banking crisis: Russian banks had extended large quantities of loans that were unlikely to be repaid. The Central Bank of Russia responded to the crisis by announcing that it would print money to subsidize those banks to save them from bankruptcy.

Alternative Monetary Institutions

A key long-run monetary policy issue concerns the *institutions* of policy. Should the Federal Reserve act as an independent agency of the government, as it does now, or should Congress or the president control the Fed more directly? What powers should the Fed have? Should the Federal Reserve exist at all? Similar questions arise in other countries. Should all the countries of Europe use the same money and have one European Central Bank rather than different moneys and different central banks? If so, how should that central bank be organized and who should control it? Should the law allow private firms such as banks to print their own money, as they did during part of the 19th century? Should people be free to use whichever money they want as long as someone else is willing to accept it? Should the government involve itself in the money business at all, or should it leave money to private producers in free markets like most other businesses?

Institutions of monetary policy could be designed to help implement policy rules, to help policy makers exercise discretion with minimal political interference, or to strengthen political control over monetary policy. Some economists argue that a monetary policy rule should be written into an explicit law, perhaps even as a constitutional amendment. This change would help to make the rule credible and guarantee adherence. Other economists argue for maximum independence of the Fed from political pressures or control. They argue that political pressures generally focus on short-run goals, while monetary policy must take long-run goals into account. Independence, according to this argument, allows the Fed to pursue the best discretionary policies.

Federal Reserve Independence

The Federal Reserve is an independent agency of the federal government, as an earlier chapter explained. This status is supposed to free its officials from political influence so they can follow the best policies without political pressures. The Fed has faced many challenges to its independence, such as proposals in Congress to require it to report to Congress or the executive branch of the federal government, or to operate under the supervision of the General Accounting Office. (It currently escapes such control.) As an earlier chapter explained, the president of the United States appoints 7 of the 12 Federal Reserve governors, while the others are Federal Reserve Bank presidents, who are appointed by the boards of directors of those banks. The Board of Governors of the Fed appoints three of the nine members of those boards of directors, but the majority, six members, are elected by private banks in each Federal Reserve Bank's district.

Some critics have argued that this procedure is undemocratic and gives too much power to private banks. For example:

> The Federal Reserve Board is indefensible in theory and indispensable in practice. Twelve unelected people have their collective finger on the second most important button in America: the one that controls the money supply,

---

IN THE NEWS

Battle with White House never ends

The Federal Reserve Board's sweeping power over the economy—and the board's independence—has inevitably produced conflict with the White House.

That's true because, while a president can influence the economy by pushing through Congress measures like tax cuts or spending programs, what ultimately happens to the economy depends to an enormous extent on what the Federal Reserve does with its day-to-day control over the nation's money supply.

Congress, hoping to influence future policy, pushes measures to curb Fed's independence

Fed cuts lending rates amid political pressure

Sources: Rochester Democrat and Chronicle, The Wall Street Journal, and New York Times

Political pressures on the Fed.

the biggest controllable factor in the equation of our economy. . . . Their decisions are made in secret and kept secret for 6 weeks. Their budget is also secret. They probably affect your life more than the Supreme Court. How many of them can you even name?[9]

Some people have proposed changes in the Fed's status, such as submission to increased control by the president or Congress; regular audits of Fed operations by the General Accounting Office; legal requirements that the Fed announce its policy decisions right away rather than 6 weeks after making them to limit secrecy; a requirement to announce its plans annually for the coming year; or a requirement to follow some specific, and perhaps very detailed, policies set by the president, Congress, or both.

More Radical Changes

Some economists favor more radical changes in monetary institutions. For example, some favor establishing a gold standard under which the Fed's main task would be to buy and sell gold to keep its nominal price fixed, as described earlier in this chapter and in Chapter 10.[10] Another radical proposal would privatize the money business; the government would stop supplying money and let private firms (banks or anyone else) print pieces of paper that people could exchange as money. Each issuing firm would put its own name on its money so people could distinguish it from other issuers' money. This idea, usually called *free banking,* would free people to choose whatever money they wanted to use, so that competition among suppliers of money could produce a currency with good properties, such as a low rate of inflation. Some proposals would let anyone issue money, providing that they back it 100 percent with gold. Another proposed reform, commonly suggested for countries that want to reduce inflation from high levels and keep it low, would establish a currency board.

Gold Standard

A gold standard is a special case of a commodity standard; the other historically important type of commodity standard is the silver standard. An earlier chapter explained the two main kinds of gold standards. In a pure gold standard, people trade gold coins as money. In a gold exchange standard, people trade paper money that is backed by gold.

The key feature of a gold exchange standard is the government's choice of a nominal money supply to keep the nominal price of gold at some fixed level, such as $350 per ounce. If something in the economy changes to reduce the price of gold below $350 per ounce, then the government increases the money supply, raising nominal prices until gold sells for $350 again. If something changes to raise the price of gold above $350 per ounce, then the government decreases the money supply, reducing nominal prices until gold sells for $350 again. The government can keep the price of gold at $350 per ounce at all times by announcing that it will act as a residual buyer and seller of gold. Precisely, it guarantees to:

1. Buy as much gold as anyone wants to sell at the price of $350 per ounce.

2. Sell as much gold as anyone wants to buy at that price.

The government buys gold by printing as much new money as it needs to pay for the purchases; it sells gold out of its storage facilities, destroying the money that it receives in payment. In this way, the money supply rises automatically whenever the government buys gold and falls whenever the government sells gold.

---

[9]Michael Kinsley, "TRB from Washington," *New Republic,* October 30, 1989, p. 4.

[10]In 1989, a Federal Reserve governor and several other people recommended to the former Soviet Union that it adopt a gold standard as part of its economic reforms. It did not follow this advice.

Because people can always buy gold from the government for $350 per ounce, they will never pay more to another seller. Because people can always sell gold to the government for $350 per ounce, they will never accept less from another buyer. In this way, the government can fix the nominal price of gold at $350.

While the government fixes the nominal price of gold, conditions of supply and demand determine its relative price. For example, the relative price of televisions in terms of gold might be 1 ounce of gold per television. With a nominal price of gold at $350 per ounce, the nominal price of a television is $350 per set. If the relative price of televisions in terms of gold falls (perhaps due to an increase in the supply of televisions) from 1 ounce of gold per television to 9/10 of an ounce of gold per television, then the nominal price of televisions falls from $350 to $315 per set, while the nominal price of gold remains at $350 per ounce. If the relative price of gold in terms of other goods and services does not change much over time, then the price level does not change much over time. Indeed, inflation averaged about zero under the gold standard of the 19th century, with varying episodes of positive and negative inflation roughly averaging out over the century.

The government has little or no discretion in monetary policy under a gold standard. It must keep the money supply at the level that guarantees the fixed nominal price of gold. If the government, or a central bank such as the Federal Reserve, were to try to raise the money supply through open market purchases, the increase in the money supply would raise the price level, which would raise the nominal price of gold above $350 per ounce. To maintain the fixed price, the government would have to reduce the money supply again. (This adjustment happens automatically if the government destroys the money that it collects in payment for gold sales.) Similarly, if the government were to try to lower the money supply through open market sales, the price level would fall, reducing the nominal price of gold below $350 per ounce. To maintain the fixed price, the government would have to raise the money supply again, which happens automatically if the government prints new money whenever it buys gold at $350 per ounce.

Debate on Free Banking

Free banking removes the government from any role in the money industry. History offers only a few cases in which governments have allowed free banking. Scotland had a form of free banking from 1716 to 1845, as did the United States in the first half of the 19th century.

Advocates of free banking argue that it removes the government almost entirely from the money business and ends political control of the money supply. It allows competition in which issuers of money can experiment with different types of products, and consumers (users of money) can choose what they prefer. Competition would encourage a high-quality money with stable and predictable purchasing power, along with innovation in the monetary and financial-payments systems.

Opponents of free banking argue that competition among private issuers' moneys would not work very well for two reasons. First, convenience dictates that people use only one kind of money instead of many different kinds. Use of many kinds of money at once would create confusion, space problems in cash registers, and costs to people who use time and resources to find out the values of the different moneys and exchange them. These problems have motivated European countries to try to adopt one money for all of Europe to replace the many national forms of money currently issued there.

Second, after a bank has printed money and some people have decided to use it, the bank then has an incentive to print *more* money. While this would create inflation, the bank could collect the inflation tax. Critics argue that banks could not easily commit to avoid this practice. Advocates of free banking respond that an offending bank's reputation would suffer, eliminating its incentive to exploit this opportunity, because a loss in reputation would hurt the bank's future profits. However, this incentive may not be strong enough to prevent some banks from inflating their currencies. Incentives to avoid inflation would be particularly weak for banks with poor financial conditions, for which reputation becomes less important.

These issues may soon arise in a new way, as governments of the world decide on policies related to electronic money for use on the Internet, or *e-money*. Will governments allow anyone to issue e-money without regulations? Will governments attempt to regulate issuance and uses of e-money? If so, what regulations will they choose and with what effects? Will people start using e-money for ordinary purchases *off* the Internet? What will be the consequences? How will government policy makers respond? How will the use of e-money affect the ability of the Fed to conduct monetary policy? These are some of the new monetary-policy questions that the world may face in coming years.

Incentives of Central Banks

While economists disagree about the best monetary-policy choices, they generally agree that central banks, like all government institutions, respond to incentives. The individual officials at the Fed may act from the best intentions, but they always operate under strong political pressures, despite the Fed's official independence. Changes in the Fed's organization, or the potential loss of its independence, would affect their incentives.

Some economists have suggested reducing the Fed's incentive to create inflation by requiring it to hold assets that lose value when inflation rises, and gain value when inflation falls. For example, the law could require the Fed to borrow money by selling bonds that are indexed to inflation, and lend money (buy bonds) without indexing to inflation. With these assets, the Fed would lose from an unexpected increase in inflation.[11]

A related proposal would force the government to replace its current, unindexed debt with indexed debt, so the federal government would not gain from inflation. Still another proposal would tie the salaries of Fed officials to inflation so that an increase in inflation would automatically reduce their salaries.

The value of these ideas depends on whether the Fed currently has an inappropriately strong incentive to produce inflation. Some economists believe it does, as the argument about the inflationary bias of discretionary policy demonstrated, but other economists believe that the Fed should emphasize inflation less and focus more on short-run changes in real GDP and unemployment.

Review Questions

13. How do Federal Reserve policy actions affect the federal funds rate? What actions does the Fed take to reduce this rate?

14. How can monetary policy maintain a fixed foreign exchange rate?

15. What is a devaluation? What happens during and after a devaluation?

Thinking Exercises

16. Discuss arguments in favor of fixed and floating exchange-rate systems.

17. After nations of Europe adopt a common currency, the Euro, what will determine the nominal supply of money held by people living in France?

---

[11]Although the Fed gives its profit back to the Treasury Department each year, the Fed gains from higher revenues because it can raise its spending on things that benefit its employees. As a result, this proposal would give the Fed an incentive to reduce inflation and keep it low.

Conclusion

Two Views of Macroeconomic Policies

Monetary and fiscal policies are the two main types of government macroeconomic policies. *Monetary policy* refers to changes in the nominal money supply through open market operations, changes in the discount rate or discount window lending policy, reserve requirement changes, or other policy actions of central banks. The Federal Reserve System conducts monetary policy in the United States.

Some economists hold an activist view about the proper role of government economic policy, believing that government policy actions can help to reduce inefficiencies in the economy. According to this view, the government should use monetary and fiscal policies to help stabilize real GDP, reducing economically inefficient fluctuations that move unemployment from its natural rate. The Fed can use monetary policy to *undo* the effects of changes in aggregate demand caused by changes in underlying conditions. The Fed can loosen monetary policy during a recession, to raise aggregate demand and therefore raise real GDP and reduce unemployment at the cost of raising inflation. The Fed can tighten monetary policy to reduce aggregate demand when inflation rises. In each case, the Fed must take care not to overreact. Most advocates of an active monetary policy favor *discretionary* policy, in which policy makers exercise their best judgment about policy actions on an ongoing basis.

Other economists hold a laissez-faire view of policy, believing that the economy usually operates efficiently on its own and that, even when it does not, active government policies usually aggravate inefficiencies and create new inefficiencies. According to this view, the economy operates best when the government plays a small role restricted to enforcing property rights and following a general set of rules for its monetary and fiscal actions.

Three Problems with Discretionary Policy

Proponents of the laissez-faire view argue for policy rules—specific statements of the policy actions that an agency will follow in the future—advancing three arguments. First, lags in the implementation and effects of policies reduce benefits of discretionary policies and create dangers of overreaction. Second, economists lack sufficient information about the economy's operation to improve its performance with activist policies.

Lack of sufficient information, combined with lags, may lead well-intentioned discretionary policies to increase the severity of business cycles and recessions. In addition, policy makers lack sufficient information about the effects of policies, partly because the effects depend on people's expectations, which change over time. The Lucas critique says that people do not always respond in the same way to a change in government policies, because changes in those policies can change their expectations, obscuring predictions about the effects of policies. These information problems create difficulties for discretionary policy making.

Third, credible rules can change incentives in ways that enhance economic efficiency. Discretionary policies affect expectations and incentives, creating an inflationary bias.

Targets of Monetary Policy

The Federal Reserve, like many other central banks, targets an interest rate (the federal funds rate) in its monetary policy. Central banks in many countries target exchange rates. Systems of fixed exchange rates require monetary policy to adjust the money supply to maintain the fixed exchange rate. Fixed exchange-rate systems are subject to problems of devaluations. Monetary policy includes decisions about the exchange-rate system, banking regulations, and the institutions for implementing policies.

Key Terms

monetary policy
activist view of policy
loose monetary policy
tight monetary policy
laissez-faire view of policy
discretionary policy

policy rule
simple policy rule
contingent policy rule
Lucas critique
credible policy rule

commitment to a policy rule
time consistent policy
time inconsistent policy
fixed (pegged) exchange rate system

floating (flexible) exchange rate system
managed-float exchange rate system
devaluation
currency board

Questions and Problems

18. Explain and contrast the activist and laissez-faire views of the role of government policy.

19. What factors influence the incentives of a central bank in its choice of monetary policy?

20. Argue the case for policy rules rather than discretion; argue the case for discretionary policy rather than rules.

21. Discuss this statement: "Improvements in computer models of the economy will increase the ability of policy makers to conduct effective discretionary monetary policy, but it will not improve the performance of policy rules."

22. How is monetary policy likely to differ between a country with a central bank that is partly independent of politics (as in the United States) and a country whose central bank is subject to more government control?

23. Discuss arguments for and against free banking. How might the creation of electronic money, or *e-money,* be similar to free banking?

24. What is a currency board, and what are its advantages and disadvantages?

25. What would happen if the United States were to abolish the Federal Reserve System and replace it with some form of free banking and privately issued money? What incentives would banks face in choosing their own monetary policies?

26. Suppose that the United States adopted a gold standard and set the nominal price of gold at $350 per ounce. Discuss the effects of the following changes:
(a) Large gold discoveries in Russia that tend to reduce the world price of gold
(b) Increase in the rate of technical progress and economic growth.

27. Discuss this statement: "Increased integration of the world economy, particularly international financial markets, reduces the effectiveness of monetary policy, because the Fed can no longer affect the interest rate."

Inquiries for Further Thought

28. Do you agree more with the activist view of policy or the laissez-faire view? Why?

29. Which guides monetary policy better: rules or discretion?
(a) If you think that rules are better, what rule best promotes appropriate goals? Should the rule be part of a constitutional amendment?
(b) If you think that discretionary policy is better than rules, who should get the discretion? How should they exercise that discretion?

30. What policy advice would you have given Asian nations facing financial crises, devaluations, and recessions in 1998?

31. If you were chairman of the Board of Governors of the Federal Reserve System, what specific data would you look at to decide when and by how much to raise or lower the federal funds rate? Be as specific as you can.

32. What incentives guide the Fed's actions? How could they be changed? How should they be changed? Should the Fed be independent of government control? Should the Federal Reserve maintain secrecy about its operations and the minutes of its meetings? Is the Federal Reserve System an undemocratic institution? Does the Fed respond to political pressures? How?

33. Should the United States adopt one of the more radical changes in monetary institutions discussed in this chapter? Why or why not?

34. How will electronic money work? How much will it be used 25 years from now? What will determine the nominal money supply? What will determine the price level? Will the government still be able to conduct effective monetary policy? Explain.

CHAPTER 14

FISCAL POLICY

In this Chapter...
Main Points to Understand

▶ Government debt shows the amount of money the government owes from past borrowing; a deficit shows current-year borrowing. Measurement and interpretation of the government's debt is controversial.

▶ Governments often try to stabilize aggregate demand by adjusting spending and taxes. Economic effects of changes in government spending depend on what the government buys and how it pays for its spending.

▶ Social security issues pose challenges for fiscal policy.

▶ Fundamental issues of fiscal policy involve the proper role of government, the effects of fiscal policy on long-run growth, and inefficiencies associated with rent seeking.

Thinking Skills to Develop

▶ Recognize the variety of channels through which government fiscal policies affect real GDP and other variables.

▶ Recognize problems involved in interpreting economic data, such as measure of the government's debt.

▶ Use the economic models developed in previous chapters to examine the effects of changes in government spending, taxes, and budget deficits or surpluses.

In 1998, the government of China announced a plan to raise government spending by $1 trillion. This policy sought to shield China from the recessions that had hit other Asian countries. By raising government spending, China sought to raise aggregate demand through *fiscal policy*.

Nearly four decades earlier, the United States had used a different kind of fiscal policy to raise real GDP. Under President Kennedy, the United States raised aggregate demand by cutting taxes. Two decades later, under President Reagan, the United States again cut taxes. This time the architects of the tax cut intended to raise real GDP by raising aggregate supply.

Only a few years ago, in 1993, the U.S. federal government spent a quarter of a trillion dollars more than it collected in taxes—it had a *budget deficit* of more than $250 billion. Since then, the deficit has fallen rapidly. In 1998, President Clinton announced the first federal budget *surplus* in nearly three decades: the government collected more tax revenue than it spent that year.

The emergence of a government budget surplus after decades of deficits ignited strong debate over government *fiscal* policy. How should the government use the surplus money? Should it cut taxes? Should it pay back some of the money it had borrowed in previous decades? (That is, should it pay off part of its *debt*?) Which policies would help prevent world economic turmoil from causing a recession in the United States? What policies would best promote long-run economic growth?

357

Looming over these debates was the potential for huge future social security deficits. The social security issue raised key questions. How should the government measure its surplus or deficit? Does the surplus or deficit, as measured, have any real meaning at all? How will our current policies affect the lives of your generation and future generations? The magnitude of the money involved staggers the imagination. The U.S. federal government has a debt of several trillion dollars. Even today, with prominent reports on these issues in daily news and public discussions, few people realize the full extent to which government budget policies will affect their lives in the coming decades.

THE GOVERNMENT BUDGET IN THE UNITED STATES

Fiscal policy involves the government budget:

> **Fiscal policy** refers to government actions that affect total government spending, tax rates and revenues, and the government budget surplus or deficit.

Federal, state, and local governments in the United States collected over $2.8 trillion in tax revenues in fiscal year 1998.[1] They spent slightly less: $2.7 trillion. The combined government budget *surplus* (excess of tax revenue over spending) amounted to about $200 billion (according to the usual measure of the surplus, which a later section of this chapter criticizes). Total government spending took 32.6 percent of GDP, and people paid 34.4 percent of GDP in taxes.

People paid $1.7 trillion in taxes to the federal government (20.5 percent of GDP), which spent just slightly less (19.9 percent of GDP), for a federal budget surplus of $71 billion. The 1998 U.S. federal government budget surplus, the first in almost 3 decades, consisted of an *off-budget* surplus of $99 billion, reflecting mainly an excess of social security tax revenue over social security payments in 1998, and an *on-budget* deficit of $28 billion. As discussed later in this chapter, some analysts view the on-budget deficit

Figure 1 | Federal Government Revenues and Expenditures, 1998

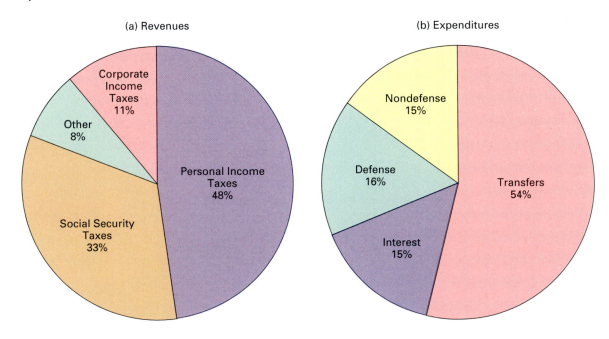

(a) Revenues

Corporate Income Taxes 11%
Other 8%
Personal Income Taxes 48%
Social Security Taxes 33%

(b) Expenditures

Nondefense 15%
Defense 16%
Interest 15%
Transfers 54%

[1]A fiscal year is an annual accounting period. The federal government's 1998 fiscal year began October 1, 1997 and ended September 30, 1998.

Figure 2 | Government Revenue as a Percentage of GDP

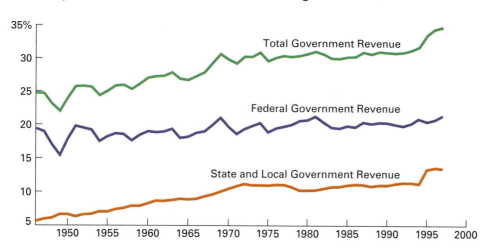

as the best indicator of the budget situation, because the off-budget surplus reflects money that the government will need in the future to meet its social security obligations.

Figure 1 shows where the federal government gets its money and how it spends money. In 1998, about 48 percent of its revenues came from personal income taxes; another 33 percent came from social security taxes. More than half of the federal government's spending covers transfer payments (mainly social security, medicare, and medicaid), 16 percent goes for defense, 15 percent goes to pay interest on its debt, and 15 percent pays for nondefense purchases of goods and services.

Figure 2 shows how government revenue has risen as a fraction of GDP in the second half of the 20th century. The fastest increase has occurred at the state-and-local government level, although the figure also shows an upward trend in federal government revenue as a fraction of GDP.

Figure 3 shows how government *spending* has risen as a fraction of GDP in the second half of the 20th century. Overall, government spending experienced a substantial increase. Figure 4 shows that the government developed a large budget deficit in the fourth quarter of the century, but that deficit has now vanished.

Figure 5 shows that increased spending on transfer payments has been the main factor behind increases in government spending in the last half-century. Decreases in government spending on national defense are the main factor behind decreases in government spending, as a fraction of GDP, in the last decade.

Latest Data Available
See the Web site for this book for the latest, up-to-date data on U.S. fiscal policy (along with other U.S. and international economic data).

Figure 3 | Government Spending as a Percentage of GDP

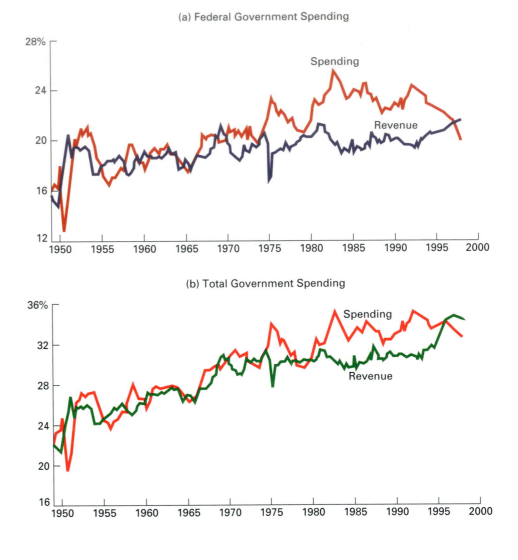

Figure 4 | Government Spending and Tax Revenues as a Percentage of GDP

(a) Federal Government Spending

(b) Total Government Spending

Debt, Deficits, and Surpluses

The government runs a *budget surplus* when it collects more tax revenue than it spends. It runs a *budget deficit* when its spending exceeds its tax revenue. It has a *balanced budget* when its tax revenue equals its spending.

> The government **budget surplus** equals tax revenue minus (smaller) government spending.

> The government **budget deficit** (a negative surplus) equals government spending minus (smaller) tax revenue.

> The government has a **balanced budget** when tax revenue equals government spending.

Figure 5 | Components of Federal Government Spending (Percentage of GDP)

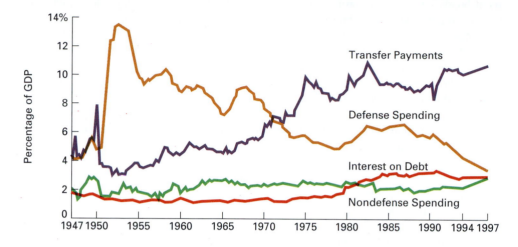

Figure 6 shows budget deficits and surpluses in the United States. A later section of this chapter discusses challenges to the usual measures of these deficits and surpluses.

When the government has a budget *deficit,* it must either borrow money or print money to spend in excess of its tax revenue.[2] The U.S. government, like governments of most developed countries, has generally *borrowed* money to finance its past deficits. However, some countries have printed money to finance budget deficits, as Russia did in the early 1990s and began doing again in 1998. The government *debt* (sometimes called the *national debt)* equals the amount of money the government currently owes due to its past borrowing.

> The **government debt** is the amount of money the government owes because it has borrowed money in the past.

Figure 6 | Government Budget Deficits as a Percentage of GDP

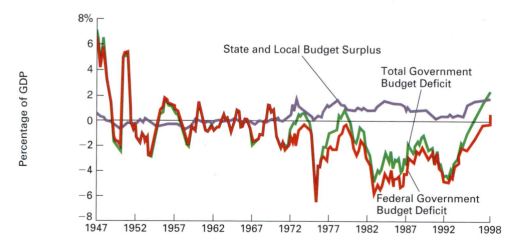

---

[2]A common mistake involves thinking that borrowing or printing money *eliminates* the deficit, but that is not true. The government has a budget deficit when it borrows or prints money to spend in excess of its income to *finance* its deficit. The amount of money it borrows or prints is the size of the deficit.

To whom does the government owe this money? It owes debts mostly to people and business firms in the United States. The government borrows money by selling government bonds—I.O.U.s that promise to repay money at future dates. People lend money to the government when they buy these bonds. People and businesses in the United States own most U.S. government bonds, so most of the government debt is money owed to them.

A budget deficit increases the government debt as the government borrows more money. A budget surplus reduces the government debt as it uses the surplus to repay part of its debt. Deficits and surpluses are *flow* variables, measured in dollars *per year*. In contrast, the debt is a *stock* variable, measured in dollars.

A government budget deficit raises the government's debt, and a surplus reduces its debt.

Figure 7 shows U.S. government debt as a fraction of GDP. Figure 8 shows the government's predictions about its *future* debt in the 21st century. The government predicts big increases in its debt as the baby-boom generation retires and begins collecting social security, creating large increases in government spending and budget deficits starting between 2010 and 2020. A later section of this chapter discusses social security.

Review Questions

1. State the approximate size of each variable in *dollars* and also as a share of GDP.
   (a) total government spending in the United States
   (b) total government tax revenue in the United States
   (c) federal government spending in the United States
   (d) federal government tax revenue in the United States

Figure 7 | U.S. Government Debt as a Percentage of GDP

Source: Congressional Budget Office

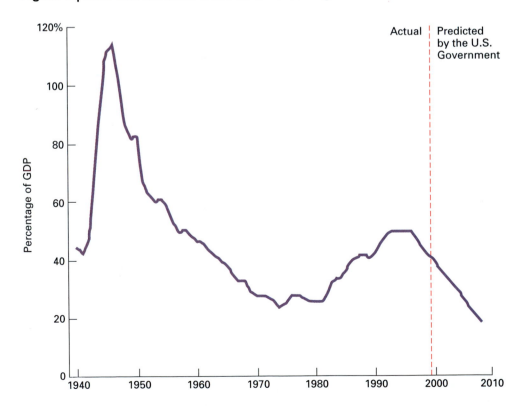

Figure 8 | Predicted U.S. Government Debt in the 21st Century

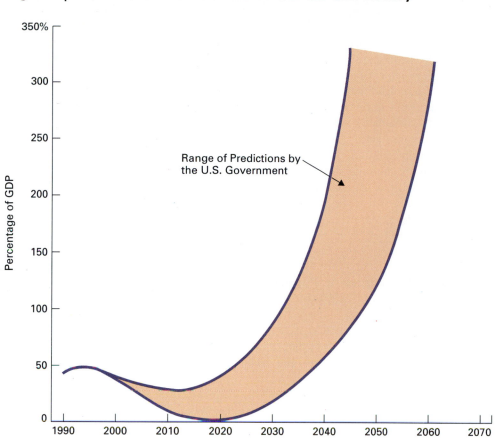

Source: Congressional Budget Office

2. Roughly how much money *per person* do units of government in the United States spend and collect in taxes?

3. What is the difference between the government's budget deficit and the government's debt? How does one affect the other? What is a government budget surplus?

Transfer payments take more than 40 cents out of every dollar of *total* (federal, state, and local) government spending in the United States. Purchases of goods and services take about half of total government spending. (The remainder of government spending covers interest payments on the government debt.) Transfer payments and government purchases of goods and services have different effects on the economy, and the effects of government purchases depend on what the government buys.

EFFECTS OF FISCAL POLICY: CHANGES IN GOVERNMENT SPENDING

Effects of Transfer Payments

Transfer payments are payments of money by the government to people. Social security is the largest transfer-payment program. Unemployment compensation payments are also transfer payments. When the government taxes one person to provide transfer payments to someone else, it redistributes income.

Transfer payments can affect demands and supplies for various goods and services. They raise demands for goods purchased by people who receive transfers, and they decrease demands for goods bought by people who pay the taxes to finance transfer payments. Aggregate demand rises if the government transfers money *from* people who *save* most of each dollar *to* people who *spend* most of each dollar. However, those transfers also reduce the supply of loans, raising the real interest rate and decreasing savings and investment.

Transfer payments, and taxes to pay for them, also affect supplies of goods, and they may affect aggregate supply. For example, the opportunity to receive social security encourages people to retire at an earlier age. It also gives them incentives to avoid actions that would reduce their payments, such as taking part-time jobs. Consequently, the social security program reduces labor supply, which decreases aggregate supply.[3]

Changes in taxes to pay for transfer payments can also affect aggregate supply. Taxes can affect aggregate supply by affecting equilibrium employment, as Chapter 7 explains. Taxes can also affect aggregate supply by affecting equilibrium investment, which affects the economy's capital stock. Because advances in technology result from investments in research and development, increases in taxes that reduce these investments may slow the growth of technology.

Effects of Government Purchases

Government purchases of goods and services directly affect aggregate demand; aggregate demand equals $C + I + G + NEX$, where G represents government purchases of goods and services (but does not include transfer payments). The effects of increases in government spending on the economy depend on several conditions:

1. What the government buys, including:
   a. How well government spending substitutes for private spending
   b. How productive the government spending is

2. How the government pays for its spending

Substitution between Government Purchases and Private Spending
Government spending can substitute for (or replace) private spending. Suppose (for now) that the government raises taxes when it raises spending, so the budget deficit does not increase. Assume that the government boosts its purchases of goods that substitute very well for spending that people already do on their own. This increase in government spending leaves aggregate demand unaffected because a fall in consumption (C) or investment (I) offsets the rise in government purchases (G). On the other hand, if the government raises spending on goods that substitute poorly for spending that people already do on their own, then aggregate demand rises. The following examples explain why.

EXAMPLE: LUNCH PROGRAM

Suppose that the government starts a free lunch program in which it buys your lunch for you. To keep the example simple, suppose that it buys exactly the same food that you would have bought for yourself, and it raises your taxes to pay for this program. (Ignore the salaries of government bureaucrats who run the program.)

This program has no effect on aggregate demand. You go through the cafeteria line and get your food, but you don't have to pay the cashier. Instead, you have to pay the tax collector, and the tax collector pays the cashier. This government program has almost

If the government buys your lunch and taxes you to pay for it, the economic effects are small—you pay the tax collector instead of the cashier, and then the tax collector pays the cashier.

---

[3]See the related discussion of tax cuts in Chapter 7.

[4]This ignores the fact that the increase in your taxes may change your incentives to work, consume, save, or invest, depending on what tax the government raises.

no effect on anything.[4] It only introduces an intermediary—the tax collector—between you and the cashier. Government spending (G) rises, but private consumption spending (C) falls, so $C + I + G + NEX$ does not change. The important feature of this example is the assumption that government spending substitutes very well (perfectly, in fact) for private spending, because the government buys exactly the same food that you would have bought for yourself.[5] The next example will consider government spending that substitutes poorly for private spending.

EXAMPLE: GOVERNMENT SPENDING ON DEFENSE

Suppose that the government raises spending on national defense, raising taxes to pay for the spending increase. Government spending on national defense is *not* a good substitute for private spending. As a result, people don't reduce their private consumption spending as in the lunch example; instead, they pay the higher taxes partly by reducing their savings. (In the lunch example, in contrast, people paid the higher taxes by reducing their private spending on lunches.) Consequently, private consumption falls by less than government spending rises. Therefore aggregate demand increases.

Types of Government Purchases

Most government purchases of goods and services fall somewhere between these two extremes; they do not substitute perfectly for private spending, as in the lunch example, but they substitute better than the spending in the national-defense example. Public schools, for example, substitute partially for spending on private schooling. (Government spending on schools exceeds $200 billion.) Government spending for police services (about $30 billion) substitutes partially for private spending to fight crime (locks and security systems on houses and businesses, private police or security guards, and so on). Government spending on natural resources, national parks, and recreation (over $100 billion) substitutes partially for private spending on recreation. Government spending for highways substitutes partially for private spending on replacement of cars, and construction of private roads or alternative transportation methods such as airlines and trains. Even government spending for courts substitutes partially for private spending on private courts and arbitration services.

Government spending on monuments, like spending on national defense (but unlike spending on lunch programs), substitutes poorly for private spending. Consequently, changes in this kind of government spending affect aggregate demand.

IN THE NEWS

China to Prime Economic Pump with Mammoth Building Outlay

BEIJING—China's leaders plan to spend $1 trillion on a huge range of public works projects in the next three years, in an ambitious effort to stop the Asian financial crisis from derailing the country's economic growth.

Huang Qifan, deputy secretary general of the Communist Party in Shanghai, said in an interview that the leadership had decided that spending money on an enormous crop of public works projects was needed to keep China's economic growth rate at 8 percent.

Source: New York Times

China uses fiscal policy by increasing government spending to raise aggregate demand.

---

[5] If the government bought different food than you would have bought for yourself, the government spending might not substitute very well for your own private spending. You might continue to buy some food for yourself. In that case, private spending on consumption would not fall by as much as government spending rises, so aggregate demand would rise.

Figure 9 uses the basic model from Chapter 7 to show the long-run effects of an increase in government purchases, financed by an increase in taxes. The figure applies to the case in which government purchases do *not* substitute well for private spending. The increases in government purchases and taxes do not affect the economy's technology, but they may affect real GDP by changing equilibrium employment.

Taxes to Pay for Government Spending

As Chapter 7 explained, taxes create a difference between before-tax wages and after-tax wages. A tax increase lowers after-tax wages, which affects workers in two ways. First, a fall in the after-tax wage can make people want to *reduce* their work hours. As the after-tax wage falls, the opportunity cost of leisure time also falls, leading people to expand leisure time and reduce time at work. In this way, a tax increase tends to reduce equilibrium employment and real GDP.

Second, a fall in the after-tax wage can make people want to *increase* their work hours. As the after-tax wage falls, people become poorer, leading them to choose less leisure time and more time at work. In this way, a tax increase tends to raise equilibrium employment and real GDP.

These conflicting forces imply that an increase in taxes can either reduce or increase equilibrium employment. For example, if you work 40 hours per week and earn $10 per hour, you earn $400 per week. If your after-tax wage were to fall to $8 per hour, you might decide to work fewer hours per week, because the hourly benefit of working has fallen. Alternatively, you might decide to increase your work time to 50 hours per week, to keep your weekly income at $400. Figure 9 shows the former case, in which an increase in taxes reduces equilibrium employment and real GDP.

Figure 10 uses the model of aggregate demand and supply to show the short-run effects of an increase in government purchases, financed by an increase in taxes. Like Figure 9, this figure applies to the case in which government purchases do *not* substitute well for private spending. The increase in government purchases raises aggregate demand. Aggregate supply falls if the tax increase reduces equilibrium employment, and rises if the tax increase raises equilibrium employment. Figure 10 shows the intermediate case in which aggregate supply remains unchanged, and the increase

As chapter 7 explained, an increase in taxes on labor income distorts incentives, and can reduce the equilibrium quantity of labor. The fall in equilibrium labor from l_0 to l_1 reduces long-run real GDP from y_0 to y_1.

When an increase in government purchases substitutes poorly for private spending, people pay part of the tax increase by reducing consumption, and part by reducing savings. This fall in savings decreases the supply of loans, reducing equilibrium investment and raising the equilibrium real interest rate. The fall in equilibrium investment reduces the economy's future capital stock, further reducing long-run equilibrium real GDP. The rise in the real interest rate raises the nominal interest rate, increasing the velocity of money, and raising the price level, since $P = MV/y$.

This figure shows that the long-run effects of an increase in government purchases (and taxes) differ from the short-run effects. In the short run, the increase in velocity raises aggregate demand, raising the real GDP along with the price level. In the long run, as this figure shows, the increase in government purchases, and taxes, lowers real GDP. (This conclusion could be reversed if government purchases are sufficiently productive, as discussed in a later section of this chapter.)

Figure 9 | Long-Run Effects of an Increase in Government Purchases and Taxes

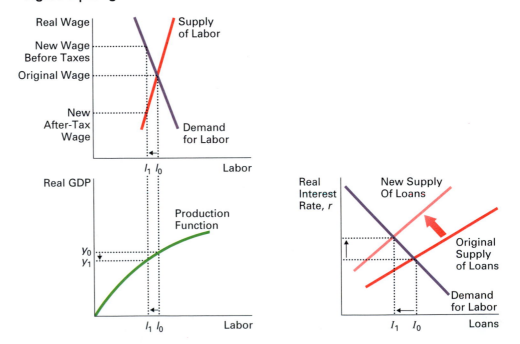

Figure 10 | An Activist View of Government Policy

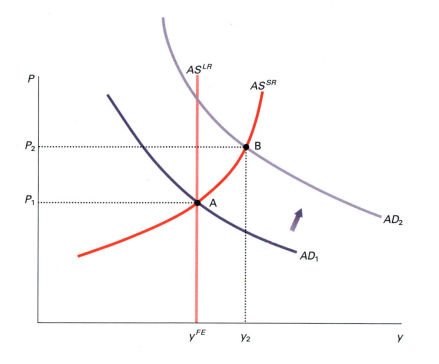

If government purchases do not substitute well for private spending, an increase in government spending raises aggregate demand from AD_1 to AD_2. If the rise in taxes and government spending does not affect aggregate supply, then the economy moves from Point A to Point B in the short run.

in government purchases raises real GDP and the price level in the short run as the economy moves from Point A to Point B.

Productivity of Government Spending

Some government spending helps private firms to produce goods. Government spending on infrastructure (transportation and communication systems, including roads, bridges, airports, mass transit, waterways, and so on) lowers private firms' costs of producing, distributing, and selling goods and services. Government spending on police and fire services, courts, hospitals, and education can also enhance productivity and reduce firms' costs of production.

An increase in government spending on productive goods or services can raise aggregate supply as well as aggregate demand. If the government spending substitutes very well for private spending (for example, if an increase in public police protection leads firms to reduce spending on their own security guards), then the increase in government spending does not have a big effect on either aggregate demand or aggregate supply.[6] If the government spending on goods and services does not substitute well for private spending, however, then it can affect both aggregate demand and aggregate supply, raising the productivity of labor and privately-owned capital.

EXAMPLE

Suppose that the government raises spending to repair bridges and roads. This outlay adds to aggregate demand; G rises while C and I do not fall, because this spending does not substitute well for private spending. This government spending also adds to aggregate supply, as improved roads and bridges allow firms to obtain inputs for production and distribute output to consumers faster and at lower cost than before.

[6] In the extreme case, in which a $1,000 increase in government spending for police leads to a $1,000 fall in private spending on security guards, the change has no effect on aggregate demand or supply.

Summary of the Effects of Changes in Government Spending

An increase in government purchases paid for by higher taxes has several effects. First, it raises aggregate demand if the government spending does not substitute well for private spending. (It has little effect on aggregate demand if they are good substitutes.) The increase in aggregate demand tends to raise real GDP (in the short run) and the price level.

Second, the increase in taxes may reduce aggregate supply if the rise in tax rates reduces the incentive to work. This fall in aggregate supply tends to reduce real GDP and raise the price level. (These effects would be reversed if the tax increase induced people to work more than before, rather than less.) In the intermediate case in which real GDP remains unchanged, the increase in government purchases leaves fewer goods and services available for other uses, so it reduces private consumption and investment.

Third, in the long run, an increase in government purchases on infrastructure may enhance productivity at private firms, tending to raise aggregate supply. Recall, however, that a tax increase (to finance the government spending) tends to reduce private investment. As a result, an increase in government purchases on infrastructure, financed by a tax increase, raises long-run aggregate supply only if the increase in government investment exceeds the fall in private investment; otherwise, it reduces long-run aggregate supply.[7]

Review Questions

4. How can transfer payments, and taxes to pay for them, affect aggregate demand and aggregate supply?

5. Why do the effects of government purchases depend on what the government buys? Explain specifically and give at least two examples.

6. Explain how a change in government purchases can affect aggregate supply.

Thinking Exercises

7. Suppose the government raises spending on national defense, and pays for the increased spending by raising taxes. Why does private consumption fall by *less* than the rise in government spending?

8. Explain how a decrease in income-tax rates affects equilibrium employment.

Borrowing to Pay for Government Spending

The effects of an increase in government spending depend on how the government pays for that spending. So far, the discussion has considered the case in which the government raises taxes to pay for a spending increase. Suppose instead that the government raises spending *without* raising taxes, so it runs a budget deficit, borrowing the money to finance the increase in spending.

The increase in government borrowing raises the government debt: it will owe more money in the future than it would have owed without the spending increase. Consequently, the government must either raise taxes in the future to repay its increased debt, with interest, or reduce its future spending. We now consider the case in which the government will respond to its increased future debt by raising future taxes. The effects of this increase in *future* taxes may differ from the effects of an increase in *current* taxes; that is, the *time path of taxes* may affect the economy.

---

[7]The relative productivity of government investment and private investment also influences the result.

Time Path of Taxes

Budget deficits and surpluses affect the time path of tax revenues. In other words, the government can cut taxes *this year* (and raise borrowing to pay for its spending) if it raises taxes *next year* to repay what it borrowed. To do this, the government must raise the *discounted present value* of future tax revenue by the amount of money it borrows this year.

EXAMPLE

Suppose that the government will spend $100 this year and $100 next year, and the nominal interest rate is 10 percent per year. The discounted present value of government spending is:

$$\$100 + \frac{\$100}{1.10} = \$191$$

where $1 + i = 1.10$.

Consider three possible time paths of taxes:

1. The government could balance its budget each year by collecting $100 in taxes both this year and next year. This policy would give it tax receipts with a discounted present value of $191, the same as the discounted present value of spending.

2. The government could collect no taxes this year and $210 in taxes next year.[8] The government would have a $100 deficit this year, which it would finance by borrowing $100. Next year the government would collect $210 in taxes to give it a $100 budget surplus. It would use $100 to pay for next year's spending and the other $110 to repay its loan with interest.

3. The government could collect $191 in taxes this year and no taxes next year. It would then have a $91 surplus this year and a $100 deficit next year. The government would use $100 for current spending and save $91, earning 10 percent interest. This would give the government $100 for next year's spending.

The government could also choose some other time path for taxes. For example, it could collect $80 in taxes this year, running a $20 budget deficit, then collect $122 in taxes next year to pay for its $100 in future spending and use $22 to repay its $20 debt with 10 percent interest.

Choosing the Time Path of Taxes

The time path of taxes affects the economy in two ways. First, the timing of tax receipts affects the size of the economic inefficiency caused by taxes. Second, it alters aggregate demand and aggregate supply, affecting real GDP and price level.

EXPLANATION

Taxes create economic inefficiencies because they affect incentives. Figure 11 shows how taxes drive a wedge between the price including tax that buyers pay, P_B, and the after-tax price that sellers receive, P_S. The difference, P_B minus P_S, is the per-unit tax. For example, with a 5 percent sales tax, buyers pay $10.50 for a good, sellers receive $10.00

---

[8]The discounted present value of this tax revenue is $210/1.1, or $191.

after taxes, and the government get \$0.50 in taxes; P_B is \$10.50, P_S is \$10.00, and the per-unit tax is \$0.50. Because buyers pay a higher price (including tax) than sellers keep (after taxes), the equilibrium quantity is Q_1 (instead of Q_0, the equilibrium quantity without any tax). Since buyers must pay P_B, they want to buy only Q_1 instead of Q_0, and since sellers keep only P_S for each good they sell, they want to sell Q_1 instead of Q_0. The tax reduces the equilibrium quantity bought and sold. This causes economic inefficiency, because it leads some people to forgo mutually advantageous trades (purchases and sales) because they can avoid the tax by not trading.

Each time the tax rate doubles, the amount of economic inefficiency more than doubles—it roughly quadruples. In fact, the economic inefficiency from a tax is roughly proportional to the tax rate squared. Raising a tax from 5 cents per unit to 10 cents per unit doubles the tax rate, but it raises the economic inefficiency about four times (5 cents squared gives 25, while 10 cents squared gives 100, which is four times larger). These relationships imply a greater benefit—less inefficiency—from a 5-cent tax for 2 years than a 10-cent tax for 1 year.[9] A 5-cent tax for 2 years also causes less economic inefficiency than an 8-cent tax for 1 year and a 2-cent tax for the other year.[10] In other words, the time path of taxes affects economic efficiency.

Analogy

Think about an analogy. The amount of gasoline a car burns per mile depends on its speed. Doubling speed *more* than doubles gasoline use. You could drive a car 80 miles by going 40 miles per hour for 2 hours. Alternatively, you could go the same distance at the same *average* speed by driving 20 miles per hour for one hour and 60 miles per hour for a second hour. However, you use less gasoline if you keep the constant speed of 40 miles per hour rather than varying between 20 and 60 miles per hour. Raising the *variation* in your speed raises the total amount of gasoline burned.

Similarly, the government could keep income taxes constant over time at 20 percent of income or vary the tax rate between 10 percent in some years and 30 percent in other

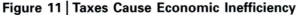

Figure 11 | Taxes Cause Economic Inefficiency

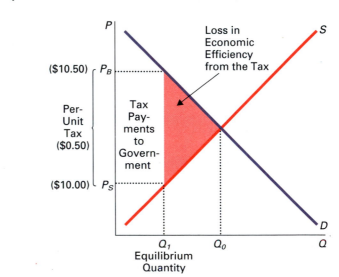

---

[9] Imposing a 5-cent tax for 2 years causes an efficiency loss proportional to \$0.25 for 2 years, so the total loss is proportional to \$0.50. Imposing a 10-cent tax for 1 year causes an efficiency loss proportional to \$1.00.

[10] A 5-cent tax causes inefficiency proportional to 25 each year for 2 years, so the inefficiency is proportional to (\$0.25)(2) = \$0.50. An 8-cent tax causes inefficiency proportional to 64, and a 2-cent tax causes inefficiency proportional to 4, so an 8-cent tax for 1 year and a 2-cent tax for the other year cause an inefficiency proportional to 64 + 4 = 68, which is larger than the inefficiency from a 5-cent tax for 2 years.

years. However, economic inefficiency is like gasoline burned. Even if this variation in taxes produced the same tax revenue for the government, an increase in the *variance* of taxes from one year to the next would raise the economic inefficiency caused by the tax.

Timing of Taxes and Aggregate Demand

The government's budget deficit rises if it cuts tax revenue without cutting spending. As an earlier chapter explained, the increase in government borrowing raises the demand for loans. Taxes fall, so people's after-tax income rises. The supply of loans increases to the extent that people save some of this extra after-tax income. However, if people spend on consumption at least *part* of the income from the tax cut, two results occur. First, the supply of loans increases by less than the demand for loans, raising the equilibrium interest rate. Second, the increase in consumption spending raises aggregate demand.

The government can attempt to stabilize aggregate demand by choosing a time path of taxes that helps *undo* changes in aggregate demand that result from changes in underlying conditions. When aggregate demand falls, the government can reduce taxes to raise aggregate demand. For example, suppose that a change in underlying conditions (such as an increase in consumer patience) reduces consumption spending, and therefore aggregate demand, from AD_2 to AD_1 as in Figure 12. By cutting taxes, the government can help raise aggregate demand back to AD_2. Similarly, when aggregate demand rises due to variations in underlying conditions, the government can raise taxes to reduce aggregate demand.

Timing of Taxes and Aggregate Supply

Changes in the time path of taxes also affect aggregate supply. A cut in the income tax rate raises the after-tax wage and increases the incentive to work. This change raises the equilibrium input of labor, raising total employment, hours worked per person, and real GDP. Economic analysis that emphasizes the incentive effects of taxes and government regulations on aggregate supply is often called *supply-side economics*. This perspective became popular in public discussions with the election of President Ronald Reagan in 1980. Although some supply-side arguments remain controversial, others receive wide agreement among economists. Their implications for government policy amount largely to emphasizing on the incentive effects of taxes and regulations when thinking about policies.

Because a tax cut can increase both aggregate demand and aggregate supply, it can potentially raise real GDP with little effect on the price level, as Figure 12 shows. Whether the price level rises or falls depends on whether aggregate supply increases by more or less than aggregate demand.

Figure 12 | Tax Cuts and Aggregate Supply and Demand

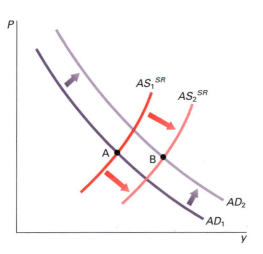

Case Studies: The Kennedy and Reagan Tax Cuts

Tax cuts proposed by President John Kennedy were enacted in 1964 and 1965, after Kennedy's assassination. Tax cuts proposed by President Ronald Reagan in 1980 took effect over the years from 1982–84. Both the Kennedy and Reagan tax cuts were followed by unusually long periods before the next recessions, which occurred in 1970 and 1990, respectively. Economists advising the government in the 1960s argued that the tax cuts helped the economy to grow during that decade by raising aggregate demand. Those advisors generally considered themselves as Keynesian economists, and they regarded the sticky-price or sticky-wage model as the best model of the economy. Economists advising the government in the 1980s, in contrast, argued that the tax cuts of that decade helped the economy to grow by raising aggregate supply. Those advisors generally regarded themselves as supply-side economists, with diverse views but a common emphasis on the effects of tax rates on incentives to work, save, and invest.

Before the Kennedy tax cuts, the top marginal federal income tax rate stood at 91 percent, although this tax rate applied only to incomes over $1 million per year in today's dollars.[11] The Kennedy tax cuts reduced taxes by about $11.5 billion in 1965. Economists at the time estimated the aggregate demand multiplier (discussed in Chapter 11) at between 1.3 and 2.0, so they expected the tax cut to increase real GDP by about $15 billion to $23 billion, through an increase in aggregate demand. GDP actually exceeded its trend rate of growth by about $28 billion.[12] If $15 billion to $23 billion of that increase in real GDP resulted from a rise in aggregate demand due to the tax cut, the remaining $5 billion to $13 billion may have resulted from an increase in aggregate supply, also caused by the tax cut.[13]

Nearly two decades later, by 1981, federal income tax rates had risen again, mainly because of bracket creep, which occurred when inflation automatically raised taxes.[14] The Reagan tax cut once again reduced federal income taxes. One study estimated that the increase in aggregate demand from the Reagan tax cut raised GDP by 3.2 percent in 1983 to 1984 and by 2.7 percent in 1985, while the increase in aggregate supply from the tax cut raised GDP by about half of this amount.[15]

Laffer Curve

Higher tax rates usually mean larger tax payments and more tax revenue for the government, but not always. The Laffer Curve shows the relationship between the marginal tax rate and the government's tax revenue.

The Laffer Curve in Figure 13 shows that the government collects no tax revenue at either a zero or a very high tax rate. If the income tax rate were 100 percent, for example, people would probably stop working for pay; without any income to tax, the government would not collect any tax revenue. At a very high tax rate (say, at Point B

---

[11]Chapter 7 discussed the difference between average tax rates and marginal tax rates.

[12]See Lawrence Lindsey, *The Growth Experiment* (New York: Basic Books, 1990). Lindsey later became a governor of the Federal Reserve System.

[13]Some economists, such as Lindsey, argue that the supply-side effects were larger than this estimate; other economists think they were smaller.

[14]To see how inflation pushes people into higher tax brackets, suppose that you are single and you earn $20,000 per year. Inflation doubles all prices and your pretax salary also doubles to $40,000. Before taxes, you have kept up with inflation. Everything costs twice as much as before, but you now earn twice as much. After taxes, however, you may have fallen behind. Suppose that you must pay a 15 percent tax on all income under $20,000 and 28 percent on all income above $20,000. Before inflation, your taxes were $3,000 (15 percent of $20,000) leaving after-tax income of $17,000. After inflation, your taxes are $8,600 ($3,000 on your first $20,000 of income and $5,600 on the rest) leaving after-tax income of $31,400. Your after-tax income did not double; it did not rise from $17,000 to $34,000. Instead, your taxes more than doubled, from $3,000 to $8,600, and your after-tax income rose from $17,000 to $31,400. The purchasing power of your after-tax income fell. This bracket creep results from inflation combined with unindexed tax rates. Starting in 1984, federal income taxes in the United States became indexed to inflation to prevent bracket creep; the tax tables now change automatically so that, if your salary keeps up with inflation before taxes, it also keeps up with inflation after federal income taxes.

[15]Lindsey, *Growth Experiment.*

Figure 13 | The Laffer Curve

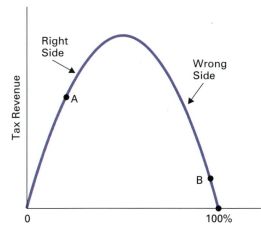

in the figure), the government would collect little tax revenue. In that case, the economy is said to be on the *wrong side of the Laffer Curve,* and the government could increase its tax revenue by reducing the tax rate.

In the early 1980s, some economists claimed that the U.S. economy was on the wrong side of the Laffer Curve and that the Reagan tax cuts would raise the government's tax revenue. Most believed, however, that the economy was on the rising (left) portion of the Laffer Curve, so that a cut in tax rates would reduce tax revenue. On balance, experience supported the majority. If the tax cut had not raised real GDP, evidence suggests that the federal government would have lost about $115 billion in tax revenue each year.[16] An increase in GDP raises the tax base, however, which helps to mitigate the fall in tax revenue. Evidence suggests that the increase in aggregate demand due to the Reagan tax cuts added about $40 billion annually to federal tax revenues, while the increase in aggregate supply from the tax cuts added about $20 billion. In addition, the decrease in tax rates raised government tax revenue by about $20 billion per year by reducing people's use of legal methods of tax avoidance.[17] While the direct effect of the tax cut may have reduced tax revenue by $115 billion per year, these three factors indirectly raised tax revenue by about $80 billion per year, so that the government had a net loss of about $35 billion annually in revenue from the tax cuts.[18]

Automatic Changes in Government Budget Deficits with GDP

Lags in the implementation of fiscal policy create difficulties for government attempts to stabilize aggregate demand through explicit changes in taxes or government spending.

---

[16] This is the estimate for 1985 from Lindsey, *Growth Experiment.*

[17] People use legal methods of tax avoidance when they choose investments that lower their taxes, even if those investments pay lower returns than others would. For example, one investment of $1,000 might return $100 of taxable income at the end of the year. If the marginal tax rate is 40 percent, people pay $40 in taxes and keep $60 for themselves. Another investment of $1,000 might pay back only $70, but in nontaxable income. If the tax rate is 40 percent, people choose the second investment, and the government gets zero tax revenue from this investment income. If the government cuts the tax rate to 25 percent, however, people choose the first investment, and they pay $25 in taxes and keep $75 for themselves. The lower tax rate leads people to change their behavior in ways that raise the government's tax revenue. (Notice that the government's revenue from a tax on investment can rise from a cut in the tax rate, even though the total amount of investment does not change. This result occurs because the type of investment changes.)

[18] Some evidence supports the claim that the tax cuts in the highest tax brackets actually raised tax revenue, so the economy was on the wrong side of the Laffer Curve for some taxes, though not for most.

However, fiscal policy can work *automatically,* without the need for explicit action by the government, through the use of automatic stabilizers.

> An **automatic stabilizer** is a feature of government policy that automatically changes taxes or spending to try to reduce fluctuations in real GDP, without any explicit actions of the government.

When aggregate demand falls, reducing real GDP, tax payments automatically fall, because people pay taxes on reduced incomes. The fall in tax payments partly offsets the fall in income. As a result, consumption spending and aggregate demand fall by less than they would if tax payments were unchanged. Similarly, when aggregate demand rises, the increase in real GDP automatically raises tax payments. Consequently, consumption spending and aggregate demand rise less than they otherwise would rise. In this way, the tax system serves as an automatic stabilizer, dampening variations in aggregate demand and real GDP.

How big is this effect? Suppose that a fall in aggregate demand reduces GDP by 1 percent. This reduces tax payments (and raises the federal government budget deficit) by about $30 billion. To see why, recall that GDP is close to $8 trillion, so a 1 percent rise in GDP amounts to an increase of about $80 billion. On average, the marginal tax rate in the United States lies between one-third and one-half, so a rise of $80 billion in GDP raises government tax revenue by between one-third and one-half of this amount, or about $30 billion. As a result, after-tax income falls by only $50 billion rather than $80 billion.

Review Questions

9. How can the government change the time path of taxes without changing its spending?

10. How does a change in the time path of taxes affect aggregate demand? How does it affect aggregate supply?

11. What is the Laffer Curve? What does it mean to be on the wrong side of the Laffer Curve?

Thinking Exercises

12. Which raises aggregate demand by a larger amount: (a) an increase in government spending financed by higher taxes, or (b) an increase in government spending without a tax increase, which raises the budget deficit as the government raises its borrowing? Explain.

13. Explain why the time path of taxes affects the level of economic inefficiency caused by taxes.

MEASURING GOVERNMENT DEBT, DEFICITS, AND SURPLUSES

Figures 6 and 7 showed the standard measures of the government's debt and the budget deficit as a percentage of GDP. However, important issues arise in measuring the debt and deficit. The first issue concerns ownership of the debt. Although the government debt in 1998 was about 5.6 trillion, the government owed part of this debt to the Social Security Trust Fund, the Federal Reserve, and other government agencies. In that sense, the government owed part of this debt to *itself*. The amount of money the government owes to other people—the government debt owned by people and business firms—is called the *privately held government debt.*

Government statistics show that the privately held government debt is about $3.8 trillion. However, that statistic raises a second measurement issue. The official government debt statistics ignore two large government liabilities: pensions for government employees, and social security benefits that the government has promised to pay in the future.

Pensions: About $1 Trillion

The official government debt figures do not include pensions that the government owes to its employees and former employees. Some of the money that the government has promised to pay as pensions is *funded:* Money has been put aside and invested to help pay the future pensions. However, about $1 trillion of the government's pension liabilities are *unfunded:* the government has no money saved or invested to cover these payments.

This $1 trillion unfunded pension debt raises the federal government's total debt from $3.8 trillion to about $4.8 trillion. This adjusted debt equals almost $18,000 for each person in the country.

Social Security: About $4 Trillion

The official government debt statistics also omit money that the government has promised to pay for social security benefits in the future. Rough estimates place the discounted present value of these payments between $3 trillion and $5 trillion. Some economists argue that the government debt statistics should include *all* liabilities of the government, regardless of type. Including the discounted present value of future social security payments raises the government's debt from $4.8 trillion to somewhere around $8 trillion: about $30,000 for every person in the country.

Other economists argue that government promises to repay loans in the future differ from government promises of future social security payments. The government can change its promises of future social security payments simply by changing the law. Many people, they argue, *expect* the government to reduce social security payments in the future, possible by raising the age at which people qualify for benefits. In contrast, the government would encounter serious legal problems if it failed to repay its explicit debt. This issue of measuring the government debt remains controversial.

Do Deficit Statistics Have *Any* Meaning?

The logic that suggests including unfunded pensions and social security obligations in government debt statistics can be extended to assets as well as liabilities. The government also owns assets such as land, mineral rights, capital equipment, and military hardware. The government collects income from some of these assets, such as lease payments on land. Perhaps the most important asset the government owns is its ability to collect taxes.

Economist Laurence J. Kotlikoff has argued that the usual measurement of the deficit, even with the corrections discussed so far, is an arbitrary and misleading guide to fiscal policy—like "driving in Los Angeles with a map of New York."[19] He argues that when the government takes money from people, it arbitrarily calls some of it *taxes* and the rest *borrowing.* When it pays money to people, it arbitrarily calls some of these payments *spending on transfer payments* and some of it *principal plus interest on the debt.* Since the *spending* and *taxes* labels are both arbitrary, their difference, the deficit, is also an arbitrary

---

[19] He suggests an entirely new way to measure fiscal policy based on its effects on people born in different years. See Laurence J. Kotlikoff, *Generational Accounting* (New York: Free Press, 1992).

figure. The pattern of taxes and government spending has important effects, however, and can affect different people (and different generations) in different ways. Kotlikoff proposes alternative statistics that measure the way government spending and taxes redistribute income from one generation to another. His proposal compares expected taxes with expected government spending for each age group. It estimates the discounted present value of *lifetime* tax payments net of lifetime receipts from the government, assuming that current government policies continue. These statistics are intended to show which age groups win and lose from the government's current fiscal policy. The main problem with the generational accounting measure centers on its need to make assumptions about future fiscal policies.

EXAMPLE

Consider social security. When the government collects money from people for social security, it labels the receipts a *social security tax*. When it makes social security payments to people, it labels this outlay *spending on transfer payments*. The government could just as well call such a payment a *loan,* though. The government could say that it borrows money from people when it collects social security taxes, and it repays the loan when it pays social security benefits. This arbitrary change in language changes the measured deficit, making the deficit a meaningless figure. Its size depends on the arbitrary language that describes what the government actually does. The government program, however, *does* redistribute income across generations. Kotlikoff proposes a way to measure that redistribution.

If this idea seems strange, consider what the government of France once did. It passed a law *requiring* people to lend money to the government. Was this a tax or a loan? If you call it a loan, you would say that the French government had a budget deficit and that its debt increased. If you call it a tax, then you would say that the program did not affect the deficit or the debt. Kotlikoff argues that this question of language has no right answer, so the measured budget deficit and debt are virtually meaningless. Nevertheless, an economist could calculate which generations pay the money to the government and which generations will pay future taxes so that the government can repay these "loans" in the future. Consequently, one can calculate the way this program redistributes wealth across generations, using assumptions about future tax policies. Issues about the best way to measure fiscal policies remain controversial.

Social Security Surplus

The $71 billion budget surplus that the U.S. federal government reported in 1998 had two parts: an *off-budget* surplus of $99 billion, reflecting mainly an excess of social security tax revenue over social security payments, and an *on-budget* deficit of $28 billion. Interpreting these numbers requires understanding the basics of the social security system.

When the government began the social security program, it began collecting social security taxes from working people and using that money to pay social security benefits to retired people. The system was *pay-as-you-go*: current taxes finance current payments. When retirees paid social security taxes during their working years, the government did not save and invest their money for them so that it could pay them social security benefits when they retired. Instead, the government distributed their money as social security payments to people who were already retired.

Recently, social security tax revenues have exceeded payments of social security benefits: a social security *surplus* has emerged. The government uses the money from this surplus to buy government bonds that it puts in the social security *trust fund*. In that sense, the government is currently saving and investing the social security surplus. However, when the social security trust fund buys government bonds, it *lends* money to the rest of the government. In 1998, the treasury department borrowed $99 billion in this way. If we count this as government borrowing rather than tax revenue, then the government had a deficit of $28 billion. This is the government's *on-budget* deficit. In contrast, the *overall* $71 billion surplus ignores this borrowing; it includes the $99 billion as part of overall tax revenue, and compares overall tax revenue with overall spending. Which is a better measure of fiscal policy? Most economists agree that no *single* number can adequately describe the government's budget situation.

Unless changes in social security soon occur, two problems will arise in the future, as the social security surplus turns into a deficit. First, when social security payments begin to exceed social security tax revenues, the government will need to use the money in the social security trust fund to cover payments. Because the government has already borrowed and spent that money, however, the overall government budget deficit will begin rising at that time. Second, the social security trust fund will not be large enough to finance future payments, because the discounted present value of expected future social security payments exceeds the discounted present value of expected future social security taxes. Both problems reflect demographic changes. The baby-boom generation (resulting from a large number of births between the end of World War II and 1960) will retire around the years 2020 to 2030, reducing social security tax revenues and raising social security payments. In 1998, the U.S. had about 3.4 workers for every social security recipient. By 2030, the U.S. is likely to have only about 2 workers per retired person. This change will have at least one of the following consequences:

1. Social security taxes will rise by about 33 percent to 50 percent.[20]

2. Social security payments will be cut by about one-third to one-half, perhaps by paying less per month, and perhaps by raising the age of eligibility.

3. The government will change its spending and taxing policies so that the social security system accumulates a larger trust fund, big enough to continue the same level of payments without higher taxes.

4. The government will make major changes in the social security program, perhaps privatizing it.[21]

All statistics on future social security problems are only rough estimates. The actual numbers will depend on issues such as overall economic growth over the next several decades, increases in life expectancy, and many other factors than are difficult to predict.

Review Questions

14. What are the main problems in measuring the size of the government debt?

15. Why does the U.S. social security system currently run a surplus? What happens to that surplus?

16. What main problems will the social security system cause in the future?

Thinking Exercise

17. Discuss the following claim: "The social security trust fund is an accounting fiction."

---

[20]Social security taxes, not including the part of the tax to cover Medicare, are currently 12.4 percent of salaries up to a certain level ($68,400 in 1998). This 12.4 percent figure includes both the employer and employee shares of the tax. A 33 percent *rise* in the tax means an increase in the tax rate from 12.4 percent to 16.5 percent (*not* an increase to 45.4 percent).

[21]Many people have advanced proposals to privatize social security. Most involve eliminating social security taxes; eliminating social security benefits entirely for people who are currently young; using general tax revenues to pay social security benefits to people who are already retired or who will retire within a decade or two; and requiring all workers to save for retirement in a government-approved manner with tax benefits for saving.

FUNDAMENTAL ISSUES OF FISCAL POLICY

Fiscal policy involves deeper issues than simply whether the government should change taxes or spending to affect aggregate demand or supply. Two fundamental types of issues underlie the main controversies and debates about fiscal policy. First, what are the proper roles of government spending and taxes in the economy? What is the optimal size of government? What are the appropriate levels of government spending, tax revenues, and budget surpluses or deficits? Second, should the government use discretionary fiscal policy to try to stabilize the economy, or should fiscal policy be guided by formal rules? What kinds of fiscal policy rules, if any, are appropriate? For example, should a rule, perhaps encoded in a constitutional amendment, require the government to balance its budget each year or to limit its taxation, its debt, or its spending?

The previous chapter discussed activist and laissez-faire views of monetary policy. Those categories also apply to fiscal policy. Economists who hold a laissez-faire view of fiscal policy tend to favor a smaller role for government spending and taxes than those who hold an activist view. Proponents of a laissez-faire view generally favor low levels of government spending and low tax rates, and they usually believe that the government should base spending and tax rates only on the merits of the programs involved and not on efforts to stabilize real GDP. Some proponents of the laissez-faire view, but not all, favor formal rules for fiscal policy, such as a balanced-budget rule or a limit on government spending as a fraction of GDP.

Proponents of an activist view of fiscal policy generally favor higher levels of government spending and higher tax rates, particularly on people with relatively high incomes. They also tend to believe that the government should vary its total spending and tax rates to try to stabilize real GDP and unemployment by offsetting, at least somewhat, other changes in aggregate demand. Most activists favor discretionary fiscal policies in addition to the automatic stabilizers discussed earlier.

Rules versus Discretion in Fiscal Policy

The three main arguments for fiscal policy rules echo the arguments for monetary policy rules:

1. Two kinds of lags complicate fiscal policies—lags in implementing policies (actual changes in tax rates or government spending) and lags in the effects of fiscal policies on the economy.[22] These lags make it difficult to improve economic performance with discretionary fiscal policy.

2. Economists and the government lack sufficient information about the economy to conduct good discretionary fiscal policy. They lack relevant information about both underlying economic conditions (including current and near-future conditions) and the likely effects of fiscal policies.

3. Credible rules for fiscal policy can improve economic performance by changing people's incentives.[23] Credible policy rules affect incentives and behavior in ways that discretionary policy cannot; rules can improve economic performance as compared to even the best discretionary policies.

The main argument for discretionary fiscal policy criticizes the inflexibility of rules. New situations might arise that call for new policy actions, and policy rules might prevent the best actions in certain situations. For example, the sticky-price model of aggregate supply

---

[22]In fact, implementing a change in fiscal policy usually takes longer than implementing a change in monetary policy.
[23]See the example of high taxes on capital in the previous chapter.

and aggregate demand from earlier chapters implies that the government can help to fight a recession by raising spending and reducing taxes, which would increase private consumption and investment spending. A policy rule that requires the government to balance its budget might prevent these actions. Because no policy rule can take into account all situations that might arise in the future, any policy rule might limit the ability of policy makers to choose the best actions in the future.

Connections between Fiscal and Monetary Policy

Some countries' governments require their central banks to print whatever money their governments need to finance budget deficits. In the United States, however, the Federal Reserve chooses monetary policy (subject to political pressures) without a requirement to finance budget deficits. The U.S. government must borrow money (sell bonds) to finance its budget deficit. It cannot directly force the Fed to print more money.

Fiscal policy can still affect monetary policy in several ways, though. For example, a government budget deficit may raise expectations of future inflation. This change raises the current nominal interest rate and velocity of money, which raises the equilibrium price level, creating temporary inflation. The new conditions may also change the incentives of the Federal Reserve. High levels of government debt may raise the incentive to create inflation to reduce the real value of this debt. High levels of debt and high budget deficits may raise political pressures on the Fed to increase the growth rate of the money supply.

Commitment and Policy Credibility

Fiscal policy, like monetary policy, can be discretionary or subject to rules. The government has had difficulty committing to policy rules in the past, though. For example, Congress passed a law in the 1980s that required a balanced budget (or surplus) by the year 1991. However, when the time came for lower deficits, the government exploited loopholes that allowed deficits to continue. Eventually, Congress changed the law and continued running deficits. Some people proposed a constitutional amendment to require a balanced government budget, arguing that such a rule is easier to enforce than a law that Congress can repeal by majority vote. When Congress voted down such an amendment in 1995, some opponents argued that it would remove the flexibility of discretionary fiscal policy, prohibiting the government from running deficits during recessions to raise aggregate demand. Others argued that enforcement of such a rule would ultimately prove an impossible task. Ultimately, the government eliminated its budget deficit (by the standard measure) in 1998. The government achieved this goal through a combination of reductions in the rate of growth of government spending, particularly military spending, and increases in tax revenue resulting from rapid growth in real GDP in the 1990s.

Fiscal policies can affect long-run economic growth by changing national savings.

FISCAL POLICIES AND ECONOMIC GROWTH

> **National savings** equals private savings plus government savings.

The government saves when it has a budget surplus; a budget deficit amounts to negative savings. Private savings equals disposable income (income after taxes, $y - T$) minus consumption spending (C). For the country as a whole, income is GDP, so disposable income is GDP minus taxes. This gives private savings as:

$$\text{Private savings} = y - T - C$$

Government savings equals the budget surplus, or tax revenue minus government spending, $T - G$. Adding private savings and government savings gives national savings:

$$\text{National savings} = (y - T - C) + (T - G)$$

$$= y - G - C$$

Chapter 5 explained that:

$$y = C + I + G + NEX$$

where NEX is net exports, which equals domestic lending to people in foreign countries. Subtracting G and C from both sides shows that national savings equals investment plus net exports:

$$\text{National savings} = I + NEX$$

This equation shows two uses for national savings:

1. Investment in the nation's economy (I)

2. Lending (investing) in foreign countries (NEX).

Investment in the nation's economy adds to its future capital stock and production, so it adds to economic growth. Investment in foreign economies (NEX) adds to the nation's future income, as foreigners pay interest or dividends on the investments. (It also adds to the foreign capital stock and promotes world economic growth.)

Deficits and National Savings

Many economists blamed government budget deficits for low rates of saving in the United States in the last quarter of the 20th century. To see why, suppose that the government cuts taxes by $100 per person without changing its spending. The government budget deficit rises by $100 per person, reducing national savings by that amount. If people save all the money they receive from the tax cut, then national savings, rises back to its original level. However, if people spend at least part of the money they receive from this tax cut, national savings falls. Because savings is essential for long-run economic growth, budget deficits could reduce growth.

Figure 14 shows national savings in the United States as a percentage of people's after-tax income. Despite reductions in the government budget deficit in recent years, the U.S. savings rate has continued its two-decade fall. Clearly, many other factors besides the government budget affect savings.

The social security program, like government budget deficits, reduces national savings. People expect to receive social security payments when they retire, so they save less than they would without the social security system. Therefore, this system reduces private savings. If the government were to save all of the money that people pay in social security taxes, then this increase in government savings would offset a fall in private savings, and the social security system would not affect national savings. (People would save less, but the government would save more.) However, the government has operated social security as a pay-as-you-go system rather than saving revenue from social security taxes. Consequently, most economists believe it has reduced overall national savings and long-run economic growth.

Current tax policies also discourage saving, and some economists favor policy changes that would reduce or eliminate the negative effects of taxes on saving. One proposal would replace the income tax with a consumption tax. This change would free people from paying income tax on money they save; government would tax only money they spend.

Figure 14 | Savings as a Percentage of Income in the United States

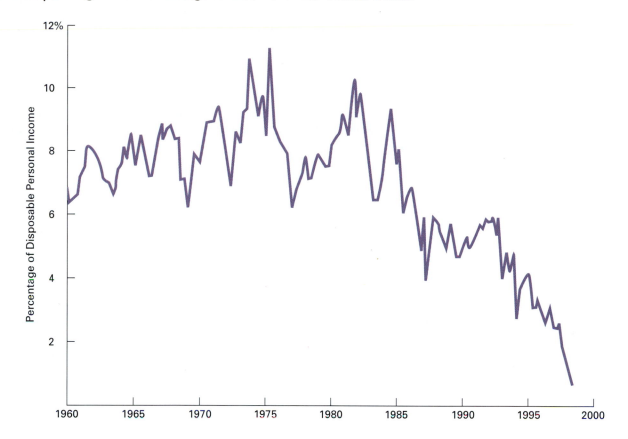

Many economists believe that a consumption tax would be more economically efficient than an income tax and, by encouraging savings, would raise long-run economic growth. Other proposals create various tax incentives for certain types of saving.

Taxes and Aggregate Supply

Some economists argue that the most important effects of taxes work on aggregate supply rather than aggregate demand. They argue that high taxes reduce savings, investment, and long-run economic growth. According to this view, a tax cut raises economic growth, even if the government does not reduce spending, that is, even if the tax cut raises the budget deficit. A reduction in marginal tax rates can raise aggregate supply by raising the incentive to work. It can also raise future aggregate supply by raising the incentives to save and invest, by raising the expected after-tax returns from investments.

Incentives and Rent Seeking

Some economists argue that discretionary fiscal policies reduce long-run economic growth in other ways. Discretionary changes in taxes create uncertainty, which reduces investment in physical and human capital, and slows technical progress by reducing investment in research and development. Discretionary changes in government spending can also create economic inefficiencies if the government spending is not justified solely by its own costs and benefits. According to this argument, government should choose its level of spending on each program (schools, roads, defense, and so on) based on those costs and benefits, and avoid spending more or less than this level in attempts to stabilize aggregate demand.

Discretionary government policies also reduce economic efficiency by encouraging *rent seeking*.

> **Rent seeking** is the use of time, money, and other resources to try to get government benefits (spending, tax changes, or regulations targeted to some special-interest group).

Rent seeking results from the very *possibility* that the government will take discretionary policy actions with benefits or harm to various special groups. Rent seeking is economically inefficient, because the resources devoted to rent seeking have an opportunity cost: they could be used to *produce* goods and services rather than redistributing them. Investing those resources in physical capital, human capital, or research and development would raise real GDP, raising the size of the economic pie rather than funding the fight about its division. Could credible policy rules reduce rent seeking? How could the government credibly commit to policy rules? Would such rules create inefficiencies by limiting policy flexibility? These are some of the fundamental issues of fiscal policy that will underlie the more immediate issues of taxes, spending, government debt, and social security reform in the coming years.

Review Questions

18. Cite arguments for rules to govern fiscal policy. Cite arguments for discretion.

19. Explain why government budget deficits may reduce national savings.

20. Explain why the social security system may reduce national savings.

21. What is rent seeking and why is it economically inefficient?

Thinking Exercise

22. Explain how the following fiscal policies may affect long-run economic growth:
  (a) An increase in government purchases for national defense, financed through an increase in income taxes
  (b) An increase in social security taxes to meet future obligations to pay social security benefits
  (c) A cut in income taxes, financed by an increase in government borrowing

Conclusion

The Government Budget in the United States

Fiscal policy refers to government actions that affect total government spending, tax rates and revenues, and the government budget deficit or surplus. Total government spending and tax payments in the United States amount to about one-third of GDP. The government runs a budget surplus when it collects more tax revenue than it spends. It runs a budget deficit when it spends more than it collects in tax revenue. It has a balanced budget when its tax revenue equals its spending. The government debt (national debt) equals the amount of money the government currently owes due to its past borrowing. A government budget deficit increases the government debt as the government borrows more money. A government budget surplus reduces the debt as government repays part of it.

Effects of Fiscal Policy: Changes in Government Spending

Transfer payments redistribute income, and affect the economy in two ways. First, people differ in their spending decisions, so redistribution may change the composition of spending, as well as aggregate demand. Second, transfer payments, (and the taxes to finance them) affect incentives, altering aggregate supply.

The effects of government purchases of goods and services depend on what the government buys. If government purchases substitute well for private spending, then changes in government purchases have little effect on aggregate demand, as in the lunch-program example. If, however, government purchases substitute poorly for private spending, then increases in government purchases raise aggregate demand, as in the defense spending example. Government spending may enhance productivity and raise aggregate supply when it does not substitute closely for similar, private spending.

Changes in taxes to finance changes in government purchases also affect the economy. A tax cut may raise or reduce equilibrium employment and real GDP, depending on how workers respond to an increase in after-tax wages. The government also affects the economy by its decision to run budget surpluses or deficits. These decisions involve choices about the time path of taxes. The government can raise economic efficiency by preventing unnecessary variations in taxes over time. However, the government can try to stabilize real GDP with fiscal policy by cutting taxes below their long-run average level when real GDP falls and raising taxes above their long-run average level when real GDP rises. Automatic stabilizers function by making these changes without direct action by the government.

Measuring Government Debt, Deficits, and Surpluses

The standard measures of government debt and the budget deficit are misleading. First, the government owes some of its debt to itself. The measure of *privately held* government debt corrects this problem. Second, the official statistics on government debt omit two large liabilities: future pensions for government employees, and social security payments that the government has promised to pay in the future. Controversies surround the measurement of the government's debt and deficit.

Social security presents two problems. The overall government surplus that emerged in 1998 includes the current social security surplus. When the current social security surplus turns into a deficit within the next 20 years, the overall government budget surplus will turn into an overall deficit. Second, the discounted present value of expected future social security taxes is less than the discounted present value of promised benefit payments, requiring either an increase in taxes or a reduction in benefits.

Fundamental Issues of Fiscal Policy

Fundamental issues of fiscal policy involve the proper roles of government spending and taxes, the optimal size of government, and issues of whether government policies should be guided by rules or discretion. The activist and laissez-faire views of monetary policy also apply to fiscal policy. Other basic issues include the effects of fiscal policy on national savings and long-run economic growth, and on inefficiencies from rent seeking.

Key Terms

fiscal policy	balanced budget	privately held government debt
budget surplus	government debt	national savings
budget deficit	automatic stabilizer	rent seeking

Questions and Problems

23. Suppose that Congress decides to build a giant pyramid in Washington, D.C., as a way to provide jobs for construction workers and stimulate the economy. Assume also that the government raises personal income taxes to pay for the additional spending. How is this project likely to affect total employment? How will it affect employment in different industries, real GDP, and the price level?

24. Summarize the effects on aggregate demand and supply of:
    (a) An increase in government spending financed by increased taxes

    (b) An increase in government spending financed by government borrowing

25. Explain the argument that the government's budget deficit or surplus is poorly measured and nearly meaningless.

26. Discuss this statement: "Large government budget deficits raise interest rates. To keep interest rates from rising, a country with rising budget deficits should loosen monetary policy." In your answer, distinguish between real and nominal interest rates, and between the short run and the long run.

27. Discuss this statement: "The government could reduce unemployment to almost zero by guaranteeing a government job to anyone who is unemployed. The people could work to clean up city streets and national parks and do other useful tasks, and everyone would benefit."

28. How are increases in government budget surpluses likely to affect:

    (a) Aggregate demand and supply?

    (b) Real GDP and employment in the short run?

    (c) Long-run economic growth?

Inquiries for Further Thought

29. Look on the Internet or in a library for information on the government budget and the economy over the last decade. Using this information, discuss (in as much detail as possible) the factors that caused the government budget deficit to vanish and turn into a surplus.

30. If the government continues to run a budget surplus (by the usual measure), what should it do with that surplus?

31. Should the government change the social security program? If so, how? If not, how should it deal with future deficits in that program?

32. Should the government exercise discretionary fiscal policy? What principles should guide the government's fiscal policy? Why?

33. What economic effects would result if the government repaid the national debt? Should it?

34. What, if anything, could the government do to reduce economic inefficiencies from rent seeking?

PART 8

ADVANCED
TOPICS IN
MACROECONOMICS

Chapter 15
Financial Markets

Chapter 16
International Trade

FINANCIAL MARKETS

In this Chapter...

Main Points to Understand

- Financial assets play important roles in allocating resources, sharing risk, and creating incentives.
- Diversification helps reduce risk.
- Stocks are shares of ownership in firms. Bonds are I.O.U.s for loans to the government or to business firms.
- Economies create many kinds of financial assets to help allocate resources and share risks.
- You can read and understand financial information in newspapers and on the Internet.

Thinking Skills to Develop

- Interpret and understand financial data.
- Understand risk and how diversification reduces risk.
- Understand the logic of equilibrium prices in financial markets and why the logic implies that stock prices follow (approximate) random walks.

Every day, television news reports, newspapers, and business magazines are filled with news about stock markets and other financial markets. Despite all this information, financial markets mystify most people. This chapter provides the basic knowledge necessary to understand these news reports and to construct informed opinions about financial matters. You can refer back to this chapter to find the background you will need for your personal and business decisions in the future.

Earlier chapters have explained how asset markets play important roles in macroeconomics. The loans market played a key role in the basic macroeconomic model developed in Chapters 6–7. Chapter 9 discussed exchange rates and their connections with inflation. Chapter 10 discussed the dual role of financial intermediaries in the money market and loans market and the problems created by that dual role. Chapter 12 discussed the role of the loans market in some recent recessions, and Chapter 13 explained how financial markets and interest rates play key roles in monetary policy

Financial markets are sets of formal or informal trading arrangements for *financial assets*.

FINANCIAL ASSETS AND MARKETS

> A **financial asset** is a right to collect some series of payments in the future.

> The **rate of return** on a financial asset is the income the owner receives from the asset over some period of time, plus the increase in its value during that period, all as a percentage of the original value of the asset:
>
> $$\text{Rate of return} = \frac{\text{Interest (or other) payments} + \text{Increase in asset price}}{\text{Beginning-of-period asset price}}$$

Suppose that General Television stock sells for $50 in October 1999 and for $52 one year later. Also suppose that each share of stock pays its owner $1 in dividends during that year. The rate of return on this stock is:

$$\text{Rate of return} = \frac{\$1 + (\$52 - \$50)}{\$50} = \frac{\$3}{\$50} = \frac{\$6}{\$100} = 6 \text{ percent per year}$$

Many types of assets are traded on financial markets. The most common are debt and equity.

> Debt is a borrower's promise to pay.

When you borrow money, you incur a debt. Similarly, a business firm or government unit incurs a debt when it borrows money. Debt is the borrower's promise to repay a loan; it is an IOU. People can buy and sell these IOUs on financial markets. Trade in debt refers to buying and selling the rights to collect money that borrowers will repay. Government bonds, corporate bonds, and Treasury bills are types of debt traded on financial markets.

> Equities (shares of stock) represent legal rights of ownership to part of a firm.

A firm's stockholders own that firm. They own its assets and liabilities, including its equipment and buildings, and legal rights to its brand names. They must pay its debts and meet its other legal obligations. A corporation's stockholders have *limited liability*, however, meaning that they cannot lose more than the value of their stock. (They cannot be required to pay a firm's debts out of their own personal funds.) A firm's stockholders choose its board of directors, who choose the firm's top management. If you own some shares of stock, you can take part in the stockholder votes through which these decisions are made.

Other common types of financial assets include futures contracts and options.

> Futures contracts are agreements to buy or sell goods at some future date at a price set today.

You might buy 5,000 bushels of corn or 5,000 shares of General Motors stock to be delivered and paid for next July, at a price set today.

> Options are legal rights, but not obligations, to buy or sell a certain amount of goods or assets in the future at a price set today.

The term *option* refers to the choice that such a contract gives to its owner. Suppose that you own an option to buy 100 shares of American Express stock at a price of $25 per share some time within the next 4 months. You can choose whether to buy that stock at the preset price of $25. Similarly, if you own an option to sell 500 shares of Xerox stock at a price of $50 per share some time within the next 2 months, you can choose whether or not to sell at that price. When people buy and sell options, they trade these rights to buy or sell at preset prices.

These assets change hands in two kinds of markets. Primary markets handle transactions where issuers sell financial assets for the first time, as when a firm issues new stock or new bonds to accumulate money to fund some investment. In secondary markets, investors (people or firms) buy and resell previously issued assets. Most financial-market trades occur on secondary markets such as the New York Stock Exchange.

Functions of Financial Markets

Financial markets promote economic efficiency in several ways. The most basic function of financial markets is to allow people to trade current goods for future goods by lending, and to trade future goods for current goods by borrowing. Financial markets allow people to borrow money to buy houses or cars, to invest in new capital, to modernize factories or start new businesses, and to finance development of new products.

Financial markets also pool resources: they allow thousands of people to pool small amounts of savings into one large sum of money to lend, giving them the highest possible return on their savings.

Financial markets allow people to reduce risks. Just as a person buys fire insurance to reduce the risk of losses in a fire, financial markets allow people to trade risks so as to reduce each person's total risk through *diversification*. People can gain from trading risks just as they gain from trading their labor services in the basic gains-from-trade examples of Chapters 1 and 3.

Financial markets help to channel the economy's resources into their most valuable uses. Chapter 7 explained how Adam Smith's metaphor of the "invisible hand" applies to the loan market as it guides the economy's response to "now or later" choices of consumers. When current resources become more valuable relative to future resources, financial markets respond with a higher interest rate, which gives consumers incentives to conserve current resources by saving and lending. Similarly, financial markets guide business firms as they judge whether to undertake risky investments: prices of financial assets reflect the willingness of savers to accept risks, and they provide incentives to businesses to undertake only the risks that consumers find worthwhile.

Because financial markets play critical roles in the economy's decisions about undertaking investments in new capital, and allocating risks, financial markets are essential for any modern economy. They are also critical for economic development of poor countries. As the 1997–1998 experiences of many Asian countries illustrate, problems in financial markets can rebound throughout the economy and may contribute to inflation and recessions.

The future is uncertain, so people's future plans rely on their *expectations*.

RISK AND INSURANCE

Expectations

An expectation is a guess about the future. A rational guess (or rational expectation) about some future variable, such as the score of a future ball game or the future price of a financial asset, is its expected value.

> The **expected value** of a variable is an average of every possible value for that variable, weighted by the chance of that value occurring.

The expected value is also called the *mean*. You can calculate an expected value in three steps:

1. Write down each possible value of the variable.

2. Multiply each value by its chance of occurring.

3. Add the answers from Step 2.

EXAMPLE 1

Suppose that you estimate a one-half chance that the rate of return on an investment will be 5 percent and a one-half chance that it will be 15 percent. The expected value of the rate of return (or the expected return, for short) is:

$$(1/2)(5\%) + (1/2)(15\%) = 10 \text{ percent}$$

EXAMPLE 2

Suppose that you lend someone $100. You estimate a 95 percent chance that the borrower will repay the loan and a 5 percent chance of default. Your expected payback is:

$$(95/100)(\$100) + (5/100)(\$0) = \$95$$

EXAMPLE 3

Suppose that you lend someone $100 for 1 year and charge 10 percent interest. The borrower owes you $110 at the end of the year. Suppose the chance that the borrower will repay you is 95 percent, and the chance that the borrower will *default* on the loan (fail to repay) is 5 percent. As a result, your expected payback is:

$$(95/100)(\$110) + (5/100)(\$0) = \$104.50$$

Notice that this loan has the same expected payback as a loan with 4½ percent interest and *no* chance of default.

Risk

Uncertainty about the future creates risks. A situation is risky for you when several things could happen, and some are better for you than others. The amount of risk you face depends on how much better or worse some of these possible outcomes are. Economists have developed a formal mathematical model of risk, but the basic ideas can be understood with examples. These examples introduce important ideas, and later discussions will refer back to them.

EXAMPLE 4

If you know for sure that your income next year will be $20,000, then your income is not risky. However, if you face a one-half chance that you will earn $30,000 and a one-half chance that you will earn $10,000, you have a risky income. If you face a one-half chance of earning $40,000 and a one-half chance of earning zero, you have an even riskier income. Notice that your expected income is the same in all three cases.

EXAMPLE 5 (PORTFOLIO RISK 1)

Suppose that you bet $10 that Team A will win a football game. If Team A wins, you win $10; if Team B wins, you lose $10. (If they tie, the bet is canceled.) The bet creates risky income. If you *also* bet $10 on Team B to win, then you can be sure of winning one bet and losing the other. Your betting income is no longer risky; you have hedged your bets. Although no sports fan would place opposing bets like this, the example shows how combining two risky investments (or bets) can reduce overall risk (to zero, in this case).

EXAMPLE 6 (PORTFOLIO RISK 2)

Larry lends someone $100 for 1 year and charges 10 percent interest. The chance that the borrower will repay Larry is 95 percent, and the chance of default is 5 percent. As a result, Larry's expected payback is $104.50 (as in Example 3).

Barb also has $100 to lend, but she lends $1 at 10 percent interest to each of 100 different people. Each loan has a 5 percent chance of default. Also, the chance that any one borrower will default is unrelated to whether any other borrowers default. Because Barb lends to a large number of separate borrowers, and each has a 5 percent chance of default, about 95 of the borrowers will repay their loans (each paying Barb $1.10) and about 5 of them will default. As a result, Barb will almost certainly collect about $104.50. Her expected payoff is the same as Larry's, but her risk is lower than Larry's. (Larry will either collect $110 or collect nothing at all.) Barb faces less risk because she *diversified* her loans. Diversification means spreading risks over many separate investments rather than "putting all your eggs in one basket" as Larry did. This example shows how diversification can reduce risk.

EXAMPLE 7 (PORTFOLIO RISK 3)

You have $100 to lend for 1 year at 10 percent interest. You could lend it all to Dave, who will repay the loan next year unless he loses his job making Silly Putty. There is a 5 percent chance that a new firm, Crazy Putty, will cut into Silly Putty's sales. If that happens, Dave will lose his job and he will default on the loan. Therefore, if you lend $100 to Dave, you have a 95 percent of collecting $110 next year and a 5 percent chance of collecting nothing.

Alternatively, you could lend $50 to Dave and $50 to Jay, who works for Crazy Putty. With these loans, you face three possible outcomes:

1. You take a 5 percent chance that Crazy Putty will put Silly Putty out of business. In this case, Dave will lose his job and default on the loan, but Jay will keep his job and repay the loan. You collect $55 from Jay and nothing from Dave.

2. You take a 5 percent chance that Crazy Putty will fail and go out of business. In this case, Dave will keep his job and repay the loan, but Jay will lose his job and default on the loan. You collect $55 from Dave and nothing from Jay.

3. You face a 90 percent chance that Crazy Putty will succeed but Silly Putty will remain in business. In this case, *both* David and Jay will repay their loans, so you collect $55 from each, for a total of $110.

You reduce your risk by lending to Dave *and* Jay rather than lending only to one of them. If you lend only to one, you face a 95 percent chance that you will collect $110 and a 5 percent chance that you will collect nothing. However, if you lend to both, you face a 90 percent chance of collecting $110 and a 10 percent chance of collecting $55. You have the same expected payback of $104.50 in either case, but a lower risk with two borrowers instead of one. Like the football-bet example, this example shows how you can reduce risk by choosing investments (bets or loans) that move out of step with each other. You can reduce your risk by choosing combinations of investments so that *some* investments have high payoffs in situations where others have low payoffs.

Diversification

The previous examples show how people can reduce the risks of their investments by diversifying.

> **Diversification** refers to the practice of spreading risks by choosing many unrelated investments or investments whose payoffs are out of step.[1]

Diversification restates the old adage, "Don't put all your eggs in one basket." This is good advice for reducing investment risk.

Insurance

Insurance is an investment specifically designed to move out of step with other investments. If you buy insurance against auto theft, the insurance company pays you only if you are robbed. If you are robbed, your investment in a car has a low payoff (because the robber takes it). However, your payoff from insurance is high in this case. On the other hand, if you are not robbed, your payoff from the car is higher but your payoff from insurance is low. In other words, your payoffs from investments in the car and in insurance move *out of step*. In the same way, you can insure against losing a bet on a football game by making another bet on the opposing team, as in Example 5. While a person who bets on a football game would not want this insurance, the logic applies to the more common situations in which people want to avoid risk through some form of insurance or diversification.[2] In Example 7, by lending money to Jay, you can partially insure against the chance that Dave will default.

Risk Aversion

People tend to be risk averse in most real-life situations.

> A **risk averse** person prefers less risk to more risk.

> A **risk neutral** person does not care about risk, only about expected return.[3]

People are usually willing to pay to reduce risk; they accept comparatively low expected returns on investments with correspondingly low risk. Risk averse people buy insurance

---

[1] In technical terms, the payoffs are negatively correlated with one another.
[2] Most people do want this insurance, so they choose not to bet on the game.
[3] A person who likes risk is said to be a *risk preferrer*.

and diversify their investments. Later sections will show that risky financial assets have higher expected returns than less risky assets; the risky assets must pay higher expected returns to get anyone to buy them.

Review Questions

1. What is a financial asset? What is its rate of return?

2. What are debts? Equities? Futures contracts? Options?

Thinking Exercises

3. If a stock price has a 4/10 chance of being at $5 next year, a 1/2 chance of being at $10, and a 1/10 chance of being at $80, what is the expected value of the stock price?

4. What is diversification? Explain how combining two risky investments can reduce overall risk.

Debt is a borrower's promise to repay a loan. When a business firm borrows money from you for 20 years, it gives you a security or I.O.U.—a written promise to repay the loan when the debt *matures* after 20 years. Before the debt matures, you can sell it to another buyer on a *secondary market*. Buying and selling debt means buying and selling the right to collect repayment on a loan.

DEBT INSTRUMENTS: BOND MARKETS AND MONEY MARKETS

Bond Markets

> A **bond** is long-term debt security, typically a loan lasting 10 years or more.

Corporate bonds are issued by corporations, government bonds by the federal government, and municipal bonds by state and local governments.[4]

Most bonds pledge to make interest payments each year called *coupon payments*.

> **Coupon payments** are payments of interest that borrowers make to bondholders.

Suppose that Walt Disney Corporation borrows money for 10 years by issuing and selling a $10,000 bond. If you pay $8,000 for the bond, you lend $8,000 to Disney for 10 years and earn $2,000 in interest when Disney repays the loan. The bond's *face value*—the money that Disney will repay in 10 years—is $10,000. The bond may also carry 5 percent coupons, which means that Disney pays you $500 every year (5 percent of $10,000). You receive these coupon payments in addition to the $10,000 repayment of the debt when the bond matures after 10 years. Some bonds, called *zero-coupon bonds*, have no coupons; they pay bondholders only at maturity.

---

[4]You may be familiar with bond issues for public schools. A vote of the community is usually required to allow a school system to borrow money by issuing bonds.

Markets for Short-Term Loans

Many kinds of short-term financial assets are available to investors. The government borrows money for several months by selling I.O.U.s called *Treasury bills,* and for longer periods by selling Treasury notes.

> **Treasury bills** (or **T-bills**) are short-term debt securities issued by the government, mostly for 3-month and 6-month loans. **Treasury notes** are similar I.O.U.s for loans of 1 year to 10 years.

A business firm can borrow money for a short period by issuing commercial paper.

> **Commercial paper** is short-term debt security (usually with a 30-day maturity) issued by a private firm.

Markets for loans of 1 year or less are sometimes called *money markets.* To simplify the discussion, the term *bond* will include these short-term assets as well as long-term assets for the remainder of this chapter.

Default Risk

The examples detailed earlier illustrated the risk of default on a loan.

> A borrower who fails to repay a loan in full **defaults.**

Note that a borrower can default by repaying some, but not all, of the loan.

The risk of default affects interest rates. Lenders demand higher interest rates to borrowers with higher chances of defaulting to compensate for that risk.

> The **risk-free interest rate** is the interest rate on a loan with no chance of default.

The interest rate on a risky loan includes a risk premium.

> A **risk premium** is an extra payment that compensates investors for risk.

The interest rate on a risky loan is the sum of the risk-free rate and a risk premium:

$$\text{Interest rate on a risky loan} = \text{Risk-free interest rate} + \text{Risk premium}$$

Riskier assets pay higher risk premiums. An increase in the risk of an asset raises its risk premium. By trading risky assets, people can buy and sell risks in financial markets. The equilibrium of supply and demand in the market for risk determines the equilibrium risk premium.

EXAMPLE

Earlier, Example 3 considered a $100 loan at 10 percent interest to someone with a 5 percent chance of defaulting. In that example, the expected payback on the loan was $104.50, giving an expected rate of return on the loan of 4½ percent per year.

Suppose that a safe borrower (one who will not default) is willing to pay you 4½ percent interest for a 1-year, $100 loan. Another person, who has a 5 percent chance of defaulting on a loan, also wants to borrow $100 from you for 1 year. If you were risk neutral (caring only about the expected return on your investment), you would be indifferent between lending to the safe borrower at 4½ percent interest and lending to the risky borrower at a 10 percent interest rate. If the equilibrium interest rate on safe loans is 4½ percent per year, then the equilibrium interest rate on loans with a 5 percent chance of default is 10 percent per year.[5] This example shows that even a risk-neutral lender charges higher interest rates to riskier borrowers. Because most lenders are risk averse, risk premiums and risky bonds pay even higher interest rates than this example indicates.

Bond Prices and Yields to Maturity

The price of a bond is the discounted present value (DPV) of its expected payments. An increase in the interest rate reduces the DPV of expected future payments, decreasing the price of bonds. For example, if the interest rate is 5 percent per year, the DPV of the $100 to be paid 1 year from now is $100/1.05, or $95.24. If the interest rate rises to 10 percent per year, the DPV falls to $100/1.10, or $90.91. For a bond with no chance of default, investors use the risk-free interest rate to calculate discounted present value. For a bond with a chance of default, investors use a higher interest rate to compensate for that chance.

EXAMPLES[6]

Example 1
A typical Treasury bill pays $10,000 after 3 months. (It makes no coupon payments.) If you pay $9,750 for this T-bill, you loan the government $9,750. When the T-bill matures in 3 months, it pays $10,000, so you get (roughly) a 2½ percent interest rate on the loan. This rate equals roughly a 10 percent annualized (per year) return on your investment, because you could reinvest your money in this way four times during 1 year, earning 2½ percent each time, for a total return of about 10 percent.[7] The equilibrium price of the T-bill is $9,750 if (and only if) the equilibrium nominal annual interest rate on T-bills is about 10 percent.

Example 2
Suppose that the nominal interest rate is 8 percent per year and people expect it to remain constant in the future. The price of a 20-year, $1,000 zero-coupon bond is $215, because the discounted present value of $1,000 to be paid 20 years in the future is:

$$\$1,000/(1 + i)^{20}$$

This equals (about) $215 if i is 0.08 (8 percent) per year.

Example 3
The price of a 20-year, $1,000 bond with 5 percent (or $50) annual interest (coupon) payment is:

$$\frac{\$50}{1 + i} + \frac{\$50}{(1 + i)^2} + \frac{\$50}{(1 + i)^3} + \ldots + \frac{\$50}{(1 + i)^{20}} + \frac{\$1,000}{(1 + i)^{20}}$$

This series sums to about $705 if the nominal interest rate is 8 percent per year.

---

[5]If the interest rate on these risky loans were lower than 10 percent, no one would lend to the risky borrowers. If the interest rate on these risky loans were higher than 10 percent, all lenders would try to lend to the risky borrowers instead of the safe borrowers, and this competition would drive the interest rate down to 10 percent.

[6]Many assets have features that complicate these calculations. For example, corporate bonds typically pay interest twice per year rather than once.

[7]This figure is not exact because it ignores compound interest, or interest earned on earlier interest income.

Holding Period Yields and Capital Gains

Another important measure of the rate of return on a bond is its holding period yield.

> The **holding period yield** on a bond is the rate of return it would provide over some specified period of time (perhaps less than the time until the bond matures).

EXAMPLE

Suppose that an asset pays $10 in interest in June 2002 and $110 when it matures in June 2003. Suppose the interest rate is 10 percent per year and there is no risk of default. The price of the asset in June 2001 equals the discounted present value, at that date, of its future payments:

$$\$10/1.10 + \$110/1.10^2 = \$100$$

so the price of the asset is $100 in June 2001.

Now suppose that the interest rate unexpectedly falls in June 2002 to 5 percent per year. The price of the asset in June 2002 equals the discounted present value, at that date, of its future payments:

$$\$110.00/1.05 = \$104.76$$

so the price of the asset in June 2002 is $104.76. The increase in the value of this asset, from $100.00 in June 2001 to $104.76 in June 2002, is called a *capital gain*.

> A **capital gain** (or **capital loss**) is an increase (or decrease) in the value of an asset.

If you bought the asset for $100 in June 2001, then you gain $14.76 in June 2002: you collect $10.00 in interest and you obtain $4.76 in capital gains because the value of your asset rises by that amount. You collect that $4.76 in cash if you *realize* your capital gain by selling the asset. Whether or not you sell the asset, your wealth rises by $14.76, and your holding period yield from 2001 to 2002 is:

$$\frac{\$14.76}{\$100.00} = 0.1476 = 14.76 \text{ percent per year}$$

Bonds generate capital gains when their prices rise. Bond prices can rise for two reasons. First, the price of a bond rises as its maturity date gets closer. An earlier example showed the price of a zero-coupon bond, 20 years before maturity when it pays $1,000, was about $215 (given an 8 percent annual interest rate). The bond price rises over time as the maturity date gets closer. Five years before the bond's maturity, its price would be:

$$\$1,000/(1 + i)^5$$

This amount equals about $681 if the interest rate remains at 8 percent per year. Therefore the bond generates a capital gain of $466 ($681 minus $215) over its first 15 years.

Changes in interest rates also affect bond prices. The previous example showed that the price of a bond rises—giving the bondholder a capital gain—if the nominal interest rate falls. An interest rate increase raises the denominator in the formula for discounted present value, reducing bond prices because those prices are the discounted present values of the future payments that bonds provide to their owners.

Default Risk and Yields

Debt securities issued by the U.S. federal government are almost completely safe from default. In contrast, all private firms have some chance of going bankrupt and defaulting on their debt, or *partially* defaulting by failing to repay full amounts on time while avoiding bankruptcy in a legal sense. Some governments also have chances of defaulting (or partially defaulting) on their bonds. For example, in 1998, the government of Russia failed to make payments on some of its bonds.

Two private firms, Standard & Poor's Corporation and Moody's Investors Services, Inc., rate bonds based on their chances of default. The best bonds, rated AAA or Aaa, have the lowest chances of default, followed by bonds rated AA or Aa, A, BBB or Baa, and so on, down to C (the riskiest bonds). Because of these risk differences, yields to maturity on Baa bonds exceed yields on Aaa bonds, which exceed yields on government bonds. The differences reflect increasing risks of default. While bonds rated below Baa often carry the pejorative label *junk bonds*, they provide an important source of finance for many small, startup firms. The long-distance telephone company, MCI, for example, was initially financed with junk bonds.[8]

Term Structure of Interest Rates

The term structure of interest rates is the relationship between interest rates on short-term loans and those on longer-term loans. Long-term interest rates are averages of the many short-term interest rates that people expect during the period of the long-term loan.

EXAMPLE

Suppose that you want to borrow $100 for 2 years. You could borrow $100 for 1 year, and then take out another 1-year loan next year to pay off the first loan. Suppose you can borrow $100 now for 1 year at an interest rate of 8 percent per year, so you will owe $108 at the end of the year. Suppose also that you believe you can borrow $108 next year for 1 year at an interest rate of 12 percent. You can use this $108 to pay off the first loan, then after 2 years you will owe $120.96 (= $108.00 plus 12 percent interest on that amount, which is $15.96).

As an alternative, you can take out a 2-year loan now. If the interest rate on a 2-year loan is 9.9818 percent per year, then at the end of 2 years you will owe:

$$(\$100)(1 + 0.099818)^2 = \$120.96$$

At this interest rate, you would owe the same amount at the end of 2 years whether you (a) take out a 1-year loan now, then take out another 1-year loan a year from now, or (b) take out a 2-year loan now. If the interest rate on 2-year loans were lower than 9.9818 percent per year, people would try to make a profit by borrowing for 2 years and lending the money for 1 year now and lending the proceeds again next year for 1 year. This activity would raise the demand for 2-year loans, and the interest rate on these loans would also rise. If the interest rate on 2-year loans were higher than 9.9818 percent per year, people would try to make a profit by borrowing now for 1 year and lending the money for 2 years, borrowing again next year to repay the first loan. This activity would

---

[8]Before the 1980s, firms encountered difficulty selling bonds rated below Baa. (In language to be discussed later in this chapter, investment banks would not underwrite bonds rated below Baa.) In 1977, Michael Milken of the firm Drexel Burnham Lambert (later sentenced to prison for violating certain federal laws governing financial markets) started helping firms to sell junk bonds by helping them to find buyers, that is, lenders willing to accept high chances of default for sufficiently high interest rates. Junk bonds helped firms with high default risk to borrow. They also became very controversial because of their use in takeovers, as discussed later in the chapter.

Figure 1 | Flat and Rising Term Structures

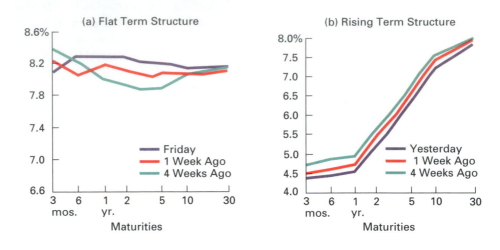

raise the supply of 2-year loans and lower their interest rate. In equilibrium, the interest rate on 2-year loans would be 9.9818 percent per year, a weighted average of the two interest rates on 1-year loans: 8 percent and 12 percent.

This example shows that if people expect short-term interest rates to rise in the future, the long-term interest rate is higher than the short-term interest rate. In the example, the short-term rate is the rate on 1-year loans and the long-term rate is the rate on 2-year loans. People expect the short-term interest rate to rise from 8 percent now to 12 percent in the future, so the long-term interest rate of 9.9818 percent per year exceeds the current short-term rate.

Figure 1 graphs the term structure of interest rates. When long-term interest rates are above short-term rates, the term structure rises. When long-term rates are below short-term rates, the term structure falls. Equal long-term and short-term rates give a flat term structure.

Reading Bond Quotes in the Financial Pages

Most bonds are traded over the counter (by telephone or computer links) among bond dealers. Figure 2 shows how to read bond tables from the financial pages of a newspaper like *The Wall Street Journal*.

Figure 3 shows quotes for various short-term interest rates, including:

▶ *Treasury bill rate*. The interest rate on Treasury bills

▶ *Commercial paper rate*. The interest rate that firms pay for short-term loans in the form of commercial paper

▶ *Federal funds rate*. The interest rate that banks charge other banks for overnight loans

▶ *Prime rate*. The interest rate banks charge their best customers for loans[9]

▶ *Federal Reserve discount rate*. The interest rate that Federal Reserve banks charge commercial banks for loans

---

[9]Sometimes, though, banks lend to very good customers at interest rates below their prime rates.

Figure 2 | Financial Page Quotes for Bonds and T-Bills

(a)

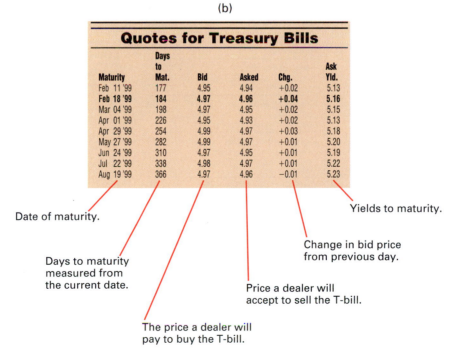

Quotes for Treasury Bonds

Rate	Maturity Mo/Yr	Bid	Asked	Chg.	Ask Yld.
5 1/8	Dec 98n	99:29	99:31	...	5.18
5 3/4	Dec 98n	100:04	100:06	−1	5.19
6 3/8	Jan 99n	100:13	100:15	...	5.17
5	Jan 99n	99:26	99:28	...	5.27
5 7/8	Jan 99n	100:07	100:09	...	5.22
5	Feb 99n	99.25	99:27	−1	5.32
8 7/8	Feb 99n	101:21	101:23	−2	5.29
5 1/2	Feb 99n	100:02	100:04	...	5.26
5 7/8	Feb 99n	100:08	100:10	−1	5.27
5 7/8	Mar 99n	100:10	100:12	...	5.24
6 1/4	Mar 99n	100:17	100:19	...	5.25
7	Apr 99n	101:01	101:03	...	5.27

Coupon Interest Rate
5 means that the annual interest payment is $5 for each $100 of the face value of the bond. *Example:* A $1,000 bond pays $50 in coupon payments every year until maturity.

Date of Maturity

Bid The price bond dealers were willing to *buy* the bond for (on August 18, 1998).
Ask The price that bond dealers were willing to *sell* the bond for (on August 18, 1998).

A price of 99:25 means $99 25/32 for each $100 of face value.

Ask Yield Yield to maturity, or the rate of return if a person buys the bond and holds it until it matures.

Change The change in the bid price from the previous day.

(b)

Quotes for Treasury Bills

Maturity	Days to Mat.	Bid	Asked	Chg.	Ask Yld.
Feb 11 '99	177	4.95	4.94	+0.02	5.13
Feb 18 '99	184	4.97	4.96	+0.04	5.16
Mar 04 '99	198	4.97	4.95	+0.02	5.15
Apr 01 '99	226	4.95	4.93	+0.02	5.13
Apr 29 '99	254	4.99	4.97	+0.03	5.18
May 27 '99	282	4.99	4.97	+0.01	5.20
Jun 24 '99	310	4.97	4.95	+0.01	5.19
Jul 22 '99	338	4.98	4.97	+0.01	5.22
Aug 19 '99	366	4.97	4.96	−0.01	5.23

Date of maturity.

Days to maturity measured from the current date.

The price a dealer will pay to buy the T-bill.

Price a dealer will accept to sell the T-bill.

Change in bid price from previous day.

Yields to maturity.

Source: The Wall Street Journal, August 18, 1998, p. C18.

Figure 3 | Quotes for Current Interest Rates

Source: The Wall Street Journal,
July 30, 1998, pp. C1, C21.

Notice that tax-exempt bonds pay lower interest rates than treasury bonds. Investors are willing to accept lower interest rates on tax-exempt bonds because they don't have to pay taxes on the interest income from them.

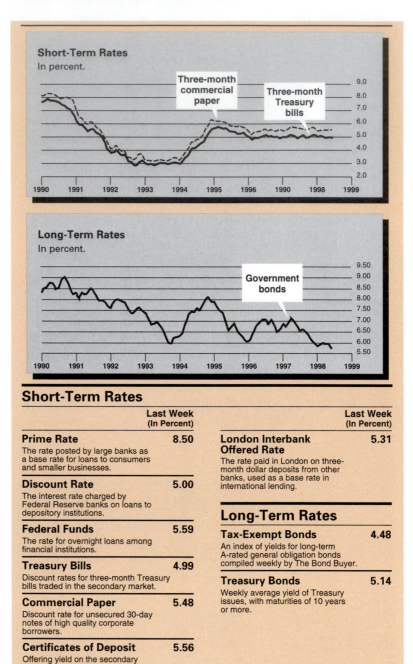

Short-Term Rates

	Last Week (In Percent)		Last Week (In Percent)
Prime Rate The rate posted by large banks as a base rate for loans to consumers and smaller businesses.	8.50	**London Interbank Offered Rate** The rate paid in London on three-month dollar deposits from other banks, used as a base rate in international lending.	5.31
Discount Rate The interest rate charged by Federal Reserve banks on loans to depository institutions.	5.00		

Long-Term Rates

Federal Funds The rate for overnight loans among financial institutions.	5.59	**Tax-Exempt Bonds** An index of yields for long-term A-rated general obligation bonds compiled weekly by The Bond Buyer.	4.48
Treasury Bills Discount rates for three-month Treasury bills traded in the secondary market.	4.99	**Treasury Bonds** Weekly average yield of Treasury issues, with maturities of 10 years or more.	5.14
Commercial Paper Discount rate for unsecured 30-day notes of high quality corporate borrowers.	5.48		
Certificates of Deposit Offering yield on the secondary market for one-month certificates of large banks in blocks of $1 million or more.	5.56		

Review Questions

5. Name some types of debt.

6. Explain why default risk affects the interest rate on a loan.

7. What is a capital gain? Why do bondholders receive capital gains if interest rates fall?

8. Governments of many developing countries have borrowed money by issuing bonds. In some cases, recessions or other economic problems in countries with large debt burdens have drastically reduced the prices of their bonds. Why would such problems cause bond prices to fall?

9. Suppose that a change in monetary policy leads people to expect inflation to rise over the next several years. (a) How would this change affect bond prices? (b) Would it be more likely to cause a rising or falling term structure of interest rates?

STOCKS AND STOCK MARKETS

A share of stock, as discussed earlier, represents a legal right of partial ownership in a company. A firm's stockholders own that firm. Stockholders earn income through dividends and capital gains on their shares.

> **Dividends** are cash payments that firms make to stockholders, usually every quarter (four times per year).

The rate of return, or holding period yield, on a share of stock is:

$$\text{Rate of return} = \frac{\text{Dividend} + \text{Increase in stock price}}{\text{Beginning-of-period stock price}}$$

where the increase in the stock price shows the capital gain on the share.

Firms pay part of their profits to stockholders as dividends, and keep part as retained earnings. They spend retained earnings to pay for investments in equipment, research, and expansion. Retained earnings increase the price of stock and generate capital gains for reasons discussed in a later section.

How Firms Issue Stock

A firm can raise money to finance new investments by borrowing from a bank, issuing bonds or commercial paper, or issuing new shares of stock. Most of the money that firms raise from external sources (as opposed to retained earnings) comes from bank loans. About one-third comes from issuing bonds and commercial paper, and only about 2 percent comes from issuing new stock. Firms often sell newly-issued stock to investment banking companies, which find buyers for the stock. Sometimes, investment bankers underwrite stock issues—they buy the stock themselves and then resell it. This practice helps the firm that issues the stock by eliminating the risk that buyers will not be willing to pay much for it. Investment bankers, of course, charge fees for their services.

Firms that have never issued stock are called *privately held firms.* *Publicly held firms* are companies that have issued stock that trades on a stock exchange When a privately held firm issues stock, it *goes public,* becoming a publicly held firm. Its first sale of stock is called an *initial public offering (IPO).* After the IPO, owners of the stock can trade it on stock exchanges. Financial pages of newspapers regularly announce IPOs.

Dividends or Retained Earnings?

A firm's stockholders want it to retain earning, rather than paying profits as dividends, only if they expect to gain sufficiently from those retained earnings. Stockholders benefit from retained earnings when they generate higher *future* profits and dividends. If an increase in the discounted present value of expected future dividends raises the current price of the stock, then stockholders benefit through a capital gain.

An Economic Puzzle
On average, IPOs appear to be underpriced. Their prices on the primary market (when people buy shares from underwriters) average about 10 to 15 percent below their eventual selling prices in the first trades on the stock exchange. Economists have not yet succeeded in explaining why. A key question is why more people don't try to profit by buying predictably underpriced IPOs.

Reading Stock Tables

The New York Stock Exchange (NYSE) is a firm that operates the world's largest equities market. The American Stock Exchange (AMEX) operates another large U.S. stock market, and smaller, regional exchanges also trade shares of stock in the United States, such as the Pacific Exchange, the Philadelphia Exchange, the Boston Exchange, and the Midwest Exchange. Important foreign stock exchanges are in Tokyo, London, Toronto, Montreal, Brussels, Hong Kong, Mexico, Paris, Amsterdam, Milan, Stockholm, Sydney, and Switzerland.

Figure 4 shows how to read stock market quotations. Look first at the table for the New York Stock Exchange. It lists abbreviated company names, for example, CampblSoup for the Campbell Soup Company. To the right of the name is the company's trading symbol, CPB. These abbreviations show up in many summaries of stock prices, such as those on the Financial News Network on television or many Internet sites. To the left of the company's name, the quote lists the highest price (Hi) and lowest price (Lo) for one share of the company's stock during the previous year (52 weeks).[10] The price of one share of Campbell Soup stock varied between 44$\frac{1}{16}$ ($44.06 per share) and 60$\frac{3}{16}$ ($60.19) in the year before this quote appeared.

The second column from the right, labeled *Close,* shows the price of the stock when the market closed at 4 P.M. eastern standard time. Campbell Soup closed at $48.75 per share of stock. The last column, labeled *Net Chg,* shows the change in the stock's closing price from the previous day; the price of Campbell Soup stock rose $0.25 from the previous day. (It had closed at $48.50 the previous day.)

Just to the left of the closing price the quote lists the high (Hi) and low (Lo) prices for the day's trading. During that day, the price of Campbell's stock varied from $46.69 to $49.50 per share. Moving further to the left, the column labeled *Vol 100s* shows the volume of trading in the stock in hundreds of shares; traders exchanged 683,800 shares of Campbell Soup stock.

Further to the left appear three columns labeled *Div, Yld %,* and *PE.* The first of these shows the annual dividend per share, $0.84 for Campbell Soup. Dividing this dividend by the stock price ($48.75) gives 0.017, or 1.7 percent per year. This figure shows the rate of return on the stock from dividends only, ignoring capital gains or losses. The column labeled *PE* shows the stock's price–earnings ratio, the stock price divided by the firm's earnings per share. To calculate the price–earnings ratio, begin by dividing the company's accounting profit by the total number of shares of stock it has issued to find earnings (or profits) per share of stock. Divide the stock price by earnings per share to get the price–earnings (PE) ratio. Campbell Soup had a PE ratio of 34, so the price of one share of stock was 34 times the amount of earnings (profit) per share of stock. In other words, the Campbell Soup Company earned profits of $1 for each $34 of its stock. Quotes for the American Stock Exchange and the NASDAQ market are similar to the New York Stock Exchange table, as is the Foreign Markets table in Figure 5.[11]

The Dow Jones Industrial Average (DJIA) index is an average of the prices of 30 industrial stocks. The Standard & Poor's 500 (S&P 500) index is an average of the prices of 500 stocks.[12] Figure 6 shows stock market indexes for major foreign exchanges. The Nikkei Average, an average of 225 stock prices on the Tokyo Stock Exchange, resembles the Dow Jones Industrial Average or the S&P 500 in the United States. Other important stock indexes include the TSE 300 Index for the Toronto exchange and the Financial Times 100-share index for the London exchange. Many Internet sites and newspapers, such as the *Financial Times* of London, report stock

---

[10] The symbols to the left of these 52-week highs are footnotes that this chapter will ignore.

[11] More details on foreign stocks are available in foreign newspapers or in publications such as the *Financial Times* of London, or on a variety of Internet sites. See the Web site for this book for additional information.

[12] The Wilshire 5,000 is an even broader average, including the prices of almost all stocks of U.S. firms.

Figure 4 | Sample Stock Market Quotations, New York Stock Exchange

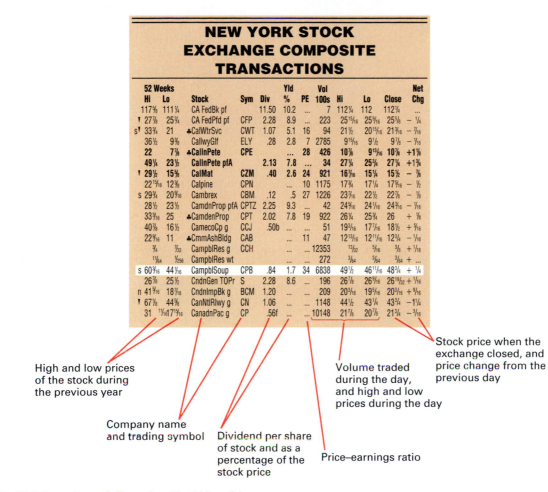

Source: The Wall Street Journal, September 11, 1998, p. C4.

market indexes for stock exchanges around the world. Some also report stock-price indexes measured in alternative currencies. For example, you can compute a stock-price index for Japanese stocks measured in either Japanese yen or U.S. dollars by converting yen prices to dollars using foreign exchange rates. Most U.S. investors are mainly interested in the dollar values of their stocks, while most investors in Japan are mainly interested in the yen values of their stocks. People who do business in other countries may be interested in both.

Mechanics of Stock Market Trades

People buy stocks through stockbrokers, who place orders to buy or to sell stocks either through their firms' New York offices or through other stock exchange members. Members of the New York Stock Exchange own seats on the NYSE; these seats can be bought and sold, sometimes at prices over $1 million each. Specialists at the New York Stock Exchange assume responsibility for trading in each stock; they match orders to buy a particular stock at some price with orders to sell it at the same price. Besides over 400 specialists, about 200 floor traders buy and sell stocks on the NYSE for their own profit. Floor traders are not allowed to trade stocks for other people.

Figure 5 | Sample Stock Market Quotations, Other Markets

AMERICAN STOCK EXCHANGE COMPOSITE TRANSACTIONS

	52 Weeks Hi	52 Weeks Lo	Stock	Sym	Div	Yld %	PE	Vol 100s	Hi	Lo	Close	Net Chg
	23 3/8	9 7/8	♣DiaMetMnl B	DMMB		...	...	10	12 5/8	11 59/64	12 5/8	+ 3/8
	10 3/4	1 9/16	DgtPwr	DPW		...	7	223	2 1/16	1 15/16	2 1/16	+ 1/8
▼	16 3/4	4	♣Diodes	DIO		...	5	471	4	3 7/8	4	− 1/8
n	14 3/4	6 13/16	DriversfCpRes	HIR		...	9	25	9 1/8	8 7/8	8 7/8	− 1/16
▼	16 15/16	10 5/8	Dixon Ti	DXT		...	10	13	10 3/4	10 1/2	10 1/2	− 1/4
▼	**50**	**38 3/4**	**DoleFd ACES**	**DLA**	**2.75**	**7.4**	**...**	**573**	**39 1/2**	**37**	**37**	**+ 3 1/4**
	15 1/8	11	♣DrewInd	DW		...	10	105	12	11 7/8	12	...
	10 15/16	8 7/8	♣DreyfMuninc	DMF	.58	6.0	...	100	9 3/4	9 11/16	9 11/16	− 1/16
	10 13/16	9 1/2	♣DreyfCalMn	DCM	.56	5.4	...	27	10 7/16	10 3/16	10 7/16	+ 3/16
	11 1/4	9 3/4	♣DreyfNYMun	DNM	.56	5.5	...	24	10 1/8	10	10 1/8	+ 1/16
n▼	25 5/8	24 7/8	EBS CapTr pf		.38p	...	...	21	25	24 3/4	24 3/4	− 1/2
n	15 1/4	9 3/4	EFC Bcp	EFC		...	...	84	10 3/4	10 3/8	10 1/2	− 1/2
▼	8	5 1/2	EtzLavud A			...	...	13	5 5/8	5 1/16	5 1/16	− 7/16
	6 1/8	1 7/16	EXX Inc A	EXXA		...	16	56	1 13/16	1 3/4	1 3/4	− 3/16

NASDAQ NATIONAL MARKET ISSUES

	52 Weeks Hi	52 Weeks Lo	Stock	Sym	Div	Yld %	PE	Vol 100s	Hi	Lo	Close	Net Chg
	4 31/32	1 19/32	♣JMAR Tch	JMAR		...	17	522	1 11/16	1 5/8	1 43/64	− 1/64
	15/16	1/16	♣JMAR Tch wt	JMARW		...	...	73	5/16	5/16	5/16	+ 1/32
	1 7/8	5/8	JMC Gp	JMCG		...	12	56	7/8	27/32	7/8	...
	27 5/8	7 3/4	JPM Co	JPMX		...	17	203	8 3/8	7 3/4	8 1/8	− 1/4
n	5 1/8	2 7/16	JPS Pack	JPSP		...	...	222	4	3 11/16	4	+ 1/8
n▼	**14 1/2**	**5 1/4**	**JPS Textile**	**JPST**		**...**	**...**	**82**	**5 1/4**	**4 3/4**	**4 3/4**	**− 1/2**
	46 1/2	22 3/4	JackHenry	JKHY	.26	.6	40	1655	44 3/4	42 1/2	44 1/8	− 5/8
	8	2 1/4	JacoElec	JACO	stk	...	12	1018	4	3 5/8	3 5/8	...
	15 3/4	**8 5/8**	**JacobsnStr**	**JCBS**		**...**	**10**	**171**	**9**	**8 11/16**	**8 11/16**	**− 13/16**
	65 1/4	**36 1/2**	**JacorComm**	**JCOR**		**...**	**dd**	**17313**	**52 7/8**	**47 7/8**	**50**	**− 4 1/8**
	8 1/4	**3 1/2**	**JacorComm wt**	**JCORZ**		**...**	**...**	**797**	**5 1/4**	**4 1/2**	**5**	**− 5/8**
	3 1/4	**1 3/8**	**JacoComm wt02**	**JCORM**		**...**	**...**	**5**	**1 3/4**	**1 3/4**	**1 3/4**	**− 5/16**
sx	26	15 53/64	JamsRvrBksh	JRBK	.40	2.2	15	26	17 13/16	17 13/16	17 13/16	− 1/16
	13 1/8	9 1/4	JamesonInns	JAMS	.92	9.7	22	313	9 3/4	9 7/16	9 7/16	...

FOREIGN MARKETS

Americas

MONTREAL in Canadian dollars

	CLOSE	NET CHG.
Bio Pha	31.35	+ 0.50
Bombrdr B	18.60	+ 0.65
Cambior	7.40	− 0.10
Cascades	9.50	− 0.05
Celanese	20.05	− 0.60
Donohue A	30.35	− 0.15
NatBk Cda	23.70	+ 0.10
Power Corp	30.75	− 0.10
Provlgo	11.00	+ 0.70
Quebecr B	31.00	+ 0.10
Quebecr P	28.85	+ 0.05
SNC-Lavalin	10.20	− 0.10
Teleglobe	39.95	+ 0.35
Videotron	19.25	− 0.35

TORONTO in Canadian dollars

	CLOSE	NET CHG.
Abitibl C	17.10	+ .35
AirCanada	8.60	+ .20
Stelco A	9.35	+ .05
TIPS	35.25	+ .85
Talisman	32.95	− .25
Teck B f	13.15	+ .20
Telus Corp	32.00	+ .45
ThomCor	39.15	+ 1.90
TorDmBk	50.20	+ 1.10
TorstarBf	19.10	− .15
TrAlt corp	22.20	+ 1.20
TrCan PL	23.75	+ .20
Trilon A	10.80	...
Trimac	9.50	+ .60
TrizecHaf	31.25	+ .55
Wcoast E	28.95	+ .25
Weston	48.05	− .15

MEXICO CITY in pesos

	CLOSE	NET CHG.
Alfa A	25.35	− 0.15
Apasco A	34.30	− 0.70
Banacci B	13.60	− 0.60
Bimbo A	16.50	+ 0.02
Cemex B	30.65	− 0.85

BRUSSELS in Belgian francs

	CLOSE	NET CHG.
Arbed	3620	− .90
BarcoNV	9770	+ 40
Bekaert	26100	− 300
CBR	3465	+ 65
Delhaize	3020	+ 20
Electrabel	11775	− 175
Fortis	10375	− 75
Gevaert	2390	− 60
GIB	2005	+ 5
Kredietbank	3060	− 55
Petrofina	13675	− 75
Solvay	2675	− 20
Tractebel	5960	− 150

FRANKFURT in marks

	CLOSE	NET CHG.
Adidas Salmn	212.00	− 12.00
Allianz	600.10	− 4.90
BASF	77.15	+ 0.65
Bayer	74.00	− 0.20
Beiersdorf	110.00	...

Source: The Wall Street Journal, August 18, 1998, pp. C12; September 11, 1998, pp. C9, C12.

Figure 6 | Foreign Stock Market Indexes

Stock Market Indexes

EXCHANGE	INDEX	9/10/98 CLOSE		NET CHG		PCT CHG		YTD NET CHG		YTD PCT CHG
Argentina	Merval Index	301.73	–	46.38	–	13.32	–	385.77	–	56.11
Australia	All Ordinaries	2526.30	–	16.20	–	0.64	–	90.20	–	3.45
Belgium	Bel-20 Index	3204.93	–	100.80	–	3.05	+	786.51	+	32.52
Brazil	Sao Paulo Bovespa	4760.00	–	895.00	–	15.83	–	5436.00	–	53.32
Britain	London FT 100-share	5136.60	–	174.70	–	3.29	+	1.10	+	0.02
Britain	London FT 250-share	4751.80	–	59.90	–	1.24	–	35.80	–	0.75
Canada	Toronto 300 Comp.	5796.77	–	75.66	–	1.29	–	902.67	–	13.47
Chile	Santiago IPSA	55.21	–	4.39	–	7.37	–	44.79	–	44.79
China	Dow Jones China 88	132.57	+	2.74	+	2.11	–	24.99	–	15.86
China	Dow Jones Shanghai	158.57	+	3.30	+	2.13	–	3.75	–	2.31
China	Dow Jones Shenzhen	157.43	+	3.17	+	2.05	–	15.84	–	9.14
Europe	DJ Stoxx (ECU)	250.71	–	11.51	–	4.39	+	14.92	+	6.33
Europe	DJ Stoxx 50 (ECU)	2914.00	–	147.69	–	4.82	+	280.37	+	10.65
Euro Zone	DJ Euro Stoxx (ECU)	264.57	–	12.77	–	4.60	+	34.71	+	15.10
Euro Zone	DJ Euro Stoxx 50 (ECU)	2903.71	–	147.78	–	4.84	+	371.72	+	14.68
France	Paris CAC 40	3589.35	–	172.78	–	4.59	+	590.44	+	19.69
Germany	Frankfurt DAX	4747.33	–	293.54	–	5.82	+	497.64	+	11.71
Germany	Frankfurt Xetra DAX	4744.05	–	214.39	–	4.32	+	519.75	+	12.30
Hong Kong	Hang Seng	7849.96	–	55.49	–	0.70	–	2872.80	–	26.79
India	Bombay Sensex	3108.67	+	11.55	+	0.37	–	550.31	–	15.04
Italy	Milan MIBtel	19719.00	–	1101.0	–	5.29	+	2913.0	+	17.33
Japan	Tokyo Nikkei 225	14666.03	–	89.51	–	0.61	–	592.71	–	3.88
Japan	Tokyo Nikkei 300	217.49	–	1.15	–	0.53	–	19.39	–	8.19
Japan	Tokyo Topix Index	1109.91	–	6.10	–	0.55	–	65.12	–	5.54
Mexico	I.P.C. All-Share	2856.10	–	311.16	–	9.82	–	2373.25	–	45.38
Netherlands	Amsterdam AEX	1021.31	–	55.28	–	5.13	+	107.64	+	11.78
Singapore	Straits Times	865.00	–	20.46	–	2.31	–	664.84	–	43.46
South Africa	Johannesburg Gold	1015.20	+	63.10	+	6.63	+	213.00	+	26.55
South Korea	Composite	338.95	+	9.73	+	2.96	–	37.36	–	9.93
Spain	Madrid General Index	710.35	–	47.63	–	6.28	+	77.80	+	12.30
Sweden	Stockholm General	3020.70	–	88.03	–	2.83	+	84.94	+	2.89
Switzerland	Zurich Swiss Market	6502.30	–	300.10	–	4.41	+	236.80	+	3.78
Taiwan	Weighted Index	6803.83	–	90.74	–	1.32	–	1383.44	–	16.90

na-Not available

Source: The Wall Street Journal, September 11, 1998, p. C14.

A buyer pays a slightly higher price for a stock than the seller receives. The difference is the bid–ask spread. Buyers pay the (higher) bid price and sellers receive the (lower) ask price. The difference covers the broker's cost of buying or selling the stock. Stockbrokers also charge commissions to place orders; some also charge for investment advice.

Profiting from Stock Price Predictions

If you could accurately predict changes in stock prices, you could become a billionaire. Suppose you expect the price of Gap Incorporated stock to rise by 10 percent over the next month. You could buy shares of Gap stock now and resell it next month for a 10-percent gain in one month. (With a 10-percent monthly return, you would more than triple your money in a year.)

Suppose you expect the price of Sony Corporation stock to *fall* by 10 percent over the next week. You can profit from this by selling your Sony stock today, before the price falls, and buying it back next week after the price has fallen. You profit because you earn more from selling the stock than you will spend next week to buy back the stock.

Suppose you expect the price of Sony stock to fall, but you don't own any Sony stock to sell. In this case, you can profit by *selling short* the stock: you borrow the stock from a broker and sell it. Next week, after the stock price has fallen, you buy the stock to repay the loan. For example, you might borrow 1000 shares of Sony stock and sell them today for $80 per share, collecting $80,000. Next week, you must buy 1000 shares to repay the loan. If the price has fallen by 10 percent, to $72 per share, you spend only $72,000 to buy the stock and repay your loan, leaving you with a profit of $8,000 (minus brokerage commission and other fees).

Many people study the stock market daily, seeking opportunities for profits. When *many* investors buy a stock because they expect its price to rise over the next month, the increase in demand for that stock raises its price *today*. The current stock price rises until it equals (approximately) the expected future price of the stock. To see why, suppose (falsely) that the current price remained below the expected future price. In that case, investors would have an incentive to *increase* their current purchases of the stock, to increase their profits. Their actions raise the current price still further. In equilibrium, the current stock price equals (approximately) the expected future price.

Similarly, when *many* investors sell a stock because they expect its price to fall over the next week, their actions reduce the stock price *today*. The current stock price falls until it equals (approximately) the expected future price.

EXAMPLE

Suppose that investors expect the price of Nike stock to rise from its current level of $40 per share to $50 per share by next month. They will try to profit by buying Nike stock now, before the price rises. Their actions raise current demand for Nike stock, immediately raising its price to $50. The investors who gain from this price increase are those who *already* owned Nike stock before investors started predicting the price increase, or those who were able to buy it *before* its price rose to $50.

Why must the stock price rise all the way to $50 today? To see why, suppose (falsely) that it rises only to $48. Investors would then expect to earn additional profits of $2 per share by buying additional shares of Nike stock today. Their actions would increase the price further. Only when today's price equals $50 would investors stop seeking to buy additional shares of the stock. As a result, the price rises today to $50 per share.

Equilibrium Stock Prices and Returns

When people expect the price of a particular stock to rise in the future, their attempts to profit by buying it today raise its current price. When people expect the price of a particular stock to fall in the future, their attempts to profit by selling it today reduce its current price. These actions of profit-seeking investors change the current price of a stock until it equals (approximately) its expected future price.

> A stock's price rises or falls each day until most investors do not predict future increases or decreases.

Economists say a variable follows a *random walk* if its changes are unpredictable. Evidence shows that stock prices are approximately random walks.

> Stock prices are (approximately) random walks.

Although investors know that stock prices will change in the future, they view the prices as (roughly) equally likely to rise or fall (aside from the slow upward drift discussed below). The logical reasoning leading to the conclusion that stock prices follow random walks is often called the *efficient markets theory*.

The **efficient markets theory** is the logical reasoning leading to the conclusion that stock prices follow (approximate) random walks.

With a few well-known exceptions, evidence strongly supports the efficient markets theory.

Stock prices reflect all publicly available information: any information that is relevant for future stock prices and is generally available to investors. Stock prices change rapidly to reflect such new information immediately after it becomes generally available. As a result, it is impossible to use publicly available information to predict changes in stock prices.

Drift in Stock Prices

Stock prices are approximately, but not exactly, random walks. The current equilibrium price of a stock does not exactly equal its expected future price, because owning stocks has an opportunity cost. For every dollar you invest in stocks, you sacrifice the interest you could have earned on other investments (T-bills, for example). People invest in stocks because they expect rates of return high enough to compensate for this opportunity cost.

For example, suppose that the interest rate is 7 percent per year. If investors expect a stock price to be $107 next year, then they might be willing to pay only $100 for the stock this year. Their expected capital gain on the stock is about 7 percent per year, so equilibrium stock prices rise predictably. Stock prices have risen, on average, about 7 percent per year over the last half century. This trend leads a rational investor to expect a stock selling for $10.00 today to sell for about $10.01 after 1 week, giving a $0.01 capital gain during the week.

For this reason, today's stock price does not exactly equal the expected stock price next week or next year, but it is a close approximation. A stock price follows a random walk with a drift. The drift is the slow, average upward movement of overall stock prices.

Implications

The fact that stock prices follow random walks has several implications. First, investors cannot expect to *beat the market* (earning a higher rate of return than average) by using past changes in stock prices to predict future changes. Because the history of a stock's price (including any trends in its price) is public information, the current price already reflects that history. Evidence confirms that so-called *technical analysis* (which looks at historical data for patterns) cannot help investors raise their profits in the stock market. However, technical analysts do earn money by selling their predictions to other people!

Second, *fundamental analysis* of a stock (efforts to predict a future stock price by examining public data such as that in an annual report about a firm's profits, sales, and costs) is unlikely to help most investors. This information is publicly available, so it is already reflected in current stock prices. The main exception applies to a person with special knowledge that is not available to everyone. A person armed with special knowledge may interpret public information better than most other investors, and may earn higher returns as a result of this special knowledge.

Third, a person with *inside information* about a firm's prospects—information unavailable to most investors—can earn high returns by buying or selling stocks before that information becomes public and affects the price of the stock. However, trading based on inside information is illegal in many cases.

What About My Uncle, Who Can Beat the Market?

Most people know someone who claims to *beat the market*—to earn higher returns than a well-diversified investor would earn. Unless that person has inside information, or special knowledge that enables a more accurate interpretation of information, that person

---

If You're So Smart, Why Aren't You Rich?

Many people have a difficult time accepting the efficient markets theory, the evidence that stock prices follow an approximate random walk, and the implication that publicly available information is not useful for beating the market. However, it is fair to ask them, "If you're so smart, why aren't you rich?" If people could effectively predict stock prices, they could become rich. Rather than working as investment advisors, they would be vacationing on their yachts.

Be careful to avoid common mistakes in thinking about these issues. One common mistake is to neglect selection bias (discussed in Chapter 2). Technical analysts who beat the market by chance are more able to attract customers and stay in business longer than other analysts. As a result, those technical analysts who remain in business tend to be the ones who happened to be lucky in their past predictions. This fact means that the past performance of technical analysts *who remain in business* is better than the *average* performance of technical analysts (some of whom have gone out of business).

may have earned high returns in the past purely by luck. Luck plays a bigger role in investment success than many people may think. If one million people invest in the stock market, a few hundred of them will very likely get rich simply by chance. (In fact, the chance that none of them get rich is quite low.) Perhaps most of the million investors begin trading with a great deal of confidence in their ability to choose good investments. The few hundred people who get rich will (incorrectly) interpret their success as the result of their ability, confirming their self-confidence. They will be even more certain than before that they know how to beat the market. Other people are likely to believe them, since the few hundred people who lost money in the stock market won't go around talking about it. (If they did, people might view them as rather stupid.)

If you flip a coin, the chance that you will flip 10 heads in a row is almost 1 out of 1,000. Because stock prices are close to random walks (with equal chances of rising or falling), think of stock prices as rising if you flip heads and falling if you flip tails. If 1 million people flip coins, about 1,000 of them will flip 10 heads in a row. (About 122 of them will flip heads 13 times in a row!) Picking 10 winning stocks in 10 tries looks impressive, but 1,000 out of every 1 million investors will do it by chance. People sometimes ridicule the efficient markets theory by telling the fable of an efficient-markets believer who wouldn't pick up a $20 bill lying on the sidewalk because he was convinced that it couldn't really be there. Considerable evidence indicates that the efficient markets theory closely approximates reality, though.[13] On the other hand, the efficient markets theory is only a model—only an approximation to real life.[14]

Ex-Dividend Stock Prices

Stock prices do change predictably immediately after stocks pay dividends. To see why, suppose that a firm will pay a $5 dividend to the owner of a share of its stock as of 3 P.M. eastern time on March 1. The stock becomes less valuable at 4 P.M. than it was at 2 P.M. because if you buy the stock at 2 P.M. you will collect the dividend, but if you buy it at 4 P.M., you are too late—the previous owner gets the dividend. This difference makes the stock worth about $5 less at 4 P.M. than it was at 2 P.M. All investors know this, so they all expect the stock price to fall $5 just after 3 P.M., when the dividend is paid. This predictable change in the price of a stock does not create any profit opportunities for investors.

Level of Stock Prices

Ultimately, stocks are valuable because they pay dividends (or they will do so at some time in the future).

> The **fundamental price** of a stock is the discounted present value of its expected future dividends.

The present value of expected future dividends is:[15]

$$\text{DPV of expected future dividends}$$
$$= \frac{d_1}{1 + i} + \frac{d_2}{(1 + i)^2} + \frac{d_3}{(1 + i)^3} + \dots \text{ forever}$$

---

[13]The efficient markets theory says that most people cannot beat the market except by luck, but it doesn't deny that people sometimes gets lucky. Someone who sees a $20 bill should not stubbornly refuse to realize that gains are possible simply by luck!

[14]For example, the model ignores the fact that if stock prices always reflected all publicly available information, investors would lose incentives to collect relevant information.

[15]This simplified formula assumes that firms pay dividends once every year at the end of the year, rather than every quarter.

where d_1, d_2, and so on, are the expected dividends after 1 year, 2 years, and so on, and i is the interest rate.

This equation gives the stock's fundamental price. In fact, the fundamental price also equals:[16]

Fundamental stock price at beginning of 2000

$$= \frac{d_{2001}}{1 + i} + \frac{\text{Fundamental stock price at beginning of 2002}}{1 + i}$$

The fundamental price of the stock rises whenever expected future dividends change. For example, suppose investors alter their beliefs about dividends to be paid 5 years from now. An increase in expected future dividends raises d_5, which increases the current fundamental price of the stock. Stock prices of firms selling condoms rose immediately after basketball star Magic Johnson reported in 1991 that he had contracted HIV, which causes AIDS. Investors expected this news to raise the future profits and dividends of condom makers.

Stocks Are Risky

Stocks are risky investments. The expected rate of return on a stock equals the risk-free rate of return plus a risk premium:

Expected rate of return on stocks = Risk-free interest rate + Risk premium

Stock prices vary substantially every day; changes of more than 1 percent per day are fairly common. (If the DJIA is 8,000, a 1 percent change is a change of 80 points.)[17] The biggest daily change in recent U.S. history was the stock market crash on Black Monday, October 19, 1987, when the DJIA fell over 22 percent.[18] More recently, it fell by 6.4 percent in one day in August, 1998. Despite these decreases, stock prices have risen dramatically over the past two decades.

Price volatility alone, however, does not make stocks risky. Instead, a stock's risk reflects the amount of uncertainty it adds to the *overall wealth* of a typical investor.

A stock is risky if owning it adds uncertainty to an average investor's wealth.

A stock can have large variability in its price without being risky, if its return moves out of step with the returns on other stocks. Stocks whose prices move *in step* with those of other stocks expose investors to more risk than stocks that move *out of step* with other stocks.[19] Stocks that move out of step can have the opposite effect, reducing the uncertainty of an investor's overall wealth. Risky stocks pay higher risk premiums than less risky stocks; they pay higher average rates of return to induce investors to accept the risk of owning them.

EXAMPLE

If this summer brings a lot of rain, Umbrellas Unlimited will earn a $1 million profit and its stock price will rise, while Picnic Supplies Incorporated will suffer a $1 million

---

IN THE NEWS

Stock prices plunge around the world as investors fear higher interest rates

*By Douglas R. Sease
Staff Reporter of
The Wall Street Journal*

Stock prices fell around the world on fears of rising interest rates.

Source: The Wall Street Journal

An increase in interest rates reduces fundamental stock prices.

---

[16] If you are mathematically inclined, you might be able to prove the equivalence of these two equations for the stock's fundamental value are equivalent. (*Hint:* Use the first equation to write the fundamental value in both 2000 and 2001, then substitute both into the second equation and try to prove the truth of the second equation.)

[17] An increase of 1 percent per day is a very large change. If such a trend were to continue for a full year, a stock selling for $1 at the beginning of the year would sell for over $37 at the end of the year, a 3,600 percent annual increase in price!

[18] It had also fallen 17 percent in the 6 weeks before the crash, so stock prices fell almost 40 percent in 6 weeks.

[19] That is, stocks whose price changes are positively correlated with those for other stocks are riskier than stocks with changes uncorrelated or negatively correlated with other stocks.

Table 1 | Annual Rates of Return, 1926–1998

Asset	Nominal Rate of Return	Real Rate of Return
Common stock	11.4%	8.3%
Corporate bonds	5.2	2.1
Government bonds	4.8	1.7
1-month Treasury bills	3.5	0.4

Source: Center for Research in Securities Prices, University of Chicago, and author's calculations.

loss and its stock price will fall. If the weather is good, the opposite will occur. Forecasters project a one-half chance of good weather and a one-half chance of a lot of rain.

If you own stock only in Umbrellas Unlimited, your wealth depends on the uncertain weather. The same is true if you own stock only in Picnic Supplies Unlimited. If you invest in both stocks, however, you reduce your risk. In fact, if you invest equally in the two stocks, you may have no risk; one of your stocks will rise in value, and the other will fall, whatever the weather. (You still gain from the upward drift in stock prices, which implies that the rise in one stock price will exceed the fall in the other price.) When you already own stock in either company, investing in the other stock reduces uncertainty in your wealth because the two stocks move out of step.

A stock's risk to an average investor depends on whether that stock moves in step or out of step with all of that investor's other investments. Risky stocks—those that move in step with other investments—pay higher rates of return on average than less risky stocks, which move out of step with other investments.

Changes in fundamentals affect stock prices.

Tradeoffs between Risk and Expected Return

From 1926 to 1998, the average nominal rate of return on the stock market exceeded 11 percent per year. The average *real* rate of return on the stock market exceeded 8 percent per year. Over this same period, the average real return on long-term government bonds was less than 2 percent per year, and the average real return on Treasury bills was less than ½ percent per year. See Table 1.

Do Stock Prices Equal Their Fundamental Prices?

Economists cannot observe the fundamental prices of stocks, because those fundamental prices depend on investor's expectations. Nevertheless, economists can estimate fundamental prices, and evidence suggests that stock prices do *not* always equal their fundamental prices. Daily changes in stock prices are often larger than changes in estimated fundamental prices. For example, most economists doubt that fundamental prices changed much on the day in 1987 when stock prices fell by 22 percent. Similarly, large increases in stock prices in the 1990s most likely exceeded increases in fundamental prices.

Most economists believe that stock prices are more volatile than their fundamental prices for two reasons.

First, stock prices may exhibit *bubbles*. A bubble occurs when people bid up the price of an asset simply because they believe that other people will be willing to pay *even more* for the asset at a future date! Federal Reserve Chairman Alan Greenspan alluded to this idea in 1998 in expressing his belief that stock prices in the late 1990s reflected "irrational exuberance" of investors.

Bubbles can burst, sending prices into sudden falls. Many economists believe that major stock market crashes, such as the 1987 crash, reflect bursting bubbles.

Second, stock prices may also move away from their fundamental prices if some investors are sufficiently irrational or poorly informed about factors affecting the value of a stock. If enough investors believe that Digmore Mining Company stock is a good deal, they may buy it and drive up its price above its fundamental value. Actions of uninformed investors may also raise the volatility of stock prices on a daily basis.

Speculation can create bubbles in stock prices, and sometimes bubbles burst.

OTHER FINANCIAL ASSETS

Mutual Funds

A mutual fund is a firm that pools money from many small investors to buy and manage a portfolio of financial assets. It then pays the earnings back to the investors. Because a mutual fund buys many assets at once, it incurs lower transactions costs than individual investors through volume discounts on commissions. A mutual fund can also fully diversify its investments, so an individual investor can achieve automatic diversification just by owning shares in the mutual fund.

In an open-end fund, people can buy or sell shares whenever they want at a price near the value of the mutual fund's assets.[20] Most open-end mutual funds are no-load funds, funds that charge no commissions for buying and selling shares. Shareholders do pay fees to cover the wages and other costs of the funds' managers.[21]

Some mutual funds own stocks, some own bonds, some own both, and some money-market mutual funds own only short-term debt securities. Prices of mutual funds are reported in financial pages of newspapers and on the Internet, and many financial magazines also rate the performance of various mutual funds.

Futures Markets

> A **futures market** is a market for trading contracts for future delivery of a good or asset.

In a futures market, you may agree today to buy or sell a certain amount of a good or asset in the future at a price set today.[22] You may buy wheat futures, contracting for 5,000 bushels of wheat to be delivered next March 1 at a price of $3.50 per bushel. Like most other people who buy these futures, you do not want 5,000 bushels of wheat, but you believe that the price of wheat will rise, giving you a chance to profit. To gain this profit, you lock in the $3.50 price today. If you are right and the price rises by March 1, you buy the wheat for $3.50 per bushel and simultaneously sell it at the higher future price without ever actually seeing any wheat.

Futures markets allow people to place bets on whether a price will rise or fall. For example, if wheat sells for $4.00 per bushel on March 1, then you earn a profit of $0.50 per bushel. On the other hand, if the price of wheat falls to $3.00 per bushel by March 1, you are stuck paying $3.50 for wheat that you can sell for only $3.00, so you lose $0.50 per bushel. When you buy futures, you are betting that the price of the good will rise, and you are said to *go long* in the good.

If you think that the price of a good will fall, you can sell futures. If you think that the price of silver will fall, you might agree to deliver 5,000 troy ounces next December 1 to someone who has agreed to pay you $4.00 per ounce. If the price of silver falls to $3.00 per ounce by December 1, you can buy the silver you have agreed to deliver for $3.00 per ounce and sell it for $4.00 per ounce, earning a profit of $1.00 per ounce. On the other hand, if the price of silver rises to $5.00 per ounce, you lose

---

[20] If you want to increase your investment in the mutual fund, you send your money and the mutual fund buys more assets. If you want to withdraw money, you redeem shares; the mutual fund sells some of its assets and sends you the money.

[21] Less common closed-end funds issue fixed numbers of shares when they begin operations. People can then buy and sell shares in such a fund, but the share price is not necessarily equal to the value of the financial assets it owns. In fact, closed-end mutual funds sell, on average, for less than the values of their assets. (The value of all the parts of the fund—the assets the mutual fund owns—are worth more than the mutual fund itself!) This apparently means that investors in such closed-end mutual funds would gain if the funds were converted to open-end funds. The fact that this conversion does not happen is an example of a situation in which a firm's managers fail to act in the interest of the firm's owners.

[22] This discussion ignores slight differences between futures markets and forward markets.

money; you must pay $5.00 per ounce for something that you have already agreed to sell for only $4.00 per ounce. When you sell futures in a good, you are said to *go short* in it.

Trading Futures

Traders buy and sell futures in commodities like soybeans, barley, pork bellies, cocoa, orange juice, and heating oil in organized futures markets like the Chicago Mercantile Exchange (CME); the Chicago Board of Trade (CBT); the Commodity Exchange (COMEX) in New York; the Coffee, Sugar, and Cocoa Exchange (NYCSCE), and many other exchanges. You can also buy and sell futures in financial assets like Treasury bills, government bonds, and many foreign currencies (like the Japanese yen). Some of these futures trade on other exchanges, like the Financial Instrument Exchange (FINEX), a division of the New York Cotton Exchange, and the International Monetary Market (IMM), a division of the CME in Chicago.

You can even buy or sell futures in stock indexes. For example, you can buy futures on the S&P 500 if you expect the index to rise, or you can sell futures on the S&P 500 if you expect it to fall. Futures exchanges also offer contracts on the Nikkei index of Japanese stock prices. Figure 7 shows how to read a futures table in a newspaper or on the Internet.

Options

Traders buy and sell two kinds of option contracts: call options (rights to buy) and put options (rights to sell).

> A **call option** is a legal right to buy some underlying asset during some specified period of time at some preset strike price.

If you own a call option, you have the choice (or option) of deciding whether to exercise it, that is, to buy the underlying asset. If you do not choose to exercise your right to buy, you let the option expire.

> A **put option** is a legal right to sell some underlying asset during some specified period of time at some preset strike price.

If you own a put option, you can decide whether to exercise it by selling the underlying asset or let it expire.

You can buy (go long) or sell (go short) in either kind of option. You need not own an option to sell one; you can simply have a broker issue the option contract and sell it for you. If you buy an option, you have the right to decide whether to exercise it. If you sell an option, the person who buys it from you has the right to decide whether to exercise it.

If you buy a call option, you are betting that the price of the underlying asset will rise. If you buy a put option, you are betting that it will fall. When you buy an option, your potential profits are unlimited, while your potential loss is limited to the price of the option contract.

If you sell a call option, you are betting that the price of the underlying asset will fall. If you sell a put option, you are betting that it will rise. When you sell an option, your potential profits are limited, but your potential loss may be unlimited. For example, if you sell a call option, nothing limits how high the price of the underlying asset may rise, so your possible loss has no limit.[23]

A simple call option with strike price $1.99.

---

[23]However, you can limit your potential loss by combining two option positions.

Because options are rights to trade other assets, they are examples of *derivative securities*—assets whose values derive from prices of other assets. Futures markets in assets are also derivative securities.

Figure 7 | Sample Futures Contract Prices

Source: The Wall Street Journal, September 11, 1998, p. C16.

FUTURE PRICES

GRAINS AND OILSEEDS

	Open	High	Low	Settle	Change	Lifetime High	Lifetime Low	Open Interest
CORN (CBT) 5,000 bu.; cents per bu.								
Sept	197	202	196¼	200½	+ 2	301	185	5,685
Dec	210¼	215	209	213	+ 2¼	299½	196	181,310
Mr99	222¾	227	221¾	225¼	+ 2	305	209½	59,085
May	230	234	229¼	232½	+ 2	299	217	21,982
July	236¼	240	235¼	238½	+ 1¾	312	223½	29,803
Sept	242	245½	242	243¾	+ 1¾	280	232	4,951
Dec	250	253	249¾	252¾	+ 2	291½	238	12,034
Dc00	264	264¾	264	264¾	+ 2¾	279½	254	329
Est vol 55,000; vol Wed 75,874; open int 315,184, – 1,220.								
OATS (CBT) 5,000 bu.; cents per bu.								
Sept	107	107	106	106	+ 1¼	177	98¼	119
Dec	110½	113¾	110½	113½	+ 1¼	177½	106¼	10,682
Mr99	119¼	122	119	121¾	+ 1¼	166½	114½	3,039
May	126¾	126¾	125¾	126	+ ½	161	119½	242
July	130	130	130	130	+ ¼	150	124½	230
COFFEE (CSCE)-37,500 lbs.; cents per lb.								
Sept	118.80	119.40	117.00	117.00	– 2.50	186.00	105.00	880
Dec	112.75	113.40	108.80	109.00	– 4.00	157.50	106.00	14,012
Mr99	110.40	110.50	107.00	107.05	– 3.45	154.00	107.00	6,294
May	111.50	111.50	108.00	108.00	– 3.20	155.50	108.00	2,836
July	112.00	112.25	109.00	109.05	– 2.55	131.00	109.00	1,286
Sept	112.00	112.00	110.75	110.75	– 2.00	123.00	110.75	1,444
Dec	113.00	113.25	112.50	112.50	– .75	123.00	112.00	245
GASOLINE-NY Unleaded (NYM) 42,000 gal.; $ per gal.								
Oct	.4115	.4360	.4115	.4285	+ .0178	.5780	.3930	38,926
Nov	.4216	.4415	.4210	.4346	+ .0157	.5585	.4005	16,605
Dec	.4335	.4490	.4330	.4420	+ .0143	.5450	.4090	9,641
Ja99	.4445	.4545	.4445	.4500	+ .0130	.5350	.4180	4,053
Feb	.4520	.4520	.4520	.4585	+ .0125	.5275	.4280	1,868
Mar	.4730	.4730	.4730	.4670	+ .0120	.5230	.4433	2,075
GOLD (Cmx. Div. NYM)-100 troy oz.; $ per troy oz.								
Sept	......	......		290.70	+ 6.30	296.50	275.60	0
Oct	285.00	292.70	285.00	291.40	+ 6.30	367.80	271.60	10,998
Dec	287.30	295.20	287.30	293.80	+ 6.40	505.00	273.80	102,040
Fb99	290.50	296.90	290.30	295.50	+ 6.40	349.50	277.50	15,060
Apr	293.50	297.60	293.50	297.20	+ 6.30	351.20	280.00	11,795
June	294.30	300.00	294.30	298.80	+ 6.20	520.00	282.00	15,349

CURRENCY

	Open	High	Low	Settle	Change	Lifetime High	Lifetime Low	Open Interest
JAPAN YEN (CME)-12.5 million yen; $ per yen (.00)								
Sept	.7310	.7485	.7310	.7439	+ .0131	.8695	.6807	72,225
Dec	.7410	.7585	.7409	.7538	+ .0133	.8445	.6890	72,011
Ju99	......	......	......	.7733	+ .0137	.7836	.7086	678

Date of delivery specified in the futures contract

High , Low High and low prices during day's trading

Settle Closing price at the end of the day's trading

Change Change in closing price from the previous day's close

Lifetime High, Low Recent high and low futures prices

Open Interest Number of futures contracts open (someone has sold and someone else has bought each contract)

Suppose that you buy a call option on stock in Levi Strauss & Company. The call option costs you $300, and it gives you the right to buy up to 100 shares of Levi stock before next March at $110 per share. Suppose that the price of Levi stock is currently $104 per share. If the stock price stays below $110 until March, you simply let the option expire; you don't buy Levi stock for $110, and you lose the $300 you paid for the call option. You cannot lose more than the money you paid for the option. If the price of Levi stock rises to $115 by March, you exercise the option; you buy Levi stock for $110 per share, and you can sell it for $115 per share, so you gain $5 per share on 100 shares, a profit of $500. Since you paid $300 for the option, your net profit is $200. Your potential profit is unlimited because the potential price of Levi stock could rise without limit; for every $1 increase in the price of Levi stock above $110, your profit rises by $100.

Suppose that you buy a put option on stock in the Boeing Corporation. The put option costs you $200 and gives you the right to sell 100 shares of Boeing stock before next February at a price of $45 per share. If the price of Boeing stock at the end of January exceeds $45 per share, you let the option expire and you lose the $200 you paid for it. If the stock price is below $45 per share, you exercise the put option. For example, if the stock price falls to $40 per share, you buy 100 shares of Boeing stock for $40 per share and exercise your option to sell it for $45 per share. You collect $500, a $300 profit (since you paid $200 to buy the option). As the stock price falls, your profit rises.

Trading Options

People can buy and sell options on stocks, bonds, and Treasury bills; options on foreign currencies and commodities like cattle and sugar; options on stock-price indexes like the S&P 500; and even options on futures contracts. Option contracts trade on the Chicago Board Options Exchange (CBOE) and other organized markets. Figure 8 shows how to read price tables for options.

Options are like bets; the seller of the option bets one way and the buyer bets the other way. The price of an option depends on what people believe might happen to the price of the underlying asset in the future. Paradoxically, an increase in uncertainty about the value of the underlying asset *raises* the value of an option to buy or sell that asset. To see why, consider a call option on Microsoft stock. Suppose that people become *less* certain about the future price of the stock—the chance rises that the price will either rise or fall by a lot. This raises the value of a call option on Microsoft stock because it

Figure 8 | Sample Option Contract Prices

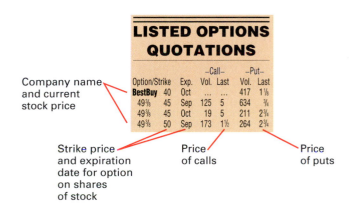

Source: The Wall Street Journal, September 11, 1998, p. C13.

PERSONAL DECISION MAKING

Investment Advice

The best investment advice is fairly simple.

Rule 1: Diversify your investments. The best and easiest way to diversify is to invest in a mutual fund that diversifies for you. Many no-load mutual funds charge low fees and provide very effective diversification—probably better than you can do on your own, and with lower transactions costs. As an alternative, you can invest on your own; choosing five or ten stocks at random usually provides a fairly high degree of diversification.

Rule 2: Buy and hold. Don't keep changing your investments. You probably won't do much better, and you might do worse than a buy-and-hold strategy. Every time you buy and sell assets, you pay commissions and other transactions costs. You can also use your time in much more valuable ways than continually following your investments. Unless you have some inside information about a firm, you are unlikely to beat the market, anyway. Take transactions costs (fees, commissions, bid–ask spreads, and the value of your time) into account.

Rule 3: Consider stocks, despite the risk. For long-term investments, remember that the average rate of return on a diversified portfolio of stocks has been much higher in the past than the average rates of return on bonds or Treasury bills. Stocks are riskier than most other investments, but they may be worth the risk, especially if you plan to hold them for a long time.

Rule 4: Plan around taxes. Some investments, such as individual retirement accounts, pay tax-deferred returns; you don't have to pay taxes on them until you take income from them in the future, for example, when you retire. Unless you think that taxes are going to be much higher then, you can gain by deferring taxes. The discounted present value of your taxes is lower if you pay them in the future than if you pay them now. (In other words, you gain the annual interest on the money you will owe in taxes.) Also, remember to focus on the after-tax, real return on your investments. Taxes and transactions costs can have big effects on the rate of return you get.

Rule 5: Remember a penny saved is no longer a penny earned. It was close in Ben Franklin's day, but today taxes are higher, so $1.00 saved is about $1.50 earned. (It is exactly

increases the chance that the option's owner will be able to profit by exercising the option. Increasing uncertainty has little effect on the investor's potential loss, however, which is limited to the cost of the option.

Review Questions

10. Discuss the claim that stock prices follow a random walk; discuss some of the implications of random-walk stock prices.

11. How large (roughly) are the average rates of return on stocks, bonds, and Treasury bills?

12. What are mutual funds? What are Treasury bill futures?

13. Suppose that you buy a call option on General Cinema stock. Under what conditions do you earn a profit? Under what conditions do you suffer a loss?

Thinking Exercises

14. The price of DullCo stock never changes by more than a few percent per year. The price of WildCorp stock is highly variable. Is WildCorp stock riskier than DullCo stock? Explain.

that much, if you are in the 33⅓ percent marginal tax bracket, including federal and state income taxes and social security tax.) If you buy a VCR for $200, you spend about $300 in before-tax income to pay for it. Every $67 you save is like earning $100 before taxes.

Rule 6: Don't waste your time and money with so-called *technical analysis* of stocks. Instead, you are probably better off spending time working toward a promotion, figuring out how to start your own business, writing the Great American Novel, producing a hot music video, or enjoying yourself.

Rule 7: Budget your time. Most people gain less from an hour spent following their investments closely than from an hour spent clipping coupons for the grocery store or driving to a distant store with low prices.

Rule 8: Diversify your investments in international markets. Stocks in different countries do not move completely in step. Consequently, you can reduce your risk through international diversification.

Rule 9: Don't pay a lot of money for investment advice. Don't put much extra faith in people with financial planning degrees or certifications. Most people who call themselves financial planners have little training, and most will recommend that you buy assets on which they earn commissions. No law prohibits conflicts of interest in this business! If you can, find a financial advisor who (a) will give you a list of customers who have stayed with that person for several years, (b) gets good recommendations from those customers, and (c) charges a flat fee or hourly rate instead of getting commissions from selling recommended assets.

Ask the financial planner what percentage of his or her revenues come from commissions (ask even "fee-only" advisors) and whether the advisor accepts any kind of payment (including free trips and gifts) from people selling specific financial assets. You can also ask outright: "How might your interests in this matter differ from mine?"

Finally, remember that the investment advice of financial advisors will not help you to beat the market. Roughly two-thirds of advisors' recommendations end up doing worse than the S&P 500. When an advisor generates an expected return higher than that of the S&P 500, it usually comes at the cost of higher risk, with higher returns in some years and lower returns in other years.

---

15. What affects the fundamental price of a stock? Why might stock prices deviate from their fundamental prices? Do economists have any way to tell if and when this happens? How?

OWNERSHIP AND CONTROL OF FIRMS

Stockholders in a firm own that firm. They collect its profits, that is, any revenue that remains after workers, suppliers of material inputs, bondholders, and so on, have been paid. Stockholders are residual income recipients—they receive the amount that remains (if anything) after the firm pays everyone else. Stockholders also have the right to make the firm's decisions and to hire and fire its managers.

Although stockholders have the right to control the firm's decisions, actual control is difficult in a big firm. One person or a few people may own and manage a small firm, as at many small retail stores and restaurants. The same people own and control these privately held firms. However, in publicly held corporations, which have issued stock, ownership is often distributed among many stockholders.[24] The stockholders do not

---

[24]Privately held firms can also be incorporated. This structure limits the liability of the owners. In a sole proprietorship or a partnership, the owners (usually) have unlimited liability; if the firm borrows money and goes bankrupt, the owners must repay the loans, or if someone sues the firm in court, the owners are legally responsible for paying any judgment. A corporation, however, becomes (legally) like a person; if the corporation borrows money, only the corporation is responsible for repaying the loan. If the corporation goes bankrupt, the owners do not have to use their own money to repay the loans. Similarly, the owners are not responsible for paying lawsuits against the firm. The only money the owners of a corporation can lose is the money they have already invested in the firm.

directly control the firm. Instead, they choose managers to run it for them. Stockholders vote—each share of stock usually gives its owner one vote—to choose the firm's board of directors, which then chooses managers who make the firm's operating decisions.

This arrangement can create a separation of ownership and control so that the owners do not fully control the firm's decisions. The managers' decisions may differ from those that the stockholders would have made; management decisions do not always serve the stockholders' best interests. Separation of ownership and control can allow the managers to make decisions that are best for themselves, even if the owners (the stockholders) lose. The managers might concentrate more on the firm's short-run profits and less on its long-run profits than owners would like, particularly if the managers do not expect to remain in their jobs for long tenures. They might simply work less hard than they would if they owned the firm.

The owners try to maintain control of a corporation in two ways. First, they monitor the managers—they watch what the managers do. Monitoring efforts confront two main problems. Managers usually have more information about details of the firm's operations and investment opportunities than owners have, which makes it hard for owners to judge whether managers are making the choices that maximize benefits to the owners. Also, monitoring takes time and resources, so each of many stockholders may prefer to wait for some other stockholders to monitor the managers rather than spending their own time and resources.

Owners also try to keep control of the firm by giving managers incentives to make the decisions that are best for the owners. They have devised many ways to do this, although none works perfectly. Rather than paying managers flat salaries, owners often increase managers' pay when the firm's profits rise. Owners might require managers to own shares of stock in the firm to make the managers part-owners and give them some of the same incentives as other owners. This requirement does not solve the problem completely, however. To see why, suppose that a manager must decide whether to spend $1 million of the firm's money on a new office building. Suppose that the new building would add $600,000 to the discounted present value of the firm's profits—$400,000 less than it costs. Stockholders would choose not to spend the money because the total value of the firm's stock—the value of the firm—would fall by $400,000. If the manager owns 0.1 percent of the firm's stock, this cost amounts to a personal loss of only $400. The manager may want a new office, however, and may be willing to pay more than $400 to get it. Consequently, the manager may spend the $1 million even though the owners would have chosen not to do so.

Another problem arises in linking managers' pay to a firm's profits: Managers do not like risk. As a manager's ownership of stock in the firm rises, the manager's wealth becomes less diversified. This reduces the manager's incentive to choose risky investments for the firm—even risky investments that other owners with diversified investments would want the firm to choose. As a result, profit-based compensation is not a perfect solution to the problems caused by separation of ownership and control; in fact, no arrangement perfectly solves the problem.

Takeovers

If managers make decisions that fail to maximize the value of a firm's stock, the stockholders have an incentive to replace them. If the owners don't replace the managers, someone who notices this situation may buy enough stock in the firm to take control of it and then try to profit by replacing the managers or by taking other actions to change their incentives and improve the firm's performance.

A **takeover** occurs when one person, a group of people, or another company buys enough stock in a firm to guarantee a majority vote at stockholder meetings.

A **leveraged buyout (LBO)** is a form of takeover financed by extensive borrowing, often pledging the assets of the takeover target as collateral for the loans.

A **merger** occurs when two firms voluntarily combine to form a single organization.

In a *hostile takeover,* the top managers of the target firm oppose the takeover, usually for fear that they will lose their jobs, which often happens. They may try to convince stockholders not to sell their stock to the would-be acquirers. They may try to use legal tricks to prevent a takeover by delaying it and imposing expenses on the potential acquirers. In some U.S. states, managers are partly protected from takeovers by antitakeover laws that add costly requirements to take over a firm. These laws tend to protect entrenched managers at the expense of stockholders.

Managers may invoke other tricks to make a takeover so expensive that no one will try. They may institute *poison pills,* provisions that raise the cost of a takeover by allowing old stockholders to buy new shares of stock at low prices if someone begins a hostile takeover. Managers may pay *greenmail,* a bribe to the acquirers to get them to abandon the takeover. Managers might establish *golden parachute* clauses in their employment contracts to pay themselves (very well, usually) if they lose their jobs in a takeover. (Despite the appearance of unfairness, golden parachutes can make top managers more willing to accept a takeover that would benefit stockholders, rather than to fight it.)

Fear of a takeover (as well as fear of being fired and replaced by the current owners) helps to give managers some incentive to act in the interests of the stockholders. A friendly takeover occurs when current managers of a firm support the takeover. (In such a case, obviously, the top managers do not expect to be replaced.) A friendly takeover can raise a firm's stock value by improving the efficiency of its operations. They can also help managers to fend off other takeovers that are not so friendly (and in which the managers might be replaced). Sometimes, managers look for *white knights*—people or firms friendly to the current managers and willing to take over the firms to preempt hostile takeovers.

Are Mergers and Takeovers Socially Wasteful?

Takeovers raise economic efficiency. Measures of productivity show that takeover targets usually have low productivity levels that improve after the takeovers. The number of managers and overhead spending usually fall after a takeover, although employment, wages, and production do not. Stock prices of takeover targets usually rise and stay high long after the takeovers. Also, the stock prices of the acquiring firms do not fall, so total stock market values—the discounted present values of expected future dividends—rise because of takeovers. Investors clearly expect firms to become more profitable after being taken over (usually including replacement of the old managers).[25]

People sometimes complain that mergers, takeovers, and leveraged buyouts harm the economy by wasting large amounts of money. These critics incorrectly believe that the money a company spends to take over another company is money that could have paid for something else, such as health care for the poor. This view is misleading. Suppose that Company A buys Company B for $100 million, that is, it buys most of the stock in Company B from that firm's previous stockholders. Company A then has less money to spend, but the previous stockholders of Company B have the money. The money does not just disappear! (The same is true if you buy stock on the New York Stock Exchange—you have less money than before, but the person who sold you the stock has

---

[25]Evidence also suggests that the increase in profitability does not result from an increase in monopoly power. However, some of the gains in stock-market value may occur because of reductions in wages paid to workers, rather than increases in productivity.

more.) Spending money for a takeover does not reduce the amount of other goods that society can afford; it does not reduce the amount of goods that society can produce.

Note one qualification to this result, though. The takeover may consume resources such as lawyers' time, preventing use of those resources in some more valuable way. Those resources are the true social cost of takeovers. Still, remember that takeovers raise the total value of stock in the firms involved by raising economic efficiency, so takeovers add to the economy's wealth.

Sometimes people say that the individuals involved in finance, takeovers, mergers, and similar activities don't produce anything useful (like cars or food), and that their activities cause problems for the economy. This argument ignores the value of services. Accountants and people in the insurance industry don't make tangible goods, either, but they provide valuable services. Without their work, production of tangible goods would be lower, not higher. Similarly, people involved in takeovers and mergers increase efficiency in the economy through their actions. The increase in total stock-market value from takeovers is a rough measure of the value of their production. (Their actions are really more valuable than this measure suggests, because the mere threat of takeovers also improves incentives for managers.)

Stockholders versus Bondholders

Stockholders and bondholders in the same firm often have different incentives and want the firm to make different decisions. One important area of disagreement concerns the riskiness of the firm's investments. Stockholders prefer riskier investments than bondholders want for a simple reason: If a firm makes a risky investment, it might win big or lose big. If it wins big, the stockholders get the benefits (profits), while the bondholders get only their usual interest payments. Bondholders usually do not gain if the risky investment succeeds. On the other hand, if the investment is a big loser, the firm may go bankrupt and bondholders may lose the chance for repayment in full. Bondholders view stockholders as saying "Heads, I win; tails, you lose" when they choose risky investments for a firm. For this reason, bondholders dislike risky investments and stockholders like them.[26]

To help protect their interests, bondholders often insist on bond covenants, special conditions in debt contracts that limit the risks the firm can take. Bond covenants help to protect bondholders from increases in risk. Conflict arises between bondholders and stockholders in many other areas, and many of the features of debt contracts and corporate law help resolve those conflicts and provide incentives for economically efficient decisions.

Review Questions

16. Explain the issue of separation of ownership and control.

17. What is a takeover? How and why does a takeover typically affect the stock price of the takeover target?

Thinking Exercises

18. Greedyblood Corporation spends $1 billion on a hostile takeover of the Goodfrus Corporation. Is this money a loss to society that it could have put to a more useful purpose? Explain.

19. What creates a conflict of interest between stockholders and bondholders?

---

[26] Stockholders like risky investments as long as they generate expected rates of return high enough to justify the risk.

Conclusion

The financial industry operates around the world, 24 hours per day, in a very competitive environment. Financial markets often innovate by creating new securities, sometimes very complicated assets, that help investors and add to economic efficiency.

Financial Assets and Markets

A financial asset is a right to collect some payment or series of payments in the future. Its rate of return is the income the asset pays, plus the increase in its price, all as a percentage of the original asset price. Financial markets increase opportunities for people and improve the economy's efficiency by helping people to borrow and lend, to diversify risk, and to direct resources toward their most economically efficient uses.

Risk and Insurance

Most people are risk averse; they dislike risk enough that they are willing to accept reduced expected rates of return in order to reduce risk. Therefore, risky assets must pay higher expected rates of return than safer assets pay. People try to reduce their risks by diversifying their investments, that is, by choosing investments whose returns move out of step with each other.

Debt Investments: Bond Markets and Money Markets

A debt is a borrower's promise to repay a loan. Bonds, Treasury bills, and commercial paper are examples of debt securities. The price of a bond is the discounted present value of its expected future payments. The discounted-present-value calculation uses a higher interest rate for bonds with higher risks of default.

Stocks and Stock Markets

Shares of stock are certificates that represent part-ownership in a corporation. The return on stock consists of dividends and capital gains. The fundamental price of a stock is the discounted present value of its expected future dividends. The discounted present value calculation uses a higher interest rate for a riskier stock. The risk of a stock depends on how much uncertainty it adds to the overall wealth of investors, which depends on whether its rate of return moves in step or out of step with other investments. Stock prices are approximately random walks; they rise slowly over time, but big changes in stock prices are not predictable with publicly available information. Stocks are riskier than bonds, but they pay much higher expected rates of return.

Other Financial Assets

A mutual fund pools investors' money to buy a diversified set of financial assets. These funds provide easy and cheap ways for individual investors to diversify. A futures market is a market for future delivery of a good or an asset. A call option is a legal right to buy an asset during some specified period of time at a preset price. A put option is a similar right to sell. Option and futures contracts allow investors to bet on a wide variety of financial events and to hedge a wide variety of risks.

Ownership and Control of Firms

Stockholders own a corporation, but they do not completely control it; they hire managers to make decisions for them, creating a separation of ownership and control. Managers' interests are not the same as stockholders' interests, so stockholders use a variety of methods to alter managers' incentives to encourage decisions that benefit the owners. If a firm has managers whose decisions differ substantially from the decisions that the owners would make, it may become the target of a takeover. A takeover raises the efficiency of the acquired firm and raises its stock market value. Managers usually oppose hostile takeovers because they are likely to lose their jobs. They have developed many ways to try to fight hostile takeovers.

Interests of bondholders and stockholders also conflict. Bondholders want the firm to make decisions that reduce its chance of bankruptcy and default, which raises the value of its bonds. Bondholders want the firm to choose less risky investments than stockholders want, even though the less risky investments pay lower expected rates of return.

Key Terms

financial asset	coupon payment	holding period yield	futures market
rate of return	Treasury bill (T-bill)	capital gain (or capital	call option
expected value	Treasury note	loss)	put option
diversification	commercial paper	dividends	takeover
risk averse	default	efficient markets theory	leveraged buyout (LBO)
risk neutral	risk-free interest rate	stock fundamental	merger
bond	risk premium	price	

Questions and Problems

20. Why do stock prices almost follow random walks? Why *almost?*

21. Suppose that a company discovers a new product that is likely to double its profits next year. What would happen to its stock price? How does your answer relate to the idea that stock prices follow random walks?

22. How would you expect reductions in government defense spending to affect the prices of stock in firms that make military equipment? What if the cuts in defense spending were already expected by investors?

23. Explain why diversifying your investments reduces your risk. Does diversification always reduce your expected profit?

Inquiries for Further Thought

24. If investment advisors are so smart, why aren't they rich? Why do they sell advice to others or write books about investing rather than earning high profits for their own benefit or for charitable contributions?

25. Why do financial markets offer so many different kinds of assets? What functions (if any) do they perform? What good (if any) do they do?

26. What are the incentives of a stockbroker? Why not compensate a broker by paying a fraction of your winnings if you win, and ask the broker to pay part of your losses if you lose? Why not pay doctors in a similar way?

27. Do you think that bubbles or fads move stock prices? Do stock prices usually equal their fundamental values?

28. Why do people work for firms? Why doesn't everyone work for himself or herself as a separate, private contractor or consultant, perhaps doing the same work?

29. Why can't you buy insurance against low grades in college?

CHAPTER 16

INTERNATIONAL TRADE

In this Chapter...

Main Points to Understand

▶ International trade creates winners and losers, but a country *as a whole* gains from international trade.

▶ A country has a trade deficit, and a current account deficit, when it spends more than its income (paying by borrowing from other countries).

▶ Restrictions on international trade create deadweight social losses.

Thinking Skills to Develop

▶ Understand the gains from international trade.

▶ Understand the causes and effects of trade deficits and surpluses.

▶ Recognize fallacious arguments about trade restrictions.

International trade conjures up images of romance and danger in foreign lands, of spices from China, tea from India, oranges from Morocco, fashions from France and Italy, and the latest consumer electronics from Japan, of established business opportunities in the European Union and entrepreneurial opportunities in developing economies. It also evokes fears of competition from foreign sellers and worries over future prospects for local jobs and family economic security.

Most of the 6 billion people in the world earn wages far below those of a typical American worker. As advances in technology, transportation, and communication create a more integrated world economy, American firms and workers will face increased competition from firms and workers in other countries. How will this competition affect the American economy and your future standard of living? Can American workers expect to earn the high incomes to which they have become accustomed when workers in other countries are willing to work for lower wages? Will American wages fall to world levels as international trade expands? What would be the consequences of shutting off the nation from the rest of the world economy? Why does the United States have a trade deficit? Is this deficit a sign that America cannot compete in the world marketplace? This chapter addresses the reasons for international trade and its economic consequences.

SCOPE OF INTERNATIONAL TRADE

International trade promotes economic efficiency; the ability to buy from foreign sellers helps consumers, and the ability to sell to foreign buyers helps producers. International trade adds to the competition facing domestic producers; it allows countries to specialize in the goods and services they can produce at lowest cost, and it helps to spread modern technology around the world, raising world output and economic growth.

Trade has two components: exports and imports.

Exports are sales of goods and services to people in other countries.
Imports are purchases of goods and services from people in other countries.

The United States exports about one-eighth of all goods and services that it produces, that is, U.S. exports are about 12 percent of GDP. People in the United States also import about one-eighth of everything they buy.[1] Figure 1 shows that the United States currently imports and exports a higher fraction of its GDP than it has in the past. Figure 2 shows that international trade is even more important for relatively small developed countries such as Italy and Canada than for large countries such as the United States and Japan.[2]

Figure 1 | U.S. Exports and Imports as a Percentage of GDP

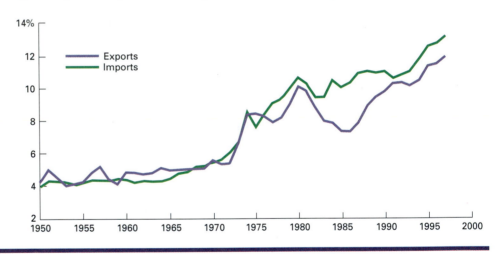

Figure 2 | International Trade as a Percentage of GDP for Selected Countries

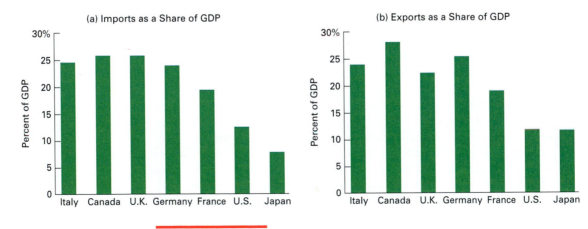

---

[1]The phrase "a country trades" means that people, business firms, or the government in that country trade. Many imports are inputs in the production of other products rather than final products themselves.

[2]*Small* and *large* refer to the relative sizes of economies (measured by total GDP), not to land areas.

A country has a trade surplus if it exports more than it imports; a country has a trade deficit if it imports more than it exports.

> A country's **balance of international trade** equals its exports minus its imports. When the balance is positive (exports exceed imports), the country has a **trade surplus;** when the balance is negative (imports exceed exports), it has a **trade deficit.**

As Figure 3 shows, the United States had a trade surplus through most of the third quarter of the 20th century, but it experienced a trade deficit throughout the final quarter of the century. Figure 4 breaks down the main categories of U.S. exports and imports.

Figure 3 | U.S. Balance of Trade on Goods and Services

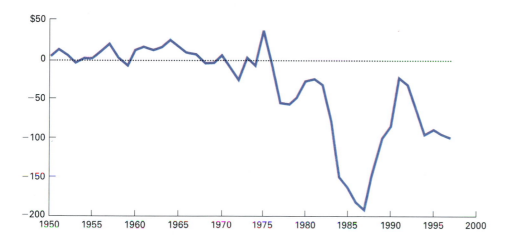

Figure 4 | Categories of U.S. Imports and Exports in 1997 ($ billions)

Total exports of merchandise and services	$932
Merchandise (excluding military goods)	678
Foods, beverages, feeds	51
Industrial supplies and materials	158
Capital goods (excluding autos)	294
Automobiles and parts	73
Nonfood consumer goods	77
Other exports	24
Services	253
Travel	74
Transportation	50
Royalties and license fees	30
Other services	99
Total imports of merchandise and services	$1,045
Merchandise (excluding miiltary goods)	877
Foods, beverages, feeds	40
Industrial supplies and materials	217
Capital goods (excluding autos)	254
Automobiles and parts	141
Nonfood consumer goods	193
Other imports	32
Services	168
Travel	52
Transportation	47
Royalties and license fees	8
Other services	61

Source: Survey of Current Business.

News reports about trade deficits can create confusion, because they report two different measures of the balance of trade. The *merchandise trade balance* refers to trade in goods only (not services). It includes international trade in food, industrial supplies, machinery and equipment, automobiles, and other consumer and industrial goods. The *balance of trade on goods and services* covers both goods *and* services, such as travel, transportation, and financial services.

The balance of trade is another name for a country's net exports, NEX.

Figure 5 shows that Canada and Japan are the two biggest trading partners of the United States, accounting for about one-third of all U.S. international trade. Mexico, the United Kingdom, Germany, South Korea, and Taiwan are also major U.S. trading partners. As Figure 6 shows, the United States is Japan's single biggest trading partner, despite rapid growth in Japanese trade with other Asian nations.

Figure 5 | U.S. Trading Partners

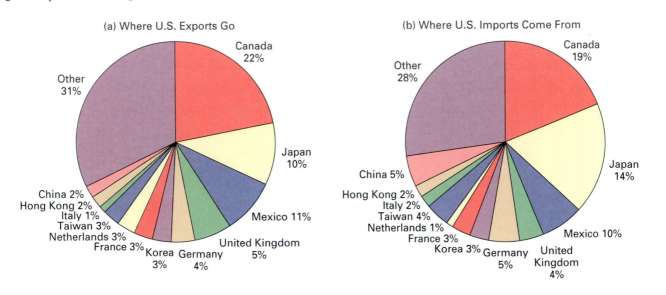

(a) Where U.S. Exports Go

Canada 22%
Other 31%
Japan 10%
Mexico 11%
United Kingdom 5%
Germany 4%
Korea 3%
France 3%
Netherlands 3%
Taiwan 3%
Italy 1%
Hong Kong 2%
China 2%

(b) Where U.S. Imports Come From

Canada 19%
Other 28%
Japan 14%
Mexico 10%
United Kingdom 4%
Germany 5%
Korea 3%
France 3%
Netherlands 1%
Taiwan 4%
Italy 2%
Hong Kong 2%
China 5%

Figure 6 | Japan's Trading Partners

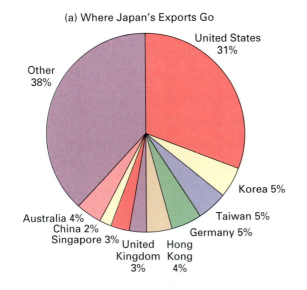

(a) Where Japan's Exports Go

United States 31%
Other 38%
Korea 5%
Taiwan 5%
Germany 5%
Hong Kong 4%
United Kingdom 3%
Singapore 3%
China 2%
Australia 4%

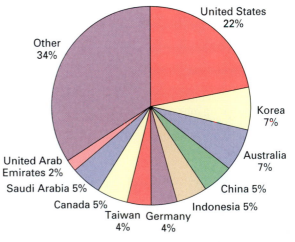

(b) Where Japan's Imports Come From

United States 22%
Other 34%
Korea 7%
Australia 7%
China 5%
Indonesia 5%
Germany 4%
Taiwan 4%
Canada 5%
Saudi Arabia 5%
United Arab Emirates 2%

International trade works like a good technology. When the U.S. loads wheat on a boat and ships it to Japan, and boats come back filled with television sets, international trade works like a technology that turns wheat into television sets. (Recall the fable in Chapter 3 about making cars from grain.)

People gain from international trade for the same reason that they gain from an improvement in technology. Of course, some people also lose from an improvement in technology. (Producers of horse-drawn carriages lost business when changes in technology led to mass production of cars.) The gains to the winners (car makers and buyers who chose cars over carriages) exceed the losses to the losers, however. Similarly, domestic car manufacturers lose when people buy foreign cars. However, while some people lose from international trade, the gains to the winners exceed the losses to the losers, just as when technology improves. That is why international trade is economically efficient.

Principle of Comparative Advantage

Trade promotes economic efficiency, because costs of production differ across countries. A country gains from trade when it exports goods in which it has a comparative advantage. As Chapter 3 explained:

> A country has a **comparative advantage** in making a product when it can produce that product at a lower opportunity cost than other countries can.

Countries gain from international trade by concentrating resources on activities that they do best. Each country produces more of the products in which it has a comparative advantage, and each produces less of other products. This raises world output and allows people to consume more of every product than they could consume without trade, a result sometimes called the *law of comparative advantage*.

EXAMPLE

Table 1 shows the hypothetical costs of producing one music video or one computer program in the United States and in Japan. The costs are measured in the number of person-days each country takes to produce one unit of each good. U.S. producers take 1 person-day of work to produce a music video; Japanese producers take 4 person-days. On the other hand, U.S. programmers take 3 person-days to write a computer program; Japanese programmers take only 2 person-days. Notice that in the United States, the cost of writing a computer program is three times the cost of producing a music video; in Japan, it is one-half the cost of a music video. The United States has a comparative advantage in music videos, because it can produce them at a lower opportunity cost than Japan can; Japan has a comparative advantage in computer programming, because the opportunity cost of computer programming is lower there than in the United States.

Table 1 | Costs of Production: Amount of Labor Time Needed to Produce 1 Unit of a Product

	United States	Japan
One music video	1 person-day	4 person-days
One computer program	3 person-days	2 person-days

Table 2 | Total World Output With and Without International Trade

	United States	Japan	World
(A) OUTPUT WITHOUT TRADE			
Music videos	24	12	36
Computer programs	12	6	18
(B) OUTPUT WITH TRADE			
Music videos	60	0	60
Computer programs	0	30	30

Note: People in each country work 60 million person-days, and buyers in each country want exactly twice as many music videos as computer programs.

These countries can gain from international trade. Suppose that each country has 60 million person-days available for work (writing computer programs or producing music videos), and that people in each country want twice as many music videos as computer programs.[3] Table 2 summarizes the results. Without international trade, Japan would spend 48 million person-days to produce 12 million music videos. Japan would spend its other 12 million person-days writing 6 million computer programs (generating twice as many music videos as computer programs, the combination that people want to buy). The United States would spend 24 million person-days to produce 24 million music videos and the other 36 million person-days writing 12 million computer programs. World output (in the United States and Japan together) would total 36 million music videos and 18 million computer programs.

With international trade, the United States would spend all 60 million person-days producing music videos, and Japan would spend all 60 million person-days working on computer programs. Total world output would rise to 60 million music videos (all produced in the United States) and 30 million computer programs (all produced in Japan). International trade would raise world output of both products. That is why international trade resembles an improvement in technology. Although no one works harder than without trade, the world produces more output. World output rises because international trade raises economic efficiency.

In real life, the United States appears to have a comparative advantage in farm products and high-tech equipment. Specific products include aircraft, computers, medicines, organic chemicals, and wheat. The United States appears to have a comparative disadvantage in goods such as auto parts, electronic components, inorganic chemicals, semiconductors, and televisions. Evidence suggests that the United States has a comparative advantage in products that use relatively large quantities of land or skilled labor as inputs. It has a comparative disadvantage in products that use relatively large amounts of unskilled labor or capital equipment.

---

[3]This means that music videos and computer programs are (perfect) complements.

Review Questions

1. What is the balance of international trade?

2. Which countries are the biggest trading partners of the United States?

3. What is comparative advantage? What is the law of comparative advantage?

4. Explain why international trade resembles a good technology.

Thinking Exercises

5. Use the data in Table 1 to calculate (a) the opportunity cost of producing music videos in the United States, (b) the opportunity cost of producing computer programs in the United States, (c) the opportunity costs of producing each good in Japan. (d) Use your answers to Questions 5a through 5c to explain why the United States has a comparative advantage in music videos and Japan has a comparative advantage in computer programs.

6. Suppose that the numbers in Table 1 change to:

Costs of Production: Labor Time to Produce 1 Unit

	United States	Japan
One music video	1 person-day	3 person-days
One computer program	2 person-days	4 person-days

Which country has a comparative advantage in which product?

7. Discuss the following claim: "Regardless of how unproductive a country is, it always has a comparative advantage in *some* product."

Production and Consumption Possibilities

Without international trade, each country is limited to consuming the goods that it can produce. International trade allows each country to increase its consumption of every good. How much does it gain? The answer depends on world equilibrium prices and the country's production possibilities frontier.

Chapter 3 explained that a country's production possibilities frontier (PPF) graphs the combinations of various goods that it can produce with its limited resources and technology. Without international trade, a country's PPF also shows its consumption possibilities. People can buy any combination of goods that the economy can produce, such as Points A, B, or C in Figure 7, but they cannot consume at points above the PPF, such as Points D or E.

International trade, however, allows people to buy more than their country can produce! To see why, look at Figure 8. The world price line shows opportunities for trading with other countries. Its slope (in absolute value) shows the world relative price of cars in terms of fabric. People can consume at any point on the world price line, such as Points B, D, or E. To consume at Point D, the country produces at Point B (30 million cars and 600 million yards of fabric), and then it trades along the world price line

GAINS FROM INTERNATIONAL TRADE: GRAPHICAL ANALYSIS

Figure 7
Production Possibilities Frontier

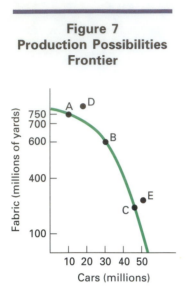

Figure 8
Consumption Possibilities with International Trade

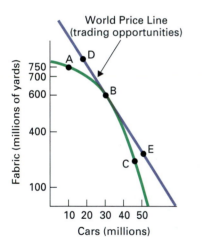

to Point D by exporting cars and importing fabric. The slope of the world price line (in absolute value) shows the amount of fabric the country can import for each car it exports. Similarly, if people in the country want to consume at Point E, they can produce at Point B, then export fabric and import cars. With international trade, people in each country can consume at any point on the world price line.

Slope of the World Price Line

The absolute value of the world price line's slope—the equilibrium relative price of the two goods—depends on world supply and demand.[4] Figure 9 summarizes equilibrium with international trade. If the United States does not trade with other countries, the equilibrium U.S. price is $12, and the equilibrium U.S. quantity is 20 units of fabric. If Mexico does not trade with other countries, its equilibrium price of fabric is $7, and its equilibrium quantity is 15 units. Without international trade, the difference in price between countries gives people an incentive to trade—to buy the good where its price is low, and to sell where its price is high.[5] With international trade, the equilibrium price is $10, and the world equilibrium quantity is 40 units. People in the United States buy 28 units of fabric, but U.S. firms produce and sell only 14 units, so the United States imports the other 14 units of fabric. Mexican firms produce and sell 26 units of fabric, while people in Mexico buy only 12, so Mexico exports 14 units of fabric; U.S. imports equal Mexican exports.

Winners and Losers: The Sizes of Gains from Trade

Some people gain from international trade, and others lose. Figure 10 summarizes the sizes of these gains and losses.

1. Consumers in the importing country gain. International trade allows them to buy the good at a price of $10 instead of $12, so they gain consumer surplus equal to Areas A + B.

2. Producers in the importing country lose. They sell the good at a price of $10 instead of $12. These losers include the owners (stockholders) of firms that face additional foreign competition and workers at those firms. They lose producer surplus equal to Area A.

3. Producers in the exporting country gain. International trade allows them to charge a price of $10 instead of $7 and to increase sales. They gain producer surplus equal to Areas C + D.

4. Consumers in the exporting country lose. They pay $10 instead of $7 to buy the good, and they buy less than they would buy without trade, losing consumer surplus equal to Area C.

On net, the importing country gains Area B, and the exporting country gains Area D. The importing country experiences a net gain, because its consumers gain more (Areas A + B) than its producers lose (Area A). Its net gain is Area B. The exporting country experiences a net gain, because its producers gain more (Areas C + D) than its consumers

---

[4]Recall that the price in a supply/demand graph is always the relative price of the good. (See Chapter 4.) The $10 equilibrium price in Figure 9 takes as given the average level of other nominal prices. The equilibrium price would be $20 if other nominal prices were to double.

[5]International trade equates relative prices across countries in situations with low transportation costs and transactions costs. High transportation and transactions costs can keep prices higher in some countries than in others. A Big Mac, for example, does not sell for the same price in all countries, or even in all cities within a country. Figure 9 ignores transportation costs and transactions costs.

Figure 9 | Equilibrium in World Markets

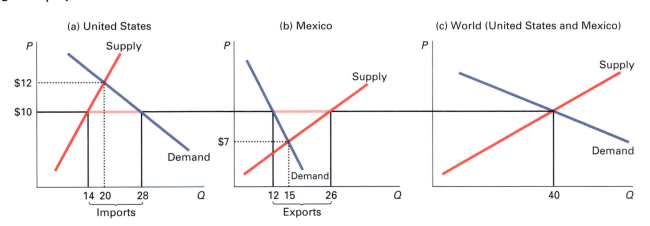

(a) United States

(b) Mexico

(c) World (United States and Mexico)

Without international trade, the equilibrium U.S. price is $12, and the United States produces and consumes 20 units of fabric. The equilibrium price is $7 in Mexico, and Mexico produces and consumes 15 units of fabric. With international trade, the world equilibrium price is $10 (that is, a unit of fabric sells for $10 in each country). The United States produces 14 units and consumes 28 units, so it imports 14 units. Mexico produces 26 units and consumes 12 units, so it exports 14 units. In equilibrium, Mexican exports of fabric equal U.S. imports. In Panel (c), world equilibrium occurs when the world quantity supplied equals the world quantity demanded.

Figure 10 | Measuring Gains from Trade

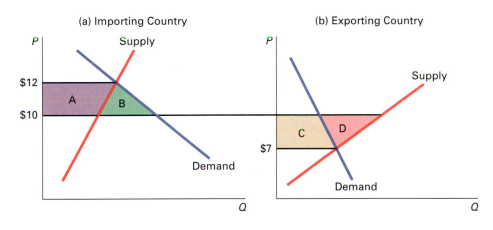

(a) Importing Country

(b) Exporting Country

Without international trade, the equilibrium price is $12 in one country and $7 in the other. With international trade, the world equilibrium price is $10. (a) Consumers in the importing country gain Areas A + B from international trade, while producers there lose Area A; on net, the importing country gains Area B. (b) Consumers in the exporting country lose Area C from international trade, but producers there gain Areas C + D; on net, the exporting country gains Area D.

lose (Area C). Its net gain is Area D. The winners in each country gain enough that they could compensate the losers for their losses and still gain from international trade. In this sense, each country, and the world as a whole, gains from international trade. Areas B + D in Figure 10 show the world's net gain.

This result on the gains from international trade is one of the most famous results in economics. It implies that (on net) countries lose when they restrict international trade.

Production and Consumption Possibilities: Example

Figure 11 shows the PPFs for the United States and Japan for the example from Table 1. Each country has 60 million person-days available for work, so the United States can produce 60 million music videos and zero computer programs, or zero music videos and

Figure 11 | Trade Expands Consumption Opportunities

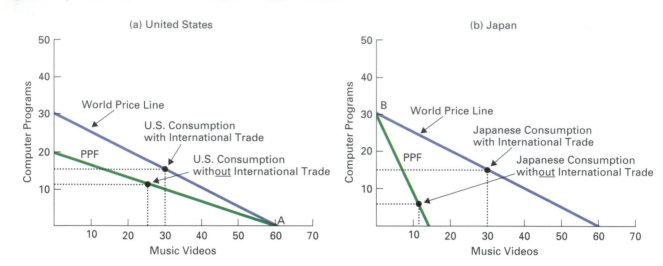

(a) Without international trade, the United States produces and consumes 24 million music videos and 12 million computer programs. With international trade, it produces 60 million music videos, exports 30 million, and imports 15 million computer programs, so the United States consumes 30 million music videos and 15 million computer programs. (b) Without international trade, Japan produces and consumes 12 million music videos and 6 million computer programs. With international trade, it produces 30 million computer programs, exports 15 million, and imports 30 million music videos, so Japan consumes 30 million music videos and 15 million computer programs.

20 million computer programs, or some combination along the PPF in Figure 11a. Japan can produce 15 million music videos and zero computer programs, or zero music videos and 30 million computer programs, or some combination along its PPF in Figure 11b.

Without international trade, people in the United States may consume 24 million music videos and 12 million computer programs, and people in Japan may consume 12 million music videos and 6 million computer programs.[6] With international trade, their opportunities depend on prices. Suppose that the world equilibrium relative price is one-half of a computer program per music video, that is, a computer program costs twice as much as a music video, as in Figure 12. This defines a slope for the world price line (in absolute value) of one-half, as in Figure 11, which shows consumption opportunities in each country. The United States produces at Point A, with 60 million music videos and no computer programs. It exports 30 million videos and imports 15 million computer programs, so people in the United States consume 30 million music videos and 15 million computer programs. Japan produces at Point B with 30 million computer programs and no music videos. It exports 15 million computer programs and imports 30 million music videos, so people in Japan consume 30 million music videos and 15 million computer programs. International trade, like an improvement in technology, allows everyone to consume more of every product.[7]

---

[6]The slopes of the PPFs show the relative prices of music videos and computer programs in the two countries without international trade. The relative price of computer programs in terms of music videos is 3 in the United States (equal to its opportunity cost); one computer program costs the same as 3 music videos. The relative price of computer programs in terms of music videos is ½ in Japan; one computer program costs half as much as one music video. Because music videos are relatively cheaper in the United States and computer programs are relatively cheaper in Japan, people in the United States may consume relatively more music videos, and people in Japan may consume relatively more computer programs.

[7]In this example, Japan gains more from international trade than does the United States. The division of the gains from international trade between the two countries depends on the world equilibrium relative price.

Figure 12 | World Equilibrium Relative Price

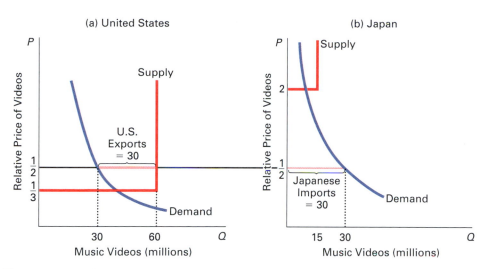

The world equilibrium relative price is one-half of a music video per computer program.

How Big Are the Gains from International Trade?

It is difficult to estimate precisely the total gains from international trade in real life, but evidence suggests that the gains are big. To see why, think about the gains from intercity trade (trade between cities in the same country). How much would your standard of living decline if you could not buy any products produced outside the city where you live? Most people would experience dramatic changes in lifestyle because each city would have to produce all of the food its people would eat, all of the materials for its housing, all of its consumer products, and so on. Most cities have few natural resources available as inputs into production of these goods. Most cities also lack sources of energy such as oil or natural gas. Trade between cities and between states clearly brings huge gains.[8]

Figure 10 may understate the gains from international trade in three ways. The economy benefits from (1) dynamic gains from trade, (2) extra gains from trade in industries with economies of scale, and (3) political gains from trade. None of these gains appear directly in the figure.

The gains shown in Figure 10 are often called the *static gains from international trade*. The benefits of international trade expand further if trade helps countries to increase their productivity. By increasing specialization, trade may raise the speed at which workers and firms improve productivity through experience. Also, the increase in competition from foreign sellers can increase incentives for firms to innovate. The benefits of increased productivity and innovation due to international trade are often called *dynamic gains from trade*. Some estimates suggest that dynamic gains from trade exceed the static gains.

In some industries, *economies of scale* reduce the average costs of producing products in large quantities. (Per-unit costs fall as the scale of operations increases.) International trade allows countries to specialize, perhaps further reducing the costs of production in these industries. This benefit adds to the gains from international trade. Increased specialization also reduces the cost of expanding the variety of sizes, colors, styles, and models available for a product. People gain from an increase in variety, because they can choose which style to buy, another addition to the gains from international trade.

[8]The gains from international trade in small countries, such as Hong Kong or Luxembourg, resemble the gains from intercity trade in large countries. People in large countries reap somewhat smaller gains from international trade than those in small countries, because they can trade with many other people within their own countries.

The *political gains from trade* refer to benefits of increased interdependencies among nations, which reinforces trust, improves communication and understanding, encourages cultural exchanges, and reduces chances of war. People are less willing to shoot other people when those other people are their customers. By encouraging economic interactions and interdependencies, increased international trade may generate many political and social benefits.

Review Questions

8. Why does international trade increase a country's consumption possibilities?

9. (a) What determines the slope of the world price line? (b) Why does the country in Figure 8 produce at Point B rather than Point A or Point C?

Thinking Exercises

10. How does international trade between two countries affect consumers and producers in each country? Draw a graph to show the sizes of the gains and losses from international trade to consumers and producers in each country.

11. Suppose that the numbers in Table 1 change to:

Costs of Production: Labor Time to Produce 1 Unit

	United States	Japan
One music video	6 person-days	1 person-day
One computer program	3 person-days	2 person-days

(a) Assume that each country has 60 million person-days available for work, as in the example in the text. Draw a production possibilities frontier for each country, and show how its consumption opportunities change if the world equilibrium relative price is *one computer program per music video*.

(b) Use your answer to help discuss whether a country gains or loses from international trade when the other country is more productive in *every* industry.

BALANCE OF TRADE AND THE CURRENT ACCOUNT

People gain from international trade in financial assets as well as trade in goods and services. Trade in financial assets allows countries to borrow and lend and to diversify investments to reduce risk. When a country lends money to other countries or invests in those countries, it creates a current account surplus.

> The **current account** measures the amount that a country lends to or borrows from other countries. A country has a **current account surplus** when it lends, and a **current account deficit** when it borrows.

The phrase "a country borrows" means that people, business firms, and units of government in one country borrow from people, business firms, and units of government in other countries.

A nation is a net debtor if it owes money on net to other countries because it has borrowed money in the past. A country to which other nations owe money is a net creditor.

Net debtor countries pay interest and make loan repayments to other countries. Net creditor countries earn income by collecting interest and repayments of past loans.

The balance of trade (or net exports, NEX) and current account are closely related. A country's current account surplus equals its trade balance surplus plus its net income from investments in other countries:

$$\text{Current account surplus} = \text{Trade balance surplus}$$

$$+ \text{ Net income from foreign investments and transfer payments}$$

In 1997, the United States exported goods and services worth $932 billion, and it imported goods and services worth $1,045 billion. U.S. GDP was $8,079 billion, so the United States exported about 12 percent (or about one-eighth) of the goods and services it produced. Because imports exceeded exports by $113 billion, the United States had a $113 billion trade deficit.[9] Other countries shipped more goods and services to the United States than it shipped to them. Other countries were willing to make those shipments, because the United States gave them financial assets in exchange (stocks, bonds, money, and other assets). In other words, the United States borrowed the money to pay for the excess of imports over exports; it borrowed to finance its trade deficit.

The United States also borrowed from other countries to make transfer payments, mainly foreign aid and gifts, to other countries. The United States gave $39 billion more to other countries as gifts and foreign aid—transfer payments to foreigners—than it received. At the same time, foreigners earned slightly more on their U.S. investments ($250 billion) than the United States earned on its investments in other countries ($236 billion), leaving net income from foreign investments of −$14 billion. On transfer payments and income on foreign investments combined, the United States paid other countries $53 billion more than it collected from them in 1997. This means that the United States owed these countries $53 billion more than it owed before that year. These countries hold U.S. financial assets that resemble IOUs from the United States. The United States owes goods and services to these countries in the future. They get these goods and services by spending the interest payments on the financial assets or selling the financial assets to buy goods from the United States.

U.S. borrowing from other countries exceeded the trade balance deficit by $53 billion:

1997 U.S. current account surplus	=	1997 U.S. trade balance surplus	+	1997 U.S. net income from foreign investments and transfer payments
−$166 billion	=	−$113 billion	+	−$53 billion

Note that a negative surplus represents a deficit; the United States had a $113 billion trade deficit and a $166 billion current account deficit. This means that the United States borrowed $166 billion from other countries.

Similarly, a country with a trade surplus lends to people in other countries. If Germany sells goods worth 20 billion Euros to other countries and imports goods worth only 16 billion Euros, then Germany lends 4 billion Euros to other countries. People in those countries receive only 16 billion Euros from German buyers, but spend 20 billion Euros, so they borrow the other 4 billion Euros to spend on German goods.

Causes of Current Account Deficits

A country has a current account deficit when it saves less than it invests. A country can invest more than it saves only by borrowing the extra money for investment from other

Advice

See the Web site (www.dryden.com) for this book for the latest statistics on international trade and other economic data. Because the government often revises its statistics as it obtains better estimates, the most recent data on the Internet may differ slightly from numbers in this book.

Don't memorize these data—use them to help learn concepts that you can apply to understand and analyze economic issues.

---

[9] In the equation, this result shows up as a negative number for the trade balance surplus.

Figure 13 | World Loan Market Equilibrium

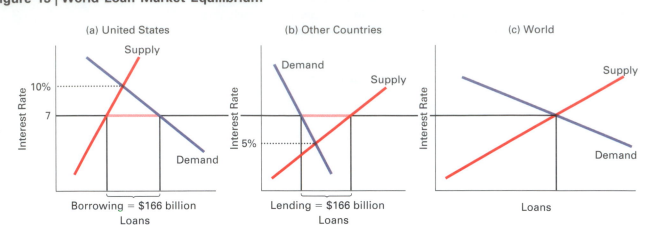

Without international borrowing and lending, the equilibrium interest rate in the United States is 10 percent per year. With international borrowing and lending, the world equilibrium interest rate is 7 percent per year and the United States borrows $166 billion from other countries (it has a $166 billion current account deficit).

countries. A country has a current account surplus when it saves more than it invests. A country can save more than it invests only by lending the extra savings to people in other countries.

Figure 13 shows three diagrams. Panel (a) shows the supply of loans and the demand for loans in the United States. Panel (b) shows the supply and demand for loans in other countries. Panel (c) shows the world supply and demand for loans. This graph resembles Figure 9, which showed exports and imports of goods. Figure 13, in contrast, shows exports and imports of loans. If the United States could not borrow from other countries in this example, the U.S. interest rate would be 10 percent per year and the foreign interest rate would be 5 percent per year. International borrowing and lending, however, gives a world real interest rate of 7 percent per year. The United States borrows $166 billion from foreign countries, so the U.S. current account deficit is $166 billion. Other countries lend $166 billion to the United States, so the rest of the world has a current account surplus of $166 billion.

The current account changes when the demand or supply of loans changes in any country. Most economists believe that U.S. government budget deficits are a main cause of U.S. current account deficits. Unless people save all the money they get from a tax cut, a government budget deficit raises the U.S. demand for loans more than the supply. Without international borrowing and lending, the deficit would raise the real interest rate in the United States. By borrowing and lending on international markets, however, the United States can meet part of its increased demand for loans. Borrowing from other countries raises the U.S. current account deficit.

The evidence on government budget deficits and current account deficits issue is mixed. U.S. current account deficits increased substantially in the mid-1980s, soon after government budget deficits increased, but the two deficits are not tightly linked in other periods. Figure 14 shows that the current account deficit appears to follow the budget deficit after a lag of about 2 years. The real U.S. government budget deficit has fallen in recent years and has recently become a surplus. If the relationship in the figure remains unaffected, a reduction in the U.S. current account deficit should soon follow.

Several other factors also affect the current account deficit. Tax policies affect supply and demand for loans by affecting investment demand. Changes in technology raise the demand for loans by increasing the demand for investment. Changes in people's tastes

Figure 14 | Twin U.S. Deficits: Government Budget Deficit and Current Account Deficit

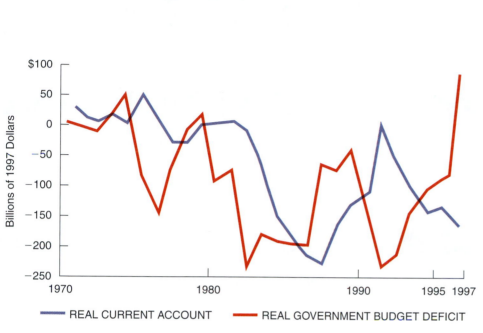

REAL CURRENT ACCOUNT REAL GOVERNMENT BUDGET DEFICIT

The graph shows the real government budget deficit measured by increases in the real value of the privately-held federal government debt. The figure also shows the real U.S. current account deficit. A larger negative number indicates a larger deficit. Notice that the U.S. government had a real budget surplus in 1997, despite news reports of a small deficit, using a less accurate measure.

for spending or saving money, or changes in expected future incomes, affect saving and the supply of loans. These and other factors affect the current account by affecting the supply or demand for loans.

Effects of Current Account Deficits

Are trade deficits good or bad? The term *deficit* sounds bad, and people often express concern about trade deficits. Some people claim that exports are good because they create jobs and that imports are bad because they destroy jobs; they conclude that trade deficits reduce domestic employment.[10] Against this view, other people argue that imports are good because they allow a country to consume certain products without producing them, while exports require people to work at producing goods for other countries to enjoy.

Both arguments are misleading. Current account deficits and surpluses occur because people borrow from and lend to people in other countries. These loans are voluntary trades, and people expect to benefit from them. If you save your money and deposit it in a bank account, the bank lends that money to someone who wants to buy a car or start a business. International lending works the same way, but on a global scale. A country runs a current account deficit when it borrows; it trades away future products to get current products. Similarly, a country runs a current account surplus when it saves and lends; it trades current products to get future products.

Trade deficits may appear to reduce the total number of jobs available, but appearances can be misleading. Both imports and exports create local jobs. Jobs supported by

---

[10]This is the argument behind buy-American campaigns.

exports are easy to identify; jobs supported by imports are difficult to identify because they are spread throughout the economy. U.S. imports create American jobs by providing foreigners with dollars to spend on American products. (When foreign sellers do not spend those dollars, they lend the dollars to other people who spend them.) For the same reason, limiting purchases to American-made goods does not encourage American job creation. It simply changes the composition of those jobs, encouraging job creation in import-competing industries and discouraging it in exporting industries and other industries.

Review Questions

12. What are the dynamic gains from trade? What are the political gains from trade?

13. What is the current account? How is it related to the balance of trade?

14. What can cause a current account deficit?

Thinking Exercises

15. Are current account deficits necessarily bad for the economy?

16. Draw a graph to show the effects of a *fall* in the U.S. government budget deficit on the U.S. current account and the world equilibrium interest rate.

PROTECTIONISM

Governments often act to restrict international trade. Because restrictions on imports protect certain domestic firms from foreign competition, a government policy to restrict imports is often labeled *protectionism*.

Allowing free international trade usually enhances economic efficiency for the reasons discussed earlier in this chapter; protectionist policies almost always cause economic inefficiency. Some people gain and some people lose from restricting imports, but the losses to the losers (such as consumers) exceed the gains to the winners (mainly domestic firms protected from foreign competition). Trade restrictions help domestic firms to maintain high prices by limiting domestic supply. The restrictions prevent consumers from buying products from foreign competitors or impose special taxes on purchases from those foreign competitors. Trade restrictions tend to occur when the groups that stand to benefit have greater political influence than the groups that stand to lose.

Types of Trade Restrictions

The two most prominent forms of restrictions on international trade are tariffs and import quotas.

> A **tariff** is a tax on imports.

> An **import quota** is a direct limit on the number of imported goods of a certain type.

Exporters and consumers, like this shopkeeper in Tokyo, lose from protectionism.

The U.S. government has imposed tariffs in recent years on computers, ball bearings, and many other goods. It has set import quotas for steel, sugar, textiles, ice cream, and many other products. Japan has set quotas for imports of beef, oranges, and rice.

Other forms of trade restrictions include voluntary export restraints (VERs), which work like unofficial quotas in which the government of a country agrees "voluntarily" to limit its exports to another country. A country may agree to limit its exports to avert a threat of trade restrictions from another country.[11] In this way, the United States induced Japan to adopt voluntary export restraints on its cars starting in 1981. According to one estimate, this action raised the U.S. prices of Japanese cars by about $2,500 each and raised the U.S. prices of American cars by about $1,000 each. U.S. pressure led Japan to reduce its automobile exports further (to 1.65 million cars per year) in 1992. Under similar pressure, other countries have established VERs on a variety of other goods.

Another form of trade restriction, a local content requirement, creates a legal minimum fraction of a good's components (perhaps parts that represent one-half of a car's value) that must come from producers in the domestic country rather than from imports. Another form of protectionism, bureaucratic (red tape) protectionism, prevents foreign producers from legally selling their goods until they complete bureaucratic procedures designed to raise costs to foreign producers. Government regulations, sometimes disguised as health and safety regulations, also serve as trade restrictions. Suppose, for example, that foreign firms and domestic firms use different types of inputs in their products. The inputs may be identical in every important respect, but a government may ban the input used by foreign firms citing questionable health or safety threats. Governments have often restricted imports in this way.

Effects of Tariffs

Figure 15 shows the effects of a tariff that does not affect the world price of the good. For example, the United States buys only a small fraction of the world's tea, so a fall in its purchases of tea reduces the world demand—and the world price—by such a small amount that economists can ignore it in practice.

Suppose that the U.S. government puts a tariff on imports of tea. P^{US} is the price including tax (that is, including the tariff) that buyers pay for imported tea. Foreign sellers receive the after-tax world price P^W. The difference, $P^{US} - P^W$, is the per-unit tariff that the government collects.

As the tariff raises the U.S. price of tea above the world price, tea producers in the United States also raise their prices to P^{US}, so they benefit from the tariff, raising their production and sales from 10 to 15 units. Area A shows the gain to U.S. producers (the increase in their producer surplus) from the tariff. The tariff hurts American consumers, because it raises the U.S. price of tea.[12] Total sales of tea in the United States fall from 34 units (10 from U.S. firms and 24 imported from foreign firms) to 24 units. Imports fall from 24 to 9 units. American consumers lose Areas A, B, C, and D from the tariff. (These areas show the fall in consumer surplus.) The U.S. government gains Area C, because people pay the government $(P^{US} - P^W)$ for each of the 14 units they continue to import.

The loss to U.S. consumers—Areas A + B + C + D—exceeds the combined gain to the government and U.S. producers—Areas A + C. The difference, Areas B + D, shows the deadweight social loss from the tariff. While the tariff creates winners and losers, the losers lose more than the winners win. The deadweight social loss measures a loss to society as a whole from the economic inefficiency created by the tariff.

Tariffs and World Prices

When a country buys a large enough fraction of total world sales of a good, a tariff imposed by its government can actually reduce the world price of that good. This benefits the country that imposes the tariff by reducing the price it pays for imports. If this benefit exceeds the deadweight social loss from the tariff, the country can gain by

---

[11] The restriction is often voluntary in the same sense that a crime victim voluntarily gives up a wallet to a mugger.

[12] Even though the tariff applies only to imports, the increase in the price of imported goods reduces the foreign competition facing U.S. producers, so U.S. producers also raise their price. The price increase applies to tea produced anywhere, not just imported tea.

Figure 15 | Effects of a Tariff

Without a tariff, the United States produces 10 units, imports 24, and consumes 34. With a tariff, the U.S. price rises from P^W to P^{US}, U.S. production rises to 15 units, U.S. imports fall to 9, and U.S. consumption falls to 24. U.S. consumers lose Areas A + B + C + D from the tariff. U.S. producers gain Area A, and the U.S. government gains Area C in tariff (tax) revenue. The difference, Area B + D, is a deadweight social loss from the tariff.

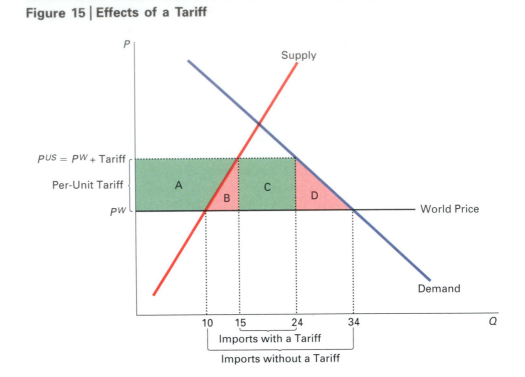

Big tariff put on sweetener

BRUSSELS, Nov. 29 (Reuters)—The European Commission today imposed large duties on cut-price imports of the low-calorie sweetener aspartame from the United States and Japan to protect the only European producer of the product.

The duties, which will add 70 percent to the imported prices almost overnight, came just days before the final phase of talks on liberalizing trade were scheduled to begin here.

Source: New York Times

Another trade restriction.

imposing a tariff. The country's gain, though, comes at the expense of even bigger losses in foreign countries, that is, a substantial fall in world economic efficiency.

Although a country can sometimes gain at the expense of other countries, evidence indicates that countries usually lose on the whole when they impose tariffs. In most real-life situations, governments impose tariffs not because their countries stand to gain overall, but because the winners (firms that want to reduce foreign competition) have more political influence than the losers (such as consumers).

Tariffs can also provoke foreign retaliation. If the United States imposes tariffs on imports of a product from the European Union (EU), the EU may in turn impose tariffs on its imports of American products. In the end, all countries are likely to lose. Even if a country could gain from some tariff considered in isolation, it may lose when foreign political forces lead to retaliatory tariffs.

Effects of Nontariff Trade Restrictions

Import quotas have effects similar to those of tariffs, but with one main difference: the government collects no tax revenue from a quota. A quota simply limits the quantity of units imported. In Figure 15, a quota that limited U.S. imports to 9 units would produce the same effects as the tariff. The interpretation of the figure requires only a slight change. Area C represents a profit to the people who are legally allowed to import the 9 units of foreign goods, instead of a gain to the government. These importers profit, because they can buy those goods at the low world price, P^W, and resell them at the higher U.S. price, P^{US}; Area C shows the profits from these resales. Otherwise, a quota has the same effect as a tariff; the United States loses Area B + D from the import quota.

A voluntary export restraint (VER) has almost the same effect as a quota, with one difference: The people who gain Area C in Figure 15 are the foreign producers whom the foreign government allows to export the 9 units of the product. The effects of bureau-

IN THE NEWS

Hong Kong agrees to limit exports of textiles to U.S.

*By Eduardo Lachica
Staff Reporter of The Wall
Street Journal*

WASHINGTON—Hong Kong agreed to sharply curb the growth of its textile and apparel exports to the U.S. through 1991.

"Obviously, we aren't happy about it, but like it or not there is a lot of protectionist pressure (in the U.S.) that forced us to make a realistic assessment of what we could get," said Hamish MacLeod, chief textile negotiator for Hong Kong.

Japanese quota extension pleases Detroit

But car-export limit is likely to hurt U.S. consumers

*By Joseph B. White
Staff Reporter of The Wall
Street Journal*

The Japanese government's decision to keep a cap on car exports to the U.S. pleased Detroit's auto makers, who will keep the benefit of trade restraint even though they may report record profits for 1988.

Detroit's gain, however, is likely to come at the expense of U.S. consumers. For them, Japan's decision announced yesterday to maintain a 2.3 million-car limit on annual exports to the U.S. means the most popular Japanese cars probably will remain expensive and in short supply.

"The impact of the quotas is quite heavy on the consumer," said a spokesman for Toyota Motor Corp.'s U.S. sales arm. "You're just making people pay more for products, and the extra money is going into Detroit's pocket, and ours."

Begun in 1981

The quotas were first established in 1981 as a device to give U.S. auto makers time to recover from the nation's deep recession. Detroit's Big Three, however, have earned near-record profits in the past 2 years, so the auto makers are using different arguments to press for continued quotas. Chief among them: the overall U.S. trade deficit is so bad that almost any measure is justified to reduce it.

Source: The Wall Street Journal

Trade restrictions imposed by the United States.

cratic restrictions are also similar to the effects of a tariff, since paying employees to handle the red tape is like paying a tax. The main difference is that the government does not collect the tariff revenue. Instead, Area C in Figure 15 represents spending by foreign firms to comply with the government's bureaucratic procedures.[13]

Scope of Protectionism

How much does protectionism cost? A recent study estimates that in 1990, protectionism cost U.S. consumers about $70 billion per year (about $270 per person each year).[14] Domestic producers gained about $35 billion from these restrictions, and they brought the government about $13 billion in revenue, so the net loss to the U.S. economy from

---

[13] Trade with some countries requires paying bribes to appropriate officials; the effects of these bribes resemble the effects of tariffs.

[14] See Gary Clyde Hufbauer and Kimberly Ann Elliott, *Measuring the Costs of Protection in the United States* (Washington, D.C.: Institute for International Economics, 1994).

Table 3 | Losses and Gains Due to Protectionism (1990 $ millions)

Protected Industry	Loss to American Consumers	Gain to American Producers	Gain to U.S. Government	Net Loss to U.S. Economy
Ceramics and tiles	$ 241	$ 63	$ 173	$ 5
Costume jewelry	103	46	51	5
Frozen concentrated orange juice	281	101	145	35
Glassware	266	162	95	9
Luggage	211	16	169	26
Rubber footwear	208	55	141	12
Women's footwear (excluding athletic shoes)	376	70	295	11
Apparel	21,158	9,901	3,545	7,712 (2,301)[a]
Textiles	3,274	1,749	632	894 (181)[a]
Canned tuna	73	31	31	10 (4)[a]
Machine tools	542	157	0	385 (35)[a]

[a]The first figure shows the net loss to the U.S. economy; the second figure (in parentheses) shows that loss after including the gains to foreign firms from U.S. protectionism.
Source: Gary Clyde Hufbauer and Kimberly Ann Elliott, *Measuring the Costs of Protection in the United States* (Washington, D.C.: Institute for International Economics, 1994).

protectionism was about $22 billion per year (about $85 per person each year). Table 3 summarizes the losses to consumers and gains to producers in certain industries.

Governments engage in less protectionism now than they did in the past. The average U.S. tariff rate in 1920 was 16 percent. It increased to 38 percent in 1922, partly because the government raised tariffs and partly because those rates rose automatically due to falling prices.[15] The Smoot-Hawley Act of 1930 and more increases in tariff rates due to falling prices raised the average U.S. tariff rate to 53 percent, though tariffs applied to only about one-third of U.S. imports.

In 1947, many countries signed the General Agreement on Tariffs and Trade (GATT) agreement to reduce trade restrictions. The GATT also established an international organization in Geneva, Switzerland, to assist trade negotiations and work to reduce restrictions on trade. The most recent round of international trade talks has renamed the GATT as the World Trade Organization (WTO).

The **World Trade Organization (WTO)** is an international organization and a series of related treaties that reduce trade restrictions.

The WTO has helped to reduce world protectionism in the last half of the 20th century. The United States reduced its tariffs to an average of about 25 percent, covering only about one-tenth of its imports, by 1960. Other countries also reduced trade restrictions. The Kennedy Round of trade talks in 1967 further reduced tariffs to an average of about 12 percent, covering only 7 percent of imports. The Tokyo Round in 1979 reduced U.S. tariff rates to 6 percent, covering only 4 percent of imports, with similar reductions in other countries.

The WTO now includes 132 countries. The latest agreement, the Uruguay Round,

[15] If a good costs $10 and the tariff is $2, then the tariff rate is 20 percent. If the price of the good falls to $5 and the tariff stays at $2, the tariff rate rises to 40 percent. Prices fell from 1920 to 1922, which automatically raised tariff rates.

emerged from 8 years of negotiations ending in 1994. In that agreement, the United States and the European Union agreed to cut tariffs on each others' goods in half (on average) and to cut tariffs on goods from other countries by a smaller amount. On average, the Uruguay Round reduced world tariffs by about one-third, and it requires countries to replace import quotas on many products with more visible tariffs. The agreement also included pioneering provisions on certain products, such as farm products and intellectual property (protection of patents, copyrights, and trademarks).[16] The agreement gave the WTO new powers to resolve trade disputes more quickly and at lower cost than previous arrangements allowed. Estimates suggest that the agreement will eventually raise U.S. real GDP by about $100 billion per year and world real GDP by about $300 billion.

Regional free trade agreements include the North American Free Trade Agreement (NAFTA) and the European Union (EU). NAFTA began with a 1989 agreement between Canada and the United States to eliminate most trade restrictions between the two countries. Its coverage was extended in 1993 to include Mexico, and it phases out most restrictions on trade with that country by 2004. In the coming years, NAFTA may expand to include other countries in the American continents, such as Chile. The EU established free trade among 15 nations of Europe and common policies toward non-EU countries. Four additional European nations have formed a European Free Trade Association (EFTA) to participate in free trade with EU countries.

The increasing economic integration of Europe has important consequences for the United States and other countries. About 400 million people live in EU and EFTA countries, roughly as many as in the United States and Japan combined. Free trade within Europe will help to raise European standards of living in the future. If trade restrictions between Europe and other countries remain low, the gains will be even larger, and most of the world will share those gains. If the European countries impose bigger trade barriers with countries outside the continent, however, the United States, Japan, and other countries could suffer. Some analysts are concerned that regional free trade agreements in Europe and North America will reduce the incentives for world free trade; other analysts see these agreements as steps toward that goal.

Review Questions

17. What are tariffs, import quotas, and voluntary export restraints?

18. What is the WTO? What is the NAFTA? What is the EU?

Thinking Exercise

19. Draw a graph to show the effects of *eliminating* a tariff. Who gains and who loses from eliminating a tariff? Show the sizes of these gains and losses on your graph.

COMMON ARGUMENTS FOR PROTECTIONISM

Groups that favor trade restrictions (usually to benefit themselves) have advanced many arguments to justify their positions. Economists generally agree that these arguments are usually incorrect, and that legitimate arguments do not apply to most real-life cases of trade restrictions. This section considers some of the most common arguments for protectionism.

[16]It failed to resolve trade disputes, however, on certain products such as movies, television shows, and music, as well as shipping and financial services.

Argument 1: Domestic Firms Need Trade Restrictions to Compete in World Markets

This argument is fallacious because every country has a comparative advantage in certain products. Domestic firms can profitably sell those products in world markets if they produce them. Firms that produce other products, those in which the country has no comparative advantage, fail to compete on world markets because their costs are higher than the costs of foreign firms. Losses at those firms, along with profits at firms producing the products at which the country has a comparative advantage, provide incentives to direct the nation's resources to their most economically efficient uses.

One form of this argument supports protection to bolster domestic competitiveness by claiming that domestic producers cannot compete on world markets because foreign countries pay lower wages in all industries. For this reason, the argument goes, no domestic producers in any industry can compete in world markets. Imagine what would happen if every domestic firm faced competition from foreign sellers who could charge lower prices based on lower costs. All domestic firms would lose most of their customers to foreign competitors. Domestic firms would lay off workers, and the demand for labor would fall. This would reduce wages until costs at some domestic firms fall to below the costs of their foreign competitors (adjusted for differences in productivity). These firms would produce the goods in which the domestic country has a comparative advantage. In summary, the level of wages adjusts so that (in equilibrium) firms in every country can compete in world markets.[17]

Argument 2: Trade Restrictions Protect Domestic Jobs

Trade restrictions save jobs in some industries, but they eliminate jobs in other industries. Suppose that the United States imposes a tariff on imports of foreign cars. This policy raises the price of cars in the United States and raises sales of American-made cars. The tariff creates jobs in the protected American car industry, but it destroys jobs in other industries for two reasons. First, American consumers spend more on cars than they would spend without the tariff, leaving them less income to spend on other products (movies, clothes, food, and so on). Sales of these other products fall, destroying jobs in those industries. Second, foreigners earn fewer dollars than they would earn without the tariff, because they sell fewer cars to U.S. buyers; this reduces their spending on American products and destroys jobs in various American industries. On net, trade restrictions have little effect on total employment.[18]

Note on Trade Deficits

What happens if foreigners do not spend the dollars they earn to buy American products? This creates a trade deficit for the United States. For example, in 1997 the United States imported $1,045 billion in goods and services from other countries and exported only $932 billion. Foreigners earned $1,045 billion by selling products in the United States (plus $53 billion from the United States in gifts, foreign aid, and net income on U.S. investments), but they spent only $932 billion of that money on American goods and services. The rest of the money—$166 billion—they loaned back to people in the United States and invested in U.S. assets (such as real estate and stocks). As a result, the Americans who borrowed this money or sold these assets acquired $166 billion for

Advice

Don't be confused by the fact that wages in the United States are higher than those in most other countries of the world. American firms can compete effectively in world markets, even when workers in many other countries earn lower wages in *every* industry, because productivity at American firms is substantially higher than productivity in those other countries. Differences in productivity result from differences in workers' education, skills, and experience, from differences in equipment per worker and in equipment quality, and from differences in technology.

---

[17] Wages in the United States are higher than those in most other countries of the world, but American firms nevertheless compete effectively in world markets, because productivity at American firms is substantially higher than the levels in most other countries.

[18] Much international trade occurs in intermediate products, which become inputs into production of other, final products. Restricting imports of intermediate products raises costs at domestic firms that use them as inputs. The cost increases reduce those firms' supplies of final products, reduce their equilibrium sales, and reduce employment at those firms.

their own spending. For this reason, a trade deficit does not necessarily affect total spending on American-made products. Foreigners spent $166 billion less on American products than Americans spent on foreign products and gave as gifts, but foreigners loaned that money back to Americans to spend.[19]

Argument 3: Trade Restrictions Raise Wages

Trade restrictions do not necessarily raise domestic wages. If a country has a comparative advantage in producing a product that requires a relatively large input of labor, then international trade tends to raise that country's wages. Trade restrictions tend to reduce its wages rather than raising them. In other cases, however, international trade can reduce wages, so restricting international trade can raise them. Even in these circumstances, however, restricting international trade reduces a country's *total* income.

While expanding international trade has benefited the United States as a whole, it has created winners and losers. Economists continue to gather and interpret evidence on the fall in wages of low-skilled U.S. workers that began in the early 1970s, and some evidence indicates that expansion of international trade has played a role (although most evidence attributes a much larger role to technological change). Trade restrictions by the United States would redistribute income, raising wages in certain industries at the expense of other people and reducing total U.S. income. Restrictions on international trade are probably a less efficient method of redistributing income than a simple program of taxing some people to fund payments to others.

Argument 4: Trade Restrictions Level the Playing Field

Some people argue for trade restrictions to keep a so-called "level playing field" in international trade. ("Other countries restrict imports, so we should, too.") International trade differs from a football game or a war, though. International trade, like all voluntary trade, occurs because both sides expect to gain, and both sides usually do. Trade restrictions reduce economic efficiency and redistribute income from domestic consumers to protected domestic producers, whether or not other countries impose their own trade restrictions.

Suppose that subsidies by the Korean government lead Korean firms to reduce the prices of goods they sell in the United States. Should the United States respond with trade restrictions to protect American firms that compete with those Korean firms? Notice that the Korean government's subsidies help American consumers, who can buy the Korean products at lower prices. The subsidies hurt American producers who compete with the Korean firms. Korean taxpayers lose, because they pay for the subsidies, while Korean firms benefit from the subsidies.

How large are these gains and losses? American consumers clearly gain more than American firms lose. To see why, notice that American firms must reduce prices to compete, but every dollar they lose by lowering prices is a gain to American buyers who pay those lower prices! In fact, American consumers gain even more, because they buy some Korean products at prices subsidized by Korean taxpayers. Therefore, the United States gains on net when a foreign government subsidizes its own producers that export to the U.S. market. Trade restrictions would prevent the domestic country from capturing those gains.[20]

---

[19] If foreigners did not lend the money back to Americans (and did not spend it on American products)—that is, if the foreigners simply kept the U.S. money—then the U.S. sellers would be in the enviable position of exporting pieces of paper (money) in return for goods and services that consumers want! Of course, most foreigners have little reason to keep U.S. money, so they do either spend it or lend it back to Americans.

[20] Sometimes people argue that a foreign government may subsidize its producers only long enough to drive domestic firms out of business, then eliminate the subsidies. Little evidence suggests that this scenario happens in real life. If domestic firms expect a foreign government to discontinue its subsidy in the future, they reduce production only temporarily and resume production when the subsidies stop. As a result, this argument provides little justification for trade restrictions.

Another version of the level playing field argument supports trade restrictions by claiming that foreign firms sometimes charge lower prices on exports than they charge for sales in their own countries. This practice, popularly called *dumping,* is illegal in the United States, and most countries restrict imports of goods from foreign firms that they find guilty of dumping. For example, in 1985, the United States required Japanese semiconductor producers to raise the prices they charged to American buyers.

Who gains and who loses from dumping? The answer resembles the case of foreign subsidies. Consumers benefit from low prices if a foreign firm dumps. Firms that compete with the foreign firm lose, because they must match its low prices or lose customers. However, domestic buyers gain every dollar that domestic firms lose by lowering their prices. In addition, buyers gain from the reduced price at which they purchase foreign products. Therefore dumping benefits domestic consumers more than it hurts domestic producers.[21] One study estimated that U.S. trade restrictions imposed in retaliation for dumping cost American consumers $2.6 billion per year and create a net annual loss to the U.S. economy of roughly $1 billion.

Argument 5: Temporary Trade Restrictions Help New Industries Get Started

Some people argue that infant industries—new industries that are not yet well-established—need protection from foreign competition until they recover high start-up costs. Without trade restrictions, the argument claims, these firms could not compete with foreign firms for the first few years, even though they could compete in the future. This argument suggests a need for temporary trade restrictions to give the new firms a chance to develop.

The main problem with this argument comes from the capital market. If investors foresee expected future profits high enough to justify the infant firms' losses for the first few years, then they would accept short-term losses in return for the prospects of future profits. If expected future profits are not high enough to compensate investors for losses in the first few years, then the infant industry is an economically inefficient use of the economy's resources. Efficiency would improve by diverting the resources to other industries. Because trade restrictions would allow infant firms to raise domestic prices high enough to profit in the short run, they essentially force buyers to subsidize infant industries by paying the high prices.

Argument 6: Trade Restrictions Help National Defense

Some people argue that free trade creates political danger, because it creates too much specialization. Suppose that a country has no comparative advantage in producing military equipment or some other product important for national defense. With free trade, the country may import these products rather than produce them. Proponents of the national-defense argument see a danger in this arrangement, because a country cannot rely on imports in wartime. (It might even fight the country from which it imports war materials.) This national-defense argument suggests that a country may benefit militarily (at the cost of some economic inefficiency) from trade restrictions in certain industries with critical importance to national defense. While this national-defense argument may apply to a few industries, it has little application to most real-life trade restrictions.

Argument 7: Strategic Trade Policy Can Move Other Nations toward Freer Trade

A strategic trade policy is a national policy to encourage other governments to reduce their trade restrictions. Strategic trade policies often involve threats to impose new trade

Dumping can provide governments with an excuse for trade restrictions.

---

[21] Dumping is illegal in most countries, presumably, because domestic firms (who are harmed by dumping) have stronger political influence on this issue than domestic consumers have.

IN THE NEWS

U.S. tariff appears to backfire

Japan is retaliating for 63% charge on computer screens

By David E. Sanger
Special to the New York Times

TOKYO, Sept. 25—A month and a half after the United States imposed a 63 percent tariff on the most advanced screens for laptop and notebook computers, the Japanese have begun to retaliate.

Some companies have said they will stop sending the screens to the United States, and the Toshiba Corporation, one of the largest Japanese companies to make computers in the United States, has said it is moving its operations abroad to obtain the screens without paying the tariffs.

Thus, the retaliation will hurt the many American computer makers that rely on the Japanese screens and could lead to a loss of American jobs. The tariff was intended to protect a nascent sector of the American computer industry.

Canada puts levies on steel sheets of U.S., 5 nations

By John Urquhart
Staff Reporter of The Wall Street Journal

OTTAWA—Canada, in a retaliatory move, placed stiff antidumping levies on steel sheet imports from the U.S. and five other countries.

The case is one of three antidumping actions that were initiated by Canadian steel producers last year after the U.S. steel industry filed unfair trade complaints against steelmakers in Canada and 18 other countries.

Sources: New York Times, The Wall Street Journal

Strategic trade policy may reduce foreign trade restrictions, but at the risk of causing a trade war.

restrictions unless other nations reduce their own restrictions. Some people believe that strategic trade policy can help to reduce worldwide trade restrictions. Others emphasize the potential danger from trade wars in which both countries raise restrictions with each other's exports, and every country loses.

Causes of Protectionism

Most restrictions on international trade result from political action by the interest groups who benefit from those restrictions. Trade restrictions, like many other government policies, create winners and losers. The winners, often relatively small, concentrated groups of people or firms, have strong incentives to lobby the government for policies that help them and to provide campaign contributions for cooperative politicians. Industry associations provide ready forums for groups to organize for effective political persuasion.

Losers from trade restrictions are usually members of large, diffuse groups who suffer relatively small per-person losses, giving each individual little incentive to spend the time and money to organize effective opposition to the trade restrictions. The losers may even be unaware of the effects of trade restrictions on the prices they pay. For these reasons, the groups that lose from trade restrictions often wield less political power than the groups that gain.

Restrictions on imports of children's pajamas may raise the price by $0.50 per pair, hardly noticeable to any one consumer. A firm selling 1 million pairs of pajamas, however, may earn an extra $500,000 from the import restrictions. The incentive for producers to lobby for restrictions is much stronger than the incentive for individual consumers to give the matter a second thought, let alone take the time to gather information, organize with other consumers, and lobby to eliminate the restrictions.

Transition to Free Trade

Eliminating trade restrictions creates losers as well as winners. Some firms lose sales, as buyers choose to import foreign products; other firms gain sales, as foreigners spend the dollars they earn from their exports. Because workers who lose their jobs need time to find new ones, the removal of trade barriers can cause short-term unemployment. Some people argue that the government should help workers who lose from the removal of trade restrictions, perhaps by providing increased unemployment compensation or job training. Some people argue that this adjustment assistance is not only fair, but that it also encourages free trade by easing the political process of removing trade restrictions. Other people argue against adjustment assistance, partly on the grounds that most changes in government policy help some people and hurt others, so they see nothing special about removing trade restrictions; these critics claim that the government could not possibly help everyone who is hurt by any change in government policies.

IN THE NEWS

As U.S. urges free markets, its trade barriers are many

By Keith Bradsher
Special to the New York Times

In comparison with Japan and America's other major trading partners, the United States is less protectionist—but many barriers to imports remain.

Quotas double the price of sugar in morning coffee and limit imports per American to no more than seven peanuts, a pound of dairy cheese, and a lick of ice cream each year. Fresh cream and milk are banned; frozen cream may be purchased only from New Zealand. And the Customs Service recently turned back a shipment of buttered croissants from France because it violated a quota on French butter shipments.

Imports of men's heavy and worsted wool suits are capped at 1.2 million, the equivalent of one for each male manager and professional every dozen years. The Commerce Department has imposed punitive duties on martial arts uniforms from Taiwan, awning window cranks from El Salvador, and the tiny pads for woodwind instrument keys from Italy after determining that they were being sold, or "dumped," at unfairly low prices.

Sprawling and Inconsistent

This sprawling and inconsistent collection of quotas, tariffs, and other barriers reflects lobbying by many industries, as well as the occasional national-security concern. The result has been higher prices for American consumers and fewer opportunities for millions of people in developing countries to escape poverty by growing crops or stitching clothes for people in wealthy countries.

Source: New York Times

Political forces, such as the relative political power of various groups, affect a country's trade policies.

20. Do some countries need trade restrictions to compete in world markets? Explain.

21. Do trade restrictions protect jobs? Explain.

22. Who loses and who gains if a foreign government subsidizes the exports of its country's producers?

23. What is a strategic trade policy? Cite one argument for and one argument against a strategic trade policy.

C o n c l u s i o n

Scope of International Trade

International trade is an important and growing part of the world economy. Imports and exports each represent about one-eighth of U.S. GDP. Some countries have trade deficits, importing more than they export, while others have trade surpluses, exporting more than they import.

Comparative Advantage and the Gains from Trade

International trade, like a good technology, expands opportunities. International trade raises economic efficiency. Because all countries can share the gains from trade, it allows every country to consume more products than it can produce.

A country gains from trade by concentrating production on products in which it has a comparative advantage—a relatively low opportunity cost—and limiting production of goods in which it has a comparative disadvantage. It then exports the former products and imports the latter. This activity raises world output and consumption in every country.

Gains from International Trade: Graphical Analysis

Without international trade, each country's consumption is limited to what it can produce. International trade allows each country to consume more of *every* good than it can produce itself. Its consumption opportunities expand beyond its production possibilities frontier (PPF), because it can trade along a world price line, exporting some products and importing others. The slope of the world price line, in absolute value, gives the world relative price of the product on the horizontal axis of the graph. Equilibrium of world supply and demand determines the relative price.

Some individual people and firms gain from international trade, and others lose. When a country imports a good, its consumers gain because international trade reduces the good's price; firms whose products compete with the imported good lose. Consumers gain more than producers lose, however, so they could compensate the losers and still gain from international trade. Foreign

exporters gain increases in sales, and foreign consumers lose because they pay a higher price for the good than they would pay without trade. Producers gain more than consumers lose, however, so on net both the importing country and the exporting country gain from trade.

Balance of Trade and the Current Account

A country runs a current account surplus if it lends money to other countries; a country that borrows experiences a current account deficit. A country's current account surplus equals its trade balance surplus plus its net income from past investments in other countries. A current account deficit results when a country saves less than it invests and borrows to finance the extra investment. A current account surplus results when a country saves more than it invests and lends the difference to people in other countries. Trade deficits are not good or bad per se; they each reflect underlying economic conditions.

Protectionism

Protectionism advocates government policies to restrict imports as protection for domestic producers from foreign competitors. Trade restrictions almost always hurt the country as a whole (ignoring the distribution of income), but they also create winners and losers. The two most prominent forms of restrictions on international trade are tariffs (taxes on imports) and import quotas (restrictions on the number of units of a particular product imported into a country). Other trade restrictions include voluntary export restraints, local content requirements, and bureaucratic (red tape) protectionism. Tariffs raise the domestic price of a product by taxing imported goods. Domestic producers benefit, but domestic consumers lose more than the producers gain. Other trade restrictions have similar effects. Trade restrictions may also provoke foreign retaliation.

The costs of protectionism are difficult to estimate. U.S. protectionism alone probably costs consumers about $70 billion per year (about $270 per person each year), while providing about a $35 billion gain to domestic producers and a $13 billion gain to the government. The U.S.

economy experiences a net loss from U.S. protectionism of about $22 billion per year (about $85 per person each year). Many countries have signed treaties to expand free international trade, and have joined the World Trade Organization (WTO). Other important agreements include the North American Free Trade Agreement (NAFTA), the European Union (EU), and the European Free Trade Association (EFTA).

Common Arguments for Protectionism

Some people argue fallaciously that domestic producers need trade restrictions to compete in world markets. In practice, the level of wages adjusts so that, in equilibrium, firms in every country can compete in world markets. Some people also claim that trade restrictions save jobs. While trade restrictions protect jobs in some industries, they eliminate jobs in other industries. Trade restrictions have little effect on overall employment.

Some people argue for trade restrictions to support high wages, because low foreign wages give cost advantages to foreign producers. In some circumstances, restrictions on international trade can keep wages higher than they would be with free trade, but even in these circumstances, restricting international trade reduces the economy's total income.

Trade restrictions are not necessary to level the playing field in international trade. International trade differs from a sporting contest or a war, because both sides win when they trade. (Everyone can gain from a voluntary trade.) Trade restrictions reduce economic efficiency and redistribute income from domestic consumers to protected domestic producers, whether or not other countries impose their own trade restrictions.

Another argument for trade restrictions urges temporary protection for infant industries with high start-up costs until they establish themselves. If investors expected future industry profits high enough to justify losses for a few years, however, they would willingly accept short-term losses in return for future profits; the industry would not need temporary protection from foreign competition. Trade restrictions essentially force buyers to subsidize economically inefficient industries.

Some people argue that trade restrictions are necessary to protect national defense. This argument may be important for a limited number of industries, but probably has little bearing on most real-life trade restrictions. Finally, some people argue that trade restrictions can help to provide leverage in bargaining with other countries to reduce their own restrictions. Such a strategic trade policy may invite further foreign retaliation and start a trade war, however, in which trade restrictions increase and every country loses.

Most real-life restrictions on international trade result from political action by the interest groups who benefit from those restrictions. The benefits of trade restrictions are usually concentrated in a small group of winners, who have an incentive to lobby for those restrictions, while the (larger) costs are spread out among many people, each of whom has little individual incentive to actively oppose the restrictions.

Key Terms

export

import

balance of international trade

trade surplus or deficit

comparative advantage

current account

current account surplus or deficit

tariff

import quota

World Trade Organization (WTO)

Questions and Problems

24. Make up a simple numerical example to show the gains from international trade.

25. Draw graphs like Figure 10 to show why the gains from trade are *larger* when trading countries are more different in the equilibrium relative prices that they would have in the absence of international trade.

26. Draw a graph to illustrate the effects of an import quota. Who gains and who loses from the quota? Show the sizes of the gains and losses on your graph. How large are the gains and losses to each country and to the world economy as a whole?

27. Consider the example from Figures 11 and 12, but suppose that the world equilibrium relative price of videos is *one* computer program per music video (that is, they have the same price).

    (a) Draw graphs like those in Figure 11 to show consumption opportunities in the United States and Japan if they trade.

    (b) Does the United States gain more from international trade if the relative price of music videos is one-half or one computer program? Explain why.

28. Suppose that the United States and Japan can produce either CD players or wheat. Each country has 60 person-days available for work. The table shows the labor required to produce each product:

Costs of Production: Labor Time to Produce 1 Unit

	United States	Japan
CD player (1 unit)	10 person-days	12 person-days
Wheat (1 ton)	1 person-day	2 person-days

(a) Draw (to scale) each country's production possibilities frontier (PPF).

(b) Which country has a comparative advantage in which product?

(c) Suppose that the world equilibrium price of a CD player is $80 and the world price of wheat is $10 per ton. What is the relative price of CD players in terms of wheat? Which country would produce which product at these prices?

(d) Add world price lines to your PPF graphs, and use those graphs to show why international trade allows each country to consume more than it could without trading.

Inquiries for Further Thought

29. What imported goods do you consume? What goods that you use have some imported parts (perhaps inside)?

30. Suppose that states in the United States could not trade with each other. What goods or services would you lose the opportunity to buy?

(a) How much would your standard of living fall? (Be sure to think about inputs into production of goods that you buy.)

(b) How much would your standard of living fall if governments were to prohibit international trade? How much would it rise if governments were to eliminate all restrictions and taxes on international trade?

31. What U.S. jobs depend on international trade?

32. When the U.S. government chooses its trade policies, should it take into account only the effects on people in the United States, or should it also consider the effects on people in other countries? For example, suppose that a policy would help the United States by $5 million and hurt people in other countries by $6 million. Should the government adopt that policy? What if it would hurt people in other countries by $60 million? What if the policy would hurt people in the United States by $5 million, but help people in other countries by $6 million or by $60 million?

33. Why would the government impose import quotas rather than levying tariffs? (It could collect revenue from tariffs, but the gains from quotas go to foreign sellers.)

34. The government of Italy subsidizes its steel industry. Italy also exports steel to the United States. How does Italy's subsidy affect U.S. consumers and steel producers? Some people say that the United States should impose an import quota or tariff in a case like this. (The U.S. government does set quotas in the form of voluntary export restraints.) Do you agree that Italian steel imports should face trade restrictions? If so, how big should they be, and who would gain and lose from the quota or tariff?

activist view of policy–the view that the economy often operates inefficiently on its own and that government macroeconomic policies can improve its efficiency (p. 330)

aggregate demand curve–a graph showing the total amount of goods and services that people, firms, and the government would buy at each possible price level, given the nominal money supply and velocity (p. 279)

aggregate demand multiplier–the ratio of the ultimate increase in aggregate demand, due to an exogenous rise in spending, to that initial increase in spending (p.310)

aggregate supply curve–a graph showing the total amount of goods and services that firms would produce and try to sell at each possible price level (p. 282)

appreciation–an increase in the value of one money in terms of another (so that the price of foreign money falls) (p. 230)

area–a number that measures the size of some specific region in a graph (p. 39)

automatic stabilizer–a feature of government policy that automatically changes taxes or spending to try to reduce fluctuations in real GDP, without any explicit actions of the government (p. 374)

average product of labor–total production divided by the number of hours worked (p. 132)

balance of international trade–the value of a country's exports minus that of its imports (p. 425)

balanced budget–when tax receipts equal spending (p. 360)

bank reserves–the deposits that banks have *not* loaned (p. 251)

bank run–when many people try at the same time to withdraw their money from a bank that lacks sufficient reserves (p. 262)

banking panic–simultaneous runs on many banks (p. 262)

bond–an IOU for a long-term debt, typically on a loan lasting 10 years or more (p. 393)

budget deficit–a negative surplus, or government spending minus (smaller) tax revenue (p. 360)

budget surplus–tax revenue minus (smaller) government spending (p. 360)

call option–a right to buy some underlying asset during some specified period of time at some preset strike price (p. 413)

capital gain (or **capital loss**)–an increase (or decrease) in the value of an asset (p. 396)

capital–the stock of equipment, structures, inventories, human skills, and knowledge available to help produce goods and services (p. 112)

central bank–a bank for banks (p. 257)

change in demand–a change in the numbers in the demand schedule and a shift in the demand curve (p. 76)

change in quantity demanded–a movement along a demand curve due to a change in price (p. 77)

change in quantity supplied–a movement along a supply curve due to a change in price (p. 84)

change in supply–a change in the numbers in the supply schedule and a shift in the supply curve (p. 83)

commercial paper–a short-term debt security (usually with a 30-day maturity) issued by a private firm (p. 394)

commitment to a policy rule–an action by a policy maker to guarantee implementation of the rule (p. 339)

comparative advantage–the ability to produce a product at a lower opportunity cost than the costs that other countries would incur (p. 54, 427)

complement–a good used in combination with another, so that a rise in the price of one decreases demand for the other (p. 79)

consumption–spending by people on final goods and services for current use (p. 111)

contingent policy rule–a rule that states specifically how policies will depend on economic circumstances (p. 334)

correlation–a measure of how closely two variables are related (p. 28)

coupon payment–an interest payment that a borrower makes to a bondholder (p. 393)

credible policy rule–a rule that people believe policy makers will follow, perhaps because they have an incentive to follow it (p. 339)

crowding out of private investment–a fall in equilibrium investment when government borrowing raises the real interest rate (p. 176)

currency board–an institution whose sole purpose is to keep a foreign exchange rate fixed by acting as a residual buyer or seller of the country's money at that price (p. 346)

currency reform–replacement of an old form of money with a new one, with automatic adjustment of all nominal values in existing contracts, such as nominal wages and nominal debts, to keep real values the same (p. 222)

currency–all the paper money and coins owned by people and business firms (p. 250)

current account deficit–net borrowing from other countries (p. 434)

current account surplus–net lending to other countries (p. 434)

current account–the amount that a country lends to or borrows from other countries (p. 434)

decrease in demand–a decrease in the quantity demanded at a given price and a leftward shift in the demand curve (p. 77)

decrease in supply–a decrease in the quantity supplied at a given price and a leftward shift in the supply curve (p. 84)

default–failure to repay a loan in full (p. 394)

demand curve–a graph of the relation between the price of a good and the quantity demanded (p. 72)

demand deposit–a balance in a bank account that you can withdraw on demand by writing a check (p. 250)

depreciation–a fall in the value of one money in terms of another (so that the price of foreign money rises) (p. 230)

devaluation–a fall in the value of a currency on foreign exchange markets (an increase in the price of foreign currency in terms of domestic currency) (p. 345)

discounted present value–the value today of a future payment of money (p. 153)

discretionary policy–choice of policy actions according to judgments of policymakers (p. 334)

disequilibrium—a situation in which the quantity demanded does not equal the quantity supplied at the current price (p. 86)

diversification—spreading risks by choosing many unrelated investments or investments whose payoffs are out of step (p. 392)

dividend—a regular cash payment from a firm to stockholders (p. 401)

economic growth—a rise in real GDP per person (p. 183)

economic model—a description of logical thinking about an economic issue expressed in words, graphs, or mathematical symbols (p. 19)

economically efficient—a situation that cannot be changed so that someone gains unless someone else loses (p. 57)

economically inefficient—a situation that can be changed so that at least one person gains while no one else loses (p. 57)

economics—the study of people's choices and what happens to make everyone's choices compatible (p. 5)

effective labor input—labor input adjusted for knowledge and skills (p. 195)

efficient markets theory—the argument that stock prices are random walks (p. 407)

equation of exchange—the equation $MV = Py$ (p. 139)

equilibrium price level—the price level that equates the quantity of money demanded with the quantity supplied (p. 219)

equilibrium price—the price at equilibrium (p. 86)

equilibrium quantity—the quantity at equilibrium (p. 86)

equilibrium rate of inflation—the growth rate of the equilibrium price level (p. 225)

equilibrium unemployment—unemployment that results from continuing changes in supplies and demands and the costs of searching for and matching jobs in labor markets (p. 142)

equilibrium—a situation in which the quantity demanded does not equal the quantity supplied at the current price (p. 86)

evidence—any set of facts that helps to convince people that a positive statement is true or false (p. 19)

excess demand (shortage)—a situation in which the quantity demanded exceeds the quantity supplied (p. 87)

excess supply (surplus)—a situation in which the quantity supplied exceeds the quantity demanded (p. 88)

exchange rate—the price of foreign money (p. 229)

exhaustible resource—a resource that cannot be physically replenished and is depleted in production (p. 196)

expected value—an average of every possible value that a variable can take, weighted by the chance of that value occurring (p. 389)

exports—goods and services sold to people and firms in other countries (p. 112, 424)

fallacy of composition—false reasoning that what is true for one person must be true for the economy as a whole (p. 25)

federal funds rate—the interest rate that banks charge each other for short-term loans of reserves (p. 259)

Federal Reserve discount rate—the interest rate that the Fed charges banks for short-term loans (p. 259)

Federal Reserve System—an independent agency of the U.S. government that serves as the country's central bank (p. 257)

fiat money—paper money that is not backed by a commodity in the sense that people cannot trade it for a particular commodity at a fixed nominal price (p. 248)

financial asset—a right to collect some payment or series of payments in the future (p. 388)

financial intermediary—an organization that accumulates money from lenders (savers) and lends it to borrowers (spenders) (p. 261)

fiscal policy—government actions that change government spending, taxes, or both (p. 358)

fixed (or pegged) exchange rate system—system in which the government buys or sells the country's currency in whatever amounts are necessary to keep its exchange rate at a particular level (p. 343)

fixed resource—a natural resource that cannot be replenished but is not depleted in production such as land (p. 195)

floating (or flexible) exchange rate system—system in which the government does not actively trade in foreign exchange markets to influence exchange rates (p. 343)

fundamental price—the discounted present value of a stock's expected future dividends (p. 408)

futures market—a market for trading contracts for future delivery of goods or assets (p. 412)

GDP deflator—nominal GDP divided by real GDP (p. 107)

gold exchange standard—a system in which people trade paper money that is backed by gold stored in a warehouse (p. 248)

government budget deficit—government spending in excess of tax receipts (p. 157)

government debt—the amount of money the government owes because it has borrowed money in the past (p. 361)

government purchases—total spending on goods and services by federal, state, and local governments (p. 112)

gross domestic product (GDP)—the value of a country's production of final market goods and services during some time period (usually a year) (p. 105)

holding period yield—the rate of return a bond would provide over some specified period of time, perhaps less than the time until the bond matures (p. 396)

import quota—a restriction on the number of imported goods of a certain type (p. 438)

imports—purchases of goods and services from people and firms in other countries (p. 113, 424)

income—money received from all sources, measured as an amount per year (p. 78)

increase in demand—an increase in the quantity demanded at a given price and a rightward shift in the demand curve (p. 76)

increase in supply—an increase in the quantity supplied at a given price and a rightward shift in the supply curve (p. 83)

inferior good—a good whose demand falls if income rises (p. 78)

inflation tax—the loss that people suffer when inflation reduces the purchasing power of their assets (p. 237)

inflation—a continuing increase in the price level (the percentage increase in the average nominal price of goods and services) (p. 214)

interest rate—the price of a loan, expressed as a *percentage per year* of the amount loaned (p. 153)

laissez-faire view—the view that the economy usually operates efficiently on its own and, even when it does not, active government policies will more likely aggravate inefficiencies and create new inefficiencies than alleviate problems (p. 333)

law of diminishing returns–the principle that raising the quantity of an input eventually reduces its marginal product, for a fixed quantity of some other input (p. 133)

leveraged buyout (LBO)–a form of takeover financed by extensive borrowing, often pledging the assets of the takeover target as collateral for the loans (p. 419)

long-run Phillips Curve–a vertical line at the natural rate of unemployment (p. 302)

looser monetary policy–Fed actions that raise the growth rate of the money supply or decrease the federal funds rate (p. 269)

looser monetary policy–a policy that increases the growth rates of the monetary base and broader measures of the money supply, decreasing the federal funds rate (p. 331)

Lucas critique–the proposition that people do not always respond the same way to changes in economic conditions or government policies, because their responses depend partly on their expectations about the future, and those expectations can change (p. 338)

M1 money multiplier–the ratio of the M1 measure of the money supply to the monetary base (p. 254)

M1–a measure of the money supply that includes currency, demand deposits, other checkable deposits, and traveler's checks (p. 250)

M2–a measure of the money supply that combines M1 with balances in savings accounts, money market mutual funds, and similar accounts (p. 251)

managed-float exchange rate system–system in which the government sometimes trades in foreign exchange markets to influence the exchange rate without maintaining a fixed rate (p. 344)

marginal product of labor–the *additional* production obtained from *increasing* labor a little, without changing the amounts of capital or natural resources (p. 132)

market demand curve–a graph of the relation between the price of a good and the market quantity demanded (p. 72)

market quantity demanded (at a given price)–the total amount of a good that all buyers in the economy would buy at that price (p. 72)

market quantity supplied (at some price)–the amount that all sellers in the economy would sell at that price (p. 82)

market supply curve–a graph of the relation between the price of a good and the market quantity supplied (p. 82)

medium of exchange–an asset that sellers generally accept as payment for goods, services, and other assets (p. 246)

merger–when two firms voluntarily combine to form a single organization (p. 419)

misleading comparison–a comparison of two or more things that does not reflect their true differences (p. 26)

monetary base–a measure of the money supply that includes currency plus bank reserves (p. 252)

monetary policy–changes in a nation's nominal money supply through open market operations, changes in the discount rate or discount-window lending policy, or bank reserve requirement changes (p. 330)

national savings–private savings plus government savings (p. 379)

natural rate of unemployment–the unemployment rate that occurs when the economy produces the full-employment level of output (p. 301)

negative correlation–a relationship between variables that tend to move in opposite directions (inversely to one another) (p. 28)

negative slope–the shape of a curve that runs downward and to the right (p. 37)

net exports, or the **balance of international trade**–exports minus imports (p. 113)

neutrality of money–the implication of an economic model that an increase in the nominal money supply raises nominal prices and wages but leaves real GDP, employment, and *relative* prices unaffected (p. 140)

nominal GDP–GDP measured in money (dollars, yen, pesos, Euros, etc.) (p. 105)

nominal interest rate–the annual dollar interest payment on a loan expressed as a percentage of the dollar amount borrowed. (p. 162)

nominal money supply–the total amount of money in the economy, measured in monetary units such as dollars or yen (p. 138)

nominal money supply–the total dollar value of all paper money and coins in the economy (p. 214)

nominal price–the money price of a good (p. 94, 213)

nominal variable–a variable measured in terms of money, such as U.S. dollars, Mexican pesos, or Japanese yen (p. 213)

nominal wages–payments for labor services, measured in monetary units like dollars or yen (p. 140)

normal good–a good whose demand rises if income rises (p. 78)

normative statement–a statement that expresses a value judgment or says what should be; such a statement cannot be true or false (p. 18)

open market operation–a Federal Reserve purchase or sale of financial assets (p. 258)

opportunity cost–the value of whatever someone must sacrifice or give up to obtain something (p. 8)

other-conditions fallacy–false reasoning that two events will always occur together in the future because they occurred together in the past (p. 26)

ownership–the right to make decisions about a scarce resource (p. 12)

policy rule–a statement of what policy an agency will follow (p. 334)

positive correlation–a relationship between variables that tend to rise or fall together (p. 28)

positive externality–a situation in which the social benefit of an action exceeds its private benefit (p. 199)

positive slope–the shape of a curve that runs upward and to the right (p. 37)

positive statement–a statement of fact, of what is or what would be if something else were to happen; such a statement is either true or false (p. 18)

positive-sum game–an environment in which everyone can gain at the same time (p. 57)

post-hoc fallacy–false reasoning that, because one event happened before another, the first event must have caused the second event (p. 25)

private benefit–the benefit of production or investment to the people who produce a good or invest (p. 199)

privately held government debt–the amount of government debt owned by people and business firms outside the government (p. 375)

production function–a mathematical description of an economy's technology, showing the total production it can obtain from its inputs of labor, capital, and natural resources (p. 132)

production possibilities frontier (PPF)–a graph of the combinations of various goods that an economy can produce with its current resources and technology (p. 46)

pure gold standard–a system in which people trade gold coins as money, and the economy includes no paper money (p. 248)

put option–a right to sell some underlying asset during some specified period of time at some preset strike price (p. 413)

quantity demanded (at a given price)–the amount that a person would buy at that price (p. 72)

quantity of money demanded–the amount of money that people would choose to own, given current conditions such as their income and wealth, the price level, the usefulness of money, and the costs and benefits of owning other assets (p. 217)

quantity supplied (at some price)–the amount that a seller would sell at that price (p. 81)

rate of job creation–the number of new workers hired each month (p. 143)

rate of job destruction–the number of people who quit or lose their jobs each month (p. 143)

rate of return–the income that an owner receives from an asset over some period of time plus the increase in its value during that period, all as a percentage of the original value of the asset (p. 388)

rational behavior–the actions of people when they do the best they can, based on their own values and information, under the circumstances they face (p. 24)

real GDP–GDP measured in the prices of a certain base year. (p. 105)

real interest rate–the interest rate *adjusted for inflation* (p. 162)

real variable–a variable that refers to a quantity of goods and services, often measured in base-year dollars (p. 213)

real wages–wages measured in *base-year* dollars (p. 140)

recession–a period in which real GDP falls for two consecutive quarters (although the official National Bureau of Economic Research definition is more complex) (p. 116)

relative price–the opportunity cost of one good in terms of other goods (equal to one nominal price divided by another or divided by a price index) (p. 213)

relative price–the opportunity cost of the first good measured in units of the second good (p. 94)

renewable resource–a natural resource that can be replenished, such as trees (p. 195)

rent seeking–the use of time, money, and other resources in pursuit of government benefits (spending, tax changes, or regulations targeted to some special-interest group) (p. 382)

required reserves–the reserves that the Fed requires banks to hold, based on their total deposits (p. 260)

risk averse–a characteristic of a person who prefers less risk to more risk (p. 392)

risk neutral–a characteristic of a person who does not care about risk, only about expected return (p. 392)

risk premium–an extra payment that compensates investors for risk (p. 394)

risk-free interest rate–the interest rate on a loan with no chance of default (p. 394)

rule of 72–a rule of thumb that a variable with a growth rate of X percent per year doubles after about $72/X$ years (p. 183)

selection bias–use of data that are not typical, but are selected in a way that biases results (p. 27)

shift–a change in the position of a curve on a graph (p. 36)

shortage–a situation in which quantity demanded exceeds quantity supplied at the current price (p. 87)

short-run Phillips Curve–a statistical relationship showing that unemployment falls temporarily when inflation rises, and unemployment rises temporarily when inflation falls (p. 301)

simple policy rule–a rule that requires a particular policy regardless of economic circumstances (p. 334)

slope–a number that shows the distance by which a curve goes up or down as it moves 1 unit to the right (p. 38)

social benefit–the benefit to everyone in society of private production or investment (p. 199)

statistical analysis–the use of mathematical probability theory to draw inferences in situations of uncertainty (p. 19)

steady state–a long-run equilibrium with constant capital per person (p. 189)

sticky price–a price that takes time to

adjust to its new equilibrium level following a change in conditions (also applies to the overall price level) (p. 279)

store of value–any good or asset that people can store while it maintains some or all of its value (p. 246)

substitute–a good that can replace another, so that a rise in the price of one increases demand for the other (p. 79)

supply curve–a graph of the relation between the price of a good and the quantity supplied (p. 82)

suppressed inflation–inflation that would occur without government controls on wages and prices, but that does not fully occur due to those controls (p. 240)

takeover–when one person, a group of people, or another company buys enough stock in a firm to guarantee a majority vote at stockholder meetings (p. 418)

tariff–a tax on imports (p. 438)

tax rate on income–the tax collected per dollar, as a percentage of income (p. 173)

technical efficiency–a situation in which an economy cannot produce more of one good without producing less of something else (p. 47)

tighter monetary policy–Fed actions that reduce the growth rate of the money supply or raise the federal funds rate (p. 269)

tighter monetary policy–a policy that reduces the growth rates of the monetary base and broader measures of the money supply, increasing the federal funds rate (p. 331)

time consistent policy–policy in which the best discretionary decisions match the decisions suggested by the best rule (p. 340)

time inconsistent policy–policy in which the best discretionary decisions differ from the decisions suggested by the best rule (p. 340)

trade deficit–imports in excess of exports (p. 425)

trade surplus–exports in excess of imports (p. 425)

Treasury bill (T-bill)–a short-term debt security issued by the U.S. government, typically for a 3-month to 6-month loan (p. 394)

Treasury note–a debt security issued by the U.S. government, typically for a loan of 1 to 10 years (p. 394)

unemployment rate–the fraction of unemployed people in the labor force. (p. 115)

unit of account–a measure for stating prices (p. 246)

variable–name of a set of numbers analyzed with a graph (ranged along the horizontal and vertical axes) or with mathematical methods (p. 32)

velocity of money–the average number of times per year that money is spent in the circular flow, equal to nominal GDP divided by the nominal money supply (p. 139)

wealth–the accumulated value of past savings, including human wealth (the value of education and skills) (p. 79)

World Trade Organization (WTO) –an international organization and a series of related treaties that reduce trade restrictions (p. 442)

zero-sum game–an environment in which one person's gain is another person's loss (p. 57)

Credits

Additional Credits (Cartoons, Figures, and Tables)

P. 90 *The Far Side*. 1987 FARWORKS, Inc. Distributed by Universal Press Syndicate. Reprinted with permission. All Rights Reserved.

P. 264 "Yeah, but who guarantees the federal government?" From *The Wall Street Journal*, August 15, 1986. Reprinted by permission of Cartoon Features Syndicate.

P. 282 "Whether the marriage lasts or not, we've certainly given the economy a boost." From *The Wall Street Journal*, October 25, 1988. Reprinted by permission of Cartoon Features Syndicate.

P. 289 ©*Richmond-Times Dispatch*. Reprinted by permission.

P. 439 James Bovard, *The Fair Trade Fraud*, New York: St. Martin's Press, 1991.

Index